T0180988

Communications in Computer and Information Science 1453

More information about this series at http://www.springer.com/series/7899

Ying Tan · Yuhui Shi · Albert Zomaya ·
Hongyang Yan · Jun Cai (Eds.)

Data Mining and Big Data

6th International Conference, DMBD 2021
Guangzhou, China, October 20–22, 2021
Proceedings, Part I

Springer

Editors
Ying Tan 🅐
Peking University
Beijing, China

Yuhui Shi
Southern University of Science
and Technology
Shenzhen, China

Albert Zomaya
The University of Sydney
Sydney, Australia

Hongyang Yan
Guangzhou University
Guangzhou, China

Jun Cai
Guangdong Polytechnic Normal University
Guangzhou, China

ISSN 1865-0929   ISSN 1865-0937 (electronic)
Communications in Computer and Information Science
ISBN 978-981-16-7475-4   ISBN 978-981-16-7476-1 (eBook)
https://doi.org/10.1007/978-981-16-7476-1

This Springer imprint is published by the registered company Springer Nature Singapore Pte Ltd.
The registered company address is: 152 Beach Road, #21-01/04 Gateway East, Singapore 189721, Singapore

Preface

The Sixth International Conference on Data Mining and Big Data (DMBD 2021) was held in Guangzhou, China, during October 20–22, 2021. DMBD serves as an international forum for researchers to exchange the latest innovations in theories, models, and applications of data mining and big data as well as artificial intelligence techniques. DMBD 2021 was the sixth event after the successful first event (DMBD 2016) in Bali, Indonesia, the second event (DMBD 2017) in Fukuoka City, Japan, the third event (DMBD 2018) in Shanghai, China, the fourth event (DMBD 2019) in Chiang Mai, Thailand, and the fifth event (DMBD 2020) in Belgrade, Serbia.

These two volumes (CCIS vol. 1453 and CCIS vol. 1454) contain papers presented at DMBD 2021 covering some of the major topics of data mining and big data. The conference received 259 submissions. The Program Committee accepted 83 regular papers to be included in the conference program with an acceptance rate of 32.05%. The proceedings contain revised versions of the accepted papers. While revisions are expected to take the referees comments into account, this was not enforced and the authors bear full responsibility for the content of their papers.

DMBD 2021 was organized by the International Association of Swarm and Evolutionary Intelligence (IASEI) and co-organized by the Guangdong Polytechnic Normal University, Pazhou Lab, Guangzhou University, and the Guangdong Provincial Engineering and Technology Research Center for Big Data Security and Privacy Preservation. It was technically co-sponsored by Peking University and Southern University of Science and Technology, and also supported by Nanjing Kangbo Intelligent Health Academy. The conference would not have been such a success without the support of these organizations, and we sincerely thank them for their continued assistance and support.

We would also like to thank the authors who submitted their papers to DMBD 2021, and the conference attendees for their interest and support. We thank the Organizing Committee for their time and effort dedicated to arranging the conference. This allowed us to focus on the paper selection and deal with the scientific program. We thank the Program Committee members and the external reviewers for their hard work in reviewing the submissions; the conference would not have been possible without their expert reviews. Finally, we thank the EasyChair system and its operators, for making the entire process of managing the conference convenient.

September 2021

Ying Tan
Yuhui Shi
Albert Zomaya
Hongyang Yan
Jun Cai

Organization

Honorary General Chair

Zhiming Zheng   Guangzhou University, China

General Co-chairs

Ying Tan   Peking University, China
Jin Li   Guangzhou University, China
Jun Cai   Guangdong Polytechnic Normal University, China
Zhendong Wu   Hangzhou Dianzi University, China

Program Committee Co-chairs

Yuhui Shi   Southern University of Science and Technology, China
Albert Zomaya   University of Sydney, Australia

Advisory Committee Co-chairs

Milovan Stanisic   Singidunum University, Serbia
Russell C. Eberhart   IUPUI, USA
Gary G. Yen   Oklahoma State University, USA

Technical Committee Co-chairs

Haibo He   University of Rhode Island, USA
Kay Chen Tan   City University of Hong Kong, Hong Kong, China
Nikola Kasabov   Auckland University of Technology, New Zealand
Ponnuthurai Nagaratnam Suganthan   Nanyang Technological University, Singapore
Xiaodong Li   RMIT University, Australia
Hideyuki Takagi   Kyushu University, Japan
M. Middendorf   University of Leipzig, Germany
Mengjie Zhang   Victoria University of Wellington, New Zealand

Special Track Co-chairs

Sheng Hong   Beihang University, China
Jingwei Li   University of Electronic Science and Technology
                              of China, China
Feng Wang   Wuhan University, China
Tianqing Zhu   University of Technology Sydney, Australia

Publication Chair

Hongyang Yan   Guangzhou University, China

Publicity Co-chairs

Nan Jiang   East China Jiaotong University, China
Weizhi Meng   Technical University of Denmark, Denmark
Yu Wang   Guangzhou University, China

Program Committee

Miltos Alamaniotis   University of Texas at San Antonio, USA
Nebojsa Bacanin   Singidunum University, Serbia
Carmelo J. A. Bastos Filho   University of Pernambuco, Brazil
Tossapon Boongoen   Mae Fah Luang University, Thailand
David Camacho   Universidad Politécnica de Madrid, Spain
Abdelghani Chahmi   Universite des Sciences et Technologie d'Oran
                              Mohamed-Boudiaf, Algeria
Vinod Chandra S. S.   University of Kerala, India
Hui Cheng   Liverpool John Moores University, UK
Jieren Cheng   Hainan University, China
Jose Alfredo Ferreira Costa   Federal University, Brazil
Bei Dong   Shanxi Normal University, China
Qinqin Fan   Shanghai Maritime University, China
A. H. Gandomi   Stevens Institute of Technology, USA
Liang Gao   Huazhong University of Science and Technology,
                              China
Shangce Gao   University of Toyama, Japan
Wei Gao   Yunnan Normal University, China
Teresa Guarda   Universidad Estatal da Peninsula de Santa Elena,
                              Ecuador
Weian Guo   Tongji University, China
Weiwei Hu   Peking University, China
Dariusz Jankowski   Wroclaw University of Technology, Poland

Mingyan Jiang	Shandong University, China
Qiaoyong Jiang	Xi'an University of Technology, China
Junfeng Chen	Hohai University, China
Imed Kacem	Université de Lorraine, France
Kalinka Kaloyanova	University of Sofia, Japan
Vivek Kumar	Università degli Studi di Cagliari, Italy
Bin Li	University of Science and Technology of China, China
Qunfeng Liu	Dongguan University of Technology, China
Jianzhen Luo	Guangdong Polytechnic Normal University, China
Wenjian Luo	Harbin Institute of Technology, Shenzhen, China
Wojciech Macyna	Wroclaw University of Technology, Poland
Katherine Malan	University of South Africa, South Africa
Vasanth Kumar Mehta	SCSVMV University, India
Yi Mei	Victoria University of Wellington, New Zealand
Efrén Mezura-Montes	University of Veracruz, Mexico
Sheak Rashed Haider Noori	Daffodil International University, Bangladesh
Endre Pap	Singidunum University, Serbia
Mario Pavone	University of Catania, Spain
Yan Pei	University of Aizu, Japan
Somnuk Phon-Amnuaisuk	Universiti Teknologi Brunei, Brunei
Pramod Kumar Singh	ABV-IIITM Gwalior, India
Joao Soares	Polytechnic Institute of Porto, Portugal
Ivana Strumberger	Singidunum University, Serbia
Yifei Sun	Shanxi Normal University, China
Hung-Min Sun	Tsing Hua University in HsinChu, Taiwan, China
Ying Tan	Peking University, China
Paulo Trigo	ISEL, Portugal
Milan Tuba	Singidunum University, Serbia
Eva Tuba	University of Belgrade, Serbia
Agnieszka Turek	Warsaw University of Technology, Poland
Gai-Ge Wang	China Ocean University, China
Guoyin Wang	Chongqing University of Posts and Telecommunications, China
Zhenzhen Wang	Jinling Institute of Technology, China
Yan Wang	Ohio State University, USA
Ka-Chun Wong	City University of Hong Kong, Hong Kong, China
Rui Xu	Hohai University, China
Zhile Yang	Shenzhen Institute of Advanced Technology, Chinese Academy of Sciences, China
Yingjie Yang	De Montfort University, UK
Wei-Chang Yeh	Tsing Hua University in HsinChu, Taiwan, China

Contents – Part I

Contents – Part II

BSMRL: Bribery Selfish Mining with Reinforcement Learning

Zhaojie Wang[1], Jianan Guo[1], Yiting Zhang[1], Ming Liu[1],
Liang Yan[1], Yilei Wang[1(✉)], Hailun Liu[2], and Yunhe Li[1]

[1] School of Computer Science, Qufu Normal University, Rizhao, China
[2] School of Information Engineering, Xizang Minzu University, Xianyang, China

Abstract. As the second valuable cryptocurrency, Ether arouses a lot of concern and discussion, leading to various potential attacks. Although the threshold of the mining power is rather high for the attackers, machine learning is accessary to a tyrant's crimes. Thus the attackers can maximize their rewards by optimizing their attacking strategies. In this paper, we propose a novel intelligent attacking strategy (aka. BSMRL). More specifically, attackers optimize, combining with bribery attacks, their strategies to maximize the rewards by utilizing reinforcement learning. Simulation results indicate that BSMRL can greatly reduce the threshold for the attackers with higher rewards. Compared with the normal selfish miners, intelligent attackers are more dangerous to the system of Ethereum.

Keywords: Blockchain · Attacking strategy · Mining reward · Reinforcement learning

1 Introduction

Bitcoin pioneered decentralized crypto-currencies. However, its inadequacies increasingly emerge with the rapid development. For example, Bitcoin is not Turing-complete, which limits the universal implementation. In 2013, Vitalik Buterin publish the white paper of the Ethereum and initiate the project[1], which solves the scalability issues of Bitcoins. Similar to Bitcoin, the operation of the Ethereum heavily relies on a consensus mechanism. More specifically, the nodes in Ethereum obtain economic rewards by solving a specific difficult problem. Same as Bitcoin, The Ethereum is also facing various strategic attacks [7,10,20]. As well known, selfish mining is a typical attack to maximize rewards by utilizing the defects of consensus mechanism [4,17]. This kind of attack has been fully studied in Bitcoin [5,11–13], but in Ethereum, the research on such attacks is still insufficient. Existing works illustrate that selfish mining can also be found, with worse harms, in Ethereum [14]. Although there are several detection methods for selfish mining, which can effectively deter such attacks, it is still necessary to study the conditions for selfish mining to take precautions [3,16,18].

© Springer Nature Singapore Pte Ltd. 2021
Y. Tan et al. (Eds.): DMBD 2021, CCIS 1453, pp. 1–10, 2021.
https://doi.org/10.1007/978-981-16-7476-1_1

1.1   Related Work

Eyal and Sirer put forward the concept of selfish mining, and pointed out that selfish miners can achieve double spending only by controlling 1/3 of the computational power, which is lower than the previously thought threshold of 1/2 [4]. Niu and Feng studied selfish mining in Ethereum, and they found that selfish mining caused more harm to Ethereum due to uncle block [14]. Ritz and Zugenmaier specifically studied the influence of uncle block on selfish mining in Ethereum [15]. They used the Monte Carlo method to quantify the effects of uncle block on selfish mining probability and system security in Ethereum. J Bonneau et al. proposed the concept of bribery attack [2,19] and conducted a quantitative analysis on bribery attack. Their results showed that compared with other attacks, the bribery attack could increase the attacker's revenue. Gao et al. first proposed the concept of bribery selfish mining (BSM) in [6] and then analyzed the feasibility of it. Moreover, they pointed out that the honest miners fell into a venal miner's dilemma when the bribery attack occurred. Yang et al. proposed an optimal bribery selfish mining strategy (IPBSM) based on the idea of reinforcement learning but did not discuss the bribery attack in Ethereum [22]. Wang et al. proposed a hybrid attack strategy based on reinforcement learning, which included BWH and FAW, but did not include bribery attack, and did not discuss the possibility of hybrid attack in Ethereum [21]. According to previous works, Ethereum is more vulnerable to selfish mining attacks, on account of the uncle and nephew blocks [14]. Therefore, we consider the BSM attack in Ethereum and utilize reinforcement learning to optimize the attacker's reward.

The main contributions of this paper include the following aspects:

1. On the basis of IPBSM, we compare the differences between Ethereum and Bitcoin and then consider the optimization of selfish mining strategy in the case of uncle block.
2. Based on the selfish mining in Ethereum, we define the environmental state and the strategy of selfish attacker, and puts forward the BSMRL algorithm.
3. We quantitatively analyzed the relative revenue of the attacker and the impact of bribery attack on his reward.

2   Preliminaries

2.1   Selfish Mining

Selfish mining is a type of Block Withholding Attack, where selfish attackers utilize protocol loopholes to obtain extra rewards through strategic attacks. Specifically, the attacker will temporarily keep the newly mined blocks to maintain a leading secret chain, and then publish them at an appropriate time (usually when the leading is only one block) to make other blocks (mined by other miners) invalid [4,14].

2.2 Bribery Attack

In the bribery attack, the attacker does not obtain mining power permanently but temporarily increases the power through leases. The attacker bribes other miners to work on his branch provisionally. And the implementations of this attack are as follows:

- In-band payment via forking: An additional fee is included in the block reward. And this fee will attract other miners to work on the attacker's branch, when the blockchain is forking.
- Outof-band payment: The attacker implements an attack through offline payment.
- Negative-fee mining pool: The attacker organizes a mining pool and then distributes rewards and bribes to pool members, thereby attracting other miners to join the pool to work for him.

2.3 Reinforcement Learning

Reinforcement learning is an influential method in the field of machine learning. The agent maximizes its rewards or achieves the expected goal by learning the optimal strategy in the process of interacting with the environment [8]. And the environment is usually defined as the Markov Decision Process (MDP). The learning process is regarded as a heuristic evaluation process. The agent chooses an action for the environment, and then the environment transfers to a new state according to the action. The environment, meanwhile, gives feedback (positive or negative) to the agent. The principle of the next action selection is to increase the probability of receiving positive feedback.

3 Modeling BSMRL

3.1 Constructing the Environment

In this section, considering the uncle reward, we redefine the system state transition to increase the attacker's relative revenue and try to keep the threshold in a low region. Similar to Bitcoin, we model the Ethereum network as a Markov Decision Process (MDP). The formal definition of MDP is a four-tuple $M = \langle S, A, P, R \rangle$. The elements respectively represent:

- S is the state space and $s_t \in S$ represents the state of MDP in time t.
- A is an action space and $a_t \in A$ represents the agent's action in time t.
- P is the transition probability matrix, $p(s_{t+1}|s_t, a_t)$ represents that the transition probability from s_t and a_t to s_{t+1}.
- R is the reward matrix, $r(s_{t+1}|s_t, a_t)$ is a direct reward to the agent in $p(s_{t+1}|s_t, a_t)$.

According to the current state, the attacker will find an optimal action from the action space. Subsequently, the environment will transfer to the next state and offer a reward. We define the reward as a two-tuples $\langle r_a, r_h \rangle$, among them, r_a represents the attacker's reward and r_h represents rational miners' reward.

Figure 1 offers the state machine in the Ethereum network to show the state transition of environment, where state 0 means that there is no fork in the current state and $0'$ indicates that there is a fork with equal length branches in the system. The numbers in other states indicate the leading of the attacker's branch than the public chain. α is the attacker's mining power, $1 - \alpha$ is rational miners' mining power, and γ is the proportion of rational miners who chose to work on the attacker's branch when the Ethereum is forking.

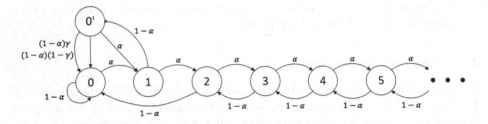

Fig. 1. The state machine of BSMRL.

3.2   The Attacker's Mining Strategy

In Algorithm 1, we describe the attacker's mining strategy in the BSMRL. Similar to SM1, the attacker will keep the excavated blocks and disclose them at the right time to invalidate the blocks of rational miners, thus increasing their relative revenue. In order to maximize the benefits, when the attacker digs out a new block, the attacker will refer to the unreferenced uncle block to obtain the nephew reward, and select the optimal action according to the environmental state. In addition, the attacker will make a bribery attack on the private chain. After the attacker chooses to take an action, the function $computingReward(\alpha, \gamma, state, action)$ is called to calculate the attacker's revenue.

In the function $computingReward(\alpha, \gamma, state, action)$, a binary search space is defined, and the value is approached by continuously narrowing the search interval. When the space gap is less than ϵ (a pre-set acceptable error range), stop searching and return the current value. The mdp_solver is an easy-to-use, freely available tool to solve Markov decision problems [9].

Algorithm 1. Bribery Selfish Mining with Reinforcement Learning (BSMRL)

1: $state \leftarrow < 0, 1, relevant, none >$
2: $actionSpace \leftarrow \{adopt, wait, override, match\}$
3: **function** MININGSTRATEGYOFATTACKER(α, γ, $state$, $action$)
4:      references an unreferenced uncle block based on the public chain
5:      performs bribery attack
6:      $l_a \leftarrow l_a + 1$
7:      **if** $l_a < l_h$ **then**
8:          $action \leftarrow adopt$
9:          $state \leftarrow < l_a, l_h, relevant, exist >$
10:     **else if** $l_a == l_h$ **then**
11:         $action \leftarrow match$
12:         $state \leftarrow < l_a, l_h, active, none >$
13:     **else if** $l_a == l_h + 1$ **then**
14:         $action \leftarrow override$
15:         $state \leftarrow < l_a, l_h, relevant, none >$
16:     **else**
17:         $action \leftarrow match$
18:         $state \leftarrow < l_a, l_h, active, exist >$
19:     **end if**
20:     $computingReward(\alpha, \gamma, state, action)$
21: **end function**
22: **function** COMPUTINGREWARD(α, γ, $state$, $action$)
23:     $i \leftarrow 0, j \leftarrow 1$
24:     **while** $j - i \geqslant \epsilon$ **do**
25:         $rev \leftarrow (i + j)/2$
26:         $mdp \leftarrow mdp\_solver(\alpha, \gamma, state, action)$
27:         **if** $mdp.v[0] > 0$ **then**
28:             $i \leftarrow rev$
29:         **else**
30:             $j \leftarrow rev$
31:         **end if**
32:     **end while**
33:     **return** rev
34: **end function**

---

4   Simulation

To verify the feasibility of our algorithm, we constructed a simulator to simulate the attack of BSMRL algorithm and original selfish mining (SM1) in Ethereum network. First of all, we simulated the SM1 algorithm in Ethereum, and the simulation results were close to [14], with only slight errors. For example, the threshold of mining power was 0.163 [14], and we got the threshold of 0.165. Then, we simulate the BSMRL and find that the mining power threshold of the attacker's extra reward was only 0.067, as shown in Fig. 2. In other words, in Ethereum, by executing the BSMRL algorithm, the attacker only needs to have more than 6.7% of the mining power and can get higher relative revenue than

honest mining. Moreover, under the same mining power, the BSMRL algorithm
has higher relative revenue than SM1 algorithm. For example, when attacker's
mining power $\alpha = 0.2$, the relative revenue of BSMRL algorithm is increased by
16.23% compared with SM1 algorithm. This shows that the BSMRL algorithm is
more harmful to Ethereum than SM1, so it is necessary to increase the detection
of such attacks.

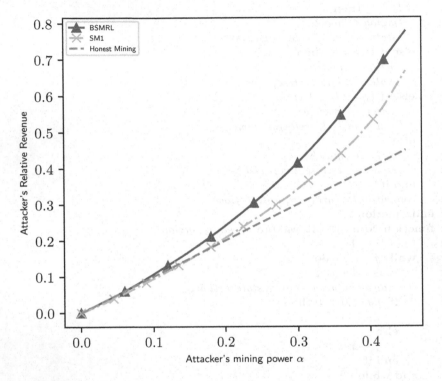

Fig. 2. The attacker's relative revenue of the BSMRL, Selfish Mining (SM1) and honest
mining in Ethereum when α changes from 0 to 0.45.

We also simulate the influence of the different γ to the revenue and threshold
of the BSMRL algorithm deeply. By Fig. 3 can be found that when $\alpha = 0.25$,
the attacker's relative revenue would be higher increased with an increased γ.
But at the same time, we also found that the revenue growth rate is gradually
reduced with the increase of γ. When $0.7 \leqslant \gamma \leqslant 1$, the trend of attacker's revenue
growth gradually slowed down. In a word, the increase of γ no longer makes the
attacker's relative revenue increase obviously. It is because that the increase of

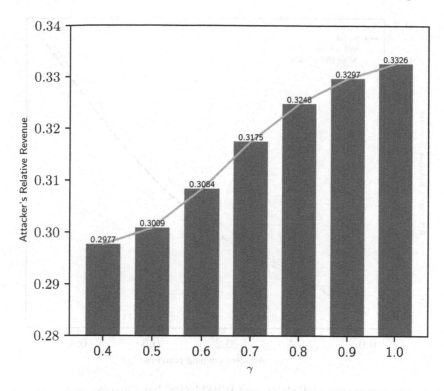

Fig. 3. The effect of γ on BSMRL yield when $\alpha = 0.25$.

the γ means that the payments of implementing the bribery attack are getting bigger, which suggests that the improvement of the revenue only by the bribery attack is limited.

We further discuss the different effects of the bribery selfish mining in Ethereum and Bitcoin. Compared to the IPBSM in Bitcoin, the BSMRL algorithm has higher relative revenue, as shown in Fig. 4. This is because the uncle rewards in Ethereum can provide additional rewards for the selfish attacker. Not only that, but the uncle rewards also make up for part of the cost of implementing selfish mining [14], which makes BSMRL have a lower threshold of mining power than IPBSM. This also shows that, compared to Bitcoin, Ethereum is more vulnerable to attacks. So it is necessary to improve the detection efficiency of such attacks.

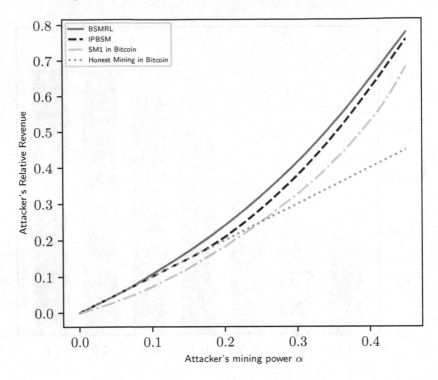

Fig. 4. The comparison of BSMRL and IPBSM (BSM in Bitcoin) on the attacker's relative revenue when $\gamma = 0.75$.

5   Conclusion and Future Work

In this paper, we consider the situation that uncle reward exists in Ethereum, and improve the IPBSM algorithm, namely BSMRL. We redefined state transitions for MDP and described the attacker's strategy in Ethereum. We also conducted simulation experiments on the BSMRL algorithm, which showed that the BSMRL algorithm has higher revenue and a lower threshold. And we illustrate the BSMRL algorithm causing more harm to Ethereum than the original selfish mining strategy. At the same time, we also found that the improvement of the relative revenue only by the bribery attack is limited. In future work, we will never fail to improve the BSMRL algorithm deeply to deal with situations where multiple attackers attack each other.

References

1. Ethereum whitepaper. https://ethereum.org/en/whitepaper/. Accessed 9 Feb 2021
2. Bonneau, J., Felten, E.W., Goldfeder, S., Kroll, J.A., Narayanan, A.: Why buy when you can rent? bribery attacks on bitcoin consensus

3. Chicarino, V., Albuquerque, C., Jesus, E., Rocha, A.: On the detection of selfish mining and stalker attacks in blockchain networks. Annals of Telecommunications, 143–152 (2020). https://doi.org/10.1007/s12243-019-00746-2
4. Eyal, I., Sirer, E.G.: Majority is not enough: Bitcoin mining is vulnerable. In: Springer, Berlin, Heidelberg (2013)
5. Eyal, I.: The miner's dilemma. In: Peisert, S. (ed.) IEEE Symposium on Security and Privacy, pp. 89–103. IEEE, Berkeley, California, USA (2015)
6. Gao, S., Li, Z., Peng, Z., Xiao, B.: Power adjusting and bribery racing: Novel mining attacks in the bitcoin system. In: Cavallaro, L., Kinder, J. (eds.) Proceedings of the 2019 ACM SIGSAC Conference on Computer and Communications Security, pp. 833–850. Association for Computing Machinery, New York, United States (2019)
7. Grunspan, C., Pérez-Marco, R.: Selfish mining in ethereum. In: Mathematical Research for Blockchain Economy, pp. 65–90. Springer (2020)
8. Hou, C., et al.: Squirrl: Automating attack analysis on blockchain incentive mechanisms with deep reinforcement learning (2019)
9. Iadine, C., Guillaume, C., Marie-Josée, C., Frédérick, G., Régis, S.: Mdptoolbox: a multi-platform toolbox to solve stochastic dynamic programming problems. Ecography **37**(9), 916–920 (2014)
10. Juels, A., Kosba, A., Shi, E.: The ring of gyges: Investigating the future of criminal smart contracts. In: Proceedings of the 2016 ACM SIGSAC Conference on Computer and Communications Security, pp. 283–295. ACM (2016)
11. Kwon, Y., Kim, D., Son, Y., Vasserman, E., Kim, Y.: Be selfish and avoid dilemmas: Fork after withholding (faw) attacks on bitcoin. In: Thuraisingham, B. (ed.) Proceedings of the 2017 ACM SIGSAC Conference on Computer and Communications Security, pp. 195–209. Association for Computing Machinery, New York, United States (2017)
12. Li, T., et al.: Rational protocols and attacks in blockchain system. Secur. Commun. Networks (2020). https://doi.org/10.1155/2020/8839047
13. Luu, L., Saha, R., Parameshwaran, I., Saxena, P., Hobor, A.: On power splitting games in distributed computation: The case of bitcoin pooled mining. In: Fournet, C., Hicks, M. (eds.) 2015 IEEE 28th Computer Security Foundations Symposium, pp. 397–411. IEEE, Berkeley, California, USA (2015)
14. Niu, J., Feng, C.: Selfish mining in ethereum. In: 2019 IEEE 39th International Conference on Distributed Computing Systems (ICDCS), pp. 1306–1316. IEEE (2019)
15. Ritz, F., Zugenmaier, A.: The impact of uncle rewards on selfish mining in ethereum. In: 2018 IEEE European Symposium on Security and Privacy Workshops (EuroS&PW), pp. 50–57. IEEE (2018)
16. Saad, M., Njilla, L., Kamhoua, C., Mohaisen, A.: Countering selfish mining in blockchains. In: 2019 International Conference on Computing, Networking and Communications (ICNC), pp. 360–364. IEEE (2019)
17. Sapirshtein, A., Sompolinsky, Y., Zohar, A.: Optimal selfish mining strategies in bitcoin. Springer, Heidelberg (2016)
18. Solat, S., Potop-Butucaru, M.: Zeroblock: preventing selfish mining in bitcoin. ArXiv abs/1605.02435 (2016)
19. Sun, H., Ruan, N., Su, C.: How to Model the Bribery Attack: A Practical Quantification Method in Blockchain (2020)
20. Wang, Y., Bracciali, A., Li, T., Li, F., Cui, X., Zhao, M.: Randomness invalidates criminal smart contracts. Inf. Sci. **447**, 291–301 (2019)

21. Wang, Y., et al.: Optimal mixed block withholding attacks based on reinforcement learning. Int. J. Intell. Syst. **35**(12), 2032–2048 (2020). https://doi.org/10.1002/int.22282
22. Yang, G., Wang, Y., Wang, Z., Tian, Y., Yu, X., Li, S.: Ipbsm: an optimal bribery selfish mining in the presence of intelligent and pure attackers. Int. J. Intell. Syst. **35**(11), 1735–1748 (2020). https://doi.org/10.1002/int.22270

The Theoretical Analysis
of Multi-dividing Ontology Learning
by Rademacher Vector

Linli Zhu[1]([✉]) [iD] and Wei Gao[2] [iD]

[1] School of Computer Engineering, Jiangsu University of Technology,
Changzhou 213001, China
zhulinli@jsut.edu.cn
[2] School of Information Science and Technology, Yunnan Normal University,
Kunming 650500, China
gaowei@ynnu.edu.cn

Abstract. Generally, to express the hierarchical and categorical relationship between concepts, the ontology structure is often expressed as a tree diagram. The multi-dividing ontology learning algorithm makes full use of the characteristics of the tree structure ontology graph, and then plays a role in the engineering field. The main contribution of this paper is to use the Rademacher vector method to perform theoretical analysis on the multi-dividing ontology learning algorithm and obtain the error bound estimate for U-statistic criterion. The main proof tricks are to use the skills of statistical learning theory and McDiarmid's inequality.

Keywords: Ontology · Learning · Multi-dividing · Rademacher vector

1 Introduction

With the improvement of hardware facilities and the development of corresponding social service algorithms, the amount of data that users or third-party manager need to represent and process is increasing. At the same time, the data structure is becoming more and more complex as well. Under these circumstances, a tool is needed to solve the problem of structured representation of data and provide effective services for various application backgrounds. As a graph structure data storage and representation model, ontology is well qualified for various data representation tasks and provides algorithmic support for corresponding application scenes. For example, multiple clients have their own data, and assume that they are willing to share data with each other. Under this setting, the data of each clinet is structured and represented by the ontology, and the ontology data of different users are communicated with each other using ontology alignment and ontology mapping, thereby establishing a connection and turning each client's small data into the entire network big data.

Y. Tan et al. (Eds.): DMBD 2021, CCIS 1453, pp. 11–22, 2021.
https://doi.org/10.1007/978-981-16-7476-1_2

Since the new century, ontology has always been a hot issue in the field of computer and related engineering applications. Osman et al. [1] provided a comprehensive overview from various ontology integration aspects. Akremi and Zghal [2] proposed a generic trick of fuzzification which permits a semantic expression of fuzzy and crisp information in a special ontology. Ben Elhadj et al. [3] presented an ontology-based healthcare surveillance system which supported the chronic diseases. Das and Swain [4] suggested a decision making system for assembly variant design in terms of ontology tricks. Dimassi et al. [5] raised ontology modelling for logical and semantic representation of transformable things and applied to application of product-process designing. Norris et al. [6] developed a trick to engage expert stakeholders in ontology development. Hastings et al. [7] studied the applicability of machine learning to structure-based classification of chemical ontology. Martin-Lammerding et al. [8] presented an ontology-based path programming adaptive system which is combined with the UAS payload that provides automatic flight replanning. Yadav and Duhan [9] introduced a partition-based ontology matching system for dealing with parallel division of ontology at multiple levels. Almendros-Jimenez and Becerra-Teron [10] raised ontology and restricting deducing based tricks for the diagnosis and discovery of error queries in SPARQL.

Since ontology is a conceptual model, various ontology algorithms and applications are developed focusing on the calculation of semantic similarity of concepts. From this perspective, the task of ontology machine learning algorithm is to get ontology concept similarity calculation function through ontology samples. Through observation, it is not difficult to notice that the concepts in the same field can be divided into several levels, and can be divided into several major categories, and the concepts in each major category can be divided into several subcategories. In this way, as the ontology of conceptual structural representation, its graph structure often presents a tree structure. For example, the famous genetics "GO" ontology and botany "PO" ontology are typical tree ontology. The multi-dividing ontology learning algorithm is a learning technique designed specifically for the tree-structured ontology graph. Its basic idea is to divide ontology concepts into several categories according to the graph structure, and the similarity between similar concepts is greater than the similarity between heterogeneous concepts. In the preprocessing process, the ontology vertices are represented by multi-dimensional vectors, so the ontology function obtained through learning is essentially a dimensionality reduction operator, which reduces the information corresponding to each ontology concept from a multi-dimensional space to a one-dimensional space. Finally, the similarity of ontology concepts is measured according to one-dimensional distance. The smaller the distance, the greater the similarity, and the greater the distance, the smaller the similarity.

Regarding the engineering application of the multi-dividing ontology learning algorithm, several related literatures have verified its accuracy. However, the theoretical research only stays within a few basic frameworks (see Gao et al. [11], Gao and Farahani [12], and Zhu and Hua [13]), and the theoretical characteristics of multi-dividing ontology learning under most settings are still to be studied. In this work, we focus on the theoretical analysis of multi-dividing ontology algorithm, and the error bound for multi-dividing ontology learning by Rademacher vector is given.

The rest of this paper is arranged as follows: the setting of the multi-dividing ontology learning problem is described in Sect. 2, including the concepts and notions; then the main results and proofs are determined in Sect. 3.

2 Ontology Learning Framework in Multi-dividing Setting and Prerequisite Knowledge

Let $V \subset \mathbb{R}^d$ $(d \in \mathbb{N})$ denote the instance space for ontology graph, and the vertices in V are drawn randomly and independently according to a certain unknown distribution $\mathcal{D}$. Given a training set $S = \{v_1, \cdots, v_n\}$ with capacity n, the purpose of ontology learning algorithms is to yield a score function $f : V \rightarrow \mathbb{R}$, which assigns a score to each vertex, and the similarity between v_i and v_j is determined in terms of $|f(v_i) - f(v_j)|$. In multi-dividing ontology setting, the vertices are divided into k categories and the learner is given examples of vertices labeled as these k classes.

Formally, the ontology sample in multi-dividing setting is denoted by $(S_1, S_2, \cdots, S_k) \in V^{n_1} \times V^{n_2} \times \cdots \times V^{n_k}$ which consists of a sequence of sub-sample sets $S_a = (v_1^a, \cdots, v_{n_a}^a)$ $(1 \leq a \leq k)$. The aim is to derive from these samples a real-valued ontology score function $f : V \rightarrow \mathbb{R}$ that orders the future S_a vertices bigger value than $S_{a'}$ where $a < a'$. Let $\mathcal{D}_a$ be the marginal distribution for $a \in \{1, \cdots, k\}$.

The ontology loss function l in this paper is a kernel function which is used to penalize the inconsistent case where $\mathrm{sgn}(f(v) - f(v'))$ is not coincided with their category relationships, where $\mathrm{sgn}(u) = \begin{cases} 1, & u > 0 \\ 0, & u = 0 \\ -1, & u < 0 \end{cases}$.

Hájek [14] introduced the Hájek projection which is stated in the following, and it will be used in the proving of our main result.

Lemma 1 (Hájek [14]). *Let $X_1, \cdots, X_n$ be independent random variables and $T_n = T_n(X_1, \cdots, X_n)$ be a real-valued square integrable statistic. The Hájek projection of T_n is denoted by $\widehat{T}_n = \sum_{i=1}^{n} \mathbb{E}[T_b | X_i] - (n-1)\mathbb{E}[T]$ which is the orthogonal projection of the square integrable random variables T_n onto the subspace of all variables with form $\sum_{i=1}^{n} g_i(X_i)$ for any measurable functions g_i satisfying $\mathbb{E}[g_i^2(X_i)] < +\infty$.*

U-statistics is a common statistical learning method, which is widely used in various algorithms and engineering applications (see Fuchs et al. [15], Goyal and Kumar [16], Benes et al. [17], Bouzebda and Nemouchi [18], and Privault and Serafin [19] for its theory and applications). Specifically, we consider an independent and identically distributed sequence $X_1, \cdots, X_n$ ($n \geq 2$ is an integer) drawn from a probability distribution $\mathcal{D}$ on a measurable space V and $\mathcal{K} : V^2 \to \mathbb{R}$ a square integrable function with respect to $\mathcal{D} \times \mathcal{D}$. The U-statistic of kernel function $\mathcal{K}$ relies on the V_i's is formulated by

$$U_n(\mathcal{K}) = \frac{1}{n(n-1)} \sum_{1 \le i,j \le n, i \neq j} \mathcal{K}(V_i, V_j). \tag{1}$$

Here, $U_n(\mathcal{K})$ is the unbiased estimator of the parameter $\theta(\mathcal{K}) = \int \mathcal{K}(v_1, v_2)\mathcal{D}(dv_1)\mathcal{D}(dv_2)$ with minimum variance, and the corresponding Hájek projection can be denoted by the following statement: the projection of $U_n(\mathcal{K}) - \theta(\mathcal{K})$ onto the space of all random variables $\sum_{i=1}^n g_i(V_i)$ with $\int g_i^2(v)\mathcal{D}(dv) < +\infty$ is $\widehat{U}_n(\mathcal{K}) = \frac{1}{n}\mathcal{K}_1(X_i)$, with $\mathcal{K}_1 = k_{1,1} + \mathcal{K}_{1,2}$, $\mathcal{K}_{1,1}(x) = \mathbb{E}[\mathcal{K}(V_1, v)] - \theta$ and $\mathcal{K}_{1,2}(v) = \mathbb{E}[\mathcal{K}(v, V_2)] - \theta$ for all $v \in V$. The U-statistic (1) is degenerated if $\mathbb{P}\{\mathcal{K}_{1,l}(V_1) = 0\} = 1$. Thus, the U-statistic (1) can be formulated as the independent and identically distributed average $\widehat{U}_n(h)$ which adds a degenerate U-statistic.

The U-statistics in multi-dividing ontology setting can be described in the following definition.

Definition 1. *Let k be an integer, $n_1, \cdots, n_k$ in $\mathbb{N}$. Consider k independent and identically distributed sequences $\{V_1^1, \cdots, V_{n_1}^1\}, \cdots, \{V_1^k, \cdots, V_{n_k}^k\}$, respectively drawn from probability distributions $\mathcal{D}_a$ on the measurable spaces V^a for $a \in \{1, \cdots, k\}$. Let $l : V^a \times V^b \to \mathbb{R}$ be a square integrable function with respect to $V^a \otimes V^b$, where $a, b \in \mathbb{N}$ and $1 \le a < b \le k$. The U-statistic of degree $(1,1)$ in multi-dividing ontology setting with loss kernel function $l(v, v')$ and ontology sample data V_i^a's ($a \in \{1, \cdots, k\}$ and $i \in \{1, \cdots, n_a\}$) is stated by*

$$U_{n_1, \cdots, n_k}(l) = \sum_{a=1}^{k-1} \sum_{b=a+1}^{k} \frac{1}{n_a n_b} \sum_{i=1}^{n_a} \sum_{j=1}^{n_b} l(f, v_i^a, v_j^b). \tag{2}$$

Furthermore, for special pair of (a, b) with $1 \le a < b \le k$, we denote

$$U_{n_1, \cdots, n_k}^{a,b}(l) = \frac{1}{n_a n_b} \sum_{i=1}^{n_a} \sum_{j=1}^{n_b} l(f, v_i^a, v_j^b).$$

For instance, the ontology loss kernel can set $l(v^a, v^b) = I\{f(v^a) > f(v^b)\} + \frac{1}{2}I\{f(v^a) = f(v^b)\}$ on $\mathbb{R}^2$ and degree $(1,1)$. In this example, the I is the truth function. The Hájek projection of (2) can be determined by calculating the orthogonal projection of the recentered random variables $U_{n_1, \cdots, n_k}(l) - \mathbb{E}[U_{n_1, \cdots, n_k}(l)]$ onto the subspace of L_2 composed of all random variables $\sum_{a=1}^{k-1} \sum_{b=a+1}^{k} \sum_{i=1}^{n_a} g_i(v_i^a) + \sum_{j=1}^{n_b} f_j(v_j^b)$ with $\int (g_i^a)^2(v^a)\mathcal{D}_a(dv^a) < +\infty$ and $\int (f_j^b)^2(v^b)\mathcal{D}_b(dv^b) < +\infty$. That is to say, $\widehat{U}_{n_1, \cdots, n_k}(l) = \sum_{a=1}^{k-1} \sum_{b=a+1}^{k} \frac{1}{n_a} \sum_{i=1}^{n_a} l_{1,1}^{a,b}(v_i^a) + \frac{1}{n_b} \sum_{j=1}^{n_b} l_{1,2}^{a,b}(v_j^b)$ with $l_{1,1}^{a,b}(v^a) = \mathbb{E}[l(v^a, v^b)] - \mathbb{E}[U_{n_1, \cdots, n_k}^{a,b}(l)]$ and $l_{1,2}^{a,b}(v^b) = \mathbb{E}[l(v^a, v^b)] - E[U_{n_1, \cdots, n_k}^{a,b}(l)]$ for all

$(v^a, v^b) \in V^a \times V^b$. The multi-dividing ontology U-statistic $U_{n_1, \cdots, n_k}(l)$ is degenerate if the random variables $\mathbb{P}\{l_{1,1}^{a,b}(v^a) = 0\} = 1$ and $\mathbb{P}\{l_{1,2}(v^b) = 0\} = 1$ for each pair of (a, b) with $1 \le a < b \le k$. Similar to (1), the recentered version of the multi-dividing ontology U-statistic of degree (1,1) (2) can be formulated by a summation of independent and identically distributed averages $\widehat{U}_{n_1, \cdots, n_k}(l)$ add a degenerate multi-dividing ontology U-statistic.

A class $\mathcal{F}$ of real-valued functions on a measurable space X is called a bounded VC-type class with parameter $(B, \mathcal{J}) \in (0, +\infty)^2$ and a positive constant $L_{\mathcal{F}}$ if for any $0 < \varepsilon < 1$, we have

$$\sup_{\mathcal{D}} \mathcal{N}(\mathcal{F}, L_2(\mathcal{D}), \varepsilon L_{\mathcal{F}}) \le \left(\frac{B}{\varepsilon}\right)^{\mathcal{J}}, \tag{3}$$

where the supremum is taken over all probability measures $\mathcal{D}$ on X and the covering number $\mathcal{N}(\mathcal{F}, L_2(\mathcal{D}), \varepsilon L_{\mathcal{F}})$ is denoted by the smallest number of $L_2(\mathcal{D})$-balls with radius less than ε which covers the function space $\mathcal{F}$.

In order to prove our main conclusions in next section, we introduce independent Rademacher variables "$\varepsilon_1^a, \cdots, \varepsilon_{n_a}^a$" for $a \in \{1, \cdots, k\}$ and define

$$T_{n_1, \cdots, n_k}(l) = \sum_{a=1}^{k-1} \sum_{b=a+1}^{k} \frac{1}{n_a n_b} \sum_{i=1}^{n_a} \sum_{j=1}^{n_b} \varepsilon_i^a \varepsilon_j^b l(f, v_i^a, v_j^b). \tag{4}$$

for all $l \in \mathcal{L}$. Specially, for each pair of (a, b) with $1 \le a < b \le k$, set

$$T_{n_1, \cdots, n_k}^{a,b}(l) = \frac{1}{n_a n_b} \sum_{i=1}^{n_a} \sum_{j=1}^{n_b} \varepsilon_i^a \varepsilon_j^b l(f, v_i^a, v_j^b).$$

3   Main Result and Proof

In this section, we aim to present the main results and we began at the following lemmas.

Lemma 2. *Let $\mathcal{D}_a$ be probability distributions on measurable spaces V^a for $a \in \{1, \cdots, k\}$. Considering the degenerate multi-dividing ontology U-statistic of degree (1,1) (2) with a bounded kernel $l : V^a \times V^b \to \mathbb{R}$ relied on the independent and identically distributed random ontology samples $v_1^a, \cdots, v_{n_a}^a$ drawn from $\mathcal{D}_a$ where $a \in \{1, \cdots, k\}$. Let ontology independent and identically distributed Rademacher variables $\varepsilon_1^a, \cdots, \varepsilon_{n_a}^a$, independent of the v_i^a's for $i \in \{1, \cdots, n_a\}$ and $a \in \{1, \cdots, k\}$, such that the randomized process (4) is defined. If the suprema is measurable and the expectations exist, then for any increasing convex function $\Psi : \mathbb{R} \to \mathbb{R}$, we have*

$$\mathbb{E}[\Psi(\sup_{l \in \mathcal{L}} |U_{n_1, \cdots, n_k}(l)|)] \le \mathbb{E}[\Psi(4 \sup_{l \in \mathcal{L}} |T_{n_1, \cdots, n_k}(l)|)] \tag{5}$$

and

$$\mathbb{E}[\Psi(\sup_{l \in \mathcal{L}} U_{n_1, \cdots, n_k}(l))] \le \mathbb{E}[\Psi(4 \sup_{l \in \mathcal{L}} T_{n_1, \cdots, n_k}(l))]. \tag{6}$$

Proof of Lemma 2. We only show the proofing details of the first inequality, and the second one can be done using the same fashion. By means of the independence of the multi-dividing ontology samples in each class, Fubini's theorem and the degeneracy property, we infer

$$\mathbb{E}[\Psi(\sup_{l\in\mathcal{L}}|U_{n_1,\cdots,n_k}(l)|)]$$

$$= \mathbb{E}[\mathbb{E}[\Psi(\sup_{l\in\mathcal{L}}|\sum_{a=1}^{k-1}\sum_{b=a+1}^{k}(\frac{1}{n_a n_b}\sum_{i=1}^{n_a}\sum_{j=1}^{n_b}l(f,v_i^a,v_j^b)$$

$$|v_1^b,v_2^b,\cdots,v_{n_b}^b)|)]]$$

$$\leq \mathbb{E}[\Psi(2\sup_{l\in\mathcal{L}}|\sum_{a=1}^{k-1}\sum_{b=a+1}^{k}\frac{1}{n_a n_b}\sum_{i=1}^{n_a}\varepsilon_i^a\sum_{j=1}^{n_b}l(f,v_i^a,v_j^b)|)]$$

$$= \mathbb{E}[\mathbb{E}[\Psi(2\sup_{l\in\mathcal{L}}|\sum_{a=1}^{k-1}\sum_{b=a+1}^{k}(\frac{1}{n_a n_b}\sum_{j=1}^{n_b}(\sum_{i=1}^{n_a}\varepsilon_i^a l(f,v_i^a,v_j^b))$$

$$|(v_1^a,\varepsilon_1^a),(v_2^a,\varepsilon_2^a),\cdots,(v_{n_a}^a,\varepsilon_{n_a}^a))|)]]$$

$$\leq \mathbb{E}[\Psi(4\sup_{l\in\mathcal{L}}|\sum_{a=1}^{k-1}\sum_{b=a+1}^{k}\frac{1}{n_a n_b}\sum_{j=1}^{n_b}\varepsilon_j^b(\sum_{i=1}^{n_a}\varepsilon_i^a l(f,v_i^a,v_j^b))|)]$$

$$= \mathbb{E}[\Psi(4\sup_{l\in\mathcal{L}}|T_{n_1,\cdots,n_k}(l)|)].$$

Notably, we also deduce that

$$\mathbb{E}[\Psi(\frac{1}{4}\sup_{l\in\mathcal{L}}|T_{n_1,\cdots,n_k}(l)|)] \leq \mathbb{E}[\Psi(\sup_{l\in\mathcal{L}}|U_{n_1,\cdots,n_k}(l)|)].$$

Thus, we complete the proof of Lemma 2.   □

The next lemma manifested an exponential bound for degenerate multi-dividing ontology U-statistics with bounded kernel ontology loss functions.

Lemma 3. *Let $\mathcal{D}_a$ be probability distributions on measurable ontology data spaces V^a for $a \in \{1,\cdots,k\}$. Considering the degenerate multi-dividing U-statistic of degree (1,1) (2) with a bounded kernel $l : V^a \times V^b \to \mathbb{R}$ relied on the independent and identically distributed random samples $V_1^a,\cdots,V_{n_a}^a$ drawn from $\mathcal{D}_a$ where $a \in \{1,\cdots,k\}$. For all $t > 0$, we then have:*

$$\mathbb{P}\{U_{n_1,\cdots,n_k}(l) \geq t\} \leq \exp\{\frac{-\binom{k}{2}n_{\min}^2 t^2}{32c_t^2}\}, \tag{7}$$

where $n_{\min} = \min\{n_1,\cdots,n_k\}$ and $c_t = \sup_{(v,v')\in V^a\times V^b, 1\leq a<b\leq k}|l(v,v')| < \infty$.

Proof of Lemma 3. Let any $t > 0$ and $\lambda > 0$, we get

$$\mathbb{P}\{U_{n_1,\cdots,n_k}(l) \geq t\} \tag{8}$$
$$\leq \exp\{-\lambda t + \log(\mathbb{E}[\exp\{\lambda U_{n_1,\cdots,n_k}(l)\}])\}$$
$$\leq \exp\{-\lambda t + \log(\mathbb{E}[\exp\{4\lambda T_{n_1,\cdots,n_k}(l)\}])\}.$$

in light of (6) with $\Psi(t) = \exp(\lambda t)$. It is almost hold that

$$\mathbb{E}[\exp\{4\lambda T_{n_1,\cdots,n_k}(l)\}]$$
$$= \prod_{a=1}^{k-1} \prod_{b=a+1}^{k} \prod_{i=1}^{n_a} \prod_{j=1}^{n_b} \frac{\exp\{\frac{4\lambda l(v_i^a,v_j^b)}{n_a n_b}\} + \exp\{\frac{-4\lambda l(v_i^a,v_j^b)}{n_a n_b}\}}{2}$$
$$\leq \prod_{a=1}^{k-1} \prod_{b=a+1}^{k} \prod_{i=1}^{n_a} \prod_{j=1}^{n_b} \exp\{\frac{8\lambda^2 l^2(v_i^a,v_j^b)}{(n_a n_b)^2}\}$$
$$\leq \prod_{a=1}^{k-1} \prod_{b=a+1}^{k} \exp\{\frac{8\lambda^2 c_t^2}{n_a n_b}\}$$
$$\leq \exp\{\frac{8\binom{k}{2}\lambda^2 c_t^2}{n_{\min}^2}\},$$

in view of the fact that $\frac{\exp\{x\}+\exp\{-x\}}{2} \leq \exp\{\frac{x^2}{2}\}$ for any $x \in \mathbb{R}$. Combining the bound over the v_i^a's and v_j^b's and putting it into (8) gets the result by selecting $\lambda = \frac{n_{\min}^2 t}{16 c_t^2}$. $\qquad\square$

For the proof of the main theorem, we still lack the following links.

Lemma 4. *Let $\mathcal{D}_a$ be probability distributions on measurable ontology spaces V^a ($a \in \{1,\cdots,k\}$). Considering the degenerate multi-dividing ontology U-statistic of degree (1,1) (2) with a bounded kernel ontology loss $l : V^a \times V^b \to \mathbb{R}$ based on the independent and identically distributed random ontology samples $V_1^a,\cdots,V_{n_a}^a$ drawn from $\mathcal{D}_a$ where $a \in \{1,\cdots,k\}$. Let sequences of independent and identically distributed Rademacher variables $\varepsilon_1^a,\cdots,\varepsilon_{n_a}^a$, independent of the v_i^a's for $i \in \{1,\cdots,n_a\}$ and $a \in \{1,\cdots,k\}$, such that the randomized process (4) is defined. Then for any $t > 0$, we get*

$$\mathbb{P}\{\sup_{l \in \mathcal{L}} |U_{n_1,\cdots,n_k}(l)| \geq 16t\} \leq 16\mathbb{P}\{\sup_{l \in \mathcal{L}} |T_{n_1,\cdots,n_k}(l)| \geq t\} \tag{9}$$

if the suprema is measurable and that the expectations exist.

Proof of Lemma 4. For any $t > 0$, we get

$$\mathbb{P}\{\sup_{l \in \mathcal{L}} |U_{n_1,\cdots,n_k}(l)| \geq 16t\}$$

$$= \mathbb{E}[\mathbb{P}(\sup_{l \in \mathcal{L}} |\sum_{a=1}^{k-1} \sum_{b=a+1}^{k} \frac{1}{n_a} \sum_{i=1}^{n_a} \{\frac{1}{n_b} \sum_{j=1}^{n_b} l(f, v_i^a, v_j^b)\}| \geq 16t)]$$

$$\leq \mathbb{E}[\mathbb{P}(\sum_{a=1}^{k-1} \sum_{b=a+1}^{k} \{\sup_{l \in \mathcal{L}} |\frac{1}{n_a} \sum_{i=1}^{n_a} \{\frac{1}{n_b} \sum_{j=1}^{n_b} l(f, v_i^a, v_j^b)\}| \geq 16t\}$$

$$|v_1^b, v_2^b, v_{n_b}^b)]$$

$$\leq 4\mathbb{E}[\mathbb{P}(\sum_{a=1}^{k-1} \sum_{b=a+1}^{k} \{\sup_{l \in \mathcal{L}} |\frac{1}{n_a} \sum_{i=1}^{n_a} \{\frac{1}{n_b} \sum_{j=1}^{n_b} \varepsilon_i^a l(f, v_i^a, v_j^b)\}| \geq 4t\}$$

$$|v_1^b, v_2^b, v_{n_b}^b)]$$

$$\leq 4\mathbb{E}[\mathbb{P}(\sum_{a=1}^{k-1} \sum_{b=a+1}^{k} \{\sup_{l \in \mathcal{L}} |\frac{1}{n_a} \sum_{j=1}^{n_b} \{\frac{1}{n_a} \sum_{i=1}^{n_a} \varepsilon_i^a l(f, v_i^a, v_j^b)\}| \geq 4t\}$$

$$|(v_1^a, \varepsilon_1^a), \cdots, (v_{n_a}^a, \varepsilon_{n_a}^a))]$$

$$\leq 16\mathbb{P}\{\sup_{l \in \mathcal{L}} |T_{n_1,\cdots,n_k}(l)| \geq t\}.$$

Hence, Lemma 4 is hold. □

Now, our main result is stated as follows which is a nonasymptotic conclusion for degenerate multi-dividing ontology U-processes of degree $(1, 1)$.

Theorem 1. *Let* $n_1, \cdots, n_k \in \mathbb{N}$. *Considering two independent and identically distributed multi-dividing ontology random samples* $\{V_1^1, \cdots, V_{n_1}^1\}$, $\cdots$, $\{V_1^k, \cdots, V_{n_k}^k\}$ *respectively drawn from the probability distributions* $\mathcal{D}_a$ *on the measurable spaces* V^a *for* $a \in \{1, \cdots, k\}$. *Let* $\mathcal{L}$ *be a class of degenerate nonsymmetrical kernels* $l : V^a \times V^b \to \mathbb{R}$ *such that* $\sup(v^a, v^b) \in V^a \times V^b |l(v^a, v^b)| \leq L < +\infty$ *and* $\int_{V^a \times V^b} l^2(v^a, v^b) \mathcal{D}_a(dv^a) \mathcal{D}_b(dv^b) \leq \sigma^2 \leq L^2$, *that defines a degenerate multi-dividing ontology U-process of degree (1,1), based on the* V_i^a, V_j^b'*s:* $\{U_{n_1,\cdots,n_k}(l) : l \in \mathcal{L}\}$. *Set* $n_{\min} = \min\{n_1, \cdots, n_k\}$. *Suppose in addition that the class* $\mathcal{L}$ *is of VC-type with parameters* $(B, \mathcal{J})$. *Then, for any* $t > 0$, *there is a constant* $K > 2$ *such that:*

$$\mathbb{P}\{\sup_{l \in \mathcal{L}} |U_{n_1,\cdots,n_k}(l)| \geq t\} \leq K2^{\mathcal{J}} (\frac{B}{L})^{2\mathcal{J}} \exp\{\frac{4}{L^2}\} \exp\{-\frac{\binom{k}{2} n_{\min} t^2}{2048 L^2}\}, \quad (10)$$

for any $\binom{k}{2} n_{\min}^2 t^2 > \max(4096 \log(2) L^2 \mathcal{J}, (\frac{\log(2) L^2 \mathcal{J}}{2})^{1+\delta}), \delta \in (1, 2)$ *is a constant.*

Proof of Theorem 1. The proof approach mainly depends on the chaining tricks applied to $U_{n_1,\cdots,n_k}(l)$ with ontology kernel loss functions $\mathcal{L}$. Introduce the random semi-metric on $\mathcal{L}$ which is formulated by

$$d^2(l_1, l_2) = \sum_{a=1}^{k-1} \sum_{b=a+1}^{k} \frac{1}{n_a n_b} \sum_{i=1}^{n_a} \sum_{j=1}^{n_b} (l_1(f, v_i^a, v_j^b) - l_2(f, v_i^a, v_j^b))^2 \qquad (11)$$

for all ontology kernel loss functions $l_1, l_2 \in \mathcal{L}$. For any $q \in \mathbb{N}$, set a number $h_q \le (\frac{B}{\varepsilon_q})^{\mathcal{J}}$ of L_2-balls with radius $\varepsilon_q \le L \le 1$ and centers $l_{q,h}$, $1 \le h \le h_q$ with respect to random probability measure $\sum_{a=1}^{k-1} \sum_{b=a+1}^{k} \frac{1}{n_a n_b} \sum_{i=1}^{n_a} \sum_{j=1}^{n_b} \delta_{v_i^a, v_j^b}$ covering the class $\mathcal{L}$. Suppose the sequence ε_q is decreasing as q increases, and hence h_q is increasing. Let $l \in \mathcal{L}$, $q \ge 1$ and $\tilde{l}_q$ be the center of a ball with $d(l, \tilde{l}_q) \le \varepsilon_q$. Given $q_0 \le q$ in $\mathbb{N}$, we yield

$$U_{n_1,\cdots,n_k}(l) = (U_{n_1,\cdots,n_k}(l) - U_{n_1,\cdots,n_k}(\tilde{l}_{q_0})) + U_{n_1,\cdots,n_k}(\tilde{l}_{q_0})$$

$$+ \sum_{\omega=q_0+1}^{q} (U_{n_1,\cdots,n_k}(\tilde{l}_\omega) - U_{n_1,\cdots,n_k}(\tilde{l}_{\omega-1})).$$

For arbitrary $l \in \mathcal{L}$, the following inequality almost hold:

$$|U_{n_1,\cdots,n_k}(l) - U_{n_1,\cdots,n_k}(\tilde{l}_q)| \le d(l, \tilde{l}_q) \le \varepsilon_q.$$

Hence, we have

$$\|U_{n_1,\cdots,n_k}(l)\|_{\mathcal{L}} \le \varepsilon_q + \max_{1 \le d \le d_{q_0}} |U_{n_1,\cdots,n_k}(l_{q_0,h})| + \sum_{\omega=q_0+1}^{q} \|U_{n_1,\cdots,n_k}(\tilde{l}_\omega) - U_{n_1,\cdots,n_k}(\tilde{l}_{\omega-1})\|_{\mathcal{L}},$$

where $\|Z\|_{\mathcal{L}} = \sup_{l \in \mathcal{L}} |Z(l)|$ for any real-valued stochastic Pprocess Z with $\mathcal{L}$. Considering positive constants η_ω and γ with $\sum_{\omega=q_0+1}^{q} \eta_\omega + \gamma \le 1$, then for any $t > \varepsilon_q$ we obtain

$$\mathbb{P}\{\|U_{n_1,\cdots,n_k}(l)\|_{\mathcal{L}} \ge 16t\} \le \sum_{h=1}^{h_{q_0}} \mathbb{P}\{|U_{n_1,\cdots,n_k}(l_{q_0,h})| \ge 16t\gamma\} \qquad (12)$$

$$+ 16 \sum_{\omega=q_0+1}^{q} h_\omega^2 \mathbb{E}[\sup_{l \in \mathcal{L}} \mathbb{P}\{|T_{n_1,\cdots,n_k}(l) - U_{n_1,\cdots,n_k}(\tilde{l}_\omega - \tilde{l}_{\omega-1})| \ge t\eta_\omega\}].$$

By means of Lemma 3, the first term on the right hand side of (12) can be bounded by

$$\sum_{h=1}^{d_{q_0}} \mathbb{P}\{|U_{n_1,\cdots,n_k}(l_{q_0,h})| \ge 16t\gamma\} \le 2h_{q_0} \exp\{-\frac{-8\binom{k}{2} n_{\min}^2 (t\gamma)^2}{L^2}\}. \qquad (13)$$

On the second term, note that

$$d(\tilde{l}_\omega, \tilde{l}_{\omega-1}) \le d(l, \tilde{l}_{\omega-1}) + d(\tilde{l}_\omega, l) \le 2\varepsilon_{\omega-1}. \qquad (14)$$

In light of the proofing process of Lemma 3, for any positive λ, we verify that

$$\mathbb{P}\{T_{n_1,\cdots,n_k}(l) - U_{n_1,\cdots,n_k}(\tilde{l}_\omega - \tilde{l}_{\omega-1}) \ge t\eta_\omega\}$$

$$\le \exp\{-\lambda t\eta_\omega + \mathbb{E}\{\exp(\lambda T_{n_1,\cdots,n_k}(l) - U_{n_1,\cdots,n_k}(\tilde{l}_\omega - \tilde{l}_{\omega-1})\}\}.$$

Using the tricks as described in the proofing of Lemma 3, the following inequality is almost true:

$$\mathbb{E}\{\exp(\lambda T_{n_1,\cdots,n_k}(l) - U_{n_1,\cdots,n_k}(\tilde{l}_\omega - \tilde{l}_{\omega-1})\}$$

$$\leq \prod_{a=1}^{k-1} \prod_{b=a+1}^{k} \prod_{i=1}^{n_a} \prod_{j=1}^{n_b} \exp\{\frac{\lambda^2(\tilde{l}_\omega - \tilde{l}_{\omega-1})^2(v_i^a, v_j^b)}{2(n_a n_b)^2}\}$$

$$\leq \prod_{a=1}^{k-1} \prod_{b=a+1}^{k} \exp\{\frac{2\lambda^2 \varepsilon_{\omega-1}^2}{n_a n_b}\}$$

$$\leq \exp\{\frac{2\binom{k}{2}\lambda^2 \varepsilon_{\omega-1}^2}{n_{\min}^2}\}.$$

Combining the two bounds above together, we get

$$\mathbb{P}\{T_{n_1,\cdots,n_k}(l) - U_{n_1,\cdots,n_k}(\tilde{l}_\omega - \tilde{l}_{\omega-1}) \geq t\eta_\omega\} \leq 2\exp\{-\frac{\binom{k}{2}n_{\min}^2(t\eta_\omega)^2}{8\varepsilon_{\omega-1}^2}\}. \quad (15)$$

In terms of (12), (13) and (15), we obtain

$$\mathbb{P}\{\|U_{n_1,\cdots,n_k}(l)\|_{\mathcal{L}} \geq 16t\} \quad (16)$$

$$\leq 2h_{q_0}\exp\{-\frac{\binom{k}{2}n_{\min}^2(t\gamma)^2}{L^2}\} + 32\sum_{\omega=q_0+1}^{q} h_\omega^2 \exp\{-\frac{\binom{k}{2}n_{\min}^2(t\eta_\omega)^2}{8\varepsilon_{\omega-1}^2}\}$$

$$\leq 2B^{\mathcal{J}}\varepsilon_{q_0}^{-\mathcal{J}}\exp\{-\frac{\binom{k}{2}n_{\min}^2(t\gamma)^2}{L^2}\} + 32B^{2\mathcal{J}}\sum_{\omega=q_0+1}^{q} h_\omega^{-2\mathcal{J}} \exp\{-\frac{\binom{k}{2}n_{\min}^2(t\eta_\omega)^2}{8\varepsilon_{\omega-1}^2}\}.$$

Selecting $\varepsilon_\omega = 2^{-\omega}L$, $\eta_\omega = \frac{2^{-\omega}\sqrt{\omega}}{8}$, and hence $\eta_{\omega+1} = \frac{\sqrt{\omega+1}\varepsilon_\omega}{16L}$, we have

$$\varepsilon_\omega^{-2\mathcal{J}}\exp\{-\frac{\binom{k}{2}n_{\min}^2(t\eta_\omega)^2}{8\varepsilon_{\omega-1}^2}\} = L^{-2\mathcal{J}}\exp\{-(\frac{\binom{k}{2}n_{\min}^2 t^2}{2048L^2} - 2V\log 2)\omega\}. \quad (17)$$

If $\binom{k}{2}n_{\min}^2 t^2 > 4096\log(2)L^2\mathcal{J}$, then the terms of the series are decreasing with respect to ω and we upperbound by $K_1 L^{-2\mathcal{J}}\exp\{-(\frac{\binom{k}{2}n_{\min}^2 t^2}{2048L^2})\omega\}$. Set $\omega \in \{q_0 + 1, \cdots, q\}$ with $\Theta(\omega) = (\frac{\binom{k}{2}n_{\min}^2 t^2}{2048L^2})\omega$, we infer

$$\sum_{\omega=q_0+1}^{q} \varepsilon_\omega^2 \exp\{-\frac{\binom{k}{2}n_{\min}^2(t\eta_\omega)^2}{8\varepsilon_{\omega-1}^2}\} \quad (18)$$

$$\leq K_1 L^{-2\mathcal{J}}\Theta'(q_0)^{-1}\exp\{-\Theta(q_0)\}$$

$$\leq K_2 L^{-2(\mathcal{J}-1)}\exp\{-\frac{n_{\min}^2 t^2}{2048L^2}q_0\},$$

where K_1, K_2 are positive constants and $n_{\min}^2 t^2 \geq 1$. For large positive number α, setting $q_0 = 2 + (\binom{k}{2}n_{\min}^2 t^2)^{\frac{1}{\alpha-1}}$ gets to the upperbound

$K_2 L^{-2(\mathcal{J}-1)} \exp\{-\frac{3n_{\min}^2 t^2}{2048L^2}\}$. Setting $\gamma = \frac{1}{2} - \frac{1}{2\binom{k}{2}n_{\min}^2 t^2}$, the upper bound is given by the similar form

$$B^{\mathcal{J}} \varepsilon_{q_0}^{-\mathcal{J}} \exp\{-\frac{8\binom{k}{2}n_{\min}^2 (t\gamma)^2}{L^2}\}$$

$$\leq (\frac{B}{L})^{\mathcal{J}} \exp\{\mathcal{J}\log 2(2 + (\binom{k}{2}n_{\min}^2 t^2)^{\frac{1}{\alpha-1}}) - \frac{2\binom{k}{2}n_{\min}^2 t^2}{L^2}(1 - \frac{1}{\binom{k}{2}n_{\min}^2 t^2})^2\}$$

$$\leq (\frac{2B}{L})^{\mathcal{J}} \exp\{\frac{4}{L^2}\} \exp\{\mathcal{J}\log 2(\binom{k}{2}n_{\min}^2 t^2)^{\frac{1}{\alpha-1}}) - \frac{2\binom{k}{2}n_{\min}^2 t^2}{L^2}\}$$

$$\leq (\frac{2B}{L})^{\mathcal{J}} \exp\{\frac{4}{L^2}\} \exp\{-\frac{2\binom{k}{2}n_{\min}^2 t^2}{L^2}\},$$

when $\binom{k}{2}n_{\min}^2 t^2 > (\frac{\log(2)L^2\mathcal{J}}{2})^{1+\delta}$, $\delta = \frac{1}{\alpha-2} \in (0,1)$ for large α. Combining with (16), we deduce

$$\mathbb{P}\{\|U_{n_1,\cdots,n_k}(l)\|_{\mathcal{L}} \geq t\} \leq K2^{\mathcal{J}+1}(\frac{B}{L})^{\mathcal{J}} \exp\{\frac{4}{L^2}\} \exp\{-\frac{3\binom{k}{2}n_{\min}^2 t^2}{2048L^2}\}, \quad (19)$$

for any $\binom{k}{2}n_{\min}^2 t^2 > \max(1, 4096\log(2)L^2\mathcal{J}, (\frac{\log(2)L^2\mathcal{J}}{2})^{1+\delta})$, and $K \geq 1 + 16K_2 e^{-4}$ constant. Finally, for any $q \geq 1$ and $\sum_{\omega=q_0+1}^{q} +\gamma \leq 1$, we have

$$8 \sum_{\omega=q_0+1}^{q} \eta_\omega \leq 8 \sum_{\omega=1}^{q} \eta_\omega \leq 1 + \int_1^{\infty} 2^{-x}\sqrt{x}\,dx \leq 4. \quad (20)$$

In all, the main result is proved. □

4 Conclusion

This paper uses the method of statistical learning theory to give the generalized bound of the multi-dividing ontology learning algorithm from the perspective of probability. The difference from the past is that the method in this paper is based on another evaluation version defined by Rademacher vector, gives the relationship between them, and finally obtains the error bound. More discussion and proof on the learning algorithm of multiple segmentation ontology needs to be further studied in the future.

Acknowledgements. This research is partially supported by Modern Education Technology Research Project in Jiangsu Province (No. 2019-R-75637).

References

1. Osman, I., Ben Yahia, S., Diallo, G.: Ontology integration: approaches and challenging issues. Inf. Fusion **71**, 38–63 (2021)

2. Akremi, H., Zghal, S.: DOF: a generic approach of domain ontology fuzzification. Front. Comp. Sci. **15**(3), 1–12 (2020). https://doi.org/10.1007/s11704-020-9354-z
3. Ben Elhadj, H., Sallabi, F., Henaien, A., et al.: Do-Care: a dynamic ontology reasoning based healthcare monitoring system. Future Gener. Comput. Syst. Int. J. Escience **118**, 417–431 (2021)
4. Das, S.K., Swain, A.K.: An ontology-based framework for decision support in assembly variant design. J. Comput. Inf. Sci. Eng. **21**(2), 021007 (2021). https://doi.org/10.1115/1.4048127
5. Dimassi, S., Demoly, F., Cruz, C., et al.: An ontology-based framework to formalize and represent 4D printing knowledge in design. Comput. Ind. **126**, 103374 (2021). https://doi.org/10.1016/j.compind.2020.103374
6. Norris, E., Hastings, J., Marques, M.M.: Why and how to engage expert stake-holders in ontology development: insights from social and behavioural sciences. J. Biomed. Semantics 12(1), 4, https://doi.org/10.1186/s13326-021-00240-6
7. Hastings, J., Glauer, M., Memariani, A., Neuhaus, F., Mossakowski, T.: Learning chemistry: exploring the suitability of machine learning for the task of structure-based chemical ontology classification. J. Cheminformatics **13**(1), 1–20 (2021). https://doi.org/10.1186/s13321-021-00500-8
8. Martin-Lammerding, D., Cordoba, A., Astrain, J.J., et al.: An ontology-based system to collect WSN-UAS data effectively. IEEE Internet Things J. **8**(5), 3636–3652 (2021)
9. Yadav, U., Duhan, N.: MPP-MLO: multilevel parallel partitioning for efficiently matching large ontologies. J. Sci. Ind. Res. **80**(3), 221–229 (2021)
10. Almendros-Jimenez, J.M., Becerra-Teron, A.: Discovery and diagnosis of wrong SPARQL queries with ontology and constraint reasoning. Expert Syst. Appl. **165**, 113772 (2021). https://doi.org/10.1016/j.eswa.2020.113772
11. Gao, W., Guirao, J.L.G., Basavanagoud, B., et al.: Partial multi-dividing ontology learning algorithm. Inf. Sci. **467**, 35–58 (2018)
12. Gao, W., Farahani, M.R.: Generalization bounds and uniform bounds for multi-dividing ontology algorithms with convex ontology loss function. Comput. J. **60**(9), 1289–1299 (2017)
13. Zhu, L., Hua, G.: Theoretical perspective of multi-dividing ontology learning trick in two-sample setting. IEEE ACCESS **8**, 220703–220709 (2020)
14. Hájek, J.: Asymptotic normality of simple linear rank statistics under alternatives. Ann. Math. Stat. **39**, 325–346 (1968)
15. Fuchs, M., Hornung, R., Boulesteix, A.L., et al.: On the asymptotic behaviour of the variance estimator of a U-statistic. J. Stat. Plann. Inference **209**, 101–111 (2020)
16. Goyal, M., Kumar, N.: Nonparametric multiple sample scale testing using U-statistics. Commun. Stat.-Simulation Comput. **49**(11), 3019–3027 (2020)
17. Benes, V., Hofer-Temmel, C., Last, G., et al.: Decorrelation of a class of Gibbs particle processes and asymptotic properties of U-statistics. J. Appl. Probab. **57**(3), 928–955 (2020)
18. Bouzebda, S., Nemouchi, B.: Uniform consistency and uniform in bandwidth consistency for nonparametric regression estimates and conditional U-statistics involving functional data. J. Nonparametric Stat. **32**(2), 452–509 (2020)
19. Privault, N., Serafin, G.: Normal approximation for sums of weighted U-statistics-application to Kolmogorov bounds in random subgraph counting. Bernoulli **26**(1), 587–615 (2020)

A Group Blind Signature Scheme for Privacy Protection of Power Big Data in Smart Grid

Xiao Li, Xueqing Sun, and Fengyin Li[✉]

School of Computer Science, Qufu Normal University, Rizhao 276826, China

Abstract. With the continuous expansion of the scale of smart grid, a large amount of data is generated during the operation of smart grid. These massive electricity data can be analyzed in detail by using big data technology to promote the construction and development of smart grid. In addition to the massive data processing generated in smart grid, one of the key factors restricting the development of smart grid is the issue of privacy leakage. In order to solve the problem of user identity information and user electricity data privacy in smart grid, we propose a conditional anonymous group blind signature scheme in smart grid, and use homomorphic tag mechanism to verify the integrity of electricity data. From the safety analysis, the results show that our scheme is safe and effective.

Keywords: Smart grid · Group blind signature · Anonymous authentication · Traceability

1 Introduction

The development of Internet technology promotes the development of various industries toward automation and intelligence. The intelligent development of the electric power industry gives birth to the smart grid. "Smart grid" is defined as the automatic transmission network that can supervise and control each node. It can ensure the two-way flow of information and power throughout the transmission and distribution process from the power plant to the end user. At this stage, the scale of the smart grid is constantly expanding, and a large amount of data is generated during the operation of the smart grid. Through the analysis of these massive user data, so as to provide users with more intelligent and rational power services is the key to distinguishing smart grids from traditional power grids. The goal of the smart grid is to provide residents and commercial users with more reliable, efficient and controllable power services. However, there are many security and privacy issues in the transmission of user data in the smart grid, such as malicious tampering of electricity consumption data, eavesdropping on user privacy data, and so on. These privacy leakage issues have affected people's information on the smart grid and seriously hindered the development of the smart grid. Therefore, how to protect the privacy of user data in the smart grid has become a top priority.

It is necessary to propose a privacy protection scheme that guarantees the conditional anonymity of user identities in the smart grid, and the control center can obtain fine-grained data on the user's electricity consumption, and at the same time verify the

Y. Tan et al. (Eds.): DMBD 2021, CCIS 1453, pp. 23–34, 2021.
https://doi.org/10.1007/978-981-16-7476-1_3

integrity of the data. The group-blind signature technology [1–3] provides a new idea for us to realize the conditional anonymity and privacy protection of users in the smart grid. It has the characteristics of group signature and blind signature at the same time. Due to the high anonymity of the group-blind signature scheme and the traceability that can guarantee conditional anonymity, more and more new practical schemes are proposed by domestic and foreign scholars [4, 5], and they are applied in various fields to ensure security [6–9].

In this paper, we apply the group-blind signature scheme to the smart grid, and propose a group-blind signature scheme that realizes privacy protection in the smart grid, ensuring the conditional anonymity of user identity information and the privacy protection of consumer data. At the same time, we use the homomorphic tag mechanism to verify the integrity of user data and achieve fine-grained data aggregation.

2 Preliminaries

2.1 Group Blind Signature

A. Lysyanskaya and Z. Ramzan combined group signature and blind signature for the first time in 1998 to design the first group-blind signature scheme-Lys98 scheme [10], and used this scheme to construct an online and anonymous electronic Cash system. The scheme usually contains three entities, including group manager, group members, and external users. A standard group-blind signature scheme consists of the following five algorithms.

(1) Setup: A probabilistic polynomial algorithm is used to generate the group public key y and the group manager's management private key S_{GM}.
(2) Join: The new member interacts with the group manager, and a probabilistic polynomial algorithm generates member keys and member certificates.
(3) Sign: Group members interact with an external user, through the message m input by the external user and the signer's private key, a probabilistic polynomial algorithm generates the signature σ.
(4) Verify: Input (m, σ, y), a probabilistic polynomial algorithm to determine the correctness of the signature σ on the message m and the group public key y.
(5) Open: A probabilistic polynomial algorithm that output identify of the signer by inputting the signature σ and group manger's private key.

2.2 Schnorr Identification Protocol

Schnorr identification protocol was proposed by Claus Schnorr in [11] and its security is based on the discrete logarithm problem. We assume that Prover(P) interactive with Verifier(V) in three-rounds protocol to prove that he owns w such that $W = g^{-w} \bmod q$. The flowchart of Schnorr identification is shown in Fig. 1.

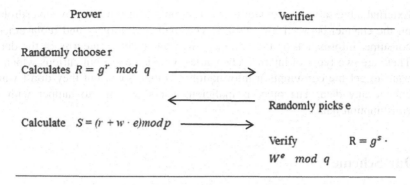

Fig. 1. The flowchart of Schnorr identification

(1) P randomly chooses number $r \in Z_q^*$ and calculates $R = g^r \; mod \; q$ then sends R to V.

(2) V randomly picks $e \in [0, 2^t - 1]$, security of the protocol is based on the parameter t, which means the protocol will be safer with the increase of t, and send e to P.

(3) P calculates $S = (r + w \cdot e) \; mod \; p$ and sends it to V.

V will verify whether the Eq. $R = g^s \cdot W^e \; mod \; q$ is set up and accept that P knows w only if the equation holds.

3 System Model and Adversary Model

3.1 System Model

The system model of the scheme in this paper involves the working relationship of the three entities. Control Center (CC), which can generate system parameters, entity registration, data validation, and conditional tracking of other entities. Smart Substation (SS), which can directly interact with the user, verify the user's identity, and generate blind signatures. Smart meters (SM), which record data in real time, regularly send a whole period consumption data, so there is a threat of data tampering. The relationship between the three entities is shown in Fig. 2. In addition, the scheme in this paper has traceability, and CC can obtain the identity of the signer or revoke the anonymity of the user when signature verification or message validation fails.

3.2 Adversary Model

The adversary of the scheme in this paper can not only eavesdrop on the channel between the user and SS, but also attempt to tamper with the data and destroy the stability of the system. There are two main types of adversaries in the adversary model, one is an external adversary who is not in the data collection model, and the other is an internal adversary who has user's identity:

(1) External adversaries can obtain user consumption information by eavesdropping on the channel between SM and SS. The malicious forgery and replacement of consumer information by the adversary will threaten the integrity of the data.

(2) There are two types of internal adversaries. One is honest but curious which they want to get the consumption information of other users, but they don't want to change any data. The other is malicious users who try to tamper with their consumption data.

4   Our Scheme

The scheme proposed in this paper includes five stages: (1) system initialization, (2) user anonymous authentication and data reporting, (3) message signatures, (4) verifying correctness of signature and integrity of data, (5) trace the signer or users. We plan to use SM_i/U_i to distinguish the different user and use the S_i to indicate the number of SS. In the phase of data reporting, for simplicity, we simulate only one case where the user reports consumption data.

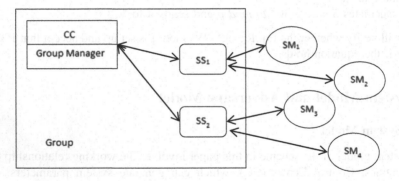

Fig. 2. Relationship between the three entities

4.1   System Initialization

(1) System parameter generation and releasing:

Step 1: CC chooses two big distinct prime p and q which satisfying $p|q - 1$ and computes $n = pq$.

Step 2: CC calculates the RSA public key pair (e, d) which satisfies $ed \equiv 1(\mod \varphi(n))$, where $\varphi(n)$ is Euler function. The group public key and group private key are e and d respectively.

Step 3: CC chooses a cyclic group $G < g >$ which is subgroup of Z_q^*. While, CC randomly chooses the element x and calculates $y = g^x \mod n$. Hence, group manager's public key and private key are y and x respectively.

Step 4: CC publicly chooses secure anti-collision hash function $H : \{0,1\}^* \rightarrow \{0,1\}^k$, $H_1 : \{0,1\}^* \rightarrow Z_q^*$.

Step 5: CC releases the public parameter $P = \{n, e, G, g, y, H, H_1\}$.

(2) The phase of registering:

Step 1: If new group member (SS) wants to join the group, SS randomly chooses the number $x_i \in Z_q^*$ and sends it to the group manager (CC). CC randomly chooses $y_i \in Z_q^*$ and calculates $C = y^{y_i}x_i \bmod n$, and $C_1 = g^{y_i} \bmod n$. The group member signed private key is y_i, the group member signed private key is C_1, Group manager Storage Group Member Certificate x_i, and returns $PK = (C, C_1)$ group member's certificate x_i and y_i to SS.

Step 2: $User_i$ opens an account in CC and gets $infor_i = (ID_i\|address\|timestack)$, CC encrypts the user information $infor_i$ to $(infor_i)^e$ with the group public key e and stores it in its own database, $User_i$ will hold the public value $gt_i = (H(infor_i)^x)$ mod n. CC installs smart meter at user's home. SM_i randomly chooses z_i to calculate $I_i = g^{z_i} \bmod n$ as his own id information and sends I_i to CC, and CC sends the value of I_i to SS.

4.2   User Anonymous Authentication and Data Reporting

(1) User anonymous authentication:

Each SM tries to convince SS that he is valid user by using Schnorr identification protocol and then send the encrypted message to SS. The detailed process is shown in the Fig. 3.

Step 1: SM_i random chooses $t_i \in Z_q^*$ and calculates $T = g^{t_i} \bmod n$ and sends to SS.

Step 2: SS calculates $c_b = H(T\|timestack)$ and sends c_b to user.

Step 3: User calculates $s_i = t_i - c_b z_i$ and sends S_i to SS.

Step 4: SS verifies the $c_b = H(g^{S_i}I_i^{c_b}\|timestack)$.

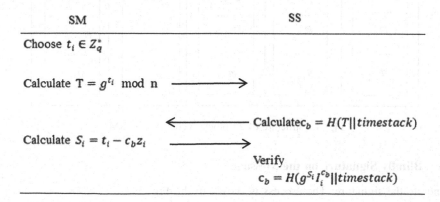

Fig. 3. User anonymous authentication

(2) Data reporting:

SS will receive the user's encrypted data after verifying the meter. Take a user $User_k$ as an example, the electricity bill data generated by one day is m.

Step 1: The number of blocks of consumption data reported per day is limited by the security parameter λ. Set the safety parameter λ to 24, SM should generate 24 data blocks a day. Structure of 24 blocks generated by SM_k shows in Fig. 4. Each block represents an hour of electricity consumption data, containing attribute values for the l dimension.

Step 2: SM generates another random number $stk \in Z_q^*$ as the secret tag key. Then SM outputs the public tag key $ptk = gt_k^{stk} \bmod n$.

Step 3: SM_k will generate l random values $\{mx_1, mx_2, mx3, \ldots \ldots, mx_l\}$ and calculate $u_j = gt_k^{mx_j} \bmod n$ for $j \in [1, l]$. For each data block m_i, it computes a data tag_i. SM_k will generate tag for every data block ($24/\lambda$/day) by calculating the $tag_i = (H(MID\|i) \cdot \prod_{j=1}^l u_j^{m_{ij}})^{stk}$, in which MID is the abstract of data and i is the block number of m_i, SM_k outputs the set of data tags Tag = $\{tag_1, tag_2, tag_3, \ldots \ldots, tag_i\}$, $i \in [1, 24/\lambda]$.

Step 4: SM encrypts (m‖tag) by using public key e. By doing so, we ensure that no other entity can learn the consumption information, other than group private key owner CC. Then SM_k calculates M = $(m\|tag)^e$ and $H_1(m)$.

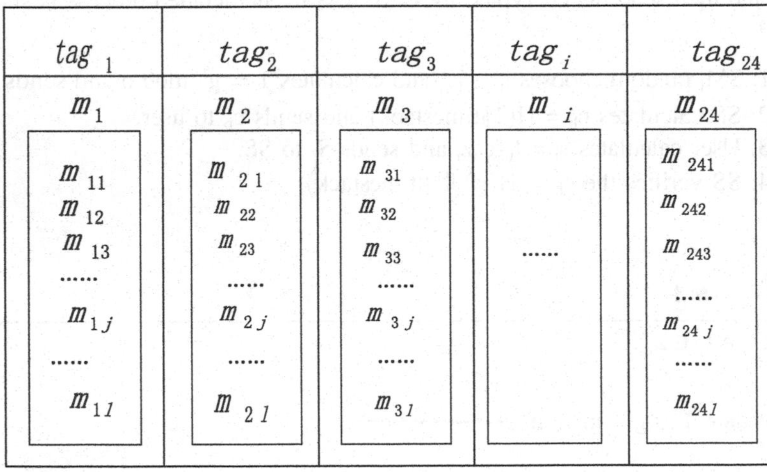

tag_1	tag_2	tag_3	tag_i	tag_{24}
m_1	m_2	m_3	m_i	m_{24}
m_{11}	m_{21}	m_{31}		m_{241}
m_{12}	m_{22}	m_{32}		m_{242}
m_{13}	m_{23}	m_{33}	....	m_{243}
....	....	....		....
m_{1j}	m_{2j}	m_{3j}		m_{24j}
....	....	....		....
m_{1l}	m_{2l}	m_{3l}		m_{24l}

Fig. 4. Structure of 24 blocks generated by SM_k

4.3   Blindly Signature on the Message

Generate the signature: The process is shown in the Fig. 5.

Step 1: Signer randomly chooses $k \in Z_p^*$, calculates $r' = g^k$ mod n, and sends the r' to SM_k, SM_k randomly chooses a, b and calculates the blind factor $r = r'^a g^b$ mod $n = g^{ak}+b$ mod n. Then calculates $H_1(m)' = a^{-1}rH_1(m)$ mod $n - 1$, sending the $H_1(m)$ to SS.

Step 2: Signers SS to calculate the signature $\sigma^* = (r, s^*, C, C_1)$ for blind messages, where $s^* = H_1(m)'y_i + k$ mod $n - 1$, $r = r'^a g^b$ mod $n = g^{ak+b}$ mod n, $C = y^{y_i}x_i$, $C_1 = g^{y_i}$.

Step 3: The SM_k extracts the $H_1(m)$'s signature from the signature of the blinded message, then gets the signature $\sigma = (r, s, C, C_1)$, and sends the M and the σ together to the CC by calculating the $s = as^* + b$ mod $n - 1$.

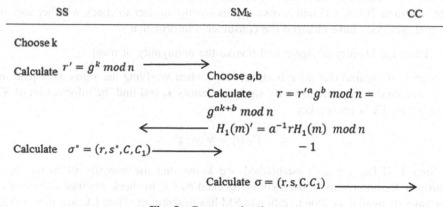

Fig. 5. Generate the signature

4.4   Verification and Traceability

(1) Verify the signature's correctness and the data's integrity:

Step 1: CC decrypts M by using group private key d and gets the consumption information (m‖Tag) and computes $H_1(m)$.

Step 2: CC verifies the correctness of the signature by judging whether or not the Eq. (1) is established. If the signature is verified correctly, it is proved that m was not tampered with during the transmission after being signed by SS.

$$g^s = rC_1^{rH_1(m)} \tag{1}$$

Step 3. If the signature is valid, verify M by using the Tag to test whether the data has been modified. CC decrypts M to get Tag, m, u_j, so CC can calculate the following values:

$$TG = \prod_{i=1}^{24/\lambda} tag_i \tag{2}$$

$$MG_j = \prod_{i=1}^{24/\lambda} m_{ij} \tag{3}$$

$$DG = \prod_{j=1}^{l} e(u_j, ptk)^{MG_j} \tag{4}$$

$$HS = \prod_{i=1}^{24/\lambda} h(MID \parallel i) \tag{5}$$

Step 4: The CC then verifies whether Eq. (6) is set up every 24 h:

$$DG \cdot e(HS, ptk) = e(TG, gt_k) \tag{6}$$

Step 5: If Eq. (6) is setting up, we can sure that the consumer's information has not been modified. If not, CC will revoke the anonymity of user to check whether user or external adversary have changed the consumer's information.

(2) Trace the identify of signer and revoke the anonymity of user:

Step 1: If we find that there is controversy when verifying the signature equation, CC can open the signature to verify signer's identity x_i and find the information of SS by using the CC's private key.

$$x_i = C/C_1^x = y^{y_i} x_i / g^{y_i x} \tag{7}$$

Step 2: If Eq. (6) isn't established, we know that the integrity of m has been destroyed, the anonymity of user will be revoked by CC to check whether adversary or user have changed data. Due to different SM has different gt, when CC acquires m‖Tag and corresponding gt. CC uses the group private key d to decrypt $(infor_i)^e$ in the database to obtain $infor_i$, and uses the decrypted information to calculate gt_i.

$$gt_i = H(infor_i)^x \bmod n = H(ID_i \| address \| timestack)^x \bmod n$$

Then, compare gt_i with the original gt to ensure the identity of user.

5   Security Analysis

The security of the proposed scheme is based on the assumption of several difficult problems, including the discrete logarithm problem and the integer decomposition problem. In addition, this scheme is based on Schnorr's identification protocol and the security of RSA encryption. The following is to prove that the proposed scheme has authentication, privacy-preserving, traceability, unforgeability and anonymity. The specific analysis is as follows:

5.1   Authenticatability

Authenticatability means that only legal users can upload their consumption information to SS. In our data reporting protocol, SS will verify the validity of consumers' identity. Only verifying successfully, SS can give a blind signature to data and send encrypted data with signature to CC. In the authenticated process, we use Schnorr identification protocol to authenticate the user's identity.

Theorem 1. The Schnorr identity protocol is an interactive protocol with the participation of certifier A and honest verifier B. If A and B successfully run the protocol, B is always convinced of A's identity.

Proof.

$$c_b = H(T||timestack)$$

$$= H(g^{t_i}||timestack)$$

$$= H(g^{S_i + c_b z_i}||timestack)$$

$$= Hg^{S_i}I_i^{c_b}||timestack)$$

SS can be calculated $g^{S_i}I_i^{c_b}$ and compared with T. Therefore, SS will accept SM's proof of identity as long as SS and SM can follow the protocol.

5.2   Privacy Protection

Theorem 2. The adversary cannot obtain the consumption information of the user in the initial and intermediate stages.

Proof. In the two phrases of data reporting and blind signature, the adversary and SS have the ability to obtain the encrypted user's consumption information M, but cannot directly obtain the private key of the CC. So the possible way is to divide the large prime number into p and q, assuming that factoring N into the correct p and q has a non-negligible possibility ϵ in the polynomial time algorithm. However, there is no effective algorithm to solve the problem of prime number factorization. Therefore, our scheme can effectively protect the privacy of user's consumption information.

5.3   Anonymity

If M is compromised, the scheme is anonymous and the adversary cannot obtain the identity of the owner of the information.

Theorem 3. Even if the adversary can crawl into the private database of CC and steal the decrypted information m and Tag, A can't infer the identity of the user by analysing the consumption information m.

Proof. If Adversary tries to infer the identify of data owner, the only way is to get gt_k from $tag_i = (H(MID||i) \cdot \prod_{j=1}^{l} u_j^{m_{ij}})^{stk}$ and compare to $H_1(infor_i)^x \mod n$. However,

Adversary has no capacity for getting gt_k because of solving the discrete logarithm problem is hard. Adversary cannot link m to user identity information, so anonymity is guaranteed.

5.4   Unforgeability

Unforgeability refer to the fact that external adversary can't forge or tamper with the file. In our scheme of data reporting, the meter will set security parameter λ in advance to control the times of reporting. If the security parameter is λ, the frequency of sending report is $24h/\lambda$. At the same time, we introduce the homomorphic tag mechanism to verify whether the original data has been modified.

Theorem 4. If our scheme has been correctly performed by all entities, the Eq. (6) will hold when the CC executes the verification.

Proof. The correctness of our verification Eq. (6) is elaborated as follows:

$$Left = DG \cdot e(HS, ptk) = \prod_{j=1}^{l} e(u_j, ptk)^{MG_j} \cdot e(HS, ptk)$$

$$Right = e(TG, gt_k) = e\left(\prod_{i=1}^{24/\lambda} tag_i, gt_k\right)$$

$$= e\left(\left(\prod_{i=1}^{24/\lambda} \left(\mathcal{H}(MID\|i) \cdot \prod_{j=1}^{l} u_j^{m_{ij}}\right)^{stk}, gt_k\right)\right)$$

$$= e\left(\left(\prod_{i=1}^{24/\lambda} \left(\mathcal{H}(MID\|i)\right)^{stk}, gt_k\right) \cdot e\left(\prod_{j=1}^{l} \prod_{i=1}^{24/\lambda} u_j^{m_{ij}stk}, gt_k\right)\right)$$

$$= e\left(HS, gt_k^{stk}\right) \cdot e\left(\prod_{j=1}^{l} u_j^{\sum_{i=1}^{24/\lambda} m_{ij}}, gt_k^{stk}\right)$$

$$= e\left(HS, gt_k^{stk}\right) \cdot e\left(\prod_{j=1}^{l} u_j, gt_k^{stk}\right)^{\sum_{i=1}^{24/\lambda} m_{ij}}$$

$$\rightarrow \prod_{j=1}^{l} e(u_j, ptk)^{MG_j} = e\left(\prod_{j=1}^{l} u_j^{\sum_{i=1}^{24/\lambda} m_{ij}}, gt_k^{stk}\right)$$

$$= \prod_{j=1}^{l} e\left(u_j^{\sum_{i=1}^{24/\lambda} m_{ij}}, gt_k^{stk}\right)$$

$$= \prod_{j=1}^{l} e\left(u_j, gt_k^{stk}\right)^{\sum_{i=1}^{24/\lambda} m_{ij}}$$

$$= e\left(\prod_{j=1}^{l} u_j, gt_k^{stk}\right)^{\sum_{i=1}^{24/\lambda} m_{ij}}$$

Left = Right

Hence, we ensure that the equation DG·e(HS, ptk) = e(TG, gt_k) will establish through the formula if all participants follow as our scheme.

5.5 Traceability

Theorem 5. If the Eq. (1) is not established, the CC executes tracking operation to get the signer's information by using $x_i = C/C_1^x$. Next, CC will revoke the anonymity of user, if the Eq. (6) is not established.

Proof. Signature correctness:

$$g^s = g^{as^* + b}$$

$$= g^{a\left(y_i H_1(m)' + k\right) + b}$$

$$= g^{a\left(y_i a^{-1} r H_1(m) + k\right) + b}$$

$$= g^{y_i r H_1(m)} g^{ak} g^b$$

$$= C_1^{r H_1(m)} r'^a g^b$$

$$= r C_1^{r H_1(m)}$$

By verifying the correctness of Eq. (1), CC can check the signature issuing from SS.

Tracking the Signer identity:

$$x_i = C/C_1^x$$

$$= y^{y_i} x_i / g^{y_i x}$$

$$= x_i$$

CC can get identity of signer by using group private key x which only group manager owns.

$$gt_i = H(infor_i)^x \bmod n = H(ID_i \| address \| timestack)^x \bmod n$$

Finally, using the registration information in the database, CC can decrypt the $(infor_i)^e$ post information stored in its own database with its own private key d to get the user information $infor_i$, and then calculate the $H(infor_i)^x$ one by one to match the results with the corresponding gt_k.

6 Conclusion

This paper proposes a group-blind signature scheme for privacy protection in smart grids. The four stages of the scheme realize the conditional anonymity of user identity information and the privacy protection of consumption data in the process of collecting electricity data. In addition, the homomorphic verifiable tag mechanism is used to ensure the verifiability of the integrity of the consumption data. The subsequent security analysis partly proves that the scheme proposed in this paper has authenticatability, privacy protection, anonymity, unforgeability and traceability.

References

1. Ramzan, Z.A.: Group blind digital signatures: theory and applications. Dissertations Massachusetts Institute of Technology (1999)
2. Mala, H., Nezhadansari, N.: New blind signature schemes based on the (elliptic Curve) discrete logarithm problem. In: ICCKE 2013, October 2013. https://doi.org/10.1109/iccke.2013.6682844
3. Khater, M.M., et al.: Blind signature schemes based on elgamal signature for electronic voting: a survey. Int. J. Comput. Appl. **975**, 8887
4. Zhao, C., Huifang, Y., Li, J.: Research on the universal composability of group-blind signatures. Appl. Res. Comput. **34**(10), 3109–3111 (2017)
5. Kong, W., et al.: A practical group blind signature scheme for privacy protection in smart grid. J. Parallel Distrib. Comput. **136**, 29–39 (2020)
6. Zhang, J., et al.: Multi-authorization electronic voting system based on group-blind signature. Favorites **8** (2015)
7. Zhang, X., Zhang, J.-Z., Xie, S.-C.: A secure quantum voting scheme based on quantum group blind signature. Int. J. Theor. Phys. **59**(3), 719–729 (2020)
8. Zhang, P., et al.: A new post-quantum blind signature from lattice assumptions. IEEE Access **6**, 27251–27258 (2018)
9. Liu, G., et al.: A novel quantum group proxy blind signature scheme based on five-qubit entangled state. Int. J. Theor. Phys. **58**(6), 1999–2008 (2019)
10. Lysyanskaya, A., Ramzan, Z.: Group blind digital signatures: a scalable solution to electronic cash. Lect. Notes Comput. Sci. 184–197 (1998). https://doi.org/10.1007/bfb0055483
11. Schnorr, C.P.: Efficient identification and signatures for smart cards. In: Brassard, G. (ed.) CRYPTO 1989. LNCS, vol. 435, pp. 239–252. Springer, New York (1990). https://doi.org/10.1007/0-387-34805-0_22

MB Based Multi-dividing Ontology Learning Trick

Meihui Lan[1][(✉)] and Wei Gao[2]

[1] School of Information Engineering, Qujing Normal University,
Qujing 6655011, China
[2] School of Information Science and Technology, Yunnan Normal University,
Kunming 650500, China
gaowei@ynnu.edu.cn

Abstract. The conceptual structure of the ontology is usually represented by a graph, and the related information of this concept is encapsulated by a vector with uniform dimension. The essence of the similarity calculation of the ontology concept is the calculation of the distance of the vector corresponding to the vertex in the high-dimensional space. This paper continues to consider the ontology learning algorithm of the multi-dividing setting, and proposes a MB based learning strategy under this framework. The experimental data verifies the effectiveness of the given new algorithm.

Keywords: Ontology · Learning · Multi-dividing ontology algorithm

1 Introduction

Concept management model like ontology has always been the focus of research in the field of database and information technology (See Mao et al. [1], Arafeh et al. [2], Rasmussen et al. [3] and Li et al. [4]). When it comes to the ontology applications, suppose the graph structure of ontology is tree-shaped, then the learning strategy of multiple partitions can be applied to deduce the optimal ontology learning function. Related theoretical and applied research can be referred to [5–9].

It is observed that a large number of ontology graph structures are tree-shaped or close to tree-shaped, hence ontology learning algorithms in multi-dividing setting have received widespread attention. It uses the characteristics of the tree structure of the ontology graph itself, and divides all vertices except the topmost virtual vertices into k categories according to branches. Domain experts determine the relationship between these categories, and then sort the k categories to specify the order relationship between the corresponding values of the vertices of each category. On the other hand, learners tend to obey the ontology function of this sorting rule.

The research is partially supported by NSFC (no. 11761083).

In order to use a mathematical model to describe the multi-dividing ontology learning method, we have to perform some preprocessing on the ontology data. For every $v \in V(G)$, use a p dimension vector to express all its semantic information. For convenience, v is used to denote the vertex v and its corresponding vector in $\mathbb{R}^p$.

Let $V \subseteq \mathbb{R}^p$ ($p \in \mathbb{N}$) be the input space (or instance space) for ontology graph G, and the vertices are drawn i.i.d. to certain unknown distribution $\mathcal{D}$. Ontology learning algorithms aim to predict an ontology function $f : V \to \mathbb{R}$ by means of ontology sample data S. In the multi-dividing ontology setting, ontology vertices are divided into k parts (corresponding to k classes or k rates) and the order of these k rates are determined by experts.

Specifically, the ontology training set $S = (S^1, S^2, \cdots, S^k) \in V^{n_1} \times V^{n_2} \times \cdots \times V^{n_k}$ consists of a sequence of ontology training samples $S_a = (v_1^a, \cdots, v_{n_a}^a) \in V^{n_a}$ ($1 \le a \le k$), and the real-valued ontology function $f : V \to \mathbb{R}$ is learned which assigns the S^a vertices larger value than S^b, i.e., $f(v^a) > f(v^b)$ for any pair of (a, b) where $1 \le a < b \le k$. Finally, the similarity between any two vertices v and v' is judged by the value $|f(v) - f(v')|$. Let $\mathcal{D}_a$ be the conditional distributions for each rate $1 \le a \le k$ and $n = \sum_{i=1}^{k} n_i$ be the capacity of ontology sample set.

2   MB Based Multi-dividing Ontology Learning Algorithm

Let $\beta \in \mathbb{R}^p$ be the optimization ontology vector, and in most settings we inquire that β is an ontology sparse vector with a large percentage of its components being zero. In this case, the ontology function is denoted by $f(v) = \beta^T v$ via ontology vector β. Let l be the ontology loss function. There are several classic ontology loss functions, such as square loss, exponential loss, logarithmic loss, ect. We aim to minimize the ontology l-risk which can be stated by

$$R_l(f) = \sum_{a=1}^{k-1} \sum_{b=a+1}^{k} \mathbb{E}_{v^a \sim \mathcal{D}_a, v^b \sim \mathcal{D}_b} \{l(f(v^a) - f(v^b))\}$$

$$= \sum_{a=1}^{k-1} \sum_{b=a+1}^{k} \mathbb{E}_{v^a \sim \mathcal{D}_a, v^b \sim \mathcal{D}_b} \{(1 - \beta^T(v^a - v^b))^2\}$$

$$= \sum_{a=1}^{k-1} \sum_{b=a+1}^{k} \{1 - 2\beta^T \mathbb{E}[(v^a - v^b)] + \beta^T \mathbb{E}[(v^a - v^b)(v^a - v^b)^T]\beta\}$$

$$= \sum_{a=1}^{k-1} \sum_{b=a+1}^{k} \{1 - 2\beta^T \mu^{a,b} + \beta^T \Sigma^{a,b} \beta\},$$

where $\mu^{a,b} = \mathbb{E}\{v^a - v^b\}$ and $\Sigma^{a,b} = \mathbb{E}\{(v^a - v^b)(v^a - v^b)^T\}$. Moreover, the corresponding ontology empirical l-risk is formulated by

$$\widehat{R}_l(f) = \sum_{a=1}^{k-1} \sum_{b=a+1}^{k} \frac{1}{2n_a n_b} \sum_{i=1}^{n_a} \sum_{j=1}^{n_b} l(f(v_i^a) - f(v_j^b)).$$

In the setting of $f(v) = \beta^T v$, the ontology empirical l-risk can be re-written by

$$\hat{R}_l(\beta) = \sum_{a=1}^{k-1} \sum_{b=a+1}^{k} \{-\beta^T [\frac{1}{n_a n_b} \sum_{i=1}^{n_a} \sum_{j=1}^{n_b} (v_i^a - v_j^b)]$$

$$+ \frac{1}{2}\beta^T [\frac{1}{n_a n_b} \sum_{i=1}^{n_a} \sum_{j=1}^{n_b} (v_i^a - v_j^b)(v_i^a - v_j^b)^T]\beta\}.$$

Redefine

$$\mu^{a,b} = \frac{1}{n_a n_b} \sum_{i=1}^{n_a} \sum_{j=1}^{n_b} (v_i^a - v_j^b)$$

and

$$\Sigma^{a,b} = \frac{1}{n_a n_b} \sum_{i=1}^{n_a} \sum_{j=1}^{n_b} (v_i^a - v_j^b)(v_i^a - v_j^b)^T.$$

Then, the ontology optimization problem in multi-dividing special setting can be solved by

$$\beta^* = \arg\min_{\beta} \{\sum_{a=1}^{k-1} \sum_{b=a+1}^{k} \{\frac{1}{2}\beta^T \Sigma^{a,b} \beta - \beta^T \mu^{a,b}\} + \lambda_1 \|\beta\|_1 + \frac{1}{2}\lambda_2 \|\beta\|_2^2\}.$$

Here, both λ_1 and λ_2 are offset parameters, and $\lambda_1 \|\beta\|_1 + \frac{1}{2}\lambda_2 \|\beta\|_2^2$ is a mixed balance term.

Now, let's describe the MB (Mini-Batch) based multi-dividing ontology learning algorithm. Let T be the total number of iterative rounds, and at each round t, there are B pairs of ontology samples in each combination (a, b). Let S_t^a be the arrays of sample indices where $a \in \{1, \cdots, k\}$, and thus there are totally $BT\frac{k(k-1)}{2}$ pairs of ontology samples. We use $S_t^{a,b}$ to denote the corresponding ontology sample pairs for each pair of (a, b) with $1 \le a < b \le k$. Set

$$\mu_t^{a,b} = \frac{1}{B} \sum_{i,j \in S_t^{a,b}} (v_i^a - v_j^b)$$

and

$$\Sigma_t^{a,b} = \frac{1}{B} \sum_{i,j \in S_t^{a,b}} (v_i^a - v_j^b)(v_i^a - v_j^b)^T.$$

Therefore, in all rounds, we get

$$\mu = \frac{1}{T} \sum_{t=1}^{T} \sum_{a=1}^{k-1} \sum_{b=a+1}^{k} \mu_t^{a,b} = \frac{1}{BT} \sum_{a=1}^{k-1} \sum_{b=a+1}^{k} \sum_{i,j \in S_t^{a,b}} (v_i^a - v_j^b)$$

and

$$\Sigma = \frac{1}{T} \sum_{t=1}^{T} \sum_{a=1}^{k-1} \sum_{b=a+1}^{k} \Sigma_t^{a,b} = \frac{1}{BT} \sum_{a=1}^{k-1} \sum_{b=a+1}^{k} \sum_{i,j \in S_t^{a,b}} (v_i^a - v_j^b)(v_i^a - v_j^b)^T.$$

The ontology optimization problem constructed by MB based multi-dividing setting is

$$\beta^* = \arg\min_{\beta}\{\{\frac{1}{2}\beta^T \Sigma \beta - \beta^T \mu\} + \lambda_1\|\beta\|_1 + \frac{1}{2}\lambda_2\|\beta\|_2^2\}.$$

Finally, the MB based multi-dividing ontology learning algorithm can be summarized as follows.

Algorithm 1: MB based multi-dividing ontology learning algorithm

Input: parameters B, T, λ_1, λ_2, and multi-dividing ontology sample data

Initialize $\mu = 0$ and $\Sigma = 0$

For $t = 1, \cdots, T$ do

For $a = 1, \cdots, k-1$ do

For $b = a+1, \cdots, k$ do

Construct index set S_t^a and S_t^b with $|S_t^a| = |S_t^b| = B$, and $S_t^{a,b} = (S_t^a(i), S_t^b(i))$ where $i = 1, \cdots, B$.

$\mu = \mu + \frac{1}{BT}\sum_{(i,j)\in S_t^{a,b}}(v_i^a - v_j^b)$

$\Sigma = \Sigma + \frac{1}{BT}\sum_{(i,j)\in S_t^{a,b}}(v_i^a - v_j^b)(v_i^a - v_j^b)^T$

End For

End For

End For

$\beta^* = \arg\min_{\beta}\{\{\frac{1}{2}\beta^T \Sigma \beta - \beta^T \mu\} + \lambda_1\|\beta\|_1 + \frac{1}{2}\lambda_2\|\beta\|_2^2\}.$

Output: ontology vector β

3   Experiments

In this section, we apply the above algorithms to three different application fields, and verify the effectiveness of proposed MB based multi-dividing ontology learning algorithm by comparing with the data obtained by other algorithms. Since the algorithm obtains the relative similarity rather than the absolute similarity value, we still use the classic $P@N$ accuracy rate to measure the efficiency of the data, and use this label to compare the experimental data with the data of other algorithms.

3.1   Experiment on Mathematics-Physics Disciplines

Very recently, Wu et al. [10] designed mathematicsCphysics ontology which records certain of the most important and frontier development directions in the fields of mathematics and physics, and the specific concepts and subject classification. It can be seen that there are 196 ontology vertices (contains virtual vertices), and the ontology sample set used in the experiment is constituted by 98 vertices.

To verify the efficiency of the algorithm in this paper, at the same time, we use the ontology learning algorithm given by Gao et al. [11], Zhu et al. [12] and [13] to act on the mathematical-physical ontology. Some data pairs are as shown in Table 1. In particular, we want to explain that the comparison data of other algorithms in the last three rows of the table are directly derived from Wu et al. [10], and our experiment only completed the first row of data, i.e., $P@N$ accuracy by means of our MB based multi-dividing ontology learning algorithm.

Table 1. Partial of ontology similarity measuring experiment data on mathematicsC-physics ontology.

	$P@1$ Average Precision Ratio	$P@3$ Average Precision Ratio	$P@5$ Average Precision Ratio	$P@10$ Average Precision Ratio
Algorithm in this work	29.59%	42.35%	54.39%	83.52%
Gao et al. [11]	27.55%	41.49%	52.04%	82.04%
Zhu et al. [12]	26.53%	40.48%	48.78%	77.35%
Zhu et al. [13]	29.59%	41.17%	52.85%	83.47%

From the data description in Table 1, it can be seen that the proposed MB based multi-dividing ontology algorithm in this paper is significantly higher than the ontology learning algorithm given in Gao et al. [11], Zhu et al. [12] and [13], and this advantage will become obvious when it gradually increases.

3.2 Ontology Mapping on Sponge City Rainwater Treatment System Ontologies

In this subsection, we use the sponge city rainwater treatment system ontologies which were introduced by Wu et al. [10]. The ontology graph structures are presented from Figs. 1, 2, 3 and 4, and all the ontology figures are taken from Wu et al. [10].

The aim of this experiment is to establish ontology mapping among the above four ontologies, that is to say, to search the most similar concepts from other ontologies. For the sample data in this experiment, we select about 1/2 of the vertices as ontology sample set, then yield the ontology function through the learner, and finally determine a similarity-based ontology mapping. To state the superiority of the given MB based multi-dividing ontology learning algorithm, we also apply the ontology learning algorithms proposed in Gao et al. [11], Zhu et al. [12] and [13] to the sponge city rainwater treatment ontologies. Some data pairs are as shown in Table 2. Again, we state that the comparison data of other algorithms in the last three rows of the table are directly derived from Wu et al. [10], and our experiment only completed the first row of data, i.e., $P@N$ accuracy by means of our MB based multi-dividing ontology learning algorithm.

From the result data in Table 2, it can be seen that our multi-dividing ontology algorithm is significantly higher than the ontology learning algorithm inferred by Gao et al. [11], Zhu et al. [12] and [13], and this advantage will become obvious when it gradually increases.

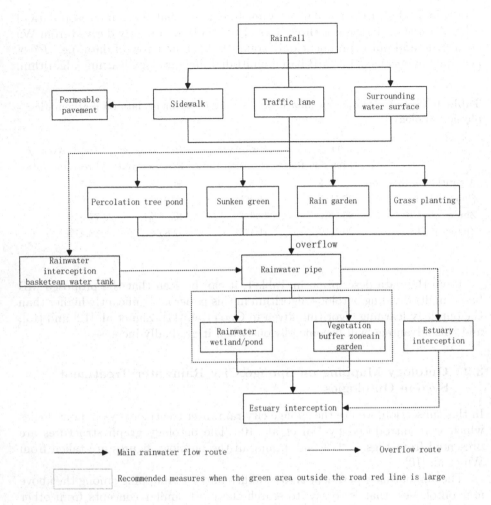

Fig. 1. Rainfall management ontology O_1 [10].

Table 2. Partial of ontology mapping data on sponge city rainwater treatment system ontologies.

	P@1 Average Precision Ratio	P@3 Average Precision Ratio	P@5 Average Precision Ratio
Algorithm in this work	27.78%	38.28%	51.89%
Gao et al. [11]	24.32%	34.68%	47.03%
Zhu et al. [12]	25.68%	36.04%	50.81%
Zhu et al. [13]	27.03%	36.49%	51.35%

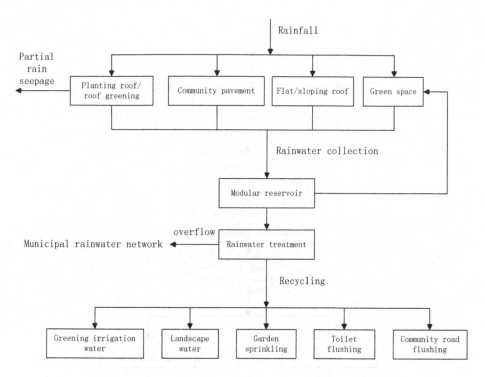

Flow chart of rainwater management in residential quarters

Fig. 2. Rainfall management ontology O_2 [10].

3.3   Experiment on Chemical Index Ontology

In the third experiment, chemical index ontology which was applied in Zhu et al. [14] is employed. The function of this ontology is to judge the redundant topological index by calculating the similarity between concepts, and the ontology graph has two branches and 840 vertices. For the parameter settings, we take $k = 2$, i.e., each part has 200 sample data and totally 400 ontology concepts as ontology sample set. Furthermore, we use the same three claims as described in Zhu et al. [14].

In order to verify the efficiency of the algorithm in our work, at the same time, we use the ontology learning algorithm given in Gao et al. [15–17] to act on the chemical index ontology. Some data pairs are as shown in Table 3. In particular, we want to explain that the comparison data of other algorithms in the last three rows of the table are directly derived from Zhu et al. [14], and our experiment only completed the first row of data, i.e., $P@N$ accuracy by means of our MB based multi-dividing ontology learning algorithm.

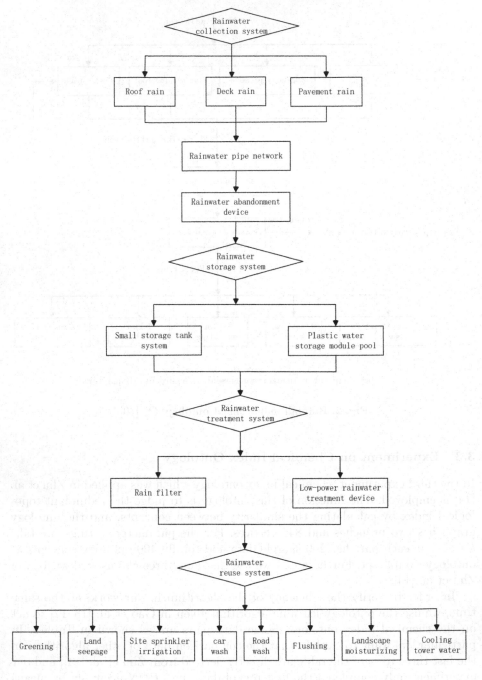

Fig. 3. Rainfall management ontology O_3 [10].

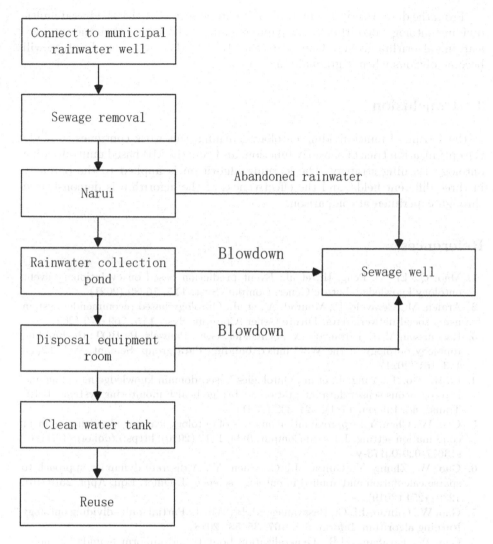

Fig. 4. Rainfall management ontology O_4 [10].

Table 3. Partial of experiment data of ontology similarity measuring on chemical index ontology.

	$P@3$ Average Precision Ratio	$P@5$ Average Precision Ratio	$P@10$ Average Precision Ratio	$P@20$ Average Precision Ratio
Algorithm in this work	0.39	0.47	0.64	0.85
Gao et al. [15]	0.30	0.36	0.55	0.73
Gao et al. [16]	0.39	0.45	0.60	0.79
Gao et al. [17]	0.28	0.37	0.54	0.78

From the data description in Table 3, it can be seen that the MB based multi-dividing ontology algorithm in this paper is significantly higher than the ontology learning algorithm given in Gao et al. [15], [16] and [17], and this advantage will become obvious when it gradually increases.

4   Conclusion

In the setting of multi-dividing ontology learning, this work continues to study the optimization trick of ontology function, and gets the MB based multi-dividing ontology learning strategy. The learning algorithm is applied to the ontology in three different fields, and the effectiveness of the algorithm is demonstrated through experimental comparison.

References

1. Mao, Q., Li, X., Peng, H., et al.: Event prediction based on evolutionary event ontology knowledge. Future Gener. Comput. Syst. **115**, 76–89 (2021)
2. Arafeh, M., Ceravolo, P., Mourad, A., et al.: Ontology based recommender system using social network data. Future Gener. Comput. Syst. **115**, 769–779 (2021)
3. Rasmussen, M.H., Lefrancois, M., Schneider, G.F., Pauwels, P.: BOT: the building topology ontology of the W3C linked building data group. Semant. Web **12**(1), 143–161 (2021)
4. Li, R., Mo, T., Yang, J., et al.: Ontologies-based domain knowledge modeling and heterogeneous sensor data integration for bridge health monitoring systems. IEEE Trans. Ind. Inform. **17**(1), 321–332 (2021)
5. Gao, W., Chen, Y.: Approximation analysis of ontology learning algorithm in linear combination setting. J. Cloud Comput. **9**(1), 1–10 (2020). https://doi.org/10.1186/s13677-020-00173-y
6. Gao, W., Zhang, Y., Guirao, J.L.G., Chen, Y.: A discrete dynamics approach to sparse calculation and applied in ontology science. J. Differ. Equ. Appl. **25**(9–10), 1239–1254 (2019)
7. Gao, W., Guirao, J.L.G., Basavanagoud, B., Wu, J.: Partial multi-dividing ontology learning algorithm. Inform. Sci. **467**, 35–58 (2018)
8. Gao, W., Farahani, M.R.: Generalization bounds and uniform bounds for multi-dividing ontology algorithms with convex ontology loss function. Comput. J. **60**(9), 1289–1299 (2017)
9. Wu, J., Yu, X., Gao, W.: Disequilibrium multi dividing ontology learning algorithm. Commun. Stat.-Theor. M. **46**(18), 8925–8942 (2017)
10. Wu, J., Sangaiah, A.K., Gao, W.: Graph learning-based ontology sparse vector computing. Symmetry **12**(1562) (2020). https://doi.org/10.3390/sym12091562
11. Gao, W., Zhu, L., Wang, K.: Ontology sparse vector learning algorithm for ontology similarity measuring and ontology mapping via ADAL technology. Int. J. Bifurc. Chaos **25** (2015). https://doi.org/10.1142/S0218127415400349
12. Zhu, L.L., Hua, G., Zafarc, S., Pan, Y.: Fundamental ideas and mathematical basis of ontology learning algorithm. J. Intell. Fuzzy Syst. **35**, 4503–4516 (2018)
13. Zhu, L.L., Hua, G., Aslam, A.: Ontology learning algorithm using weak functions. Open Phys. **16**, 910–916 (2018)

14. Zhu, L., Hua, G., Baskonus, H.M., Gao, W.: Multi-dividing ontology learning algorithm and similarity measuring on topological indices. Front. Phys. **8**(547963) (2020). https://doi.org/10.3389/fphy.2020.547963
15. Gao, W., Zhu, L.L., Wang, K.Y.: Ranking based ontology scheming using eigenpair computation. J. Intell. Fuzzy Syst. **31**, 2411–2419 (2016)
16. Gao, W., Guo, Y., Wang, K.: Ontology algorithm using singular value decomposition and applied in multidisciplinary. Clust. Comput. **19**(4), 2201–2210 (2016). https://doi.org/10.1007/s10586-016-0651-0
17. Gao, W., Baig, A.Q., Ali, H., Sajjad, W., Farahani, M.R.: Margin based ontology sparse vector learning algorithm and applied in biology science. Saud J. Biol. Sci. **24**, 132C138 (2017)

Application of LSTM Model Optimized Based on Adaptive Genetic Algorithm in Stock Forecasting

Yong He, Huan Li, and Wenhong Wei[✉]

School of Computer, Dongguan University of Technology,
Dongguan 523808, China
weiwh@dgut.edu.cn

Abstract. The need to predict stock price arises in the quantitative financial transaction field is a challenging problem. Long-short term memory (LSTM) neural network has shown a good effect on this problem. There are two main issues when implementing this method. One, it always suffers from huge attempts of constructing the neural network and adjustments of the hyper-parameter. Two, it often fails to find an excellent solution. We propose an AGA-LSTM algorithm, which uses an adaptive genetic algorithm to automatically optimize the network structure and hyper-parameters of the LSTM neural network. The simulation results show that the accuracy of the rise and fall of the stock outperforms LSTM as well as other previously machine learning models. Moreover, attempts are significantly less than other tuning methods.

Keywords: Stock price prediction · Long short-term memory · Adaptive genetic algorithm · Machine learning

1 Introduction

The prediction of stock prices is an important issue in the financial field. Through the prediction of price fluctuation trends, financial risks can be minimized. Obtaining the characteristics of price fluctuations and their trends have significant impacts, on individuals to choose investment, government to control the financial market, and the securities market to promote the sustainable and healthy development. The current predictive analysis technology can be roughly divided into two categories: forecasting and clustering [1]. Specifically, we centered on forecasting, as forecasting methods are divided into two categories: the traditional forecasting model based on statistical theory, and the commonly used method of exponential smoothing. With the increase in the amount of data and the continuous development of the stock market, traditional non-intelligent methods have gradually decreased [2]. The second type of intelligent method, forecasting models based on gray theory and neural networks, are more and more common in stock price forecasting due to its powerful learning ability and self-adaptive ability [3].

Among prediction methods of machine learning, artificial neural network (ANN) is a commonly used method, since it is suitable for dealing with complex relationship

© Springer Nature Singapore Pte Ltd. 2021
Y. Tan et al. (Eds.): DMBD 2021, CCIS 1453, pp. 46–58, 2021.
https://doi.org/10.1007/978-981-16-7476-1_5

problems. But the testing and training speed is relatively slow, and it is easy to fall into local extreme values and over-fitting. In order to avoid the black box problem of neural networks, Li-Ping Ni, Zhi-Wei Ni, Ya-Zhuo Gao used support vector machines (SVM) with strict mathematical proofs, but there is a problem of obtaining the optimal number of features in feature selection [4]. So this method is not easy to generalize. Yang Su, Yao-yuan Shi, and Heng Song used the genetic algorithm to optimize the kernel function of SVM, and got better results on the stock index prediction of the Chinese stock market [5]. Yakup Kara, Melek Acar Boyacioglu, Ömer Kaan Baykan compared the SVM model and BP neural network to predict the trend of the stock index, and found that the prediction effect of BP neural network is better than SVM model [6].

Christopher Krauss, Xuan Anh Do and Nicolas Huck applied Random Forest (RF) to the stock price prediction problem. Comparing with the random forest, SVM, BP neural network, and naive Bayes models, the overall performance of the random forest was the best. Although the accuracy of random forest is higher than most individual algorithms, the RF model is prone to over-fitting on sample sets with large noise such as stock price sequence [7]. Long short-term memory (LSTM) has always been one of the most popular methods in time series prediction. LSTM is an improvement of RNN, which can memorize important state information of longer time series, and will not have the problem of gradient disappearance or gradient explosion. Although it is seldom used for financial time series forecasting, the characteristics of this model are highly compatible with stock forecasting problems. Fischer and Krauss [8] used LSTM to predict the sample return based on the S&P 500 constituent stocks. Although this method performed better than random forest (RF), deep neural network (DNN) and logistic regression (LOG), its accuracy is between 51% and 54%. Reasons for the lower accuracy rate may be the feature samples are not appropriate, the neural network structure is not suitable, and the model is unable to jump out of local extremes. The hyper-parameter selection in LSTM mostly uses grid search algorithms and fine-tuning control variables, but their computational overhead is huge. This article proposes a stock price prediction method based on the AGA-LSTM recurrent neural network for the stock price time series. The adaptive genetic algorithm is used to optimize the hyper-parameters of LSTM. With the goal of maximizing test accuracy, the experiment is carried out with US stock data, The experimental results show that the AGA-LSTM model has good forecasting performance in the test data.

The contribution of this work includes: (1) The use of the AGA-LSTM algorithm, slightly improves performance compared with other models. (2) Real number coding and adaptive methods are implemented for computationally efficient. (3) The automatically building optimal network model is much faster than manual trial, error method and grid search method.

2   Algorithm Background

Long short-term memory neural network (LSTM) is a neural network structure that connects the LSTM unit as a directed graph [9]. The characteristic of the LSTM neural network is to store the input of the neuron at the current time and the output at the previous time. The LSTM is an improvement of Recurrent Neural Network (RNN). RNN neural network can store the relationship between the current input of the neuron and the previous output [10]. By introducing the LSTM module in the chain structure, the LSTM has a complex internal structure, which can learn long-term calculation and memory information from input data (Fig. 1). It has been widely used in the prediction of nonlinear time series data in recent years [11].

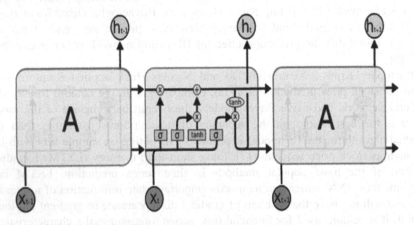

Fig. 1. The internal structure of the LSTM calculation unit.

First, the A gate is an optional way to let information through. It consists of a Sigmoid layer and a point multiplication operation. LSTM has three gates to protect and control the state of a single computing unit. The forget gate determines the information that needs to discard, which can be expressed as:

$$f_t = \sigma\big(W_f * [h_{t-1}, x_t] + b_f\big) \tag{1}$$

W_f represents the connection weight of the previous output, h_{t-1} as the previous output, x_t as current input, b_f as bias vector, and σ as activation function. The input gate determines the information needs to be updated, which is obtained by multiplying the two vectors created by the input gate layer and the tanh layer. It can be described as:

$$i_t = \sigma\big(W_f * [h_{t-1}, x_t] + b_i\big) \tag{2}$$

$$\tilde{C}_t = \tanh(W_c * [h_{t-1}, x_t] + b_c) \tag{3}$$

The output gate provides information of the input gate and the forget gate. It can be defined as:

$$C_t = f_t * C_{t-1} + i_t * \tilde{C}_t \tag{4}$$

The calculation unit outputs the result after the above operation. It contains two processes. First, the Sigmoid layer determines the output. The cell state passes through the Tanh layer to normalize the value to between −1 and 1, and then performs dot multiplication. The output of this process determines the part of the output, which can be expressed as:

$$o_t = \sigma(W_o * [h_{t-1}, x_t] + b_o) \tag{5}$$

$$h_t = o_t * \tanh(C_t) \tag{6}$$

Connecting each computing unit into a chain structure can get a neural network (Fig. 2).

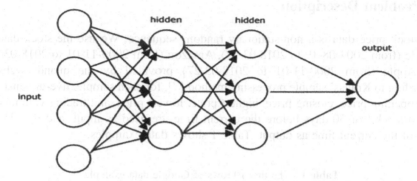

Fig. 2. A typical network structure.

The training method of the LSTM model is to calculate the output value of the LSTM unit according to the forward propagation method first. Second step is to propagate the error value of the LSTM unit back, and calculate the weight gradient according to the error value. Then use the optimization algorithm to perform gradient descent. Last step to continuously Update weight.

Most optimization algorithms use the stochastic gradient descent (SGD), the adaptive gradient algorithm (AdaGrad), and the adaptive moment estimation algorithm (Adam). The Adam algorithm is different from the stochastic gradient descent. The Stochastic gradient descent maintains a single learning rate, while the Adam algorithm calculates first-order moment estimation and second-order moment estimation for parameter to obtain an independent adaptive learning rate [12].

As the number of network layers increases, it often leads to long training time and over-fitting problems. The integrated learning method is used to train a different model to improve the generalization ability. By adding a dropout layer, randomly omitting a certain ratio of feature detectors in each training case to reduce the over-fitting phenomenon [13].

The Adaptive genetic algorithm is a heuristic search algorithm based on the improvement of genetic algorithm, by dynamically changing the crossover probability (P_c) and the mutation probability (P_m). When the fitness of each individual is lower than the average fitness of the group, P_c and P_m increase to jump out of the local optimum. When the fitness of each individual of the population is lower than the average fitness of the group, P_c and P_m are reduced to ensure the survival probability of excellent individuals.

The prediction accuracy of the LSTM model is closely related to the value of the hyper-parameters. The number of layers in the LSTM need to be optimized in the search space that includes the dense layer, the number of neurons, the forgetting rate of the dropout layer and the number of iterations. The grid search algorithm and the fine-tuning method are essentially traversal optimization of the search space. This paper used adaptive genetic algorithm (AGA) to adjust the LSTM hyper-parameters to obtain the optimal solution in the search space to form a composite AGA-LSTM model.

3 Problem Description

The stock price data is a non-stationary random sequence. We use the stock data of Google (from 2004-08-19 to 2018-03-27), Amazon (from 2000-11-01 to 2018-03-27) and Apple (from 2000-11-01 to 2018-03-27) provided by the quandl website. According to Krauss' sample processing method [7], for each sample, five-dimensional data (opening price, closing price, highest price, lowest price, and trading volume of a certain stock.) of 50 days before the current time are used as input, and the closing price of the current time as output. Table 1 shows data examples.

Table 1. The first 10 rows of Google data example

Date	Open	High	Low	Close	Volume
2004/08/19	100.01	104.06	95.96	100.35	44659000
2004/08/20	101.01	109.08	100.50	108.31	22834300
2004/08/23	110.76	113.48	109.05	109.40	18256100
2004/08/24	111.24	111.60	103.57	104.87	15247300
2004/08/25	104.76	108.00	103.88	106.00	9188600
2004/08/26	104.95	107.95	104.66	107.91	7094800
2004/08/27	108.10	108.62	105.69	106.15	6211700
2004/08/30	105.28	105.49	102.01	102.01	5196700
2004/08/31	102.32	103.71	102.16	102.37	4917800
2004/09/01	102.70	102.97	99.67	100.25	9138200

Table 1 shows the data examples. Here are the first 10 rows of the Google data example.

In order to eliminate the influence of different dimensions of the above characteristic, this article normalized the data. The data is mapped to (0, 1).

$$x_{norm} = \frac{x - x_{min}}{x_{max} - x_{min}} \tag{7}$$

The original data sequence is x = {$x_1, x_2,..., x_n$}, and the x norm is the normalized value. We obtain a new data sequence D = {$d_1, d_2,..., d_n$}. There are training set and test set, d_{tr} = {$d_1, d_2,..., d_m$} and d_{te} = {$d_{m+1}, d_{m+2},..., d_n$}. Seting the timestamp of the data to 50 as S, the input data is:

$$X = \{X_1, X_2, ..., X_n\} \tag{8}$$

$$X_i = \{d_i, d_{i+1}, ..., d_{(m-S+p-1)}\} \quad s.t 1 \leq i \leq S; S \in N \tag{9}$$

The output data is converted into the rise or fall of stock price, which is a classification label calculated based on the closing price. C_{t+1} represents the closing price on day t + 1, and the classification label on day t is calculated by the following formula:

$$y_t = \begin{cases} 1, & C_{t+1} > C_t \\ -1, & others \end{cases} \tag{10}$$

The actual and predicted values are:

$$Y = \{Y_{m+1}, Y_{m+2}, ...Y_n\} \tag{11}$$

$$y_i = \{y_{m+1}, y_{m+2}, ...y_n\} \tag{12}$$

In order to quantitatively analyze the model performance of AGA-LSTM, model accuracy is used as a measurement index and compared with models such as SVM, BP, random forest, and LSTM. Those indicators are calculated based on true-TP, true-negative-TN, false positive-FP, false negative-FN, and the prediction accuracy. It is expressed as:

$$acc = \frac{TP + TN}{TP + FP + TN + FN} \tag{13}$$

4 Algorithm Description

4.1 Genes Code

The coding method of the genetic algorithm adopted in this paper is real number coding, and directly performs genetic operations on the phenotype of the solution. There are 8 genes in one sample. The first gene represents the number of LSTM layers (1–2, and the step size is 1). The second gene indicates the number of dense layers (1–2, with a step size of 1). The third and fourth genes represent the number of neurons in each layer of the LSTM layer (32–128, and the step size is 1). If the indicated layer does not exist, the number of neurons is coded as 0. The fifth and sixth gene represents the number of neurons in the dense layer. Similarly, if the represented layer does not exist, the number of neurons is coded as 0. The seventh and eighth genes represent the dropout layer forget rate (0.1–0.5, the step size is 0.1) and the number of network iterations (20–60, and the step size is 20).

4.2   Crossover Operator

This paper adopts the adaptive single-point crossover method, and randomly sets a crossover point in the individual string. When the crossover operator is performed, the genes are at the corresponding positions of the individual cross. The first and second digits do not cross, because they represent the number of layers. After the crossover, it will affect the number of neurons in the back. If the third to sixth digits have exchanged genes of 0, they should not be crossed. The adaptive crossover probability is expressed as:

$$p_c = \begin{cases} k_3, & f_c \leq f_{avg} \\ \frac{k_1(f_{max}-f_c)}{f_{max}-f_{avg}}, & f_c \geq f_{avg} \end{cases} \tag{14}$$

In the formula, f_c is the larger fitness value of the two individuals to be crossed. For individuals with higher fitness, the smaller p_c is in line with the setting of "preserving good individuals". When the individuals with lower fitness are bigger, they are in line with the setting of "changing bad individuals". Set $k_1 = 1$ and $k_3 = 1$.

4.3   Mutation Operator

The mutation method used in this paper is an adaptive mutation single-point operator, which only adjusts the value of the individual after the two genes. It randomly selects the value according to the corresponding range. The third to sixth digits are randomly selected from (32, 128), and the seventh value is randomly selected from (0.1, 0.5). The last bit is randomly selected from (1, 3), where the adaptive mutation probability is expressed as:

$$p_m = \begin{cases} k_4, & f_m \leq f_{avg} \\ \frac{k_2(f_{max}-f_m)}{f_{max}-f_{avg}}, & f_m \geq f_{avg} \end{cases} \tag{15}$$

In this formula, f_m is the fitness value of the individual to be mutated. For the individual with the highest fitness, the crossover probability is 0. If the mutation probability is also 0, it will lead to mass reproduction and produce "premature" phenomenon. Therefore, the individual with lower fitness is used to search for the global optimal solution. Set $k_2 = 0.5$, $k_4 = 0.5$.

4.4   Steps of the Algorithm

The specific steps of the algorithm are as follows: The first step is to initialize the population and determine the value of each chromosome. Neural networks are determined according to the genes of the chromosomes, the number of network layers, the number of hidden neurons and the number of iterations of the LSTM. Then, the neural network is trained to calculate the fitness value. Drawing on formula (13), the accuracy of model prediction is used as a fitness function. Further, roulette generates the next generation. Adaptive crossover and mutation operations on the solved individuals generate new individuals. Repeating the above steps until reaches the maximum number of iterations, and the best individual would emerge among them. Last is to train the LSTM neural network with the best hyper-parameter combination. Input test samples, output prediction are compared with true values (Fig. 3).

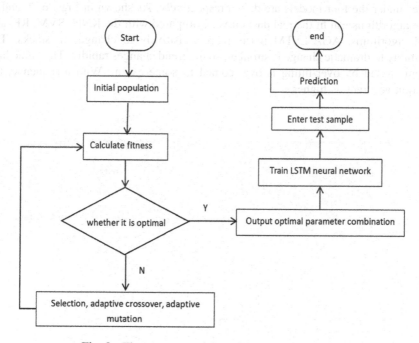

Fig. 3. The summary of the AGA-LSTM algorithm.

5 Experimental Result

The computer configuration and software environment used in the experiment are as follow: The processor is Intel Xeon E3–1230 v6, with 16.0 GB memory and NVIDIA Quadro M2000 graphics card; the system is Windows 10 (64-bit); the programming language version is Python 3.6.2; IDE is Pycharm 2020.3 in the Anaconda package. AGA-LSTM and LSTM are implemented in the Keras library with Tensorflow as the backend. The SVM, random forest, and KNN model used for the comparison of prediction are implemented in the scikit-learn library. The hyper-parameters of the genetic algorithm are as follow: the number of populations in each generation is 20, the length of individual genes is 8, and the number of iterations is 100.

After the data is trained with the AGA-LSTM model, it is possible to quickly find better solutions and approximately optimal solutions in the search space than the sub-optimal model (Fig. 4).

A neural network is constructed by setting the parameters of the optimal solution. As the number of iterations increases, the verification error converges quickly. The mean square error in the LSTM neural network is reduced to achieve the optimal solution in the search space (Fig. 5).

In order to show the experimental result, this article uses the fitting curve of the verification set to compare with the true curve of the test set. The test set data is from 82%–100% of the price series of the total data set. The horizontal axis is time, and the vertical axis is the normalized stock price. The prediced effects of the three data samples under the four models are drawn respectively. As shown in Figs. 6, 7, and 8, all five algorithms can fit the real data curve. Compared with the KNN, SVM, RF, and LSTM algorithms, AGA-LSTM reacts more sensitively to changes in stocks. The adaptability to dramatic change is stronger, so the trend changes rapidly. The "time lag" problem caused by over-fitting is over comed to some extent. With a sequence, the prediction accuracy is higher.

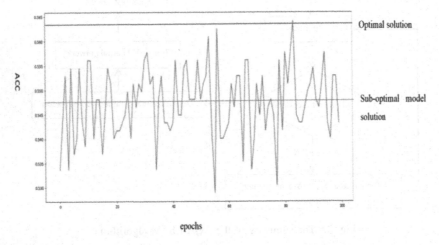

Fig. 4. The best accuracy of each generation.

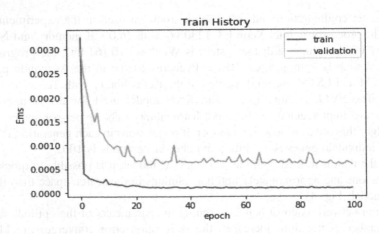

Fig. 5. The mean square error of the optimal solution is decreasing, and the optimal solution in the search space is realized.

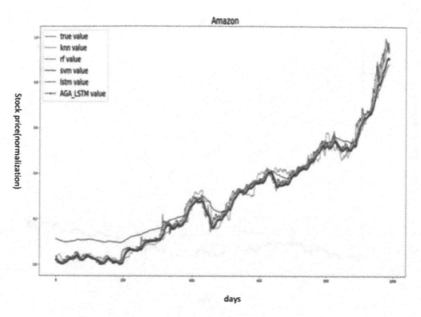

Fig. 6. Amazon stock price prediction in five models

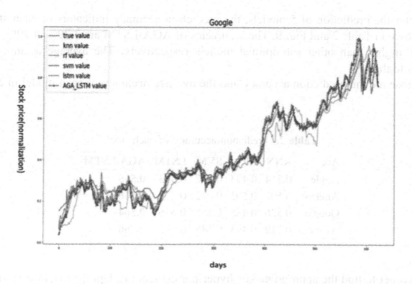

Fig. 7. Google stock price prediction in five models

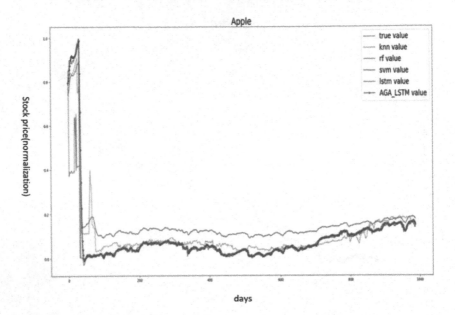

Fig. 8. Google stock price prediction in five models

After the prediction of 5 models, the prediction accuracy indicators of each stock are shown in Table 2 and Fig. 9. The accuracies of AGA-LSTM are 3.29%, 4.79%, and 1.43% higher than other sub-optimal models respectively. The average accuracy is 3.28% higher.

Those are the prediction accuracy and the average accuracy of each model in each stock.

Table 2. Prediction accuracy of each stock

Acc	KNN	RF	SVM	LSTM	AGA-LSTM
Apple	0.514	0.493	0.547	0.533	**0.565**
Amazon	0.507	0.502	0.542	0.521	**0.568**
Google	0.536	0.485	0.556	0.516	**0.564**
Average	0.519	0.493	0.548	0.523	**0.566**

In order to find the appropriate key hyper-parameters to adapt the machine learning model, a grid search (GS) or random search (RS) method is used. In this question, the time of each model training is set to t. GS can be regarded as an exhaustive search, and the model training time is $(2 * 2 * 96 * 96 * 96 * 96 * 5 * 3) * t = 5096079370t$. This time consuming is undoubtedly very huge. Although RS method can avoid excessive training time in a small area with poor performance, it does not use the previously well-performing parameter combination. If the RS method is used in a sufficiently large configuration space, the time performance of this method is relatively poor. The AGA-LSTM algorithm has strong early local search capabilities, adaptively adjusts the crossover, and mutation probability. However it is not easy to fall into the local extreme value in the early stage and maintain good individuals in the later stage, As shown in Fig. 4 the 50th round of iteration. To obtain a parameter combination (individual) close to the optimal solution, the model training time required is only $(50 * 20) * t = 1000t$, which is $1.96 * 10–7$ of the time required by the grid search algorithm.

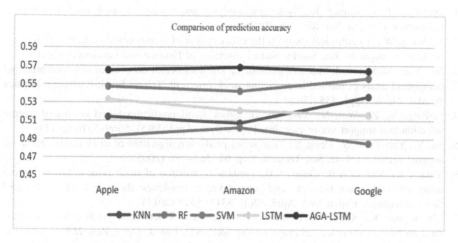

Fig. 9. Prediction accuracy of each stock and the average accuracy of each model.

6 Conclusion

The main contribution of this research is that we build a model with a high prediction accuracy. It can automatically adjust network structure and parameter combination, which significantly reduced the number of parameter adjustments. We conducted a quantitative analysis of the three stocks. The result demonstrates not only our model produces better performance than using LSTM, but also performs better than other four machine learning models. Our approach includes using actual codes to directly find the optimal solution in the solution space, adaptive crossover and mutation probability to accelerate the speed of finding the optimal solution. The found parameter combinations can achieve better prediction goals. Furthermore, comparing with grid search (GS) method and random search (RS) method, the efficiency of parameter tuning is higher. In order to get better accuracy, there are still more directions for future exploration. The use of more features of big data might be a good choice for yielding a better prediction accuracy. In this research, the disparities of fitness of each individual are not that huge, and using an adaptive algorithm based on individual order might augment the speed of finding the optimal solution.

Acknowledgement. This work was supported by the Key Project of Science and Technology Innovation 2030 funded by the Ministry of Science and Technology of China (No. 2018AAA0101301), the Key Projects of Artificial Intelligence of High School in Guangdong Province (No. 2019KZDZX1011) and The High School innovation Project (No. 2018KTSCX222).

References

1. Dattatray, P.G., Kumar, K.: Systematic analysis and review of stock market prediction techniques. Comput. Sci. Rev. **34** (2019)
2. Jin-Song, W.: An empirical study on the effectiveness of commonly used technical analysis methods in stock market. Southwestern University of Finance and Economics (2010)
3. Javad, Z., Mohammad, M.R.: Application of artificial neural network models and principal component analysis method in predicting stock prices on Tehran Stock Exchange. Physica A: Stat. Mech. Appl. **438** (2015)
4. Li-Ping, N., Zhi-Wei, N., Ya-Zhuo, G.: Stock trend prediction based on fractal feature selection and support vector machine. Expert Syst. Appl. **38**(5), 5569–5576 (2011)
5. Su, Y., Yao-Yuan, S., Heng, S.: Time series prediction algorithm of stock market based on support vector machine. Sci. Technol. Eng. **02**, 381–386 (2008)
6. Yakup, K., Melek, A.B., Ömer, K.B.: Predicting direction of stock price index movement using artificial neural networks and support vector machines: the sample of the Istanbul Stock Exchange. Expert Syst. Appl. **38**(5), 5311–5319 (2011)
7. Christopher, K., Xuan, A.D., Nicolas, H.: Deep neural networks, gradient-boosted trees, random forests: statistical arbitrage on the S&P 500. Eur. J. Oper. Res. **259**(2), 689–702 (2016)
8. Thomas, F., Christopher, K.: Deep learning with long short-term memory networks for financial market predictions. Eur. J. Oper. Res. **270**(2), 654–669 (2018)
9. Pascanu, R., Gulcehre, C., Cho, K.: How to construct deep recurrent neural networks. In: International Conference on Learning Representations, pp. 1–13. IEEE Press, Piscataway (2014)
10. Dong, Y., Li, D.: Automatic Speech Recognition, vol. 237. Springer Verlag, London (2015)
11. Ma, X., Tao, Z., Wang, Y.: Long short-term memory neural network for traffic speed prediction using remote microwave sensor data. Transp. Res. Part C: Emerg. Technol. **54**, 187–197 (2015)
12. Kingma, D., Ba, J.: Adam: a method for stochastic optimization. In: 2014 IEEE International Conference on Learning Representations. IEEE (2014)
13. Srivastava, N., Hinton, G., Krizhevsky, A.: Dropout: a simple way to prevent neural networks from overfitting. J. Mach. Learn. Res. **15**(1), 1929–1958 (2014)

A Network Based Quantitative Method for the Mining and Visualization of Music Influence

Jiachen Zheng$^{(\boxtimes)}$, Xinning Chi, and Siyang Weng

School of Data Science and Engineering, East China Normal University,
Shanghai 200062, China

Abstract. In the era of big data, the quantitative analysis of music influence has become an indispensable dimension. This paper focuses on the quantitative representation of the artist's influence value and proposes an AR (*ArtistRank*) value to quantify the influence value, which is obtained during the construction of Influencer-Follower network. Then, Louvain based Music Influencer-follower Network Construction model (LMIFNC) is developed and utilized to construct directed weighted Influencer-Follower network. Experimental results indicate that the AR can quantify the influence value and Influencer-Follower network based on LMIFNC can embody the relationship of different artists.

Keywords: Music influence · Quantitative analysis · Network analysis · Louvain method

1 Introduction

Music is a key cultural expression that has captured listener's attention for ages. Like language, it is a human universal involving perceptually discrete elements displaying organization and has penetrated into our lives. Since music is the gem of human civilization, the connections analysis between artists plays a major role in unveiling the impacts of music on human society and culture. Such emphasis on their producers can help us better understand them [1]. The development of society and technology gives us handful music data to especially analyze in a specific quantitative way despite the fact that researches on how music affects our cultural society in a cultural aspect have been in-depth a lot. However, this has become an indispensable and original dimension and can help us go further in this field [2].

Born from human productive activities, music has a long history just as the humankind. It is music that has distinctive features of the times. The mainstream music of different times has separate styles and genres. Moreover, it is the artists that use their wits to compose music. Thus, the characteristics of music mirrors their producers' thoughts. All the variations of music can be ultimately dated to the people behind them [3]. Therefore, this paper centers around those music producers and probes the evolution and revolution of music over 90 decades by building network based on the connection between the influences and those being affected.

© Springer Nature Singapore Pte Ltd. 2021
Y. Tan et al. (Eds.): DMBD 2021, CCIS 1453, pp. 59–72, 2021.
https://doi.org/10.1007/978-981-16-7476-1_6

Nowadays, machine learning has been widely applied to many different fields, for examples healthcare, marketing, security, and information retrieval and achieved many inspiring results [4]. However, to the best of our knowledge, researches on network based quantitative method for music influence are not found although many machine learning methods are used in music retrieval and classification [5].

For example, with the growth of online music databases and easy access to music content, it is difficult for listeners to select and manage the songs. Tzanetakis and Cook studied the features of the music such as rhythmic structure, harmonic content and instrumentation and used them to categorize and organize songs. The supervised machine learning approaches such as Gaussian mixture model and k-nearest neighbor classifiers are employed [6]. Mandel and Ellis studied Support Vector Machines (SVMs) with different distance metrics and applied to classify genre [7]. Wyse used the spectrogram of a signal to capture both time and frequency information. Spectrograms can be considered as images and used to train Convolutional Neural Networks (CNNs) [8]. Li et al. developed a CNN to predict the music genre using the raw MFCC matrix as input [9].

In this paper, a network based quantitative method for music influence is proposed to study the relationship between influencer and followers. Firstly, an AR (*ArtistRank*) is proposed to quantify the influence value, which is obtained during the construction of Influencer-Follower network. Secondly, Louvain based Music Influencer-follower Network Construction (LMIFNC) model is developed and utilized to construct directed weighted Influencer-Follower network. Finally, several experiments are conducted and results indicate that the AR can quantify the influence value and Influencer-Follower network based on LMIFNC can embody the relationship of different artists.

The rest of the paper is organized as follows. Section 2 defines the notation used in this paper. Section 3 details the definition of AR and LMIFNC Model for Influencer-Follower Network while Sect. 4 presents the experimental results analysis and visualization. At last, Sect. 5 concludes the papers and discusses the future work.

2   Notations

We defined the symbols used in this paper and their explanations in Table 1. Other non-frequent-used symbols will be introduced once they are used.

Table 1. Notations

Symbol	Definition
i	The i_{th} id
a_i	The artist of i_{th} id
v_{a_i}	The vertex of $artist_i$
v_{a_j}	The vertex of $artist_j$, made up of the followers of $artist_i$
$N(v_{a_i})$	The set of neighbour vertices of $artist_i$
n	The number of artists (vertices)
m	The number of edges of the network
$in(v_{a_j})$	The indegree of $artist_j$ as a vertex
$out(v_{a_i})$	The outdegree of $artist_i$ as a vertex, same logic as $in(v_{a_j})$
$W_{n \times m}$	The network weight matrix with n artists
$AR_O(v_{a_j})$	initial influence of $artist_j$
$AR(v_{a_i})$	The final influence of $artist_i$ after correction
C	The correction coefficient considering both start-time
Com_x	The community (music genre) item(musician) x belongs to

3 LMIFNC Model for Influencer-Follower Network

This section describes the whole process of building the Influencer-Followers network in detail. Such network plays an important role in the music over-time evolution study, because the network between influencer and follower can effectively help us to study music evolution over time. We propose the LMIFNC model to build the whole network and subnetwork accordingly. Our method will help us quantify the 'music influence' between both artists and artists groups clearly and reasonably, through which we can study the over-time music evolution.

3.1 Features of "Music Influence"

Basic features that capture "music influence" include start-time of influencers and followers, artists or vertices, linkage or relationship between artists (vertices), weights and so on. Then, they are incorporated into 2 conclusive ones, namely influence of the artist vertex (general donated as *ArtistRank*) and linkage weights between artists.

3.2 The Influence of Artist

For an artist, to explore its influence, we not only explore the number of its followers, but also consider the influence ability of its followers. The linkage between artists can be analogous to the user linkage on the web. Therefore, the method of ranking related pages can be used for reference. PageRank algorithm [10] is a method used by Google to measure the importance of web pages and mark the rank of web pages. PageRank value marks the relevance and quality of a web page. Here, we can draw lessons from the idea of voting system in PageRank algorithm as a quantification of the "music influence" of individual artists.

Different from the randomness of users' autonomous jump on the web pages, this 'music influence' is determined by default when one artist believes that I was indeed influenced by him and thus the connection relationship is existed. What is more, due to the obsolescence of PageRank's theme, we introduce the time parameter, and consider it as a very indispensable one.

3.2.1   The Initial Influence of Artist Drawn from Linkage

In this study, we have assumed to ignore the impact of uneven sample distribution on link results, that is, a small number of samples are understood as less famous genres, and the influence of artists belonging to them will naturally be much smaller than that of larger schools. Therefore, the initial influence of artist can be described based on connection by only considering the connection relationship. As shown in Fig. 1 (A, B, C, D, E, F stands for $artist_A$ to $artist_F$), directed edges (A, C) and (B, C) are chains to $artist_C$. Then, (C, D), (C, E), (C, F) are links from $artist_C$ to other artists.

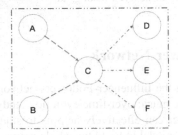
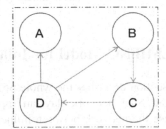

Fig. 1. Artist network   **Fig. 2.** Artistrank leakage

Intuitively, in Fig. 1, $artist_C$ should be the most influential artist, because it has multiple entering and leveling edges at the same time. Therefore, two assumptions to measure the "music influence" of artists (*ArtistRank*) are as follows. (1) If many artists point to an artist at the same time, the pointed artist will be more influential, and its corresponding *ArtistRank* value is higher; (2) If a very influential artist points to an artist, the pointed artist will also be relatively important, and its corresponding *ArtistRank* value is higher. Based on the above assumptions, the initial influence of artist based on connection $AR_O(v_{a_i})$ is defined as Formula (1):

$$AR_O(v_{a_i}) = \sum_{a_j \in N(v_{a_i})} \frac{AR_O(v_{a_j})}{in(v_{a_j})} \tag{1}$$

In fact, among all the artists given in the data set apart from the 2010s artist, some artists also don't have followers and therefore lack entering edges. *ArtistRank* of these artists will gradually reduce to 0 or be lost in a certain process of iterative calculation (as shown in the algorithm process in the pseudocode), resulting in "ranking leakage". Considering the above problems, we adjust the algorithm as follows.

Firstly, the weight adjacent matrix $W_{n \times n}$ is defined as follows:

$$
W_{4 \times 4} = \left\{ \begin{array}{cccc} 0 & 0 & 0 & 0 \\ 0 & 0 & 1 & 0 \\ 0 & 0 & 0 & 1 \\ 0.5 & 0.5 & 0 & 0 \end{array} \right\}
$$

$W_{n \times n}$ describes the connections between artists simplified as following figures.

Secondly, Fig. 2 describes the cases that some artists do not point to the other artists. If we calculated *ArtistRank* according to the above method, *ArtistRank* value will leak. Therefore, we adjusted the method of calculating *ArtistRank* as follows where local parameter γ work as a modification in Formula (2):

$$
W_{n \times n} = \gamma W_{n \times n} + (1 - \gamma) \left[\frac{1}{n} \right] n \times n \tag{2}
$$

If the rounds of iteration are increased, some *ArtistRank* values can also be lost because some sum of rows of matrix are not 1. In this sense, there will still be leakage, but just the speed of leakage is a little bit slower. Therefore, to avoid leakage, another parameter s is introduced to solve this leakage at the end of each iteration. At the end of each iteration, the sum of the *ArtistRank* values of all vertices is calculated as s, and the leakage value of this iteration is $1-s$. In order to avoid leakage, the leakage part equally is assigned to each vertex, that is $\frac{1-s}{n}$ for each vertex.

Finally, the ultimate *ArtistRank* value of each vertex is divided into three parts as Formula (3). The first part is obtained according to the connection relationship of the original network; The second part is the initial modification parameter γ to prevent leakage; The last part is to evenly allocate the leakage value $1-s$ to n vertices.

$$
AR_O(v_{a_i}) = \gamma \sum_{a_j \in N(v_{a_i})} \frac{AR_O(v_{a_j})}{in(v_{a_j})} + (1 - \gamma)\frac{1}{n} + \frac{1-s}{n} \tag{3}
$$

Algorithm 1 is the pseudocode description of ArtistRank Algorithm.

Algorithm 1: ArtistRank

1: Initialization vector $r^{old} = (0, 0, \cdots, 0)$;

2: Initialization vector $r^{new} = \left(\frac{1}{n}, \cdots, \frac{1}{n}\right)$;

3: while $\sum_j |r_j^{new} - r_j^{old}| > \varepsilon$ do

4:      $r^{old} \leftarrow r^{new}$;

5:      $S \leftarrow 0$;

6:      for j=1, 2, $\cdots$, n do

7:          if the indegree of vertex j == 0 then

8:              $r_j^{new} \leftarrow 0$;

9:          else

10:             $r_j^{new} \leftarrow \sum_{i \to j} \frac{r_i^{old}}{n_i}$;

11:             $S \leftarrow S + r_j^{new}$;

12:     for j=1, 2, $\cdots$, n do

13:         $r_j^{new} \leftarrow \beta r_j^{new} + \frac{1-\beta S}{n}$;

14: return r^{old};

3.2.2 Logarithm Function for Time-Offset Correction Coefficient C

When exploring the development of music over time, we cannot ignore the time parameter. Musicians in different periods have various aesthetic understanding of music creation means as well as music style. We will not discuss "music influence" quantification from the perspective of rigorous music theory and cultural knowledge, but consider the influence of time parameters of different artists' start-time from two perspectives. For the earlier artists, we would be confident to suggest that the number of followers affected by them will increase over time, so we appropriately reduce their *ArtistRank* values. For the later artists, we have reason to suggest that the number of followers affected by them will decrease because timepoint has always have an end, so we therefore increase their *ArtistRank* values. Therefore, we introduce a refinement parameter *C* to make above ideas into formula. Time refinement parameter *C* is defined as Formula (4):

$$C = \log\left(\frac{\left(T_{influencer} - T_0 + \alpha\right)}{\beta} + 1\right) \tag{4}$$

Where T_0 denotes the earliest year in the dataset (1930); α denotes the year span interval, also same as the data set (10 years); β denotes scaler; +1 denotes add-one smoothing method.

The earliest one in the data is selected as the benchmark and the start-time of other artists is subtracted so as to eliminate the influence of time accumulation. At the same time, an interval of 10 is added here, which is the same as the data year span interval to prevent the effect that the numerator is 0 which renders the correction discussion meaningless. Then we add scaler to the denominator, the value of which is taken 100 to ensure that the value is within the range of. What is more, because the span interval of the dataset is 10-year, such time span is very large and could be very sensitive compared with other fine-grained timespan. Finally, a real number 1 is added inside the logarithm function as add-one smoothing, which satisfies the domain of logarithm so that all corrections with this formula must be positive.

We compare the modification of log function, power function and linear function. The definition of function is shown in the Table 2.

Table 2. Definitions of different C

Name of correction function	Definition of C
Power function	$2^{\frac{\left(T_{influencer}-T_0+\alpha\right)}{\beta}}+1$
Linear function	$\frac{\left(T_{influencer}-T_0+\alpha\right)}{\beta}+1$
Logarithm function	$\log(\frac{\left(T_{influencer}-T_0+\alpha\right)}{\beta}+1)$

The following experiments show that power function and linear function can make the results of top10 *ArtistRank* concentrate in 2010s significantly as shown in Table 3.

Table 3. Comparison of different methods

power_method		linear_method		log_method	
start_time	Count	start_time	Count	start_time	Count
1930	7	1930	3	1930	4
1950	1	2010	7	1940	1
1960	2			1950	2
				1960	3

So, the log function is selected as the final refinement coefficient and normalized to get the final *ArtistRank* value of each musician. We define the final *ArtistRank* calculation Formula (5):

$$AR_O(v_{a_i}) = C \times AR_O(v_{a_i}) \tag{5}$$

3.2.3 Assigning Weight to the Edges of Influencer-Follower Network
According to the calculation of final value of *ArtistRank* of $artist_i(AR_O(v_{a_i}))$, the weight of edge of *artist$_i$* pointing to *artist$_j$* is defined as Formula (6):

$$w_{v_{a_i}} \rightarrow v_{a_j} = \frac{AR(v_{a_i})}{out(v_{a_i})} \tag{6}$$

3.3   Deriving Influencer-Follower Network and Subnetwork

After the first three steps (Sect. 3.2.1 to Sect. 3.2.3), weighted Influencer-Follower network matrix $W_{n \times n}$ can be attained. This section describes the last step of LMIFNC (Louvain based Music Influencer-Follower Network Construction) model.

3.3.1   Definition of Modularity and Increment of Modularity

The change of modularity is often utilized to judge the effect of community division. Newman defined the modularity of undirected graphs and it is easy to extend the modularity of undirected graph to directed graph and weight graph. We define modularity as Q:

$$Q = \frac{1}{2m} \sum_{i,j} (W_{i,j} - \frac{k_{a_i} k_{a_j}}{2m}) \delta(Com_{a_i}, Com_{a_j}) \tag{7}$$

Where k_{a_i} denotes the degree of vertex v_{a_i}, Com_{a_i} denotes the community of $artist_i$, Com_{a_j} denotes the community of $artist_i$, and $\delta(x, y)$ denotes the indicator function with detailed following definition.

Since k_{a_i} denotes the degree of vertex v_{a_i}, it is derived from the following equation:

$$k_{a_i} = out_{a_i} + in_{a_i} \tag{8}$$

The equation $Com_{a_i} = Com_{a_j}$ means that $artist_i$ and $artist_j$ belong to the same community. Thus, function $\delta(x, y)$ is defined in Formula (9):

$$\delta(Com_{a_i}, Com_{a_j}) = \begin{cases} 1, & Com_{a_i} = Com_{a_j} \\ 0, & Otherwise \end{cases} \tag{9}$$

After the nodes are compressed according to the community, the number of edges and nodes will be greatly reduced. When the community of $artist_i$ is changed, the change of modularity will only be affected by their neighbors $artist_j$.

Such change is formally defined as the change of modularity as Formula (10):

$$\Delta Q = \Delta Q(v_{a_i} \rightarrow Com_{new}) + \Delta Q(Com_{old} \rightarrow v_{a_i}) \tag{10}$$

Modularity Increment can be calculated as Formula (11):

$$\Delta Q(v_{a_i} \rightarrow Com_{new}) = Q_{new + v_{a_i}} - (Q_{new} + Q_{v_{a_i}}) \tag{11}$$

Modularity Decrement can be calculated as Formula (12):

$$\Delta Q(Com_{old} \rightarrow v_{a_i}) = -\Delta Q(v_{a_i} \rightarrow Com_{old}) \tag{12}$$

The change of modularity shown in Fig. 3 can be vividly understood when we move v_{a_j} from Com_{old} to Com_{new} where Com_{old} was made up of 3 vertices (later it only had 2) and Com_{new} was made up of 4 vertices (later it only owned 4 vertices).

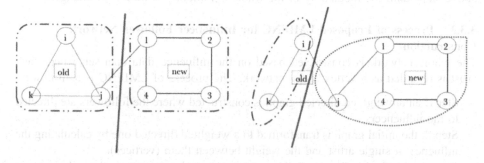

Fig. 3. Modularity increment

3.3.2 Louvain Method

Louvain algorithm is a common and fast heuristic community discovery algorithm [1]. It is a bottom-up community method, which is very consistent with the logic that we regard each artist as a vertex and a small community. It can identify all sets of communities by constantly merging small ones and obtains the final community structure. The object function of Louvain method is to maximize the modularity and find the optimal community partition. Figure 4 shows the general process of Louvain method.

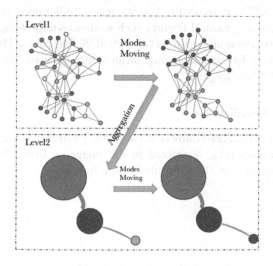

Fig. 4. Louvain method

At Level 1, each vertex v is added to the community of its neighbors and ΔQ is calculated. Then ΔQ before and after the change of the community division is compared. For each vertex v, our goal is to find the maximum ΔQ_{max}. If ΔQ_{max} is positive, vertex v is added to the community where the adjacent vertex is located. At Level 2, all the vertices belonging to the same community is compressed into a new "super vertex" (which is marked in color and the size of the icon is bigger than that in level 2). Repeat above steps until the modularity of the whole community is no longer changes.

3.3.3 Process of Proposed LMIFNC for Influencer-Follower Network Construction

The whole network is constructed based on the influence_data data set, where each artist is regarded as a vertex in the network. The process of LMIFNC is as follows:

Step1: an unweighted directed graph is constructed where the followers are directed to the influencers.

Step 2: the initial graph is transformed to a weighted directed one by calculating the influence of single artist and the weight between them (vertices).

Step 3: the final influencer-follower network and subnetwork through Louvain community detection method is achieved.

4   Experimental Results and Discussion

4.1   Data Set

Data set used in this study is provide by Integrative Collective Music (ICM) Society. "influence_data" represents musical influencers and followers, as reported by the artists themselves, as well as the opinions of industry experts. These data contain influencers and followers for 5,854 artists in the last 90 years. "full_music_data" provides 16 variable entries, including musical features such as danceability, tempo, loudness, and key, along with *artist_name* and *artist_id* for each of 98,340 songs. These data are used to create two summary data sets, including: mean values by artist "*data_by_artist*" and means across years "*data_by_year*".

4.2   Results and Visualization

Figure 5 shows the Influencer-Follower network by LMIFNC model. The communities, that is, the subnetworks, is marked in the image as lines. The representative *ArtistRank* (AR) greater than 0.1 is labelled in the figure.

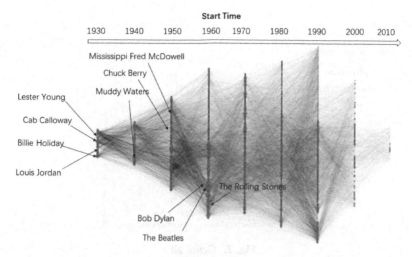

Fig. 5. Top star

Some representative musicians are marked in the Fig. 5. For each artist, the size of the point is used to represent the number of people affected which is group by given main genre or the community by LMIFNC Model.

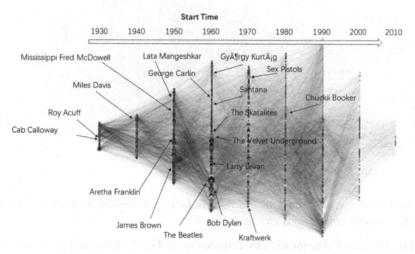

Fig. 6. Community all

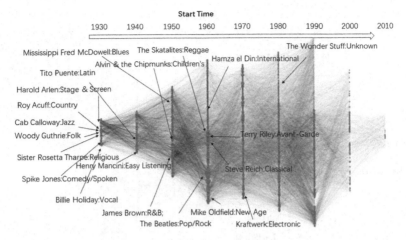

Fig. 7. Genre all

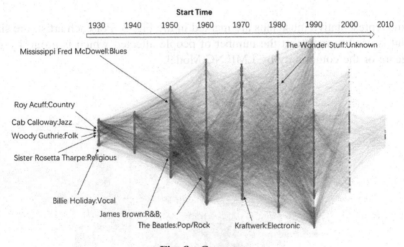

Fig. 8. Genre top

Based on the visualization of the final Influencer-Follower network and its sub-networks, several conclusions can be drawn:

(1) For the case of classification by community, in Fig. 6, different colors are used to indicate the community they belong to. It can be seen that in the 1950s and 1960s, with the great changes in popular genre, community is also changed to a certain extent.

(2) In Fig. 7, we plot the artist with the largest *ArtistRank* value in each genre. It can be seen that they are mainly concentrated in 1930 and 1960 which is consistent with the fact of music development.

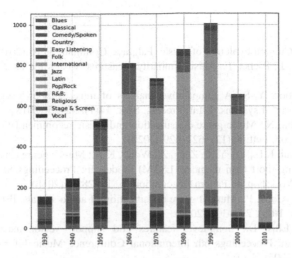

Fig. 9. Genre_year

(3) In Fig. 7, we also plot the artist with the largest *ArtistRank* value in each community. It can be seen that they are mainly concentrated around 1960. Compared with genre classification, top star in community appears later.

(4) In Fig. 8, we remove the artist whose *ArtistRank* value is smaller than the previous figure. At this time, we can see that artist is more concentrated around 1930 than in the previous figure.

(5) For artists of the same time, we arrange them in the same column. In Fig. 9, we can see that there are more data in 1950–1980 which means more counts of the artists and the number of people generally affected by early artists is more than that of late artists (post-90s).

5 Conclusion and Future Work

By weighting and iterating the influencer-follower network, influence factors for the artists are identified, and can be tuned according to the time difference so as to better adjust the influence deviation across different periods. When calculating the influence value, ArtistRank algorithm similar to Page Rank is developed to calculate the influence value of follower to influencer. The indirect influence on follower within the network based on the iteration algorithm are analyzed. However, this work is primary and need to be elaborated further. The dynamic evolution process will be studied by adopting deep learning method as recurrent neural network, long-short term memory network and the results should be verified by more artists in the field of music.

References

1. Savage, P.E.: Cultural evolution of music. Palgrave Commun. **5**, 16 (2019)
2. Aucouturier, J.-J., Pachet, F.: Music similarity measures: what's the use? Ismir **9**(1), 105–106 (2003)
3. Gurjar, K., Moon, Y.-S.: A comparative analysis of music similarity measures in music information retrieval systems. J. Inf. Process. Syst. **14**(1), 32–55 (2018)
4. Elbir, A., Aydin, N.: Music genre classification and music recommendation by using deep learning. Electron. Lett. **56**(12), 627–629 (2020)
5. Tang, C.P., Chui, K.L., Yu, Y.K., Zeng, Z., Wong, K.H.: Mu-sic genre classification using a hierarchical long-short term memory (LSTM) model. In: Proceedings SPIE 10828, Third International Workshop on Pattern Recognition, p. 108281B (2018)
6. Tzanetakis, G., Cook, P.: Musical genre classification of audio signals. IEEE Trans. Speech Audio Process. **10**(5), 293–302 (2002)
7. Mandel, M., Ellis, D.: Song-level features and support vector machines for music classification. In: Proceedings 6th International Conference Music Information Retrieval, pp. 594–599 (2005)
8. Wyse, L.: Audio spectrogram representations for processing with convolutional neural networks. In: Proceedings of the First International Conference on Deep Learning and Music, Anchorage, US, May, 2017, pp. 37–41 (2017).
9. Li, T.L., Chan, A.B., Chun, A.H.: Automatic musical pattern feature extraction using convolutional neural network. Lect. Notes Eng. Comput. Sci. **2180**(1), 11 (2010)
10. Page, L., Brin, S., Motwani, R., Winograd, T.: The pagerank citation ranking: Bringing order to the web. Stanford InfoLab, pp. 1–14 (1998)

Research on Off-Path Exploits of Network Protocols

Falin Hou[1], Xiao Yu[2(✉)], Kefan Qiu[1], Junli Liu[1], Zhiwei Shi[3],
and Yuanzhang Li[1]

[1] School of Computer Science,
Beijing Institute of Technology, Beijing 100081, China
{kfqiu,junli,popular}@bit.edu.cn
[2] Department of Computer Science and Technology,
Shandong University of Technology, Zibo 255022, China
marquis@bit.edu.cn
[3] China Information Technology Security Evaluation Center,
Beijing 100085, China

Abstract. With the rapid development of the Internet industry, from a global perspective, the risks brought by network security are becoming increasingly prominent, and continue to penetrate into political, economic, cultural, social, national defense and other fields. Network security has attracted more and more researchers' attention. This paper first analyzes the two types of network protcol attacks, reviews the development history and current status of off-path attacks, analyzes and summarizes the domestic and foreign literature from the morris TCP injection attacks inwa 1985 to the present. Finally, relying upon the reviewed work, we prospect the future development direction and research focus of off-path attacks.

Keywords: Network security · Off-path · Protocol

1 Introduction

While the Internet has become an important achievement and innovation highland for human civilization in the information age, it will also become a place where security risks converge and a new source of national conflicts. The network not only has its own security risks, but also provides conditions and media for the interweaving and transmission of various traditional and non-traditional threats, which may lead to the catalytic amplification of security incidents and bring new challenges to national security in the information age.

Network protocol vulnerability is the use of protocol defects to enable attackers to access or damage the system without authorization. It has the characteristics of wide distribution, large impact and high degree of harm. From the perspective of vulnerability distribution, there are IP address spoofing, TCP-RST attacks, TCP session hijacking, ICMP attacks, IP fragment attacks, UDP spoofing etc. From the perspective of the impact and the degree of the vulnerability, for example, Callstrider vulnerability (CVE-2020–12695) allows an attacker to evade the data leakage prevention system (DLP) of the intranet, which can lead to sensitive data leakage, and even hijack the device for distributed denial of service (DDoS) attacks.

Y. Tan et al. (Eds.): DMBD 2021, CCIS 1453, pp. 73–80, 2021.
https://doi.org/10.1007/978-981-16-7476-1_7

2 Background Theory

2.1 MITM

Limited by the development of attack capability and attack technology, the traditional network attack and defense technology usually has strong assumptions and restrictions on the attack resources or conditions of the protocol. It is generally assumed that the attacker is on the path between the two sides of the session, that is, the man in the middle (MITM) [7]. These attacks can be divided into in-path or on-path models, the attacker pretends to be the communicating party, deceives the other party by forging the source address, and hijacks th network session of the communicating party.

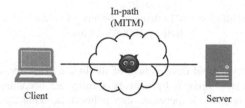

Fig. 1. In-path threat model.

Figure 1 illustrates the in-path attack model. The attacker is located between the network paths of the communicating parties, can monitor, intercept, tamper, and discard all data traffic between the server and the client. At this time, the attacker is a MITM.

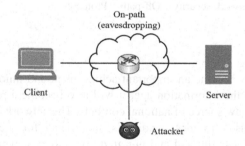

Fig. 2. On-path threat model.

Figure 2 illustrates the on-path attack model. The attacker controlled a router or switch in the communication link between the two parties, cannot intercept and discard the original normal packet between the server and the client, but the attacker can monitor and tamper with terminal packets between the server and the client.

2.2 Off-Path

The side-channel attack allows the attacker to infiltrate the target network connection off the communication path of the two parties. It usually exploits the vulnerabilities in the protocol stack to detect the sensitive information of the network connection (such as the port number and TCP sequence number under the protection of randomization, confirmation Number, etc.) to detect, and then inject forged packets to attack the target network connection, achieving the effect of blocking, tampering, hijacking connections, and network services.

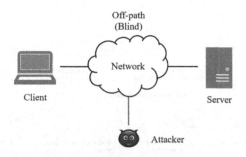

Fig. 3. Off-path threat model.

Figure 3 illustrates the off-path attack model [11]. The attacker can send a packet to the server on its own connection, or send a spoofed packet with the victim client's IP address or the the victim server's IP address. Different from a MITM attack, the off-path attacker is completely off the path of the target communication parties, unable to monitor, intercept, tamper with, and discard the network traffic between the server and the client, and can only forge one party to send a packet to the other party. It attempts to exploit a side-channel vulnerability to infer the state of the victim connection. By inferring the port number, the attacker can determine if there is an established victim connection between the server and the client. By inferring the port number and the SEQ number expected by the server, the attacker can initiate a DoS attack by sending a packet with the RST flag (and the correct SEQ) to terminate the victim's connection. If all three attributes are inferred, the attacker can hijack the victim connection and inject malicious payloads [15].

Table 1 illustrates four different types of side-channels that have been exploited to initiate off-path TCP attacks.

Table 1. Different types of off-path TCP side-channels attacks.

Side channel	Requirement	Affected OS	Patch/Mitigation
Global IPID count [1]	Pure/Javascript	Windows	Global IPID counter eliminated
Direct browser page read [8]	Javascript	Any old OS	RFC 5961
Global Challenge ACK rate limit [11]	Pure	Linux	Global rate limit eliminated
Packet counter [3, 4]	Malware	Linux,macOS	Namespace/macOS* patch
Wireless contention [12]	Javascript	Any	Wi-Fi full-duplex

3 Research on Off-Path Attacks

More and more researchers pay attention to network protocol security under off-path conditions. These studies not only involve IP protocol, TCP protocol, UDP protocol and ICMP Protocol, but also attempts to verify the attack capability in the scenario with weak attack resources and attack conditions.

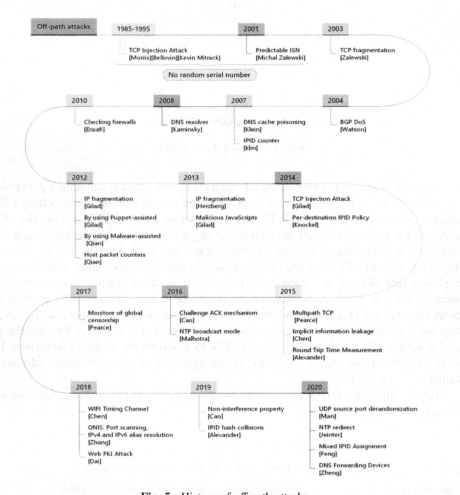

Fig. 5. History of off-path attacks.

Figure 5 illustrates the timeline of important off-path attacks and protocol security improvements. The timeline begins with morris TCP injection attacks in 1985 and Bellovin's seminal paper in 1989. Both studies have shown that predictable sequence numbers allow off-path attacks on TCP communications.

In 1995, Shimomura et al. launched a TCP injection attack on Tsutomi shimomura.

In 2001, Zalewski et al. proposed that most implementations are still sufficiently predictable ISNs to allow off-path attacks.

In 2003, Zalewski et al. proposed that the use of fragmented TCP traffic may lead to injection attacks. The piggybacking attack has been improved and is used for DNS poisoning.

In 2004, Watson et al. proposed that the first off-path injection attack against random ISNs. This attack injects RST packets to disconnect, to solve this prob-lem, many TCP implementations have also begun to use unpredictable client ports.

In 2007, Klein et al. proposed that a weakness in the pseudo random number generator in use to produce random DNS transaction IDs and random IP fragmentation IDs. This technique can be used to conduct DNS cache poisoning attack on OpenBSD DNS server in caching mode. klm et al. proposed that a TCP injection attack and a DNS poisoning attack using a random number generator in Phrack magazine. Among them, TCP attacks only target Windows machines directly connected to the Internet, and do not handle concurrent connections.

In 2008, Kaminsky et al. proposed that a more important DNS poisoning attack, which allowed most DNS resolvers at that time to achieve effective off-path poisoning. The response to this attack is to quickly adopt additional patches, increase the length of random attacks.

In 2010, Ensafi et al. proposed to use idle scanning modeling of the non-interference property of the network protocol stack, the attacker can port scan the network from outside the firewall on ports blocked by the firewall.

In 2012, Gilad et al. [5] proposed that the use of the fragmentation mechanism in the IP protocol can achieve pollution attacks on network traffic, including DNS cache pollution, traffic hijacking in NAT scenarios, and traffic blocking and discarding. In addition [1], a puppet running on the victim's client is used to inject data into a TCP connection between two peers. It allows non path attackers to effectively understand the serial numbers of clients and servers in TCP connections and perform XSS, CSRF and site spoofing without web browser or server vulnerabilities. Qian et al. [3, 4] proposed to use the firewall's filtering mechanism for traffic, installing unprivileged malware on the victim, knowing the target quadruple (source/destination IP and port), the attacker can use the deception target quadruple to detect, To infer the effective sequence number, complete the TCP sequence number inference attack.

In 2013, Herzberg et al. [6] proposed to use UDP to retrieve long DNS responses, which leads to IP fragmentation. Attackers inject forged "toxic" records into legitimate DNS responses to avoid widely deployed challenge response defense and implement out of path DNS cache poisoning attack. Gilad et al. [7, 8] proposed to exploit mali-cious JavaScripts for webcache poisoning, allow longterm control over connections to the victim server. TCP injections suffice to circumvent the SOP, hijack cookies, and cause malicious script (XSS, CSRF, and phishing) execution.

In 2014, Gilad et al. [2] proposed that when the global IPID counter client sends a packet to another destination, an offline attacker can communicate with the victim. Knockel et al. [9] proposed that the information flow between the per-destination counters of Linux machines is used to cache the fragments of machine M and L, and it can be inferred whether there is ICMP, UDP, and TCP communication between L and M, and calculate the given time The number of packets sent in the segment.

In 2015, Pearce et al. proposed that the impact of multi-path TCP (MPTCP) network security: MPTCP is prone to fragmentation of traffic. Chen et al. [10] proposed the concept of implicit information leakage controlled by attacker, designed and implemented an accurate static pollution analysis tool, PacketGuardian, to comprehensively check the packet processing logic implemented by various network protocols, and the Six popular protocol implementations including RTP are analyzed, revealing two new vulnerabilities in the Linux kernel TCP and three RTP implementations. Alexander et al. proposed that a new off-path roundtrip time estimation technique to infer the roundtrip time between hosts at any two ends.

In 2016, Cao et al. [11] discovered a newly discovered side channel vulnerability (CVE-2016–5696). The attacker uses the global challenge ack rate limit to obtain the correct TCP serial number, reset or even hijack the previous TCP connection, hijack unencrypted web traffic, or interrupt encrypted communication (such as tor connection). Malhotra et al. proposed that in the encrypted and authenticated broadcast mode of NTP, an off-path attacker sends a badly formatted broadcast packet to the client every query interval to prevent the broadcast client from updating its system clock. DoS attack.

In 2017, Pearce et al. [14] proposed that use TCP/IP auxiliary channels to measure the reachability between two Internet locations without directly controlling the measurement advantage points of any location, and achieve Corresponding systems that can continuously monitor global inspections.

In 2018, Chen et al. [12] proposed to use the half-duplex transmission mechanism of the wireless network to infer the correct TCP sequence number based on the RTT difference of the packet, breaking the security restriction of TCP sequence number randomization. Zhang et al. [13] present ONIS, a new scanning technique that can perform network measurements. Dai et al. proposed to exploits DNS Cache Poisoning and tricks the CA into issuing fraudulent certificates for domains the attacker does not legitimately.

In 2019, Cao et al. [15] proposed to research and design an automatic SCENT tool to detect TCP side-channel vulnerability by detecting violations of non-interference properties between connections. Alexander et al. [20] proposed to take advantage of side-channel present in the Linux kernel's handling of the values used to populate an IPv4 packet's IPID field, detecting the presence of an active TCP connection between a remote Linux server and an arbitrary client machine.

In 2020, Jeitner et al. [17] proposed to use the insecurity of DNS to implement off-path time-shifting attacks, and to enhance NTP attacks against the Man-In-The-Middle (MITM) security schedule, redirecting the NTP client to the attacker's control server. Man et al. proposed to quickly scan open UDP ports by using a flaw in the method of restricting ICMP packet responses in the Linux kernel function, so that remote users off the path can effectively bypass the source port UDP randomization. Kaminsky's vulnerability can be reused to cause DNS poisoning attacks. Feng et al. [16] proposed to determine the existence of a TCP connection by observing the global shared IPID counterchange, and then infer the sequence number and confirmation number of the connection based on the IPID side-channel, to interrupt the connection or inject forged traffic. Zheng et al. propose a cache poisoning attack against DNS forwarders. Through this attack, the adversary can use the controlled domain name to inject the DNS records of any victim domain name and bypass the current cache poisoning defense.

The advantages of off-path attacks are: 1) the attacker is not on the path of both parties in communication, nor does it need to implant additional privileged malicious programs in the server and client to assist in the attack; 2) from the point of view of the attack steps, the attacker Without a lot of interaction with the attacked object, the attacker can perform the attack. 3) Compared with on-path attacks, off-path attacks have a strong limitation on the ability of the attacker and the degree of network resources he has mastered. There is no need to reserve a backdoor for the target network, which means that the preconditions of the attack are greatly reduced, its concealment is greatly improved, the harm is higher, and it is more difficult to prevent.

4 Conclusions and Future Work

Many network side-channels are for specific operating systems and even specific system versions. Different versions of Linux kernel have different IPID assignment policies, and the available side-channels are different [16]. Therefore, studying off-path attacks that span different system versions of the same operating system or even between different operating systems will be a new direction.

With the increasing adoption of IPv6, more and more machines will use IPv6 to communicate. Zhang et al. [14] proposed that both IPv4 and IPv6 of Linux 3.16 or higher kernel use the same 2048 IPID global counter, and demonstrate by using multiple IPv6 addresses in the measurement machine. Therefore, studying off-path attacks under IPv6 or even under the mixture of IPv4 and IPv6 will be a new direction.

In the context of the era of the Internet of Everything, the Internet of Things, the Internet of Vehicles, and the Internet of Ships, as products of the in-depth integration of a new generation of information technology and manufacturing, will face greater security risks while developing rapidly, and will surely become new ones [18, 19]. Attack targets, cross-system, cross-version, and cross-platform off-path network offensive and defensive technologies under the new form have also attracted more and more researchers' attention.

Acknowledgments. This work was supported by the National Natural Science Foundation of China (no. 61876019, U1936218 and 62072037).

References

1. Gilad, Y., Herzberg, A.: Off-path attacking the web. In: WOOT, pp. 41–52 (2012)
2. Gilad, Y., Herzberg, A.: Off-path TCP injection attacks. ACM Trans. Inf. Syst. Secur. (TISSEC) **16**(4), 1–32 (2014)
3. Qian, Z., Mao, Z.M., Xie, Y.: Collaborative TCP sequence number inference attack: how to crack sequence number under a second. In: Proceedings of the 2012 ACM Conference on Computer and Communications Security, pp. 593–604 (2012)

4. Qian, Z., Mao, Z.M.: Off-path TCP sequence number inference attack-how firewall middleboxes reduce security. In: 2012 IEEE Symposium on Security and Privacy, pp. 347–361. IEEE (2012)
5. Gilad, Y., Herzberg, A.: Spying in the dark: TCP and Tor traffic analysis. In: Fischer-Hübner, S., Wright, M. (eds.) privacy enhancing technologies, pp. 100–119. Springer Berlin Heidelberg, Berlin, Heidelberg (2012). https://doi.org/10.1007/978-3-642-31680-7_6
6. Herzberg, A., Shulman, H.: Fragmentation considered poisonous, or: One-domain-to-rule-them-all. In: 2013 IEEE Conference on Communications and Network Security (CNS), pp. 224–232. IEEE (2013)
7. Gilad, Y., Herzberg, A., Shulman, H.: Off-path hacking: the illusion of challenge-response authentication. IEEE Secur. Priv. 12(5), 68–77 (2013)
8. Gilad, Y., Herzberg, A.: When tolerance causes weakness: the case of injection-friendly browsers. In: Proceedings of the 22nd International Conference on World Wide Web, pp. 435–446 (2013)
9. Knockel, J., Crandall, J.R.: Counting packets sent between arbitrary internet hosts. In: 4th {USENIX} Workshop on Free and Open Communications on the Internet ({FOCI} 14) (2014)
10. Chen, Q.A., Qian, Z., Jia, Y.J., et al.: Static detection of packet injection vulnerabilities: a case for identifying attacker-controlled implicit information leaks. In: Proceedings of the 22nd ACM SIGSAC Conference on Computer and Communications Security, pp. 388–400 (2015)
11. Cao, Y., Qian, Z., Wang, Z., et al.: Off-Path {TCP} exploits: global rate limit considered dangerous. In: 25th {USENIX} Security Symposium ({USENIX} Security 16), pp. 209–225 (2016)
12. Chen, W., Qian, Z.: Off-path {TCP} exploit: how wireless routers can jeopardize your secrets. In: 27th {USENIX} Security Symposium ({USENIX} Security 18), pp. 1581–1598 (2018)
13. Zhang, X., Knockel, J., Crandall, J.R.: Onis: inferring tcp/ip-based trust relationships completely off-path. In: IEEE INFOCOM 2018-IEEE Conference on Computer Communications, pp. 2069–2077. IEEE (2018)
14. Pearce, P., Ensafi, R., Li, F., et al.: Toward continual measurement of global network-level censorship. IEEE Secur. Priv. 16(1), 24–33 (2018)
15. Cao, Y., Wang, Z., Qian, Z., et al.: Principled unearthing of TCP side-channel vulnerabilities. In: Proceedings of the 2019 ACM SIGSAC Conference on Computer and Communications Security, pp. 211–224 (2019)
16. Feng, X., Fu, C., Li, Q., et al.: Off-path TCP exploits of the mixed IPID assignment. In: Proceedings of the 2020 ACM SIGSAC Conference on Computer and Communications Security, pp. 1323–1335 (2020)
17. Jeitner, P., Shulman, H., Waidner, M.: The impact of DNS insecurity on time. In: 2020 50th Annual IEEE/IFIP International Conference on Dependable Systems and Networks (DSN), pp. 266–277. IEEE (2020)
18. Wang, K., Teng, Y., Wang, Q., et al.: Research on the application of SM algorithms of implicit certificate. Netinfo Secur. 21(5), 74–81 (2021)
19. Liu, J., Han, Y., Liu, B., Yu, B.: Research on 5G network slicing security model. Netinfo Secur. 20(4), 1–11 (2020)
20. Alexander, G., Espinoza, A., Crandall, J.: Detecting TCP/IP connections via IPID hash collisions. Proc. Priv. Enhancing Technol. 2019(4), 311–328 (2019)

Building a Covert Timing Channel over VoIP via Packet Length

Zhibin Zhang[1], Xiaosong Zhang[2(✉)], Yuan Xue[3], and Yuanzhang Li[1]

[1] School of Computer Science, Beijing Institute of Technology,
Beijing 100081, China
popular@bit.edu.cn
[2] Department of Computer Science and Technology, Tangshan University,
Tangshan 063000, China
[3] Academy of Military Science, Beijing 100091, China

Abstract. With the rapid development of the Mobile Internet, the application of instant messaging technology has become increasingly abundant, among which Voice over Internet Protocol (VoIP) has played an important role. However, in the VoIP-based instant messaging scene, there is a risk of illegal eavesdropping by a third party. For this problem, we consider building a covert timing channel (CTC) to hide user messages and improve the security of instant messaging. At present, the existing methods of building covert timing channels (CTCs) are mainly applied to traditional Ethernet, and there is a lack of relevant methods for mobile networks, especially VoIP networks. In order to improve the transmission capacity of the CTC and improve the transmission security of user information, the research of this article focus on the method of building covert timing channel over VoIP according to the characteristics of packet length. And a prototype is established based on Linphone, which is an open-source VoIP application. Through reality transmission tests, covert messages are delivered effectively, which proves that the CTC based on packet length are feasible.

Keywords: Covert timing channel · VoIP · Packet length

1 Introduction

According to a report [1] by Global System for Mobile Communications Association (GSMA), as of December 2020, more than 990 million people in China have used Mobile Internet services. With the popularization of 4G networks and the gradual deployment of 5G networks, the application and development of instant messaging technology on the Mobile Internet is on the rise. However, due to some security problems in the network system, it is often maliciously attacked by a third party, which affects the security and confidentiality of instant messaging. Therefore, how to transmit data safely and reliably has become the focus of research.

The definition of covert channels is proposed by Lampson in 1973 [2]. The covert channel can realize the hiding transmission under the condition of being monitored. With the continuous expansion of the Mobile Internet, the covert channel provides a

© Springer Nature Singapore Pte Ltd. 2021
Y. Tan et al. (Eds.): DMBD 2021, CCIS 1453, pp. 81–88, 2021.
https://doi.org/10.1007/978-981-16-7476-1_8

secure and covert transmission solution between terminals, which meets the transmission needs in specific scenarios [3].

This article proposes a method of building a covert timing channel over VoIP via packet length, which provides covert and robust data transmission capabilities to complete the transmission of covert data. In addition, a prototype is developed based on the Linphone, and the feasibility and transmission performance of the method are evaluated.

The contribution of this article is as follows:

We propose a method of building a covert timing channel over VoIP via packet length. Firstly, the covert data need to be grouped to construct packet data frames. In the precoding stage, referring to the design of High-Level Data Link Control (HDLC), frame header and CRC code are added before and after each packet data, so that the receiver can judge whether the received data is complete in time. Then, use the parity characteristics of packet length to encode and decode the covert data, and the data packets are reordered to achieve modulation and demodulation, which has better transmission performance and robustness.

We build a prototype of the covert timing channel on Linphone. Adding control interface in the UI layer, used to receive and process user control instructions, and return the response results. Adding message transmission interface in the SDK layer, used to transfer data and control commands between the control interface and the execution component. Adding execution component in the SDK layer, used to monitor and control the voice packets, and realize the transmission logic of the covert timing channel. Through the reality test and evaluation, the feasibility of this method is verified.

The rest of this paper is organized as follows: Sect. 2 gives a brief introduction to the related work and background. Section 3 discusses the design process of this method and issues to be addressed. Section 4 describes implementation details in a specific environment. Section 5 evaluates the performance of the prototype. Section 6 gathers the conclusion and future work.

2 Related Work and Background

2.1 VoIP Technology

The communication process of VoIP includes multiple core technologies such as voice encoding and decoding, real-time transmission protocol, and packet switching. Research on its core technologies is the premise and foundation for building CTCs. Under normal circumstances, during VoIP communication, the analog signal of the input voice data is converted into a digital signal for processing [4]. The digital processing of audio usually requires three steps of sampling, quantization and encoding to convert continuous analog signals into discrete digital signals, so that digital data packets can be transmitted through the network.

Real-time Transport Protocol (RTP) is the application layer protocol for VoIP communication, which provides end-to-end network transmission of real-time data, including audio and video. Since the payload of RTP packets generally does not exceed 1440 bytes [5], in the process of VoIP communication, data frames must be subcontracted for transmission, which greatly increases the number of packets.

2.2 Covert Timing Channels

In the network environment, CTCs refer to the covert communication mechanism constructed by embedding secret information in the time sequence of network data packets [6]. CTCs have good concealment and are suitable for scenarios with strict concealment requirements [7, 8]. However, they are limited by the channel resources and network noise of the host channel, so they are more suitable for the transmission of a small number of messages.

Covert timing channels over traditional Ethernet has been explored in multiple ways. Cabuk et al. [9] proposed the first Internet Protocol CTC and investigated many design issues. Gianvecchio et al. [10] proposed a model-based CTC, which endeavored to evade detection by modeling and mimicking the statistical features of legitimate traffic. Tan et al. [11] built a covert timing channel over IOT networks via Inter-Packet Delay (IPD).

Some CTCs have been proposed for VoIP and other VoLTE applications. Tan et al. [12] proposed a covert channel over VoLTE via packet dropout, and robustness was guaranteed by additional packet dropout. Zhang et al. [13] proposed a two-way covert channel based on VoLTE, which modulates covert messages by actively discarding data packets. Liang et al. [14] proposed a payload-dependent CTC over mobile networks, where the hash checksum of a packet was extracted as the feature, and the covert message was embedded into the feature values of packet reorder. Zhang et al. [15] proposed the CTC scheme via adjusting silence periods called silence-period based covert channel (SPCC). Li et al. [16] proposed a robust packet-dropout covert timing channel (RPDCTC) over VoLTE via parity cascade coding.

In addition, we also need to refer to relevant research on network slicing and data encryption. Liu et al. [17] proposed a research on 5G network slicing security model. Wang et al. [18] proposed a research on the application of SM algorithms of implicit certificate.

3 Design

In this section, we will introduce design ideas based on the main problems to be solved during the implementation process, including architecture design, and modulation-demodulation method.

3.1 Architecture Design

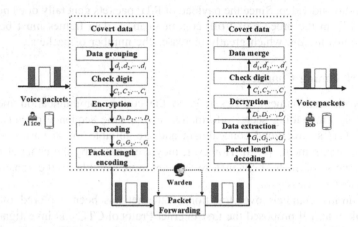

Fig. 1. The architecture of the covert timing channel based on packet length

The architecture of the CTC is shown in Fig. 1. Users Alice and Bob transmit covert data through the covert timing channel, and the warden monitors the VoIP communication between the two parties in the network.

3.2 Modulation-Demodulation Method

In this section, we introduce how to modulate and demodulate the covert data via the length characteristics of voice packets from two aspects: precoding method and packet length encoding method.

3.2.1 Precoding Method

In the precoding stage, we need to use the encrypted message block D_i and the check value C_i corresponding to the message block to construct the packet data frame G_i. However, since there may be a bit string in the data part of G_i that conflicts with the frame header, the receiver cannot accurately judge the beginning mark of the data frame, which is prone to ambiguity.

Therefore, referring to the bit stuffing in HDLC, since the frame header is set to "01111110", we need to look for the conflicting bit string in the data part of G_i, and add a bit to distinguish the frame header from the data part. Specifically, once it appears that all 5 consecutive bits are "1", one bit "0" is filled in the back, that is, the new data is "111110".

3.2.2 Packet Length Encoding Method

In the process of VoIP communication, Opus encoding is a currently popular encoding algorithm. It provides a coding method named VBR mode. The voice data encoded by this mode is constantly changing in unit time, that is, the length of the voice packet is constantly changing. The packet length encoding method just uses this feature of constant change of data packet length to modulate the covert data.

In general, the length characteristics of data packets can be considered from two aspects: length and parity. We capture the voice packets within 2 s of the voice call on Linphone as samples to analyze the length characteristics of voice packets. Figure 2 shows the variation of length characteristics and parity characteristics in the samples. It can be seen that the parity distribution of packet length is relatively uniform and dispersed, with better data distribution characteristics.

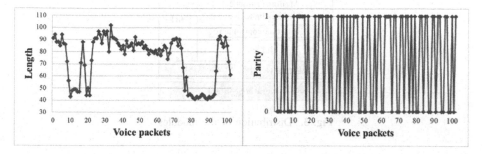

Fig. 2. Length distribution and parity distribution of voice packets

Therefore, this article uses the parity of the packet lengths to encode the covert data. That is, when the length of the voice packet is an even number, the encoding is "0"; when the length of the voice packet is an odd number, the encoding is "1".

The encoded voice packets need to be reordered according to the covert data before being sent to the receiver. Here we need to create a buffer to store and sort the voice packets.

4   Implementation

This section discusses the implementation of this method. We develop a CTC prototype with Linphone, and verify the CTC method based on packet length in the Linphone environment. The Android version of Linphone used in this article is 4.2.3, and SDK version is 4.3.0.

As shown in Fig. 3, the CTC prototype includes the following three modules:

1. control interface
2. message interface
3. execution component

The control interface is located in the UI layer of Linphone, used to receive and process user control instructions, and return the response results; the message interface is located in the Mediastreamer2 layer of the Linphone SDK, used to transfer data and control commands between the control interface and the execution component; the execution component is located in the Opus module of the Mediastreamer2 layer, which is used to monitor and control the voice packets encoded and decoded by Opus, and realize the transmission logic of the CTC.

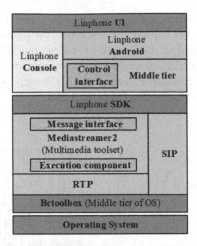

Fig. 3. Distribution of the modules

5   Test Evaluation

In this section, we evaluate the feasibility and transmission performance of the prototype.

5.1   Feasibility Test

We set three network environments for testing, namely WIFI-WIFI, 4G-WIFI and 4G-4G. Each time, 16 bytes of covert data were transmitted, and the testing time was 1 min. Ten tests were conducted in a group, and a total of 10 groups were conducted to determine whether the receiver could receive and accurately restore covert data within the testing time.

Table 1. Transmission success rate.

Network	Success rate	Packet loss rate
WIFI-WIFI	95%	0.41%
WIFI-4G	83%	2.36%
4G-4G	81%	1.05%

The test results under different network environments are shown in Table 1, the transmission success rate all exceeds 80%. When accessing a 4G network, due to the increase of network complexity, the link is unstable. As the packet loss rate increases, the transmission success rate decreases.

5.2   Transmission Performance Test

Assuming that the length of the covert data to be transmitted is K bits, and the number of voice packets used to modulate the covert data is N, the transmission capacity of the CTC is defined as $C = K/N$. Assuming that the time used to transmit covert data is T, the transmission rate of the CTC is defined as $S = K/T$.

In this section, a test is performed with 16 bytes of covert data, and the length of the data slice in the packet data frame is set to 4 bytes, 6 bytes, 8 bytes, 10 bytes, and 12 bytes, respectively. The test results of transmission rate and transmission capacity are shown in Fig. 4.

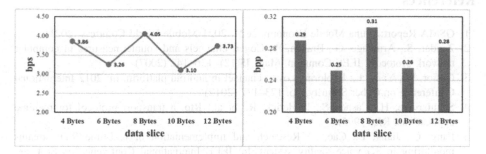

Fig. 4. The test result of transmission rate and transmission capacity

It can be seen from the figure that when the length of data slice is set to 8 bytes, the transmission performance of the CTC is the highest. This is because the longer the data slice, the smaller the proportion of the frame header and the check value, and the higher the transmission rate, but the number of discontinuous transmissions will increase, thereby affecting the transmission rate.

The comparison of transmission rate between the CTCs are summarized in Table 2. According to the result, the CTC behaves well in transmission rate.

Table 2. The comparison of transmission rate.

CTC via packet length	SPCC [15]	RPDCTC [16]
4.05 b/s	0.8–3.0 b/s	1.0–2.0 b/s

6   Conclusion and Future Work

In this article, we propose a secure transmission method over VoIP. According to the parity characteristics of packet length, we build a covert timing channel and develop a prototype based on the Linphone platform. Through the test of the prototype, the feasibility of this method is verified. The results show that this method can efficiently and stably transmit covert data under the premise of protecting the concealment of data.

However, there are still some limitations. First, the covert timing channel has a weak ability to deal with packet loss. The method in this article can only check the error of covert data, but cannot correct and modify the error. Secondly, the transmission rate needs to be improved, and there is still a big gap compared with the covert storage channel. In the future work, we will study related methods for correcting errors in the covert data, and improve the capability of error handling to achieve high reliability.

Acknowledgments. This work was supported by the National Natural Science Foundation of China (no. 62072037).

References

1. GSMA Report: China Mobile Economy 2021. 2021 Mobile World Congress (2021)
2. Zander, S., Armitage, G., Branch, P.: Covert channels and countermeasures in computer network protocols. IEEE Commun. Mag. **45**(12), 136–142 (2007)
3. Gasior, W., Yang, L.: Exploring covert channel in android platform. In: 2012 International Conference on Cyber Security, pp. 173–177 (2012)
4. Schulzrinne, H., Casner, S., Frederick, R., et al.: Rtp: a transport protocol for realtime applications. Rfc (1995)
5. Fang, C., Jiang, L., Cao, J.: Research and implementation of real-time RTP streams monitoring in 3G voice quality system. In: IEEE International Conference on Software Engineering & Service Science. IEEE (2012)
6. Zseby, T., Vázquez, F.I., Bernhardt, V., et al.: A network steganography lab on detecting TCP/IP covert channels. IEEE Trans. Educ. **59**(3), 224–232 (2016)
7. Kaur, J., Wendzel, S., Meier, M.: Countermeasures for covert channel-internal control protocols. In: International Conference on Availability, pp. 422–428 (2015)
8. Elsadig, M.A., Fadlalla, Y.A.: Network protocol covert channels: countermeasures techniques. In: 2017 9th IEEE-GCC Conference and Exhibition (GCCCE). IEEE (2018)
9. Cabuk, S., et al.: IP covert timing channels: design and detection. In: ACM Conference on Computer & Communications Security. ACM (2004)
10. Gianvecchio, S., et al.: Model-based covert timing channels: automated modeling and evasion. In: Recent Advances in Intrusion Detection (2008)
11. Tan, Y.A., Zhang, X., Sharif, K., et al.: Covert timing channels for IOT over mobile networks. IEEE Wirel. Commun. **25**(6), 38–44 (2018)
12. Tan, Y.A., Xu, X., Liang, C., et al.: An endtoend covert channel via packet dropout for mobile networks. Int. J. Distrib. Sens. Netw. **14**(5), 1550147718779568 (2018)
13. Zhang, X., et al.: A two-way VoLTE covert channel with feedback adaptive to mobile network environment. IEEE Access (99), 1 (2019)
14. Liang, C., et al.: A payloaddependent packet rearranging covert channel for mobile VoIP traffic. Inf. Sci. **465**, 162–173 (2018)
15. Zhang, X., Tan, Y.A., Liang, C., et al.: A covert channel over VoLTE via adjusting silence periods. IEEE Access **6**, 9292–9302 (2018)
16. Li, Y., Zhang, X., Xu, X., et al.: A robust packet-dropout covert channel over wireless networks. IEEE Wirel. Commun. **27**(3), 60–65 (2020)
17. Liu, J.W., Han, Y.R., Liu, B., Yu, B.Y.: Research on 5G network slicing security model. Netinfo Secur. **20**(4), 1–11 (2020)
18. Wang, K.X., Teng, Y.J., Wang, Q.X., et al.: Research on the application of SM algorithms of implicit certificate. Netinfo Secur. **21**(5), 74–81 (2021)

Bone Marrow Cell Segmentation Based on Improved U-Net

Lingmin Jin[1], Zhaochai Yu[2], Haoyi Fan[3], Shenghua Teng[1(✉)],
and Zuoyong Li[2(✉)]

[1] College of Electronic and Information Engineering,
Shandong University of Science and Technology, Qingdao 266590, China
shteng@sdust.edu.cn
[2] Fujian Provincial Key Laboratory of Information Processing and Intelligent
Control, College of Computer and Control Engineering, Minjiang University,
Fuzhou 350121, China
[3] School of Information Engineering, Zhengzhou University,
Zhengzhou 450001, China

Abstract. Automatic segmentation of bone marrow cells plays an important role in the diagnosis of many blood diseases such as anemia and leukemia. Due to the complex morphology and wide variety of bone marrow cells, their segmentation is still a challenging task. To improve the accuracy of bone marrow cell segmentation, we propose an end-to-end U-shaped network based on the pyramid residual convolution and the attention mechanism. Specifically, the standard convolution and dilated convolution are combined as its feature encoder, which designs a pyramid residual convolution block to extract multi-scale features. Then, the attention gating mechanism is introduced into each skip connection module for fusing the shallow and deep information. Finally, the proposed method combines convolution and deconvolution for feature decoding to achieve the final segmentation of bone marrow cells. Experiments with quantitative and qualitative comparisons are carried out on a self-built bone marrow smear dataset. Experimental results demonstrate the superiority of the proposed method over several state-of-the-art methods.

Keywords: Bone marrow cell · Image segmentation · Pyramid convolution · Attention gating mechanism

1 Introduction

Bone marrow is the main hematopoietic system of the human body. Bone marrow cells, including myeloid stem cells and lymphoid stem cells, exhibit complex morphology and a wide variety of types. For example, the myeloid lineage cells can be divided into erythroid cells, granular cells and megakaryocytic cells, with more than 20 subtypes. The number and proportion of various types of cells in the bone marrow smear is an important clue for the diagnosis of acute leukemia. Traditional blood cell microscopy is manually operated by physicians through a microscope, which is usually time and energy consuming and suffers from human subjectivity. Therefore, it is necessary to

© Springer Nature Singapore Pte Ltd. 2021
Y. Tan et al. (Eds.): DMBD 2021, CCIS 1453, pp. 89–99, 2021.
https://doi.org/10.1007/978-981-16-7476-1_9

study the automatic segmentation of bone marrow cells to facilitated the diagnosis of some related diseases.

Researchers have developed some computer-aided methods for bone marrow cell segmentation. These methods are initially based on features of gray level, color or texture, roughly divided into three categories: edge based methods, region based methods, and the hybrid methods combining region-based and edge-based approaches. For instance, a two-level thresholding method by color feature weighted filter was proposed to separate the nucleus and cytoplasm of bone marrow cells [1]. Zhou et al. [2] used adaptive histogram threshold and color component to locate the blood cell, and then extracted the entire cell by contour detection. Besides, some machine learning methods are applied in bone marrow cell segmentation, such as Maximum a Posteriori (MAP) estimation [3], K-means clustering [4–6], support vector machine (SVM) [5, 8] and extreme learning machine (ELM) [7] classification, etc. It should be noted that all these methods rely on optimal handcraft features.

In recent years, deep learning has made significant progress in the fields of computer vision and medical image processing. Deep learning based semantic segmentation is appropriate for medical imaging. The classic method wherein is the U-Net [9] network with encoder-decoder structure, followed by some improved deep convolutional neural networks [10–14] applied in the field of medical image segmentation. As for bone marrow cell segmentation, a fully convolutional neural network (FCNN) was proposed by Eekelen et al. [15] to segment six different types of cells in bone marrow biopsy sections. Wu et al. [16] developed a network model by adding a residual module to the U-Net network to realize the segmentation and classification of bone marrow red granulocytes.

Inspired by the network structure of U-Net [9], this paper proposes a U-shaped network based on pyramid residual convolution and attention mechanism to realize an end-to-end segmentation of bone marrow cells. The main contributions of this work are summarized below.

(1) Following the U-shaped segmentation framework, we use the pyramid convolution block in the encoder to enlarge the receptive field, capture different levels of information, and reduce feature loss.
(2) The attention gating mechanism is introduced into the skip connection process of the encoder-decoder to better integrate the shallow and deep information.
(3) Quantitative and qualitative experiment comparisons among our method and several state-of-the-art methods are carried out on a self-built dataset, demonstrating the effectiveness of the proposed method.

The rest of this paper is organized as follows. Section 2 describes the principle and implementation of the proposed method, then Sect. 3 introduces the experimental results and analysis. And finally, Sect. 4 draws the conclusion.

2   Proposed Method

Our goal is to automatically segment the bone marrow cells from the complex background of the stained bone marrow smears for subsequent identification and classification. For this, we propose an end-to-end U-shaped segmentation network for bone marrow cells, termed BM-net, by using pyramid convolution and attention mechanism. As illustrated in Fig. 1, the architecture of BM-Net consists of three stages: feature encoder, feature fusion, and feature decoder. The detailed descriptions for them will be in the following sections.

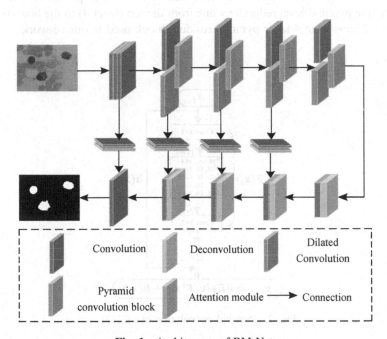

Fig. 1. Architecture of BM-Net.

2.1   Feature Encoder Module

The encoder stage comprises an input module and 4 down-sampling modules. The input module is composed of three convolutions with the size 3×3. GN (Group Normalization) [18] and PReLU (Parametric Rectified Linear Unit) activation function are applied after each convolutional layer. GN divides channels into different groups, calculates the normalized mean and variance in each group, and finally combines the results of all groups, avoiding the influence by batch size of the model. Using PReLU activation function can solve the neuron necrosis in negative space neurons.

The down-sampling module consists of a convolution block and a pyramid convolution block. The convolution block combines the standard convolution and dilated convolution to extract shallow features, followed by a pyramid convolution block [17] composed of n levels of different types of convolution kernels. At each level of pyramid, the convolution kernel contains different spatial resolutions. The size of the convolution kernel continues to increase from the bottom of the pyramid to the top, and the depth of the kernel gradually decreases from the bottom to the top. Different size of convolution kernels can capture different levels of information and help improve the segmentation performance of the network. We use grouped convolution that input feature is divided into different numbers of groups and the convolution kernel is used to process the input feature in parallel. Finally, the outputs of different convolution kernels are merged into the final output that enhancing the connectivity between the convolution kernels. In this paper, we use four levels convolution kernels (level-1 to level-4): 3×3, 5×5, 7×7, 9×9. When the network performs one downsampling, the pyramid level reduces by one from the top (level-4) to the bottom (level-1). Figure 2 shows the 4-layer pyramid residual block used in our network.

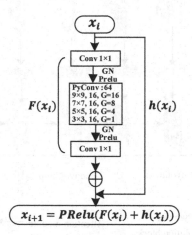

Fig. 2. Pyramid convolution block [17].

2.2   Feature Fusion Module

The information obtained by the encoder is shallow, and that by the decoder belongs to deep information. To deal with the semantic gap between them, we add residual connection and an attention mechanism in connecting them. By assigning different weights for input features, we can filter out the important information. The attention gating mechanism (AG) [19] used in this paper is shown in Fig. 3. First, the feature x_l of the encoding stage and the feature g of the corresponding decoding stage pass through 1×1 convolution respectively. Their results are added in an element-wise manner, and then undergoes a non-linear change through the PReLU activation function. Second, the 1×1 convolution and Sigmoid activation function are consecutively applied to get the attention weight map. Finally, the attention weight map is multiplied by the encoder feature x_l to generate the attention weighted vector which is fed to the decoder.

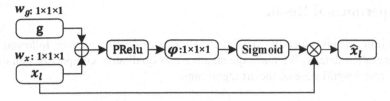

Fig. 3. Attention gating mechanism [19].

2.3 Feature Decoder Module

After the feature encoder stage, the size of the bone marrow cell feature map will reduce. To achieve the end-to-end segmentation, we use a decoder to gradually restore the original image size. The decoder consists of four up-sampling blocks and one output block. The up-sampling block is composed of convolution and deconvolution. After each convolution layer, Group Normalization and PReLU activation are applied. Finally, the output block undergoes a 1×1 convolution to restore the original image size.

2.4 Loss Function

Being an important factor to determine the network performance, the loss function evaluates the difference between the model's output and the true label. Due to the complex morphology of bone marrow cells, we combine binary cross entropy [9] and Dice [12] loss function to guide the network training. The loss function is:

$$L = \lambda L_{BCE} + L_{Dice},\tag{1}$$

where L_{BCE} and L_{Dice} are binary cross entropy and Dice loss function respectively, and λ is an adjustable parameter.

$$L_{BCE} = -\sum\nolimits_{i=1}^{N} \left(y_i \log(\sigma(p_i)) + (1 - y_i)\log(1 - \sigma(p_i)) \right),\tag{2}$$

$\sigma()$ is the Sigmoid function, N represents the number of pixels, y_i is the true label of the input image x_i, and p_i is the probability that the category of the predicted input image x_i is 1.

$$L_{Dice} = 1 - \frac{2\sum_{i=1}^{N} y_i \cdot p_i}{\sum_{i=1}^{N} y_i + \sum_{i=1}^{N} p_i},\tag{3}$$

λ is set to 0.5 in practice.

3 Experimental Results

This section first introduces the dataset and various evaluation metrics, followed by the implementation details. We make quantitative and qualitative comparisons among our method and several state-of-the-art algorithms.

3.1 Dataset and Evaluation Metrics

The bone marrow smear dataset used in this paper is collected by the Third People's Hospital of Fujian Province. The dataset contains 227 bone marrow smear images including lymphoid and myeloid cells with the size 512×512 pixels. To prevent over-fitting and improve the generalization ability and accuracy of the network model, data enhancement is applied to expand the dataset, including color dithering, rotation, and flipping.

To quantitatively evaluate the segmentation accuracy, the following six measures, Precision [20], Dice (Dice coefficient) [21], mIoU (mean Intersection over Union) [22], ME (Misclassification Error) [23], FPR (False Positive Rate), FNR (False Negative Rate) [24] are introduced. These metrics are defined as:

$$Precision = \frac{|G_b \cap P_b|}{|P_b|}, \tag{4}$$

$$Dice = \frac{2|G_b \cap P_b|}{|G_b| + |P_b|}, \tag{5}$$

$$mIoU = \frac{1}{2} \left(\frac{|G_n \cap P_n|}{|G_n \cup P_n|} + \frac{|G_b \cap P_b|}{|G_b \cup P_b|} \right), \tag{6}$$

$$ME = 1 - \frac{|G_n \cap P_n| + |G_b \cap P_b|}{|G_b| + |G_n|}, \tag{7}$$

$$FPR = \frac{|G_n \cap P_b|}{|G_n|}, \tag{8}$$

$$FNR = \frac{|G_b \cap P_n|}{|G_b|}, \tag{9}$$

Among them, G_b and G_n represent bone marrow cell and non-marrow cell region of the ground truth labels; P_b and P_n are bone marrow cell and non-marrow cell region of the predicted segmentation results.

3.2 Implementation Details

The experiment runs in the environment of NVIDIA GeForce GTC 1650Ti GPU, 16 GB RAM, Windows10 operating system. The model is implemented by using Pytorch framework. The ratio of the training set, validation set, and test set is 7:1:2. We expand the training set with data enhancement, initial learning rate 0.0001, and iterative training is performed 200 times. We employ Adam algorithm [25] to optimize the network model.

3.3 Results and Analysis

To verify the effectiveness of the BM-Net segmentation method, it is compared qualitatively and quantitatively with the methods Zhou [2], U-Net [9], Resnet++ [10], Att U-Net [19] and Ternausnet [11].

Quantitative Results. To quantitatively compare the segmentation accuracy of these methods, we compute and list the corresponding metrics of Precision, Dice, mIoU, ME, FPR, and FNR in Table 1. It can be seen that the proposed method is superior to other methods in Precision, Dice, mIoU, and ME. Although the FPR of the method by Zhou [2] is the lowest, its FNR is the highest, indicating serious under-segmentation. Resnet++ [10] has the lowest FNR and relatively high FPR, revealing its over-segmentation. The FNP of the Ternausnet [11] network is slightly higher than that of the BM-Net, indicating that our network has a little under-segmentation problem, but other indicators of our network are higher than Ternausnet. In summary, the segmentation method proposed in this paper is superior to these competing methods and improves the segmentation accuracy of bone marrow cells.

Table 1. Quantitative comparison of bone marrow cell segmentation results.

Method	Precision	Dice	mIoU	ME	FPR	FNR
Zhou [2]	0.9200	0.8655	0.4771	0.0193	**0.0015**	0.1344
U-Net [9]	0.9678	0.9680	0.9646	0.0082	0.0049	0.0311
Resnet ++ [10]	0.9614	0.9666	0.9632	0.0084	0.0057	**0.0271**
Att U-Net [19]	0.9743	0.9685	0.9651	0.0081	0.0041	0.0361
Ternausnet [11]	0.9770	0.9711	0.9678	0.0072	0.0035	0.0341
BM-Net(ours)	**0.9776**	**0.9750**	**0.9720**	**0.0063**	0.0033	0.0272

As shown in Fig. 4, we further draw the cumulative distribution of these six evaluation indicators in the test set. The blue line represents U-Net [9], the green line represents Resnet++ [10], the black line represents Ternausnet [11], and the purple line represents Att U-Net [19], the red line represents the algorithm of BM-Net proposed in this paper. By observation, BM-Net has higher values of Dice and mIoU, and lower ME, FPR, and FNR. In the aspect of Precision, the Att U-Net algorithm appears to be slightly higher than our algorithm but relatively less stable. Hence, it can be further seen that our proposed method is superior in the segmentation of bone marrow cells.

Qualitative Results. To qualitatively compare the effectiveness of different methods in bone marrow cell segmentation, Fig. 5 shows some visualization results of cell image segmentation. From top to bottom are the results by Zhou [2], U-Net [9],

Resnet++ [10], Att U-Net [19], Ternausnet [11] and BM-Net. In order to facilitate observation, we have marked on the original image: red curve represents the prediction result, and green for the ground truth label. It can be seen from Fig. 5 that Zhou [2] showed serious under-segmentation. Several competing methods based on deep learning show slight over-segmentation and under-segmentation. For example, the background impurities are incorrectly classified into the cytoplasm and the cell contour is not detected accurately. As a contrast, the cell segmentation results by our proposed BM-Net improve obviously, and the problems of over-segmentation and under-segmentation are effectively handled. It can also be concluded that our proposed method exhibits good segmentation performance for bone marrow cells.

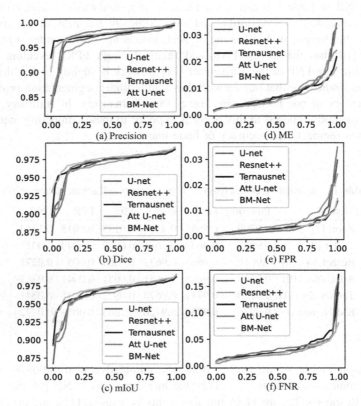

Fig. 4. Cumulative distributions of six measures of segmentation accuracy: (a) Precision, (b) Dice, (c) mIoU, (d) ME, (e) FPR, (f) FNR. (Color figure online)

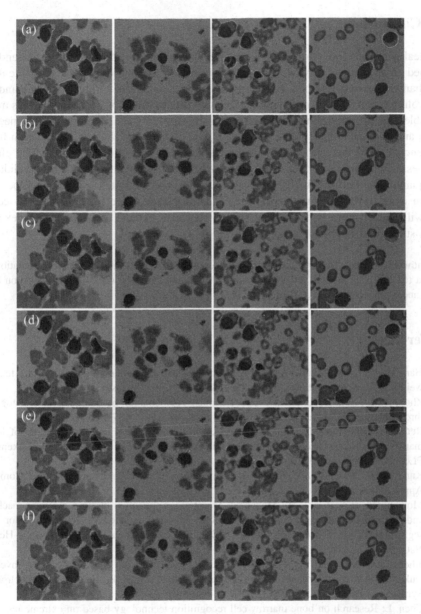

Fig. 5. Qualitative comparison of bone marrow cell segmentation results. From top to bottom: (a) Zhou [2], (b) U-Net [9], (c) Resnet ++ [10], (d) Att U-Net [19], (e) Ternausnet [11], (f) BM-Net. (The red color represents segmentation result, and the green color represents the label). (Color figure online)

4   Conclusion

To deal with the bone marrow cell segmentation problem, we propose an end-to-end U-shaped deep neural network based on pyramid convolution block and attention mechanism, termed BM-Net. In its feature encoder stage, the combination of standard convolution and dilated convolution, together with pyramid convolution block, is more capable of extracting abundant information. By applying the attention gating mechanism and residual connection in the feature fusion stage, the shallow information from the encoder and the deep one from the encoder can be better integrated. The effectiveness of the proposed method for bone marrow cell segmentation has been validated by quantitative and qualitative comparisons with several state-of-the-art methods. In future work to further improve the segmentation performance for bone marrow cells, we will collect more bone marrow smear images to expand the dataset and develop semi-supervised learning methods.

Acknowledgments. This work is partially supported by National Natural Science Foundation of China (61972187), Natural Science Foundation of Fujian Province (2020J02024), Fuzhou Science and Technology Project (2020-RC-186).

References

1. Han, Y., Yang, N., Miao, Y., et al.: Bone marrow cell segmentation based on color feature weighted filter. Comput. Sci. **38**(7), 283–286 (2011). (in Chinese)
2. Zhou, X., Li, Z., Xie, H., et al.: Leukocyte image segmentation based on adaptive histogram thresholding and contour detection. Curr. Bioinform. **15**(3), 187–195 (2020)
3. Reta, C., Altamirano, L., Gonzalez, J.A., et al.: Segmentation and classification of bone marrow cells images using contextual information for medical diagnosis of acute leukemias. PLoS ONE **10**(6), e0130805 (2015)
4. Kandil, A.H., Hassan, O.A.: Automatic segmentation of acute leukemia cells. Int. J. Comput. Appl. **133**(10), 1–8 (2016)
5. Mohammed, E.A., Far, B.H., Mohamed, M., et al.: Application of support vector machine and k-means clustering algorithms for robust chronic lymphocytic leukemia color cell segmentation. In: Proceedings of the IEEE 15th International Conference on e-Health Networking, Applications and Services, pp. 622–626 (2013)
6. Khomairoh, N., Sigit, R., Harsono, T., et al.: Segmentation system of acute myeloid leukemia (AML) subtypes on microscopic blood smear image. In: International Electronics Symposium (IES), pp. 565–570 (2020)
7. Chen, L: Research on bone marrow cell recognition technology based on extreme learning machine. China Jiliang Univ. (2014). (in Chinese)
8. Ramoser, H., Laurain, V., Bischof, H., et al.: Leukocyte segmentation and classification in blood-smear images. In: IEEE Engineering in Medicine and Biology 27th Annual Conference, pp. 3371–3374 (2005)
9. Ronneberger, O., Fischer, P., Brox, T.: U-Net: convolutional networks for biomedical image segmentation. In: Navab, N., Hornegger, J., Wells, W.M., Frangi, A.F. (eds.) Medical Image Computing and Computer-Assisted Intervention – MICCAI 2015: 18th International Conference, Munich, Germany, October 5-9, 2015, Proceedings, Part III, pp. 234–241. Springer International Publishing, Cham (2015). https://doi.org/10.1007/978-3-319-24574-4_28

10. Jha, D., Smedsrud, P.H., Riegler, M.A., et al.: Resunet++: an advanced architecture for medical image segmentation. In: IEEE International Symposium on Multimedia (ISM), pp. 225–2255 (2019)
11. Iglovikov, V., Shvets, A.: Ternausnet: U-net with VGG11 encoder pre-trained on imagenet for image segmentation (2018). arXiv preprint arXiv:1801.05746
12. Lu, Y., Qin, X., Fan, H., et al.: WBC-Net: a white blood cell segmentation network based on UNet++ and ResNet. Appl. Soft Comput. **101**, 107006 (2021)
13. Fan, H., Zhang, F., Xi, L., et al.: LeukocyteMask: an automated localization and segmentation method for leukocyte in blood smear images using deep neural networks. J. Biophoton. **12**(7), e201800488 (2019)
14. Zhou, C., Fan, H., Li, Z.: Tonguenet: accurate localization and segmentation for tongue images using deep neural networks. IEEE Access 7, 148779–148789 (2019)
15. Eekelen, L., Pinckaers, H., Hebeda, K.M., et al.: Multi-class semantic cell segmentation and classification of aplasia in bone marrow histology images. Proc. SPIE Med. Imaging **11320**, 113200B (2020)
16. Wu, F., Lu, L., Lu, D., et al.: Deep learning model for automatic identification of bone marrow red granulocytes. J. Jilin Univ. (Inf. Sci. Ed.) **38**(6), 729–736 (2020). (in Chinese)
17. Duta, I.C., Liu, L., Zhu, F., et al.: Pyramidal convolution: rethinking convolutional neural networks for visual recognition (2020). arXiv preprint arXiv:2006.11538
18. Wu, Y., He, K.: Group normalization. In: Ferrari, V., Hebert, M., Sminchisescu, C., Weiss, Y. (eds.) ECCV 2018. LNCS, vol. 11217, pp. 3–19. Springer, Cham (2018). https://doi.org/10.1007/978-3-030-01261-8_1
19. Oktay, O., Schlemper, J., Folgoc, L.L., et al.: Attention U-Net: learning where to look for the pancreas (2018). arXiv preprint arXiv:1804.03999
20. Pont-Tuset, J., Marques, F.: Measures and meta-measures for the supervised evaluation of image segmentation. In: Proceedings of the IEEE Conference on Computer Vision and Pattern Recognition, pp. 2131–2138 (2013)
21. Zhou, C., Fan, H., Zhao, W., et al.: Reconstruction enhanced probabilistic model for semisupervised tongue image segmentation. Concurr. Comput. Pract. Exp. **32**(22), 5844 (2020)
22. Fan, H., Zhang, F., Li, Z.: AnomalyDAE: dual autoencoder for anomaly detection on attributed networks. In: Proceedings of the IEEE International Conference on Acoustics, Speech and Signal Processing, pp. 5685–5689 (2020)
23. Tian, C., Yong, X., Zuo, W., et al.: Coarse-to-fine CNN for image super-resolution. IEEE Trans. Multimedia **23**, 1489–1502 (2021)
24. Fawcett, T.: An introduction to ROC analysis. Pattern Recogn. Lett. **27**(8), 861–874 (2006)
25. Kingma, D., Ba, J.: Adam: a method for stochastic optimization (2015). arXiv preprint arXiv:1412.6980

An Improved Unsupervised White Blood Cell Classification via Contrastive Learning

Yuning Zhong[1], Maoye Huang[2], Haoyi Fan[3], Rong Hu[1(✉)],
and Zuoyong Li[2(✉)]

[1] College of Computer Science and Mathematics,
Fujian University of Technology, Fuzhou 350118, China
[2] Fujian Provincial Key Laboratory of Information Processing and Intelligent
Control, College of Computer and Control Engineering, Minjiang University,
Fuzhou 350121, China
[3] School of Information Engineering, Zhengzhou University,
Zhengzhou 450001, China

Abstract. The classification and counting of white blood cells (WBCs, leukocytes) in blood smears are of great significance for clinicopathological diagnosis. Therefore, the classification of WBCs in the images is a basic task. Most of the existing WBCs classification methods are based on supervised learning, which highly depends on a large number of image labels. To cope with the challenge of image annotation, in this paper, we propose an unsupervised WBCs classification method, which combines the advantages of contrastive learning and a deep clustering algorithm. Specifically, the proposed method firstly employs contrastive learning to pre-train the feature encoder, which is able to improve the similarity of feature coding among the same kind of cell categories. Then, the classical clustering algorithm is used based on the pre-trained image features for unsupervised classification of WBCs. Finally, the high confidence clustering results are fed back to the pre-trained feature encoder, which can be used as the pseudo labels to form a closed loop. Experimental results on a dataset containing 574 leukocyte images demonstrate the effectiveness of the proposed method.

Keywords: Cluster · Unsupervised classification · White blood cells

1 Introduction

As the principal components of immune cells, white blood cells (WBCs) play a significant role in disease diagnosis such as leukemia, hepatitis, and acquired immune deficiency syndrome (AIDS) [1]. WBCs are colorless, spherical, and nucleated blood cells, which can pass through the capillary wall by transshaping when the body is invaded by viruses. WBCs contain five types that could be differentiated by their shape and size. Specifically, WBCs can be divided into neutrophils, basophils, eosinophils, monocytes, and lymphocytes. Among them, neutrophils, basophils, and eosinophils contain granules, monocytes and Lymphocytes do not contain granules. Figure 1 shows the differentiation in WBCs between normal blood and blood with Leukemia.

© Springer Nature Singapore Pte Ltd. 2021
Y. Tan et al. (Eds.): DMBD 2021, CCIS 1453, pp. 100–109, 2021.
https://doi.org/10.1007/978-981-16-7476-1_10

When the human body suffers from certain diseases, the WBC number and the proportion of different WBC types in the blood will change significantly. Therefore, correctly classifying and counting the WBCs in the blood is helpful for blood diseases diagnosis. However, due to the challenges of background interference, large inter-class differences and small extra-class differences in WBC datasets, WBC classification is still an open problem.

At present, the accuracy of WBC classification highly depends on the practitioners' experiences, and the classification has subjective time-consuming limitations. To solve this problem, some WBC classification methods based on image processing have emerged. Most of these methods are based on traditional machine learning and heavily relied on labeled data [3–13]. However, since the labeling of medical data requires professional domain knowledge and lots of manpower, it is difficult to obtain a large number of labels.

To cope with the aforementioned challenges, in this paper, we propose a new unsupervised method that consists of two parts of iteration execution: pre-training contrastive learning module and unsupervised clustering module. To increase the feature similarity of the same type of WBCs, the contrastive learning model is used to enhance the image representation in a self-supervised manner. Then, an unsupervised cluster module is used as a classifier for final classification, from which, the classification results can be used as the pseudo-labels to assist the training of the contrastive learning modules. We conducted extensive experiments on the WBC dataset and the experimental results demonstrate the effectiveness of the proposed method.

In sum, the main contributions for this paper are as follows:

- We propose a method of unsupervised WBC classification based on contrastive learning and clustering, which does not require any data labeling.
- We introduce a contrastive learning module to guide the clustering process, generating better performance compared with traditional clustering.

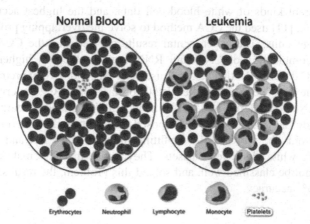

Normal Blood   **Leukemia**

Erythrocytes   Neutrophil   Lymphocyte   Monocyte   Platelets

Fig. 1. This image illustrates an abnormal number of WBC in blood with leukemia disease. In most circumstances, the number of WBC in the blood stays a dynamic balance (Normal Blood). Relatively leukemia [2] patients have a higher proportion of WBC.

2 Related Work

Recent years have witnessed a rapidly increasing interest in classification techniques based on computer-assisted methods. The classification methods used in WBCs data sets can be roughly divided into two categories: traditional machine learning methods and deep learning methods.

The traditional machine learning methods usually first used feature extraction technology to obtain WBC's features, and finally utilizes a classifier to achieve final classification. For example, Yampri et al. [3] extracted features from the concept of the eigenface and then using 50 WBC images to classify that reach 92% accuracy. Falcon et al. [4] take the difference from the method of dividing the whole cell and the method of dividing the nucleus is adopted, and extracted contour-based and region-based shape features from manually segmented images of a nucleus Multi-Layer Perceptron, pair-wise Support Vector Machine, K-Nearest Neighbors, PART and C4.5 are used for classification. The experiment results show under a situation of the shape features of a nucleus can achieve over 96% accuracy for all classifiers. Zhao et al. [5] use a micro-image blood cell detection algorithm to locate, and classify WBCs by using the granularity feature with SVM to reach an accuracy rate of 92.6%. Kurniadi et al. [6] applied the VGG-16 model with the Local Binary Pattern (LBP) together for feature extraction. Using K-Nearest Neighbor (KNN) [7] and XGBoost [8] for classification, they successfully reached an accuracy rate of 92.93% in the test dataset. Racikumar et al. [9] applied relevance vector machine (RVM) in the WBCs test dataset and achieved 91% accuracy.

In recent years, with the development of deep learning, the deep learning-based WBCs classification has become a new research hotspot. For example, Shain et al. [10] proposed two methods by transfer learning: The first was the fine-tuning of the existing deep network, and the second was the transfer learning model based on the deep activation function. A new network specially designed for the WBC classification task was established which was called WBC-Net. After the network pretraining, it is divided into three different kinds of white blood cell data, and the highest accuracy reaches 96.1%. Patil et al. [11] used the CCA method to solve the overlapping problem of white blood cell image units. The experimental results showed that the CCA base model which was a combination of CNN and RNN could achieve a higher accuracy of 95.89% in WBC datasets. Kutlu et al. [12] used R-CNN and several pretrained models: Google-Net, Alexnet, VGG16, and ResNet50 to classify WBCs, experimental results show that ResNet50 had the best performance in the previous learning, reaching 99.52% accuracy. Baydilli et al. [13] proposed the lightweight network capsule network, which avoids the problem of over-fitting in traditional CNN and TL models in order to classify white blood cell datasets. They notice that the small sample WBCs data set could not be classified well, and solved this problem, the results of the test set achieved 96.86% accuracy.

3 Method

In this section, the WBC dataset and the proposed method are introduced. Inspired by two unsupervised models [14, 15], we proposed a novel model which combined SimCLR and DeepCluster. Specifically, the SimCLR network pre-training the feature encoder, where the ResNet18 is the backbone, to improve the similarity of feature coding among the same kind of categories. Then, K-means is used for unsupervised classification of WBCs features. Finally, some high confidence clustering results are fed back to the SimCLR as pseudo labels to form a closed loop. The architecture of the proposed method is shown in Fig. 2.

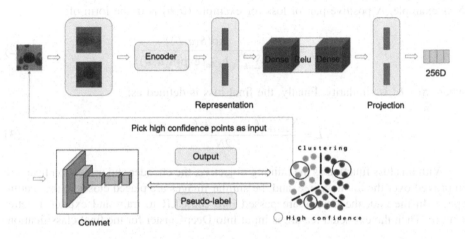

Fig. 2. The architecture of the proposed model.

3.1 Dataset Preprocessing

During the training, we take a random batch of N samples and define a data augmentation operation as *Aug* including random crop, color jitter, and Gaussian blur, etc. Then we apply *Aug* to each image to obtain two correlated views, which results in a total of 2N samples. Finally, all 2N images are fed into the feature encoder to obtain the representation of the images.

3.2 Feature Extraction via SimCLR

The first step in this process is to use SimCLR to learn the representation of each image in the latent space that makes the similarity between the same classes is increased, and the similarity between different classes is reduced to obtain better features. The process is illustrated in Fig. 3. We choose ResNet18 as a base of our neural network encoder $f(\cdot)$ and this network architecture is not limited in ResNet18. We define X as the input image. Each image is operated Aug, then we get two different augmentation views a and b and pass them into $f(\cdot)$, to obtain representation r_a and r_b respectively. To get the views, the representations are mapped on a projection head $g(\cdot)$ that consists of one hidden layer of MLP. We use cosine similarity to calculate the similarity between two enhanced images, which is defined as:

$$S(a,b) = \frac{v_a^T v_b}{\tau \|v_a\| \|v_b\|} \tag{1}$$

where τ is an adjustable parameter. It can scale the input and expand the range of cosine similarity $[-1, 1]$, $\| . \|$ is modulus of vector, $a \in \{1, ..., 2N\}$ and $b \in \{1, ..., 2N\}$ where N is example. A positive pair of loss for example (a, b) is in the form of:

$$\ell_{(a,b)} = -\log \frac{\exp(S(a,b))}{\sum_{k=1}^{2N} l_{[k \neq a]} \exp(S(a,b))} \tag{2}$$

where $S(a, b)$ is similarity. Finally, the final loss is defined as:

$$L = \frac{\sum_{k=1}^{N} \left[\ell_{(2k,2k-1)} + \ell_{(2k-1,2k)} \right]}{2N} \tag{3}$$

With this loss function as the training objective, the encoder and projection head are improved over the training time, and the similar images are placed closer in the feature space. In the end, the images are passed into SimCLR to train and extract a better feature. Then the extracted feature is input into DeepCluster for the final classification.

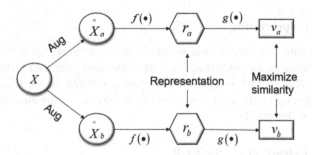

Fig. 3. The process of contrastive learning to obtain representations. The same data augmentation action applied in each data example to generate two correlated views. Encoder $f(\cdot)$ aim to obtain representation. Afterwards a projection head $g(\cdot)$ is trained and through contrastive loss to maximize the similarity between two views.

3.3   Training of DeepCluster and SimCLR Update

A convolutional network such as Alexnet or VGG16 is used to extract features in DeepCluster. Then, the dimension of feature vectors is reduced by PCA to perform the whiten and L2 normalization at the same time. Finally, the handled features are passed into the K-means cluster, and the pseudo label are assigned based on the reduced feature. However, the operation of PCA is replaced by SimCLR in our method, because that the features from SimCLR have the better performance in cluster assignments. The feature extraction process is described in Sect. 3.2. Following equation explained how pseudo-labels are produced:

$$P = \min_{c \in \mathbb{R}^{i \times k}} \frac{\sum_{n=1}^{N} \min_{y_n \in \{0,1\}^k} \|f_\theta(x_n) - Cy_n\|_2^2}{N} \tag{4}$$

where $f_\theta(x_n)$ denotes the features produce from extractor, k is the number of clusters. To get the pseudo-labels, the feature matrix C of $i \times k$ isclustered into k groups based on geometric criterion to execute the cluster assignments y_n. Then, these assignments are used as pseudo-labels. To get a better feature vector, we re-cluster with the top 10 percentage of confidence data every 20 epochs.

3.4   Clustering

In the end, the final network model is saved and performs the clustering to get the last result. The process of clustering is as follows: Firstly, the number of cluster center is determined. Secondly, produce k clusters and choose the center of each cluster randomly. Third, calculate the distance of each data points from the center points to determine which class it belongs to. Finally, repeatedly allocate data points until reaching the maximum iterations. We use Euclidean distance to measure the range between each data points and central points, which is defined as follows:

$$D = \sqrt{d_1^2 + d_2^2 + ... + d_n^2} \tag{5}$$

where d denotes the difference between each dimension of the data point and each dimension of the center point.

4   Experiments

In this section, we evaluate the proposed method on real white blood cells dataset. Firstly, we compare it with two existing unsupervised methods. Then, we discuss the results of its ablation experiments. Finally, because there are no previous unsupervised methods for WBC classification, in the experiment, we choose to compare the traditional k-means clustering and contrastive cluster [16] on WBCs. The results of the experiments are shown in Fig. 5.

4.1   Dataset

The dataset used in this paper is from the People's Hospital affiliated with Fujian University of Traditional Chinese Medicine. The white blood cell dataset consists of 84 Basophils, 99 Eosinophils, 165 lymphocytes, 83 Monocytes, and 143 Neutrophil images, with a total of 574 white blood cell microscopic images. The size of image is of 256 × 256. Five types of white blood cells are showed in Fig. 4.

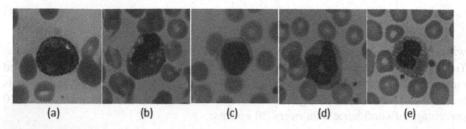

Fig. 4. Five types of WBC; (a) Basophil, (b) Eosinophil, (c) Lymphocyte, (d) Monocyte, (e) Neutrophil.

4.2   Parameter Settings

In our experiments, we use Python 3.6, Pytorch 1.8 as the deep learning framework, and Intel Xenon Silver 4208 is set as the processor of the experimental equipment, Nvidia Quadro RTX 4000 is selected as the graphics card, and we use Ubuntu16 as the operating system. Finally, we select the 4, 8, 16, and 32 as the batch sizes of our experiment, the learning rate of SimCLR with Deepcluster is set as 0.0003, the weight of decay is set as 1e–4, and the temperature of SimCLR is set as 1. The training epoch is set as 100.

4.3   Evaluation Metric

Accuracy is a common evaluation metric for image classification. A higher value means the result is better, and a lower value is the opposite. Accuracy is defined as follows:

$$ACC = \frac{(TP + TN)}{(P + N)} \tag{6}$$

where TP denotes the number of positive samples judged to be correct, TN denotes the number of negative samples judged to be correct, $P + N$ denotes the total number of samples.

4.4   Experimental Results

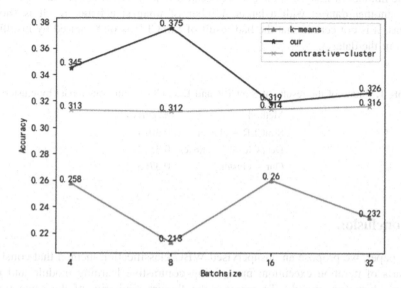

Fig. 5. Experimental results of our model compared with traditional k-means and contrastive-cluster.

Figure 5 shows the experiment results that the accuracy of our method is higher than the other two unsupervised methods at least 0.5% points. Among the k-means clustering and contrastive clustering, note that the performance of the traditional k-means clustering is the worst. Three reasons cause the difference in performance between k-means and ours. Firstly, the random selection of cluster centers makes the fluctuation of results. Secondly, the k-means clustering algorithm is insensitive to the data points that are far away from the cluster centers, and consequently cannot properly classify points at boundaries of different classes. Thirdly, the images in the WBC dataset are significantly similar, which makes the classification task harder.

We also find that the contrastive cluster is also worse than the result of our model, one possible reason behind this might be that the WBC dataset has only 574 pictures, which is too little to learn for contrastive cluster and consequently causes the poor experiment results.

4.5   Ablation Experiment

Table 1 shows the result of our method with the other two methods. Note that the performance of the WBC dataset cluster is worse than our method, whether it uses separate SimCLR or DeepCluster. One reason behind this might be caused by the different architectures used in SimCLR. The network used in SimCLR is Resnet18, which is not deep enough that makes the feature from it is not well. However, the feature is extracted in our model comes from Resnet18 and Alexnet that makes the result of our method is better than SimCLR. The result of DeepCluster is also lower than the result of our method. The reasons are not clear but it may have something to do with the number of images in the dataset because if we give SimCLR a larger batchsize or use another dataset with a larger number of images, a better result is showed. Whereas, it is not certain that the bad result of SimCLR is only caused by insufficient images in the dataset.

Table 1. Show of the results of SimCLR and DeepCluster and our model by clustering

Method	Accuracy
SimCLR + cluster	0.3014
DeepCluster + cluster	0.3502
Our + cluster	0.3763

5 Conclusion

In this paper, we propose an unsupervised WBC classification method that consists of two parts of iteration execution: pre-training contrastive learning module and unsupervised clustering module. To increase the feature similarity of the same type of WBCs, the contrastive learning model is used to enhance the image representation in a self-supervised manner. Then, an unsupervised clustering module is used as a classifier for final classification, where, the classification results can be used as the pseudo-labels to assist the training of the contrastive learning module. We conducted extensive experiments on the WBC dataset. Experimental results show that the proposed method has higher accuracy and stability than the existing unsupervised classification methods.

Acknowledgments. This work is partially supported by National Natural Science Foundation of China(61972187)。 Natural Science Foundation of Fujian Province (2020J02024), Fuzhou Science and Technology Project(2020-RC-186).

References

1. Fan, H., Zhang, F., Xi, L., et al.: LeukocyteMask: an automated localization and segmentation method for leukocyte in blood smear images using deep neural networks. J. Biophoton. **12**(7), e201800488 (2019)
2. Laboratory info. https://laboratoryinfo.com/mpv-blood-test/, Accessed 11 Nov 2019
3. Yampri, P., Pintavirooj, C., Daochai, S., et al.: white blood cell classification based on the combination of eigen cell and parametric feature detection. In: 2006 1ST IEEE Conference on Industrial Electronics and Applications, pp. 1–4 (2006)
4. Falcón-Ruiz, A., Taboada-Crispí, A., Orozco-Monteagudo, M., et al.: Classification of white blood cells using morphometric features of nucleus. In: Cuba-Flanders Workshop on Machine Learning and Knowledge Discovery (2010)

5. Habibzadeh, M., Krzyżak, A., Fevens, T.: Comparative study of shape, intensity and texture features and support vector machine for white blood cell classification. J. Theor. Appl. Comput. Sci. **7**(1), 20–35 (2013)
6. Kurniadi, F.I., Putri, V.K.: A comparison of human crafted features and machine crafted features on white blood cells classification. J. Phys. Conf. Ser. **1201**, 012045 (2019)
7. Song, K., Yan, F., Ding, T., et al.: A steel property optimization model based on the XGboost algorithm and improved PSO. Comput. Mater. Sci. **174**, 109472 (2020)
8. Ma, Z.F., Tian, H.P., Liu, Z.C., et al.: A new incomplete pattern belief classification method with multiple estimations based on KNN. Appl. Soft Comput. **90**(4), 106175 (2020)
9. Ravikumar, S., Shanmugam, A.: WBC image segmentation and classification using RVM. Appl. Math. Sci. **8**(45), 2227–2237 (2014)
10. Shahin, A.I., Guo, Y., Amin, K.M., et al.: White blood cells identification system based on convolutional deep neural learning networks. Comput. Methods Progr. Biomed. **168**, 69–80 (2017)
11. Patil, A.M., Patil, M.D., Birajdar, G.K.: White blood cells image classification using deep learning with canonical correlation analysis. IRBM **42**, 377–389 (2020)
12. Kutlu, H., Avci, E., Özyurt, F.: White blood cells detection and classification based on regional convolutional neural networks. Med. Hypotheses **135**, 109472 (2020)
13. Ravikumar, S.: Image segmentation and classification of white blood cells with the extreme learning machine and the fast relevance vector machine. Artif. Cells Nanomed. Biotechnol. **44**(3), 985–989 (2016)
14. Chen, T., Kornblith, S., Norouzi, M., et al.: A simple framework for contrastive learning of visual representations (2020)
15. Caron, M., Bojanowski, P., Joulin, A., Douze, M.: Deep clustering for unsupervised learning of visual features. In: Ferrari, V., Hebert, M., Sminchisescu, C., Weiss, Y. (eds.) Computer Vision – ECCV 2018. LNCS, vol. 11218, pp. 139–156. Springer, Cham (2018). https://doi.org/10.1007/978-3-030-01264-9_9
16. Li, Y., Hu, P., Liu, Z., et al.: Contrastive clustering. In: 2021 AAAI Conference on Artificial Intelligence (AAAI) (2021)

High-Altitude Pedestrian Detection Based on Improved YOLOv3

Qing Tian[1], Pengfei Cao[2], Haoyi Fan[3], Rong Hu[1(✉)],
and Zuoyong Li[4(✉)]

[1] School of Computer Science and Mathematics,
Fujian University of Technology, Fuzhou 350118, China
[2] The Higher Polytechnic School (EPS), University of Sevilla, Sevilla, Spain
[3] School of Computer Science and Technology, Harbin University of Science
and Technology, Harbin 150080, China
[4] Fujian Provincial Key Laboratory of Information Processing
and Intelligent Control, College of Computer and Control Engineering,
Minjiang University, Fuzhou 350121, China

Abstract. As one of the main tasks in the field of computer vision, pedestrian detection aims to find out all pedestrians in the image or video. The existing YOLOv3 is a relatively mature object detection method. However, for the long-distance pedestrian detection task in high-altitude scenes, YOLOv3 has the limitations of low detection speed and low detection accuracy. This paper proposes an improved YOLOv3 method briefly called YOLOv3-M for the high-altitude pedestrian detection, which replaces the feature extraction module called darknet53 in YOLOv3 with MobileNetv1. Specifically, YOLOv3-M first constructs the dataset with the small objects of high-altitude pedestrians as the detection object. Then, it uses the K-means + + algorithm to re-cluster the high-altitude pedestrian dataset. Next, it uses the Distance Intersection over Union (DIoU) loss function to alleviate the problem of high-altitude pedestrian overlapping. Experimental results show that the proposed YOLOv3-M improves the detection precision and the detection speed compared to YOLOv3.

Keywords: High-altitude pedestrian detection · YOLOv3 algorithm · Loss function · MobileNet algorithm

1 Introduction

Since various objects in an image have different shapes and appearances, as well as the interference of vision during imaging, object detection has always been a challenging problem in the field of computer vision. Object detection mainly includes two steps [1]: object positioning and classification. Object positioning is responsible for identifying the position of the object and positioning it with a circumscribed rectangle. Object classification is responsible for judging whether the input image contains the required object. Object detection usually needs to introduce pre-defined rectangular boxes (i.e., anchor boxes) on the convolution feature map. These anchor boxes are evenly distributed according to the area and aspect ratio, which is convenient for detecting objects

Y. Tan et al. (Eds.): DMBD 2021, CCIS 1453, pp. 110–121, 2021.
https://doi.org/10.1007/978-981-16-7476-1_11

of different proportions. This type of method is called anchor-based object detection. Anchor-based detection methods are usually divided into two-stage (such as Faster R-CNN [2] and Feature pyramid networks (FPN) [4–4]), and one-stage (such as You Only Look Once (YOLO) series [5] and Single-shot multi-box detector (SSD) [6]) methods. In anchor-based detection methods, a large number of predefined anchor point boxes are firstly tiled on the image. Then, the anchor point box category is predicted. Finally, the appropriate anchor point box is selected as the output result, and the regression operation is performed.

Pedestrian detection belongs to object detection, and aims to detect pedestrians in images or videos. The existing pedestrian detection methods mainly include the following three categories:

The first category is traditional machine learning-based methods, such as Support Vector Machine (SVM), Histogram of Oriented Gradients (HOG) [7], and Deformable Parts Model (DPM). These methods [8] usually use regional gradient features and geometric constraint filtering to extract pedestrian spots. Then, they use a linear SVM with a hybrid descriptor to classify the detected spots. Finally, they use the mixer to convert the HOG combined with discrete cosine transform (DCT) function to achieve accurate detection.

The second category is Two-stage methods, such as R-CNN and Fast R-CNN methods. These methods usually contain four main steps. Firstly, several convolutional layers are used to extract the feature maps of the image. Secondly, Region Proposal Networks (RPN) are used to generate region proposals. Thirdly, ROI (Region of Interest) pooling layers are used to determine the object category. Finally, proposal feature maps and bounding box regression are used to calculate the category of the proposal and obtain the final precise position of the detection box with a priori box obtained by the SSD model.

The final category is the One-stage methods proposed by Redmon, et al. [5]. This method abandons the candidate frame extraction mechanism and completes both of object positioning and object classification tasks at the same time. Moreover, it improves the detection speed. Based on YOLO, Redmon et al. also proposed YOLO 9000 [9] and YOLOv3 [10]. Early object detection methods usually use manual extraction of features to construct complex models, and thus the detection accuracy is difficult to improve. However, since the YOLOv3 detection method takes the accuracy and the detection speed into account, the detection effect is improved.

Compared with other two category methods, the YOLO based network has two shortcomings. The first is that the accuracy of identifying objects is low, and the other is that the detection speed is slow. Motivated by YOLOv3, due to the slow speed of YOLOv3, we proposed an improved YOLOv3 method (YOLOv3-M), which replaces the YOLOv3 backbone feature extraction network darknet with MobileNetv1 [11] to greatly improve the model detection speed. In addition, we use the Distance Intersection over Union (DIoU) loss function [13] instead of the Intersection Over Union (IoU) loss function [12] of YOLOv3 for effectively alleviating the pedestrian overlapping problem in the high-altitude pedestrian detection task.

The main contributions of this paper are as follows:

(1) Motived by the YOLOv3, we proposed an improved YOLOv3 method for high-altitude pedestrian detection (called YOLOv3-M). YOLOv3-M replaces the feature extraction module darknet53 of YOLOv3 with MobileNetv1.

(2) The proposed YOLOv3-M first utilizes the small high-altitude pedestrian object as the detection object to reconstruct the dataset. Then, it uses the k-means + + algorithm to re-cluster the high-altitude pedestrian dataset, and replaces the Backbone of the network to increase the speed. Finally, it uses the Distance Intersection over Union (DIoU) loss function to alleviate the problem of high-altitude pedestrian overlapping.

(3) Experimental results show that the proposed YOLOv3-M improves the detection precision and the average detection speed compared to YOLOv3. This reduces the equipment requirements for detecting high-altitude pedestrians and simplifies the model, which is conducive to industrial applications.

2   Related Work

2.1   YOLOv3

To achieve end-to-end object detection, convolutional neural networks (CNNs) [13] is proposed to directly predict the bounding box and category probabilities of objects from the input image. Based on CNNs, YOLO [5] is proposed to overcome the drawbacks (i.e., overfitting and low accuracy) of CNNs. For further improving the detection performance, Joseph Redmon et al. proposed YOLOv2 and YOLOv3 object detection algorithms for higher accuracy and faster speed in 2017 and 2018, respectively.

The basic idea of the YOLOv3 algorithm can be summarized as follows: Firstly, it extracts the feature maps of the input image through the feature extraction network, and divides the input image into 13×13, 26×26, 52×52 grids. Then, the grid, to which the object's real box center coordinate belong, is used to detect this object. To sum up, YOLOv3 reuses the classifier or locator to perform the detection task. It applies the model to multiple locations and scales [15] of one image, and those areas with higher scores can be regarded as the test results. Compared to the existing object detection methods [16], YOLOv3 has some advantages over classifier-based [17] methods. Firstly, since YOLOv3 looks at the entire image during the testing, its prediction can use the global information of the image. Secondly, it applies a single neural network [18] for the entire image [19] to divide the image into different regions. Thirdly, it predicts the bounding box and probability for each region. Finally, these bounding boxes are weighted by the predicted probability.

2.2   MobileNet

MobileNet uses a deep separable convolution structure to construct a lightweight deep neural network model. As shown in Table 1, the depth separable convolution decomposes the standard convolution into a $D_K \times D_K$ deep convolution and a 1×1 point-by-point convolution. For given the convolution kernel size D_K, the convolution channels M, the number of convolution kernels N, and the input feature map size D_F, both the standard convolution cost ($Cost_s$) and the depth-wise separable convolution computational cost ($Cost_d$) can be calculated as Eq. (1) and Eq. (2), respectively.

$$Cost_s = D_K \cdot D_K \cdot M \cdot D_F \cdot D_F. \tag{1}$$

$$Cost_d = D_K \cdot D_K \cdot M \cdot D_F \cdot D_F + M \cdot N \cdot D_F \cdot D_F. \tag{2}$$

After obtaining both of the deep convolution and standard convolution costs, the quantity is compared as,

$$\frac{D_K \cdot D_K \cdot M \cdot D_F \cdot D_F + M \cdot N \cdot D_F \cdot D_F}{D_K \cdot D_K \cdot M \cdot N \cdot D_F \cdot D_F} = \frac{1}{N} + \frac{1}{D_K^2}. \tag{3}$$

According to Eq. (3), it can be observed that the computational cost of the depth-wise separable convolution of MobileNet is much cheaper than that of the standard convolution. For instance, given a convolutional kernel size of 3×3, the calculation amount of the depth-wise separable convolution is about 1/9 of the standard convolution.

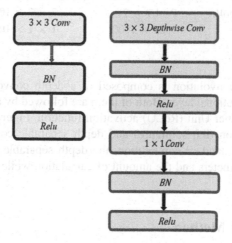

Fig. 1. Standard convolution (left) and depth separable convolution (right).

Table 1. MobileNet body architecture.

Type/Stride	Filter shape	Input size
Conv/s2	3 × 3 × 3 × 32	224 × 224 × 3
Conv dw/s1	3 × 3 × 32dw	112 × 112 × 32
Conv/s1	1 × 1 × 32 × 64	112 × 112 × 32
Conv dw/s2	3 × 3 × 64dw	112 × 112 × 64
Conv/s1	1 × 1 × 64 × 128	56 × 56 × 64
Conv dw/s1	3 × 3 × 128dw	56 × 56 × 128
Conv/s1	1 × 1 × 128 × 128	56 × 56 × 128
Conv dw/s2	3 × 3 × 128dw	56 × 56 × 128
Conv/s1	1 × 1 × 128 × 256	56 × 56 × 128
Conv dw/s1	3 × 3 × 256dw	28 × 28 × 256
Conv/s1	1 × 1 × 256 × 256	28 × 28 × 256
Conv dw/s2	3 × 3 × 256dw	28 × 28 × 256
Conv/s1	1 × 1 × 256 × 512	14 × 14 × 256
5 × Conv dw/s1	3 × 3 × 512dw	14 × 14 × 512
5 × Conv/s1	1 × 1 × 512 × 512	14 × 14 × 512
Conv dw/s2	3 × 3 × 512dw	14 × 14 × 512
Conv/s1	1 × 1 × 512 × 1024	7 × 7 × 512
Conv dw/s2	3 × 3 × 1024dw	7 × 7 × 1024
Conv/s1	1 × 1 × 1024 × 1024	7 × 7 × 1024
Avg Pool/s1	Pool 7 × 7	7 × 7 × 1024
FC/s1	1024 × 1000	1 × 1 × 1024

Depth separable convolution is composed of a depth convolutional layer and a point-by-point convolutional layer. Both of them are followed by a batch normalization (BN) and Rectified Liner Unit (ReLU) activation function. Figure 1 gives an example of standard convolution (left subfigure) and depth separable convolution (right subfigure). Compared to standard convolution, the depth separable convolution can significantly reduce parameters and the amount of calculation while without reducing the detection accuracy.

3   The Proposed Method

In the paper, we proposed a method briefly called YOLOv3-M to alleviate the limitations of YOLOv3. We replaced YOLOv3's feature extraction network using MobileNetv1 [11]. The MobileNet structure is built with depth-wise separable convolution proposed in Subsect. 2.2. However, its first layer is replaced with a full convolution. By defining the network in such a simple change, we can easily explore network topologies to find a better object detection network. Specifically, the detailed designs of MobileNet architecture are listed in Table 1.

Since the a priori box scale of network detection is not suitable for the high-altitude pedestrian dataset, using MobileNetv1 as the backbone feature extraction network can speed up the speed of finding a suitable a priori box scale.

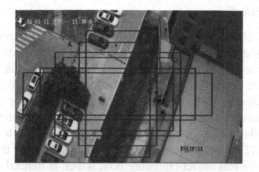

Fig. 2. SSD model prediction box.

The six blue prior boxes can be used to adjust the gap between the default bounding box and the real bounding box, and can help us to determine the width and height of target objects, which are beneficial to target prediction. Specifically, those objects identified in a priori box can obtain higher confidence, i.e., higher IoU values, so the prediction box can approach the real box through translation and transformation, as shown in Fig. 2.

3.1 YOLOv3-M Architecture

The proposed YOLOv3-M replaces the feature extraction network of the YOLOv3 with MobileNetv1. Figure 3 shows the entire architecture of the YOLOv3-M. Firstly, the feature extraction step of YOLOv3-M is composed of MobileNetv1 for improving the

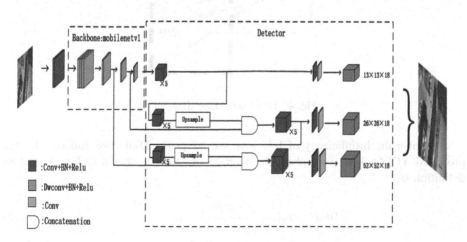

Fig. 3. YOLOv3-M architecture.

object detection speed. Secondly, its detection step has the same network structure as YOLOv3. Finally, by fusing the obtained feature detection results under different scales, it can output the final object detection result.

3.2   DIoU Loss Function

The loss function of the YOLOv3 [10] consists of three items, i.e., coordinate regression loss, confidence loss, and classification loss. The coordinate regression loss is calculated by the mean square error, and the confidence loss and classification loss are calculated by the cross-entropy. However, the accuracy of coordinate regression performance is affected by object scales, and the mean square error cannot deal with the sensitivity of the detection object scale problems. DIoU can effectively handle the above issues, thus this paper uses DIoU, we designed our first loss item with DIoU based on the IoU [13]. IoU is the intersection ratio between the predicted object bounding box and the real object bounding box, which is defined as,

$$IoU = \frac{|B \cap B^{gt}|}{|B \cup B^{gt}|},$$ (4)

where B and B^{gt} denote the bounding boxes of both the predicted object and the real object, respectively.

Although IoU loss has the advantage of better reflect overlapping degree than the mean square error, it tends to a fixed value when the prediction box and real box are inclusive. Therefore, it makes that the detection effect exist large difference. On the contrary, the value of IoU loss tends to zero when the prediction box and real box are non-intersect, which will lead to that the optimization cannot be performed.

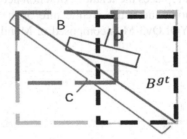

Fig. 4. DIoU schematic diagram.

To solve the insufficiency of IoU loss, we adopt the DIoU loss function for the proposed YOLOv3-M. The schematic diagram of DIoU is shown in Fig. 4, and its definition is,

$$DIoU = IoU - \frac{\rho^2(B, B^{gt})}{c^2} = IoU - \frac{d^2}{c^2},$$ (5)

where $d = \rho^2(B, B^{gt})$ denotes the distance between the two center points of the predicted frame and the real object box, c denotes the diagonal length of the minimum bounding rectangle of the two object bounding boxes, B^{gt} and B denote the center coordinates of the real object bounding box and the predicted object bounding box, respectively. Therefore, the DIoU loss function is defined as,

$$L_{DIoU} = \sum_{i=0}^{S^2} \sum_{j=0}^{B} I_{ij}^{obj} \times (1 - DIoU), \tag{6}$$

where s^2 is the total number of grids, B is the total number of bounding boxes, I_{ij}^{obj} denotes the j-th bounding box in the i-th grid. DIoU loss [14] can adapt to both of the inclusive and non-intersect situations between predicted object bounding box and real object bounding box.

The confidence loss L_{conf} and the classification loss L_{class} are based on the cross-entropy loss function. They are defined as follows,

$$\begin{aligned} L_{conf} = &-\sum_{i=0}^{S^2} \sum_{j=0}^{B} I_{ij}^{obj} \left[\widehat{C}_i^j log(C_i^j) + \left(1 - \widehat{C}_i^j\right) log(1 - C_i^j) \right] \\ &-\lambda_{noobj} \sum_{i=0}^{S^2} \sum_{j=0}^{B} I_{ij}^{noobj} \left[\widehat{C}_i^j log(C_i^j) + \left(1 - \widehat{C}_i^j\right) log(1 - C_i^j) \right] \end{aligned} \tag{7}$$

$$L_{class} = -\sum_{i=0}^{S^2} I_{ij}^{obj} \sum_{cclasses} [\hat{P}_i^j log(P_i^j) + (1 - \hat{P}_i^j) log(1 - P_i^j)], \tag{8}$$

where C_i^j and $\widehat{C}_i^j$ denote the confidence of the predicted object bounding box and the real object bounding box, respectively. P_i^j and $\widehat{P}_i^j$ denote the class probabilities of the j-th predicted object bounding box and the real object bounding box in the i-th grid, respectively.

In the paper, we defined the final total loss function as the sum of DIoU loss, confidence loss and classification loss, i.e.,

$$Loss_{total} = L_{DIoU} + L_{conf} + L_{class}. \tag{9}$$

4   Experimental Results

4.1   Parameters Setting and Datasets

In our experiments, we used our high-altitude pedestrian image dataset for networking training. The dataset contains 1691 training images and 188 testing images. The input image resolution was resized to 416 × 416. The initial learning rate, batch size and training epoch were set to 0.001, 16 and 100, respectively. The maximum number of iterations is determined according to the model evaluation index. In order to enhance the robustness of the model to images of different input sizes, we adopted a multi-scale training strategy. Additionally, the processor of the experimental equipment is Intel

Xenon Silver 4208, the graphics card is Nvidia Quadro RTX 4000 [20], and its Video memory is 8G.

4.2 Quantitative Results

To quantitatively evaluate the object detection performances of the proposed YOLOv3-M, we use Precision, Recall, and Mean Average Precision (MAP) to measure image object detection results. Specifically, Precision is defined as,

$$Precision = \frac{TP}{TP + FP}, \tag{10}$$

where TP denotes the number of correctly recognized target objects, and FP denotes the number of non-target objects incorrectly recognized as target objects of the image. The Recall and Average Precision (AP) are defined as follows,

$$Recall = \frac{TP}{TP + FN}, \tag{11}$$

$$AP = \int_0^1 P(r)dr, \tag{12}$$

where FN denotes the number of unrecognized target objects, and $P(r)$ denotes a function of recall rate r. Mean Average Precision value denotes the integration under different confidence with the recall as the abscissa and the precision as the ordinate. Higher values of all the above indexes indicate better image object detection results.

Table 2. Quantitative comparison results of two methods.

Algorithm	Precision	Recall
YOLOv3 [10]	55.46%	46.33%
YOLOv3-M	58.88%	49.53%

As shown in Table 2, we quantitatively compared the proposed YOLOv3-M with YOLOv3 on the high-altitude pedestrian dataset. The data listed in Table 2 shows that the YOLOV3-M achieves a better object detection performance with both a higher Precision value of 58.88% and a Recall value of 49.53%. Additionally, to further verify the efficiency of the YOLOv3, we use Mean Average Precision (MAP), Frames Per Second (FPS), and detection speed to measure the efficiencies of different methods, and compared results are shown in Table 3. It can be observed that the proposed YOLOv3-M has a great advantage in image object detection speed indicating more practical.

Table 3. Comparison results of object detection efficiency of different methods.

Algorithm	MAP(%)	FPS(Frames/s)	Speed(s)
Faster R-CNN [2]	5.76	2.74	0.365
CenterNet [21]	6.76	19.26	0.052
SSD [6]	20.16	13.02	0.077
YOLOv3 [10]	40.31	8.52	0.117
YOLOv3-M	**41.87**	**30.26**	**0.033**

4.3 Qualitative Results

To qualitatively evaluate the object detection performances of the YOLOv3-M, Figs. 5 and 6 show the object detection results of the YOLOv3 and the proposedYOLOv3-M on the same testing dataset, respectively. From Figs. 5 and 6, it can be observed that the proposed YOLOv3-M can detect more high-altitude pedestrians indicating better object detection performance.

Fig. 5. The high-altitude pedestrian detection results of YOLOv3 [10].

Fig. 6. The high-altitude pedestrian detection results of the YOLOv3-M.

5   Conclusion

In order to solve the problems that low detection speed and accuracy of the existing YOLOv3 in image object detection tasks, this paper proposes an improved deep neural network model based on YOLOv3 (briefly called YOLOv3-M). YOLOv3-M replaces the feature extraction network of the initial YOLOv3 with MobileNetv1, whose deep separable convolution can greatly reduce the number of training parameters and simplify the model. Additionally, YOLOv3-M uses the DIoU loss function to alleviate the problem of high-altitude pedestrian overlapping for improving object detection accuracy. Extensive experimental results show that YOLOv3-M obtains faster object detection speed and higher target detection accuracy than the YOLOv3, which is more suitable for pedestrian detection tasks at high altitude and non-laboratory scenes.

Acknowledgments. This work is partially supported by National Natural Science Foundation of China (61972187), Natural Science Foundation of Fujian Province (2020J02024), Fuzhou Science and Technology Project (2020-RC-186).

References

1. Zou, Z., Shi, Z., Guo, Y., et al.: Object detection in 20 years: a survey. arXiv preprint arXiv: 1905.05055 (2019)
2. Ren, S., He, K., Girshick, R., Sun, J.: Faster R-CNN: towards teal-time object detection with region proposal networks. IEEE Trans. Pattern Anal. Mach. Intell. **39**(6), 1137–1149 (2015)
3. Lin, T.Y., Dollar, P., Girshick, R., He, K., Hariharan, B., Belongie, S.: Feature pyramid networks for object detection. In: IEEE Conference on Computer Vision and Pattern Recognition (CVPR), pp. 936–944 (2017)
4. Yim, J. G., Lee, G.Y., Lee, T.G.: Improving the efficiency of the FPN. In: International Conference on Electronics, Informations and Communications, pp. 20–23 (1995)
5. Redmon, J., Divvala, S., Girshick, R., et al.: You only look once: unified, real-time object detection. In: IEEE Conference on Computer Vision and Pattern Recognition (CVPR), pp. 779–788 (2016)
6. Liu, W., et al.: SSD: single shot multibox detector. In: Leibe, B., Matas, J., Sebe, N., Welling, M. (eds.) ECCV 2016. LNCS, vol. 9905, pp. 21–37. Springer, Cham (2016). https://doi.org/10.1007/978-3-319-46448-0_2
7. Michele, A., Colin, V., Santika, D.D.: Mobilenet convolutional neural networks and support vector machines for palmprint recognition. Procedia Comput. Sci. **157**, 110–117 (2019)
8. Ma, Y., Wu, X., Yu, G., Xu, Y., Wang, Y.: Pedestrian detection and tracking from low-resolution unmanned aerial vehicle thermal imagery. Sensors. **16**(4), 446 (2016)
9. Redmon, J., Farhadi, A.: YOLO 9000: better, faster, stronger. In: IEEE Conference on Computer Vision and Pattern Recognition (CVPR), pp. 6517–6525 (2017)
10. Redmon, J., Ali, F., YOLOv3: an incremental improvement. In: IEEE Conference on Computer Vision and Pattern Recognition (CVPR), pp. 1–6 (2018)
11. Howard, A.G., et al.: MobileNets: Efficient Convolutional Neural Networks for Mobile Vision Applications. ArXiv abs/1704.04861 (2017)
12. Zhou, D., Fang, J., Song, X., et al.: Iou loss for 2d/3d object detection. In: International Conference on 3D Vision (3DV), pp. 85–94 (2019)

13. LeCun, Y.: LeNet-5, convolutional neural networks. http://yann.lecun.com/exdb/lenet20.5: 14 (2015)
14. Zheng, Z., Wang, P., Liu, W., et al.: Distance-IoU Loss: faster and better learning for bounding box regression. arXiv preprint arXiv: 2019: 08287.
15. Fan, H., Zhang, F., Li, Z.: AnomalyDAE: Dual autoencoder for anomaly detection on attributed networks. In: IEEE International Conference on Acoustics, Speech and Signal Processing (ICASSP), pp. 5685–5689 (2020)
16. Li, J., Liang, X., Wei, Y., et al.: Perceptual generative adversarial networks for small object detection. In: IEEE Conference on Computer Vision and Pattern Recognition, pp. 1222–1230 (2017)
17. Krizhevsky, A., Sutskever, I., Hinton, G.E.: ImageNet classification with deep convolutional neural networks. Neural Inf. Process. Syst. (NIPS) **25**, 1097–1105 (2012)
18. Wang, R.J., Li, X., Ling, C.X.: Pelee: A real-time object detection system on mobile devices. arXiv preprint arXiv: 1804.06882 (2018)
19. He, K., Zhang, X., Ren, S., Sun, J.: Deep residual learning for image recognition. In: IEEE Conference on Computer Vision and Pattern Recognition (CVPR), pp. 770–778 (2016)
20. De Ruvo, P., Distante, A., Stella, E., Marino, F.: A GPU-based vision system for real time detection of fastening elements in railway inspection. In: 16th IEEE International Conference on Image Processing (ICIP), pp. 2333–2336 (2009)
21. Duan, K., et al.: Centernet: keypoint triplets for object detection. In: Proceedings of the IEEE/CVF International Conference on Computer Vision (2019)

Automatic Identification for Projector Brand and Model Number

Zuoyong Li[1], Weice Wang[2], Fuquan Zhang[1], and Haoyi Fan[1,3(✉)]

[1] Fujian Provincial Key Laboratory of Information Processing and Intelligent Control, College of Computer and Control Engineering, Minjiang University, Fuzhou 350121, China
[2] College of Computer and Information Sciences, Fujian Agriculture and Forestry University, Fuzhou 350002, China
[3] School of Computer Science and Technology, Harbin University of Science and Technology, Harbin 150080, China

Abstract. The projector production process needs to pack manufactured projectors. The key step of projector packing is to check whether the brand and model number of the projector is correct or not, for avoiding the projector's packing error. To achieve automation of identifying projector brand and model number for improving the efficiency of the projector packing, we proposed an automatic identification method by using image processing, character recognition, and string matching. Specifically, image grayscale processing, image gradient calculation, morphological operations, and image thresholding are sequentially performed to determine candidate target regions located by a projector's brand and model number. Then, two shape prior-based image features are designed to perform target region screening, i.e., excluding fake target regions as far as possible. Next, the character recognition technology is used to extract the texts in the target regions. Finally, string matching is performed to obtain identification results of the projector's brand and model number. Experimental results on several projectors demonstrate the effectiveness of the proposed method on automatic identification of projector brand and model number. The proposed method provides a general framework for identifying the brand and model number of other similar electronic products.

Keywords: Projector · Image processing · Character recognition · String matching

1 Introduction

In the industrial production process of projectors, it is indispensable to pack the produced projectors. The general packing process of a projector is as follows: (1) check its appearance for defects; (2) paste factory label; (3) check whether its brand and model number are correct or not; (4) put it into a plastic bag; (5) put it in a box. The key step in the above packing process is to check whether the brand and the model number are correct or not. Traditional practice is to identify the brand and the model number on the projector's plastic fuselage by the human eyes, which has the limitations of low efficiency and high labor consumption.

© Springer Nature Singapore Pte Ltd. 2021
Y. Tan et al. (Eds.): DMBD 2021, CCIS 1453, pp. 122–137, 2021.
https://doi.org/10.1007/978-981-16-7476-1_12

To achieve automatic identification of the brand and the model number on the surface of a projector's plastic fuselage, we presented a novel method by using several technologies such as morphological operations [1–4], image thresholding [5–8], character recognition [9–12], and string matching [13–15]. In the proposed method, several image processing technologies are first sequentially used to determine candidate target regions located by the brand and the model number. Then, two image features based on a shape prior are designed to exclude fake target regions and remain true target regions as far as possible. Finally, the character recognition and the string matching on the target regions are sequentially performed to identify the brand and the model number.

The rest of this paper is organized as follows. Section 2 introduces related works. Section 3 describes the theory and implementation of the proposed method. Section 4 reports our experimental results. Section 5 draws conclusions.

2 Related Works

This work was done to meet an actual need for industrial production automation from a projector production factory in Fujian Province, China. To our knowledge, there are no related works for automatic identification of a projector's brand and model number. The proposed method is specifically developed to achieve this goal, and also provides a novel framework for identifying the brand and model number of other similar electronic products.

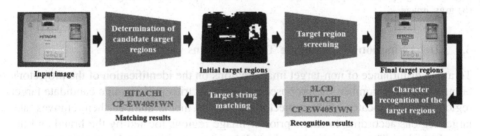

Fig. 1. Automatic identification system integrated by projector brand and model number recognition.

3 The Proposed Method

The proposed method aims to automatically and quickly identify the brand and the model number of a projector for avoiding the packing error in the production line. The proposed method is composed of four key steps, i.e., determination of candidate target regions, target region screening, character recognition of the target regions, and target string matching. The flowchart of the proposed method is given in Fig. 1. The contributions of our proposed method are as follows.

(1) We innovatively propose a scheme to determine the target regions of a projector's brand and model number by using several image processing technologies and a shape prior. The target region determination narrows the scope of subsequent character recognition and string matching, which improves their accuracy and efficiency.
(2) We propose an automatic identification method for projector brand and model number. The proposed method also provides a novel framework for identifying the brand and model number of other similar electronic products.

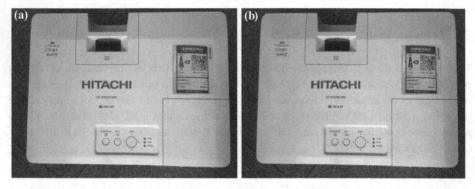

Fig. 2. Image grayscale processing result of the first projector's image: (a) original image, (b) gray image.

3.1 Determination of Candidate Target Regions

To avoid disturbance of non-target image regions on the identification of the projector's brand and model number, the proposed method first tries to determine candidate target regions possibly located by the projector's brand and model number, then removes fake target regions according to shape prior of image regions located by the brand and the model number. The determination of candidate target regions includes four sub-steps, i.e., image grayscale processing, image gradient calculation, morphological operations, and image thresholding. The theory and implementation of each sub-step will be described in detail by the following subsections.

3.1.1 Image Grayscale Processing

Based on the weights used in the Matlab function termed as rgb2gray, a color projector image I can be transformed into a gray image I_{gray}, i.e.,

$$I_{gray} = 0.299R + 0.587G + 0.114B \qquad (1)$$

where R, G, and B indicate the red, green, and blue color component of the image, respectively. Figure 2 exhibits the grayscale processing result of the first projector's image with the brand (HITACHI) in our experiments, where Fig. 2(a) shows the original color image, and Fig. 2(b) shows its corresponding gray image.

3.1.2 Image Gradient Calculation

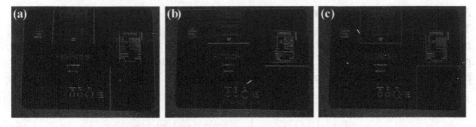

Fig. 3. Gradient calculation results of the first projector's image: (a) image gradient on X direction, (b) image gradient on Y direction, and (c) total image gradient.

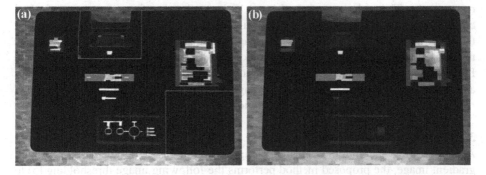

Fig. 4. Morphological operation results of the first projector's gradient image shown in Fig. 3(c): (a) the morphological closing operation result, (b) the morphological opening operation result.

To approximately calculate image gradient values on X (horizontal) direction and Y (vertical) direction, two Sobel operators [16] on both directions are first used to filter the projector's gray image, respectively. The Sobel operators on X direction and Y direction are defined as,

$$S_X = \begin{bmatrix} -1 & 0 & 1 \\ -2 & 0 & 2 \\ -1 & 0 & 1 \end{bmatrix}, S_Y = \begin{bmatrix} -1 & -2 & -1 \\ 0 & 0 & 0 \\ 1 & 2 & 1 \end{bmatrix} \tag{2}$$

Then, the approximate value of the total image gradient can be calculated as,

$$G(i,j) = |\Omega(i,j) * S_X| + |\Omega(i,j) * S_Y| \tag{3}$$

where $\Omega(i,j)$ indicates a 3×3 local image window centered at pixel (i, j), the star symbol indicates image convolution, and $G(i,j)$ is the calculated gradient value at the pixel (i, j). Taking Fig. 2(b) as an example, its gradient calculation results on X direction and Y direction are visually shown in Fig. 3(a) and Fig. 3(b), respectively. The total image gradient of Fig. 2(b) is visually shown in Fig. 3(c).

3.1.3   Morphological Operations

To accurately find the target regions located by the first projector's brand and model number, morphological operations are implemented on its gradient image to refine possible target regions. First, the proposed method constructs a rectangular structure element E, which is a $m \times n$ matrix with definition,

$$E = \begin{bmatrix} 1 & \cdots & 1 \\ \vdots & \ddots & \vdots \\ 1 & \cdots & 1 \end{bmatrix}_{m \times n}, n = \lceil \frac{H}{48} \rceil, m = \frac{n}{2} \tag{4}$$

where H indicates the total number of image rows (i.e., the image height), m and n indicate the total numbers of rows and columns in the structure element matrix E, respectively. Then, the structure element E is used to perform the morphological closing operation [1] on the total gradient image shown in Fig. 3(c), aiming at filling the inner holes and concave corners of image regions, and connecting adjacent image regions. The morphological closing operation result of Fig. 3(c) is shown in Fig. 4(a). Finally, the morphological opening operation is performed to eliminate small regions and burrs, and to disconnect thinner image regions for smoothing possible target regions. The morphological opening operation result of Fig. 4(a) is shown in Fig. 4(b).

3.1.4   Image Thresholding

After obtaining the morphological opening operation result of the first projector's gradient image, the proposed method performs the following image thresholding [5] to obtain an image binarization result, i.e.,

$$B(i,j) = \begin{cases} 1, & \text{if } \tilde{G}(i,j) > T \\ 0, & \text{otherwise} \end{cases} \tag{5}$$

where,

$$T = \text{Otsu}(\tilde{G}) \tag{6}$$

$\tilde{G}$ indicates the gradient image after performing the morphological closing and opening operations, and T is the optimal threshold determined by the classic image thresholding method called Otsu [5]. Figure 5 shows the image binarization result after performing image thresholding on the gradient image shown in Fig. 4(b). After comparatively analyzing the white regions in Fig. 5 and the locations of the projector's brand and model number in Fig. 2(b), one can conclude that the white regions not only include the target regions located by the projector's brand and model number, but also include other non-target regions.

3.2 Target Region Screening

After obtaining the image binarization result shown in Fig. 5, those white regions are regarded as the initial target regions located by the projector's brand and model number. Unfortunately, the white regions include some non-target regions. To avoid disturbance of these non-target regions on the identification of the projector's brand and model number, based on a shape prior of the target regions, the proposed method extracts two image features to exclude non-target regions and remain true target regions as far as possible. The specific target region screening steps are as follows.

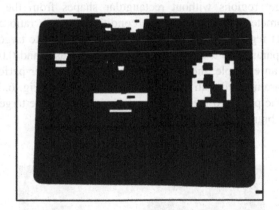

Fig. 5. Image thresholding result of the first projector's gradient image.

(1) For each candidate target region indexed by i, the proposed method extracts two image features related with the geometric properties of its smallest outer rectangle, i.e., aspect ratio (R_i) and area ratio (R_{Area_i}), according to the following equations.

$$R_i = \frac{W_i}{H_i} \tag{7}$$

$$R_{\text{Area}_i} = \frac{\text{Area}_i}{A} \tag{8}$$

$$W_i = \max\{N_{Rows_i}, N_{Columns_i}\} \tag{9}$$

$$H_i = \min\{N_{Rows_i}, N_{Columns_i}\} \tag{10}$$

$$\text{Area}_i = W_i \times H_i \tag{11}$$

where W_i and H_i indicate the width and the height of the smallest outer rectangle termed as Recti corresponding to the i-th candidate target region, N_{Rows_i} and $N_{Columns_i}$ are the total numbers of rows and columns of the smallest outer rectangle Recti, and A is the area of the whole image, i.e., the total number of image pixels.

(2) The above two image features are used to exclude fake target regions and construct the set of true target regions, S_{TR}, by the following target region screening scheme, i.e.,

$$S_{TR} = \begin{cases} Rect_i, & \text{if } R_i > \alpha \text{ and } R_{\text{Area}_i} > \beta \\ \varnothing, & \text{otherwise} \end{cases} \tag{12}$$

where $Rect_i$ is the smallest outer rectangle of the i-th candidate target region. In addition, the parameter α is the restriction condition for aspect ratio, which is used to remove fake target regions without rectangular shapes from the candidate target regions. The parameter β is the restriction condition for area ratio, which is used to remove fake target regions with small areas from the candidate target regions. In our experiments, the parameters α and β are empirically set as 4 and 0.001, respectively. Taking Fig. 5 as an example, the remained target regions after performing the target region screening are marked with two red rectangular lines in Fig. 6. From Fig. 6, one can observe that the proposed method accurately determines the target regions located by the projector's brand and model number.

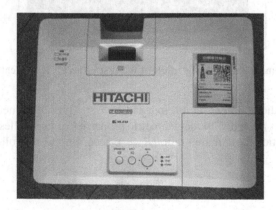

Fig. 6. Target region determination result of the first projector's image.

3.3   Character Recognition of the Target Regions

After determining the target regions located by the projector's brand and model number, different OCR (Optical Character Recognition) technologies can be used to recognize the characters in the target regions. In the proposed method, we use Tesseract-OCR engine [9] to achieve character recognition. Taking both target regions depicted by two red rectangles in Fig. 6 as examples, the character recognition results are shown in Fig. 7, and the time consuming is 0.42 ms.

Fig. 7. Character recognition result of the first projector's target image regions.

HITACHI   CP—EX5001WN   (3LCD   STANDBY/ON   INPU   T   MENU
0   &   A   8   (amp   M   +g
cosin   6b   c   it   carea   horsey   #ak   unxnce
B   \   N(ig/R)   mAE   linu   d   on   dE   z.

Fig. 8. Character recognition result of the first projector's whole image.

To explain the necessity of determining the target regions located by the projector's brand and model number in the proposed method, Fig. 8 shows the character recognition result on the first projector's whole image without the target region determination for its brand and model number, and the time consuming is 1.82 ms. After comparing the character recognition results of the target regions and those of the whole image, one can obviously observe that the character recognition result of the whole image not only takes more time, but also obtains a worse recognition result containing a lot of undesirable non-target characters, as compared with the character recognition result on the target regions extracted by the proposed method. This example demonstrates the superiority of determining target regions located by the projector's brand and model number in terms of target character recognition accuracy and efficiency. Accordingly, accurate character recognition is beneficial to subsequent target string matching of the projector's brand and model number.

3.4   Target String Matching

The above character recognition step only extracts the strings of the projector's brand and model number from the target image regions located by them. However, the projector's packing process in its production line requires checking whether the texts of the projector's brand and model number are correct or not. To achieve this goal, the proposed method will perform target string matching for the projector's brand and model number, respectively. Therefore, we will describe string matching of the brand and the model number in following two subsections, respectively.

Fig. 9. String matching result of the character recognition on the first projector's target regions.

Fig. 10. String matching result of the character recognition on the first projector's whole image.

3.4.1   String Matching of Brand

The previous character recognition step uses spaces to separate recognized characters from different image regions, as shown in Fig. 7 and Fig. 8. Since the projector's brand and the projector's model number are located at two different image regions represented by two white regions in Fig. 5 or two red rectangles in Fig. 6, their character recognition results construct two strings corresponding to the brand and the model number, respectively.

To achieve string matching of the projector's brand, each string in the previous character recognition result is matched one by one with strings in the previously constructed database of projector brands until the matching succeeds, or fails on the whole database. Taking the character recognition results shown in Fig. 7 and Fig. 8 as examples, their respective string matching results of the brand and the model number is shown in Fig. 9 and Fig. 10, and their respective string matching time is 0.44 ms and 1.42 ms. Figure 9 and Fig. 10 show that string matching operations on the character recognition results of the target regions and those of the whole image obtain the same correct results, i.e., "HITACHI". This demonstrates that an inaccurate character recognition result shown in Fig. 8 also generates an accurate brand string matching result. However, luck is not always there. In addition, the brand string matching on the character recognition result of the whole image takes more time than the brand string matching on the character recognition result of the target regions, because the former contains a lot of non-target strings.

3.4.2   String Matching of Model Number

Once the brand string matching fails, string matching of the model number is not needed, and the warning information of unmatched brand will generate a signal to trigger certain automatic control in the real production line. When the brand string matching succeeds, each remained string in the character recognition result will continue to be matched with strings in a previously constructed database of model numbers corresponding to the matched brand, until the matching succeeds, or fails on the whole database. If string matching of both the brand and the model number is successful, the matched strings could be displayed to indicate the success; otherwise, the matched brand could be displayed for convenient observation, and the warning information of the unmatched model number will generate a signal to trigger certain automatic control in the real production line. Also taking the character recognition results shown in Fig. 7 and Fig. 8 as the examples, their respective string matching results of the model number is shown in Fig. 9 and Fig. 10. Being similar to string matching of the brand in the above subsection, an inaccurate character recognition result also generates an accurate string matching result of the model number, i.e., "CP-EX5001WN". However, luck is not always there, and the fourth projector's image will demonstrate this misfortune in Sect. 4. In addition, the string matching on the character recognition result of the target regions takes less time than the string matching on the character recognition result of the whole image, because the former provides fewer candidate strings for matching the model number.

4 Experimental Results

To validate the effectiveness of the proposed method on identifying projector brand and model number, we used four projectors as samples. The first projector's brand is HITACHI from Japan, and the projector is used to acquire a clean testing image without sticky strips on the projector's surface. Figures 2, 3, 4, 5, 6, 7, 8, 9, 10 already show the first projector's original color image and its intermediate processing results obtained by the proposed method. For convenient reading, Fig. 11 again exhibits the first projector's original color image and its main intermediate processing results. The second projector also has the same brand (HITACHI) and different model number with the first projector. In addition, there is a sticky strip with many texts on the surface of the second projector, which adds to the difficulty of identifying the projector's brand and model number. Figure 12 shows the second projector's original color image and its main intermediate processing results. The third and fourth projectors have the same brand (EPSON) and different model numbers. Figure 13 and Fig. 14 show their original color images and their main intermediate processing results, respectively. The proposed method was coded by using Python, and experiments were run on a laptop with 2.6 GHz Intel Core TM i7-4720HQ CPU and memory.

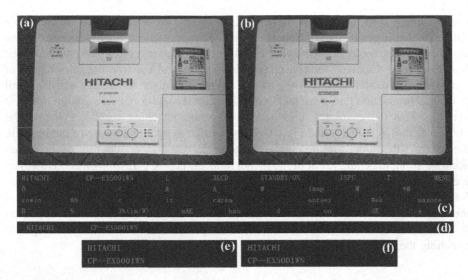

Fig. 11. Experimental results on the first projector's image: (a) original image, (b) target regions (i.e., red rectangles) determined by the proposed method, (c) character recognition result of the whole image, (d) character recognition result of the target regions, (e) string matching result of the character recognition on the whole image, (f) string matching result of the character recognition on the target regions. (Color figure online)

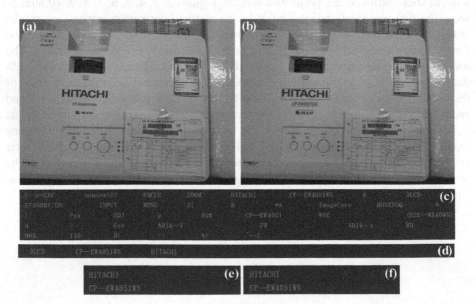

Fig. 12. Experimental results on the second projector's image: (a) original image, (b) target regions (i.e., red rectangles) determined by the proposed method, (c) character recognition result of the whole image, (d) character recognition result of the target regions, (e) string matching result of the character recognition on the whole image, (f) string matching result of the character recognition on the target regions. (Color figure online)

4.1   Results of Qualitative Evaluation

For the first projector, Fig. 11(b) shows the determination result of the target regions located by its brand and model number. In addition, Fig. 11(d) and Fig. 11(f) show the character recognition result and the string matching result of the target regions located by the brand and the model number, respectively. From Fig. 11(b), one can observe that the proposed method accurately determines the target regions of the projector's brand and model number as depicted by using two red rectangles. Accordingly, as shown in Fig. 11(d), the character recognition result of the target regions only contains the characters of the brand and the model number, which makes subsequent successful string matching be a piece of cake. Without the determination of the target regions, the character recognition result and the string matching result of the whole image are shown in Fig. 11(c) and Fig. 11(e), respectively. As compared with the character recognition result of the target regions shown in Fig. 11(d), the character recognition result of the whole image contains a lot of undesirable non-target characters. Fortunately, these undesirable non-target characters do not cause the failure of the string matching on the brand and the model number, as illustrated in Fig. 11(e). However, it consumes more time on the string matching, as described in Sect. 3.4.

For the second projector, Figs. 12(a)-(f) show its original color image, target region determination result of its brand and model number, character recognition result of the whole image, character recognition result of the target regions, string matching result of the character recognition on the whole image, and string matching result of the character recognition on the target regions, respectively. The second projector has the same brand (HITACHI) and different model number (CP-EX4051WN) with the first projector. There is a sticky strip on the second projector's surface, and a plastic tape with reflective interference in the image background. This adds the difficulty of determining the target regions, subsequent character recognition and target string matching. Figure 12(b) shows that the proposed method successfully finds the target regions of the brand and the model number, but also determine a fake target region. Figure 12(d) shows that the character recognition on three target regions generates three strings (i.e., 3LCD, CP-EW4051WN, HITACHI), where the string (3LCD) is from the fake target region. Figure 12(f) shows that the target string matching operation successfully matches the brand (HITACHI) and the model number (CP-EW4051WN). Similar to the first projector's image, the character recognition directly on the second projector's whole image generates a lot of undesirable non-target characters for identifying its brand and model number, as illustrated in Fig. 12(c). Fortunately, the string matching of the brand and the model number are successful, as illustrated in Fig. 12(e).

For the third projector, Figs. 13(a)-(f) show its original color image, target region determination result of its brand and model number, character recognition result of the whole image, character recognition result of the target regions, string matching result of the character recognition on the whole image, and string matching result of the character recognition on the target regions, respectively. As compared with the previous two projectors, the third projector has different brand (EPSON) and model number (CB-UO5). The design style and text layout of the projectors with different brands are very different, which adds the difficulty of determining target regions located by the third projector's brand and model number. Figure 13(b) shows that the proposed method determines five target regions, where only two regions are true target regions. From Figs. 13(c)-(f), one can draw the following conclusions. 1) The character recognition result of the target regions contains several undesirable non-target characters, and subsequent target string matching obtains the correct results, i.e., the brand (EPSON) and the model number (CB-UO5). 2) The character recognition result of the whole image contains a lot of undesirable non-target characters. Fortunately, subsequent target string matching also obtains the correct results. Of course, more characters will consume more time for string matching.

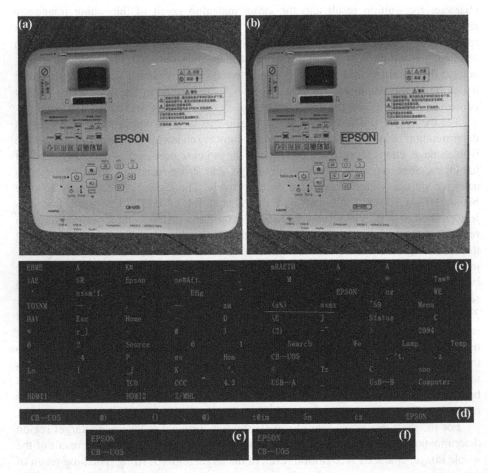

Fig. 13. Experimental results on the third projector's image: (a) original image, (b) target regions (i.e., red rectangles) determined by the proposed method, (c) character recognition result of the whole image, (d) character recognition result of the target regions, (e) string matching result of the character recognition on the whole image, (f) string matching result of the character recognition on the target regions. (Color figure online)

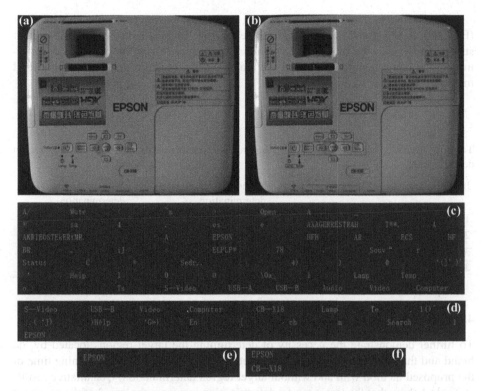

Fig. 14. Experimental results on the fourth projector's image: (a) original image, (b) target regions (i.e., red rectangles) determined by the proposed method, (c) character recognition result of the whole image, (d) character recognition result of the target regions, (e) string matching result of the character recognition on the whole image, (f) string matching result of the character recognition on the target regions. (Color figure online)

For the fourth projector, Figs. 14(a)-(f) show its original color image, target region determination result of its brand and model number, character recognition result of the whole image, character recognition result of the target regions, string matching result of the character recognition on the whole image, and string matching result of the character recognition on the target regions, respectively. The projector has the same brand (EPSON) and different model number (CB-X18) as the third projector. In addition, the text layout of the fourth projector slightly differs from that of the third projector. This adds a little difficulty in determining target regions located by the projector's brand and model number. Figure 14(b) shows that the proposed method determines seven target regions, where only two regions are true target regions. From Figs. 14(c)-(f), one can draw the following conclusions. 1) The character recognition result of the target regions contains some undesirable non-target characters, and subsequent target string matching obtains correct results, i.e., the brand (EPSON) and the model number (CB-X18). 2) The character recognition result of the whole image contains a lot of undesirable non-target characters.

Fortunately, subsequent string matching of the brand also obtains the correct result (EPSON), as illustrated in Fig. 14(e). However, Fig. 14(e) also shows that subsequent string matching of the model number fails. This demonstrates the necessity of determining the target regions located by the brand and the model number in the proposed method.

Table 1. Running time (millisecond) of the proposed method with and without target region determination.

Image number	Image size	Without target region determination	With target region determination
1	3264 × 2448	3.24	0.86
2	4000 × 3000	4.77	0.96
3	2448 × 2448	6.54	1.05
4	3648 × 2736	5.22	1.51

4.2   Results of Quantitative Evaluation

To further demonstrate the necessity of determining the target regions located by the brand and the model number in the proposed method, Table 1 lists the running time of the proposed method with and without target region determination. Quantitative results in Table 1 show that the target region determination increases the speed of the proposed method by 3 to 5 times, which helps our proposed method more suitable for real-time application of the projector industrial production line.

5   Conclusions

The key step of packing a projector in a real industrial production line is to check whether the projector's brand and model number are correct or not, for avoiding the projector's packing error. To achieve automation of identifying projector brand and model number, we developed an automatic identification method in this paper. The main feature of the proposed method includes target region determination of a projector's brand and model number by using image processing technologies and shape prior. Accurate target region determination narrows the scope of subsequent character recognition and target string matching, which improves their accuracy and efficiency. Experimental results on four projectors with different brands and model numbers demonstrate the effectiveness of the proposed method. In addition, our proposed scheme of target region determination can be generalized for achieving similar automation tasks in other industrial applications. The proposed method also provides a general framework for identifying the brand and model number of other similar electronic products.

Acknowledgments. This work is partially supported by National Natural Science Foundation of China (61972187), Natural Science Foundation of Fujian Province (2020J02024), Fuzhou Science and Technology Project (2020-RC-186).

References

1. Vincent, L.: Grayscale area openings and closings, their efficient implementation and applications. In: First Workshop on Mathematical Morphology and its Applications to Signal Processing, pp. 22–27 (1993).
2. Wang, Z.: A new clustering method based on morphological operations. Expert Syst. Appl. **145**, 113102 (2020)
3. Parida, P., Bhoi, N.: 2-D gabor filter based transition region extraction and morphological operation for image segmentation. Comput. Electr. Eng. **62**, 119–134 (2017)
4. Li, M., Wang, Q., Zhang, D., Li, P., Zuo, W.: Joint distance and similarity measure learning based on triplet-based constraints. Inf. Sci. **406–407**, 119–132 (2017)
5. Otsu, N.: A threshold selection method from gray-level histograms. IEEE Trans. Syst. Man Cybern. **9**(1), 62–66 (1979)
6. Lei, B., Fan, J.: Image thresholding segmentation method based on minimum square rough entropy. Appl. Soft Comput. **84**, 105687 (2019)
7. Martino, F.D., Sessa, S.: PSO image thresholding on images compressed via fuzzy transforms. Inf. Sci. **506**, 308–324 (2020)
8. Zhang, Z., Liu, L., Shen, F., Shen, H.T., Shao, L.: Binary multi-view clustering. IEEE Trans. Pattern Anal. Mach. Intell. **41**(7), 1774–1782 (2019)
9. Kay, A.: Tesseract: an open-source optical character recognition engine. Linux J. **159**, 2 (2007)
10. Robby, G.A., Tandra, A., Susanto, I., Harefa, J., Chowanda, A.: Implementation of optical character recognition using tesseract with the javanese script target in android application. Procedia Computer Science **157**, 499–505 (2019)
11. Yang, C.S., Yang, Y.H.: Improved local binary pattern for real scene optical character recognition. Pattern Recogn. Lett. **100**, 14–21 (2017)
12. Lee, Y.G.: Novel video stabilization for real-time optical character recognition applications. J. Vis. Commun. Image Represent. **44**, 148–155 (2017)
13. Ryu, C., Park, K.: Improved pattern-scan-order algorithms for string matching. J. Discrete Algorithms **49**, 27–36 (2018)
14. Ibanez, R., Soria, A., Teyseyre, A., Rodriguez, G., Campo, M.: Approximate string matching: a lightweight approach to recognize gestures with Kinect. Pattern Recogn. **62**, 73–86 (2017)
15. Zhao, L., Lin, T., Zhou, K., Wang, S., Chen, X.: Pseudo 2D string matching technique for high efficiency screen content coding. IEEE Trans. Multimedia **18**(3), 339–350 (2016)
16. Sobel, I., Feldman, G.: A 3 × 3 isotropic gradient operator for image processing. a Talk at the Stanford Artificial Project, pp. 271–272 (1968)

SC-VDM: A Lightweight Smart Contract Vulnerability Detection Model

Ke Zhou[1,3], Jieren Cheng[2,3(✉)], Hui Li[4(✉)], Yuming Yuan[4],
Le Liu[2,3], and Xiulai Li[1,3,5]

[1] School of Cyberspace Security (School of Cryptology), Hainan University,
Haikou 570228, China
[2] School of Computer Science and Technology, Hainan University,
Haikou 570228, China
[3] Hainan Blockchain Technology Engineering Research Center,
Haikou 570228, China
[4] Hainan Huochain Tech Company Limited, Haikou 570100, China
lihui0729@huochain.com.cn
[5] Hainan Hairui Zhong Chuang Technol Co Ltd, Haikou 570100, China

Abstract. The smart contract technology of blockchain is being applied in many industries, but its security issues have also caused huge economic losses, so it is very important to conduct security audits on them before smart contracts' deployment. The existing smart contract security audit methods rely heavily on the rules formulated by experts based on their own knowledge and experience, require high hardware resources and the detection procedure is time-consuming. To address these problems mentioned above, we propose a lightweight smart contract vulnerability detection model(SC-VDM) based on Convolutional Neural Networks(CNN), which can automatically detect the vulnerabilities in the smart contract on a lightweight computer without expert knowledge. We first convert the smart contract bytecode into smart contract bytecode grayscale matrix pictures and then use CNN for vulnerability detecting. We test SC-VDM on two datasets which each contain four types of smart contract vulnerabilities. The experimental results show that the accuracy and F1-score can reach more than 81% and 86% on two datasets. It performs best on the Reentrancy vulnerability which had caused The DAO attack in 2016, and the accuracy and F1-score is 89.52% and 93.96%. Moreover, the detection time is greatly shortened than traditional tools, it costs only 0.021 s for each smart contract.

Keywords: Blockchain · Smart contract · Lightweight · Vulnerability detection

1 Introduction

The blockchain technology which is represented by Bitcoin [1] and Ethereum [2] has developed rapidly, and received increasing attention because of its non-tamperable and decentralized nature. The smart contract is a program on the blockchain which can automatically respond to requests and store assets. Blockchain-based smart contracts are trying to be applied to a variety of industries, such as the Internet of Things [3],

© Springer Nature Singapore Pte Ltd. 2021
Y. Tan et al. (Eds.): DMBD 2021, CCIS 1453, pp. 138–149, 2021.
https://doi.org/10.1007/978-981-16-7476-1_13

medical [4], supply chain management [5], finance [6], energy [7]. Smart contracts have the same non-tamperable characteristics with blockchains [8] and cannot be modified once deployed. However, as a program, there may be vulnerabilities in smart contract, and these vulnerabilities can not be modified due to its non-tamperable characteristic which may cause huge economic losses. A classic case is The DAO attack [9], where hackers used the Reentrancy vulnerability of The DAO contract to steal nearly 50 million U.S. dollars in ether. There are many similar incidents and the security issues of smart contracts have drawn public attentions [10], so it is necessary to make vulnerabilities detection before the smart contract is deployed.

Most of the existing smart contract analysis methods are inspired by traditional program vulnerabilities detection methods, such as symbolic execution: OYENTE [11], theorem proving: ZEUS [12] and dynamic execution: ContractFuzzer [13]. These methods have some obvious shortcomings. Firstly, these methods rely heavily on the vulnerability rules defined by experts. The experts are required to analyze the vulnerabilities and pre-define the vulnerabilities to detect smart contracts, but if the vulnerability rules are wrong, the detection results will also be wrong. Secondly, with the development of blockchain technology, the number of smart contracts is increasing rapidly and the detection efficiency of fewer experts is limited. Therefore, a large number of smart contracts will be deployed which without vulnerabilities detection and may cause huge economic losses. Finally, these methods require high hardware resources and the detection procedure is time-consuming.

In order to solve these problems, we propose a lightweight smart contract vulnerability detection model(SC-VDM) based on CNN, which is contain two part: "Making smart contract bytecode grayscale matrix pictures(SC-BGMPs)" and "Smart Contract Spatial Pyramid Pooling Convolutional Neural Networks(SC-SPP-CNN)". During the vulnerability detection, we first use "Making SC-BGMPs" to convert the different length smart contracts bytecode into different size SC-BGMPs, and then we put them in SC-SPP-CNN directly without resizing. The convolution kernel in CNN can better associate the opcodes with the operands to allow the network learn local features better. So we built a shallow special CNN called SC-SPP-CNN which without pooling layer between convolutional layers. We adjust the feature maps with spatial pyramid pooling(SPP) [14] layer before fully connected layers. Finally, the SC-SPP-CNN will give the result whether there is vulnerability in smart contract. Comparing with OYENTE [11], ZEUS [12] and ContractFuzzer [13], SC-VDM is automated and does not require expert knowledge, and it is suitable for multiple types of smart contract vulnerabilities which means it can be used to the detection of a variety types of smart contract vulnerabilities after vulnerability dataset training. Moreover, SC-VDM is a lightweight model which can run on a lightweight computer and greatly shorten the vulnerability detection time.

In general, our main contributions are:

1) We propose a method to construct the SC-BGMPs. We divide two bits smart contract bytecode into a group and construct bytecode matrix. Then we convert each group of bytecode from hexadecimal to decimal and convert it into SC-BGMP.

2) We propose a lightweight smart contract vulnerability detection model called SC-VDM. We put the smart contract bytecode with different length into SC-VDM and it will automatically detecet smart contract vulnerabilitiy in very little time.
3) We propose a lightweight smart contract vulnerability detection method suitable for multiple types of smart contract vulnerabilities. After our model is trained on a certain type of smart contract vulnerability dataset, it can efficiently detect this vulnerability.

2 Related Work

2.1 Smart Contract Vulnerability Detection

The security of smart contracts is one of the foundations of blockchain security, so smart contract security analysis is also a hot issue in blockchain. Luu et al. [11] use symbolic execution methods, focusing on the transaction order dependency, reentrancy, timestamp dependency and unhandled exceptions of smart contracts. CF Torres et al. [15] proposed Osiris, which combines symbolic execution with taint analysis to detect integer problems in smart contracts. Zeus [12] will convert the smart contract written in solidity into a low-level intermediate representation, and then determine the security of the smart contract through static analysis and verification engine. ContractFuzzer [13] is a smart contract detection tool that uses fuzz testing. It defines seven test primitives to support the detection of security vulnerabilities.

2.2 Program Vulnerability Detection Using CNN

With the successful application of neural networks in various fields [16, 17], CNN has also received a lot of attention. In terms of security, Yuxin Ding et al. [18] converted the software bytecode into a two-dimensional byte matrix, and then used CNN for malware detection. Jieren Cheng et al. [19] proposed a multi-scale network flow gray matrix feature DDoS attack detection method based on CNN. Tobiyama et al. [20] proposed a malware process detection method based on process behavior, which uses long-term short-term memory(LSTM) for feature extraction, and then uses CNN for classification.

3 Our Method

3.1 Method Overview

The SC-VDM model is mainly composed of two parts:

1) Making SC-BGMPs: Preprocessing the smart contract bytecode and convert it into the SC-BGMPs. The SC-BGMPs can be trained and tested by SC-SPP-CNN.
2) SC-SPP-CNN: Puting the SC-BGMPs of the training dataset into SC-SPP-CNN model for training. After the model is trained, putting the SC-BGMPs of the testing dataset into SC-SPP-CNN model for testing.

The SC-VDM model structure is shown in Fig. 1. When a smart contract bytecode is putted in SC-VDM, the "Making SC-BGMPs" part will first convert it into SC-BGMP. Then the SC-BGMP will be putted in "SC-SPP-CNN" part directly. Finally, "SC-SPP-CNN" part will give the result whether there is vulnerability in smart contract.

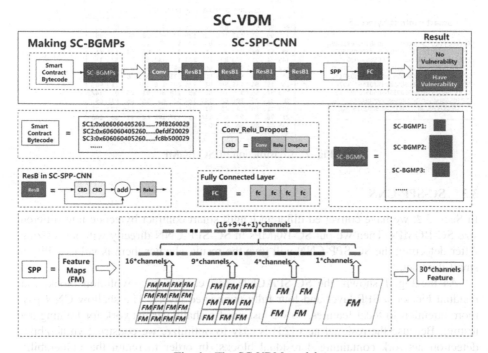

Fig. 1. The SC-VDM model

3.2 Making SC-BGMPs

First of all, we need to preprocess the smart contract bytecode, and convert the smart contract bytecode into the SC-BGMP. In the EVM, the smart contract code is written in Solidity [21], and it will be converted into bytecode [22] which is hexadecimal number and consists of three parts: deployment code, running code and auxdata. We only focus on the running code part. The opcodes in EVM is represented by two-digit hexadecimal number, so we first divide two bits bytecode into a group for dividing the opcodes, and make a matrix by using bytecode groups (the empty part at the end is filled with number 0). Then we convert each group of bytecode from hexadecimal to decimal, so that each group of data is in the range of $0 \sim 255$. The pixel value range of traditional grayscale image is $0 \sim 255$, so we can convert the matrix to grayscale image. At this time, we have already convert the smart contract running bytecode into the SC-BGMPs. Because of many smart contracts bytecode have different length, many SC-BGMPs have different size.

We take the smart contract "0xd8f1da4a236c4d6f310c02dedc049b69277b7c80" as an example to construct SC-BGMP. The smart contract bytecode in the red and blue frame are 60 and 50, whom are converted to 96 and 80 in the smart contract bytecode matrix. The construction process is shown in Fig. 2.

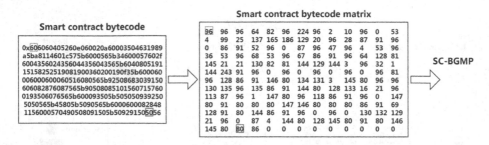

Fig. 2. Construction of SC-BGMP

3.3   SC-SPP-CNN

In Sect. 3.2, we have converted different length smart contract bytecode into different size SC-BGMPs. Then we put SC-BGMPs in SC-SPP-CNN directly without resizing. After detecting, the SC-SPP-CNN will give the result whether there is vulnerability in smart contract.

As the Fig. 1 shown, the SC-SPP-CNN part contain a convolution block, four residual blocks, a SPP layer and four fully connected layers. The shallow CNN pays more attention to local features, so we just need a shallower network for training and testing. Because the residual nets [23] is easy to optimize, we construct vulnerability detection network containing 4 residual blocks. In order to retain the vulnerability information in the smart contract as much as possible, we don't perform additional operations on the SC-BGMP, and input the SC-BGMPs of different sizes into SC-SPP-CNN directly. And there is no pooling layer between convolutional layer in SC-SPP-CNN. However, the size of SC-BGMP is different, so the fully connection layer of the network will get many feature maps of different size, which can not be learned and classified by fully connected layer. Therefore, we conduct SPP [14] layer before the fully connected layer, which make the feature maps of different size into a unified measure. Finally, the features will be putted in fully connected layer and get the final result.

4   Experiments

4.1   Dataset and Experimental Environment

In this article, we will focus on Ethereum smart contracts, which were written in Solidity [21]. We test our model on two datasets, the first dataset contain nearly 18000 smart contracts called small dataset (SD), the second dataset contain nearly 45000 smart contracts called big dataset(BD). Both in SD and BD, we use label = 0 to indicate that there is no vulnerability, and label = 1 to indicate that there is a vulnerability.

SD: We collect nearly 20000 smart contracts from Etherscan [24]. After excluding duplicate and very small smart contracts, we used OYENTE [11] and Remix [25] to verify the dataset and add vulnerability labels. There are four vulnerabilities in SD: Assert Fail (AF), Block Timestamp(BT), Check Effects(CE) and Unchecked Low-Level Calls(ULLC). We randomly selected 80% of the contracts as the training dataset and 20% of the contracts as the testing dataset. The number of four vulnerabilities in SD is shown in Table 1.

Table 1. The number of four vulnerabilities in SD

Vulnerability type	Number					
	Train dataset			Test dataset		
	Vulnerable	Invulnerable	Total	Vulnerable	Invulnerable	Total
AF	6000	6000	12000	1500	1500	3000
BT	4400	8800	13400	1100	2200	3300
CE	5440	8160	13600	1360	2040	3400
ULLC	4240	9760	14000	1060	2440	3500

BD: We use the dataset which is provided by the paper [26]. It uses Mythril [27], Slither [28] and Smartcheck [29] and other tools to verify the dataset and add vulnerability labels. There are four vulnerabilities in BD: Denial of Service(DoS), Reentrancy(Re), Unknown Unknowns(UU) and Unchecked Low-Level Calls(ULLC). We randomly selected 80% of the contracts as the training dataset and 20% of the contracts as the testing dataset. The number of four vulnerabilities in BD is shown in Table 2.

Table 2. The number of four vulnerabilities in BD

Vulnerability type	Number					
	Train dataset			Test dataset		
	Vulnerable	Invulnerable	Total	Vulnerable	Invulnerable	Total
DoS	8616	27047	35663	2153	6762	8915
Re	6328	29335	35663	1581	7334	8915
UU	10533	25131	35664	2633	6281	8914
ULLC	9154	26507	35661	2288	6629	8917

4.2 Evaluation Index

In order to reasonably judge the test results of the model, we use some evaluation indicators to fully explain its detection performance, including Accuracy, Recall, Precision and F1-score. Accuracy is one of the measurement indexes of classification model. In addition, F1-score is an index used in statistics to measure the accuracy of two-classification(or multitask two-classification) model, which takes into account the precision and recall of classification model at the same time.

$$Accuracy = \frac{true\,positive + true\,naegtive}{Number\,of\,total\,samples} \tag{1}$$

$$Recall = \frac{true\,positive}{true\,positive + false\,negative} \tag{2}$$

$$Precision = \frac{true\,positive}{true\,positive + false\,positive} \tag{3}$$

$$F1 - score = 2 \times \frac{Recall \times Precision}{Recall + Precision} \tag{4}$$

4.3   Experimental Result

After constructing SC-BGMPs, we used a traditional CNN to compare with SC-SPP-CNN. In traditional CNN, we first resize all SC-BGMPs to 128*128, and also use four residual blocks, but we add a max-pooling layer after each residual block. Finally, we remove the SPP layer.

In Table 3, we show the test results of CNN and SC-SPP-CNN for the four vulnerabilities in SD. From Table 3, we can see that SC-SPP-CNN is higher than traditional CNN in terms of accuracy. But in terms of F1-scores, for Unchecked Low-Level Calls vulnerabilities, traditional CNN is 0.16% higher than SC-SPP-CNN, although the F1-score of the other three vulnerabilities are lower than SC-SPP-CNN.

Table 3. The test results on SD

Vulnerability	SC-SPP-CNN				CNN			
	A(%)	R(%)	P(%)	F1(%)	A(%)	R(%)	P(%)	F1(%)
AF	**85.83**	**87.27**	**84.83**	**86.03**	81.27	82.67	80.42	81.53
BT	**81.33**	**90.32**	**83.14**	**86.58**	79.48	88.00	82.42	85.12
CE	**85.82**	**89.95**	**86.88**	**88.39**	83.89	87.75	85.73	86.72
ULLC	**85.63**	93.85	**86.64**	90.10	85.20	**98.32**	83.41	**90.26**

In Table 4, we show the test results of CNN and SC-SPP-CNN for the four vulnerabilities in BD. From Table 4, we can see that on the four vulnerabilities SC-SPP-CNN is better than traditional CNN in terms of accuracy and F1-scores. But on Reentrancy vulnerability and Unchecked Low-Level Calls vulnerabilitiy, SC-SPP-CNN is a little worse than traditional CNN in terms of Recall. On Denial of Service vulnerabilitiy, SC-SPP-CNN is a little worse than traditional CNN in terms of Precision.

Table 4. The test results on BD

Vulnerability	SC-SPP-CNN				CNN			
	A(%)	R(%)	P(%)	F1(%)	A(%)	R(%)	P(%)	F1(%)
DoS	**84.48**	**92.46**	87.74	**90.03**	84.10	91.51	**88.00**	89.72
Re	**89.52**	99.03	**89.38**	**93.96**	89.30	**99.58**	88.78	93.87
UU	**83.59**	**95.00**	**83.85**	**89.08**	83.23	94.68	83.67	88.83
ULLC	**87.28**	96.53	**87.62**	**91.86**	86.90	**96.92**	86.95	91.67

In the paper [26], the author run Mythril [27], Slither [28], Smartcheck [29] and OYENTE [11] on BD, the results show that Slither [28] takes 5 s on average to analyze each smart contract, Smartcheck [29] takes 10 s on average to analyze each smart contract, OYENTE [11] takes 30 s on average to analyze each smart contract and Mythril [27] takes 64 s on average to analyze each smart contract. Our experimental result shows that SC-VDM can greatly shorten the detection time, it takes about 0.021 s on average to detect each smart contract in BD. In Table 5, we show the running time of some tools and SC-VDM.

Table 5. The running time on BD

Tools	Mythril	OYENTE	Smartcheck	Slither	SC-VDM
Detection time	64 s	30 s	10 s	5 s	**0.021 s**

Both SD and BD have Unchecked Low-Level Calls vulnerability. In Fig. 3, we show four evaluation indexes for Unchecked Low-Level Calls vulnerability in BD.

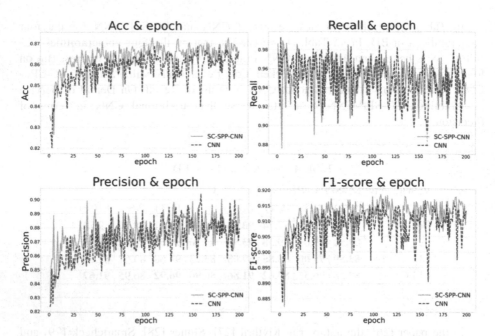

Fig. 3. Four evaluation indexes for Unchecked Low-Level Calls vulnerability

5   Discussion

5.1   Making SC-BGMPs

We expect to use the convolution kernel in CNN to associate the opcodes and operands in the smart contract bytecode to learn local features better, so we convert the smart contract bytecode to SC-BGMPs. In the construction of the SC-BGMPs, we don't introduce additional information, and don't do too much conversion, because we want the SC-BGMPs to retain the semantic information and vulnerability information in the smart contract as much as possible. In theory, the more information the SC-BGMPs retain the higher accuracy SC-VDM will have. From the experimental results in Table 3 and Table 4, we can see that SC-VDM can detect whether there are vulnerabilities in the smart contract, which proves that the SC-BGMPs can partially retain the vulnerability information of the smart contract. In addition, in traditional CNN, we resize all SC-BGMPs to a size of 128*128, and there are too many pooling layers in the model, whom lead to the detection results worse than SC-SPP-CNN. The experimental result indicates that if operate the SC-BGMPs too much will introduce additional information to destroy the vulnerability information of the smart contract. At the same time, excessive pooling layer may lose vulnerability information.

However, the information involved in some opcodes in the smart contract will be related to the current transaction status, which is not considered by our "Making SC-BGMPs". At the same time, different type of vulnerabilities may be related to different opcode, which also requires a lot of research and correlation analysis. Therefore, the next step of our research is to improve the most suitable SC-BGMPs construction method for different vulnerabilities.

5.2   SC-SPP-CNN

In terms of vulnerability detection, from Table 3 and Table 4 we can see that the accuracy and F1-score of SC-SPP-CNN can reach more than 81% and 86% on two datasets, and it perform best on Reentrancy vulnerability which has caused The DAO attack in 2016. So if there is a vulnerability dataset, SC-VDM can automatically detect vulnerabilities without expert knowledge, which is fast and efficient. But from another point of view, there is some limitations in SC-VDMas well. For example, SC-VDM need the corresponding vulnerability dataset for learning, and we can't work without vulnerability dataset.

In addition, the model is pay attention to the high-level feature maps after four residual blocks. We find that most of the smart contracts are relatively short programs and the SC-BGMPs are small, so the high-level feature maps after four residual blocks are small, which may not be able to represent the vulnerability information of the smart contract. Therefore, in the next step, we will optimize the SC-SPP-CNN by considering both shallow feature maps and high-level feature maps for vulnerability detection of smart contracts.

5.3   Running Time

From Table 5, we can see that compared with traditional tools, SC-VDM greatly shortens the detection time of vulnerabilities. In the experiment, we run SC-VDM on a lightweight computer which have i5 Processor with 16 GB of RAM and GeForce GTX 1080 Ti with 12 GB of RAM. During the detection, the "Making SC-BGMPs" takes 0.015 s and the "SC-SPP-CNN" takes 0.006s. We think the reason is that SC-VDM only detects the vulnerabilities trained and cannot detect unknown vulnerabilities without training. Although traditional tools are time-consuming, they can analyze unknown vulnerabilities.

6   Conclusion

We propose a lightweight smart contract vulnerability detection mode(SC-VDM) based on CNN, which can automatically detect smart contract vulnerabilities on a lightweight computer. SC-VDM first convert the smart contract bytecode into SC-BGMP, and then use SC-SPP-CNN for vulnerability detecting. We test SC-VDM on two datasets, the experimental results show that SC-VDM has good detection ability and it takes very little time. And it performs best on Reentrancy vulnerability.

In the future, we will try to associate different vulnerabilities with the SC-BGMP, and explore the most suitable construction method for different vulnerabilities. We will optimize SC-SPP-CNN by considering both shallow feature maps and high-level feature maps for vulnerability detection of smart contracts as well.

Acknowledgements. This work was supported by the Key Research and Development Program of Hainan Province(Grant No.ZDYF2020040), Major science and technology project of Hainan Province(Grant No.ZDKJ2020012), Hainan Provincial Natural Science Foundation of China (Grant Nos. 2019RC098) and National Natural Science Foundation of China (NSFC)(Grant No.62162022, 62162024 and 61762033), Young Talents'Science and Technology Innovation Project of Hainan Association for Science and Technology(Grant No. QCXM202007), Key project of College Students' innovation and Entrepreneurship of Hainan University(Grant No.20210110), Innovative scientific research project of Postgraduates in Colleges and universities in Hainan Province(Grant No. Hyb2020–01).

References

1. Nakamoto, S.: Bitcoin: A peer-to-peer electronic cash system. 2008. https://bitcoin.org/bitcoin.pdf
2. Wood, G.: Ethereum: a secure decentralised generalised transaction ledger. Ethereum Proj. Yellow Paper **151**, 1–32 (2014)
3. Bahga, A., Madisetti, V.K.: Blockchain platform for industrial internet of things. J. Softw. Eng. Appl. **9**(10), 533 (2016)
4. Mettler, M.: Blockchain technology in healthcare: the revolution starts here. In: 2016 IEEE 18th International Conference on e-Health Networking, Applications and Services (Healthcom), pp.1–3. IEEE (2016)
5. Chen, S., Shi, R., Ren, Z., Yan, J., Shi, Y., Zhang, J.: A blockchain based supply chain quality management framework. In: 2017 IEEE 14th International Conference on e-Business Engineering (ICEBE), pp. 172–176. IEEE (2017)
6. Eyal, I.: Blockchain technology: transforming libertarian cryptocurrency dreams to finance and banking realities. Computer **50**(9), 38–49 (2017)
7. Knirsch, F., Unterweger, A., Eibl, G., Engel, D.: Privacy-preserving smart grid tariff decisions with blockchain-based smart contracts. In: Rivera, W. (ed.) Sustainable Cloud and Energy Services, pp. 85–116. Springer, Cham (2018). https://doi.org/10.1007/978-3-319-62238-5_4
8. Tsankov, P., Dan, A., Drachsler-Cohen, D., et al.: Securify: practical security analysis of smart contracts. In: Proceedings of the 2018 ACM SIGSAC Conference on Computer and Communications Security (CCS), USA, Association for Computing Machinery, pp. 67–82 (2018)
9. Sergey, I., Hobor, A.: A concurrent perspective on smart contracts. In: Brenner, M., et al. (eds.) Financial Cryptography and Data Security. FC 2017. Lecture Notes in Computer Science, Springer, Cham, vol. 10323, pp. 478–493 (2017). https://doi.org/10.1007/978-3-319-70278-0_30
10. Atzei, N., Bartoletti, M., Cimoli, T.: A survey of attacks on ethereum smart contracts (SoK). In: Maffei, M., Ryan, M. (eds.) POST 2017. LNCS, vol. 10204, pp. 164–186. Springer, Heidelberg (2017). https://doi.org/10.1007/978-3-662-54455-6_8
11. Luu, L., Chu, D.H., Olickel, H., Saxena, P., Hobor, A.: Making smart contracts smarter. In: Conference on computer and communications security, pp. 254–269. ACM (2016)
12. Kalra, S., Goel, S., Dhawan, M., et al.: ZEUS: analyzing safety of smart contracts. In: 25th Annual Network and Distributed System Security Symposium, NDSS 2018, San Diego, California, USA, 18–21 February 2018

13. Jiang, B., Liu, Y., Chan, W.: Contractfuzzer: fuzzing smart contracts for vulnerability detection. In: Proceedings of the 33rd ACM/IEEE International Conference on Automated Software Engineering, pp. 259–269 (2018)
14. He, K., Zhang, X., Ren, S., et al.: Spatial pyramid pooling in deep convolutional networks for visual recognition. IEEE Trans. Pattern Anal. Mach. Intell. 37(9), 1904–1916 (2015)
15. Torres, C.F., Schütte, J., State, R.: Osiris: hunting for integer bugs in ethereum smart contracts. In: Proceedings of the 34th Annual Computer Security Applications Conference, pp. 664–676 (2018)
16. Kankanhalli, M.: MMALFM: explainable recommendation by leveraging reviews and images. ACM Trans. Inf. Syst. 37(2), 16:1–16:28 (2019)
17. An-An, L., Ning, X., Hanwang, Z., et al.: Multi-level policy and reward reinforcement learning for image captioning (2018)
18. Ding, Y., Zhang, X., Hu, J., et al.: Android malware detection method based on bytecode image. J. Ambient Intell. Humanized Comput. 1–10 (2020)
19. Cheng, J., Liu, Y., Tang, X., et al.: DDoS attack detection via multi-scale convolutional neural network. Comput. Mater. Continua 62(3), 1317–1333 (2020)
20. Tobiyama, S., Yamaguchi, Y., Shimada, H., et al.: Malware detection with deep neural network using process behavior. In: 2016 IEEE 40th Annual Computer Software and Applications Conference (COMPSAC), vol. 2, pp. 577-582. IEEE (2016)
21. Ethereum Foundation. 2018. The solidity contract-oriented programming language. https://github.com/ethereum/solidity
22. Wohrer, M., Zdun, U.: Smart contracts: security patterns in the ethereum ecosystem and solidity. In: 2018 International Workshop on Blockchain Oriented Software Engineering (IWBOSE), pp. 2–8. IEEE (2018)
23. He, K., Zhang, X., Ren, S., et al.: Deep residual learning for image recognition. In: Proceedings of the IEEE Conference on Computer Vision and Pattern Recognition, pp. 770–778 (2016)
24. Etherscan. https://cn.etherscan.com/ Access (2021)
25. Remix, Ethereum-IDE. https://remix.ethereum.org/. Access (2021)
26. Durieux, T., Ferreira, J.F., Abreu, R., et al.: Empirical review of automated analysis tools on 47,587 Ethereum smart contracts. In: Proceedings of the ACM/IEEE 42nd International Conference on Software Engineering, pp. 530–541 (2020)
27. Mueller, B.: Smashing ethereum smart contracts for fun and real profit. In: 9th Annual HITB Security Conference (HITBSecConf). HITB, Amsterdam, Netherlands, vol. 54 (2018)
28. Josselin, F., Gustavo, G., Alex, G.: Slither: a static analysis framework for smart contracts. In: Proceedings of the 2Nd International Workshop on Emerging Trends in Software Engineering for Blockchain (WETSEB 2019). IEEE Press, Piscataway, NJ, USA, pp. 8–15 (2019). https://doi.org/10.1109/WETSEB.2019.00008
29. Sergei, T., Ekaterina, V., Ivan, I., et al.: Smartcheck: static analysis of ethereum smart contracts. In: 2018 IEEE/ACM 1st International Workshop on Emerging Trends in Software Engineering for Blockchain (WETSEB). IEEE, Gothenburg, Sweden, Sweden, pp. 9–16 (2018)

Intrusion Detection Based on GA-XGB Algorithm

Ruizhe Zhao, Yingxue Mu$^{(\boxtimes)}$, and Xiumei Wen$^{(\boxtimes)}$

Hebei Institute of Architecture and Civil Engineering, Big Data Technology
Innovation Center of Zhangjiakou,
13 Chaoyang West Street, Zhangjiakou, China

Abstract. With the development of network technology, the importance of intrusion detection has gradually increased. At the same time, due to the continuous increase in the number of network connections, the efficiency of traditional intrusion detection technologies is low. In order to solve this problem, this article uses GA-XGB algorithm for intrusion detection. The model uses genetic algorithm for feature selection, remove redundant and low-relevant features and XGBoost algorithm for final classification. Experiments conducted with the KDD data set prove that the accuracy, recall, F1 score and ROC score of the GA-XGB algorithm are improved compared to other traditional machine learning algorithms.

Keywords: GA-XGB · Data mining · Intrusion detection

1 Introduction

In recent years, machine learning has produced good results in disease prediction and can be used as a more efficient screening method. With the continuous development of Internet technology, network traffic has increased significantly, and at the same time, intrusion methods and intrusion techniques have been more improved, which has brought greater losses to network users and companies. Traditional intrusion detection methods cannot cope with unknown types of intrusion attacks. With the continuous development of machine learning technology, more and more scholars apply machine learning algorithms to intrusion detection. These algorithms have certain reasoning capabilities, can process massive amounts of traffic data, and use data to train models. They also have a certain detection effect for unknown patterns of attacks, and have a high accuracy rate.

The main purpose of this article is to use the GA-XGB algorithm to establish an intrusion detection model. The KDD CUP dataset was be used to evaluate and compare it with traditional classification algorithms such as logistic regression, SVM and KNN.

X. Wen—Project Fund: Research Project of Fundamental Scientific Research Business Expenses of Provincial Colleges and Universities in Hebei Province 2021QNJS04.

© Springer Nature Singapore Pte Ltd. 2021
Y. Tan et al. (Eds.): DMBD 2021, CCIS 1453, pp. 150–157, 2021.
https://doi.org/10.1007/978-981-16-7476-1_14

In this article, we explore the actual performance of the algorithm model in intrusion detection, hope to find out new model to detect the malicious link reliable and efficacious.

2 Research Review

Holger Fröhlich, Olivier Chapelle [1] proposed a new way to select features for SVM by using genetic algorithm. They use the CHC algorithm with a more aggressive search strategy to optimize the choice of kernel function in the SVM. They used decimal encoding to replace the usual binary encoding. Recursive feature elimination algorithm has the lowest error estimate and reduces overfitting when number of features to select is not known beforehand.

Yongguo Liu, Kefei Chen, Xiaofeng Liao and Wei Zhang [2] proposed the Intrusion Detection Basedon Genetic Clustering (IDBGC) algorithm. The algorithm first uses the nearest neighbor method to cluster the data set, then uses the genetic algorithm to combine the original clusters, uses the simulated annealing algorithm to escape the local minimum, and obtains a near-optimal result. The algorithm is tested on the KDD data set, which proves that the IDBGC algorithm is effective.

Il-Seok Oh, Jin-Seon Lee, and Byung-Ro [3] proposed a novel hybrid genetic algorithm based on local search. The algorithm uses the size of the feature subset as a penalty item, calculates the fitness of the chromosome, and improves the running speed of the genetic algorithm to search for the local best by deleting the least significant feature or adding the most significant feature.

Peng Wei, Zhen Zhang, and Diyang Liu [4] used the fish school idea to optimize the particle swarm algorithm. They disrupted the smoothness of all historical extremum positions, so that the algorithm can better find the extremum of a single particle, and avoid the individual extremum of particles from falling too quickly into the local optimal solution.

3 Future Selection

Feature selection is a very important data preprocessing step, and the dimensionality disaster problem can be alleviated by selecting important features. In this article, for the features with low redundancy and low correlation in the data, the features are first filtered by calculating the similarity between the features. Secondly, logistic regression combined with adaptive genetic algorithm is used to search for a subset of features with good classification effect, which improves the detection effect of intrusion detection and shortens the detection time of XGBoost. The algorithm of the feature selection process is shown in Fig. 1.

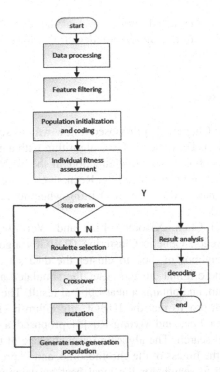

Fig. 1. Feature selection flowchart

3.1 Population Individual Coding

After filtering the features with low relevance for intrusion detection, randomly initialize the population on the remaining feature data set, and use binary coding to encode the population individuals. There are 41 features in the intrusion detection data, so the size of the chromosome is 41. The value of each gene on the chromosome can be 0 or 1. 0 means not selecting the feature corresponding to the gene; 1 means selecting the feature corresponding to the gene.

3.2 Fitness Function Calculation

Genetic algorithm itself can be used as a feature selection algorithm, which can find and eliminate redundant features, but the performance of genetic algorithm often depends on the definition of fitness function. The greater the fitness of an individual, the more likely the individual's genes are to be passed on to the next generation. In order to reduce features to a greater extent and obtain features with better classification results, the accuracy of the XGBoost algorithm after cross-validation can be used as the result of the fitness function of GA to evaluate the impact of different features on the final classification result.

3.3   Operator Selection

In this experiment, the selection operator adopts a roulette strategy. The roulette strategy can avoid the premature concentration of resources to individuals in a well-adapted population and maintain the diversity of the population [5]. The specific operations are as follows:

(1) Calculate the accuracy rate of each individual in the group.
(2) Calculate the probability that each feature is still selected in the next-generation population.

$$p(x_i) = \frac{f(x_i)}{\sum_{j=1}^{n} f(x_j)} \tag{1}$$

(3) Statistically sum the probabilities of the features in the population.

$$q_i = \sum_{j=1}^{i} p(x_j) \tag{2}$$

3.4   Crossover and Mutation

Crossover means selecting one position of two individuals randomly from the population, start from a random bit of their genes, exchange all subsequent gene fragments, and generate two new individuals. The purpose of crossover is to inherit the excellent genes, and reorganize and concentrate good genes to generate better individuals. Mutation is to exchange the 0–1 value in the individual's genes randomly according to the probability. The purpose of mutation is to prevent the genetic algorithm from converging prematurely and to make the genetic algorithm stronger in local random search. The crossover rate and mutation rate need to be selected according to the actual situation.

3.5   Algorithm Termination Condition

When the algorithm reaches 80 times (max time), or the current population fitness value reaches 0.999, the algorithm stops.

4   Experiment

4.1   Algorithm Involved

Data mining is the use of algorithms to transform the high-dimensional data that are not closely related in the data set into a usable structure, and use the rules to predict unknown data. As a typical classification problem, intrusion detection can use machine learning algorithms to process large amounts of data, detect and search for abnormal data, and deal with problems efficiently and timely.

Logistic Regression

Logistic Regression is a machine learning method used to solve two classification (0or1) problems [6]. The logistic distribution curve is an S-shaped curve. The curve grows fastest near the center and grows slowly at both ends. Logistic regression uses a hypothetical function to estimate the actual value. In order to constrain the estimated value between 0 and 1, logistic regression uses the Sigmoid function to convert the linear prediction function into a non-linear function. Logistic regression algorithm divides the parts into two categories.

SVM

The SVM algorithm uses the separation hyperplane with the largest geometric interval to realize the two class of the data set [7]. The basic function of SVM is to classify samples. The boundary values of the two types of samples are called support vectors. [8] The final classification result of the model is only related to the support vector. The farther the distance between the two types of samples is, the better the classification effect. Therefore, the plane with the largest sum of the distances to all support vectors is the best division hyperplane.

XGBoost

XGBoost is a gradient boosting decision tree, which belongs to boosting algorithm family [9, 10]. The algorithm uses a tree-based parallel strategy to speed up iteration and can handle sparse data at the same time. The algorithm proposes an algorithm to estimate the split point, which accelerates the construction of the CART tree. Each time it learns a new function to fit the residual of the last prediction, and calculates the score corresponding to each node according to the characteristics of the sample. The sum of all the scores is worked as the final output.

4.2   Dataset

The experiment uses the KDD CUP 99 dataset. [11] Each record in the data set has 42 attributes. 41 attributes represent the characteristic attributes of the data, and 1 attribute represents the class of the connection. Among the 41 characteristic attributes of the data, nine characteristic attributes are discrete, and the others are continuous. The labels include normal data and 4 abnormal types [12].

4.3   Experimental Setup

Genetic algorithm was used to select the features. Hyperparameters setting in genetic algorithm are shown in Table 1.

Table 1. Genetic algorithm parameter setting

Parameter name	Parameter symbols	Parameter value
Population size	N_population	50
Number of genes	N_features	35
Maximum algebra	N_generations	70
Crossover rate	Crossover_proba	0.5
Mutation rate	Mutation_proba	0.05

The population size of the genetic algorithm in Table 1 is generally between 20 and 50. The number of chromosome genes is consistent with the number of features in the incoming data set, and the value is 35. The crossover rate and mutation rate of the adaptive genetic algorithm are set according to empirical data [13], but should not be too large. When the maximum evolutionary algebra is 80, the population evaluation fitness value is the best, as shown in Fig. 2.

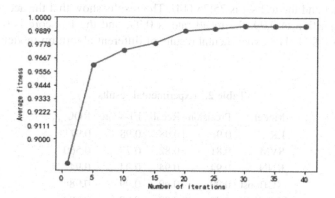

Fig. 2. Genetic algorithm evolution curve

One-hot encoding is adopted to map character features to digital features. The up-sampling method is used to solve the problem of uneven sample distribution. In the experiment, the log1p function is used to transform the data to make it obey the Gaussian distribution. The experiment first calculates the similarity between features, compare the correlation between all features and label features, and discard the features with a correlation less than 0.1. Then the remaining features are used as the genes of the population. Adjust the hyperparameters of the genetic algorithm and the number of output features, and finally obtain multiple feature groups with different feature numbers, and then input the feature groups into the XGBoost algorithm model for intrusion detection. The mean normalization is used in this experiment. The data can be mapped into the interval from −1 to 1, which can make the changes between the various dimensional features can be directly compared. The normalization formula is shown in formula (3):

$$x_{norm} = \frac{x - \mu}{x_{\max} - x_{\min}} \tag{3}$$

The processed data is randomly divided according to the ratio of 3–1, the data is passed into the model, and the ROC score is used to evaluate the detection effect of the model.

5 Experimental Results

In order to verify the effect of GA-XGB algorithm in intrusion detection, traditional classification algorithms such as Logistic regression, KNN and SVM were used for comparison. The experiment used precision rate, recall rate, F1-score and ROC score to evaluate the hepatitis prediction results of each model.

The experiment was carried out under the version of python 3.8.3. The split ratio of the training set and the test set is 75:25 [14]. The results show that the accuracy rate of GA-XGB algorithm is 0.99, the recall rate is 0.99, and the F1-score is 0.99 and the ROC score is 0.994. The experimental results of different algorithm models are shown in Table 2.

Table 2. Experimental results

Model	Precision	Recall	F1-score	ROC
LR	0.98	0.98	0.98	0.971
SVM	0.81	0.82	0.77	0.560
KNN	0.94	0.94	0.94	0.94
XGBoost	0.99	0.99	0.99	0.986
GA-XGB	0.99	0.99	0.99	0.994

It can be seen that GA-XGB has obvious advantages compared with traditional machine learning models in terms of accuracy, recall, F1 score, ROC and other performance indicators. Compared with the XGBoost algorithm, which does not use genetic algorithm for feature selection, GA-XGB algorithm improves the ROC score, while reducing the value of the features of the incoming model, speeding up the calculation time of the model, and increasing the intrusion in the case of large traffic data [15].

6 Conclusion and Future Work

In this article, we experimented all above-mentioned models. This article used the GA-XGB algorithm to intrusion detection. By comparing with a variety of traditional classification models, it was confirmed that the GA-XGB algorithm has the best performance in the intrusion detection. It can use high-dimensional features more efficiently and reduce the number of features as well as running time of the model.

For further study, genetic algorithm will be considered to combine with other filtering algorithms to process different types of data features and further improve the feature reduction capabilities of the algorithm. In addition, the algorithm can be implemented on the Hadoop platform, and MapReduce can be used to achieve parallel detection.

References

1. Frohlich, H., Chapelle, O., Scholkopf, B.: Feature selection for support vector machines by means of genetic algorithm. In: Proceedings of 15th IEEE International Conference on Tools with Artificial Intelligence, IEEE (2003). https://doi.org/10.1109/tai.2003.1250182
2. Yongguo, L., et al.: A genetic clustering method for intrusion detection. Pattern Recogn. 37 (5), 927–942 (2004)
3. Il-Seok, O., Jin-Seon, L., Byung-Ro, M.: Hybrid genetic algorithms for feature selection. IEEE Trans. Pattern Anal. Mach. Intell. 26(11), 1424–1437 (2004)
4. Yongguo, L., et al.: A genetic clustering method for intrusion detection. Pattern Recogn. 37 (5), 927–942 (2004)
5. Gong, M., et al.: Bio-inspired Computing–Theories and Applications (2016)
6. Dreiseitl, S., Ohno-Machado, L.: Logistic regression and artificial neural network classification models: a methodology review. J. Biomed. Inf. 35(5–6), 352–359 (2002)
7. Schuldt, C., Ivan, L., Barbara, C.: Recognizing human actions: a local SVM approach. In: Proceedings of the 17th International Conference on Pattern Recognition, 2004. ICPR 2004, vol. 3, IEEE (2004)
8. Moraes, R., Valiati, J.F., Neto, W.P.G.: Document-level sentiment classification: an empirical comparison between SVM and ANN. Expert Syst. Appl. 40(2), 621–633 (2013)
9. Chen, T., Carlos, G.: Xgboost: a scalable tree boosting system. In: Proceedings of the 22nd acm sigkdd international conference on knowledge discovery and data mining (2016)
10. Chen, T., et al.: Xgboost: extreme gradient boosting. R package version 0.4–2 1.4 (2015)
11. Tavallaee, M., Bagheri, E., Lu, W., Ghorbani., A.: Detailed analysis of the KDD CUP 99 data set. In: 2009 IEEE Symposium on Computational Intelligence for Security and Defense Applications, pp. 1–6. IEEE (July 2009)
12. Liu, M., et al.: Learning based adaptive network immune mechanism to defense eavesdropping attacks. IEEE Access 7, 182814–182826 (2019)
13. Xu, J., et al.: Stochastic multi-objective optimization of photovoltaics integrated three-phase distribution network based on dynamic scenarios. Appl. Energy 231, 985–996 (2018)
14. Ding, S., Genying, W.: Research on intrusion detection technology based on deep learning. In: 2017 3rd IEEE International Conference on Computer and Communications (ICCC), IEEE (2017)
15. Hajian-Tilaki, K.: Receiver operating characteristic (ROC) curve analysis for medical diagnostic test evaluation. Caspian J. Internal Med. 4, 627 (2013)

A Video Axle Counting and Type Recognition Method Based on Improved YOLOv5S

Liubin Li[1], Jiawei Wu[2], Haibo Luo[3], Rongteng Wu[3(✉)], and Zuoyong Li[3(✉)]

[1] College of Mathematics and Computer Science, Fuzhou University, Fuzhou 350108, China
[2] College of Mechanical and Electrical Engineering, Fujian Agriculture and Forestry University, Fuzhou 350002, China
[3] Fujian Provincial Key Laboratory of Information Processing and Intelligent Control, College of Computer and Control Engineering, Minjiang University, Fuzhou 350121, China
rongtengwu@aliyun.com

Abstract. The number of axles of the vehicle and the type of tires can reflect the information of the vehicle to a certain extent, and the load capacity can be calculated according to the number of axles of the truck and the type of axles. Therefore, the identification of the axle is of great significance for judging whether the truck is overweight. At present, the method of calculating the axles is carried out by the method of Laser Radar or grating for axle counting. In the prior art, the method of axle counting is complicated to deploy and the cost is high. Some computer vision-based axle statistics methods have emerged in recent years, but complete vehicle sideways pictures are required. However, due to the long body of the truck and the limited space factor, it is difficult to obtain the complete vehicle in an original image. Although image stitching can solve this problem, the current video image stitching methods have a relatively high time cost. To solve this issue, we propose an object detection and tracking method based on YOLOv5s for axle counting and tire type identification. Experimental results show that the proposed method has extremely high accuracy and can meet real-time requirements even without GPU.

Keywords: YOLOv5S · Axle counting · Type recognition

1 Introduction

In recent years, with the rapid development of China's economy, all kinds of civil trucks can be seen everywhere in our daily life and work. Traffic accidents caused by overweight often occur. Therefore, before the truck is on the road, we should judge whether it is overloaded or not by comparing the standard load and actual load of the truck which can be implied by the number of axles and the type of tire. The manual detection method is inefficient. Moreover, due to the uncertainty of the departure time of goods, the staff is required to work around the clock, and the labor cost is higher than that of people for a long time. Although there are also some automatic counting devices

© Springer Nature Singapore Pte Ltd. 2021
Y. Tan et al. (Eds.): DMBD 2021, CCIS 1453, pp. 158–168, 2021.
https://doi.org/10.1007/978-981-16-7476-1_15

with laser or grating, these methods are cumbersome and have high cost yield, and are not used widely.

With the development of computer vision and digital image technology, a lot of one-stage and two-stage object detection methods with high accuracy have emerged in recent years. The most representative two-stage object detector is the R-CNN [1] series, including fast R-CNN [2], faster R-CNN [3], R-FCN [4], and Libra R-CNN [5]. The most representative one-stage object detector is YOLO [6–8]. In recent years, anchor-free one-stage object detectors are developed. The detectors of this sort are CenterNet [11]. These networks can be used for tire type identification and axle statistics, which requires a complete side view of the truck. However, it is difficult to obtain a complete picture of the truck body due to the long car body and the limited scope of the visual equipment. The real-time panoramic video stitching algorithm [11] can solve this problem, but GPU must be used to meet the real-time requirements. We propose a method, uses YOLOv5S to detect, track and count the detected targets (axles in this paper). The main contributions of this article are as follows:

- We propose an object detection and tracking method based on YOLOv5S to axle counting and tire type identification. The experimental results show that our method has extremely high accuracy and can meet real-time requirements without GPU.
- We use CIOU Loss as bounding box Loss to guide YOLOv5S training. The experimental results show that it can improve YOLOv5S detection performance.
- We setup a dataset for axle counting and type recognition. The dataset includes 23 videos of a struck passing the weighbridge captured by our camera. In future, someone who wants to engage in related research can ask us to take the datasets and save the time of labeling the data.

2   The Proposed Method

The flow chart of the proposed real-time axle counting and type recognition method is shown in Fig. 1. The network consists of two modules, namely detection module and tracking module. The following sub-sections will describe the two modules in details.

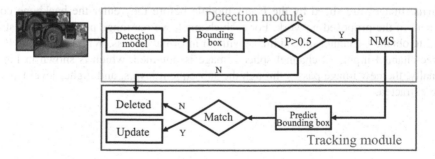

Fig. 1. Flow chart of the proposed method.

2.1   Detection

The proposed method uses Tracking-By-Detector (TBD) strategy, so the accuracy of target detection is closely related to the tracking performance, and a detection model with high detection accuracy is required. In recent years, there are many high-precision networks of target detection, such as Faster RCNN [3], DETR [13], and Swin Transformer [14]. Good results have been achieved on many datasets by them. However, these networks are not lightweight and cannot meet the real-time requirement. Compared with networks mentioned above, YOLOv5S has competitive detection accuracy, faster inference speed, and fewer parameters. Considering the tradeoff between the detection precision and efficiency, we choose YOLOv5S as the target detection network. The following tricks are used by our method.

Mosaic. Mosaic is a kind of data enhancement method. This data enhancement method is to splice the training pictures by random scaling, planting, subtraction, and arrangement when training the model. Mosaic enriches the background and small targets of the object. Moreover, it can reduce the difficulty of training the network. Even small batch size can be used for training Batch Normalization layer effectively. Some mosaic enhanced images are shown in Fig. 2.

Fig. 2. Mosaic enhancement images

Focus. Images are sliced by the Focus module before they enter the backbone component of the proposed network. For each channel, we rearrange pixels with the stride of 2 to obtain 4-channel spliced image without information loss. With the original RGB three-channel input, 12-channel spliced image is obtained, which is shown in Fig. 3. Finally, the new image passes through the subsequent layers, and higher-level features are extracted.

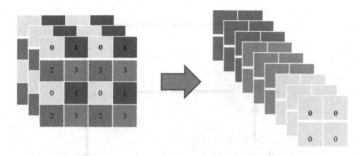

Fig. 3. Focus operator.

SPP. Since the Spatial Pyramid Pooling (SPP) module [15] outputs a one-dimensional feature vector, it is infeasible to be applied in Fully Convolutional Network (FCN). Thus YOLOv3 [6] improves the SPP module to the concatenation of max-pooling outputs with multiple kernel sizes k × k, where k = {1, 5, 9, 13}, as shown in Fig. 4. This design enables the network to effectively enlarge the receptive field and concatenate multi-scale information.

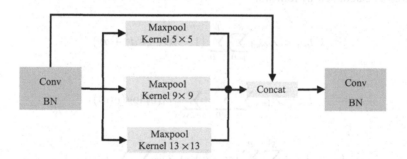

Fig. 4. Spatial Pyramid Pooling.

Neck Structure. YOLOv5S's neck network still uses the Pixel Aggregation Network (PAN) [20] + Feature pyramid networks (FPN) [21] structure, as shown in Fig. 5, but some improvements have been made based on it. In YOLOv4's neck structure, an ordinary convolution operation is used. In the neck network of YOLOv5S, the CSPnet structure designed by CSP2 is used to enhance the ability of network feature fusion.

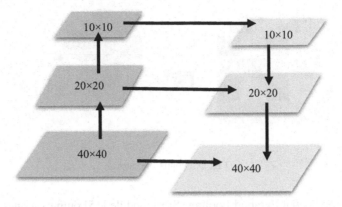

Fig. 5. PAN + FPN.

Loss. Yolov5 uses GIOU loss [16] to calculate bounding box loss. Through experiments, it is found that replacing GIOU loss with CIOU loss [17] improves the detection performance of the model, so we use CIOU loss as the bounding box loss of the model. The loss is calculated as follows:

$$l_{box} = \lambda_{coord} \sum_{i=0}^{S^2} \sum_{j=0}^{B} (1 - IOU + d^2 + \alpha v) \tag{1}$$

$$l_{cls} = \lambda_{class} \sum_{i=0}^{S^2} \sum_{j=0}^{B} \sum_{c \in classes} p_i(c) \log(p(\hat{c})) \tag{2}$$

$$l_{obj} = \lambda_{noobj} \sum_{i=0}^{S^2} \sum_{j=0}^{B} (c_i - \hat{c}_i)^2 + \lambda_{obj} \sum_{i=0}^{S^2} \sum_{j=0}^{B} (c_i - \hat{c}_i)^2 \tag{3}$$

$$loss = l_{box} + l_{cls} + l_{obj} \tag{4}$$

Where l_{box} is bounding box loss, l_{cls} is class probability score loss, and l_{obj} is objectness score loss. B is the number of anchors. S is width of feature map. c_i is the confidence score, and $\hat{c}_i$ is the intersection of the prediction bounding box. When there is a target in the cell of the feature map, λ_{obj} is equal to 1, and λ_{noobj} is equal to 0, otherwise λ_{obj} is equal to 0, and λ_{onobj} is equal to 1.

2.2   Tracking

In recent years, there are many excellent neural networks that can do tracking task well, e.g., DeepSORT [18] and fairMOT [19]. High performance computing power is necessary in those tracking methods to deal with complicated scene. However, our tracking task is relatively simple. On the scenario of the truck driving on the weighbridge, one of the detected targets moves from left to right or from right to left, and there is no mutual occlusion. As long as the performance of the detection model is stable, the traditional tracking method can perform well in this task, and will not occupy too many computer resources. Here is our tracking process.

Object Representation. Here we describe the object model, i.e. the representation and the motion model used to propagate a target's identity into the next frame. We approximate the inter-frame displacements of each object with a linear constant velocity model which is independent of other objects and camera motion. The state of each target is modeled as:

$$X = [top, bottom, left, right, class, ID] \qquad (5)$$

where (top, left) represents the coordinate of the upper left point of the bounding box, and (down, right) represents the coordinate of the lower right point. The *class* represents the target category and *ID* uniquely represents the identity of each target.

Counting Area. When the target enters and leaves the counting area, it needs to create and destroy a unique ID for the target. As shown in Fig. 6. The Predict Bounding Box (PBB), which is the output of the detection model, can be represented by a vector as the state of target model.

$$PBB = [top, bottom, left, right, class] \qquad (6)$$

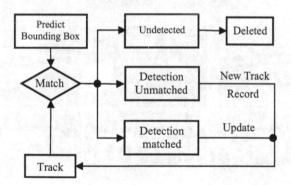

Fig. 6. Flow chart of tracking.

In the counting area, the target of the current frame is matched with the previous frame, and the distance between the target detected in the current frame and the previous frame is calculated. If a target can be detected in the current frame, and the distance between them is less than the *threshold*, then the target is considered to exist and the target state is updated. If the distance between any target in the previous frame and the target in the current frame is not less than the threshold, then the target is regarded as a new target, thus an *ID* is assigned to the target, and the counter of the corresponding category is incremented by 1. If there is one in the previous frame and the target does not find a matching target in the current frame, it is considered that the target has left the detection area, and the *ID* assigned to the target is destroyed. The *threshold* can be formulated as:

$$threshold = \frac{(right - left) + (bottom - top)}{2} + 10 \tag{7}$$

3 Results

3.1 Dataset

We collected 23 videos of a truck passing the weighbridge captured by our camera to form the dataset for axle counting and type recognition. 6 videos are selected for training, another 2 videos for validation, and the rest 15 videos for test. LabelImg (code is available at: https://github.com/tzutalin/labelImg) is used to mark the pictures. Some frames from the dataset are shown in Fig. 7.

Fig. 7. Some frames selected from the dataset.

More information of the dataset is shown in Table 1. The training data includes video NO.1–6 and the validation data includes video NO.7–8.

Table 1. The information of the training and validation dataset.

Video	Number of frames	Recording time	Single-axle single tire	Single-axle twin tire
NO.1	86	Night	1	1
NO.2	130	Daytime	2	1
NO.3	173	Daytime	1	3
NO.4	216	Daytime	1	4
NO.5	173	Night	1	3
NO.6	87	Daytime	1	1
NO.7	90	Night	1	3
NO.8	100	Daytime	1	4

3.2 Experimental Results

Performance Evaluation Standard. To evaluate the performance of the object detection algorithm, this paper uses COCO mAP [22] and AP50 in common with previous methods [10].

Parameter Selection. Here are some hyperparameters when we train the model. The optimizer used in this paper is SGD and the initial learning rate is 0.01, optimizer weight decay is 5×10^{-4}, and batch size is 16. Input image size is 320×320. Although the accuracy of using 640×640 as the input image size will be higher, the time to process an image on the CPU will increase by 37.5%.

Object Detection Results and Analysis. Our proposed network YOLOv5S (CIOU) and some representative one-stage object detection networks are trained using our training dataset, which include YOLOv3, YOLOv3-SPP, YOLOv3-tiny, YOLOv4, YOLOv4-tiny, CenterNet (resNet50), YOLOv5S (GIOU). The results are shown in Table 2.

From Table 2, one can see that YOLOv3-SPP obtains highest mAP (0.718) and CenterNet gets highest AP_{50} (0.982), In other words, YOLOv3-SPP and CenterNet outperform other models in detection accuracy. However, the model sizes (62.58M and 32.67M) are too large so that these models cannot be deployed in embedded devices. The model size of YOLOv3 (61.53M) is still large and the performance drops marginally. Other models, including YOLOv3-tiny, YOLOv4, YOLOv4-tiny have much smaller size than YOLOv3-SPP, CenterNet and YOLOv3. However, these models perform worse than our YOLOv5S (CIOU). YOLOv5S (CIOU) has the same model size as YOLOv5S (GIOU), but the performance of YOLOv5S (CIOU) is better than that of YOLOv5S (GIOU). To balance the weight and accuracy, YOLOv5S (CIOU) is selected as our detection network, its mAP and AP_{50} are relatively high, which can reach 0.670 and 0.954, and the model size is only 6.86M.

Table 2. Results of different object detection models.

Model	mAP	AP$_{50}$	Model size
YOLOv3	0.691	0.961	61.53M
YOLOv3-SPP	**0.718**	0.955	62.58M
YOLOv3-tiny	0.587	0.947	8.67M
YOLOv4	0.664	0.949	63.94M
YOLOv4-tiny	0.617	0.968	5.92M
CenterNet (resNet50)	0.578	**0.982**	32.67M
YOLOv5S (GIOU)	0.659	0.952	6.86M
YOLOv5S (CIOU)	0.670	0.954	6.86M

Fig. 8. The results of the proposed method on test data. Noting that only 9 frames are shown instead of all frames of the video because of the limited length. (Color figure online)

We test our model in test dataset on CPU (i7–8700) and GPU (GTX1050ti), and record the inference speed in Table 3. The results of the algorithm are shown in Fig. 8. In the Fig. 8, count1 is the single-axis single tire counter, count2 is the single-axis twin tire counter and Count is the total counter. It is worth noting that the green rectangle is the counting area.

Based on the analysis of the results in Table 3. we draw a conclusion that our algorithm is very fast. Its inference speed can up to reach about 50 fps when running in GPU and 17 fps when running in CPU. That is to say, our model can meet real-time requirement.

Table 3. The inference speed of the proposed algorithm running in CPU/GPU (Unit: fps).

Video	Detection (CPU)	Tracking (CPU)	Total (CPU)	Detection (GPU)	Tracking (GPU)	Total (GPU)
NO.1	23.4	67.9	17.4	123.9	90.7	46.6
NO.2	22.7	75.6	17.4	121.1	109.8	51.6
NO.3	22.7	65.8	16.9	123.0	83.1	45.2
NO.4	23.0	65.0	17.0	129.7	100.9	49.6
NO.5	23.4	71.9	17.7	123.0	91.7	49.0
NO.6	23.0	69.5	17.3	123.5	96.6	51.2
NO.7	22.8	63.0	16.7	118.9	71.0	40.6
NO.8	23.4	85.0	18.4	124.0	121.2	58.6
NO.9	22.9	65.6	17.0	122.6	92.5	47.9
NO.10	22.9	66.2	17.1	123.6	105.9	50.2
NO.11	22.6	69.0	17.0	119.8	98.5	48.8
NO.12	22.9	64.7	16.9	120.0	84.1	45.1
NO.13	22.8	65.9	16.9	120.9	85.7	45.5
NO.14	25.1	76.6	18.9	135.7	106.0	53.4
NO.15	22.9	67.8	17.1	120.4	88.9	46.6

4   Conclusion

In this paper, we propose a new computer vision based video axle counting and type recognition methods based on improved YOLOv5S. Our proposed method not only performs well in detection accuracy and inference speed, but also is lightweight. This makes our algorithm can be easily transplanted to various embedded devices, and can be directly applied in industrial applications.

Acknowledgments. This work is partially supported by National Natural Science Foundation of China (61972187, 61902167), Natural Science Foundation of Fujian Province (2020J02024, 2020J01824), Fuzhou Science and Technology Project (2020-RC-186).

References

1. Girshick, R., Donahue, J., Darrell, T., Malik, J.: Rich feature hierarchies for accurate object detection and semantic segmentation. In: Proceedings of the IEEE Conference on Computer Vision and Pattern Recognition (CVPR), pp. 580–587 (2014)
2. Girshick, R.: Fast r-cnn. In: Proceedings of the IEEE International Conference on Computer Vision(ICCV), pp. 1440–1448 (2015)
3. Ren, S., He, K., Girshick, R., Sun, J.: Faster R-CNN: towards real-time object detection with region proposal networks. IEEE Trans. Pattern Anal. Mach. Intell. **39**(6), 91–99 (2016)
4. Dai, J., Li, Y., He, K., Sun, J.: R-FCN: object detection via region-based fully convolutional networks. In: Advances in Neural Information Processing Systems (NIPS), pp. 379–387 (2016)

5. Pang, J., Chen, K., Shi, J., Feng, H., Ouyang, W., Lin, D.: Libra R-CNN: towards balanced learning for object detection. In: Proceedings of the IEEE Conference on Computer Vision and Pattern Recognition (CVPR), pp. 821–830 (2019)
6. Redmon, J., Divvala S., Girshick, R., Farhadi, A.: You only look once: unified, real-time object detection. In: Proceedings of the IEEE Conference on Computer Vision and Pattern Recognition (CVPR), pp. 779–788 (2016)
7. Redmon, J., Farhadi, A.: YOLO9000: better, faster, stronger. In: Proceedings of the IEEE Conference on Computer Vision and Pattern Recognition (CVPR), pp. 7263–7271 (2017)
8. Redmon, J., Farhadi, A.: YOLOv3: An incremental improvement. arXiv:1804.02767 (2018)
9. Bochkovskiy, A., Wang, C.Y., Liao, H.Y.M.: Yolov4: Optimal speed and accuracy of object detection. arXiv:2004.10934 (2020)
10. Duan, K., Bai, S., Xie, L., Qi, L., Huang, Q., Tian, Q.: CenterNet: keypoint triplets for object detection. In: Proceedings of the IEEE International Conference on Computer Vision (ICCV), pp. 6569–6578 (2019)
11. Du, C., Yuan, J., Dong, J., Li, L., Chen, M., Li, T.: Gpu based parallel optimization for real time panoramic video stitching. Pattern Recogn. Lett. **133**, 62–69 (2020)
12. Gan, M.G., Chen, J., Liu, J., Wang, Y.N.: Moving object detection algorithm based on three-frame-differencing and edge information. J. Electron. Inf. Technol. **32**(4), 894–897 (2016)
13. Carion, N., Massa, F., Synnaeve, G., Usunier, N., Kirillov, A., Zagoruyko, S.: End-to-end object detection with transformers. In: Vedaldi, A., Bischof, H., Brox, T., Frahm, J.-M. (eds.) ECCV 2020. LNCS, vol. 12346, pp. 213–229. Springer, Cham (2020). https://doi.org/10. 1007/978-3-030-58452-8_13
14. Liu, Z., et al.: Swin transformer: hierarchical vision transformer using shifted windows. arXiv:2103.14030 (2021)
15. He, K., Zhang, X., Ren, S., Sun, J.: Spatial pyramid pooling in deep convolutional networks for visual recognition. IEEE Trans. Pattern Anal. Mach. Intell. **37**(9), 1904–1916 (2014)
16. Rezatofighi, H., Tsoi, N., Gwak, J., Sadeghian, A., Reid, I., Savarese, S.: Generalized intersection over union: a metric and a loss for bounding box regression. In: Proceedings of the IEEE Conference on Computer Vision and Pattern Recognition (CVPR), pp. 658–666 (2019).
17. Zheng, Z., et al.: Distance-iou loss: Faster and better learning for bounding box regression. In: Proceedings of the AAAI Conference on Artificial Intelligence, pp. 12993–13000 (2020)
18. Wojke, N., Bewley, A., Paulus, D.: Simple online and realtime tracking with a deep association metric. In: IEEE International Conference on Image Processing (ICIP), pp. 3645–3649 (2017)
19. Zhang, Y., Wang, C., Wang, X., Zeng, W., Liu, W.: FairMOT: on the fairness of detection and re-identification in multiple object tracking. arXiv:2004.01888 (2020)
20. Liu, S., Qi, L., Qin, H., Shi, J., Jia, J.: Path aggregation network for instance segmentation. In: Proceedings of the IEEE Conference on Computer Vision and Pattern Recognition (CVPR), pp.8759–8768 (2018)
21. Lin, T. Y., Dollár, P., Girshick, R., He, K., Hariharan, B., Belongie, S.: Feature pyramid networks for object detection. In: Proceedings of the IEEE Conference on Computer Vision and Pattern Recognition (CVPR), pp. 2117–2125 (2017).
22. Lin, T.-Y., et al.: Microsoft COCO: common objects in context. In: Fleet, D., Pajdla, T., Schiele, B., Tuytelaars, T. (eds.) ECCV 2014. LNCS, vol. 8693, pp. 740–755. Springer, Cham (2014). https://doi.org/10.1007/978-3-319-10602-1_48

An Anonymous Communication Scheme Between Nodes Based on Pseudonym and Bilinear Pairing in Big Data Environments

Pei Ren, Bo Liu, and Fengyin Li[✉]

School of Computer Science, Qufu Normal University, Rizhao 276826, China

Abstract. In recent years, Big data has attracted more and more attention. The strategic significance of big data technology is not to master huge data information, but to professionally process these meaningful data. The emergence of big data technology has made the Internet of Things a reality. Among them, wireless sensor networks (WSNs) have been widely used in military, medical and other fields. WSNs can be used to realize data collection, processing and transmission. However, in the process of message forwarding and data aggregation in WSNs, there are problems such as node's real identity, key and data leakage. The adversary can use this information to disrupt communication and attack important nodes. In resource-constrained WSNs, we propose an anonymous communication scheme between nodes based on pseudonyms and bilinear pairing. Firstly, we use pseudonyms instead of real identities to receive and forward messages to achieve node anonymity. Secondly, based on bilinear mapping operation and hash-based message authentication code (HMAC), we achieved key agreement between nodes and verification of message integrity to protect data security. In addition, we propose the energy-based link direction selection protocol, which ensures that the message can reach the base station without passing too many nodes, thus saving network resources to a certain extent. The anonymous communication scheme between nodes based on pseudonyms and bilinear pairing ensures the anonymity, reliability and security of communication in WSNs, and ensures low overhead in storage, computation and communication.

Keywords: Anonymous communication · Pseudonym · Bilinear pairing · Message integrity · WSNs

1 Introduction

Big data, like computer technology and the Internet, has universal applicability and versatility. It is needed by all walks of life. It is not only required by traditional industries, but also supported by emerging industries. The emergence of big data technology has made the Internet of Things, cloud computing, and artificial intelligence a reality. Data that originally seemed difficult to collect

© Springer Nature Singapore Pte Ltd. 2021
Y. Tan et al. (Eds.): DMBD 2021, CCIS 1453, pp. 169–182, 2021.
https://doi.org/10.1007/978-981-16-7476-1_16

and use is beginning to be easily utilized. The wireless sensor network is a kind of distributed sensor network, which is composed of a large number of stationary or moving sensor nodes in a self-organizing and multi-hop manner. These sensor nodes cooperatively sense, collect, process and transmit the information of the sensed object, and finally send this information to the sink node of the network [1,2], so as to realize the function of sensing and inspecting the external world. From military to civilian use [3], sensor nodes have been widely deployed and used to detect various phenomena in the surrounding environment, including temperature and humidity and so on.

However, in the process of message forwarding in WSN, if a node directly informs its real identity when forwarding the message, and receives and forwards the message by using its constant identity, the adversary can track and selectively compromise important nodes by analyzing the identity when intercepting and tampering with the data packet.

In recent years, the issue of anonymous communication authentication and privacy in WSNs [4] has received attention and a lot of research has been done. Chen et al. [5] proposed an efficient anonymous communication protocol for wireless sensor networks. The EAC scheme provides the anonymity of senders, communication relationships, and receivers, and prevents the adversary from identifying important nodes and attacking them. Boukerche et al. [6] proposed a novel distributed routing protocol, which encrypts the routing data packet header and avoids the use of unreliable intermediate nodes, allowing trusted intermediate nodes to participate in the path construction protocol without Endanger the anonymity of communication nodes.

Abuzneid et al. [7] proposed the enhanced anonymous communication protocol in WSN through a modular approach, which expanded the key solutions required for end-to-end location privacy, namely anonymity, observability, capture possibility and The security period provides solutions for end-to-end anonymity and location privacy against multiple local and global adversaries. Jebri et al. [8] proposed a secure and trusted anonymous communication protocol for IOT-STAC protocol, which is based on a lightweight key agreement protocol, identity-based encryption and pseudonym-based encryption, in the resource-constrained devices of the Internet of Things and Wireless Sensor Networks, the trust management of anonymity and hiding the real identities of nodes is realized, and security and privacy are guaranteed.

In this paper, in order to further ensure the communication security in wireless sensor networks, ensure anonymity and security in the process of data aggregation, this paper proposes an anonymous communication protocol based on pseudonyms and bilinear pairing. The contribution points are as follows:

(1) Use a one-time pseudonym to replace the real identity of the node to forward the message to ensure that the identity of the node is not leaked, so that the scheme can forward the message anonymously, ensuring identity privacy.
(2) Based on the bilinear pairing operation and HMAC, the security key agreement between nodes is realized, and the integrity of the message and the authenticity of the source are verified. Ensure the privacy of the key and prevent information leakage.

(3) An energy-based link direction selection protocol is proposed to ensure that the message can reach the base station without consuming too much network resources.

This anonymous communication scheme realizes the confidential transmission of messages in WSNs and provides anonymous communication. The use of bilinear pairing and HMAC realizes the function of key agreement and authentication message. The rest of this article is organized as follows: The second part introduces the basics knowledge of cryptography used in secure anonymous communication scheme. The third part describes the three models of the scheme. Next, the proposed scheme is described in detail in the fourth part. In the fifth part, the safety analysis of the scheme is given. Finally, in the sixth part, we summarize the paper.

2   Preliminaries

2.1   Message Authentication Code

In an open computing and communication world, we will use unreliable media to transmit and store information. The verification of information integrity is very important in some scenarios. The method of integrity verification based on the key is called Message Authentication Code (MAC). Generally, MAC is used to verify the information passed between the two parties sharing the key. Among them, HMAC is a method that uses a one-way hash function to construct a message authentication code, where H in HMAC means Hash.

The principle of using MAC between two communicating parties is as follows: assuming that both communicating parties share a key K, one party uses the message authentication code algorithm to calculate the message verification code Mac from K and the message M, and then sends Mac and M together to the other party. After the other party receives it, it uses M and K to calculate a new verification code Mac^*. If Mac^* and Mac are equal, the verification is successful, proving that the message has not been tampered with. In this process, the adversary does not have the key K. We give the calculation procedure of HMAC (see Fig. 1).

Among them, $ipadkey$ and $opadkey$ are bit sequences that have the same packet length as the one-way hash function and are related to the key. The combination with the message in step (3) refers to attaching the $ipadkey$ to the beginning of the message. The combination with the hash value in step (6) means that the hash value of (4) is appended to the back of the $opadkey$.

It can be seen from the above process that the finally obtained MAC value must be a fixed-length bit sequence related to the input message and the key.

2.2   Bilinear Pairings

Roughly speaking, a bilinear pairing provides a bilinear map that maps two group elements in elliptic curve groups to a third group element in a multiplicative

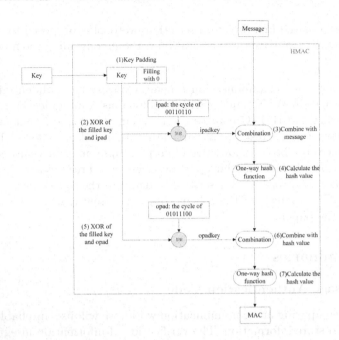

Fig. 1. The process of using HMAC to calculate the MAC value.

group without losing its isomorphism property. We use symmetric pairing here, let G_1 and G_2 are two groups of prime order q, and let $PG = (G_1, G_2, g, q, \hat{e})$ is a symmetric pair group. We denote G_1 using additive notation and G_2 using multiplicative notation. Furthermore, $|G_1| = |G_2| = q$, g is the generator of G_1, $\hat{e}: G_1 \times G_1 \to G_2$ is a mapping that satisfies the following three properties:

(1) Bilinear: For all $u, v \in G_1$, $a, b \in Z_p^*$, we have $\hat{e}(au, bv) = \hat{e}(u, bv)^a = \hat{e}(au, v)^b = \hat{e}(u, v)^{ab}$.

(2) Non-degeneration: If g is a generator of G_1, then $\hat{e}(g, g)$ is a generator of G_2.

(3) For all $u, v \in G_1$, there are effective algorithm $\hat{e}(u, v)$.

3   System Model

3.1   Network Model

Assume a multi-hop wireless sensor network composed of hundreds of small wireless sensor nodes, which are randomly and evenly distributed in an area. We assume that there is a sink node (base station) in the network to collect information (see Fig. 2).

3.2   Adversary Model

(1) The adversary has more abundant energy resources than ordinary sensor nodes, as well as stronger computing power.

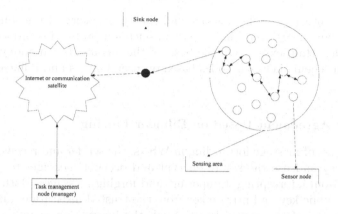

Fig. 2. Network model.

(2) Passive attack. The adversary can be distributed in all possible locations throughout the wireless sensor network, eavesdropping on communication between nodes;

(3) Active attack. The adversary can physically capture the sensor node and launch denial-of-service, replay and other attacks [9].

3.3 Energy Model

In the process of message forwarding in WSNs, for each node, sending and receiving data will consume its own stored energy. Here we only consider the energy consumption when sending and receiving a certain number of data [10,11]. Assuming that the initial energy of each node is I_e, the transmission distance is d, and the forwarded data size is n bits, the energy consumed for sending and receiving n bits of data is defined as:

$$E_{Tx}(n, d) = E_{Tx-elec}(n) + E_{Tx-amp}(n, d) = E_{elec}n + \varepsilon_{amp}nd^k \qquad (1)$$

$$E_{Rx}(n) = E_{Rx-elex}(n) = E_{elec}n \qquad (2)$$

Among them, E_{elec} represents the energy consumption per unit bit sent or received by the sender and the receiving circuit [12], and this value is related to the distance d between the sender and the receiver. k is the propagation attenuation index, usually in the range of [2, 4], which is determined by the surrounding environment and is directly proportional to the degree of obstacles in the environment.

4   Anonymous Communication Scheme Between Nodes Based on Pseudonym and Bilinear Pairing

In this part, we proposed key agreement based on bilinear pairing and message verification based on HMAC, completed the key agreement between nodes, and verified the integrity of the message and the authenticity of the source. At the same time, an energy-based link direction selection protocol is proposed to save energy to a certain extent. On the basis of these contents, an anonymous communication scheme between nodes based on pseudonyms and bilinear pairing is proposed.

4.1   Key Agreement Based on Bilinear Pairing

In the process of message forwarding in WSNs, the sender and receiver negotiate a session key and use the key to encrypt and decrypt messages to prevent the adversary from intercepting, tampering, and forging messages. Both parties get their own public key and private key from the trusted institution, and complete the negotiation of the shared key through the interaction of public key information. This method has better fairness and security [13]. We implement the key agreement between two nodes based on the bilinear pairing operation. The specific process is as follows:

(1) Parameter initialization
The trusted institution will generate the pairing parameters $(q, g, G_1, G_2, \hat{e})$, and choose two cryptographic hash functions $H_1: \{0,1\}^* \rightarrow G_1$ and $H_2: G_2 \times \{0,1\}^* \rightarrow \{0,1\}^n$. Also choose a random number $r_{ms} \in Z_q^*$ as the master secret in the entire network.

(2) Generate public and private keys
After the node (set as x) sends its ID number to the trusted institution, the trusted institution will use formula (3) and formula (4) to generate a public key and a private key for node x and send private key to node x.

$$PK_x = H_1(ID_x) \tag{3}$$

$$SK_x = r_{ms}PK_x \tag{4}$$

There is interaction process between node x and trusted institution (see Fig. 3).

(3) Calculate the shared key and encrypt the message If node i wants to forward a message to node j. Nodes i and j have obtained their own public key and private key respectively. Node i will randomly select an integer $r_{i \leftrightarrow j} \in Z_n^*$ shared between the two, generate two parameters: $V_{i \leftrightarrow j} = r_{i \leftrightarrow j}PK_i$, $E_{V_{i \leftrightarrow j}} = r_{i \leftrightarrow j}SK_i = r_{ms}V_{i \leftrightarrow j}$. Then calculate the shared key $k_{i \leftrightarrow j} = \hat{e}(r_{ms}V_{i \leftrightarrow j}, PK_j) = \hat{e}(PK_i, PK_j)^{r_{ms}r_{i \leftrightarrow j}}$ between i and j, and use this key to encrypt the message to be forwarded.

(4) Message decryption
After node j receives the message, it calculates the session key shared with i: $k_{i \leftrightarrow j} = \hat{e}(V_{i \leftrightarrow j}, SK_j) = \hat{e}(PK_i, PK_j)^{r_{ms}r_{i \leftrightarrow j}}$, to decrypt the message and get the plaintext.

4.2 Message Verification Based on HMAC

In order to further prevent the message from being maliciously tampered with by the adversary during the forwarding process, while ensuring that the source of the message is authentic. We add a verification in the message forwarding process, that is, every time a node is reached, the message must be verified from two aspects before forwarding. Two aspects refer to: One is whether the content of the message has been changed, and the other is whether the source of the message is true.

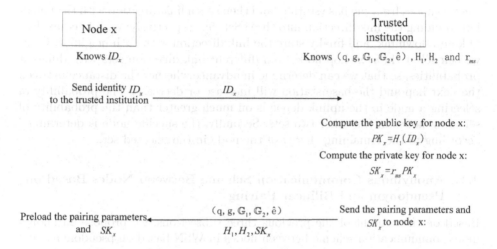

Fig. 3. The interaction process between node and trusted institution.

Message verification can be achieved through message authentication code or signature [14]. By comparing the difficulty of the two, the amount of calculation and the effect that can be achieved respectively, we choose a more lightweight [15, 16] message authentication code HMAC that can realize the verification function. In the process of forwarding messages, HMAC is added to the message. Still assuming that node i forwards a message to j, and the content to verify is set to y, the verification process of HMAC is as follows:

(1) Calculate $HMAC$

After node i calculates the shared key $k_{i \leftrightarrow j}$ with j, it calculates $HMAC(k_{i \leftrightarrow j}, y) = H(k_{i \leftrightarrow j} \oplus opad || H(k_{i \leftrightarrow j} \oplus ipad || y))$ and appends the result to the message to be forwarded.

(2) Verify $HMAC$

Node j first calculates the session key $k_{i \leftrightarrow j}$ to decrypt the payload to obtain y, then calculates a $HMAC^* = HMAC(k_{i \leftrightarrow j}, y)$, and compares whether the newly obtained $HMAC^*$ is the same as the $HMAC$ in the message. If they are the same, it proves that the message has not been tampered with and the source of the message is authentic.

4.3 Energy-Based Link Direction Selection Protocol

In order to prevent messages from passing through the random walk strategy, most of them have to pass through most nodes in the network to be sent to the base station, which wastes resources. Meanwhile, in order to avoid forwarding the message to the base station through the shortest path routing strategy, which is conducive to the adversary locate the next hop. We propose an energy-based link direction selection scheme (EBLD).

In the network initialization process, after each node receives the neighbor's single-hop broadcast message, it compares the minimum number of hops between the two nodes from the base station, and then sets a link direction with the neighbor, dividing the link direction into three Set [5], respectively: uplink, equivalent link and downlink, and finally store the link direction with each neighbor. First, we can select the next hop node from different link direction sets with different probabilities, so that we can determine in advance whether the distance between the next hop and the base station will increase or decrease. The probability of selecting a node in the uplink depends on much greater than the probability of selecting nodes in the other two sets. Secondly, the specific node is determined according to the remaining energy of the node in the selected set.

4.4 Anonymous Communication Scheme Between Nodes Based on Pseudonym and Bilinear Pairing

Based on the content of the previous three subsections, we propose an anonymous communication scheme between nodes in WSN based on pseudonyms and bilinear pairs in this subsection. Including two stages of network initialization and anonymous data forwarding.

Network Initialization. (1) Node pre-deployment: Each sensor node i needs to preload several parameters, including the random number α_i, the identity of the node i ID_i, etc., and then deploy it to the WSN. At the same time, the trusted institution will generate the pairing parameters $(q, g, G_1, G_2, \hat{e})$ and choose two cryptographic hash functions $H_1: \{0,1\}^* \to G_1$ and $H_2: G_2 \times \{0,1\}^* \to \{0,1\}^n$, and also choose a random number $r_{ms} \in Z_q^*$ as the master secret in the entire network.

(2) Parameter initialization: Using the existing broadcast scheme from the base station, each node i in the network can get the minimum number of hops between itself and the base station $Hop_{i,bs}$ [17], and save it in the node information. Each node i will also create a neighbor information table, which contains the information of all one-hop neighbor nodes of node i.

$V_{i \leftrightarrow j} = r_{i \leftrightarrow j} PK_i$ In this stage, each node i will calculate a global anonymous identity GAI_i according to formula (5) and save it in the node information, which is only known by node i and the base station [3].

$$GAI_i = H_1(ID_i \oplus \alpha_i) \tag{5}$$

In addition, each node i also obtains its own public key PK_i and private key SK_i through the scheme described in 4.1 at this stage: $PK_i = H_1(ID_i)$, $SK_i = r_{ms}PK_i$.

(3) Single-hop broadcast process: Then, each node i exchanges information with its one-hop neighbors through a single-hop broadcast message. The message format is as follows:

$SHBM = BF\|h\|ID_i\|\alpha_i\|Hop_{i,bs}\|RE_i$ The various parts in the message respectively represent: broadcast flag BF, broadcast hop count (here $h = 1$), identity of i, random number, minimum hop count between i and the base station, and remaining energy of i.

We assume that j is one of i's one-hop neighbors. After j receives the single-hop broadcast message $SHBM = BF\|h\|ID_i\|\alpha_i\|Hop_{i,bs}\|RE_i$ from i, it performs the following operations:

Calculate the random number shared between i and j: $\alpha_{j\leftrightarrow i} = H_1(ID_i \oplus ID_j)$;

Establish a single-hop anonymous identity shared between i and j: $SHAI_{j\leftrightarrow i} = H_1(\alpha_i \oplus \alpha_j)$;

Determine the number of hops between the two nodes and the base station, and set the link direction $Link_{j\rightarrow i}$ from j to i: If $Hop_{j,bs} > Hop_{i,bs}$, set $Link_{j\rightarrow i}$ to $link_{upward}$; if $Hop_{j,bs} = Hop_{i,bs}$, set $Link_{j\rightarrow i}$ to $link_{equal}$; if $Hop_{j,bs} < Hop_{i,bs}$, set $Link_{j\rightarrow i}$ to $link_{down}$.

After that, node j stores the information of node i in its neighbor information table T_j:

$SHAI_{j\leftrightarrow i}, \alpha_{j\leftrightarrow i}, Link_{j\rightarrow i}, RE_i$

The following figure depicts single-hop broadcast process from node i to node j (see Fig. 4).

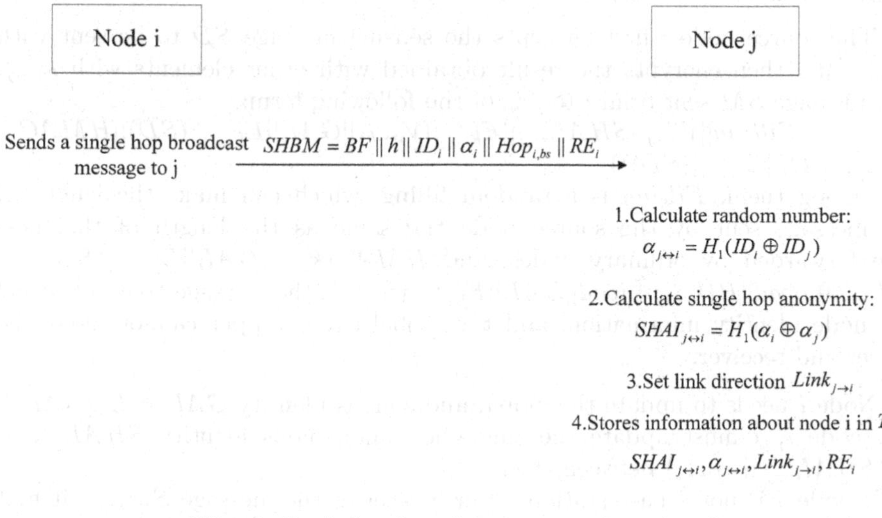

Fig. 4. Single-hop broadcast process from i to j.

After the single-hop broadcast process in the entire network ends, the neighbor information table T_i of each node i will contain the information of all one-hop neighbor nodes of node i. In order to save storage space and protect private information, after i receives the broadcast message from each neighbor and leaves a record in the neighbor information table, it deletes the broadcast message.

Anonymous Data Forwarding. When the source node wants to send a message to the base station, it follows the hop-by-hop sending mechanism, during which it will pass through the multi-hop node [18]. In this process, the source node will use a global anonymous identity to represent its real identity, and change the global anonymous identity after each message is sent. At the same time, in the process of hop-by-hop message sending, each two adjacent nodes will also use a single-hop anonymous identity for message forwarding, and the single-hop anonymous identity will be updated after each message forwarding.

Assuming that the source node is i, it selects the next hop node through the EBLD protocol described in Sect. 4.3, assuming that node j is selected. Node i performs the following operations:

(1) Uses the scheme mentioned in Sect. 4.1, i randomly selects an integer $r_{i \leftrightarrow j} \in Z_n^*$, generates a random data value based on the public key between i and j: $V_{i \leftrightarrow j} = r_{i \leftrightarrow j} PK_i$, and a random encrypted value based on the private key: $EV_{i \leftrightarrow j} = r_{i \leftrightarrow j} SK_i = r_{ms} V_{i \leftrightarrow j}$. Then node i calculates the shared key between i and j: $k_{i \leftrightarrow j} = \hat{e}(r_{ms} V_{i \leftrightarrow j}, PK_j) = \hat{e}(PK_i, PK_j)^{r_{ms} r_{i \leftrightarrow j}}$.

(2) Repeat the above process, the source node i randomly selects an integer $r_{i \leftrightarrow bs} \in Z_n^*$ again, generates random data value based on the public key: $V_{i \leftrightarrow bs} = r_{i \leftrightarrow bs} PK_i$, random encrypted value based on private key: $EV_{i \leftrightarrow bs} = r_{i \leftrightarrow bs} SK_i = r_{ms} V_{i \leftrightarrow bs}$, and then calculates the shared key between i and the base station: $k_{i \leftrightarrow bs} = \hat{e}(r_{ms} V_{i \leftrightarrow bs}, PK_{bs}) = \hat{e}(PK_i, PK_{bs})^{r_{ms} r_{i \leftrightarrow bs}}$.

(3) The source node i first encrypts the sensing message SD to be sent with $k_{i \leftrightarrow bs}$, and then encrypts the result obtained with other elements with $k_{i \leftrightarrow j}$. The message SM sent from i to j is of the following form:
$SM_{i \rightarrow j} = Filling||V_{i \leftrightarrow j}||SHAI_{i \leftrightarrow j}||E_{k_{i \leftrightarrow j}}(V_{i \leftrightarrow bs}||GAI_i||E_{k_{i \leftrightarrow bs}}(SD)||HMAC$
$(k_{i \leftrightarrow j}, GAI_i||E_{k_{i \leftrightarrow bs}}(SD)))$
Among them, $Filling$ is a random filling, which can make the length of the message sent by the source node the same as the length of the message forwarded by ordinary nodes, and $HMAC(k_{i \leftrightarrow j}, GAI_i||E_{k_{i \leftrightarrow bs}}(SD)) = H(k_{i \leftrightarrow j} \oplus opad||H(k_{i \leftrightarrow j} \oplus ipad||GAI_i||E_{k_{i \leftrightarrow bs}}(SD)))$, the message does not reveal any node identity information, and the global eavesdropper cannot judge the sender and receiver.

(4) Node i needs to update the global anonymous identity $GAI_i = H_1(GAI_i \oplus \alpha_i)$, node i, j must update the single-hop anonymous identity $SHAI_{i \leftrightarrow j} = H_1(SHAI_{i \leftrightarrow j} \oplus \alpha_{i \leftrightarrow j})$ between them.

If node j is not a base station, after j receives the message $SM_{i \rightarrow j}$, it first compares whether the $SHAI_{i \leftrightarrow j}$ and anonymous identities stored in T_j match.

If they do not match, it means that the message is not sent to j, j discards the message. If it matches, node j performs the following operations:

(1) Calculate the session key $k_{i\leftrightarrow j} = \hat{e}(V_{i\leftrightarrow j}, SK_j) = \hat{e}(PK_i, PK_j)^{r_{ms}r_{i\leftrightarrow j}}$ shared with i to decrypt the message, get $V_{i\leftrightarrow bs}||GAI_i||E_{k_{i\leftrightarrow bs}}(SD)$.

(2) Node j use the session key to calculate an $HMAC^*$, and compare whether $HMAC^*$ is the same as the $HMAC$ in the message. If they are the same, execute (3);

(3) Select the next hop node r. After selection, j calculates the session key $k_{j\leftrightarrow r}$ shared with node r, and then uses this key to encrypt $GAI_i||E_{k_{i\leftrightarrow bs}}(SD)$, and calculate the $HMAC$ value. Get the message:
$SM_{j\rightarrow r} = Filling||V_{j\leftrightarrow r}||SHAI_{j\leftrightarrow r}||E_{k_{j\leftrightarrow r}}(V_{i\leftrightarrow bs}||GAI_i||E_{k_{i\leftrightarrow bs}}(SD)||HMAC$
$(k_{j\leftrightarrow r}, GAI_i||E_{k_{i\leftrightarrow bs}}(SD)))$

(4) Node j sends the message to node r.

(5) Node j updates $SHAI_{i\leftrightarrow j}$ and $SHAI_{j\leftrightarrow r}$.
We take the communication between source nodes i and j as an example, give the specific process (see Fig. 5).

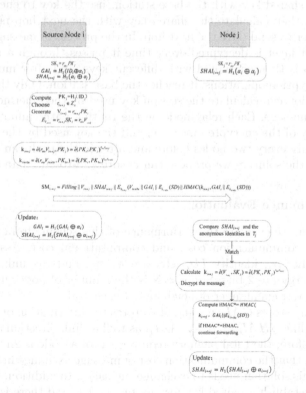

Fig. 5. Source node i forwards the message to node j

5   Security Analysis

5.1   Anonymous Communication

In this scheme, each time a message is transmitted, an anonymous identity is used, that is, a one-time pseudonym is used to identify the other party, and any two messages use different pseudonyms during transmission, and no pseudonym is used multiple times. This ensures that the relay node on the path does not know who its previous hop is, only to whom the next hop is to be sent to. After each hop, the message will be re-encrypted with a different key. After each hop, the message will have a different appearance. Anonymous data forwarding is realized, the anonymity of the forwarding node is ensured, and the data forwarding relationship between adjacent nodes is hidden. In addition, for global passive adversary, they can only observe the transmission in the network, but cannot capture the source node and communication relationship.

5.2   End-to-End Data Security

If the source node wants to send a message to the base station, it must first calculate the shared key with the base station, use the key to encrypt the original message, then calculate the shared key with the next hop node, and then encrypt a layer to send Give the next hop. In the process of message forwarding, the outermost layer is decrypted every time it passes through a node, and the required data is then encrypted with different keys, and after multiple encryption and decryption operations, it reaches the base station. Only the source node and base station can calculate the session key used by the innermost encryption layer of the message. Each relay node on the routing path cannot calculate the innermost key of the encrypted message, and the key used by the outer encryption layer. Only every two nodes before and after in the path can be calculated. In summary, the solution we propose can ensure end-to-end data security.

5.3   Performance Evaluation

In this section, we evaluate the performance of this scheme from three aspects: storage cost, communication cost, and computational cost. Assume that the random number α_i, identity ID_i, etc. are n bits, and the link direction and remaining energy are 2 bits. Suppose N is the number of nodes in the network, and C is the average number of neighbors of each node.

Each node i stores GAI_i, α_i, and also stores the information of each neighbor node j, including $SHAI_{i\leftrightarrow j}$, $\alpha_{i\leftrightarrow j}$, AAI_j, as well as link direction and remaining energy. Therefore, the total memory requirement of a node is 2n+3nC+4.

Assuming that the communication cost of message exchange in the entire network is W, this solution needs to exchange messages. In addition, both SAS and this scheme establish a paired key for any two nodes, and there is an additional communication overhead P.

Table 1 compares the storage, calculation, and communication costs between our scheme and several existing anonymous communication protocols. γ refers to the communication cost of the confirmation message. According to Table 1, ESAC has the smallest storage overhead, but it cannot achieve end-to-end data confidentiality and anti-counterfeiting attacks. SAS creates anonymous identities from pseudonymous spaces, so it has low computational cost.

Table 1. Comparison of performance.

Scheme	Storage overhead (bytes)	Computation overhead (clock cycles)	Communication overhead (number of messages)
SAS [20]	2nN+4nC+16	Generating anonymous IDs from pseudonym space	P+W
ESAC [19]	3n	Two hashing operations and two bilinear pairing	P+W
EAC [5]	6n+7nC+2	Four hashing operations	W+γ
This scheme	2n+3nC+4	Two bilinear pairing and four hashing operations	P+W

6 Conclusion

The intensive deployment of wireless sensor networks has led to the generation of big data. Through the deployed sensor nodes, the data is sent to the base station in a hop-by-hop manner to achieve the purpose of collecting data. In the process of receiving and forwarding data by the node, if the real identity is used, if the adversary obtains the real identity of the source node, it will attack and compromise the communication. In this paper, we propose an anonymous communication scheme based on pseudonym and bilinear pairing. This scheme uses pseudonyms to hide the identities of important nodes, provides node anonymity, and prevents adversary from identifying important nodes, such as source nodes and base station. At the same time, it implements secure key agreement between nodes based on bilinear pairing operation and HMAC, and verifies the integrity of the message and whether the source is authentic, ensuring key privacy and preventing information leakage. The energy-based link direction selection protocol ensures that the message can reach the base station faster and saves network resources. Security analysis shows that this scheme can realize anonymous communication, strengthen end-to-end privacy, and ensure the security and reliability of communication in WSNs.

References

1. Abuzneid, A.S., Sobh, T., Faezipour, M., et al.: An enhanced communication protocol for anonymity and location privacy in WSN. In: Wireless Communications & Networking Conference Workshops, pp. 91–96. IEEE (2015)

2. Nia, M.A., Ruiz-Martnez, A.: Systematic literature review on the state of the art and future research work in anonymous communications systems. Comput. Electr. Eng. **69**, 497–520 (2018)
3. Nezhad, A.A., Miri, A., Makrakis, D.: Location privacy and anonymity preserving routing for wireless sensor networks. Comput. Netw. **52**(18), 3433–3452 (2008)
4. Li, X., Niu, J., Kumari, S.: A three-factor anonymous authentication scheme for wireless sensor networks in internet of things environments. J. Netw. Comput. Appl. **103**, 194–204 (2018)
5. Chen, J., Du, X., Fang, B.: An efficient anonymous communication protocol for wireless sensor networks. Wirel. Commun. Mob. Comput. **12**(14), 1302–1312 (2012)
6. Boukerche, A., El-Khatib, K., Xu, L., et al.: An efficient secure distributed anonymous routing protocol for mobile and wireless ad hoc networks. Comput. Commun. **28**(10), 1193–1203 (2005)
7. Abuzneid, A.S., Sobh, T., Faezipour, M., et al.: Fortified anonymous communication protocol for location privacy in WSN: a modular approach. Sensors **15**(3), 5820–5864 (2015)
8. Jebri, S., Abid, M., Bouallegue, A. et al.: STAC-protocol: secure and trust anonymous communication protocol for IoT. In: 2017 13th International Wireless Communications and Mobile Computing Conference (IWCMC). IEEE, pp. 365–370 (2017)
9. Yao, L., Kang, L., Shang, P., et al.: Protecting the sink location privacy in wireless sensor networks. Pers. Ubiquit. Comput. **17**(5), 883–893 (2013)
10. Ren, J., Zhang, Y.X., Liu, K., et al.: An energy-efficient cyclic diversionary routing strategy against global eavesdroppers in wireless sensor networks. Int. J. Distrib. Sens. Netw. **9**(4), 834245 (2013)
11. Zhou, L., Shan, Y., Chen, X.: An anonymous routing scheme for preserving location privacy in wireless sensor networks. In: 2019 IEEE 3rd Information Technology, Networking, Electronic and Automation Control Conference (ITNEC), pp. 262–265. IEEE (2019)
12. Zhang, Z.D., Sun, Y.G., Liu, Y., et al.: Energy model for wireless sensor networks. J. Tianjin Univ. Natural Sci. Eng. Technol. Edition **40**(9), 1029–1034 (2007)
13. Chen, T.M., Ye, M.K., Cai, J.M.: Journal of Tianjin University: Natural Science and Engineering Technology Edition (2008)
14. Semple, J., Rose, G. G., Paddon, M., et al.: Mutual authentication with modified message authentication code. U.S. Patent 8,260,259 (2012)
15. Anita, X., Bhagyaveni, M.A., Martin Leo Manickam, J.: Collaborative lightweight trust management scheme for wireless sensor networks. Wireless Pers. Commun. **80**(1), 117–140 (2014). https://doi.org/10.1007/s11277-014-1998-2
16. Li, C.T., Hwang, M.S.: A lightweight anonymous routing protocol without public key en/decryptions for wireless ad hoc networks. Inf. Sci. **181**(23), 5333–5347 (2011)
17. Chen, J., Fang, B., Yin, L., et al.: A source-location privacy preservation protocol in wireless sensor networks using source-based restricted flooding. Chinese J. Comput. **33**(9), 1736–1747 (2010)
18. Sengupta, J., Ruj, S., Das, B.S.: An efficient and secure directed diffusion in industrial wireless sensor networks. In: Proceedings of the 1st International Workshop on Future Industrial Communication Networks, pp. 41–46 (2018)

A Novel Complex Pignistic Belief Transform for Conflict Measure in Complex Evidence Theory

Yangyang Zhao[1,2] and Fuyuan Xiao[2(✉)]

[1] School of Computer and Information Science, Southwest University,
Chongqing 400715, China
[2] School of Big Data and Software Engineering, Chongqing University,
Chongqing 401331, China
xiaofuyuan@cqu.edu.cn

Abstract. Information fusion has received extensive attention in the past decades, in which the handing of uncertain information is still an open issue. Complex evidence theory (CET) can effectively deal with uncertain information. However, in CET, the measurement of conflict is still a problem to be solved. Therefore, this paper proposes a novel method of measurement method for CET. Firstly, we divide the belief into power sets and propose a complex pignistic belief transform. Then the betting commitment function is designed. Finally, a new betting distance based on betting commitment function is proposed, and some properties of the betting distance are analyzed, including the non-negativeness, nondegeneracy, symmetry, and triangle inequality. The betting distance can be used to measure the conflict between CBBAs. In addition, an example is given to show the advantage of betting distance compared to the conflict coefficient.

Keywords: Complex evidence theory · Complex pignistic belief transform · Conflict measure · Betting commitment · Betting distance

1 Introduction

In the process of information fusion, uncertain information processing has been widely concerned in recent years [1–3]. Consequently, many methods have been put forward, including evidential reasoning [4–6], Z number [7], entropy-based [8], fuzzy set [9], and Dempster-Shafer evidence theory [10]. They have been widely used in many fields, including classification [11], target recognition [12], complex network [13,14], uncertainty-based multidisciplinary design optimization [15,16],reliability evaluation [17], parrondo effect [18,19], and decision-making [20].

Supported by the National Natural Science Foundation of China (No. 62003280).

Y. Tan et al. (Eds.): DMBD 2021, CCIS 1453, pp. 183–191, 2021.
https://doi.org/10.1007/978-981-16-7476-1_17

As is well known, since basic belief assignment (BBA) represents uncertainty more flexibly than probability distribution, Dempster-Shafer evidence theory has more advantages in dealing with uncertain information. In addition, Dempster-Shafer evidence theory also provides a method to fuse multiple BBAs, namely Dempster combination rule, which is helpful to reduce the uncertainty in the process of fusion. Therefore, D-S evidence theory has been widely studied [21–23]. In particular, the complex evidence theory (CET) proposed by Xiao [24,25] recently can be used to deal with more complex uncertainty problems.

In CET, BBA is extended to complex basic belief assignment (CBBA), and the mass function is modeled by complex number, not a positive real number. What's more, a method of fusing CBBAs is proposed based on the Dempster combination rule. Because CET uses the amplitude and phase of complex number to model, it can better express and deal with the uncertainty in fusion process. This gives CET the ability to solve more complex problems, such as combining with quantum mechanics to build new models to predict the impact of inference on human decision-making behavior [26]. When CBBAs degrade to classical BBAs, CET reduces into Dempste-Shafer theory when the conflict coefficient is less than 1. Therefore, CET provides a more generalized framework compared with Dempster-Shafer evidence theory.

In Dempster-Shafer evidence theory, conflict measure plays an important role in the process of information fusion. In the past few decades, many researchers have worked to solve this problem. But there are few methods can be used to measure the difference between CBBAs that use complex number modeling in CET [27]. And in some cases, the conflict coefficient will be counter-intuitive. Therefore, we propose a novel conflict measure for CBBAs in CET.

In this article, we first propose a complex pigistic belief transform (CPBT). It distributes the belief equally to the power set, so it can not only transform the single subset, but also act on multiple subsets. Then on the basis of CPBT, a betting commitment function is designed. Finally, based on the betting commitment function, the betting distance is proposed, which can be used to measure conflict, and several properties of betting distance are analyzed, including non-negativeness, nondegeneracy, symmetry, and triangle inequality. In addition, an example is given to show the advantage of betting distance compared to the conflict coefficient.

The rest of the paper is organized as follows. In Sect. 2, we introduce the conflict coefficient and discuss its deficiency. In Sect. 3, the novel proposed complex pignistic belief transform and betting commitment function are introduced. Then, the betting distance is proposed based on betting commitment function, and an example is given to show the advantage of betting distance compared with the conflict coefficient in Sect. 4. Finally, the conclusion is given in Sect. 5.

2 $|\mathbb{K}|$ Versus Conflict

Conflict coefficient is an effective method to measure conflict in CET, but it is counter intuitive in some cases [27]. This section will discuss the deficiency of conflict coefficient.

Definition 1. *Let* $\mathbb{M}_1$ *and* $\mathbb{M}_2$ *be two independently CBBAs in* Ω. *The complex Dempster's rule of combination, defined by* $\mathbb{M} = \mathbb{M}_1 \oplus \mathbb{M}_2$, *is represented as:*

$$\mathbb{M}(C) = \begin{cases} \frac{1}{1-\mathbb{K}} \sum_{A \cap B = C} \mathbb{M}_1(A)\mathbb{M}_2(B), & C \neq \emptyset, \\ 0, & C = \emptyset, \end{cases} \tag{1}$$

with

$$\mathbb{K} = \sum_{A \cap B = \emptyset} \mathbb{M}_1(A)\mathbb{M}_2(B), \tag{2}$$

where $A, B \in 2^\Omega$ *and* $\mathbb{K}$ *is the conflict coefficient between* $\mathbb{M}_1$ *and* $\mathbb{M}_2$. $|\mathbb{K}|$ *is used to measure the conflict between* $\mathbb{M}_1$ *and* $\mathbb{M}_2$.

Generally, the value of $|\mathbb{K}|$ reflects the degree of conflict between evidences. When $|\mathbb{K}| = 0$, it means that it is completely consistent and there is no conflict. Conversely, the greater the value of $|\mathbb{K}|$, the greater the conflict between the evidences. But in some cases, the value of $|\mathbb{K}|$ will be counter-intuitive, as shown in Example 1 [27].

Example 1. $\mathbb{M}_1$ and $\mathbb{M}_2$ are two CBBAs in FOD $\Omega = \{A, B, C, D\}$:

$$\mathbb{M}_1 : \mathbb{M}_1(\{A\}) = \frac{1}{4}, \mathbb{M}_1(\{B\}) = \frac{1}{4}, \mathbb{M}_1(\{C\}) = \frac{1}{4}, \mathbb{M}_1(\{D\}) = \frac{1}{4};$$

$$\mathbb{M}_2 : \mathbb{M}_2(\{A\}) = \frac{1}{4}, \mathbb{M}_2(\{B\}) = \frac{1}{4}, \mathbb{M}_2(\{C\}) = \frac{1}{4}, \mathbb{M}_2(\{D\}) = \frac{1}{4}.$$

By using Eq. (2), the result of $|\mathbb{K}|$ calculation is:

$$|\mathbb{K}| = 0.75.$$

As can be seen from Example 1, $\mathbb{M}_1$ and $\mathbb{M}_2$ have the same support for hypothesis $\{A\}$, $\{B\}$, $\{C\}$, and $\{D\}$, both are $\frac{1}{4}$. This indicates that $\mathbb{M}_1$ and $\mathbb{M}_2$ are exactly the same, there is no conflict between them, therefore, $|\mathbb{K}|$ should be zero. However, the value of $|\mathbb{K}|$ calculated by Eq. (2) is 0.75, which is obviously counter-intuitive.

Therefore, we propose a novel conflict measure for CBBAs in CET.

3   The Proposed Complex Pignistic Belief Transform

In this section, we will introduce the complex pignistic belief transform, and by taking the absolute value of CPBT, we define the betting commitment function.

In order to avoid the false claims caused by using only $|\mathbb{K}|$, we propose a new alternative method to measure conflict. Firstly, *CBBA* is divided into two parts: (1) belief from a subset of A, namely $B \subseteq A$; (2) belief from those that are not contained in A, that is, $C \nsubseteq A$. For the first part, *CPBT* is obtained by adding the beliefs directly. For the second part, we distribute the belief of the set to its power set, and then divide these sets into the following two parts according to whether the power set is a subset of set A: (2.1) $E \subseteq C, E \subseteq A$; (2.2) $D \subseteq C, D \nsubseteq A$.

When the belief of set C is assigned to its power set, since the cardinality of the set and the proportion of the intersection of the sets may be different, we define the following asymmetric similarity measure as the weight for calculating the second part.

Definition 2. *We define the asymmetric similarity measure between set A and B as below:*

$$Sim(A, B) = \frac{2^{|A \cap B|} - 1}{2^{|A|} - 1},\tag{3}$$

where $|A|$ represents the cardinality of set A.

For part 2.1, in fact, the essence of set E is the power set of $A \cap C$. Consequently, $2^{|A \cap C|} - 1$ is used to denote the cardinality of set $A \cap C$.

For part 2.2, we use the quotient of $Sim(A, D)$ and $Sim(A, C)$ to represent the degree of relevance between A and D, and regard it as the assigned weight. The belief of D is evenly assigned to its power sets and then multiplied by the assigned weight. Finally, the $CPBT$ of the second part is obtained by adding parts 2.1 and 2.2 together. Thence, the $CPBT$ is defined as below.

Definition 3. *According to the previous discussion, we define the complex pignistic belief transform (CPBT) as follows:*

$$CPBT(A) = CPBT_1(A) + CPBT_2(A).\tag{4}$$

It consists of two parts, the first part $CPBT_1(A)$ is:

$$CPBT_1(A) = \sum_{B \subseteq A} \mathbb{M}(B),\tag{5}$$

and the second part $CPBT_2(A)$ is denoted as:

$$CPBT_2(A) = \sum_{C \nsubseteq A} \frac{\mathbb{M}(C)}{2^{|C|} - 1} \cdot \left(\sum_{E \subseteq C, E \subseteq A} \frac{|E \cap C|}{|E \cap A|} + \sum_{D \subseteq C, D \nsubseteq A} \frac{|A \cap D|}{|D|} \cdot \frac{Sim(A, D)}{Sim(A, C)} \right)$$

$$= \sum_{C \nsubseteq A} \frac{\mathbb{M}(C)}{2^{|C|} - 1} \cdot \left(2^{|A \cap C|} - 1 + \sum_{D \subseteq C, D \nsubseteq A} \frac{|A \cap D|}{|D|} \cdot \frac{2^{|A \cap D|} - 1}{2^{|A \cap C|} - 1} \right).\tag{6}$$

When $|A| = 1$, the first part becomes:

$$CPBT_1(A) = \mathbb{M}(A),\tag{7}$$

the second part becomes:

$$CPBT_2(A) = \sum_{C \nsubseteq A, A \cap C \neq 0} \frac{\mathbb{M}(C)}{2^{|C|} - 1} \cdot \left(1 + \sum_{D \subseteq C, D \nsubseteq A} \frac{1}{|D|} \right)$$

$$= \sum_{C \nsubseteq A, A \cap C \neq 0} \frac{\mathbb{M}(C)}{|C|}.\tag{8}$$

Proof. Now, we prove the Eq. (8). First, we define the operation of the symbol $F(n,j)$ as follows:

$$F(n,j) = \frac{n!}{j! * (n-j)!},\tag{9}$$

where $n! = 1 * 2 * 3 * \ldots * n$.

In addition, using the binomial expansion, we can get:

$$(x+y)^n = \sum_{j=0}^{n} F(n,j) * x^j * y^{n-j},\tag{10}$$

when $x = 1$ and $y = 1$, substituting in the above formula, we get:

$$(1+1)^n = \sum_{j=0}^{n} F(n,j) * 1^j * 1^{n-j} = \sum_{j=0}^{n} F(n,j).\tag{11}$$

Since $F(n,0) = 1$, we can get the following relationship from Eq. (11):

$$\sum_{j=1}^{n} F(n,j) = 2^n - 1,\tag{12}$$

besides,

$$F(n-1,j) \cdot \frac{1}{j+1} = \frac{(n-1)!}{(n-1-j)! \cdot (j+1)!} = \frac{F(n,j+1)}{n}.\tag{13}$$

Thus,

$$
\begin{aligned}
CPBT_2(A) &= \sum_{C \not\subseteq A, A \cap C \neq 0} \frac{\mathbb{M}(C)}{2^{|C|} - 1} \cdot (1 + \sum_{D \subseteq C, D \not\subseteq A} \frac{1}{|D|}) \\
&= \sum_{C \not\subseteq A, A \cap C \neq 0} \frac{\mathbb{M}(C)}{2^{|C|} - 1} \cdot (1 + \sum_{j=1}^{|C|-1} \frac{F(|C|-1,j)}{j+1}) \\
&= \sum_{C \not\subseteq A, A \cap C \neq 0} \frac{\mathbb{M}(C)}{2^{|C|} - 1} \cdot (\frac{F(|C|,1)}{|C|} + \sum_{j=1}^{|C|-1} \frac{F(|C|,j+1)}{|C|}) \\
&= \sum_{C \not\subseteq A, A \cap C \neq 0} \frac{\mathbb{M}(C)}{(2^{|C|} - 1) \cdot |C|} \cdot (\sum_{j=1}^{|C|} F(|C|,j)) \\
&= \sum_{C \not\subseteq A, A \cap C \neq 0} \frac{\mathbb{M}(C)}{(2^{|C|} - 1) \cdot |C|} \cdot (2^{|C|} - 1) \\
&= \sum_{C \not\subseteq A, A \cap C \neq 0} \frac{\mathbb{M}(C)}{|C|}.
\end{aligned}\tag{14}
$$

According to Definition 3, we define the betting commitment function of set A as follows.

Definition 4. *Let Ω be the FOD, we define the betting commitment to A as:*

$$BetC(A) = |CPBT(A)|, \qquad \forall A \subseteq \Omega, \tag{15}$$

where $|CPBT(A)|$ represents the absolute value of $CPBT(A)$.

4   Conflict Measure

Based on the betting commitment function, we define a novel conflict measure in this section.

Definition 5. *Given two CBBAs $\mathbb{M}_1$ and $\mathbb{M}_2$, we define the betting distance between $\mathbb{M}_1$ and $\mathbb{M}_2$ as below:*

$$d_{BetC}(\mathbb{M}_1, \mathbb{M}_2) = \max_{A \subseteq \Omega}\{|BetC_{\mathbb{M}_1}(A) - BetC_{\mathbb{M}_2}(A)|\}, \tag{16}$$

where $|\cdot|$ represents the absolute value function. The value of $d_{BetC}(\mathbb{M}_1, \mathbb{M}_2)$ can be used to measure the conflict.

Property 1. Consider three *CBBAs* $\mathbb{M}_1$, $\mathbb{M}_2$ and $\mathbb{M}_3$ on *FOD* Ω. The betting distance d_{BetC} holds the following properties:

P1 Nonnegativity: $d_{BetC}\{\mathbb{M}_1, \mathbb{M}_2\} \geq 0$;
P2 Nondegeneracy: $d_{BetC}\{\mathbb{M}_1, \mathbb{M}_2\} = 0 \iff \mathbb{M}_1 = \mathbb{M}_2$;
P3 Symmetry: $d_{BetC}\{\mathbb{M}_1, \mathbb{M}_2\} = d_{BetC}\{\mathbb{M}_2, \mathbb{M}_1\}$;
P4 Triangle inequality: $d_{BetC}\{\mathbb{M}_1, \mathbb{M}_3\} \leq d_{BetC}\{\mathbb{M}_1, \mathbb{M}_2\} + d_{BetC}\{\mathbb{M}_2, \mathbb{M}_3\}$.

Proof.(1) Let $\mathbb{M}_1$ and $\mathbb{M}_2$ be two *CBBAs*. According to Eq. (16), it is obviously that $d_{BetC}\{\mathbb{M}_1, \mathbb{M}_2\} \geq 0$, due to the absolute value function.
(2) Assuming two *CBBAs* $\mathbb{M}_1$ and $\mathbb{M}_2$, we can get:

$$d_{BetC}(\mathbb{M}_1, \mathbb{M}_2) = \max_{A \subseteq \Omega}\{|BetC_{\mathbb{M}_1}(A) - BetC_{\mathbb{M}_2}(A)|\} = 0.$$

Next, suppose $d_{BetC}\{\mathbb{M}_1, \mathbb{M}_2\} = 0$, then:

$$\max_{A \subseteq \Omega}\{|BetC_{\mathbb{M}_1}(A) - BetC_{\mathbb{M}_2}(A)|\} = 0.$$

Therefore, for $\forall A \subseteq \Omega$, we can get:

$$\mathbb{M}_1(A) = \mathbb{M}_2(A).$$

Consequently, it is proven that $d_{BetC}\{\mathbb{M}_1, \mathbb{M}_2\} = 0 \iff \mathbb{M}_1 = \mathbb{M}_2$.
(3) Consider two *CBBAs* $\mathbb{M}_1$ and $\mathbb{M}_2$, it is easy to obtain:

$$\max_{A \subseteq \Omega}\{|BetC_{\mathbb{M}_1}(A) - BetC_{\mathbb{M}_2}(A)|\} = \max_{A \subseteq \Omega}\{|BetC_{\mathbb{M}_2}(A) - BetC_{\mathbb{M}_1}(A)|\}.$$

Hence:

$$d_{BetC}\{\mathbb{M}_1, \mathbb{M}_2\} = d_{BetC}\{\mathbb{M}_2, \mathbb{M}_1\}.$$

(4) Considering three $CBBAs$ $\mathbb{M}_1$, $\mathbb{M}_2$ and $\mathbb{M}_3$, according to the triangle inequality of real numbers, we can get:

$$|BetC_{\mathbb{M}_1}(A) - BetC_{\mathbb{M}_3}(A)| \leq |BetC_{\mathbb{M}_1}(A) - BetC_{\mathbb{M}_2}(A)| + |BetC_{\mathbb{M}_2}(A) - BetC_{\mathbb{M}_3}(A)|.$$

Then, it is obviously that:

$$\max_{A \subseteq \Omega}\{|BetC_{\mathbb{M}_1}(A) - BetC_{\mathbb{M}_3}(A)|\} \leq \max_{A \subseteq \Omega}\{|BetC_{\mathbb{M}_1}(A) - BetC_{\mathbb{M}_2}(A)|\} +$$
$$\max_{A \subseteq \Omega}\{|BetC_{\mathbb{M}_2}(A) - BetC_{\mathbb{M}_3}(A)|\}.$$

Thus:

$$d_{BetC}\{\mathbb{M}_1, \mathbb{M}_3\} \leq d_{BetC}\{\mathbb{M}_1, \mathbb{M}_2\} + d_{BetC}\{\mathbb{M}_2, \mathbb{M}_3\}.$$

Now, consider the case of Example 1 to verify the effectiveness of the betting distance expression conflict.

Example 2. Consider two $CBBAs$ $\mathbb{M}_1$ and $\mathbb{M}_2$ defined in Example 1. Though Eq. (15), the following result is obtained:

$$BetC_{\mathbb{M}_1}(\{A\}) = 0.25, BetC_{\mathbb{M}_1}(\{B\}) = 0.25,$$
$$BetC_{\mathbb{M}_1}(\{C\}) = 0.25, BetC_{\mathbb{M}_1}(\{D\}) = 0.25;$$

and:

$$BetC_{\mathbb{M}_2}(\{A\}) = 0.25, BetC_{\mathbb{M}_2}(\{B\}) = 0.25,$$
$$BetC_{\mathbb{M}_2}(\{C\}) = 0.25, BetC_{\mathbb{M}_2}(\{D\}) = 0.25.$$

Then by calculating the absolute value of the difference between the results obtained above, we can get:

$$|BetC_{\mathbb{M}_1}(\{A\}) - BetC_{\mathbb{M}_2}(\{A\})| = 0, |BetC_{\mathbb{M}_1}(\{B\}) - BetC_{\mathbb{M}_2}(\{B\})| = 0,$$
$$|BetC_{\mathbb{M}_1}(\{C\}) - BetC_{\mathbb{M}_2}(\{C\})| = 0, |BetC_{\mathbb{M}_1}(\{D\}) - BetC_{\mathbb{M}_2}(\{D\})| = 0.$$

Thus, the betting distance between $\mathbb{M}_1$ and $\mathbb{M}_2$ is the maximum value of the above results:

$$d_{BetC}\{\mathbb{M}_1, \mathbb{M}_2\} = 0. \tag{17}$$

According to the analysis of Example 1, $\mathbb{M}_1$ and $\mathbb{M}_2$ are exactly the same, there is no conflict between them, so $\mathbb{K} = 0.75$ is counter-intuitive. While $d_{BetC}\{\mathbb{M}_1, \mathbb{M}_2\} = 0$ indicates that there is no conflict, which is in line with our expected value.

5   Conclusion

In this paper, we propose a novel method to measure conflict in CET. First of all, we propose the complex pignistic belief transform. It distributes the belief equally to the power set, so it can not only transform the single subset, but also act on multiple subsets. Then, by taking the absolute value of CPBT, we define the betting commitment function. Finally, the betting distance is proposed based on the betting commitment function, and some properties of the betting distance are analyzed, including the non-negativeness, nondegeneracy, symmetry, and triangle inequality. The betting distance can measure the conflict between CBBAs, and an example is given to show the advantage of the proposed betting distance compared with the conflict coefficient.

References

1. Deng, J., Deng, Y.: Information volume of fuzzy membership function. Int. J. Comput. Commun. Control **16**(1), 4106 (2021). https://doi.org/10.15837/ijccc.2021.1.4106
2. Meng, D., Li, Y., He, C., Guo, J., Lv, Z., Wu, P.: Multidisciplinary design for structural integrity using a collaborative optimization method based on adaptive surrogate modelling. Mater. Design **206**, 109789 (2021)
3. Lai, J.W., Chang, J., Ang, L., Cheong, K.H.: Multi-level information fusion to alleviate network congestion. Inf. Fusion **63**, 248–255 (2020)
4. Zhou, M., Liu, X.-B., Chen, Y.-W., Qian, X.-F., Yang, J.-B., Wu, J.: Assignment of attribute weights with belief distributions for MADM under uncertainties. Knowl.-Based Syst. **189**, 105110 (2020)
5. Fu, C., Xue, M., Chang, W., Xu, D., Yang, S.: An evidential reasoning approach based on risk attitude and criterion reliability. Knowl.-Based Syst. **199**, 105947 (2020)
6. Z.-G. Liu, L.-Q. Huang, K. Zhou, T. Denoeux, Combination of transferable classification with multisource domain adaptation based on evidential reasoning, IEEE Transactions on Neural Networks and Learning Systems
7. Jiang, W., Cao, Y., Deng, X.: A novel Z-network model based on Bayesian network and Z-number. IEEE Trans. Fuzzy Syst. **28**(8), 1585–1599 (2020)
8. Babajanyan, S., Allahverdyan, A., Cheong, K.H.: Energy and entropy: Path from game theory to statistical mechanics. Phys. Rev. Res. **2**(4), 043055 (2020)
9. Pan, L., Gao, X., Deng, Y., Cheong, K.H.: The constrained pythagorean fuzzy sets and its similarity measure. IEEE Trans. Fuzzy Syst
10. Deng, Y.: Uncertainty measure in evidence theory. Sci. China Inf. Sci. **63**(11), 210201 (2020)
11. Xu, X., Zheng, J., Yang, J.-B., Xu, D.-L., Chen, Y.-W.: Data classification using evidence reasoning rule. Knowl.-Based Syst. **116**, 144–151 (2017)
12. Pan, L., Deng, Y.: An association coefficient of a belief function and its application in a target recognition system. Int. J. Intell. Syst. **35**(1), 85–104 (2020)
13. Zhao, J., Deng, Y.: Complex network modeling of evidence theory. IEEE Trans. Fuzzy Syst
14. Wen, T., Cheong, K.H.: The fractal dimension of complex networks: a review. Inf. Fusion **73**, 87–102 (2021)
15. Meng, D., Xie, T., Wu, P., Zhu, S.-P., Hu, Z., Li, Y.: Uncertainty-based design and optimization using first order saddle point approximation method for multidisciplinary engineering systems, ASCE-ASME Journal of Risk and Uncertainty in Engineering Systems. Part A: Civil Eng. **6**(3), 04020028 (2020)

16. Meng, D., Xie, T., Wu, P., He, C., Hu, Z., Lv, Z.: An uncertainty-based design optimization strategy with random and interval variables for multidisciplinary engineering systems. Structures **32**, 997–1004 (2021)
17. Meng, D., Hu, Z., Wu, Zhu, S.-P., Correia, J.A., De Jesus, A.M.: Reliability-based optimisation for offshore structures using saddlepoint approximation. In: Proceedings of the Institution of Civil Engineers-Maritime Engineering, vol. 173, pp. 33–42. Thomas Telford Ltd. (2020)
18. Cheong, K.H., Koh, J.M., Jones, M.C.: Paradoxical survival: examining the parrondo effect across biology. BioEssays **41**(6), 1900027 (2019)
19. Lai, J.W., Cheong, K.H.: Parrondo effect in quantum coin-toss simulations. Phys. Rev. E **101**, 052212 (2020)
20. Liu, P., Zhang, X., Pedrycz, W.: A consensus model for hesitant fuzzy linguistic group decision-making in the framework of dempster-shafer evidence theory. Knowl.-Based Syst. **212**, 106559 (2021)
21. Deng, Y.: Information volume of mass function. Int. J. Comput. Commun. Control **15**(6), 3983 (2020)
22. Song, Y., Zhu, J., Lei, L., Wang, X.: A self-adaptive combination method for temporal evidence based on negotiation strategy. Sci. China Inf. Sci. (2020). https://doi.org/10.1007/s11432-020-3045-5
23. Liu, Z., Liu, Y., Dezert, J., Cuzzolin, F.: Evidence combination based on credal belief redistribution for pattern classification. IEEE Trans. Fuzzy Syst. **28**(4), 618–631 (2020)
24. Xiao, F.: Generalization of Dempster-Shafer theory: a complex mass function. Appl. Intell. **50**(10), 3266–3275 (2019)
25. Xiao, F.: Generalized belief function in complex evidence theory. J. Intell. Fuzzy Syst. **38**(4), 3665–3673 (2020)
26. Xiao, F.: CEQD: a complex mass function to predict interference effects. IEEE Trans. Cybern. (2020). https://doi.org/10.1109/TCYB.2020.3040770
27. Xiao, F.: Complex pignistic transformation-based evidential distance for multisource information fusion of medical diagnosis in the IoT. Sensors **21**(3), 840 (2021)

A Secure Aggregation Routing Protocol with Authentication and Energy-Saving on Data Mining and Big Data

Ying Wang, Bo Liu, and Fengyin Li[✉]

School of Computer Science, Qufu Normal University, Rizhao 276826, China

Abstract. In the era of big data, with the mining of the value of big data, wireless sensor network has been more and more widely used. However, due to the limited and uneven resource distribution of the sensor equipment, the service life of the wireless sensor is seriously affected. Moreover, the problem of privacy leakage in wireless sensor networks is becoming more and more serious. In order to solve the resource-constrained and privacy-leaking problems of nodes, we propose a secure convergent routing protocol with authentication and energy-saving. First, a new cost function calculation method is proposed. Aiming at the resource limitation of sensor nodes, the communication cost calculation function of each node is designed by synthesizing the residual energy of the node, the distance from the sink node and the current link quality, to measure the communication cost of wireless sensor nodes dynamically. The data transmission path is designed by changing the cost function. Secondly, a key agreement protocol with authentication function is designed. In order to solve the problem of privacy leakage in the communication process, a trusted registration node is used to register the node and distribute the authorization information, mutual authentication and session key negotiation are carried out, a key agreement scheme with authentication function is designed for safe and efficient key distribution. Finally, through performance analysis, we verify that our protocol consumes less total energy than the other two related protocols.

Keywords: Big data · Wireless sensor network · Energy saving · Authentication · Key agreement

1 Introduction

With the rapid development of social network and mobile Internet technology, the collection, storage, analysis and release of all kinds of data become convenient and fast. Organizations such as health care, insurance companies, e-commerce companies, social networking sites, and telecom operators publish industry data for research, and a variety of big data analytics companies, big data analytics competitions, and more. In the era of big data, businesses are hard at work

© Springer Nature Singapore Pte Ltd. 2021
Y. Tan et al. (Eds.): DMBD 2021, CCIS 1453, pp. 192–204, 2021.
https://doi.org/10.1007/978-981-16-7476-1_18

mining data to analyze usage patterns and improve product features or user experience [3].

With the value mining of big data, the information related to individuals and enterprises will increase significantly. Data transmission and data privacy protection in big data and data mining have also aroused widespread concern. In big data environments, data is collected by sensors, which collect data to make more informed decisions that help organizations develop in an internet environment. Wireless technology enables sensors to be connected to each other to form a "Large network" [9]. Sensors with sensing data, communication and processing capabilities are connected to each other, which is a typical wireless sensor network. Wireless sensor networks are used in many fields, such as agriculture to monitor environmental temperature and humidity, traffic network, traffic flow and so on. They can also be deployed in many places where people can not reach, such as deserts, so there's a military component [6].

However, wireless sensor networks also have some limitations [10], mainly facing the following two challenges:

(1) Sensor equipment has the characteristics of micro-size and therefore also has the nature of limited resources. Energy consumption is a very outstanding problem in WSN communication.
(2) In some cases in a real-time data environment, external adversaries can directly access real-time data from sensor nodes.

In recent years, many people have made some research contributions on how to save energy consumption of sensor nodes. In 2019, Arpita Mallick et al. proposed a multi-hop routing protocol that transfers data from body area sensor networks (BAN) to cellular devices or display coordinators. In the hospital scenario, there can be multiple display coordinators near one of Ban's coordinators. In addition, in a hospital, multiple patients may have wearable or implantable sensors and form multiple BAN configurations nearby [4]. In 2020, Muhammad Ilyas et al. proposed a three-tier cluster-based routing protocol for wireless sensor networks. This protocol utilizes three-layer clustering mechanism, which is a center-based clustering protocol [1]. Researchers have also done some technical research on the issue of data privacy breach. In 2020, Naswan S et al. proposed an anonymous access authentication scheme for wireless sensor networks in large data environments, using a set of lightweight symmetric encryption and hash function to prevent existing known attacks, perfect forward secrecy provides two way authentication and complete anonymity [7]. 2021, Inam ul haqa et al. have proposed an efficient multi server architecture based on Hasche's authenticated key protocol scheme, which uses a simple hash operation to achieve key sharing and identity authentication [2].

All of the above studies give rise to the enlightenment of our scheme. In order to solve the problem of unbalanced energy consumption of sensor nodes, some nodes have to bear the problem of high energy consumption resources, and the problem of privacy leakage in data transmission between sensor nodes, we propose a secure converged routing protocol with authentication and energy-saving functions. The main contributions of this article are as follows.

(1) A new calculation method of cost function is proposed.
    The cost function proposed in this paper can be used to effectively classify the cost consumption level of a sink node when transmitting data by selecting a node from all sensor nodes as a cluster "Leader" node, a reasonable path is planned for the realization of energy-saving converging routing protocol based on cost function.
(2) A new key agreement scheme with authentication function is proposed.
    The proposed key agreement protocol is used for efficient key distribution in communication between two parties, which realizes data privacy of communication between nodes and ensures data security.
(3) The performance of the proposed protocol and other existing schemes is analyzed.
    We compare the performance of the proposed scheme with the existing schemes, and clearly verify the efficiency of our proposed protocol in terms of total energy consumption.

This article is organized as follows. In Sect. 2, we introduce the basics used in this article. In Sect. 3, a new multi-layer energy-saving convergent routing protocol with authentication key agreement is proposed. In Sect. 4 provides a performance comparison of the proposed scheme with existing related schemes. In Sect. 5 summarizes the full text.

2   Preliminary

2.1   WSN

The network environment itself has the openness, if can not carry on the effective supervision to the network environment, the entire Internet system will certainly be disorderly [5]. Based on this, it is necessary to implement constraint management for the load network environment. Wireless Sensor Networks (WSN) is a kind of distributed Sensor Networks, the end of which is the Sensor that can sense and examine the outside world. Sensors in WSN communicate wirelessly, so network settings are flexible, device locations can be changed at any time, and wired or wireless connections can be made with the Internet. A multi-hop self-organizing network formed by wireless communication. The wireless sensor network (WSN) not only connects the wireless network with the wired network, but also senses and checks the state of the external sensors through flexible network settings, and then makes device changes, it's also a great way to avoid the dangers of the internet. Wireless network sensors can also collect and transfer data in the internet environment, not only reduce the cost of network transmission, but also simplify the form of network deployment. In the process of data transmission, the dynamic collection and detection of network resource information can be realized through the operation of internal sensor nodes, and the online monitoring of information transmission can be realized [11].

2.2   Cluster Structure in WSN

In wireless sensor networks, cluster-based routing protocol is called hierarchical routing protocol. The idea of hierarchy-based or cluster-based routing protocol is to divide the network into many different clusters based on certain attributes, including cluster head (CLH) and cluster member node (CM), cluster heads can communicate directly with Sink nodes or form a higher-level network, in which each cluster head node is regarded as a normal node and then clustered until the last node is left in the network. The cluster head node is responsible for the management of the cluster members and acts as the leader or coordinator. The collection and processing of the data of the cluster members are also carried out at the cluster head node. Meanwhile, the cluster head is responsible for the data transmission between clusters, data is taken from a cluster member node (CM), aggregated and forwarded to a base station (BS) or Sink node. The choice of CLH is based on important parameters such as residual energy and the distance to the sink node (SN). The CLH role rotates according to the level of the node. The level of a node is determined by the increase or decrease of important parameters. Now the most popular algorithm is to improve the energy balance of the network, the energy consumption of the network is evenly distributed to all nodes, the network is divided into periodic rounds. The advantage of hierarchical routing protocol is that it is scalable, can adapt to the dynamic changes of the network, and is suitable for large-scale networks [8]. Cluster-based WSN is divided into two-tier and three-tier hierarchies as shown in Fig. 1.

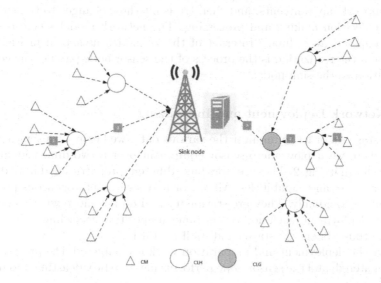

Fig. 1. Cluster-based WSN two-level structure and three-level structure.

3   Proposed Protocol

In order to solve the problems of high power consumption, network lifetime, low network throughput and privacy leakage in secret data transmission, we propose an energy-saving routing protocol with authentication and agreement key. This paper is organized as follows, in Sect. 3.1 gives the network model of the scheme, our scheme is implemented on the ordinary Internet of Things Network, in Sect. 3.2 we carry out the network deployment of the sensor nodes, and collected deployment information for the sink node. In Sect. 3.3, we first design a cost function to calculate a cost for each sensor node. The sensor node is chosen for its high energy and good link quality. The node near the sensor node becomes CLH (Cluster Head), CLG (Cluster Gateway) node. In Sect. 3.4, after selecting CLH node and CLG node, we use K-means clustering algorithm to divide sensor nodes near CLH node into the same cluster, and these cluster member nodes send information to CLH node, CLH then sends the aggregated information to the CLG node, and finally the CLG node sends the information to the Sink node to construct a three-layer cluster structure in Sect. 3.5. In Sect. 3.6, we design a communication scheme based on authenticated key agreement for two-node secret data transmission. Finally, a secure aggregation routing protocol with authentication and energy-saving functions is implemented.

3.1   Network Model

The sensor nodes monitor the physical and chemical reaction from various intelligent network environments, and then transmit these changes to the sink node (SN) for decision making and processing. The network model scenario studied in this paper is an ordinary Internet of things model, as shown in Fig. 2. The function of the realization is the process of the sensor node passing the collected information to the sink node.

3.2   Network Deployment and Initializing

At this stage, in order to monitor the various data, we begin with sensor deployment, where we deploy micro-sensor equipment over a two-dimensional target area, as shown in Fig. 2. These sensors have different properties and have different capacities, sizes and capabilities. All sensor nodes with heterogeneous properties are deployed randomly. They are stationary and do not move when deployed.

After deployment, each node determines its position according to its latitude and longitude, its energy status and its link status.

After the deployment and preparation work is completed, the pre-processing stage is entered, and the sensor node performs message broadcasting and message reply.

After the sensor nodes are deployed, the Sink node (SN) communicates with all the deployed nodes via a broadcast initiated greeting packet ($Init\_Hello_{Pkt}$). $Init\_Hello_{Pkt}$ contains information about the SN node, such as SN_{id} and its own location.

Fig. 2. General structure model of wireless sensor networks.

After receiving $Init\_Hello_{Pkt}$ from SN, each node calculates the distance to SN node dtance and packages its remaining energy R.E, link quality LQ into the $Reply_{pkt}$ for response. $Reply_{pkt}$ contains important information about all deployed nodes, such as N_{id}, residual energy R.E, link mass LQ, distance to SN node d_{tance}.

After receiving the $Reply_{pkt}$ from the node, SN responds with the confirmed packet (Ack_{Pkt}), which ensures that the message has been successfully received. Ack_{Pkt} contains the information of SN node, such as SN_{id} and its own location.

Therefore, at this stage, SN obtains important information of the deployed node (N_{id}, residual energy R.E, link quality LQ, distance to SN node d_{tance}).

3.3   Cost Function

After SN obtains the information, the cost function (C.F) for each deployed node is calculated based on the information obtained from the deployed node. Based on the results of C.F, the decisions of CLH, CLG and CN are made. Sink nodes identify CLH, CLG nodes, broadcast to all nodes, send a notification packet, notify all nodes which nodes are selected, and public at the Sink node. In addition, SN deploys a CN (Check-up Node) to monitor CLH and CLG. If the number of forwards for CLH and CLG does not exceed a fixed number of packets, CN broadcasts messages in the cluster to stop responding to them and blacklists the relevant CLH or CLG. CN node should also monitor the energy consumption of CLH and CLG nodes in real time. If these two nodes run out of energy, SN node will be notified to update CLH and CLG nodes dynamically to ensure the effective implementation of the protocol. CN is selected from CLH by Sink nodes based on the cost function C.F chooses CN according to the game theory, compares two games in the selected CLH node, chooses the low cost as the CN node.

In addition, due to CLH, CLG nodes need to consume a lot of energy, in order to extend the service time of the nodes, we provide an energy collection module for CLH, CLG nodes, that allows them to harvest energy from their surroundings or from radio signals around them.

The cost function (C.F) is calculated in three parts, including the distance from each node to Sink node, the residual or total energy of each node, and the quality of each node in the overall network node (link quality).

3.4   Cluster Construction Based on Cost Function

According to the above four sections, Sink node calculates the cost function of all nodes based on the results of the preprocessing section. According to the cost function, CLH and CLG nodes are selected. Next we build the cluster. The Clustering Method is used to cluster all the data elements, and then the three-layer cluster routing protocol is formed, which can reduce the data transmission cost of large-scale WSN.

In order to classify the network into hierarchical clusters, we adopt the idea of K-means clustering algorithm, and take the distance as the standard of similarity measurement between data objects, that is, the smaller the distance between data objects, the higher the similarity between them, the more likely they are in the same cluster.

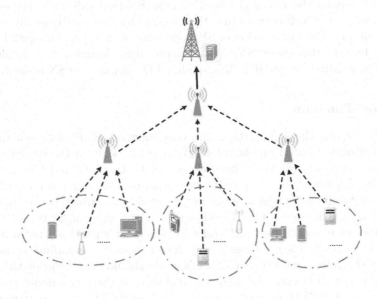

Fig. 3. Three-tier cluster structures.

3.5   Energy-Saving Aggregation Routing Protocol Based on Cost Function

Finally, our system model is constructed as shown in Fig. 3.

In this paper, we construct a three-layer cluster routing protocol. The sensor node wants to transmit data to the Sink node. The sensing data is forwarded by CM (Cluster Member) to CLH, which forwards it to CLG, and then the aggregated data is further forwarded to SN.

3.6   Anonymous Communication Scheme Based on Energy-Saving Routing Protocol

After clustering, the idea of on-demand routing discovery can be used when CM nodes want to send secret information to CLH nodes. When the CM node needs to send packets to the CLH node, it sends a routing request message RREQ to all its neighbors. When an intermediate node receives it, the intermediate node adds its address to the packet, sends it to its neighbor, and so on. When a request reaches the destination CLH node, it generates the route reply message RREP. The reply is unicast along the reverse path already built by the intermediate node to the CM source node. The CM node thus gets a multi-hop link to the CLH node, see Fig. 4.

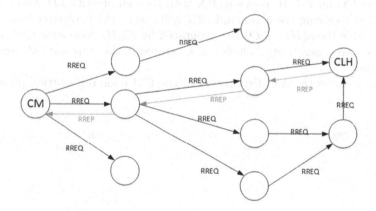

Fig. 4. The communication process between the CM node and the CLH node.

But when the two communicate, because the Internet is a public channel, malicious users can intercept ongoing communications and wreak havoc. In order to reduce such activities and ensure the security of the online communication, we design an identity authentication key protocol scheme to protect the privacy and security of the node communication. With this mechanism, two communication entities validate each other and then build a session key to protect future communication between them.

Registration of CLH. During this process, CLH_j node is registered in RN node. CLH_j sends a registration request and RN feeds back to CLH_j two keys, h(Q) and $h(HID_j||Q)$.

Figure 5 shows the detailed process of the CLH node registration phase.

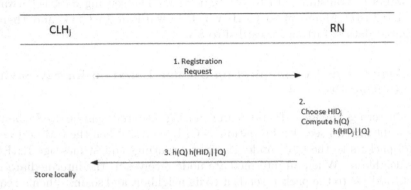

Fig. 5. Registration of CLH.

Registration of CM. This process is the CM_i node registration phase, in the Secure Channel, CM_i provides RN with its own identity ID_i and password PW_i. After receiving the command, RN will merge the two parts into a smart chip, and hide the $h(HID_j||Q)$ key generated by CLH_j node with CM_i identity information to generate A_{ij}, which will be stored in the chip and fed back to the CM_i node.

Figure 6 shows the detailed process of the CM node registration phase.

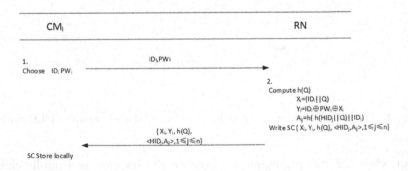

Fig. 6. Registration of CM.

Validation of CM. The process is to verify the validity of CM_i node with password for smart chip. Before the CM_i request begins communication, the smart chip first validates the CM_i node by providing its own $< ID_i^*, PW_i^* >$. The smart chip computes $X_i^* = Y_i \oplus ID_i^* \oplus PW_i^*$ and verifies $X_i^* \overset{?}{=} X_i$. If the condition is met, the CM_i node password and identity information is consistent with the registered node in RN, the node is valid and verified. If the condition is not met, the smart card rejects the CM_i node.

Key Agreement with Authentication. If the smart chip is verified, the smart chip provides the CM_i node with the A_{ij}, which contains the $h(HID_j||Q)$ key. The CM_i finds the CLH_j it wants to communicate with and encrypts a random number α_i. This ensures that only CLH_j can decipher the random number. At the same time, the identity information is sent to CLH_j together with the verification message V_1 generated by the random number. After receiving the message, CLH_j decrypts the random number α_i with its own key and verifies the correctness of the message V_1. If the verification is successful, a random number α_j is generated for the later session key SK calculation. Similarly, a validation message, V_2, will be passed to CM_i. CM_i carries out the identification of CLH_j and the calculation of session key SK, and finally the confirmation of SK.

Figure 7 shows the detailed process of authentication and key agreement between CM and CLH nodes.

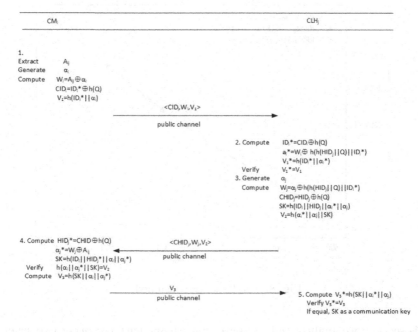

Fig. 7. Key agreement with authentication function.

4   Security Analysis

We assume that we have compromised a pair of cluster head node CLH_j^C and cluster member node CM_i^C. Using these leaked confidential information nodes, the enemy can not impersonate any other node, nor can it compute the session key of any other participant, as follows: Adversary A can get $\{h(Q), h(HID_j\|Q)\}^c$ from cluster head, and adversary A can get HID_j from cluster member.

Can not impersonate any legitimate CLH node: In all nodes, $h(Q)$ is known, but $h(HID_j\|Q)$ is different. To know $h(HID_j\|Q)$, A either knows Q from RS (which is impossible), or it can reverse-deduce it from $A_{ij}^c = h(h(HID_j\|Q)\|ID_i^c)$ (which is also impossible).

Can not impersonate any legitimate CM node: To impersonate a member of the legal cluster, adversary A needs to calculate the A_{ij}. Suppose the adversary obtains $< CID_i, W_i, V_1 >$ from the landing phase, relevant to the calculation of A_{ij}, of these four parameters only W_i, $W_i = A_{ij} \oplus \alpha_i$. Because of the unavailability of α_i, A_{ij} is not computable.

Can not calculate any session key: The session key is calculated as $SK = h(ID_i\|HID_j\|\alpha_i\|\alpha_j)$. A_{ij} is not obtainable, so α_i and α_j are not obtainable.

5   Performance Analysis

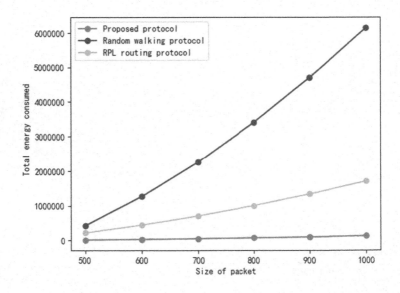

Fig. 8. Total energy consumed.

In this section, we analyze and compare this scheme with the other two schemes. We set all the member nodes at the bottom to send packets to the SN node, the completion of the transmission is considered as the end of a round of data transmission. We calculate the total energy consumption of each node from the total energy consumption, according to the established routing protocol, calculate the total energy consumption of all member nodes to SN node.

Figure 8 shows the energy consumption of a round trip from all the member nodes we calculated to the sink node. As can be seen from Fig. 8, the difference in total energy consumption between protocols increases as the number of packets to be transmitted increases after the information is transmitted. When the packet reaches 1000 bits, as can be seen from the graph, the total energy of RPL is 200 times that of our proposed protocol, and the total energy consumption of RPL is 66 times that of our proposed protocol. To sum up, in terms of total energy consumption, our proposed protocol is lower than other protocols.

6   Conclusion

With the advent of the big data era, it is conceivable that the collection and analysis of data is very important. As a data collection device, wireless sensor network has greatly promoted the development of big data and data mining technology. This paper focuses on a secure convergent routing protocol with authentication and energy-saving functions. This paper proposes a solution to the problems of excessive energy consumption, unbalanced resource consumption and data privacy leakage in wireless sensor networks. The designed cost function selects a suitable "Leader" node of the data transmission cluster by calculating the communication loss, helps to plan the data transmission path, and solves the problem that some nodes consume too much energy due to the uneven resource consumption. The key agreement protocol is designed by using one-way Hasche function and XOR operation to hide and restore the parameters, using these parameters to calculate the shared key. The privacy protection of the secret data is realized, and the problem that the secret data is easy to be divulged when two nodes communicate is solved. The key agreement protocol with authentication function is designed. We authenticate first and then negotiate to prevent the third party from maliciously impersonating. Through the implementation of the above three parts, we construct a secure converging routing protocol with authentication and energy-saving functions. At last, through the performance analysis, the total energy consumption of the proposed protocol is compared with that of the two related protocols. Our work extends the network lifetime to some extent, increases the number of active nodes, reduces energy consumption, and increases the privacy of secret data transmission to some extent.

References

1. Ilyas, M., Ullah, Z., Khan, F.A., Chaudary, M.H., Durrani, H.: Trust-based energy-efficient routing protocol for internet of things-based sensor networks. Int. J. Distrib. Sens. Netw. **16**(10), 155014772096435 (2020)

2. Iuh, A., Jian, W.A., Yz, A., Sm, B.: An efficient hash-based authenticated key agreement scheme for multi-server architecture resilient to key compromise impersonation. Digital Commun. Networks **7**(1), 140–150 (2021)
3. Lekhwar, S., Yadav, S., Singh, A.: Big data analytics in retail (2019)
4. Mallick, A., Saha, A., Chowdhury, C., Chattopadhyay, S.: Energy efficient routing protocol for ambient assisted living environment. Wireless Personal Commun. **109**(3), 1333–1355 (2019)
5. Mishra, P.K., Verma, S.K.: Ffmcp: feed-forward multi-clustering protocol using fuzzy logic for wireless sensor networks (wsns). Energies **14**(10), 2866 (2021)
6. Moon, S.H., Park, S., Han, S.J.: Energy efficient data collection in sink-centric wireless sensor networks: a cluster-ring approach. Comput. Commun. **101**, 12–25 (2016)
7. Nashwan, S.: Aaa-wsn: anonymous access authentication scheme for wireless sensor networks in big data environment - sciencedirect. Egyptian Informatics Journal (2020)
8. Ullah, M.F., Imtiaz, J., Maqbool, K.: Enhanced three layer hybrid clustering mechanism for energy efficient routing in IoT. Sensors **19**(4) (2019)
9. Ullah, Z., Ahmed, I., Ali, T., Ahmad, N., Niaz, F., Cao, Y.: Robust and efficient energy harvested-aware routing protocol with clustering approach in body area networks. IEEE Access, p. 1 (2019)
10. Wei, L., Yuwang, Y.: Energy-efficient routing protocol in mobile ad hoc networks. Comput. Eng. Design **039**(010), 3013–3017 (2018)
11. Wenkang Zhou, X.W.: WSN routing algorithm based on AHP and FIS. In: Computer Engineering, pp. 1–11 (2020)

Enity Relation Extraction of Industrial Robot PHM Based on BiLSTM-CRF and Multi-head Selection

Songhai Lin[1], Hong Xiao[1(✉)], Shaofeng Liu[1], Wenchao Jiang[1,2],
Meng Xiong[2], and Zhongtang He[2]

[1] School of Computer Science and Technology,
Guangdong University of Technology, Guangzhou 510006, China
[2] Cloud Computing Center, Chinese Academy of Sciences, Dongguan 523808,
Guangdong, China

Abstract. This paper extracted the entity relation from unstructured text in the industrial robot prognostics and health management (PHM) data for the construction of a knowledge graph. Traditionally, there is a disadvantage of error propagation in the pipeline method. At the same time, the industrial robot PHM corpus has a relation overlap problem, which reduces the accuracy of relations extraction. To solve this problem, we proposed a joint entity relations extraction model combining BiLSTM-CRF and multi-head selection. In this model, the encoding layer is shared by entity extraction tasks and relations extraction tasks. Moreover, BiLSTM-CRF is introduced for named entity recognition tasks, and the entity recognition information is utilized by the multi-head selection structure to solve the problem of overlapping relations. The results show that the model can effectively extract the entity relations of unstructured text in the robot PHM data, and the overall F1-score for entity relations extraction reaches 87.64. It is an increase of 2.92% and 13.5%, compared with the BiLSTM-ED-CNN model and the pipeline method using the same model.

Keywords: Prognostics and health management · Joint extraction · Named entity recognition · Entity relation extraction

1 Introduction

With the popularization of the industrial robot applications, numerous data of PHM (Prognostics and Health Management) for industrial robots have been accumulated in enterprises, and they are mainly unstructured text. The effective use of these PHM text data is of great significance to the health maintenance of industrial robots and the intelligent management of robots. Information extraction is one of the key technologies for the effective use of PHM data. It can automatically extract the named entities and their relations from massive unstructured text [10], and use them to compose a triplet: "{entity, relation, entity}". The triplet is composed of structured data, which is the basis for constructing a knowledge graph in this field. Information extraction includes the named entity recognition (NER) and the relation extraction (RE). With the

© Springer Nature Singapore Pte Ltd. 2021
Y. Tan et al. (Eds.): DMBD 2021, CCIS 1453, pp. 205–217, 2021.
https://doi.org/10.1007/978-981-16-7476-1_19

development of deep learning and knowledge graph technology, information extraction based on deep learning is popular currently.

At present, there are two kinds of information extraction techniques based on deep learning: the pipeline method and the joint extraction method [2]. The traditional pipeline method carries out two subtasks in sequence, named entity extraction and relation extraction. However, this method has some flaws: First, the error of entity extraction will accumulate and affect the performance of the next relational extraction. Second, this segmentation ignores the relation and internal relation between the two subtasks, resulting in the lack of interaction. Third, there is no relation between the candidate entities identified in the named entity recognition task and the results, it will bring redundant information, increase the error rate and the computational complexity, which is the reason of entity redundancy. The joint extraction method unifies entity extraction and relation extraction, which can make better use of the potential information between the two subtasks, to reduce the impact of error propagation in the pipeline method. Zheng et al. [4] proposed a hybrid neural network model to extract entities and their relations. The model includes a Bi-LSTM-ED for entity extraction and a CNN module for relation classification. Experiments on the dataset ACE05 verify the effectiveness of the method. Miwa et al. [5] annotated the data with BILOU coding scheme, extracted the pair of entity by Bi-LSTM and softmax. Then, the SPTree (shortest path dependency tree) covering the entity pair was found in the current sentence.and the vector representation corresponding to subtree was generated by TreeLSTM. Finally, according to TreeLSTM vector corresponding to root node of subtree, softmax relation classification is carried out. Zheng et al. [7] proposed a new method of data annotation. Firstly, the named entity recognition and relation classification task are converted into a problem of sequence annotation, and then the entity relations triples are directly obtained by the proposed model.

Although many scholars and research institutions have studied the joint extraction of entity relations and achieved some results, the research on the information extraction of knowledge graph in the field of industrial robot or intelligent manufacturing is less and simple. In addition, the problem of relation overlapping appears in PHM unstructured text, one entity overlaps with multiple entities at the same time. This problem will affect the data annotation method of dataset and the selected joint extraction model. How to extract accurate entity relations triples efficiently is a big challenge for information extraction in this field. To solve the above problems, this paper proposed a joint entity relation extraction model based on the fusion of Bi-LSTM-CRF and multi-head selection [1]. The overall F1-score of entity relations extraction of this model reached 87.64. The experimental results showed that the model can extract the entities and relations in the PHM text of industrial robots efficiently and accurately.

2 Semantic Annotation

In the process of fault detection and maintenance of industrial robots, a large amount of text information will be recorded in the enterprise system in unstructured forms such as document corpus. This paper studies the information extraction in the field of industrial robot PHM. Therefore, the data mainly comes from the fault maintenance documents recorded by the enterprise, supplemented with part of the text crawled from the Internet in this field, a total of 1,300 sentences, about 30,000 words. The raw data is cleaned to remove special characters and extra spaces and the preprocessed text corpus is shown in Fig. 1.

电机的电源电压过高，表现为电机的温度过热
电机的电源电压不对称，表现为电机的温度过热
电机的负载功率过大，表现为电机运行温度过高
电机的定子绕组短路，表现为电机运行温度过高
机壳带电、控制线路失控、绕组短路发热，致使电机无法正常运行
离子的磁场分布不均，三相电流不平衡而使电机运行时振动和噪声加剧
电机某一相熔丝断路，缺相运行，表现为不能起动或起动困难，且有嗡嗡声
电源电压太低，使电机起动困难或不能起动
定子绕组或转子绕组断路，致使电机起动困难
定子绕组相间短路或接地，致使电机不能起动
电机风道阻塞，通风不畅，进风量减小，导致电机温度过高
轴承损坏或磨损过大，使电机温度过高
电机风道阻塞，表现为电机温度过高
电机不转且没有声音，原因是绕组有两相或两相以上断路
电机绕组烧毁大多数是由于电机缺相运行造成的
定子绕组接地导致通电后电机熔丝烧断
定子绕组相间短路表现为通电后电机熔丝烧断
绕组存在匝间短路、线圈反接等故障导致电机空载电流不平衡，三相相差大
造成运行中电机振动较大原因是转子不平衡
电机过载或缺相运行导致电机运行转速过低
电机缺相运行，表现为电机运行振动异常
电机过载或缺相运行导致电机运行温度过高
电机定子绕组存在断路、短路或接线错误，造成电机运行振动异常
电机起动频繁导致电机运行温度过高
电机的外壳没有可靠接地致使电机外壳带电
定子绕组连接错误，局部短路或接地，造成电机运行声音不正常

Fig. 1. Preprocessed text corpus

In this paper, the semantic annotation of PHM field information of industrial robots is carried out, and the structured knowledge is extracted from unstructured data. We annotated text corpus by crowdsourcing semi-automatic semantic annotation which includes two kinds.

(1) Entity classes annotation. This part annotates the entities in the PHM document of the industrial robot, including entity type and entity boundary. Specifically, entities are classified into 7 categories: equipment (EQUI), sub-equipment (SEQUI), component (BJ), part (LJ), attribute (ATT), attribute value (VAL), state value (ZTZ). We annotated the entity classes with BIO coding scheme which "B" indicates that the element is the beginning of the entity word, "I" indicates that the element is located in the middle or the end of the entity word, and "O" indicates that the element does not belong to the part of entity word.

(2) Relation type annotation. This part annotates the possible relation between the entities annotated in (1) above. Specifically, the relations types are classified into 4 categories: (Consist_Of), Existence Attribute Relation (Has_Attributes), Appearing Relation (Appear), and Lead to Relation (Lead_To). To eliminate redundancy, we annotated the relation with the method that the last word of an entity word is labeled as the head of this entity word. For example, "电机" (motor) and "轴承" (bearing), instead of linking all the labels of the entity, we link only "机-Containment Relation (Consist_OF)-承" (There is an inclusive relation between

"motor" and "bearing"). Moreover, the "N" label is introduced to annotate words that have no relation with others. In addition, the following two situations may exist in the process of relation annotation.

(1) If the relation between the two entities is clear, it will be marked directly.
(2) If the relation between the two entities does not exist, it will be retained by the annotators and determined through discussion by all annotators.

The preconditions for semantic annotation are as follows.

(1) Annotated object: maintenance document of robot failure recorded by enterprise;
(2) Annotation tool: YEDDA annotation tool [3], which is a Chinese natural language processing annotation tool.
(3) Participants: annotation manager, annotator

The process of the crowdsourcing semantic annotation [9] is divided into the following parts. First, the annotation administrator determines the annotation scheme, divides the data, and distributes it to the annotators. Second, the annotator annotates the data. Third, the results from the annotator are collected and reviewed by the annotation administrator. Finally, the results are exported by YEDDA. An example of entity BIO annotation is shown in Fig. 2(a). The figure shows that the word "电机" (motor) is labeled with "电 B-EQUI" and "机 I-EQUI", which means that the "电机" (motor) is an equipment entity while the beginning word of the entity is "电" and the end word of the entity is "机". An example of relation annotation is shown in Fig. 2(b). For example, there is a "Consist_Of" (containment) relation between "电机" and "轴承", and the link should be "机-Containment Relation (Consist_OF)-承", which is shown row 1 of Fig. 2: "机 I-EQUI ['Consist_of'] [3]", where "[3]" is the position index of "承" in the sentence.

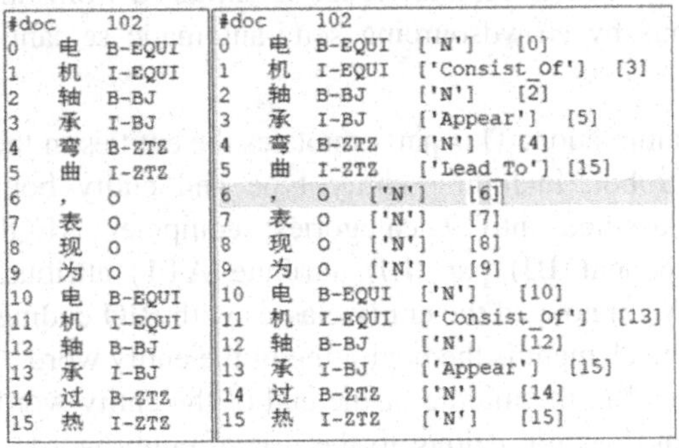

```
#doc    102          #doc    102
0    电   B-EQUI      0    电   B-EQUI   ['N']      [0]
1    机   I-EQUI      1    机   I-EQUI   ['Consist_Of']   [3]
2    轴   B-BJ        2    轴   B-BJ     ['N']      [2]
3    承   I-BJ        3    承   I-BJ     ['Appear']   [5]
4    弯   B-ZTZ       4    弯   B-ZTZ    ['N']      [4]
5    曲   I-ZTZ       5    曲   I-ZTZ    ['Lead_To']   [15]
6    ，   O           6    ，   O        ['N']      [6]
7    表   O           7    表   O        ['N']      [7]
8    现   O           8    现   O        ['N']      [8]
9    为   O           9    为   O        ['N']      [9]
10   电   B-EQUI      10   电   B-EQUI   ['N']      [10]
11   机   I-EQUI      11   机   I-EQUI   ['Consist_Of']   [13]
12   轴   B-BJ        12   轴   B-BJ     ['N']      [12]
13   承   I-BJ        13   承   I-BJ     ['Appear']   [15]
14   过   B-ZTZ       14   过   B-ZTZ    ['N']      [14]
15   热   I-ZTZ       15   热   I-ZTZ    ['N']      [15]
```

(a)   (b)

Fig. 2. Example of entity relation annotation

3 Joint Model

The overview of the joint extraction model of entity relation combining BiLSTM-CRF [6] and multi-head selection is illustrated in Fig. 3. The model mainly consists of four representation layers: a word embedding layer (Embedding Layer), a bidirectional LSTM layer (BiLSTM Layer), a CRF layer [8], and finally a label embeddings layer based on sigmoid. During encoding, word embedding layer encodes the PHM corpus of the industrial robot and represents each word into a word vector. In the intermediate network layer, BiLSTM is introduced to encode the input sequence vector via a bidirectional hidden state information transfer method to extract sentence features. The third layer is the CRF layer, which calculates labels for named entity recognition tasks, and it means that each word from the features will get a label here. The sigmoid layer produces the outputs of the relation extraction task, which determines whether two entities have a relation and what relation they have.

3.1 Word Embedding Layer

Given a sentence $w = w_1, w_2 \cdots w_n$ as a sequence of word, the word embedding layer (based on word2vec [11]) is responsible to convert each sparse word vector with a dimension of 1 (the size of the dictionary) into a low-dimensional dense word vector with a dimension of d.

3.2 Bidirectional LSTM Layer

Long short-term memory (LSTM) is a kind of RNNs. Because of its characteristics, LSTM is very suitable for modeling temporal data, such as text data. **Bidirectional LSTM** is composed of the forward LSTM and backward LSTM, which can better capture bidirectional semantic dependency than LSTM. In this work, we use BiLSTM as the encoder to encode the input features of the embedding layer, which can not only capture the long dependence information but also obtain bidirectional information of the past and future. This way, we can get a combination of hidden state sequence $\{h_1, h_2, \cdots, h_n\}$ by the forward $\{\overrightarrow{h_1}, \overrightarrow{h_2}, \cdots, \overrightarrow{h_n}\}$ and the backward $\{\overleftarrow{h_1}, \overleftarrow{h_2}, \cdots, \overleftarrow{h_n}\}$ output at timestep i, $i \in \{1, 2, \cdots n\}$.

3.3 CRF Layer

CRF layer produces the predicted label of each word by processing the output of the BiLSTM. In this part, we combined the CRF layer and the softmax layer to calculate the outputs $\{h_1, h_2, \cdots, h_n\}$, where h_i is the prediction vector corresponding to the character i label score matrix is defined as.

$$P_i = W h_i + b, \quad i = 1, 2, \cdots n \tag{1}$$

Each P_{ij} of P_i can be regarded as the probability of classifying the i-th word into the j-th label in the sentence, as the dimension of W and b is {Numbers of label type, dimension of word vector} and label types respectively.

In the sequential tagging for named entity recognition task, there exists the problem that the labels of neighboring words affect the labels of specific words (e.g., the beginning of a sentence should be "B-" or "O-" instead of "I-"). For the corpus trained in this paper, "I-EQUI" can only be followed by "B-EQUI", like "B-EQUI, I-EQUI, I-EQUI" is correct, whereas "B-EQUI, I-SEQUI, I-SEQUI" is incorrect. Such restrictions for label prediction will be learned and optimized by the CRF. We supposed the input X and possible label sequence $Y = \{y_1, y_2, \ldots y_n\}$, the CRF score is defined as.

$$s(X, y) = \sum_{i=1}^{n} P_{i,y_i} + \sum_{i=0}^{n} A_{y_i, y_{i-1}} \tag{2}$$

where matrix P is the output of the BiLSTM layer, the matrix A is the matrix of the label transfer score of the CRF layer. A_{ij} represents the probability of the label i transferred to the label j. Then the conditional probability of the correct predicted label given the input X is as follows.

$$p(y|X) = \frac{e^{s(X,y)}}{\sum_{\tilde{y} \in Y} e^{s(X,\tilde{y})}} \tag{3}$$

During training, we take the negative logarithm of $P(y|X)$ as the loss function, and minimize the loss function to continuously adjust the parameters of the model.

$$L_{REL} = -\log(P(y|X)) = -s(X, y) + \log\left(\sum_{\tilde{y} \in Y} e^{s(X,y)}\right) \tag{4}$$

After training, the Viterbi algorithm is utilized for decoding, and this way, the optimal predicted sequence label is obtained.

$$y^* = arg\, max_{\tilde{y} \in Y}\, s(X, \tilde{y}) \tag{5}$$

3.4   Relation Extraction Based on Multi-head Selection

In this subsection, we regard the relation extraction subtask as a multi head selection problem (each word can have multiple relations with others). The input of this layer is $z_i = [h_i, g_i]$ which concatenates the h_i and the label g_i, both of which from the named entity recognition task. Particularly, the label g_i is obtained by learning label embeddings. The problem is summarized as given a sequence $w = \{w_1, w_2, \ldots, w_n\}$ and a relation label set R, for each $w_i, i \in (0, n)$, we calculate the most likely head entity w_j and the most likely relation label r_k. Given a label r_k, the calculation formula of the score between tokens w_i and w_j is as shown in formula.

$$s^{(r)}\left(z_j, z_i, r_k\right) = Vf\left(Uz_j + z_i + b\right) \tag{6}$$

where the superscript (r) represents the relation extraction task, $f(\cdot)$ is the activation function (i.e., $relu$(7), $tanh$(8)). V, W, U, and b are parameter matrixes.

$$Relu(x) = \max(0, x) \tag{7}$$

$$tanh(x) = \frac{e^x - e^{-x}}{e^x + e^{-x}} \tag{8}$$

The score obtained from Eq. (6) is processed by the sigmoid function to obtain the probability (9) of the existence relation between entity token w_j and w_i.

$$P_{r\left(head=w_j, label=r_k | w_i\right)} = \sigma\left(s^{(r)}\left(z_j, z_i, r_k\right)\right) \tag{9}$$

where $\sigma(\cdot)$ is the sigmoid activation function, and the cross-entropy loss L_{REL} is minimized as follow.

$$L_{REL} = \sum_{i=0}^{n} \sum_{m}^{j=0} -\log P_{r\left(head = t_{i,j}, relation = r_{i,j} | w_i\right)} \tag{10}$$

where $t_i \subseteq w, r_i \subseteq R$ are the real head vector and the relation label vector of w_i respectively, and m is the number of relations corresponding to w_i. We set the lowest probability calculated from all true label values as the threshold. During predicting, as long as the score of $P_{r(wi,rk,wj)}$ exceeds the threshold, we are able to produce a pair of relation of $\{w_i, r_k, w_j\}$. Introducing the relation extraction method based on multi-head selection can not only identify whether there is a relation between entities, but also identify multiple pairs of relations between entities, effectively solving the problem of entity relation overlapping.

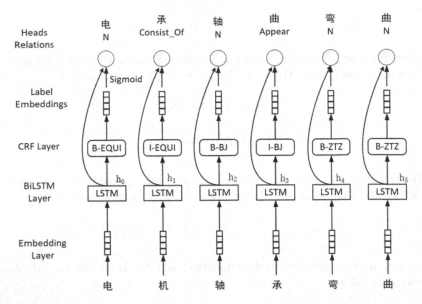

Fig. 3. The joint entity relations extraction model combining BiLSTM-CRF and multi-head selection

4 Results and Discussion

4.1 Experimental Evaluation

The strict evaluation is utilized to report the results of the joint extraction task. Specifically, only if the type and boundaries of the entity are both correct, an entity is considered to be correct and only if both the entity and the relation are correct, a predicted relation is considered correct.

Standard precision(P), and recall(R), overall F1 score is used as the evaluation metrics to report the performance of the model, which can be calculated by the following formulas.

$$P = \frac{The\ nums\ of\ entities(relations)\ extracted\ correctly}{Number\ of\ entities(relations)\ extracted} \tag{11}$$

$$R = \frac{The\ nums\ of\ entities(relations)\ extracted\ correctly}{Number\ of\ entities(relations)\ in\ the\ dataset} \tag{12}$$

$$F1 = \frac{2 * P * R}{P + R} \tag{13}$$

4.2   Experimental Settings

In this paper, we obtain the annotated dataset by carrying out the semantic annotation of PHM information of industrial robots. Then, the dataset is divided at a ratio of 7:1.5:1.5, of which consists of 910 training instances, 195 for validation and 195 for testing.

The model in this article is implemented by using TensorFlow [12]. We train our model with the Adam Optimizer [13], with a learning rate of 0.001, and character (belong to a word) vector dimension of 100. Early stopping is employed on the model, with the threshold of nepoch_on_imrv is set to 30. We also apply dropout to the input embedding layer and hidden layer to reduce over-fitting problem, hidden layer size, character embedding size, and label embedding size impact the model performance observably. Table 1 gives the comparison of different LSTM hidden layer, character embedding and label embedding settings on the performance of the model. It shows that the overall F1 of the model is the best when the LSTM hidden layer size is 128, the character embedding size is 15, and the tag embedding size is 25, indicating that the model has the best ability of entity recognition and relations extraction under this condition. In general, the hyperparameter setting does not have a great impact on the model performance as expected. We conclude that the PHM data set of the industrial robot used in this paper is not rich enough to fully demonstrate the performance differences of the model.

4.3   Experimental Hyperparameter

After a series of testing, it is found that the LSTM hidden layer size, character embedding size, and label embedding size impact the model performance observably. Table 1 gives the comparison of different LSTM hidden layer, character embedding and label embedding settings on the performance of the model. It shows that the overall F1 of the model is the best when the LSTM hidden layer size is 128, the character embedding size is 15, and the tag embedding size is 25, indicating that the model has

Table 1. Comparison of experimental results of the impact of different LSTM hidden layers, character embedding, and label embedding settings on model performance

Hyper-parameter	Parameter setting	Entity recognition			Relation extraction			F1-score
		P	R	F1	P	R	F1	
LSTM size	32	89.98	90.70	90.34	77.24	78.94	78.08	84.21
	64	92.42	92.42	92.42	82.53	81.78	82.15	87.28
	128	92.36	93.00	**92.68**	82.12	83.07	**82.60**	**87.64**
Embeddings size of char	**15**	92.36	93.00	**92.68**	82.12	83.07	**82.60**	**87.64**
	25	90.95	92.31	91.62	79.05	81.91	80.46	86.04
	50	91.55	92.08	91.81	79.95	80.36	80.15	85.95
Embeddings size of label	0	91.43	91.85	91.64	80.94	80.10	80.52	86.08
	15	91.55	92.08	91.81	81.81	80.75	81.27	86.54
	25	92.36	93.00	**92.68**	82.12	83.07	**82.60**	**87.64**

the best ability of entity recognition and relation extraction under this condition. In general, the hyperparameter setting does not have a great impact on the model performance as expected. We conclude that the PHM data set of the industrial robot used in this paper is not rich enough to fully demonstrate the performance differences of the model.

4.4 Baselines

For a comprehensive comparison, we compare our method against the classical pipeline method (e.g., BiLSTM-CRF for NER, BiLSTM-softmax for RE) and joint extraction method, both of which are based on the industrial robot PHM dataset.

(1) BiLSTM-CRF for NER [15] convert characters into low-dimensional dense character vectors by Word2vec. Then it used BiLSTM as an encoder to extract the features and CRF layer to mark labels for each character to identify the entities;

(2) BiLSTM-attention for RE [14] marks the entities in the dataset, and extracts the features of the corresponding vector-matrix in the sentence using BiLSTM. Finally, the attention layer is utilized to merge features and the softmax layer is utilized to classify the entities, and the relations between the entities are extracted by the last layer;

(3) Hybrid network BiLSTM-ED-CNN joint extraction model [4] uses the BiLSTM as the shared encoding layer, and then the model combines the LSTM-decode layer and softmax layer into the entity recognition, combines CNN layer and softmax layer into the relation extraction. Note that this model only predicts two entities in the sentence and their relation in a sentence each time.

The traditional entity relation extraction model uses the pipeline method, which first identifies the entities and then extracts the relation between entities. The overall F1-score of the pipeline method is the product of the value of the entity recognition F1 and the relation extraction F1. In our case, the overall-F1 of the joint extraction model using the pipeline method is 74.14, while the overall-F1 of the joint extraction model used in this paper is 87.64. As can be seen from Table 2, our model performs better than the joint extraction model using the pipeline method. The end-to-end joint model can optimize the shared parameters, improve the performance of the model, reduce the loss caused by error propagation between the two subtasks of the pipeline model, and

Table 2. Experimental results of different entity relation extraction models

Model	F1 of entity recognition	F1 of relation extraction	Comprehensive F1
BiLSTM-CRF entity recognition model	92.27	–	92.27
BiLSTM-softmax relation extraction model	–	80.36	80.36
BiLSTM-ED-CNN	90.87	78.57	84.72
BiLSTM-CRF + multi-head selection	92.68	82.60	87.64

enhance the interaction and connection between the two subtasks. Compared with the joint extraction model based on the hybrid network (e.g., BiLSTM-ED-CNN), the overall F1-score of the model we used (combined BiLSTM-CRF and multi-head selection joint model) has increased by 2.92, indicating that the multi-head selection is suitable for solving the problem of relation overlap.

4.5 Analysis

Table 3 and Table 4 show the experimental results of seven entity recognition and four relation extraction. It can be seen from Table 4 that in the named entity recognition subtask, most of the F1-score of the entity type are more than 90%, and the "EQUI equipment" even reaches 100%, indicating that the model is effective on "equipment" entity recognition. However, the F1-score of the "LJ parts" and the "ZTZ state" is significantly lower than the average, which is also an important factor for reducing the performance of the named entity recognition subtask. We analyzed the corpus data and results of "ZTZ state", and found that there are many compound words in "ZTZ state" words, such as "频繁启动" (frequent start), "啮合不规则" (irregular mesh), "冷却不到位" (poor cooling), etc., which lead to the error of entity boundaries prediction. As can be seen from Table 3, in the relation extraction subtask, the performance of "LEAD_TO cause" is worse than other relation types, which influenced the performance of the relation extraction task. By the analysis of the corpus corresponding to the "LEAD_TO cause" relation and the experimental results, it is found that the entity pairs linked by the "LEAD_TO cause" appeared in each clause of the compound sentence. Illustrating with sentence, "减速机齿轮啮合间隙过大, 表现为减速机运行时产生噪声" (the gear meshing clearance of the reducer is too large, which shows that the reducer produces noise when it is running). Among the sentence, because of the large word distance between "过大" (too large) and "产生噪声" (produces noise), the semantic information can be lost, which leads to unpredictable problems and affects to the prediction of the model relation extraction.

4.6 Example of Experimental Results

We used the entity relation joint extraction model proposed in this paper to experiment on the testing dataset. "[]" represents the entity, and the subscript represents the tag of the entity and the tag of the relation with the entity. For the example sentence "电机线圈组接反, 导致电机接法错误" (The motor coil set is connected reversely, resulting in wrong motor connection), with the extraction result obtained by the model proposed in this paper, "[电机]$_{equipment\ entity,\ consist\_of}$ [线圈组]$_{sub\text{-}equipment}$" means that "[电机]$_{device\ entity}$" (motor) is an equipment entity, "[线圈组]$_{sub\text{-}device\ entity}$" (coil set) is a sub-equipment entity. Besides, there is a relation of "Consist_of" between "电机" (motor) and "线圈组" (coil set).

Table 3. Experimental results of each relation extraction using the joint entity relation extraction model that combines BiLSTM-CRF and multi-head selection

Relation type	P	R	F1
APPEAR	81.50	82.28	81.89
CONSIST_OF	87.05	88.42	87.73
HAS_ATTRIBUTES	89.22	88.35	88.78
LEAD_TO	73.37	75.15	74.25
Overall	82.12	83.07	**82.60**

Table 4. Experimental results of entity recognition using joint entity relation extraction model that combines BiLSTM-CRF and multi-head selection

Entity type	P	R	F1
ATT	91.18	93.94	92.54
BJ	96.45	94.44	95.44
EQUI	100.0	100.0	100.0
LJ	81.40	81.40	81.40
SEQUI	90.63	95.08	92.80
VAL	91.09	90.20	90.64
ZTZ	85.98	87.62	86.79
Overall	92.36	93.00	**92.68**

5   Conclusions

For the entity relation extraction problem of unstructured text in industrial robot fault prediction and health management PHM data, this paper proposed a joint entity relation extraction model. Combined with BiLSTM-CRF and multi-head selection, this model can identify the entities and extract the relations simultaneously. Experimental results showed that the model in this paper is better than that of the contrast model in extracting entity relation. This method has been successfully applied to entity recognition and relation extraction in the unstructured text of industrial robot PHM, which shows the feasibility of this method.

Acknowledgement. This paper is supported by the Key Technology Project of Foshan City in 2019 (1920001001367), National Natural Science and Guangdong Joint Fund Project (U2001201), Guangdong Natural Science Fund Project (2018A030313061, 2021A1515011243), Research and Development Projects of National Key fields (2018YFB1004202), Guangdong Science and Technology Plan Project (2019B010139001) and Guangzhou Science and Technology Plan Project (201902020016).

References

1. Bekoulis, G., Deleu, J., Demeester, T., Develder, C.: Joint entity recognition and relation extraction as a multi-head selection problem. Expert Syst. Appl. **114** (2018)
2. Sun, C.: Joint entity relation extraction with deep learning. East China Normal University (2019). (in Chinese)
3. Jie, Y., Yue, Z., Linwei, L., Xingxuan, L.: YEDDA: a lightweight collaborative text span annotation tool. In: Proceedings of the 56th Annual Meeting of the Association for Computational Linguistics (2018)
4. Suncong, Z., Yuexing, H., Dongyuan, L., et al.: Joint entity and relation extraction based on a hybrid neural network. Neurocomputing **257**(9), 59–66 (2017)
5. Miwa, M., Bansal, M.: End-to-end relation extraction using LSTMs on sequences and tree structures. In: Proceedings of the 54th Annual Meeting of the Association for Computational Linguistics 2016, pp. 1105–1116 (2016)
6. Lample, G., Ballesteros, M., Subramanian, S., Kawakami, K.: ChrisDyer: Neural Architectures for Named Entity Recognition. HLT-NAACL 2016, pp. 260–270 (2016)
7. Suncong, Z., Feng, W., Hongyun, B., et al.: Joint extraction of entities and relations based on a novel tagging scheme. In: Proceedings of the 55th Annual Meeting of the Association for Computational Linguistics 2017, pp. 1227–1236 (2017)
8. Lafferty, J., McCallum, A., Pereira, F.C.N.: Conditional randomfields: probabilistic models for segmenting and labeling sequence data (2001)
9. Yang, Y.J., Xu, B., Hu, J.W., Tong, M.H., Zhang, P., Zheng, L.: Accurate and efficient method for constructing domain knowledge graph. Ruan Jian Xue Bao/J. Softw. **29**(10), 2931–2947 (2018). (in Chinese)
10. Cowie, J., Lehnert, W.: Information extraction. Commun. ACM **39**(1), 80–91 (1996)
11. Mikolov, T., Chen, K., Corrado, G., et al.: Efficient Estimation of Word Representations in Vector Space. Comput. Sci. (2013)
12. Abadi, M., Barham, P., Chen, J., et al.: TensorFlow: a system for large-scale machine learning. In: 12th {USENIX} symposium on operating systems design and implementation ({OSDI} 16) 2016, pp. 265–283 (2016)
13. Kingma, D.P., Ba, J.: Adam: a method for stochastic optimization. arXiv preprint arXiv: 1412.6980 (2014)
14. Zhou, P., Shi, W., Tian, J., et al.: Attention-based bidirectional long short-term memory networks for relation classification. In: Proceedings of the 54th annual meeting of the association for computational linguistics, vol. 2: Short papers 2016, pp. 207–212 (2016)
15. Zhiheng, H., Xu, W., Yu, K.: Bidirectional LSTM-CRF models for sequence tagging. arXiv preprint arXiv:1508.01991 (2015)

An Agricultural Traceability Permissioned Blockchain with Privacy-Aware

Xueqing Sun, Xiao Li, and Fengyin Li[(✉)]

School of Computer Science, Qufu Normal University, Rizhao 276826, China

Abstract. As the blockchain technology maturing, data publishing platform based on blockchain also more and more. However, the privacy of the blockchain becomes one of the key problems. In order to solve the problem of privacy protection, the paper proposed a privacy-awake aggregate signature scheme based on the bilinear mapping. This signature scheme aggregates the signatures of multiple users, shortens the signature verification time and reduces the use of memory space. At the same time, in order to protect the privacy of users, this signature scheme uses pseudonyms to protect the real identity of users. In this paper, the privacy-awake aggregate signature scheme is applied to the permissioned blockchain, and a traceable permissioned blockchain data publishing platform with privacy-awake is designed. The platform can be applied to agricultural product traceability, realizing product traceability and the anonymous release of agricultural product and trading records.

Keywords: Agricultural product traceability · Permissioned blockchain · Digital signature

1 Introduction

Blockchain technology originated in Satoshi Nakamoto's 2008 paper Bitcoin: A Peer-to-Peer Electronic Cash System. This paper elaborates the architecture concept of electronic cash system based on P2P network technology, encryption technology, timestamp technology, blockchain technology, etc., which marks the birth of Bitcoin. However, blockchain technology should not only be applied to Bitcoin. Because storing data in large, centralized data centers often has performance, availability, and scalability issues, as well as high capital or operating expenses. Moreover, centrally stored data is highly vulnerable to network attacks [1]. Blockchain, as a distributed shared ledger and database, in which records are copied and shared among its members, has the characteristics of decentralization, immutability, whole-process traces, traceability, collective maintenance, openness and transparency. These characteristics have brought great advantages to blockchain, making blockchain technology gradually applied in financial services, supply chain management, culture and entertainment, public administration and other fields [2].

In the area of product traceability, we typically use permissioned blockchain rather than the public blockchain. A permissioned blockchain is not the same as a public blockchain. In a public blockchain, such as Bitcoin, all users in the network are allowed to participate without third-party approval. Users in the permissioned blockchain to be

Y. Tan et al. (Eds.): DMBD 2021, CCIS 1453, pp. 218–229, 2021.
https://doi.org/10.1007/978-981-16-7476-1_20

verified by the permissioned blockchain server before they can join the permissioned blockchain network. The permissioned blockchain servers are administrators in the permissioned blockchain who are considered trust worthy by other nodes, which may not trust each other. There are two types of permissioned blockchain, private blockchain and consortium blockchain, a private blockchain consisting of a private blockchain server and many users, and a consortium blockchain consisting of a consortium blockchain server and many private blockchains [3].

Blockchain can provide a strong support for the design of distributed systems, however, in the process of using blockchain, privacy issues cannot be ignored in terms of protecting users' benefit, such as preventing leakage of users' real identity and transaction data. When the permissioned blockchain is applied in a supply chain management (SCM) system, if the relationship between the various suppliers or each transaction information in the permissioned blockchain is not protected, the trade secrets of the suppliers may be disclosed [4]. The competitors can analyze transaction records to estimate the price of products from different suppliers. In this way, the profit of suppliers will be damaged, and the motivation of suppliers to use the blockchain-based traceability platform will be greatly reduced, which will seriously limit the wide application of blockchain in SCM system [5]. Therefore, the study of privacy protection in permissioned blockchain has become one of the key issues to be urgently solved.

Anonymity in a public blockchain as part of the privacy protection in a blockchain means that even if a message is made public on the blockchain, the public key is not related to an individual's true identity. Even with information about a person, that person's identity cannot be identified or inferred. Anonymity requirements in a permissioned blockchain are somewhat different from those in a public blockchain. While ensuring the anonymity of users, the traceability of users should be satisfied between users.

2 Preliminary

2.1 Bilinear Pairings

$\mathbb{G}_1$ and $\mathbb{G}_2$ are two multiplicative cyclic groups of prime order p.g_1 is a generator of $\mathbb{G}_1$, g_2 is a generator of $\mathbb{G}_2$. ψ is a computable isomorphism from $\mathbb{G}_2$ to $\mathbb{G}_1$, $\psi(g_2) = g_1$. A bilinear pairing is defined to be $\delta = (n, \mathbb{G}_1, \mathbb{G}_2, \mathbb{G}_T, e, g_1, g_2)$, where $\mathbb{G}_1 = \langle g_1 \rangle$, $\mathbb{G}_2 = \langle g_2 \rangle$, $\mathbb{G}_T$ are multiplicative groups of order n. Let $e : \mathbb{G}_1 \times \mathbb{G}_2 \to \mathbb{G}_T$ be a map with the following properties:

(1) Bilinear: $\forall u \in \mathbb{G}_1, v \in \mathbb{G}_2$ and $a, b \in \mathbb{Z}_n : e(u^a, v^b) = e(u, v)^{ab}$.
(2) Nondegenerate: $\exists u \in \mathbb{G}_1, v \in \mathbb{G}_2$ $e(u, v) \neq \mathcal{O}$, where $\mathcal{O}$ means the identity of $\mathbb{G}_T$.
(3) Computability: for all $u \in \mathbb{G}_1, v \in \mathbb{G}_2$, there is an efficient algorithm to compute $e(u, v)$ [6].

2.2 Digital Signatures

A digital signature is a fundamental tool in cryptography that has been widely applied to authentication and non-repudiation. Take authentication as an example. A party, Alice, wants to convince all other parties that a message m is published by her. To do so, Alice generates a public/secret key pair (pk,sk) and publishes the ublic key pk to all verifiers. To generate a signature σ_m on m, she digitally signs m with her secret key sk. Upon receiving (m, σ_m), any receiver who already knows pk can verify the signature σ and confirm the origin of the message m [7].

A digital signature scheme consists of the following four algorithms.

System Generate: The system parameter generation algorithm takes as input a security parameter λ. It returns the system parameters SP.

Key Generate: The Key Generate algorithm takes as input the system parameters SP. It returns a public/secret key pair (pk, sk).

Sign:The signing algorithm takes as input a message m,the secret key sk, and the system parameters SP. It returns a signature of m denoted by σ_m.

Verify: The verification algorithm takes as input a message-signature pair (m, σ_m), the public key pk, and the system parameters SP. It returns "accept" if σ_m is a valid signature of m signed with sk; otherwise, it returns "reject".

Correctness. Given any (pk, sk, m, σ_m), if σ_m is a valid signature of m signed with sk, the verification algorithm on (m, σ_m, pk) will return "accept".

Security. Without the secret key sk, it is hard for any probabilistic polynomial-time (PPT) adversary to forge a valid signature σ_m on a new message m that can pass the signature verification.

3   A Privacy-Aware Aggregate Signature Scheme

3.1   Aggregate Signature

System Generate: The System Generate algorithm select a bilinear pairing $\mathbb{PG} = (\mathbb{G}_1, \mathbb{G}_2, \mathbb{G}_T, g_1, g_2, p, e)$ and a hash function $H : \{0,1\}^* \to \mathbb{G}_1$. $\mathbb{G}_1$ and $\mathbb{G}_2$ are two multiplicative cyclic groups of prime order p, g_1 is a generator of $\mathbb{G}_1$, g_2 is a generator of $\mathbb{G}_2$. Let $e\mathbb{G}_1 \times \mathbb{G}_2 \to \mathbb{G}_T$ be a map, p is a prime number. Return the system parameters $SP = (\mathbb{PG}, H)$.

Key Generate: The Key Generate algorithm takes as input the system parameters $SP = (\mathbb{PG}, H)$. Select a random number $\alpha \in \mathbb{Z}_p$. Return public/secret key

$$(pk, sk) = (g_2^\alpha, \alpha).$$

Sign: The Sign algorithm takes as input a message $m \in \{0,1\}^*$, the secret key sk and the system parameters SP. It returns a signature of m, $\sigma_m = H(m)^\alpha$.

Verify: The Verify algorithm takes as input a message-signature pair (m, σ_m), the public key pk, the hash $H(m)$, and the system parameters SP. It returns "accept" if $e(\sigma_m, g_2) = e(H(m), pk)$, σ_m is a valid signature of m signed with sk; otherwise, it returns"reject".

The correctness proof of the Verify algorithm:

$$e(\sigma_m, g_2) = e(H(m)^\alpha, g_2) = e\big(H(m), g_2^\alpha\big) = e(H(m), pk).$$

Aggregate Sign: The Aggregate Sign algorithm takes as input $\sigma_{m_1} \ldots \sigma_{m_n}$. It returns a aggragate signature of $m_1 \ldots m_n$, $\sigma = \prod_{i=1}^{n} \sigma_{m_i}$.

Aggregate Verify: The Aggregate Verify algorithm takes as input a aggregate signature σ, the public key pk_i, the hash $H(m_i)$, and the system parameters SP. It returns "accept" if $e(\sigma, g_2) = \prod_{i=1}^{n} e(H(M_i), pk_i)$, σ is a valid aggregate signature of $m_1 \ldots m_n$; otherwise, it returns "reject".

The correctness proof of the Aggregate Verify algorithm:

$$e(\sigma, g_2) = e\left(\prod_{i=1}^{n} \sigma_{m_i}, g_2\right) = e\left(\prod_{i=1}^{n} H(M_i)^\alpha, g_2\right) = e\left(\prod_{i=1}^{n} H(M_i), g_2^\alpha\right)$$

$$= e\left(\prod_{i=1}^{n} H(M_i), pk_i\right) = \prod_{i=1}^{n} e(H(M_i), pk_i).$$

3.2   Security Proof

Theorem 1. Suppose the hash function H is a random oracle. If the CDH problem is hard, the BLS signature scheme is provably secure in the EU-CMA security model with reduction loss $L = q_H$, where q_H is the number of hash queries to the random oracle.

Proof. Suppose there exists an adversary A who can (t, q_s, ε)-break the signature schemes in the EU-CMA security model. We construct a simulator B to solve the CDH problem. Given as input a problem instance (g_2, g_2^a, g_2^b) over the pairing group $\mathbb{PG} = (\mathbb{G}_1, \mathbb{G}_2, \mathbb{G}_T, g_1, g_2, p, e)$, B controls the random oracle, runs A, and works as follows.

Setup. Let $SP = \mathbb{PG}$ and H be the random oracle controlled by the simulator. B sets the public key as $h = g_2^a$, where the secret key α is equivalent to a. The public key is available from the problem instance.

Query. The adversary makes hash queries in this phase. Before receiving queries from the adversary, B randomly chooses an integer $i^* \in [1, q_H]$, where q_H denotes the number of hash queries to the random oracle. Then, B prepares a hash list to record all queries and responses as follows, where the hash list is empty at the beginning. Let the i-th hash query be m_i. If m_i is already in the hash list, B responds to this query following the hash list. Otherwise, B randomly chooses $w_i \in \mathbb{Z}_p$ and sets $H(m_i)$ as

$$H(m_i) = \begin{cases} g_2^{b+w_i}, & if\, i = i^* \\ g_2^{w_i}, & otherwise \end{cases}.$$

The simulator B responds to this query with, $H(m_i)$ and adds $(i, m_i, w_i, H(m_i))$ to the hash list.

Query. The adversary makes signature queries in this phase. For a signature query on m_i, if m_i is the i^*-th queried message in the hash list, abort. Otherwise, we have $H(m_i) = g_2^{w_i}$. B computes $\sigma_{m_i} = (g_2^a)^{w_i}$. According to the signature definition and simulation, we have $\sigma_{m_i} = H(m_i)^\alpha = (g_2^{w_i})^a = (g_2^a)^{w_i}$. Therefore, σ_{m_i} is a valid signature of m_i. B return the signature σ_{m_i} to A.

Forgery. The adversary returns a forged signature σ_{m^*} on some m^* that has not been queried. If m^* is not the i^*-th queried message in the hash list, abort. Otherwise, we have $H(m^*) = g^{b + w_{i^*}}$.

According to the signature definition and simulation, we have

$$\sigma_{m^*} = H(m^*)^\alpha = (g_2^{b + w_{i^*}})^a = g_2^{ab + aw_{i^*}}.$$

The simulator B computes g^{ab} as the solution to the CDH problem instance.

$$g^{ab} = \frac{\sigma_{m^*}}{(g_2^a)^{w_{i^*}}} = \frac{g_2^{ab + aw_{i^*}}}{(g_2^a)^{w_{i^*}}}$$

Theorem 2. The CDH problem is hard, there no adversary A who can (t, q_s, ε)-break the signature scheme in the EU-CMA security model.

The security of an aggregation signature scheme means that no adversary can forge an aggregation signature on a message of his choice [8].

Setup. An aggregate signature forger is provided with a randomly generated public key PK_1.

Queries. The aggregate signature forger queries the selected message m using the public key PK_1. The simulator responds to this query with σ_m. The aggregate signature forger gets the message signature σ_m, choice $(PK_2, SK_2)...(PK_k, SK_k)$, randomly selected message $m_2...m_k$, queries the selected message $m_i (2 \leq i \leq k)$ using the public key $PK_i (2 \leq i \leq k)$. The simulator responds to $i^* (2 \leq i \leq k)$ query with $\sigma_i (2 \leq i \leq k)$.

Response. Finally, the aggregate signature forger forge the signature σ_1 on message $m_1 (m_1 \neq m)$, and generate aggregate signature $\sigma = \prod_{i=1}^{k} \sigma_i$.

If the aggregate signature σ is a valid signature of the message $m_1...m_k$, the aggregate signature forger wins.

Theorem 2 shows that the aggregate signature forger cannot generate a valid signature σ_1 for the message m_1, the aggregated signature σ generated by the adversary cannot be satisfied $e(\sigma, g_2) = \prod_{i=1}^{n} e(H(m_i), pk_i)$. The aggregation signature cannot be verified by the aggregate verify algorithm. The aggregate signature forger cannot generate a valid aggregate signature.

4   An Agricultural Product Traceability Platform with Privacy-Aware

4.1   The Model and Entity of Protocol

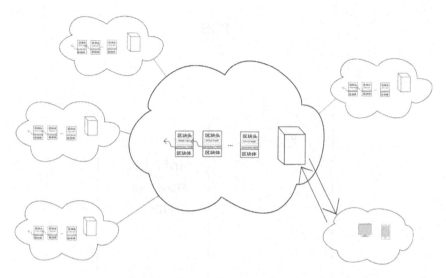

Fig. 1. The model-entity of protocol

The proposed protocol consists of a permissioned blockchain and consumers in the Internet, where the permissioned blockchain consists of a consortium blockchain server and some private blockchains. A private blockchain consists of a private blockchain server and some users (see Fig. 1) [9].

Consortium blockchain server(CBS): CBS as the server of the agricultural product traceability platform, which is responsible for verifying the private blockchain server to be joined and responding to consumers' inquiries about related agricultural products on the Internet.

Private blockchain server(PBS): PBS as a server controlled by an agricultural company, which is responsible for managing the information of the agricultural products produced by the agricultural company, verifying the users who will join the private blockchain managed by the server, packaging the signatures on the consortium blockchain, and responding to the queries of the consortium blockchain server about the relevant agricultural products.

User(u): Employees of agricultural companies, who work in agriculture-related production and responsible for uploading information about agricultural products.

Consumers on the Internet: Consumers of agricultural products can use the Internet to request information about agricultural products from the agricultural products traceability platform.

4.2   Workflow of Protocol

Protocol Creation Phase. In the protocol creation phase, the protocol is initialized, each entity selects and calculates relevant parameters (see Fig. 2).

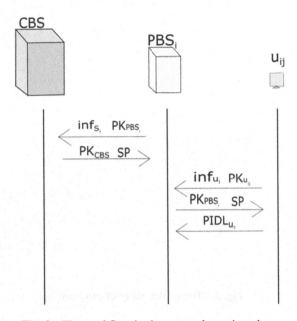

Fig. 2. The workflow in the protocol creation phase.

CBS creates three groups $\mathbb{G}_1, \mathbb{G}_2, \mathbb{G}_T$ and the bilinear map $e : \mathbb{G}_1 \times \mathbb{G}_2 \to \mathbb{G}_T$. $\mathbb{G}_1$ and $\mathbb{G}_2$ are two multiplicative cyclic groups of prime order p. g_1 is a generator of $\mathbb{G}_1$. g_2 is a generator of $\mathbb{G}_2$. CBS choices a hash function $H:\{0, 1\}^* \to \mathbb{G}_1$. CBS randomly choices $r \in Z_p$, computes $g_2^r \in \mathbb{G}_2$. The public key of CBS is $PK_{CBS} = g_2^r \mathrm{mod} p$, the public key of CBS is $PK_{CBS} = r$.

CBS publishes system parameter $SP = (H, g_1, g_2, p, e, PK_{CBS})$.

Each PBS_i choice $x_i \in Z_p$, computes $g_2^{x_i} \in \mathbb{G}_2$. The public key of PBS_i is $PK_{S_i} = g_2^{x_i} \mathrm{mod} p$. The secret key of PBS_i is x_i. PBS_i sends own public key $PK_{S_i} = g_2^{x_i}$ and information inf_{S_i} to CBS. CBS adds PK_{S_i} and inf_{S_i} to the PBS-public key-information-table.

The CBS stores a PBS-public key-information-table, numbering each private blockchain server according to the order in which it receives the private blockchain server's public keys. The i-th PBS, designated by CBS as S_i, is responsible for managing the i-th private blockchain. CBS records the corresponding public key of each PBS PK_{S_i}, and the identity information corresponding to each PBS inf_{Si} in the PBS-public-key-information-table. The CBS stores the PBS-public key-information-table shown in Table 1.

Table 1. The PBS-public key-information-table

PBS'number	Public key	Information
S_1	PK_{S_1}	inf_{S_1}
S_2	PK_{S_2}	inf_{S_2}
...	...	...
S_n	PK_{S_n}	inf_{S_n}

PBS_i, $1 \leq i \leq |PBS|$, where $|PBS|$ is the number of private blockchain servers in the private blockchain at the current point in time, publish their public keys PK_{S_i} and system parameters SP to all users in the private blockchain.

Each user u_{ij} randomly choice $y_{u_{ij}} \in Z_p$ The public key of user u_{ij} is

$$PK_{u_{ij}} = g_2^{y_{u_{ij}}} \bmod p.$$

The secret key of user u_{ij} is $SK_{u_{ij}} = y_{u_{ij}}$. In private bolckchain PB_i, user u_{ij} sends own public key and information $inf_{u_{ij}}$ to PBS_i. PBS_i adds the public key of u_{ij} and information $inf_{u_{ij}}$ to user-public key-information-table.

PBS_i stores a user-public key-information-table, numbering each user according to the order in which it receives the private user's public keys. The j-th user in PB_i, designated by PBS_i as u_{ij}. PBS_i records each user's public key $PK_{u_{ij}}$. Meanwhile, PBS_i records each user's information $inf_{u_{ij}}$. PBS_i stores the user-public key-information-table shown in Table 2.

Table 2. The user-public key-information-table

User's number	Public key	Information
u_{i1}	$PK_{u_{i1}}$	$inf_{u_{i1}}$
u_{i2}	$PK_{u_{i1}}$	$inf_{u_{i1}}$
...	...	...
u_{in}	$PK_{u_{i1}}$	$inf_{u_{i1}}$

PBS_i creates a user-one-time-key-table, records all one-tine-key of user in private blockchain. The one-time key pairs created for u_{ij} are recorded in $PIDL_{u_{ij}}$. PBS_i stores the user-one-time-key-table shown in Table 3.

PBS_i creates 10 one-time-key pairs for each user in PB_i. PBS_i selects 10 different random integers $d_{u_{ij},1} \ldots d_{u_{ij},10}$ as the one-time secret keys $sk_{u_{ij},1} \ldots sk_{u_{ij},10}$ of user u_{ij}. Where, $d_{u_{ij},1} \ldots d_{u_{ij},10}$ are different from the secret key of other users recorded in the user-one-time-key-table. PBS_i computes the one-time public key of user u_{ij}

$$pk_{u_{ij},1} = g_2^{d_{u_{ij},1}} \bmod p, ..., pk_{u_{ij},10} = g_2^{d_{u_{ij},10}} \bmod p.$$

PBS_i sends $PIDL_{u_{ij}}$ to user u_{ij}.

Table 3. The user-one-time-key-table

User's number	One-time key pairs
u_{i1}	$PIDL_{u_{i1}} = \left\{ \left(sk_{u_{i1,1}}, pk_{u_{i1,1}} \right) \cdots \left(sk_{u_{i1,10}}, pk_{u_{i1,10}} \right) \right\}$
u_{i2}	$PIDL_{u_{i2}} = \left\{ \left(sk_{u_{i2,1}}, pk_{u_{i2,1}} \right) \cdots \left(sk_{u_{i2,10}}, pk_{u_{i2,10}} \right) \right\}$
...	...
u_{in}	$PIDL_{u_{in}} = \left\{ \left(sk_{u_{in,1}}, pk_{u_{in,1}} \right) \cdots \left(sk_{u_{in,10}}, pk_{u_{in,10}} \right) \right\}$

Joining Phase. When a new agribusiness company wants to join the agricultural product traceability platform, the company's private blockchain server needs to apply to CBS to join the consortium blockchain.

When a private blockchain server PBS_{new} wants to join the consortium blockchain, it sends an application to CBS to join the consortium blockchain.

The application received by CBS, after confirming that the identity of PBS_{new} is valid, CBS publishes the system parameter SP and the public key PK_{CBS} to PBS_{new}.

PBS_{new} sends its public key $PK_{PBS_{new}}$ and identity information $inf_{PBS_{new}}$ to consortium blockchain server CBS.

CBS numbering PBS_{new} as PBS_{n+1}, and records $PK_{PBS_{new}}$ and $inf_{PBS_{new}}$ in the PBS-public key-information-table.

When a new employee u_{inew} joins an agribusiness company, the user u_{inew} needs to apply to the agribusiness company's private blockchain server PBS_i to join the private blockchain PB_i.

PBS_i receives the application of u_{inew}, after confirming that the identity of u_{inew} is valid, PBS_i publishes the system parameter SP and the public key PK_{S_i} to u_{inew}.

u_{inew} sends the public key $PK_{u_{inew}}$ to PBS_i. PBS_i adds the public key of u_{inew} $pk_{u_{inew}}$ and information of $inf_{u_{inew}}$ as a new tuple to the user-public key-information-table.

PBS_i randomly selects 10 integers $d_{u_{inew,1}} \ldots d_{u_{inew,10}}$ as the one-time secret key of user u_{inew}, where, $d_{u_{inew,1}} \ldots d_{u_{inew,10}}$ are different from the secret key of other users recorded in the user-one-time-key-table, computes $g_2^{d_{u_{inew,1}}} \bmod p \ldots g_2^{d_{u_{inew,10}}} \bmod p$ as the one-time public key of u_{inew}. PBS_i creates $PIDL_{u_{inew}} = \left\{ \left(sk_{u_{inew,1}}, pk_{u_{inew,1}} \right) \cdots \left(sk_{u_{inew,10}}, pk_{u_{inew,10}} \right) \right\}$ for user u_{inew}. PBS_i sends $PIDL_{u_{inew}}$ to user u_{inew}.

PBS_i adds the number of u_{inew} and $PIDL_{u_{inew}}$ as a new tuple to the user-one-time-key-table stored in PBS_i. The user-one-time-key-table shown in Table 4.

Table 4. The new user-one-time-key-table

User's number	One-time key pairs
u_{i1}	$PIDL_{u_{i1}} = \left\{ \left(sk_{u_{i1,1}}, pk_{u_{i1,1}} \right) \cdots \left(sk_{u_{i1,10}}, pk_{u_{i1,10}} \right) \right\}$
u_{i2}	$PIDL_{u_{i2}} = \left\{ \left(sk_{u_{i2,1}}, pk_{u_{i2,1}} \right) \cdots \left(sk_{u_{i2,10}}, pk_{u_{i2,10}} \right) \right\}$
...	...
u_{in}	$PIDL_{u_{in}} = \left\{ \left(sk_{u_{in,1}}, pk_{u_{in,1}} \right) \cdots \left(sk_{u_{in,10}}, pk_{u_{in,10}} \right) \right\}$
u_{inew}	$PIDL_{u_{in}} = \left\{ \left(sk_{u_{inew,1}}, pk_{u_{inew,1}} \right) \cdots \left(sk_{u_{in,10}}, pk_{u_{inew,10}} \right) \right\}$

Sign In Private Blockchain Phase. When a user u_{ij} needs to publish a transaction in private blockchain, the user u_{ij} sends a signature request $\{SG\}$.

User u_{ij} computes $H(M_{u_{ij}})$, randomly choice one of the one-time secret keys $sk_{u_{ij,s}}$ sign for $H(M_{u_{ij}})$, get the signature $\sigma_{u_{ij}} = H(M_{u_{ij}})^{d_{u_{ij,s}}}$, $\sigma_{u_{ij}} \in \mathbb{G}_1$. User u_{ij} sends signature $\sigma_{u_{ij}}$, brief $a_{M_{u_{ij}}}$ and message $M_{u_{ij}}$ to PBS_i.

PBS_i use the bilinear map $e(\sigma_{u_{ij}}, g_2) = e\left(H(M_{u_{ij}}), pk_{u_{ij,s}} \right)$ to verify user signature, where $pk_{u_{ij,s}}$ is one of the one-time public key of u_{ij} recorded in $PIDL_{u_{inew}}$.

After successful verification, PBS_i records signature $\sigma_{u_{ij}}$, brief $a_{u_{ij}}$ and message $M_{u_{ij}}$ as transaction $\{tx_{u_{ij}}\}$ in transaction list. After PBS_i received k transactions ($k \in 2^q, q \in Z_p$, q depended on the size of the block), hash each transaction, store the hash value in the leaf node, calculate the root hash value layer by layer, and finally generate a complete Merkle tree.

PBS_i records Merkle tree in block body, connects block header and block body, generates a new block, broadcasts the block to private blockchain CB_i.

Sign In Consortium Blockchain. PBS_i creats aggregate subset of users U'_i, aggregates k signatures, generate aggregate signature σ_{PBS_i}.

$$\sigma_{PBS_i} = \prod_{j=1}^{k} \sigma_{u_{ij}} \left(u_{ij} \in U'_i \right).$$

PBS_i send the aggregate signature σ_{PBS_i}, message $M_{u_{i1}} \ldots M_{u_{ik}}$, brief $a_{u_{i1}} \ldots a_{u_{ik}}$ and the one-time public key of user $pk_{u_{i1,s}} \ldots pk_{u_{ik,s}}$ to CBS.

CBS use bilinear map e to verify aggregate signature.

$$(\sigma_{PBS_i}, g_2) = \prod_{j=1}^{k} e(H(M_{u_{ij}}), g_2^{d_{u_{ik,s}}}), \text{ where } g_2^{d_{u_{ij,s}}} \text{ is the pseudonym of user } u_{ij}$$

After successful verification, CBS records signature σ_{PBS_i}, brief $a_{u_{i1}} || \ldots || a_{u_{ij}}$ and message $M_{u_{ij}} || \ldots || M_{u_{ik}}$ as a transaction $\{tx_{PBS_i}\}$ in transaction list. After CBS received k transactions($k \in 2^q, q \in Z_p$, q depended on the size of the block), hash each transaction, store the hash value in the leaf node, calculate the root hash value layer by layer, and finally generate a complete Merkle tree.

CBS records Merkle tree in block body, connects block header and block body, generates a new block, broadcasts the block to consortium blockchain.

User Tracking Stage. In the user tracking stage, consumers in the Internet want to inquire about the information of agricultural products, including the production company, production date and other relevant production, logistics and sales information of agricultural products. Consumers submit the brief of the agricultural products to be searched to the consortium blockchain server. The consortium blockchain server searches the information related to the brief in consortium blockchain, finds the corresponding production company according to the signature in the transaction list, sends the brief to the corresponding PBS, and obtains the identity information of the production personnel. The specific information of the production company, the information of the production personnel and the relevant information of the agricultural products will be sent to the consumers in the Internet.

Consumers in the Internet log on to relevant websites or apps, scan the QR code or enter the serial number, and submit the serial number, where the serial number is brief a_{M_F}, of the agricultural products to be querying to CBS.

CBS received brief a_{M_F}, based on the brief a_{M_F} finding the messages in the transaction list. (There may be more than one message, one brief a_{M_F} can correspond to multiple messages).

CBS verifies the signature σ_F, searches the private blockchain server PBS_F that signed the message, records the PBS's identity information inf_{PBS_F}, sends {FTP} and the brief a_{M_F} to PBS_F.

After receiving the query application {FTP} and the brief a_{M_F}, PBS_F searches the relevant transaction {tx_F} in the transaction list of the private blockchain, finds the user u_F signed a_F, and finds the user u_F with the pseudonym in the user-one-time-key-table. PBS_F returns user u_F related information inf_{u_F} to CBS.

CBS connects PBS identity information inf_{PBS_F}, user identity information inf_{u_F}, messages M_F and returns them to consumers on the Internet.

Consumers get the relevant production logistics sales information of the agricultural products to be inquired.

Analysis. Aggregate Signing Time. In a single signature, one hash operation, one modular power multiplication are implemented. Let σ be an aggregate signature of the signatures $\sigma_1, ..., \sigma_k$. The time to generate the aggregate signature σ is linear in k. And k-1 multiplications with aggregation is implemented [10].

Aggregate Verification Time. In a single signature, one bilinear map operation is implemented. Let σ be an aggregate signature of the signatures $\sigma_1, ..., \sigma_k$. In the aggregate signature verification, k bilinear map operations and k-1 multiplications are implemented. The time to verify the aggregate signature σ is linear in k [11].

Signature Space. Let σ be an aggregate signature of the signatures $\sigma_1, ..., \sigma_k$. The space of the signature will be 1/k of the normal k signatures [12].

5   Conclusions

In this paper, we propose a privacy-aware aggregate signature scheme, and then, according to the privacy-aware aggregate signature scheme, we propose a privacy-aware anonymous protocol on the permissioned blockchain, which meets the user's anonymity requirements and provides the user's tracking function. We use pseudonym mechanism to guarantee the anonymity of the agreement anonymity requirement. In the pseudonym mechanism, a user has more than one pseudonym, users use pseudonyms to release information. The pseudonym mechanism hide the identity of the users requirements. However, for a controversial transaction, we have provided the user tracking function, can be traced to the controversial transaction is released by which users.

References

1. Chao, Y., Mi-xue, X., Xue-ming, S.: Research on a New Signature Scheme on Blockchain. Security and Communication Networks (2017)
2. Fuchun, G., Willy, S., Yi, M.: Introduction to Security Reduction. Springer, Switzerland (2012)
3. Boneh, D., Gentry, C., Lynn, B., Shacham, H.: Aggregate and verifiably encrypted signatures from bilinear maps. In: Biham, E. (ed.) EUROCRYPT 2003. LNCS, vol. 2656, pp. 416–432. Springer, Heidelberg (2003). https://doi.org/10.1007/3-540-39200-9_26
4. Mingxiao, D., Qijun, C., Jieying, C., Xiaofeng,M.: An Optimized Consortium Blockchain for Medical Information Sharing. IEEE Transactions on Engineering Management, (2020).
5. Feng, Q., He, D., Zeadally, S., et al.: A survey on privacy protection in blockchain system[J]. J. Netw. Comput. Appl. **126**, 45–58 (2019)
6. Wang, R., He J., Liu, C., et al. A privacy-aware pki system based on permissioned blockchains. In: IEEE 9th International Conference on Software Engineering and Service Science (ICSESS), vol. 2018, pp. 928–931. IEEE (2018)
7. Lin, C., He, D., Huang, X., et al.: PPChain: A privacy-preserving permissioned blockchain architecture for cryptocurrency and other regulated applications. IEEE Syst. J. **15**, 4367–4378 (2020)
8. Dubovitskaya, A., Xu, Z., Ryu, S., et al.: Secure and trustable electronic medical records sharing using blockchain[C]AMIA annual symposium proceedings. American Medical Informatics Association **2017**, 650 (2017)
9. Zhu, X., Su. Y., Gao, M., et al.: Privacy-preserving friendship establishment based on blind signature and bloom filter in mobile social networks. In: IEEE/CIC International Conference on Communications in China (ICCC), vol. 2015, pp. 1–6. IEEE (2015)
10. AitzhanN, Z., Svetinovic, D.: Security and privacy in decentralized energy trading through multi-signatures, blockchain and anonymous messaging streams. IEEE Trans. Dependable Secure Comput. **15**(5), 840–852 (2016)
11. Zhang, A., Lin, X.: Towards secure and privacy-preserving data sharing in e-health systems via consortium blockchain. J. Med. Syst. **42**(8), 1–18 (2018)
12. Ezure, T., Inamura, M.: Proposal and performance evaluation of an order-specified aggregate authority-transfer signature. In: Mori, P., Furnell, S., Camp, O. (eds.) Information Systems Security and Privacy, ICISSP 2019, Communications in Computer and Information Science, vol. 1221, pp. 121–136. Springer, Cham.(2020). https://doi.org/10.1007/978-3-030-49443-8_6

Trust Evaluation Mechanism of Service Nodes Based on Blockchain

Wen Feng[1,2], Jieren Cheng[1,2(✉)], Yuming Yuan[3(✉)], Xinbin Xu[1,2],
Yuqing Kou[1,2], Yuanshen Li[1,2], and Xiulai Li[1,2,4]

[1] Hainan Province Blockchain Technology Engineering Research Center,
Hainan University, Haikou 570228, China
[2] School of Computer Science and Technology,
Hainan University, Haikou 570228, China
[3] Hainan Huochain Tech Company Limited, Haikou 570100, China
yuanyuming@huochain.com.cn
[4] Hainan Hairui Zhong Chuang Technol Co. Ltd,
Haikou 570228, Hainan, China

Abstract. The blockchain is a modern digital ledger that not only records currency transactions, but also records anything of value. Once the transaction is verified and submitted to the blockchain, it is difficult to recover. Therefore, in order to prevent malicious behavior, there should be a mechanism to evaluate the trust between participants before any transaction, which can effectively reduce the malicious behavior of malicious nodes. There are some nodes that provide low-quality services to quickly get rewards, and even malicious nodes may appear to deliberately provide extremely low-quality or invalid services. This paper proposes a blockchain-based trust mechanism for service nodes, which takes into account the privacy and security of the nodes, and is used to evaluate the confidence situation between the task assignment node and the task participating node. Experiments show that the mechanism we proposed can not only improve the service quality of service nodes, but also effectively distinguish high-quality nodes, low-quality nodes and malicious nodes, which provides an effective reference for selecting high-quality and credible service nodes

Keywords: Trust · Blockchain · Data acquisition

1 Introduction

Nowadays, technologies such as the Internet of Things are developing rapidly and widely used, trust establishment is very important to strengthen cooperation and security [1]. Therefore, more and more trust estimation methods are proposed so as to accurately evaluate the trust relationship between nodes. Based on the VANET architecture, Shahid et al. [2] proposed a new technology of malicious node detection based on weighted trust evaluation, which detects the victim nodes by monitoring the reported data. Desai et al. [3] proposed a trust evaluation method that uses the internal resources of the node to assess the node-level trust, which keeps the integrity of the node unchanged and achieves inter-node verification for specific attacks. FWu et al. [4]

© Springer Nature Singapore Pte Ltd. 2021
Y. Tan et al. (Eds.): DMBD 2021, CCIS 1453, pp. 230–239, 2021.
https://doi.org/10.1007/978-981-16-7476-1_21

proposed a trust evaluation algorithm based on node behavior, which integrates the method of node behavior strategy and modified evidence theory, which can effectively identify malicious nodes. However, the existing service node trust evaluation methods still have the problems of long evaluation period and unstable detection quality. Therefore, there is an urgent need to propose an accurate and efficient service node trust evaluation method. Anwar et al. [5] proposed a belief-based effective trust evaluation mechanism (BTEM) to isolate malicious nodes from trustworthy nodes and resist malicious, shutdown, and denial of service (DoS) attacks. Desai et al. [6] proposed a method for trust evaluation using the intrinsic properties of node memory in a multi-hop scenario. Simultaneously, this method evaluates the route. The proposed method works with the trusted nodes in the route to establish a trusted destination. node. Mo et al. [7] proposed an Active and Verifiable Trust Evaluation (AVTE) method for determining the reliability of IoT devices, thereby ensuring reliable data collection for advanced computing at low cost. Kim et al. [8] proposed a blockchain-based trust management model to increase the trust relationship between beacon nodes and remove malicious nodes in wireless sensor networks. This complex trust evaluation includes trust based on behavior and trust based on data.

In this paper, we propose a blockchain-based service node trust evaluation mechanism. After transactions and interactions between nodes, based on the transaction records in the blockchain, using the service node trust evaluation method, the service quality of the service node and the trust relationship between the corresponding nodes can be obtained. Compared with previous work, we added the feedback mechanism of the service node, and designed a service node evaluation model based on the blockchain, which dynamically evaluates the trust relationship of the service nodes through the trust mechanism. In addition, by using the feedback mechanism based on the blockchain, securely record and share the node's reputation value.

The main work and innovation of this paper is to propose a service node trust model based on blockchain, which distinguishes participating nodes through a trust evaluation method. The structure of the rest of this paper is as follows: Sect. 2 introduces the current working status of the blockchain-based trust evaluation mechanism for service nodes, Sect. 3 introduces related background knowledge such as blockchain technology and smart contracts, and Sect. 4 explains the trust evaluation mechanism we proposed. Finally, Sects. 5 and 6 present our experimental results and conclusions.

2 Related Work

2.1 Blockchain-Based Distributed Data Collection Architecture

Hu et al. [9] proposed a new blockchain-based mobile group perception framework, which realizes the privacy protection and security defense of the perception process and incentive mechanism through the emerging blockchain technology. Gan et al. [10] proposed a blockchain-based access control scheme for electronic health systems, in which patients play a supervisory role, allowing medical institutions to legally use their medical data without prior authorization. Have the right to manage medical data; at the same time, the program also includes an incentive mechanism to encourage patients to actively share their medical data. Zhang et al. [11] proposed a platform architecture of a blockchain-based federated learning system, which enables client data to have verifiable integrity and can be used for fault detection in the industrial Internet of Things. Huang et al. [12] proposed a blockchain-based mobile group perception system (BMCS) that uses miners to verify perception data; and designed a dynamic reward ranking incentive mechanism to reduce the imbalance of multiple perception tasks. Liu et al. [13] proposed a blockchain-based mobile edge computing video streaming framework (MEC) with adaptive block size, which includes an incentive mechanism to promote content creators, video transcoders Collaboration with consumers.

2.2 Feedback Mechanism

Data quality is the most important indicator to measure how the participating nodes complete the assigned tasks, but this may not be enough, because the data quality cannot fully reflect the satisfaction of the task publishing node with the service participating nodes [14]. Therefore, it is necessary to increase the evaluation factor to supplement the evaluation of the completed results of the participating node services, and feedback is an important evaluation factor. Information feedback can be divided into implicit feedback and explicit feedback according to its manifestation; it can be divided into artificial feedback and non-artificial feedback according to the degree of personnel participation [15]. After the service is provided, feedback can be obtained through direct user consultation. This method has been applied to many e-commerce that require huge efforts to attract users' expectations, such as Alibaba, Amazon, and NetEase [16]; opinions are sometimes incomplete. The implicit method of result estimation based on a calculation model with pre-defined criteria usually does not require human involvement, which usually does not require human involvement [17]. For example, in some network protocols, this is used as a confirmation message to indicate the success or failure of a data packet or file transfer. However, this data type feedback is not within the scope of this paper. We ignore information feedback now, and the indirect interaction results of users only depend on data quality [18]. However, user feedback can be a key element in improving the quality of service of the Internet of Things, and we will consider it in future research on evaluation algorithms [19].

3   Background

3.1   Blockchain Technology

Blockchain is a distributed ledger with a decentralized chain structure, which combines data blocks in order and maintains them through all nodes in the blockchain [20], It has the characteristics of decentralization, traceability and anti-tampering [21]. Blockchain combines point-to-point transmission, cryptography, distributed systems and other technologies into a new type of applied model [22], including public chain, private chain and alliance chain, etc., which realizes the transformation of the Internet from informationization to value, so as to better play the value of the Internet [23]. As more and more researchers join the research of blockchain technology, blockchain has gradually become another high-tech following artificial intelligence, big data, etc. [24]. Without the introduction of third intermediation, blockchain has no central system, which can trace past data and has the advantage of tamper-proof [25]. Therefore, for third party guarantee trust agency, blockchain technology can create huge benefits for them [26]. The rapid development of blockchain has led to the expansion of blockchain from the currency field to finance, Internet of Things, industrial manufacturing and other fields, government officials and industry people also began to pay attention to blockchain [27]. Botello et al. [28] proposed BlockSIEM, a distributed security information and event management solution framework based on blockchain, which relies on blockchain technology to safely store and access security events. Chen et al. [29] proposed a framework for sharing data services based on blockchain, focusing on the implementation plan that does not depend on any untrusted the third party characteristics, and can realize the secure storage and privacy protection of the accessed data.

3.2 Smart Contract

Ethereum is one of the best systems using blockchain technology, which integrates a distributed computing platform and operating system [30]. Smart contracts [31] is a piece of code that is deployed on Ethereum and can be automatically executed when certain conditions are met. Smart contracts define operating rules, and external applications call smart contracts to perform various operations and access blockchain data [32]. The operation data is recorded in the blockchain, and the contract execution result is recorded in the state database [33]. Ahmed S. et al. [34] proposed the FarMed framework, which will implement Ethereum's reputation system based on smart connections and develop a reliable blockchain-based protocol to transfer reputation values from one provider to another. business. The wrong operation of smart contracts will bring huge losses to people, but formal verification can effectively avoid the wrong operation of smart contracts and escort blockchain smart contracts. Sun [35] proposed a complete formalized verification method for Binance Coin (BNB) contracts, and designed a formal verification framework for blockchain intelligent contracts to effectively verify security vulnerabilities. Lucas M [36] proposed a transparent model related to blockchain, which uses Brazilian public critical infrastructure for student identity management, records information of students and their credits in the blockchain of record, verifies historical databases and uses smart contracts to trigger transactions. So as to improve the reliability of students' certificate issuance, and realize the decentralized issuance of degree certificates.

4 Trust Evaluation Mechanism

4.1 Trust Model of Service Node Based on Blockchain

Trust plays an important role in how to choose participating nodes. In the blockchain system, whether a participating node (i.e., Participate Node) provides a high-quality service for the service requested by a task release node (i.e., Task Release Node), we can use a trust model to predict.As shown in Fig. 1, a reliable trust relationship is established between the participating nodes and the task issuing node. After each sensing task is completed, indirect interaction occurs. The result calculated by the trust model is uploaded to the chain and returned. The data is publicly shared, credible and traceable. The experience relationship between any two nodes is created and changed through an interactive integration model.

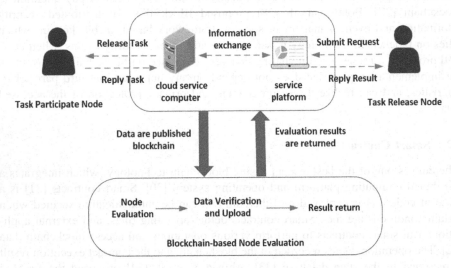

Fig. 1. Trust model of node based on block chain

4.2   Trust Model

Reputation is an individual attribute of a service node, reflecting the overall evaluation of the service node by the entire service cluster. In the distributed data collection service scenario, only a few service nodes directly interact with other nodes. The lack of direct trust conditions between task publishing nodes and participating nodes makes it difficult for them to establish cooperative service relationships. Therefore, the reputation of a node is an important factor in trust evaluation.

The reputation of service node i is marked as P_i, $i \in (0, 1, \cdots, m)$, where m is the number of nodes in the service cluster. P_i is an integer parameter in a set $(0, 1, \ldots, P_{max})$, where P_{max} is the maximum value of the reputation. In our paper, QoD_{Trust} (Quality of Data, QoD) is an important factor in trust evaluation, $QoD_i(j)$ represents the data quality score generated by the interaction between the service node i and other nodes j. The comprehensive data quality score i of the service node QoD_T is expressed as:

$$QoD_T = \frac{\sum_{j=1}^{m} QoD_i(j)}{P_i} \tag{1}$$

The reputation value of the service node depends on the evaluation of the requester. If the task requester affirms the task solution and gives a positive evaluation, the reputation value of the service node will increase. P_a represents the average reputation of all nodes in the service cluster, and e represents the result of reputation evaluation. h represents the high-level reputation threshold, and l represents the low-level reputation threshold. Therefore, the reputation value of service node i is calculated as follows:

$$P_i = \begin{cases} \min\left(P_i^{max}, P_i + 1\right), & \text{if } e = h \text{ and } P_i \geq P_a \\ P_i + 2, & \text{if } e = h \text{ and } P_i < P_a \\ P_i - 1, & \text{if } e = l \text{ and } P_i \geq P_a \\ \max(P_a, P_i - 2), & \text{if } e = l \text{ and } P_i < P_a \end{cases} \tag{2}$$

The node trust evaluation mechanism not only helps to encourage service nodes to provide high-quality data, but also effectively distinguishes high-level credibility and low-level credibility through QoD [37].

5   Results and Analysis

5.1   Set Up

The experimental hardware devices in this paper are 8G memory and i7 processor, which are implemented in the windows10 64-bit system and Matlab 2016(64-bit) environment to establish the simulation environment. This paper uses Crowd Temperature data set. Conduct multiple sets of comparative experiments to compare with existing methods. Experiments are compared with other methods to distinguish node service quality, test the effect of node service quality improvement, and mainly compare node service quality, data reliability and data processing speed.

5.2   Smart Contract

Storage contract should have the following functions to manage internal data:

- Upload data(): This method is used to upload the trust evaluation data information of nodes.
- Get data(): This method is used to obtain the trust evaluation data information of a node.
- Delete Contract(): This method is used to delete the contract so that the contract cannot be called again.

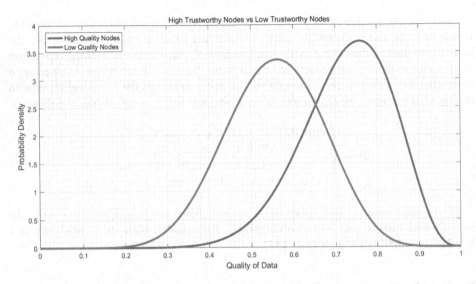

Fig. 2. High trustworthy nodes vs low trustworthy nodes

5.3   Result and Analysis

High trustworthy nodes and low trustworthy nodes are divided by data quality, as shown in Fig. 2, so that we can select the content provided by highly reliable nodes. Data quality assessment value trust mechanism shown in Fig. 3. As the number of services increases, it quickly stabilizes and is higher than the average method. Figure 4 shows the degree of malicious nodes when the number of node services is 40, 80, 120, and 160. The results show that the trust evaluation mechanism can improve the quality of nodes, with faster processing speed and higher reliability.

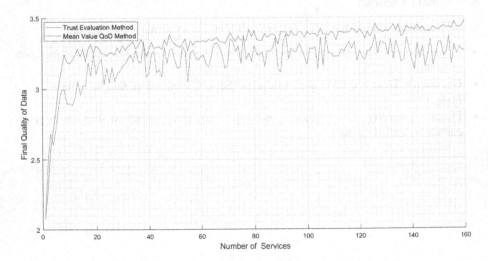

Fig. 3. Final quality of data for different methods

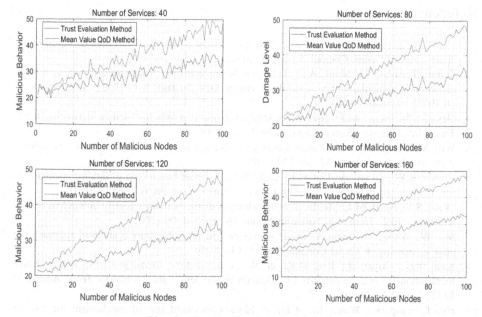

Fig. 4. The degree of malicious nodes

6 Conclusions

This paper proposes a trust evaluation mechanism for service nodes based on block-chain, taking into account the privacy and security of nodes. Our method is verified by related experiments. The experimental results show that the trust evaluation mechanism we proposed can not only improve the service quality of service nodes, but also effectively distinguish high-quality nodes, low-quality nodes and malicious nodes. Due to the small number and types of experimental samples, the experimental results may not be comprehensive. Therefore, we will increase the types and numbers of experimental samples in our future work to make the experimental results more comprehensive. And we will continue to improve the trust evaluation mechanism algorithm to achieve better node privacy information protection effect.

Acknowledgements. This work was supported by the Key Research and Development Program of Hainan Province (Grant No. ZDYF2020040), Major science and technology project of Hainan Province(Grant No. ZDKJ2020012), Hainan Provincial Natural Science Foundation of China (Grant Nos. 2019RC098) and National Natural Science Foundation of China (NSFC) (Grant No. 62162022, 62162024 and 61762033), Young Talents' Science and Technology Innovation Project of Hainan Association for Science and Technology (Grant No. QCXM202007), Key project of College Students' innovation and Entrepreneurship of Hainan University (Grant No. 20210110), Innovative scientific research project of Postgraduates in Colleges and universities in Hainan Province (Grant No. Hyb2020-01).

References

1. Liu, Y.H., Zhang, S.: Information security and storage of Internet of Things based on block chains. Future Gener. Comput. Syst. **106**(2020), 296–303 (2020)
2. Sultan, S., Javaid, Q., Malik, A.J., et al.: Collaborative-trust approach toward malicious node detection in vehicular ad hoc networks. Environ. Dev. Sustain. 1–19 (2021). https://doi.org/10.1007/s10668-021-01632-5
3. Desai, S.S., Nene, M.J.: Node-level trust evaluation in wireless sensor networks. IEEE Trans. Inf. Forensics Secur. **14**(8), 2139–2152 (2019)
4. Wu, X., Liang, J.: A blockchain-based trust management method for internet of things. Pervasive Mob. Comput. **72**, 101330 (2021)
5. Anwar, R.W., Zainal, A., Outay, F., et al.: BTEM: belief based trust evaluation mechanism for wireless sensor networks. Future Gener. Comput. Syst. **96**, 605–616 (2019)
6. Desai, S.S., Nene, M.J.: Multihop trust evaluation using memory integrity in wireless sensor networks. IEEE Trans. Inf. Forensics Secur. **16**, 4092–4100 (2021)
7. Mo, W., Wang, T., Zhang, S., et al.: An active and verifiable trust evaluation approach for edge computing. J. Cloud Comput. **9**(1), 1–19 (2020)
8. Kim, T.H., Goyat, R., Rai, M.K., et al.: A novel trust evaluation process for secure localization using a decentralized blockchain in wireless sensor networks. IEEE Access **7**, 184133–184144 (2019)
9. Hu, J., Yang, K., Wang, K., et al.: A blockchain-based reward mechanism for mobile crowdsensing. IEEE Trans. Comput. Soc. Syst. **7**(1), 178–191 (2020)
10. Gan, C., Saini, A., Zhu, Q., et al.: Blockchain-based access control scheme with incentive mechanism for eHealth systems: patient as supervisor. Multimedia Tools Appl. 1–17 (2020). https://doi.org/10.1007/s11042-020-09322-6
11. Zhang, W., Lu, Q., Yu, Q., et al.: Blockchain-based federated learning for device failure detection in industrial IoT. IEEE Internet Things J. **8**(7), 5926–5937 (2020)
12. Huang, J., Kong, L., Dai, H.N., et al.: Blockchain-based mobile crowd sensing in industrial systems. IEEE Trans. Industr. Inf. **16**(10), 6553–6563 (2020)
13. Liu, M., Yu, F.R., Teng, Y., et al.: Distributed resource allocation in blockchain-based video streaming systems with mobile edge computing. IEEE Trans. Wireless Commun. **18**(1), 695–708 (2018)
14. Cui, Y., Qian, Q., Guo, C., et al.: Towards DDoS detection mechanisms in software-defined networking. J. Netw. Comput. Appl. **68** (2021)
15. Wang, M., Lu, Y., Qin, J.: A dynamic MLP-based DDoS attack detection method using feature selection and feedback. Comput. Secur. **88**, 1–14 (2019)
16. Kejriwal, M., Shen, K., Ni, C.C., et al.: An evaluation and annotation methodology for product category matching in e-commerce. Comput. Ind. **131**, 1–12 (2021)
17. Brotsis, S., Limniotis, K., Bendiab, G., et al.: On the suitability of blockchain platforms for IoT applications: Architectures, security, privacy, and performance. Comput. Netw. **191**, 1–29 (2021)
18. Yw, A., Zw, B., Ym, C., et al.: Deep reinforcement learning for blockchain in industrial IoT: a Survey. Comput. Netw. **191**, 1–15 (2021)
19. Wang, H., He, D., Yu, J., et al.: RDIC: a blockchain-based remote data integrity checking scheme for IoT in 5G networks. J. Parallel Distrib. Comput. **152**, 1–10 (2021)
20. Perdana, A., Robb, A., Balachandran, V., et al.: Distributed ledger technology: its evolutionary path and the road ahead. Inf. Manage. **58**(3), 1–15 (2021)

21. Gimenez-Aguilar, M., Fuentes, J.M.D., Gonzalez-Manzano, L., et al.: Achieving cybersecurity in blockchain-based systems: a survey. Future Gener. Comput. Syst. **124**(6), 91–118 (2021)
22. Truong, N., Lee, G.M., Sun, K., et al.: A blockchain-based trust system for decentralised applications: when trustless needs trust. Future Generation Comput. Syst. **124**, 68–79 (2021)
23. Maesa, D., Mori, P.: Blockchain 3.0 applications survey. J. Parallel Distrib. Comput. **138**, 99–114 (2020)
24. Sanka, A.I., Irfan, M., Huang, I., et al.: A survey of breakthrough in blockchain technology: adoptions, applications, challenges and future research. Comput. Commun. **169**(10), 179–201 (2021)
25. Kumar, R.L., Pham, Q.V., Khan, F., et al.: Blockchain for securing aerial communications: potentials, solutions, and research directions. Phys. Commun. **47**(9), (2021)
26. Zhou, Z., Wang, M., Yang, C.N., et al.: Blockchain-based decentralized reputation system in E-commerce environment. Future Generation Comput. Syst. **124**, 155–167 (2021)
27. Wang, J., Wei, B., Zhang, J., et al.: An optimized transaction verification method for trustworthy blockchain-enabled IIoT. Ad Hoc Netw. **119**(1) (2021)
28. Ozyilmaz, K.R., Yurdakul, A.: Designing a blockchain-based IoT with Ethereum, swarm, and LoRa: the software solution to create high availability with minimal security risks. IEEE Cons. Electron. Mag. **8**(2), 28–34 (2019)
29. Botello, J.V., Mesa, A.P., Rodríguez, F.A., et al.: BlockSIEM: protecting smart city services through a blockchain-based and distributed SIEM. Sensors **20**(16) (2020)
30. Vivar, A.L., Orozco, A., Villalba, L.: A security framework for Ethereum smart contracts. Comput. Commun. **172**, 119–129 (2021)
31. Chen, Y., Ding, S., Xu, Z., Zheng, H., Yang, S.S.: Blockchain-Based medical records secure storage and medical service framework. J. Med. Syst. **43**(1), 5–14 (2019)
32. Zheng, Z., Xie, S., Dai, H.-N., et al.: An overview on smart contracts: challenges, advances and platforms. Future Generation Comput. Syst. **105**, 475–491 (2020)
33. Vacca, A., Sorbo, A.D., Visaggio, C.A., et al.: A systematic literature review of blockchain and smart contract development: techniques, tools, and open challenges. J. Syst. Softw. **174**, 1–19 (2020)
34. Taylor, P.J., Dargahi, T., Dehghantanha, A., et al.: A systematic literature review of blockchain cyber security. Digital Commun. Netw. **6**(2), 147–156 (2020)
35. Almasoud, A.S., Hussain, F.K., Hussain, O.K.: Smart contracts for blockchain-based reputation systems: a systematic literature review. J. Netw. Comput. Appl. **170** (2020)
36. Sun, T., Yu, W.: A formal verification framework for security issues of blockchain smart contracts. Electronics **9**(2), 1–23 (2020)
37. Truong, N.B., Lee, G.M., Um, T.W., et al.: Trust evaluation mechanism for user recruitment in mobile crowd-sensing in the Internet of Things. IEEE Trans. Inf. Forensics Secur. **14**(10), 2705–2719 (2019)

Irregular Flight Timetable Recovery Under COVID-19: An Approach Based on Genetic Algorithm

Tianwei Zhou[1,2], Junrui Lu[1,2(✉)], Wenwen Zhang[1,2], Pengcheng He[1], and Ben Niu[1,2]

[1] College of Management, Shenzhen University, Shenzhen 518060, China
junrui.lu@muc.edu.cn
[2] Greater Bay Area International Institute for Innovation, Shenzhen University, Shenzhen 518060, China

Abstract. With the growing demands on civil aviation transportation in post-pandemic of COVID-19, irregular flight has become a headache problem for both airlines and passengers. This paper considers the large-scale irregular flight timetable recovery problem for the airline with temporarily closed airport. First, a mathematical model with the objective of minimizing total delay time of passengers under several realistic constraints is constructed. Second, both improved genetic algorithm for the irregular flight timetable recovery problem and encoding scheme are proposed based on problem characteristics. Finally, a large-scale data set from contest is chosen and both optimal solution and recovery scheme are obtained to illustrate the feasibility of our recovery algorithm for irregular flight timetable recovery problem.

Keywords: Irregular flight timetable recovery · Genetic algorithm · Large-scale data · COVID-19

1 Introduction

Irregular flight timetable recovery is an important part in civil aviation. The COVID-19 and inclement weather lead to unavoidable delayed and cancelled flights—called irregular flights. Among the existing conventional solutions, the commonly utilized manual recovery approach is time-consuming and laborious. Moreover, the professional recovery software is expensive and incompatible with real situation. The occurrence of irregular flights brings losses to both airlines and passengers, bringing an urgent need for the intelligent recovery approach.

Most recovery approaches of irregular flight belong to the traditional mathematical optimization methods, such as column generation and branch and bound method [1–4]. Eggenebrg et al. [5] proposed a column generation algorithm based on a time-band network, considering aircraft maintenance, flight delay and aircraft exchange. Zhang et al. [6] designed a rolling horizon based algorithm to effectively solve the integrated airline schedule recovery problem. Delgado et al. [7] proposed a matheuristic approach based on column generation for short-run cargo flight schedule recovery problem.

© Springer Nature Singapore Pte Ltd. 2021
Y. Tan et al. (Eds.): DMBD 2021, CCIS 1453, pp. 240–249, 2021.
https://doi.org/10.1007/978-981-16-7476-1_22

However, in view of the NP-hard characteristics and the recovery time requirements, those approaches take too long to solve the large-scale irregular flight timetable recovery problem (IFTRP).

To overcome the above problem, metaheuristics approach, like genetic algorithm (GA) [8–10], has gradually become a useful tool with the intrinsic characteristics and can quickly obtain one or more feasible solutions. Liu et al. [11] proposed a multi-objective optimization evolutionary computation approach using the evaluation preference GA to deal with the flight schedule recovery problem under short-haul flight schedule disturbance. Jeng [12] designed an inequality-based multi-objective GA to recover the disturbed flight schedule in a short time. Liang et al. [13] proposed a hybrid algorithm based on the mutation characteristics of GA and ant colony algorithm to minimize the total flight delay time. Zhang et al. [14] applied multi-objective GA to solve the departure flight scheduling recovery problem.

Based on the above analysis, to deal IFTRP under COVID-19, this paper aims to propose the recovery approach using metaheuristics. Our contributions involve:

- Construct the model of IFTRP under COVID-19 with the objective of minimizing total delay time of passengers.
- Design the improved GA for IFTRP (GA-IFTRP) and propose the encoding scheme.
- Design the experiment based on real data from contest, and provide the recovery scheme.

The remainder of this paper is organized as follows. Section 2 introduces our IFTRP and its mathematic model, including the objective function and reasonable constraints. Section 3 proposes recovery approach designed based on GA. Section 4 designs the experiment based on real data from contest, and provides the recovery scheme. Section 5 provides the conclusion and future research directions.

2 Problem Formulation

2.1 Problem Description

This paper focuses on IFTRP, where airport is temporarily closed due to the disruption of bad weather or emergency incidents. Therefore, in view of flight replacement and cancellation, how to build an irregular flight timetable recovery model considering both flights and passengers recovery, and how to design an approach to get the recovery solution, including the sequence of takeoff and landing of flights with specific time, are our main concern.

2.2 Problem Modeling

Model Variables and Parameters. On account of the suggestions from airlines, for clearer model introduction, Table 1 listed the parameters and variables, and Table 2 represents the variable sets.

Table 1. Model variables and parameters

Decision Variables	Descriptions	Value Coefficients	Descriptions
$x_{f,\rho}^{\alpha^d,\alpha^a}$	Value is 1 when flight f flies by plane ρ from airport α^d to airport α^a, otherwise is 0	c_{cancel}	Unit cancellation cost of flight
$\tau_{f,\rho}^{\alpha^d,\alpha^a}$	Actual departure time of flight f by plane ρ from airport α^d to airport α^a	c_{delay}	Unit delay cost of flight
γ_f	Value is 1 when flight f is cancelled, otherwise is 0	$\bar{c}_\rho$	Number of seats in plane ρ
γ'_f	Value is 1 when flight f is executed, otherwise is 0	$\tau_{f,\rho^p}^{\alpha^d,\alpha^a}$	Planned departure time of flight f by planned plane ρ^p from airport α^d to airport α^a

Other Variables	Descriptions	Time Parameters	Descriptions
α^d	Actual departure airport	$\tau_{\alpha^c}^{start}$	Start time of closure in airport α^c
α^a	Actual arrival airport	$\tau_{\alpha^c}^{end}$	End time of closure in airport α^c
α^c	Closed airport	τ_ρ^{early}	Earliest available time of plane ρ
α^s	Stopover airport	τ_ρ^{late}	Latest available time of plane ρ
ρ^p	Planned plane for flight	$\Delta\tau_{\alpha^d \to \alpha^a}$	Flight duration from airport α^d to airport α^a
ρ	Actual plane used for flight	$\tau_{f,\rho}^{\alpha^c,\alpha^a}$	Departure time of flight f by plane ρ from airport α^c to airport α^a
ρ'	Available plane that can replace the planned plane ρ^p for flight	$\tau_{f^{last},\rho}^{\alpha^d,\alpha^s}$	Arrival time of the last flight f^{last} by plane ρ from airport α^d to airport α^s
$f(\tau_{f,\rho^p}^{\alpha^d,\alpha^a}, \tau_{f,\rho}^{\alpha^d,\alpha^a}, \alpha^d, \alpha^a, \rho, \rho^p, \bar{c}_p)$	Flight information	$\tau_{f^{next},\rho}^{\alpha^s,\alpha^a}$	Departure time of the next flight f^{next} by plane ρ from airport α^s to airport α^a
k_1	Value is 1 when the type of plane ρ and ρ' are different, otherwise is 0	t_1	Time cost of plane replacement related to plane's type
k_2	Value is 1 when the number of seats of plane ρ^p and ρ' are different, otherwise is 0	t_2	Time cost of plane replacement related to the number of plane's seats

Table 2. Variable sets

Sets	Descriptions	Sets	Descriptions
A	All airports	F	All flights
A^c	All closed airports	F^{α^d}	All departure flights in airport α^d
P	All planes		

Model Formulation. With the parameters listed in Table 1 and Table 2, the specific expressions of the objective function and its constraints are shown in formula (1)–(8).

$$\min\ Time = \left(c_{delay}\bar{c}_\rho\right) \sum_{f \in F} \sum_{\rho \in P} \sum_{\alpha^d,\alpha^a \in A} x_{f,\rho}^{\alpha^d,\alpha^a} \left(\tau_{f,\rho}^{\alpha^d,\alpha^a} - \tau_f\right) + \left(c_{cancel}\bar{c}_\rho\right) \sum_{f \in F} \gamma_f \qquad (1)$$

$$s.t. \qquad\qquad\qquad\qquad \gamma'_f + \gamma_f = 1 \quad \forall f \in F \qquad\qquad (2)$$

$$0 \leq x_{f,\rho}^{\alpha^d,\alpha^a} \left(\tau_{f,\rho}^{\alpha^d,\alpha^a} - \tau_{f,\rho^p}^{\alpha^d,\alpha^a} \right) \leq 300 \quad \forall f \in F^{\alpha^d}, \alpha^d, \alpha^a \in A, \rho, \rho^p \in P, \gamma_f' = 1 \quad (3)$$

$$x_{f,\rho}^{\alpha^d,\alpha^a} \left(\tau_{f,\rho}^{\alpha^d,\alpha^a} + \Delta\tau_{\alpha^d \to \alpha^a} - \tau_{\rho}^{late} \right) \leq 0 \quad \forall f \in F^{\alpha^d}, \alpha^d, \alpha^a \in A, \rho \in P, \gamma_f' = 1 \quad (4)$$

$$x_{f,\rho}^{\alpha^d,\alpha^a} \left(\tau_{f,\rho}^{\alpha^d,\alpha^a} - \tau_{\rho}^{early} \right) \geq 0 \quad \forall f \in F^{\alpha^d}, \alpha^d, \alpha^a \in A, \rho \in P, \gamma_f' = 1 \quad (5)$$

$$\sum_{\rho \in P} x_{f,\rho}^{\alpha^c,\alpha^a} = 0 \quad \forall f \in F, \alpha^a \in A, \alpha^c \in A^c, \tau_{\alpha^c}^{start} \leq \tau_{f,\rho}^{\alpha^c,\alpha^a} \leq \tau_{\alpha^c}^{end} - \Delta\tau_{\alpha^c \to \alpha^a} \quad (6)$$

$$\sum_{\rho \in P} x_{f,\rho}^{\alpha^d,\alpha^c} = 0 \quad \forall f \in F, \alpha^d \in A, \alpha^c \in A^c, \tau_{\alpha^c}^{start} \leq \tau_{f,\rho}^{\alpha^d,\alpha^c} + \nabla\tau_{\alpha^d \to \alpha^c} \leq \tau_{\alpha^c}^{end} \quad (7)$$

$$\tau_{f^{next},\rho}^{\alpha^s,\alpha^a} - \tau_{f^{last},\rho}^{\alpha^d,\alpha^s} \geq 45 \quad \forall \rho \in P, \alpha^d, \alpha^a, \alpha^s \in A, f^{next}, f^{last} \in F \quad (8)$$

The Objective function (1) and constraint conditions (2)–(8) are described as follows.

(1) The objective is to minimize the total cost of flight delay and flight cancellation.
(2) Each flight has two states: the executed state and the cancelled state.
(3) The actual departure time should not be earlier than the planned one and the delay time period should be within 300 min [15].
(4) The planned arrival time should be earlier than the latest time.
(5) The scheduled departure time should be later than the available earliest one.
(6) When the airport is closed, all of the scheduled departure flights should be changed from executive status to cancelled status until the airport reopens.
(7) When the airport is closed, all flights scheduled to land at the airport should be changed from executive status to cancelled status until the airport reopens.
(8) The waited time between two neighbor flights should be at least 45 min [15].

This paper also considers the situation of plane replacement for flights. If flights meet the conditions of takeoff and landing, flights' executing time should be checked whether the available time of flights' planes are met. For flights which their planes are not ready to take off, it is necessary to check whether their planes can be replaced.

If the planned planes can be replaced and there are other available planes which can be used to replace the planned planes of flights, define the function of plane replacement solution, which contains the flight delay cost and other cost caused by the difference of planes' types and number of planes' seats. Choose the available plane belonging to the minimum value of the function to replace the planned plane of the flight, which is set as a value coefficient in the objective function.

The function of the plane replacement solution is described as follows.

$$\bar{c}_\rho = \left\{ \bar{c}_{\rho'} \Big| \min \left[\left(\tau_{\rho'}^{early} - \tau_{f,\rho^p}^{\alpha^d,\alpha^a} \right) \bar{c}_{\rho'} + k_1 t_1 \bar{c}_{\rho'} + k_2 t_2 \left(\bar{c}_{\rho^p} - \bar{c}_{\rho'} \right) \right] \right\} \quad (9)$$

3 Recovery Approach

In view of the NP-hard characteristic of the IFTRP, it is necessary to design the recovery approach by heuristic [16]. GA is an effective approach to deal with the mixed integer programming. Therefore, the recovery approach GA-IFTRP is designed based on GA.

3.1 Algorithm Design

Encoding. Irregular flight timetable recovery is the process of arranging departure and arrival timetable for each flight. In this paper, a five-bit binary string is designed to characterize different delay durations given to each flight. This paper also considers whether the flight has replaceable plane, which is represented in a one-bit binary string. Therefore, these two binary strings are integrated in a total six-bit binary string to characterize the delay duration and replacement states of each flight.

The delay duration and replacement states of a flight directly determine the real departure and landing time of a flight, so the six-bit binary string directly corresponds to a gene in GA, and the number of individual genes in GA equals to the number of flights involved in the problem. In GA, our solution is finally obtained through continuous iterations. Encoding scheme is shown in Fig. 1.

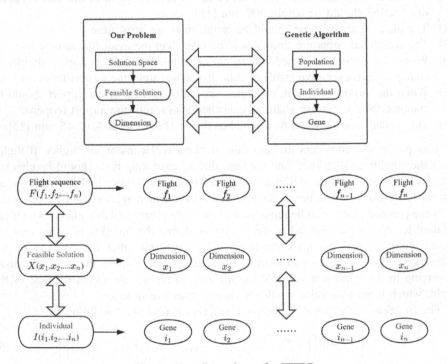

Fig. 1. Encoding scheme for IFTRP

In this paper, GA-IFTRP is designed based on the characteristics of IFTRP, and both selection and mutation approaches have been improved compared with original GA.

Selection. A selection probability is used to generate a fixed positive integer, and a random number conforming to the probability density of the normal distribution is generated. Individuals in the population are sorted according to the values of fitness. The fitness of each individual corresponds to the independent variable interval of the probability density of the normal distribution function. Individuals who compose the next generation population are selected according to a certain probability.

Mutation. The long delay duration to some flights or the requests for flights that can not replace planes is detrimental to overall recovery results. In this paper, two random numbers are set to be generated for each iteration. One of the random numbers has three numbers, representing three different possible flight states. The flight can not be replaced only when the random number is one of the specific set numbers. If the other random number is positive, the flight delay time will increase by 10 min. If the other random number is negative, the flight delay time will decrease by 10 min. When the flight delay time is 0, operations above are terminated.

3.2   Recovery Steps

Figure 2 shows the designed irregular flight timetable recovery process based on GA-IFTRP. Among them, process a-g represents the process of importing the planned flight information and presenting the corresponding optimal solution. Process 1–8 represents the iterative evolution about the flight information and objective function value acquisition.

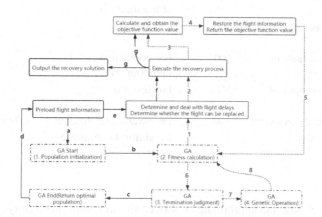

Fig. 2. Irregular flight timetable recovery process based on GA-IFTRP

4 Experiment Implementation

In this part, an experiment with parameters listed in Table 3 is utilized to test our designed recovery scheduling process. Experimental data is borrowed from a contest [15], including 749 flights, 151 planes and about 5500 passengers. The delay duration of each flight is 10 min, and the maximum delay duration of each flight is 300 min, which means there are 30 different delay durations for each flight. The flight should be cancelled when it delays more than 300 min [15].

Table 3. Related Parameters

Parameters	Values	Description	
Unit delay cost of flight	10 min	k_{de}	Irregular flight timetable recovery model
Maximum delay time of flight	300 min	Equation (3)	
Unit cancellation cost of flight	800 min	k_{can}	
Minimum layover time in legs	45 min	Equation (8)	
Maximum delay cost	10^{11}s	Infinity in fitness function	
Time cost of plane replacement related to plane's type	30 min	t_1	
Time cost of plane replacement related to the number of plane's seats	120 min	t_2	
Maximum proportion of optimal individual in population	60%	One of the conditions to determine the termination of iteration	GA-IFTRP
Maximum number of iteration	100		
Number of individuals in population	100	For population initialization	
Protection rate of optimal individual	5%	For selection	
Number of particles in swarm	100	For swarm initialization	DPSO
Number of iteration	31	Condition to terminate iteration	

In order to choose the appropriate crossover and mutation probability, based on the ideal range of crossover and mutation operator, three different combinations of genetic operator (GA-IFTRP I ~ III) are compared. Each genetic operator combination is utilized to run for 20 times respectively and Table 4 lists the average results.

Table 4. Experiment results

Algorithm	Probability of crossover	Probability of mutation	Computing duration(s)	Objective function value(s)	Iterations
GA-IFTRP I	0.8	0.1	3009	110806500	40
GA-IFTRP II	0.8	0.2	2136	111189000	37
GA-IFTRP III	0.9	0.1	1835	110463360	31
DPSO	N/A	N/A	1935	196611465	31

Figure 3 shows the objective value (left) and proportion of the optimal individual (right) changing with iterations under different parameters.

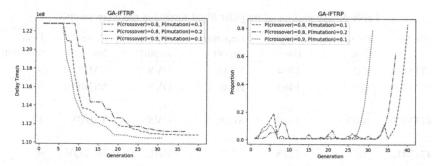

Fig. 3. Evolution process of GA-IFTRP I~III

Through careful comparison in Fig. 3, when crossover probability is 0.9 and mutation probability is 0.1, the optimal solution is obtained: total passenger delay time is 110463360 s and the number of iteration is 31.

Besides, a discrete particle swarm optimization (DPSO) is used in IFTRP to compare with the optimal GA-IFTRP III and Table 4 also lists their average results. Figure 4 shows the objective value of only DPSO (left) and DPSO and GA-IFTRP III (right) changing with the same iterations.

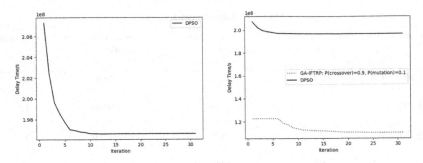

Fig. 4. Iteration process of DPSO and GA-IFTRP III

Through comparison with DPSO in Fig. 4, GA-IFTRP III is the better approach with shorter computing duration and iterations to obtain the optimal solution. An excerpt of its recovery scheme is shown in Table 5.

Table 5. An excerpt of irregular flight timetable recovery solution

Flight No.	Departure time	Arrival time	Departure airport	Arrival airport	Plane No.	Delay time(min)
174774174	870	1494	NAH	OVS	VMBQV	0
174773530	872	1463	KKB	OVS	MQBQV	0
......	......	......	......	......	......	......
174773809	1460	1639	SUD	OVS	TSBQV	10
......	......	......	......	......	......	......
174777410	3025	3275	OVS	RHL	NCBQV	0

5   Conclusion and Future Research

This paper focuses on the irregular flight timetable recovery problem with flight cancellation and plane replacement caused by airport temporary closure under COVID-19. An irregular flight timetable recovery model is constructed with the objective of minimizing the total delay time for passengers. Moreover, GA-IFTRP approach is designed based on GA and the encoding process is subtly proposed. The effectiveness of our approach is tested by the experiment with real data from contest.

In the future, the paralleled recovery algorithm based on GA will be designed to strengthen calculation speed. Moreover, crew and passenger integrated recovery problem will be considered.

Acknowledgement. The study was supported in part by Natural Science Foundation of China (No. 62103286, 71971143, 71571120, 71702111), in part by Social Science Youth Foundation of Ministry of Education of China under Grant (No. 21YJC630181), in part by Natural Science Foundation of Guangdong Province (No. 2020A1515010749), in part by Guangdong Basic and Applied Basic Research Foundation (No. 2019A1515110401), in part by Key Research

Foundation of Higher Education of Guangdong Provincial Education Bureau (No. 2019KZ DXM030), and in part by Natural Science Foundation of Shenzhen (No. JCYJ201908081 45011259).

References

1. Bratu, S., Barnhart, C.: Flight operations recovery: new approaches considering passenger recovery. J. Sched. **9**, 279–298 (2006)
2. Maher, S.J.: Solving the integrated airline recovery problem using column-and-row generation. Transp. Sci. **50**(1), 216–239 (2016)
3. Zhu, B., Clarke, J.P., Zhu, J.F.: Real-time integrated flight schedule recovery problem using sampling-based approach. J. Comput. Theor. Nanosci. **13**(2), 1458–1467 (2016)
4. Woo, Y.B., Moon, I.: Scenario-based stochastic programming for an airline-driven flight rescheduling problem under ground delay programs. Transp. Res. Part E **150**, 102360 (2021)
5. Eggenberg, N., Bierlaire, M., Salani, M.: A column generation algorithm for disrupted airline schedules. In: Technical report, Ecole Polytechnique Federale de Lausanne (2007)
6. Zhang, D., Lau, Y.K.: A rolling horizon based algorithm for solving integrated airline schedule recovery problem. J. Autom. Control Eng. **2**(4), 332–337 (2014)
7. Delgado, F., Mora, J.: A matheuristic approach to the air-cargo recovery problem under demand disruption. J. Air Transp. Manag. **90**, 101939 (2021)
8. Lee, L.H., Lee, C.U., Tan, Y.P.: A multi-objective genetic algorithm for robust flight scheduling using simulation. Eur. J. Oper. Res. **177**(3), 1948–1968 (2007)
9. Hu, Y.Z., Song, Y., Zhao, K., et al.: Integrated recovery of aircraft and passengers after airline operation disruption based on a GRASP algorithm. Transp. Res. Part E **87**, 97–112 (2016)
10. Cacchiani, V., Salazar-Gonzalez, J.-J.: Heuristic approaches for flight retiming in an integrated airline scheduling problem of a regional carrier. Omega **91**, 102028 (2020)
11. Liu, T.K., Liu, Y.T., Chen, C.H., et al.: Multi-objective optimization on robust airline schedule recover problem by using evolutionary computation. In: 2007 IEEE International Conference on Systems, Man and Cybernetics. IEEE, Montreal (2007)
12. Jeng, C.R.: Airline schedule recovery with an environmental consideration. In: 12th World Conference on Transport Research, WCTR, Lisbon, pp. 1–14 (2010)
13. Liang, W.K., Li, Y.: Research on optimization of flight scheduling problem based on the combination of ant colony optimization and genetic algorithm. In: 2014 IEEE 5th International Conference on Software Engineering and Service Science. Beijing, pp. 296–299. IEEE (2014)
14. Zhang, H.F., Hu, M.H.: Optimization method for departure flight scheduling problem based on genetic algorithm. Trans. Nanjing Univ. Aeronaut. Astronaut. **32**(4), 477–484 (2015)
15. Problem C: 14th China Post-graduate Mathematical Contest in Modeling (2017)
16. Liu, Q., Li, X.F., et al.: Multi-objective metaheuristics for discrete optimization problems: a review of the state-of-the-art. Appl. Soft Comput. J. **93**, 106382 (2020)

A Transfer Learning Method Based on ResNet Model

Le Liu[1], Jieren Cheng[1,3(✉)], Luyi Xie[1], Jinyang Song[2(✉)], Ke Zhou[2], and Jingxin Liu[1]

[1] School of Compute Science and Technology, Hainan University, Haikou 570228, China
[2] School of Cyberspace Security (School of Cryptology), Hainan University, Haikou 570228, China
[3] Hainan Blockchain Technology Engineering Research Center, Hainan University, Haikou 570228, China

Abstract. As countries around the world improve their garbage recycling and processing policies, the intelligently and efficiently garbage classification and identification has become a key point for implementing policies. However, traditional image recognition methods still have disadvantages, for instance, it needs a large amount of data annotation and a long time is required to train the model. In response to these drawbacks, this paper proposes a transfer learning method based on ResNet model, which aims to solve the problem of efficient classification of small-scale garbage image data sets. For the small sample image data set, after the data augmentation, the pre-training model ResNet50 is migrated to the data set through two migration learning methods of fine-tuning and pre-training model as the feature extractor, so as to realize the training of the target model. The experimental results show that the model classification effect after fine-tuning method and hyperparameter adjustment is better than the model without transfer learning, which can effectively improve the training speed and accuracy, and reduce the impact of over-fitting.

Keywords: Transfer learning · Image recognition · Garbage classification · Convolution neural network

1 Introduction

With the development of social economy and the improvement of residents' living standards, the output of domestic waste in the world is increasing day by day. Unsorted garbage mainly relies on landfill incineration, which deteriorates the ecological environment. Facing the complicated types and nature of garbage, people's awareness of the specific classification of garbage needs to be improved. It is very important to adopt efficient and intelligent technologies to improve the efficiency and accuracy of garbage classification when refining garbage categories.

To perform intelligent garbage classification, the first task is to accurately identify the acquired images. Image recognition technology includes feature extraction and classification recognition of images. This technology has undergone technological

© Springer Nature Singapore Pte Ltd. 2021
Y. Tan et al. (Eds.): DMBD 2021, CCIS 1453, pp. 250–260, 2021.
https://doi.org/10.1007/978-981-16-7476-1_23

changes such as artificial neural networks and deep learning, and has now been widely used in practical scenarios such as image retrieval [1], face recognition [2], driverless driving [3], license plate recognition [4] and other practical scenarios. And the technology is used in military, agriculture, public security and other fields. From the cumbersome manual design of image features to the early learning and extraction of image features by convolutional neural networks, and from the optimization of convolutional neural network structures to deep learning algorithms that can automatically learn features from large-scale image data sets, the accurate and generalization ability of image recognition have been greatly improved. However, many machine learning algorithms mainly rely on the assumption that training data and test data must have the same feature space and distribution, which may not meet this premise in a large number of practical applications. In addition, the deep learning model requires a large amount of labeled data, which has the problems of large network scale, many parameters, and high training overhead. Aiming at the above drawbacks of deep learning, transfer learning can use trained deep neural networks to transfer them to a given task, and can build a reliable machine learning model with relatively little training data, so as to shorten the training time and reduce the cost of computing resources. Because the transfer learning model can transfer knowledge in different tasks, it expands the application field of deep learning.

The garbage image recognition method based on transfer learning proposed in this paper applies transfer learning to the field of image recognition for small-scale data sets to solve the problem of intelligent garbage recognition and classification. By applying the parameters and network structure of the ResNet model pre-trained on a large image data set to the garbage image data set for training, the learned target model not only reduces the impact of overfitting, but also improves the generalization ability and image recognition, as well as the robustness of the model.

The organization structure of this paper is as follows: Sect. 2 introduces the related research work of image recognition and transfer learning. Section 3 describes the garbage identification method based on transfer learning and the optimization method of the model. The knowledge learned by the pre-training model is transferred to a small-scale sample data set for training. Section 4 visually analyzes the experimental results through comparative experiments. Section 5 summarizes the full text and proposes prospects for future research directions.

2 Related Work

Scholars at home and abroad have conducted in-depth research in the field of image recognition. Deep learning models can be trained through a large amount of data and automatically learn features, and the classification effect is more accurate and stable. However, the good performance of deep neural networks depends on a sufficiently large data set. However, for actual scenes, large-scale image datasets with labels are more scarce. In the case of a small sample data set, the application of a deep learning model is prone to overfitting, that is, the generalization ability of the trained model is insufficient. Therefore, the application of transfer learning to small-scale image recognition has become a research hotspot.

Duan Meng et al. [5] migrated the pre-trained model to small samples for image recognition and made full use of the convolutional features and parameters of the pre-trained model to improve the classification and recognition effect. Aiming at the overfitting phenomenon caused by a small number of data set training models, Wang Jingxian [6] and others constructed and integrated 6 different depths of convolutional neural network models to complete image feature extraction, which improved the accuracy of crop diseases, insect pests and weed recognition. Chang Liang et al. [7] described the application of convolutional neural networks in the field of image recognition.

In the research field of transfer learning, Zhuang et al. [8] reviewed and summarized representative transfer learning methods based on previous research on transfer learning and compared the performance of different methods through experiments. The transfer learning model is discussed. Different from the traditional method of optimizing two independent objective functions to explore the potential common factors of the source domain and the target domain, Long et al. [9] proposed a graph cooperative regularization transfer learning method, which integrates the two objective functions into an optimization problem. Effectively improve the accuracy of the model. Wang et al. [10] proposed a weighted balanced distribution adaptation method (W-BDA) for the problem of unbalanced data set categories in actual situations, which can adaptively adjust the weights of categories.

3 Junk Image Recognition Method Based on Transfer Learning

3.1 Data Augmentation

The sample data set used in the experiment is the Kaggle garbage classification data set, and each picture has 584 384 pixels. The data set is divided into six categories: glass (393 sheets), paper (491 sheets), cardboard (400 sheets), plastic (584 sheets), metal (472 sheets), and general garbage (127 sheets), with a total of 2467 sheets. Part of the images in the data set are shown (see Fig. 1).

Due to the complexity of deep learning models, the training of model parameters relies on a large amount of data. Especially in the case of a small sample size, data enhancement methods can be used to avoid the problem of overfitting. In terms of image processing, data enhancement is achieved by means of cropping, rotation, scale scaling, and translation. Through this method, the number of images in each category can be expanded, and the generalization ability of the model can be effectively enhanced.

In addition, normalizing and standardizing pixel values can improve the stability of data distribution and speed up the convergence speed of the model. The image is normalized according to the given mean and variance, the purpose is to eliminate the dimensional difference, so that the pixel mean value of the RGB channel after normalization is 0, and the standard deviation is 1. A typical method is Z-score standardization, as shown in Eq. 9, where μ is the mean and σ is the standard deviation.

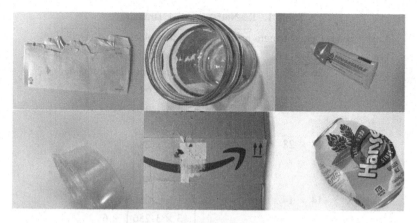

Fig. 1. Part of the garbage image data set

The training set and the test set are divided into the garbage image data set according to the ratio of 8:2. The training set is used to train the network weight parameters, and the test set is used to adjust the hyperparameters in the model. In order to adapt the image to the input of ResNet, the image is reduced to 224 * 224 pixels, and each batch contains 32 3-channel 224 * 224 images. This experiment performed random aspect ratio reduction, RGB channel pixel normalization, random horizontal flip, and data standardization operations on the image. The effect is shown in Fig. 2.

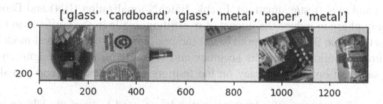

Fig. 2. Sample image after data enhancement

3.2   Network Structure

The pre-training model used in this paper is a ResNet50 model trained on ImageNet, which can avoid the problem of excessive time-consuming training of the model from scratch. Its structure is shown in Table 1. After 224 × 224 input images are pooled in the first layer as the convolutional layer and the second layer, the feature map with an output of 56 × 56 is obtained. The convolutional layer of the second layer is composed of 3 groups 1 × 1, 3 × 3, and 1 × 1 The convolutional layers of is stacked, and the rest of the layers are in turn.

Table 1. ResNet50 network structure.

Layer name	Output feature map size	Residual block structure
conv1	112×112	$7 \times 7, 64$, Step size is 2
conv2_x	56×56	3×3max pooling, Step size is 2
		$\begin{bmatrix} 1 \times 1, 64 \\ 3 \times 3, 64 \\ 1 \times 1, 256 \end{bmatrix} \times 3$
conv3_x	28×28	$\begin{bmatrix} 1 \times 1, 128 \\ 3 \times 3, 128 \\ 1 \times 1, 256 \end{bmatrix} \times 4$
conv4_x	14×14	$\begin{bmatrix} 1 \times 1, 256 \\ 3 \times 3, 256 \\ 1 \times 1, 1024 \end{bmatrix} \times 6$

3.3   Transfer Learning Model for Junk Image Recognition

The method proposed in this paper first loads the ResNet50 model and its pre-trained parameters, and converts the classification number of the fully connected layer into 6 categories through linear mapping. The cross-entropy function is used to measure the difference between the expected output and the real output, and the parameters are updated by back propagation. The training of the model is divided into two stages: train (training) and eval (test/evaluation). Enable BatchNormalization (BN) and Dropout in the training phase to reduce the impact of overfitting, while in the verification phase of the test set, disable BN and Dropout to test the performance of the trained model. After each training iteration, record the accuracy and loss rate of model recognition on the test set, save the optimal accuracy on the training set and test set, and visualize the results.

In this paper, two transfer learning methods are used to train models on garbage data sets. The first fine-tuning method is to train the data set of the parameters of all layers. The second type of pre-training model as a feature extractor is to freeze the convolutional layer, and only train the parameters of the last layer of the fully connected layer. Both methods achieve the convergence of the model by adjusting the optimizer and hyperparameters. Finally, the accuracy of the model performance and the change of the loss function on the training set and the test set are used to evaluate the performance of the model. This realizes the migration from a model trained on a large-scale image data set to a small-scale garbage image data set.

3.4   Model Training and Optimization

The pre-training model ResNet50 used in this paper uses the powerful feature expression and automatic learning advantages of the deep learning model to transfer the knowledge learned in the large image data set ImageNet to the target task, avoiding the time-consuming training of the model from scratch Long question. With the deepening of the network depth, the learned features deepen from the general features to the specific features of the training set, so that the pre-training model can achieve better training effects on the target samples. The following experiments are conducted in two ways: fine-tuning and pre-training the model.

Fine-Tuning. The first part of the experiment uses the method of fine-tuning the model to train the parameters of all layers. Table 2 shows the effect of the optimizer SGD on model performance under different hyperparameter conditions. The results show that when the optimizer is set to SGD, the momentum is set to 0.9, and the learning rate is 0.001, the model has the highest recognition accuracy on the test set, reaching 86.75%.

Table 2. Comparison of experimental results of different hyperparameters

Optimizer	Learning rate	Test	Training set accuracy	Test set accuracy
SGD	0.001	0.9	95.32%	86.75%
SGD	0.001		70.49%	65.66%
SGD	0.01	0.9	96.27%	84.94%

When the learning rate is set to be large, the convergence process is prone to oscillating, and it takes a longer iteration period to converge to the optimal accuracy rate (see Fig. 3 and Fig. 4). It can be seen from Table 2 that the introduction of a momentum factor in the gradient descent process can significantly improve the prediction accuracy of the model. The performance of the model on the training set is better than the accuracy on the test set, indicating that the generalization ability of the model needs to be improved.

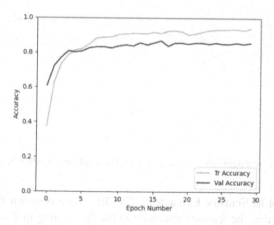

Fig. 3. The accuracy of lr = 0.001 when the optimizer is SGD

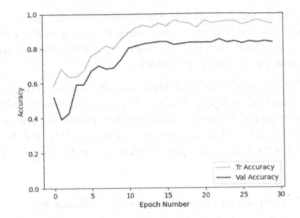

Fig. 4. The accuracy of lr = 0.01 when the optimizer is SGD

In order to better reflect the effect of transfer learning, this paper also uses the ResNet50 model to directly train the model. Under the condition of setting the optimizer to SGD and lr = 0.01, the classification accuracy rate on the test set is only 59.04%. It is significantly lower than the case of setting the same classifier and hyperparameters when using the transfer learning method, and the effect is shown in Fig. 5.

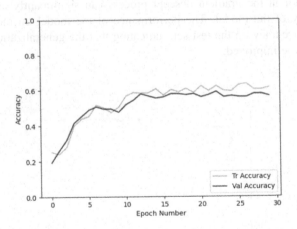

Fig. 5. Recognition accuracy of directly applying ResNet50 model

Pretrained Model as Feature Extractor. The difference between the method of pre-training model used as the feature extractor and the fine-tuning in the second part of the experiment is that it sequentially freezes the parameters of the last layer, and only optimizes the parameters of the last layer. After the optimizer, this experiment also sets lr_scheduler, so that the learning rate can be adjusted as the number of iterations epoch increases, so as to achieve better training results. Table 3 shows the influence of SGD and Adam optimizers on the accuracy of the training set and the test set.

Table 3. Comparison of experimental results of different optimizers

Optimizer	Learning rate	Test	Training set accuracy	Test set accuracy
SGD	0.1	0.9	89.72%	80.72%
SGD	0.01	0.9	90.01%	82.53%
SGD	0.001	0.9	82.71%	80.12%
Adam	0.001		86.89%	82.53%
Adam	0.003		90.01%	83.13%
SGD (ours)	0.01	0.9	**96.27%**	**84.94%**
SGD (ours)	0.001	0.9	**95.32%**	**86.75%**

When the optimizer is SGD and lr = 0.01, the model converges faster, and reaches a relatively stable accuracy rate after approaching the 10th epoch). In addition, in the case of the same learning rate, compared to the fine-tuning method in Experiment 1, the training time was shortened from 1 min and 31 s to 1 min and 1 s. From the comparison of Fig. 9 and Fig. 7, it can be seen that when the optimizer is Adam, the performance of the trained model is better than that of the optimizer is SGD. At the same time, from the comparison of Fig. 8 and Fig. 6, it can be seen that the difference between the model's recognition accuracy on the test set and the training set is reduced, indicating that the impact of overfitting has been reduced.

4   Experiments

4.1   Experimental Environment

The experimental environment is python3.6 and Ubuntu20.04.2 LTS operating system. The open-source deep learning framework Pytorch is used to complete the experiment, and GPU GeForce RTX 2080 is used to greatly improve the training speed of the model.

4.2   Visualization of Experimental Results

For the classification model, the recognition accuracy, recall, and F1 can be used to evaluate the pros and cons of the model recognition. The classification performance indicators of the model obtained in this training in each category are shown in Table 4. The total accuracy of model recognition is 86.03%. Among them, the recognition accuracy of cardboard is the highest, reaching 92.51%, reflecting the proportion of the number of cases predicted to be correct for this category in all cases predicted to be of this category. The total recall rate is 82.54%, which reflects the proportion of the number of cases where the model predicts that the image category is correct in the

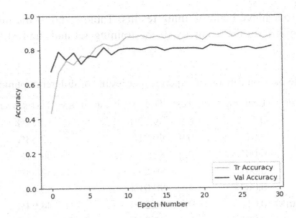

Fig. 6. The accuracy of lr = 0.01 when the optimizer is SGD

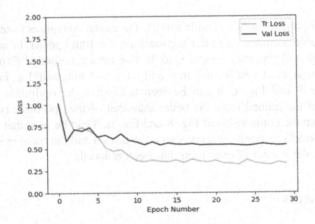

Fig. 7. The loss rate of lr = 0.01 when the optimizer is SGD

number of samples in that category. The model has the lowest recall rate on general garbage, only 58.26%. The total F1 score is taken as the harmonic mean of precision and recall, and the result is 84.24%.

Load the saved optimal model, convert the predicted labels into category names, and output the specified number of pictures in the test set and the predicted results. The visualization results are shown in Fig. 10.

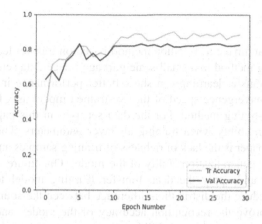

Fig. 8. The accuracy of lr = 0.003 when the optimizer is Adam

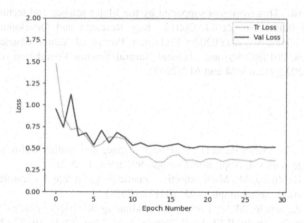

Fig. 9. The loss rate of lr = 0.003 when the optimizer is Adam

Table 4. Comparison of experimental results of different optimizers

	Cardboard	Glass	Metal	Paper	Plastic	General trash
Accuracy	92.51%	83.89%	83.72%	86.76%	83.86%	86.45%
Recall rate	90.37%	84.38%	84.83%	93.72%	83.65%	58.26%
F1	91.43%	84.14%	84.27%	90.11%	83.75%	69.61%

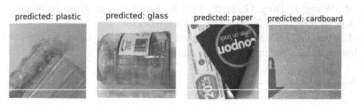

Fig. 10. Test set image category prediction results

5 Conclusions

This paper studies an image recognition method based on transfer learning, and applies the transfer learning method to a small-scale garbage image data set. The experimental results show that transfer learning can show better performance in the case of small samples, and the convergence speed of the pre-trained model as a feature extractor is faster than the fine-tuning method. For the data set used in this paper, the model has stronger recognition ability when training all layer parameters. The limitation of the experiment in this paper is the lack of richness of training samples and the lack of noise data to enhance the generalization ability of the model. Our future work will combine the latest research and apply the deep transfer learning model to realize adaptive transfer learning, reduce the distribution difference between the source domain and the target domain, improve the recognition accuracy of the model, and make the model have stronger feature expression capabilities.

Acknowledgement. This work was supported by the Major science and technology project of Hainan Province (Grant No. ZDKJ2020012), Key Research and Development Program of Hainan Province (Grant No. ZDYF2020040),Hainan Provincial Natural Science Foundation of China (Grant Nos. 2019RC098) and National Natural Science Foundation of China (NSFC) (Grant No. 62162022, 62162024 and 61762033).

References

1. Sajid, M., Ali, N., Dar, S.H., et al.: Short search space and synthesized-reference re-ranking for face image retrieval. Appl. Soft Comput. **99**, 106871 (2021)
2. Bi, Y., Xue, B., Zhang, M.: Multi-objective genetic programming for feature learning in face recognition. Appl. Soft Comput. **103**, 107152 (2021)
3. Ma, Y., Li, Z., Sotelo, M.A.: Testing and evaluating driverless vehicles' intelligence: the Tsinghua lion case study. IEEE Intell. Transp. Syst. Mag. **12**(4), 10–22 (2020)
4. Ma, L., Zhang, Y.: Research on vehicle license plate recognition technology based on deep convolutional neural networks. Microprocess. Microsyst. **82**, 103932 (2021)
5. Duan, M., Wang, G., Niu, C.: Small sample image recognition method based on convolutional neural network. Comput. Eng. Des. **39**(1), 224–229 (2018)
6. Wang, J.: Research on image recognition of crop diseases and weeds based on convolutional neural network and transfer learning (2019)
7. Chang, L., Deng, X.M., Zhou, M.Q., et al.: Convolutional neural networks in image understanding. Acta Automatica Sinica **42**(9), 1300–1312 (2016)
8. Zhuang, F., Qi, Z., Duan, K., et al.: A comprehensive survey on transfer learning. Proc. IEEE 1–34 (2020)
9. Long, M., Wang, J., Ding, G., et al.: Transfer learning with graph co-regularization. IEEE Trans. Knowl. Data Eng. **26**(7), 1805–1818 (2014)
10. Wang, J., Chen, Y., Hao, S., et al.: Balanced distribution adaptation for transfer learning. In: IEEE International Conference on Data Mining (2017)

Performance Prediction and Fine-Grained Resource Provision of Virtual Machines via LightGBM

Jia Hao[1,2], Jun Wang[1,2(✉)], and ZhaoXiang OuYang[3]

[1] Key Laboratory of Education Informatization for Nationalities,
Ministry of Education, Yunnan Normal University, Kunming 650500, China
[2] Yunnan Key Laboratory of Smart Education, Yunnan Normal University,
Kunming 650500, China
[3] School of Information, Dehong Teachers' College, Mangshi 678400, China

Abstract. It is significant to accurately predict the performance of virtual machines (VMs), and then provide the corresponding fine-grained resources according to users' requirements for both users and cloud resource providers in IaaS cloud computing. In this paper, based on the idea of LightGBM, we first analyze the hardware/software, configuration and then runtime environmental features that may have impacts on the VM performance, and then propose a VM performance prediction model with Gradient-based One-side Sampling (GOSS) method, called VPGB. VPGB pays more attentions on the data instances that with the larger gradients so as to speed up the model training process and then predicts the VM performance accurately. In addition, based on the prediction results, we apply the genetic algorithm to find the optimal fine-grained resources configuration and then provide for users. Experimental results show that VPGB-based method can predict the VM performance accurately and provide the fine-grained VM resources for users effectively.

Keywords: Virtual machine · Performance prediction · Fine-grained resource provision · LightGBM · Genetic algorithm

1 Introduction

Cloud computing aims to provide the resources via a pay-as-you-go manner [1]. Infrastructure as a Service (IaaS) is one of the service modes of cloud computing, and it provides a certain number of CPU cores, memory capacity, hard disk capacity and network bandwidth in the form of virtual machines (VMs) [2]. Services providers deploy their applications like online games and websites on the VMs and then pay according to their own needs. But this kind of coarse-grained resource provision has some limitations. First, the IaaS providers usually avoid the service level agreements (SLAs) violation via overprovision, which will inevitably cause the resources wastage [3, 4]. Furthermore, users cannot adapt their applications flexibly, which may lead the resources under-utilized. Therefore, the ideal way for resource provision is to accurately predict the performance of the VMs and then allocate the corresponding resources to the user based on the prediction results [5].

© Springer Nature Singapore Pte Ltd. 2021
Y. Tan et al. (Eds.): DMBD 2021, CCIS 1453, pp. 261–272, 2021.
https://doi.org/10.1007/978-981-16-7476-1_24

However, predicting the performance of VMs has some difficulties. First of all, in addition to the quantified resources, there are many VM-related environmental features will affect its performance, like the capacity of the last-level cache (LLC), the types of hypervisor, and the CPU scheduling algorithm, etc. The prediction error might occur if these features are ignored. In addition, the relationships between the various VM-related features are non-linear [6]. For example, the sharing manner of LLC is affected by the CPU type, and this kind of relationship is hard to quantified.

LightGBM, a new implementation of GBDT, proposes to pay more attentions to the data instances with large gradients by a Gradient-based One Side Sampling method (GOSS), and then bundles the mutually exclusive features together, so as to speed up the GBDT training processes [7]. Therefore, in order to quantify the non-linear relationships among the VM-related features and then achieve the efficient prediction, we employ the framework of LightGBM, and then build a VM Performance prediction Gradient Boosting model, i.e. VPGB. In addition, based on the performance prediction results of VPGB, we further propose a method that uses genetic algorithms [8] to search for the best VM configuration which consists of some fine-grained resources, including memory type, LLC size, and CPU scheduling algorithm, so as to meet the personal requirements of cloud users.

Experiments results show that our proposed VPGB model can predict the performance of the VMs accurately. In addition, the genetic algorithm based fine-grained resource provision method can allocate the corresponding resource that is closer to the target performance effectively.

The remainder of this paper is organized as follows: Sect. 2 introduces related work. Sections 3 gives the method of constructing the VM performance prediction model of VPGB. Section 4 presents the details of fine-grained resources provision. Section 5 shows the experimental results and Sect. 6 concludes and discusses the future work.

2 Related Works

2.1 VM Performance Prediction

One of the main ways to predict the performance of VMs is to analyze the relationships between the used resources and the VM performance, so as to evaluate its performance effectively. Zhang et al. [9] first selected multiple features that may have effects on the performance of VMs, and then use the random forest to construct the VM performance prediction model. Hao et al. [10] used an XGboost-induced Bayesian Network to quantified the relationships among the VM-related features, and then measure the response time of VMs accurately. Li et al. [11] collected the four hardware resource characteristics of CPU time cycle weight, virtual CPU core number, memory size, and I/O competition, and used their impact on application performances as the modeling parameters. Then, they used Singular Values Decomposition (SVD) method to analyze the relationships between the hardware and the corresponding VM performance. Gandhi et al. [12] proposed a Kalman filtering based Dependable Compute Cloud

(DC2), which can automatically scale the infrastructure to meet the user-specified performance requirements.

Our proposed method pays more attention to the quantification of non-linear relationships among the environmental features and the corresponding VM performance.

2.2 VM Resource Provision

Due to the uncertainty and the dynamics of IaaS deployed applications, a great number of efforts have been dedicated to evaluate the status of the applications, and then allocate the corresponding fine-grained resources to VMs. Eli et al. [13] first analyzed the resource requirements during the day and the week, and then proposed a dynamic CPU scheduling algorithm. Li et al. [14] modeled the cloud resource allocation as a dynamic bin packing process, and then proposed a modified any fit (MAF) method to minimize the number of physical hosts used. Hadary et al. [15] set several rules that should be meet during the resource allocation, and then selected the best allocation to offer the VM resources. Qiu et al. [5] proposed to profile the dynamic behavior of micro services, and then applied an actor-critic reinforcement learning framework to allocate the CPU, memory bandwidth, LLC capacity and I/O bandwidth to the users.

These methods can allocate the resources dynamically, but our work focus more on the fine-grained VM resources.

3 VPGB Construction and Performance Prediction

3.1 VM-Related Feature Selection

There are mainly four types of features having impacts on the performance of VMs, i.e. hardware/software features, configuration features, and the runtime environmental features. We list the selected VM-related features in Table 1.

Table 1. VM-related features

Hardware	Software	Configuration	Runtime environment
CPU type	Type of hypervisor	Number of vCPU cores	Co-located VMs
CPU frequency	Type of CPU virtualization	vCPU-pCPU pinning	Type of application
Memory type	Type of memory virtualization	Memory capacity	Resource usage rate
Hard disk type	Type of I/O device virtualization	Hard disk capacity	...
Network bandwidth	CPU scheduling algorithm	Virtual network bandwidth	...
...	...	...	...

We select N features from Table 1 and then get several VMs with different configurations. Then, we run the benchmarks on these VMs n times, and then record the corresponding results as the performance of VMs. Thus, the VM feature-performance training set consist of n instances, and the i-th one is denoted as $D_i(x, y)$, where $x = \{x_1, x_2, \ldots x_N\}$. denotes the features and y represents the VM performance.

3.2   The Construction of VPGB

The conventional implementation of GBDT needs to scan all of the n training instances to estimate the information gain of all the possible splits of VM-related features. These processes are very time consuming while dealing with big data. Inspired by the idea of LightGBM that the instances with greater gradients can provide us with more useful information, we adopt a Gradient-based One-side Sampling (GOSS) method to reduce the number of training instances. The VM performance prediction model with GOSS is the VPGB, denoted by $f_{\mathrm{VPGB}}(x)$.

The loss between the i-th ($i \in \{1, 2, \ldots n\}$.) prediction result of f_{VPGB} (x_i) and its true performance value y_i is denoted by Eq. (1), the corresponding gradient is $g_i = \frac{dL}{dx}$.

$$L(y_i, f_{\mathrm{VPGB}}(x_i)) = (y_i - f_{\mathrm{VPGB}}(x_i))^2. \tag{1}$$

Aording to the idea of GOSS [7], VPGB first sorts all of the training instances according to their absolute values of the gradients, and then select the top $a\%$ (including $|A|$ pieces) of instances. Then, the $b\%$ (including $|B|$ pieces) instances are selected from the rest randomly, but each of them are amplified by a constant $\frac{1-a}{b}$. when calculating the information gain, so as to balance the data distribution. According to the ($|A|+|B|$) pieces of instances, the information gain of a split candidate d for VM-related feature j is calculated by Eq. (2).

$$V_j(d) = \frac{1}{n} \left(\frac{\left(\Sigma_{x_i \in A_l} g_i + \frac{1-a}{b} \Sigma_{x_i \in B_l} g_i \right)^2}{n_l^j(d)} + \frac{\left(\Sigma_{x_i \in A_r} g_i + \frac{1-a}{b} \Sigma_{x_i \in B_r} g_i \right)^2}{n_r^j(d)} \right) \tag{2}$$

where A_l and A_r represent the sets which are less and greater than d in set A separately, B_l and B_r represent the sets which are less and greater than d in set B.

VPGB consist of M trees. In the m step, by calculating the split points with the maximum information gain of N VM-related features via Eq. (2), we can get a tree denoted by $T_m(x, \theta_m) = \sum_{j=1}^{N} V_j(d)$ θ_m is the parameter of T_m and is denoted by Eq. (3).

$$\theta_m = argmin \left(\sum_{m=1}^{M} (y_i - f_{\mathrm{VPGB}-1}(x_i) - T_m(x, \theta_m)) \right)^2 \tag{3}$$

Thus, the VPGB is represented as $f_{VPGB}(x) = \sum_{m=1}^{M} T_m(x, \theta_m)$ and the construction of VPGB is given in algorithm 1.

Algorithm 1. Construction of VPGB

Input: $D(x, y)$: training data with n instances

    M: number of trees included in VPGB

    a: the sampling ratio of larger gradients data

    b: the sampling ratio of small gradients data

    L: the loss function defined by Equation (1)

Output: $f_{VPGB}(x)$

Steps:

1. $f_0=0, f_{VPGB}(x)=f_0$ //initialization of $f_{VPGB}(x)$

2. for $m=1$ to M do:

    $preds=f_{VPGB}(x)$.predict($D(x,y)$) //use VPGB to predict VM performance

    $g=L(D(x,y), preds)$ //apply Equation (1) to calculate the gradients of all instances

    $sorted=$ GetSortedIndices(abs(g)) //sort the gradients g in descending order

    $A=sorted$ [1:top $a\%$] //select the A instances with larger gradients

    $B=RandomPick(sorted[$top $a\%$: n]) //select B instances with smaller gradients

    $V_j(d) =SelectBestSplit()$ //apply Equation (2) to calculate the split point d

    $T_m(x, \theta_m) = \sum_{j=1}^{N} V_j(d)$ // use $V_j(d)$ and the θ_m to construct the m-th tree

    $f_{VPGB-m}(x)=f_{VPGB-(m-1)}(x)+ T_m(x, \theta_m)$ //update the VPGB model

---

During the running of algorithm 1, the number of training instances and the VM-related features are $(A + B)$ and N respectively. Thus, the time complexity of algorithm 1 is $O((A + B) * N)$. Compared with applying all of the n VM feature-performance instances to implement GBDT, our proposed VPGB can reduce the time cost of model construction to a great extent.

3.3   VPGB-Based Performance Prediction

Supposed that the VM-related feature set is $x = \{x_1, x_2, \ldots x_N\}$, whose corresponding performance y is to be predicted. Starting from the root node of the j-th ($j \in \{1, 2, \ldots M\}$) tree in VPBN, if x_i $i \in \{1, 2, \ldots N\}$ is less than or equal to the split value of the current node, then it will be put into its left subtree, otherwise it will be put into the right subtree until x_i reaches a certain leaf node. Then, we add the residuals of M trees to get the final VM performance prediction results.

Figure 1 illustrates a tree constructed with the VM-related features of memory capacity, the number of vCPU, and the hard disk capacity. Figure 2 is an example of predicting the final performance value based on the VPBG model with 4 trees.

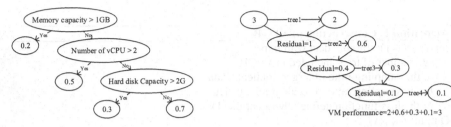

Fig. 1. A tree in VPGB   **Fig. 2.** Performance prediction of VPGB

4 Fine-Grained Resource Provision Based on the Prediction Results of VPGB

Based on the VPGB-based VM performance prediction results, we further use the genetic algorithms to provide users with fine-grained resources. The baeas are: we first randomly generate a set of VM resources and use them as the initial population.

For example, suppose that we use 1 and 2 to denote that the *CPU type* is Intel and AMD; and for feature *CPU scheduling algorithm*, 1 and 2 represent the CPU scheduling algorithm are Credit and SEDF respectively; for feature *pinning*, 1 and 2 represent that virtual CPU uses the physical CPU in a sharing or exclusively manner. So, the configuration $X = \{CPU\ type = 1,\ CPU\ scheduling\ algorithm = 1,\ pinning = 1,\ memory\ capacity = 500\ MB,\ number\ of\ CPU\ cores = 2,\ disk\ capacity = 1\ GB\}$ can be a compose of the initial population.

Secondly, we use VPGB to predict the performance of each VM in this population, and then compare the prediction results with the target performance values. Next, we select the resource configurations with the greater fitness as the fine-grained resources candidates; then, after the crossover and variation, we can get the next-generation population. The above operations are iterated until the fine-grained VM resources are closest to the target performance value.

The function for calculating the fitness between the true VM performance y_i and the VPGB-based prediction result y_{pred} is defined in Eq. (4).

$$\text{fitness}(i) = \left(y_i - y_{pred}\right)^2 \tag{4}$$

where the target performance is denoted as y_{target}, so the probability of a chromosome i being selected is calculated by Eq. (5).

$$P_i = \frac{1 - \frac{\text{fitness}(i)}{y_{target}}}{\sum_{i=1}^{|population|}\left(1 - \frac{\text{fitness}(i)}{y_{target}}\right)}. \tag{5}$$

The fine-grained resource provision method is given in algorithm 2.

Algorithm 2. Fine-grained resource provision based on VPGB

Input: y_{target}: VM performance target
     P: the size of population
     X_N: N sets of resource configuration
     I: number of iterations
     S: the number of chromosomes in the population
     Q: the number of crossover chromosomes
     V: the number of variation chromosomes
     Candidate: the set consists of candidate chromosomes
Output: $x = \{x_1, x_2, ... x_N\}$: a set of fine-grained VM resources
Steps:
1. *Candidate* ← *Initial*(P, I, y_{target}, S) //get the initial population
2. for i=1 to I
2. *fitness*(*Candidate*) //calculate the fitness by Equ. (4) for each chromosome
3. for s=1 to S do
crossoverProb(s)←P_s // calculate the crossover probability by Equ. (5)
cumulatedProb(s)←$\Sigma_{s=1}^{S} P_s$ //calculate the cumulated probability of s
if *random*() < *cumulatedProb*(s) //use Russian Roulette to select the candidates
  Candidate = *Candidate* ∪ *cumulatedProb*(s)
Else
  when ($\Sigma_{l=1}^{L-1} P_l$<*random*() <$\Sigma_{l=1}^{L} P_l$) do
    Candidate = *Candidate* ∪ *cumulatedProb*(l)
4. *Crossover*(Q)← Candidate //select Q chromosomes in Candidate for crossover
5. *Variation*(V)← Candidate // select V chromosomes in Candidate for variation
5. *bestFit*← *Crossover*(Q) ∪ *Variation*(V) // select the best fit chromosome
6. $x = \{x_1, x_2, ... x_N\}$← *bestFit* // provide the users the fine-grained resources

---

According to Algorithm 2, after I times iterations, we can provide the user a set of fine-grained VM resource configuration which can meet with the target performance with the best fitness. The running time of algorithm 2 is within our acceptable range.

5 Experiments

5.1 Experimental Setup

The details of the two hosts we used for physical hosts simulation are given below. The first is configured with an AMD-A10 7850k Quad-Core 3.6 GHz processor, 16 GB 1866 GHz DDR3 memory, 500 GB SATA hard drive and 120 GB SSD. The second is configured with an Intel i5-6600 Quad-Core 3.3 GHz processor, 16 GB 2133 GHz DDR4 memory, 500 GB SATA hard drive and 120 GB SSD.

Both physical hosts run Xen-4.6, and each of them hosts two VMs. Each VM runs Centos-7 with Linux kernel 3.18.34-20.el7.x86_64. We select six main properties which influence VM performance and list the details in Table 2.

Table 2. Properties and their value ranges

Properties	CPUTYPE	HDD	vCPUNUM	vCPU-pinning	MEM	LoadTYPE
Range	AMD	SATA	1	None	512	CPU-intensive
	Intel	SSD	2	Competitive	1024	Memory-intensive
			3	Noncompetitive	2048	

We set up VMs according to the configurations which are combinations of these properties. Then we select some programs in benchmark PARSEC[1] to stimulate different applications. They are *bodytrack*, *freqmine*, *x264* and *streamcluster*. We use their wall clock execution time to represent the VM performance. We run each program 100 times on each VM and collect all the property values and corresponding performance results as a training set D to construct a VPGB.

5.2 VPGB-Based Performance Prediction Accuracy

We used the Adaboost [16], XGboost [17], random forest [18] and decision tree as the baseline methods. The numbers of trees for the first three algorithms were set as 200, and the maximum depth of a tree was 4 for all of the methods. We randomly selected 16 VM configurations, denoted as $c_1, c_2, \ldots, c_{16}$, and then used all of the algorithms for accuracy comparisons. The results are shown in Fig. 3.

It can be seen that the average accuracy via VPGB is higher than 95%, but the metric ranges between 75% and 90% for the rest of the baselines. In addition to VPGB, XGboost can also can predict the VM performance with relatively higher accuracy. Thus, it can be concluded that among all the four algorithms, the highest value of accuracy is achieved by VPGB while decision tree corresponds to the lowest.

---

[1] PARSEC: http://parsec.cs.princeton.edu/overview.html.

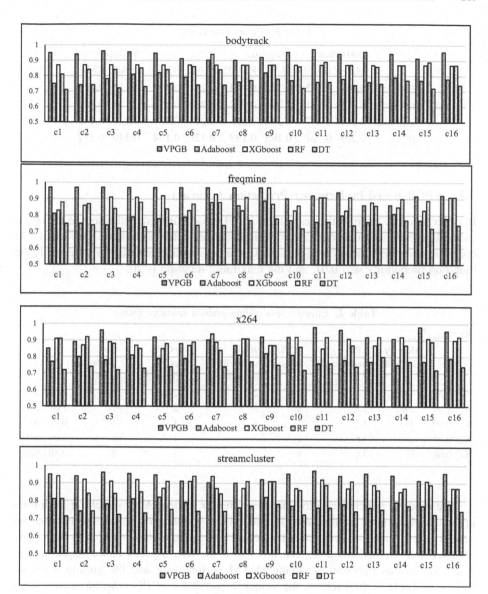

Fig. 3. Accuracy comparison of VM performance prediction

Furthermore, we calculated the MAE and RMSE for the VM performance prediction results, and shown the results in Table 3.

It can be concluded from Table 3 that among the four performance prediction algorithms, the results predicted by VPGB can reach smaller error values in most cases. In addition, the errors based on the random forest are also small, which is consistent with the results shown in Fig. 3. However, the VM performance prediction results based on Adaboost have the largest errors.

Table 3. Errors evaluation

	Bodytrack		Freqmine		x264		Streamcluster	
	MAE	RMSE	MAE	RMSE	MAE	RMSE	MAE	RMSE
VPGB	**0.114**	**0.233**	**0.191**	**0.174**	0.191	0.297	**0.114**	**0.278**
Adaboost	0.301	0.331	0.154	0.272	0.286	0.358	0.304	0.422
XGboost	0.219	0.347	0.287	0.355	0.271	0.321	0.321	0.445
RF	0.208	0.361	0.195	0.193	**0.126**	**0.194**	0.349	0.377

5.3   VPGB-Based Performance Prediction Accuracy

In order to verify the effectiveness of the VPGB-based fine-grained resource provision method, we set the initial conditions of the genetic algorithm as follows. The initial VM configuration population S was set as 200, the crossover probability was set as 1, the mutation probability was 0.01, and the maximum iteration is 20.

Table 4. Effectiveness of fine-grained resource search

ID	y_{target}	y_{target}						y_{pred}	y_i
		Memory size/MB	CPU frequency/HZ	vCPU number	vCPU scheduling algorithm	vCPU-pCPU pinning	Co-located VMs		
X_1	2.30	450	3.3	3	2	2	1	2.36	2.37
X_2	1.00	698	3.3	2	2	2	1	1.01	1.14
X_3	0.90	1193	3.3	2	1	1	1	0.91	0.92
X_4	0.95	530	3.6	2	2	1	0	0.99	0.97
X_5	0.68	1531	3.6	4	1	1	0	0.68	0.65

We used the benchmark x264 and freqmine for testing. After searching for a fine-grained VM resource configuration that meets the performance requirements based on genetic algorithms, we predicted its performance and compared that whether the obtained fine-grained resources can meet with the user's performance requirements. The comparisons between the predicted VM performance and the ground truth are shown in Table 4. In Table 4, the values 1 and 2 for *vCPU scheduling algorithm* represent Credit and SEDF respectively. For *vCPU-pCPU pinning*, 1 and 2 represent the virtual CPU cores use the physical CPU cores in a shared or exclusive manner. For *Co-located VMs*, 1 and 0 represent the VM use the physical resources in a shared or exclusive manner.

It can be concluded from Table 4 that when given a certain VM performance requirement, the genetic algorithm can find a fine-grained VM resource configuration that is closer to the target performance value. Furthermore, the corresponding performance values predicted by VPGB can also accord with the targets, which shows the effectiveness of our proposed method.

6 Conclusion and Future Work

Focusing on that the current coarse-grained resources provision of the IaaS platform cannot provide the resources to users according their needs, we propose a fine-grained resources provision method. Firstly, we propose a VM performance prediction model with gradient-based one-side sampling method, i.e. VPGB. VPGB can use the data instances with larger gradients to speed up the model training process, and have a higher accuracy in predicting the performance of the VMs. Based on the prediction results of VPGB, we further propose a fine-grained resource provision method based on genetic algorithm. This method can find the resource configuration which can meet with the specific requirements of users. The experimental results show that our method is effective and accurate.

In the future, we will consider using some public datasets to improve the predictive accuracy of VPGB. Moreover, we will try to use the parallel and incremental approaches to construct the VPGB model efficiently and predict the performance of VMs in and online manner.

Acknowledgement. This work is supported by National Natural Science Foundation of China (No. 61862068), Yunnan Expert Workstation of Xiaochun Cao, and Scientific Technology Innovation Team of Educational Big Data Application Technology in University of Yunnan Province.

References

1. Danilov, A., Molodkina, J., et al.: The NIST definition of cloud computing. Communications of the ACM, vol. 53, p. 50 (2011)
2. Gavvala, S.K., et al.: QoS-aware cloud service composition using eagle strategy. Future Gener. Comput. Syst. **90**, 273–290 (2019)
3. Emeakaroha, V.C., et al.: SLA-aware application deployment and resource allocation in clouds. In: International Computer Software and Applications Conference, pp. 298–303 (2011)
4. Syu, Y., Wang, C.-M., Fanjiang, Y.-Y.: Modeling and forecasting of time-aware dynamic QoS attributes for cloud services. IEEE Trans. Netw. Serv. Manag. **16**(1), 56–71 (2019)
5. Qiu, H., et al.: FIRM: An Intelligent Fine-grained Resource Management Framework for SLO-Oriented Microservices, pp. 805–825 (2020)
6. Hao, J., et al.: Measuring performance degradation of virtual machines based on the Bayesian network with hidden variables. Int. J. Commun. Syst. **31**(13), e3732 (2018)
7. Ke, G., et al.: LightGBM: A Highly Efficient Gradient Boosting Decision Tree, pp. 3146–3154 (2017)
8. Keshavarzi, A., Haghighat, A.T., Bohlouli, M.: Clustering of large scale QoS time series data in federated clouds using improved variable Chromosome Length Genetic Algorithm (CQGA). Expert Syst. Appl. **164**, 113840 (2021)
9. Zhang, B., Wang, J., Yue, K., Wu, H., Hao, J.: Performance prediction and configuration optimization of virtual machines based on random forest. Comput. Sci. **46**(9), 85–92 (2019)
10. Hao, J., Yue, K., Duan, L., Zhang, B., Fu, X.: Predicting QoS of virtual machines via Bayesian network with XGboost-induced classes. Cluster Comput. **24**(2), 1165–1184 (2020). https://doi.org/10.1007/s10586-020-03183-2

11. Li, F., Yang, D., Zhou, P., et al.: Modeling application performance in a virtualized environment **24**(9), 9–15 (2015)
12. Gandhi, A., et al.: Providing performance guarantees for cloud-deployed applications. IEEE Trans. Cloud Comput. **8**(1), 269–281 (2020)
13. Cortez, E., et al.: Resource central: understanding and predicting workloads for improved resource management in large cloud platforms. In: ACM Symposium on Operating Systems Principles, pp. 153–167 (2017)
14. Li, Y., Tang, X., Cai, W.: Dynamic bin packing for on-demand cloud resource allocation. IEEE Trans. Parallel Distrib. Syst. **27**(1), 157–170 (2016)
15. Hadary, O., et al.: Protean: VM allocation service at scale, pp. 845–861 (2020)
16. Collins, M., Schapire, R., Singer, Y.: Logistic regression, AdaBoost and Bregman distances. Mach. Learn. **48**(1–3), 253–285 (2002)
17. Chen, T., Guestrin, C.: XGBoost: a scalable tree boosting system. In: Proceedings of the 22nd ACM SIGKDD International Conference on Knowledge Discovery and Data Mining, pp. 785–794 (2016)
18. Breiman, L.: Random forests. Mach. Learn. **45**(1), 5–32 (2001)

A Semantic Retrieval Method Based on the Knowledge Graph of Ethnic Clothing Culture

Lin Cui[1,2], Shu Zhang[1(✉)], Jun Wang[1,2], and Ken Chen[1,3]

[1] Key Laboratory of Education Informatization for Nationalities,
Ministry of Education, Yunnan Normal University, Kunming 650500, China
zhangshu@ynnu.edu.cn
[2] Yunnan Key Laboratory of Smart Education, Yunnan Normal University,
Kunming 650500, China
[3] Logistics Support Service Center, Yunnan Normal University,
Kunming 650500, China

Abstract. There is no mature ontology construction method in the field of ethnic costume culture. Based on the analysis of the existing ontology construction methods and the characteristics of ethnic clothing cultural information, this paper combines the seven-step method and IDEF-5 (ICAM DEFinition method, IDEF) to propose an ontology construction method suitable for the ethnic clothing cultural field, and completes the ethnic clothing cultural knowledge graph construct. On the basis of the knowledge graph, in order to solve the problem of inaccurate retrieval results caused by the lack of semantic information in traditional information retrieval, a semantic retrieval model based on the knowledge graph is proposed, which realizes a full understanding of user retrieval intentions by adding semantics in the retrieval process. Finally, it is evaluated by experiments that this model can return accurate retrieval results to users.

Keywords: Knowledge graph · Semantic retrieval · Ethnic costume culture

1 Introduction

There are 55 ethnic minorities in our country, and the costumes of each ethnic group are different. The costume culture embodies almost all the characteristics of the ethnic group [1]. Clothing is the crystallization of human wisdom and the product of the integration of many factors such as history, culture, ideology, religious and cultural beliefs. Currently, the digitalization of ethnic minority costume culture mainly appears in the form of ethnic cultural resource websites and encyclopedia websites. There are problems such as scattered resources, easy content of digital resources, small coverage of knowledge, and inconvenience for scholars to study in depth [2]. At the same time, the retrieval method of the above-mentioned traditional websites is keyword matching. This retrieval method has the disadvantage of different quality of the information obtained by the retrieval, and it needs to be identified before it can be used.

© Springer Nature Singapore Pte Ltd. 2021
Y. Tan et al. (Eds.): DMBD 2021, CCIS 1453, pp. 273–286, 2021.
https://doi.org/10.1007/978-981-16-7476-1_25

The knowledge graph is a semantic network graph that stores entities and their relationships. The process of constructing a knowledge graph is to distill data of different structures into a structured knowledge base [3]. Therefore, this article aims to carry out research on the construction and application of the knowledge graph of ethnic costume culture by using the advantages of knowledge graph in the construction of knowledge system and knowledge expression. At the same time, in view of the problem of inaccurate retrieval results caused by the lack of semantic information in traditional information retrieval, this paper uses word segmentation, semantic expansion, knowledge reasoning and other technologies to propose a semantic retrieval model based on knowledge graphs, which is realized by adding semantics in the retrieval process A full understanding of the user's search intent also improves the depth and breadth of the search.

2 Related Work

Knowledge graph, as its name implies, is a technical method to describe the attributes of an entity and the relationship between entities in the form of a graph. At present, the more well-known knowledge graphs abroad include MetaWeb's FreeBase [4], Wikipedia-based DBpedia [5], Wikimedia Foundation's Wikidata [6], and Max Planck Institute's YAGO [7]. Domestic relatively systematic general knowledge graphs with a certain scale include XLore [8] established by Tsinghua University based on Wiki and Baidu Encyclopedia, ZhiShi.Me [9] established by Shanghai Jiao Tong University based on Interactive Encyclopedia, and Sogou Knowledge Cube [10] established by Sogou Company. and Baidu Knowledge Graph [11].

The above-mentioned knowledge graphs are general knowledge graphs with wide coverage of knowledge, but their accuracy is not as good as that of industry knowledge graphs. Therefore, in order to improve the accuracy of retrieval results, the primary task of this paper is to construct the knowledge graph in the field of ethnic minorities.

In the field of ethnic minorities, Li Qiuao [12] constructed the knowledge graph of ethnic information resources to provide users with triple query. However, this knowledge graph covers a wide range but is not precise, and lacks a certain length of text description of the concept, which has some defects in popularizing ethnic minority culture. Wang Haining [13] constructed the knowledge graph of ethnic festivals, and on this basis carried out the application of intelligent question answering. However, as long as the user's questions have certain complexity or the questions are not in the knowledge graph, they cannot give accurate answers. Pan Peipei [14] constructed the ontology of national festivals and conducted semantic path retrieval research. This project is to extract the events of Guangxi ethnic festivals and construct the ontology of ethnic festivals. This project mainly provides the query of semantic path between Guangxi ethnic festivals, which also has the problem of low popularity of ethnic knowledge.

To sum up, most of the existing knowledge graphs or ontology in the field of ethnic minority culture only contain brief triad information. The lack of a certain text description of the concept led to the project's failure to meet the requirements of popular science work. Therefore, this article adds textual descriptions to the knowledge graph to improve the science performance and application value of the knowledge graph. At the same time, research on the application of semantic retrieval is carried out on the basis of knowledge graph to meet the retrieval needs of users. At the same time, in terms of the application of knowledge graphs, the coverage of question and answer templates and event templates of the aforementioned knowledge graphs is limited, which leads to poor retrieval effects. Therefore, this article uses semantic expansion technology to improve retrieval results on the basis of knowledge graphs.

3 The Construction of Cultural Knowledge Graph of Ethnic Costumes

The first step of constructing the knowledge graph in this paper is to use ontology technology to complete the construction of the knowledge system structure of ethnic costume culture, and then complete the construction of the knowledge graph of ethnic costume culture on the basis of ontology.

3.1 The Construction of Ethnic Minority Costume Cultural Ontology

The Concept of Ontology. The concept of ontology originated in the field of philosophy [15]. In philosophy, ontology is defined as "the systematic description of the objective existence in the world" [16]. It was introduced into the computer field in the 1980s to describe concepts and the relationship between them. It is the model layer of most knowledge graphs [17]. The goal of constructing ontology is to obtain recognized concepts in the field, and to provide definitions of concepts and relationships between concepts to build a knowledge system for the construction of knowledge graphs. At present, common ontology construction methods are: the METHONTOLOGY method used in the chemical field [18], the skeleton method used in the commercial field [19], the IDEF-5 [20] method and the TOVE method [21], and the method developed by Stanford Medical School seven-step method [22], the following focuses on the seven-step method and IDEF-5.

The seven-step method was originally used to build ontologies in the medical field, but now it has been moved to other fields. The seven-step method is divided into 7 steps: (1) Determine the purpose and scope of the ontology. (2) Find the existing ontologies in the field and reuse them appropriately existing ontology. (3) List the terminology in this field, and define the classes of the ontology according to the terms; (4) Clarify the structural hierarchical relationship of the ontology and determine the hierarchical relationship between the classes. (5) Determine the attributes of the classes. (6) Determine the subject and object of the attribute. (7) Filling examples.

IDEF-5 is divided into 5 steps: (1) Define the scope and team members of the ontology. (2) Collect raw data. (3) Analyze the data. (4) Preliminary development of the ontology. (5) Ontology optimization and verification.

Seven-step method and IDEF-5 are one of the most commonly used methods for ontology construction in their respective fields. Both methods have their own advantages and disadvantages and cannot be directly used for the construction of ethnic costume culture ontology. Table 1 lists the shortcomings of the two methods in the ontology construction of ethnic minority costume culture.

Table 1. Defects of seven-step method and IDEF-5.

Ontology construction method	Shortcomings
Seven-step method	(1) There is a lack of data collection and data analysis links (2) There is no ontology evaluation link in the ontology construction process, and the quality of the ontology cannot be guaranteed
IDEF-5	(1) Without ontology structure design, it is impossible to guarantee whether the structure of ontology is perfect or not (2) No reuse of existing resources

Based on the problems in Table 1, this article improves the seven-step method and the IDEF-5 method, combines the two methods to learn from each other's strengths, and proposes a method for constructing ethnic minority costume culture ontology. This method adds data analysis, ontology structure design, ontology evaluation and other stages on the original basis, making the ontology knowledge structure of ethnic clothing more scientific and complete.

The Construction of Ethnic Minority Costume Cultural Ontology. According to the improved process of constructing ethnic costume culture ontology in this article, the specific steps for constructing ethnic costume culture ontology in this section are as follows:

(1) Determine the scope of ontology. The research content of this paper is to build the knowledge graph of minority costume culture, and the focus of ontology content should also be minority costume culture.
(2) Collection and analysis of ethnic costume cultural information. This article summarizes the data from books and the Internet, uses the published authoritative book structure as the main reference basis, compares and analyzes data from multiple sources, and supplements and improves the knowledge description.
(3) Ontology analysis. According to the analysis of the cultural data of ethnic costumes, taking ethnic costumes as the center and referring to the national standard clothing terminology, this paper determines the relevant concepts, divides these concepts into different levels, and determines the attributes and relationships of the concepts (see Fig. 1).

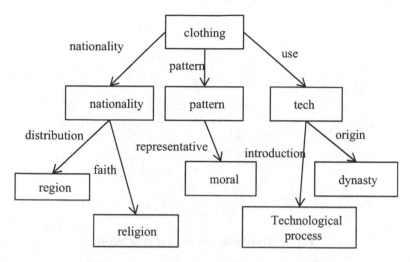

Fig. 1. Main concepts and relations of ontology

(4) Build and reuse ontology. In this section, Protégé software is used to construct the cultural ontology of ethnic minority costumes. The OWL ontology description language is used to model the above-mentioned concepts, relationships, and attributes.

(5) Ontology evaluation. In the ontology evaluation stage, the opinions of experts are consulted to evaluate the ontology of ethnic costume culture. At the same time, Jena inference engine is used to verify the logic relationship between concepts. For example: "tie dye" is also called "twisted dye", the logical relationship between the two should be equivalent. If I deliberately set "tie dye" and "twisted dye" as the relationship between the parent class and the child class, the inference engine will prompt a logic error. From this, to verify whether the ontology we created meets the requirements.

(6) Complete the preliminary construction of ontology. After the evaluation, the preliminary construction of ethnic costume culture ontology is completed.

(7) Iterative upgrade. Ontology is a continuous and dynamic process. After the initial completion of ontology, we need to correct the ontology according to the practical application. We cannot collect all the data of ethnic minority clothing culture at one time, so we need to continuously obtain the data of ethnic minority clothing field, and constantly iterate and upgrade the content of ontology.

3.2 Knowledge Storage of the Cultural Knowledge Graph of Ethnic Costumes

After data processing according to ontology structure, the structured data is stored in Neo4j graph database (see Fig. 2).

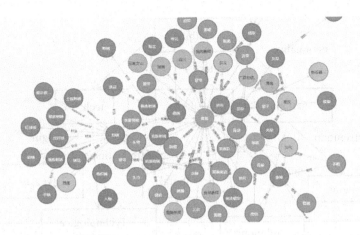

Fig. 2. Visualization of some data in Neo4j

The original intention of this article to establish a knowledge graph of minority costume culture is to promote and popularize minority costume culture. In the original data collected in this article, some of the knowledge contained in the descriptive text cannot be refined into triples. In the existing knowledge graph, the content of the knowledge graph generally only contains the domain concepts and entities in the form of triples. The explanation and description of the concepts and the entities themselves are lacking, but a concept in the field of ethnic clothing culture often requires a paragraph of descriptive text explains and expands it to strengthen users' understanding of the concept, so as to better spread and popularize the knowledge of the field of ethnic minority clothing. Therefore, this article will do the following processing for this part of the data:

STEP 1: Document parsing, parsing documents in PDF, DOC and other formats into plain text and storing them in MySql database;

STEP 2: Segment the parsed text data into paragraphs;

STEP 3: Use TF-IDF (Term Frequency - Inverse Document Frequency) method to extract keywords from text;

STEP 4: Take the top three keywords as the text index value;

To sum up, structural data is stored in Neo4j, descriptive text is stored in MySql, then the construction of knowledge graph is completed.

4   Research on Semantic Retrieval Model Based on Knowledge Graph

In the previous article, we have completed the construction of the minority clothing culture knowledge graph. At this stage, this paper will realize semantic retrieval on the basis of the knowledge graph. Traditional retrieval methods can not take into account the situation of multiple words in one meaning, and can not expand knowledge. To solve the above problems, this paper uses word segmentation technology to obtain keywords. Synonym dictionary is used to replace synonyms to reduce the workload of semantic input and reduce the error of retrieval results caused by the ambiguity of retrieval words. Finally, semantic similarity calculation technology and knowledge reasoning technology are used to realize semantic expansion. Integrate the above modules to build a semantic retrieval model to improve the retrieval efficiency. Make up for the shortcomings of traditional retrieval. Semantic retrieval model (see Fig. 3).

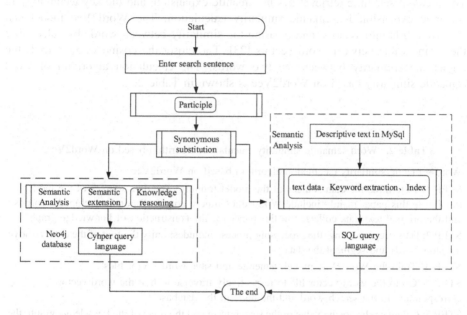

Fig. 3. Semantic retrieval model

The workflow of the semantic retrieval model is as follows:

STEP 1: Perform word segmentation on the user's search sentences, and convert a sentence into a search term. Use the Jieba.load_userdict() function in the Jieba word segmentation tool to load a custom domain dictionary to segment the search sentence, and at the same time to tag the segmented words. In order to better capture the keywords of the search sentence, this article only retains noun search words and verb search words.

STEP 2: Use the thesaurus to synonymously replace the search terms, and replace the non-standard words entered by the user with the standard words in the knowledge graph. This can reduce the workload of semantic input before retrieval, and to a certain extent reduce the retrieval result errors caused by the ambiguity of retrieval words.

STEP 3: Graph the search term to the entities and keywords in the knowledge graph. If the search term is contained in the knowledge graph, the search result will be displayed. If the search term is not in the knowledge graph, then jump to STEP 4.

STEP 4: Use the semantic similarity calculation method based on Word2Vec to calculate the semantic similarity between the search term and the entities and keywords in the knowledge graph, find the words similar to the search term, search and return the result for the user.

4.1   Semantic Extension Based on Word2Vec

The focus of semantic retrieval lies in semantic expansion, and the key technology in semantic expansion is semantic similarity calculation. The Word2Vec model can convert words into vectors, and measure the similarity between words by calculating the cosine value between word vectors [23]. The closer the cosine value is to 1, the higher the similarity between the two words. The calculation algorithm of word semantic similarity based on Word2Vec is shown in Table 2.

Table 2. Word semantic similarity calculation algorithm based on Word2Vec.

Word semantic similarity calculation algorithm based on Word2Vec
STEP 1: Determine the data sources of the model training. The data sources of the model training in this paper mainly include Wikipedia Chinese corpus, Baidu Encyclopedia corpus and the original text data collected in this paper for the construction of knowledge graph
STEP 2: Data preprocessing, the processing process includes: unify the font of the data, remove the stop words and segment the data
STEP 3: Train the Word2Vec model, generate and save word vector files
STEP 4: Go to the word vector file to respectively traverse to find the word vector corresponding to the search word and the node in the database
STEP 5: Calculate the cosine value of the search term and the node of the knowledge graph, the calculation formula is as follows: $$sim(A,B) = \frac{\sum_{i=1}^{n} A_i \times B_i}{\sqrt{\sum_{i=1}^{n} A_i} \times \sqrt{\sum_{i=1}^{n} B_i}} \quad (1)$$
STEP 6: Reverse sort the cosine values
STEP 7: Use the node corresponding to the largest cosine value as the search term and output the search result

4.2   Knowledge Reasoning

Knowledge reasoning is to reason about the implicit knowledge in the field of ethnic costume culture through the rules and constraints between ontology concepts (such as equivalence relations between concepts, inheritance relations, etc.).

Different from traditional retrieval, this module uses Jena inference engine to map keywords to ontology for reasoning, which expands the retrieval results to a certain extent. The cultural ontology of ethnic minority clothing in this article uses OWL as the description language, uses Jena to read the ontology OWL file, and defines rules to reason about the meaning of clothing patterns.

For example, define an inference rule as: [ruleclothermaen: (?A: pattern 'hook flower') -> (? A: meaning 'strong')], which means that the pattern "hook flower" represents strong, if clothes A the pattern is a hook flower, so this dress has a strong symbolic meaning. The specific reasoning process is shown in Table 3.

Table 3. Jena reasoning process.

Jena reasoning process:
STEP 1: Create an inference engine and define rules through jena.reasoner.Reasoner.   [ruleclothermaen: (? A: the pattern " hook flower ") - > (? A: it means "strong")

STEP 2: load ontology.
 //Coat is a subclass of clothing
     \<owl:Class rdf:about=" coat ">
       \<rdfs:subClassOf rdf:resource=" clothing "/>
     \</owl:Class>
 //Plant pattern is a subcategory of pattern collection
     \<owl:Class rdf:about=" Plant pattern ">
        \<rdfs:subClassOf rdf:resource=" pattern collection "/>
     \</owl:Class>
 //Tujia brocade coat belong to coat, the pattern is hook flower
   \<owl:NamedIndividual rdf:about="Tujia Brocade coat">
      \<rdf:type rdf:resource=" coat "/>
        \<pattern rdf:resource="hook flower"/>
     \</owl:NamedIndividual>
 //The pattern belongs to the plant pattern in the pattern collection, and the hook flower symbolizes strong.
     \<owl:NamedIndividual rdf:about=" hook flower ">
       \<rdf:type rdf:resource="plant pattern "/>
       \<rdf:type rdf:resource="pattern collection"/>
       \<meaning rdf:resource="strong"/>
       \<pattern name> hook flower \</pattern name>
   \</owl:NamedIndividual>

STEP 3: After the Jena inference engine infers:
 //The Tujia brocade top is a piece of clothing, and the hook flower pattern on it symbolizes strong.
     \<owl:NamedIndividual rdf:about="Tujia Brocade coat">
       \<rdf:type rdf:resource="Clothing"/>
   \<rdf:type rdf:resource="coat"/>
     \<pattern rdf:resource=" hook flower"/>
   \<meaning rdf:resource="strong"/>
     \</owl:NamedIndividual>

Through the above reasoning, when the user searches for clothes with strong meaning, the knowledge related to the Tujia brocade coat will be returned to the user as the answer.

5   Experiment and Discussion

5.1   Experimental Comparison of Calculation Methods for Word Semantic Similarity

At present, the semantic similarity algorithms of Chinese vocabulary are mainly divided into two categories: one is the calculation of vocabulary similarity based on "HowNet" and "Synonyms Cilin"; the other is the calculation of semantic similarity of words based on Word2Vec.

In this paper, the calculation method of semantic similarity based on "HowNet" is recorded as method A; the calculation method of semantic similarity based on "Synonym Cilin" is recorded as method B; combining "HowNet" and "Synonym Cilin" The calculation method of semantic similarity of vocabulary is recorded as method C; the calculation method of semantic similarity of vocabulary based on Word2Vec is recorded as method D, and the experiment is compared. The group of words in Table 4 was given to 20 subjects for semantic similarity judgment, and finally the average value of 20 human judgments was taken as the artificial evaluation value. The comparison results are shown in Table 4.

Table 4. Comparison of experimental results

Word group	A	B	C	D	Manual evaluation
Long skirt | Hui nationality	0.000000	No long skirt	0.083149	0.075190	0.083140
Hui people | Hui nationality	0.000000	0.358899	0.000000	0.618080	0.789359
Bird | Dog	0.762140	0.000000	0.762140	0.309886	0.378158
Skirt | Pants	1.000000	0.870000	1.000000	0.837494	0.722807
Embroidery | Tie dye	No tie dye	No Tie Dye	−1.000000	0.730776	0.512046

According to the experimental comparison, for the phrase "long skirt" and "Hui nationality", method A can accurately judge that there is no similarity between the two; method B cannot calculate the similarity because the word "long skirt" is not included; method C calculates the calculated similarity is about 0.083; the similarity calculated by the D method is about 0.075, and the values calculated by the two methods are in line with the expected value of human judgment.

"Hui people" and "Hui nationality" phrases, the similarity calculated by method A is 0.0, but in our common sense, the Hui nationality can be regarded as a subset of the

Hui people, or as the same collective, so this result is not accurate; the similarity calculated by method B is about 0.35, and the value is slightly smaller, which does not meet the expected value of manual judgment; the similarity calculated by method C is about 0.0, which does not meet the expected value of manual judgment; the similarity calculated by method D the degree is about 0.61, which is in line with the expected value of human judgment.

"Bird" and "Dog" phrases, the similarity calculated by method A is 0.76, but in our common sense, although birds and dogs are animals, but birds belong to poultry, and dogs belong to livestock, so this result is too high. The similarity calculated by method B is about 0.0, and the value is too small to meet the expected value of manual judgment; the similarity calculated by method C is about 0.76, and the value is too large to meet the expected value of manual judgment. The similarity calculated by D method is about 0.30, which is in line with the expected value of human judgment.

The phrase "Pants" and "Skirt". The similarity calculated by the A method is 1.00; the similarity calculated by the B method is about 0.87; the similarity calculated by the C method is about 1.00; the similarity calculated by the D method is about 0.83. Although the four methods have different values but they are basically in line with the expected value of human judgment.

The phrases "Embroidery" and "Tie Dye" are not included in "Synonyms Cilin" and "HowNet", so the first three methods cannot calculate the similarity; the similarity calculated by the D method is about 0.73, embroidery and tie dyeing are both techniques, basically in line with the expected value of human judgment.

To sum up, in order to avoid the embarrassment caused by the small coverage of the dictionary and the lack of detailed classification of dictionary vocabulary attributes, this paper chooses the Word2Vec based vocabulary semantic similarity calculation method with relatively higher accuracy as the core method of semantic expansion in this paper.

5.2 Evaluation of Semantic Retrieval Model

For the evaluation of the retrieval model, the precision, the recall and the F1 value are generally used to evaluate the quality of the retrieval results. The Precision is mainly used to evaluate the precision of the system, and the recall is used to evaluate the recall of the system.

The calculation formula is:

$$P = \frac{\text{Relevant documents retrieved}}{\text{The total number of files retrieved by the system}} \tag{2}$$

$$R = \frac{\text{Relevant documents retrieved}}{\text{The total number of all related files in the system}} \tag{3}$$

$$F1 = \frac{2 * P * R}{P + R} \tag{4}$$

This article selects 5 groups of search terms to test the evaluation model.

The precision, recall and F1 values of each group of search terms are shown in Table 5:

Table 5. Experimental results.

Search sentence	Number	P	R	F1
Pleated skirt	104	93.75%	71.43%	81.08%
Miao embroidery	256	98.00%	96.00%	93.95%
Flower pattern	107	92.85%	81.25%	86.66%
Flower-patterned bodice	67	88.00%	80.73%	84.20%
Auspicious meaning clothing	323	75.00%	60.00%	66.66%

It can be seen from Table 5 that the semantic retrieval model based on the knowledge graph of ethnic minority clothing has relatively good performance in precision and recall. For "Pleated skirt", "Miao embroidery", and "Flower pattern" containing a single keyword, which can be directly graph to the search sentence in the knowledge graph, the precision is about 90%. But for "Pleated skirts", due to the many classifications of pleated skirts and their description methods, some information related to pleated skirts has not been retrieved, resulting in a low recall rate; for "Flower-patterned bodice" in the knowledge graph the search sentence of the same concept cannot be found directly in, and the precision reaches 88%. Compared with the search sentence that can be found directly through the knowledge graph mapping, the precision is lower. As for the "Auspicious meaning clothing" search sentence that requires semantic analysis to get the search result, the precision and recall are relatively low because it cannot be directly mapped to the knowledge graph, but it can basically meet the search requirements from the search results. Finally, based on the F1 value, the semantic retrieval model based on the ethnic clothing knowledge graph can bring users a better retrieval experience in practical applications.

6   Conclusion

This paper aims to spread the excellent minority costume culture. Firstly, this paper makes a comparative analysis of the ontology construction methods; The seven- step method and IDEF-5 ontology construction method are improved, and the ontology construction is completed. Then, the knowledge graph of ethnic minority clothing culture is constructed on this basis. Compared with other knowledge graphs, this knowledge graph adds a large number of descriptive texts to meet the supplementary needs of users for knowledge. Thirdly, a semantic retrieval model is designed based on the knowledge graph. Compared with traditional retrieval, the model uses synonym dictionary to replace synonyms to reduce the workload of semantic input, and extracts keywords from descriptive text to establish index values to improve the retrieval speed. Finally, semantic similarity calculation technology and knowledge reasoning technology are used to realize semantic expansion, which solves the problem of "not find, the result is wrong" to a great extent. After experimental evaluation, the accuracy of the semantic retrieval model proposed in this paper can reach more than 90%, which can meet the daily retrieval needs of users.

Acknowledgments. This work is supported by Major Science and Technology Project of Yunnan Province (No. 202002AD080001), Yunnan Expert Workstation of Xiaochun Cao, Kunming Key Laboratory of Education Informatization, and Doctoral research initiation program of Yunnan Normal University (No. 2019XJLK21).

References

1. Peng Shengqiong, F.: Research on the construction technology of ethnic costume characteristic resource database. Manuf. Autom. **37**(08), 44–47 (2015)
2. Lu Na, F.: Digital exploration of Yugu costume culture protection. China Packaging **38**(06), 46–48 (2018)
3. Liu Qiao, F.: Summary of knowledge graph construction technology. Comput. Res. Dev. **53** (03), 582–600 (2016)
4. Bollacker, K.D.F.: Freebase: a collaboratively created graph database for structuring human knowledge. In: SIGMOD Conference. ACM (2008)
5. Bizer, C.F.: DBpedia - a crystallization point for the web of data. J. Web Semant. **7**(3), 154–165 (2009)
6. WMF. Wikidata. https://www.wikidata.org/wiki/Wikidata:Main_Page. Accessed 10 Marc 2021
7. Suchanek, F.: Yago - a large ontology from Wikipedia and WordNet. Web Semant. Sci. Serv. Agents World Wide Web **6**(3), 203–217 (2008)
8. Jin, H.F.: XLORE2: large-scale cross-lingual knowledge graph construction and application. Data Intell. **1**(1), 77–98 (2019)
9. Niu, X., Sun, X., Wang, H., Rong, S., Qi, G., Yu, Y.: Zhishi.me - weaving Chinese linking open data. In: Aroyo, L., et al. (eds.) ISWC 2011. LNCS, vol. 7032, pp. 205–220. Springer, Heidelberg (2011). https://doi.org/10.1007/978-3-642-25093-4_14
10. Baidu Baike. Baidu Knowledge Graph. https://baike.baidu.com/item/. Accessed 10 Mar 2021
11. Sogou Encyclopedia. Sogou Knowledge Cube. https://baike.sogou.com/. Accessed 10 Mar 2021
12. Li, Q.: Construction and application of knowledge grap in the field of information resources of ethnic minorities. Yunnan Normal University (2020)
13. Wang, H.: Research on the Construction and Application of Ethnic Festival Knowledge Graph. Yunnan Normal University (2020)
14. Pan, P.: Research on the Semantic Path of Ethnic Festival Event Ontology. Guangxi Normal University (2016)
15. Gan Jianhou, F., Jiang Yue, S., Xia Youming, T.: Ontology method and its application. Beijing Science Press (2011)
16. Lin, Y.: Research and implementation of key technologies for the construction and retrieval of cultural relics knowledge graphs. Zhejiang University (2017)
17. Huang Hengqi, F.: A review of knowledge graph research. Comput. Syst. Appl. **28**(06), 1–12 (2019)
18. Juristo, N.F.: METHONOLOGY: form ontological art towards ontological engineering. AAAI Technical report, vol. 97, no. 06, pp. 33–40 (1997)

19. Yu Fan, F.: Domain Ontology Construction Method and Empirical Research, pp. 39–40. Wuhan University Press, Wuhan (2015)
20. Yan Ye, F.: Ontology-based semantic models for supply chain management. Int. J. Adv. Manuf. Technol. **37**(11), 1250–1260 (2008)
21. Hu Zhaoqin, F.: Ontology and Knowledge Organization, pp. 65–66. Beijing China Literature and History Publishing House (2013)
22. Zhang, K.F.: An approach for named entity disambiguation with knowledge graph, pp. 138–143 (2018)
23. Sun Lili, F.: The calculation method of concept semantic similarity based on WordNet. Stat. Decis. **23**, 79–82 (2017)

Fine-Grained Semantic Segmentation of National Costume Grayscale Image Based on Human Parsing

Di Wu[1,2], Jianhou Gan[1,2(✉)], and Wei Zou[1,2]

[1] Key Laboratory of Education Informatization for Nationalities, Ministry of Education, Yunnan Normal University, Kunming 650500, China
ganjh@ynnu.edu.cn
[2] Yunnan Key Laboratory of Smart Education, Yunnan Normal University, Kunming 650500, China

Abstract. In order to enhance the image understanding of different regions for national costume grayscale image automatic colorization, let coloring tasks take advantage of semantic conditions, also let it can apply the human parsing semantic segmentation method to the national costume grayscale image for semantic segmentation task. This paper proposes a semantic segmentation model for context embedding based on edge perceiving. Aiming at the features of national costume grayscale image, more optimizing the model and loss function. The national costume grayscale image semantic segmentation is different from semantic segmentation of the color image, this task is more difficult for the grayscale image has no color feature. In this paper, edge information and edge consistency constraints are used to improve the national costume grayscale image coloring effect. The experimental results show that the model designed in this paper can obtain more accurate fine-grained semantic segmentation results for the national costume grayscale image.

Keywords: Semantic segmentation · National costume grayscale image · Human parsing · Fine-grained semantic

1 Introduction

Semantic segmentation task has always been a hot research topic in the field of computer vision, which can give different regions of the image corresponding semantic information, and provide support for the subsequent higher-level tasks. The human parsing task belongs to a branch of semantic segmentation task which is a kind of fine-grained semantic segmentation task, the purpose is to identify the pixel level regions of the human body image, each human body region of the target image can be the fine-grained level of semantic segmentation, get to the various body regions of image intensification of semantic information.

For the grayscale image coloring task of the national costume, the fine-grained semantic information of different regions of the costume can be used to assist

© Springer Nature Singapore Pte Ltd. 2021
Y. Tan et al. (Eds.): DMBD 2021, CCIS 1453, pp. 287–299, 2021.
https://doi.org/10.1007/978-981-16-7476-1_26

the grayscale image coloring task of the national costume, making the grayscale image coloring effect of national costume more outstanding. In order to make provide accurate and refined semantic information conditions for the subsequent tasks better, it is necessary to execute fine-grained semantic segmentation operation for the grayscale images of national costume. At present, for semantic segmentation tasks, the input image is generally a color image, while the input in this paper is a grayscale image. Due to the difference in color features between the two, the grayscale image as the input will increase the difficulty of semantic segmentation, especially for semantic segmentation at the fine-grained level.

This paper studies the semantic segmentation method of fine-grained national costumes with national costumes as the target object. The semantic segmentation model of the national costume grayscale image has been designed. Referring to the CE2P [10] human parsing model, a high-resolution embedded module is used to amplify the feature image to recover more details. A larger model network allows more details to be retained, which is conducive to subsequent operations. The global context embedded module is introduced to encode multi-scale context information, and the multi-scale context information is used to supplement more details and optimize feature extraction. The edge perceiving module is introduced to further use semantic segmentation information to supplement the object contour information, integrate the corresponding features of the object contour, and sharpen the predicted boundary.

2   Related Work

For the task of semantic segmentation, researchers have proposed different methods for more accurate segmentation of images. At present, the mainstream semantic segmentation methods can be roughly divided into two kinds. The first is the idea of high-resolution preservation. Since the semantic segmentation at the fine-grained level needs to achieve a more refined effect, many methods try to use the feature information of low dimension to achieve refined semantic resolution by using the feature information of high resolution. The general semantic segmentation model includes a large number of convolution and pooling operations, which caused the key feature information to obviously be lost. There are two main solutions to this problem. One is to remove several downsampling operations [1], and another one is to introduce low-dimensional feature information [2]. The second is contextual information embedding, which uses the feature information of multiple scales to solve the problem of refined semantic segmentation. The two structures of ASPP [3] and the PSP [12] are used to effectively solve various problems caused by various scales. Combine local features with global features to achieve more reliable predictions.

As for the human parsing task, more and more researchers devote themselves to it because of its wide application. The earliest explorations and attempts were the analytical method [4,11] based on CRF and the prediction of segmentation results based on the information of human post estimation [6]. Liang et al. [9] proposed that the Co-CNN structure integrates local features and global features, which significantly improves the performance of segmentation. SSL [5] introduces a self-supervised structure perceived loss function, which restricts the consistency between the parsing results and the human connection structure, it helps the human body to resolve the task. JPPNet [8] integrates two tasks of human post estimation and human parsing. CE2P framework proposes a semantic segmentation method of context embedding based on edge perceiving. A-CE2P [7] framework has been further improved on the basis of the previous framework.

3 Method

3.1 Context Embedding with Edge Perceiving

Human parsing is a fine-grained semantic segmentation task that aims to identify the individual components (e.g., clothing and body parts) of a human image at the pixel level. The human parsing task is actually a category analysis of each pixel in the target image. Context embedding human parsing method based on edge perceiving, its model includes context embedding module, high-resolution embedding module and edge perceiving module. The model integrates the three functional modules, and finally realizes the human parsing model that integrates contextual embedding features, low-dimensional features, and semantic boundary information. This model can train the fine-grained semantic results end-to-end.

Compared with general semantic segmentation tasks, the challenge of human parsing is to produce more detailed predictions of various regions of the human body. The Context Embedding with Edge Perceiving (CE2P) method uses ResNet-101 as the backbone of feature extraction. The whole model is composed of three main modules, which will be described in detail in the following paragraphs.

Context Embedding Module. For the human parsing task, the global context embedding module is mainly helpful to predict the fine-grained category information. For example, if two relatively similar regions are been judged, the category needs to be further referred to and combined with the global features to help the fine-grained category judgment. The module performs four adaptive average pooling operations on the features extracted from the feature extraction network to generate multi-scale context features with dimensions of 1×1, 2×2, 3×3 and 6×6, respectively. The four groups of context features adopt upsampling operation, and the size of the original feature image is kept consistent with the size of the original feature image through the bilinear interpolation sampling method, so as to generate features that can be further concatenated with the original feature image. Then 1×1 convolution operation is adopted to reduce the number of feature channels and further integrate multi-scale context feature information. Finally, the output of the context embedded module is fed into the subsequent high-resolution embedded module as the global prior context information.

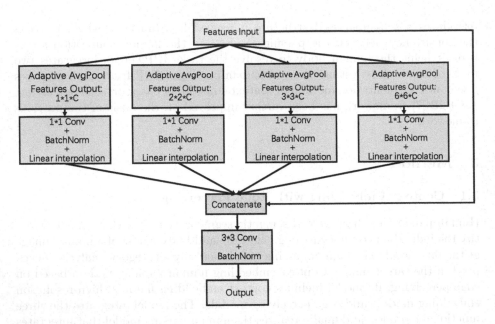

Fig. 1. Diagram of context embedding module.

Context embedded module is as shown in Fig. 1, the detailed structural features were input into four groups of adaptive average pooling, four groups of features output channel respectively 1×1, 2×2, 3×3, 6×6, and then into 1×1 of convolution and batch of normalized linear interpolation operation, then the results of four groups and input features of the original data to concatenate, In the next step, the concatenated feature map is input to the 3×3 convolution layer and the batch normalization layer for processing, and the new feature map is finally output.

High-Resolution Embedding Module. The main purpose of the high-resolution embedded module is to restore the feature map and make it contain more information. For fine-grained semantic segmentation and parsing tasks, some segmentation contents take a small proportion in the image, such as shoes, gloves, and other semantics. The general deep neural network is used to extract features. After multiple convolutional pooling operations, the detailed information is seriously lost, which makes the segmentation task of small targets difficult. Therefore, the introduction of a high-resolution embedded module is very important for the semantic segmentation of fine-grained small targets. As the depth of the network increases, the convolution and pooling operations reduce the detail representation of the feature graph. In order to recover the missing details of the features, the low-order visual features embedded in the middle layer of the convolutional neural network are used to supplement the higher-order semantic features. The schematic diagram of the high-resolution embedded module is shown in Fig. 2.

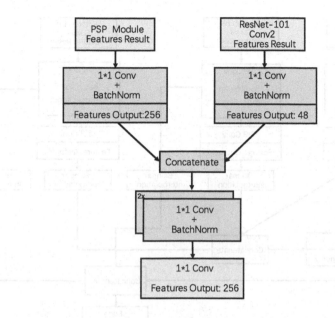

Fig. 2. Diagram of high-resolution embedding module.

The module is divided into two parts. The first input is the feature result output by the PSP module, and the second input is the feature result output by the Conv2 layer of the ResNet-101 feature extraction network. Both feature results are input into the 1 × 1 convolution layer respectively, and before that batch normalization is executed. After the feature map of the PSP, the module is convolved, the dimension of the feature output channel becomes 256, and the dimension of the special channel output result after the convolution of ResNet-101 Conv2 becomes 48. After that, the two are concatenated and then input into two continuous 1 × 1 convolution layers and batch normalization layer as a whole. Finally, the dimension of the feature output channel becomes 256 after passing through 1 × 1 convolution layer.

Edge Perceiving Module. The edge Perceiving module uses the interface of each semantic of the semantic dataset to form an edge graph and further assist semantic segmentation tasks. The purpose of the module is to learn the representation of the contour boundary and further sharpen the proximity to improve the prediction of fine-grained semantic segmentation results. The module adopts the multi-scale semantic edge detection of three groups, which can predict the edge information and get better prediction results.

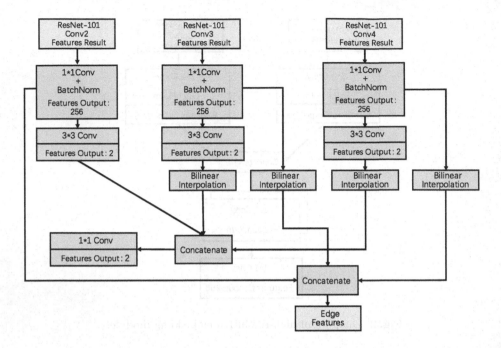

Fig. 3. Diagram of edge perceiving module.

As shown in Fig. 3, 1×1 convolution operation and batch normalization operation is executed for the output feature graphs of Conv2, Conv3, and Conv4 layers in the feature extraction module of ResNet-101, and the dimension of feature output channel is 256. Then, 3×3 convolution layer is executed for the three branches, and the dimension of the output feature channel is 2. The second branch and the third branch are concatenated after bilinear interpolation to generate the final feature map. At the same time, the feature output channel dimension of the other way is 2, and then the stitching operation is executed to output the edge graph with the feature channel dimension of 2.

Loss Function. For deep learning methods, the architecture of the whole model and the design of the loss function is crucial, and each module should cooperate with each other. The loss function in this chapter is composed of three parts, each corresponding to the respective parts of the network model. The three components of the loss function are cumulative cross-entropy loss functions. The formula of the cross-entropy loss function is shown in Eq. 1. The overall loss function of the network model is shown in Eq. 2.

$$H(p,q) = -\sum_{i=1}^{n} p(x_i) \log(q(x_i)) \tag{1}$$

$$\mathcal{L} = \mathcal{L}_{Parsing} + \mathcal{L}_{Edge} + \mathcal{L}_{Edge-Parsing} \tag{2}$$

where represents the weighted cross-entropy loss function between the edge graph detected by the edge module and the binary edge label graph; Represents the cross-entropy loss function between the parsing result of the high-resolution module and the parsing label; Represents the cross-entropy loss function between the final parsing result predicted from the edge perception branch and the parsing label.

3.2 Improved Semantic Segmentation Method Based on Grayscale Image of National Costume

Context embedding model CE2P based on edge perception has excellent human parsing segmentation performance. It combines edge parsing with human parsing to accurately predict semantic edge regions. The three branches of CE2P can be briefly understood as a parsing branch, edge branch, and fusion branch. It is worth noting that edge branching is used to generate boundaries between fine-grained classes. All the semantic features of the fusion branch are from the parsing branch, and the edge features are from the edge branch. In this way, fine-grained semantic segmentation is carried out.

Although CE2P is very powerful, there are some aspects that can be improved. Firstly, $MIoU$ can be indirectly optimized by the cross-entropy loss function. Secondly, CE2P implicitly influences the segmentation results through edge prediction and does not make explicit use of boundary features in the parsing results. Based on the key functions, the parsing branch of CE2P is divided into the backbone module, the context encoding module, and the decoding module. Specifically, the backbone module can segment the semantic network based on the residual network structure, and the context coding module can use the global feature information to execute fine-grained semantic classification, which can adopt the pyramid multi-scale method or the attention mechanism method.

Different from color images, the semantic segmentation of grayscale images is faced with the problem of lack of color features and fuzzy semantics. In order to improve the semantic segmentation performance and solve the problem of CE2P, based on A-CE2P, this paper studies and improves the fine-grained semantic segmentation method of national costume grayscale images. Through A large number of experiments and analyses, the optimal solution for fine-grained semantic segmentation of national costume grayscale images is found. The overall structure of the network model is shown in Fig. 4.

The target image is first inputted into the parsing branch, and then features are extracted through the five-layer convolution layer of ResNet-101. Different levels of features are obtained through different convolution layers, and then input into the decoding unit through context embedding and upsampling concatenated. Edge branch, the features extracted from the backbone network are connected to the decoding unit for upsampling and edge result prediction. The fusion branch inputs the features extracted from the backbone network to its branch decoding unit by upsampling and concatenated the results of the parsing branch decoding unit and the edge decoding unit. Finally, the results of the parsing branch decoding unit and the fusion branch decoding unit are connected to

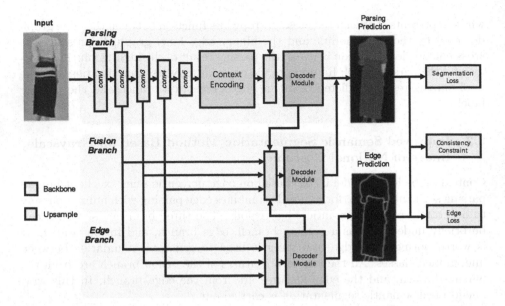

Fig. 4. Diagram of edge perceiving module.

get the semantic segmentation prediction results. The loss function of the model consists of three parts, as shown in Eq. 3. Among them, λ_1, λ_2, and λ_3 are three hyper-parameters, which are used to control the contribution degree of three loss functions. $L_{Parsing}$ is the deviation between the predicted result of edge branch and the real edge information, L_{Edge} is the deviation between the result of parsing branch prediction and the real semantic information, $L_{Edge-Parsing}$ is the deviation between the result of branch prediction and that of edge prediction after the result of branch prediction is transformed into edge information

$$\mathcal{L} = \lambda_1 \mathcal{L}_{Parsing} + \lambda_2 \mathcal{L}_{Edge} + \lambda_3 \mathcal{L}_{Edge-Parsing} \tag{3}$$

where $\mathcal{L}_{Parsing}$ is composed of two parts, and the loss functions of the two parts are superimposed together, as shown in Eq. 4, where $\mathcal{L}_{cls}$ uses the common convolutional cross-entropy loss function to evaluate the effect of neural network classification, as shown in Eq. 5. $\mathcal{L}_{miou}$ adopts $Lovász$-$Softmax$ [?] for calculation, which specifically targets the loss function involving IoU and is proved to have excellent performance in semantic segmentation tasks.

$$\mathcal{L}_{parsing} = \mathcal{L}_{cls} + \mathcal{L}_{miou} \tag{4}$$

$$\mathcal{L}_{cls} = -\frac{1}{N} \sum_k \sum_n \hat{y}_k^n \log p\left(y_k^n\right) \tag{5}$$

4   Experiments and Discussion

4.1   Database

This article main researched the content of national costume grayscale image color, because there is temporarily no public dataset on the national costume, so this article previously use previously built minority costume image dataset, launches the research, the collected in Yunnan province within the scope of common four national high-definition clothing dataset, including Dai, Hani, Wa, Yi. There is also a lot of work after the image collection, especially for high-definition image resources. The dataset used in this paper is a uniform and standard fine-grained semantic dataset of national costume constructed for the research content. The quality of each image in the dataset constructed is guaranteed, and it is all taken by professional equipment and background. According to the shape features of national costume images, the ratio of length to width of images in the dataset is set to 2:1, and the resolution reaches up to 2048×1024. The dataset used in this paper contains a total of 340 sets of images of national costume, each of which contains 3 to 4 images from multiple angles including front, back, and side, etc. About 1200 images are included.

According to the features of national costume, the semantics can be roughly divided into 8 categories. The dataset contains a total of about 4,000 labels. An example of semantic annotation of images in the dataset is shown in Fig. 5. In the figure, the first column is the original image of the national costume, the second column is the visual effect of the integration of the original image and semantic of national costume, and the third column is the visual effect picture of the separate semantic of national costume.

4.2   Experimental and Setting

The Experimental Software Configuration Is as Follows:

1) Operating system: Ubuntu 16.04
2) Programming language: Python 3.7.6
3) Image processing library: opencv-python 4.3.0.36
4) Deep learning framework: Pytorch 1.5.1

The Experimental Hardware Configuration Is as Follows:

1) Central processing unit (CPU): Intel Xeon Silver; 4210
2) Graphics processing unit (GPU): 2*NVIDIA GeForce RTX 2080 Ti
3) Memory: 128 GB

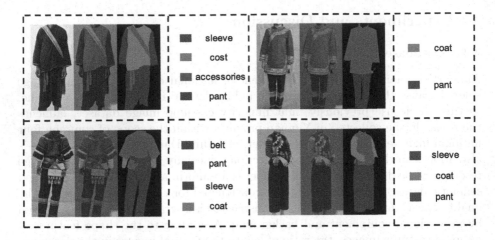

Fig. 5. Example of semantic annotation of a dataset image.

4.3   Evaluation Metric

For semantic segmentation tasks, the commonly used evaluation indexes include PA (pixel accuracy), MPA (average pixel accuracy) and $mIoU$. Where PA refers to the proportion of the correctly classified pixel points and all pixel points in the image, and the calculation method is shown in Eq. 6.

$$PA = \frac{\sum_{i=0}^{k} p_{ii}}{\sum_{i=0}^{k} \sum_{j=0}^{k} p_{ij}} \tag{6}$$

MPA is to calculate the proportion of the correct number of pixel points in each category to all the pixel points in this category and then average it. The calculation method is shown in Eq. 7.

$$MPA = \frac{1}{k+1} \sum_{i=0}^{k} \frac{p_{ii}}{\sum_{j=0}^{k} p_{ij}} \tag{7}$$

The $mIoU$ is the IoU for each class and then the average. The calculation method is shown in Eq. 8.

$$mIoU = \frac{1}{k+1} \sum_{i=0}^{k} \frac{p_{ii}}{\sum_{j=0}^{k} p_{ij} + \sum_{j=0}^{k} p_{ji} - p_{ii}} \tag{8}$$

4.4   Training Parameter Setting

Firstly, the dataset constructed in this paper is divided into the training set and verification set, with a partition ratio of 9:1. The image size of model input is set to 256 × 512. The semantic information is read through the png image format to ensure the accuracy of semantic categories after scaling in the preprocessing stage. 150 *epochs* were set in the training stage, and model parameters were updated for a total of 3750 iterations.

In terms of parameter setting, ResNet101 is used as the backbone network, and the parameters trained in ImageNet are used as the pre-training model. The number of categories for semantic segmentation is 8, of which 0 is required for the label as the background, and the rest 1–7 corresponds to the semantics of each region. The training batch size is set as 50, the learning rate is set as 0.0007, the optimizer adopts SGD, and the momentum parameter is set as 0.9. For the loss function designed in this paper, the corresponding loss coefficients, λ_1, λ_2, and λ_3 are set as 1, 1 and 0.1 respectively.

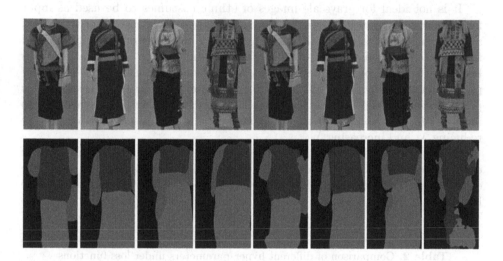

Fig. 6. Comparison of visual effects.

4.5 Experimental Comparison and Analysis

For general semantic segmentation tasks, color images are often input into the model, while the research in this paper focuses on the semantic segmentation method of grayscale images. We compared the semantic segmentation performance of color images and grayscale images, and the results are shown in Table 1.

Through CE2P and A-CE2P two groups of experiments, it can be seen that the semantic segmentation effect of grayscale images is not as good as that of color images. The main reason is that the grayscale images do not contain color features, and the semantic boundaries of each region are blurred, so the real boundary situation cannot be determined. Secondly, it can be seen that the performance of A-CE2P is better than that of CE2P in the three evaluation indexes, whether the color image is used as the input or the grayscale image is used as the input. The semantic segmentation effect is shown in Fig. 6. It can be seen that the grayscale image as the output of semantic segmentation has the problem of be unable to distinguish the local parts.

Table 1. Comparison of different methods under different conditions

Method	Pixel Acc	Mean Acc	MIoU
CE2P Colour	91.238	65.371	62.125
CE2P Grayscale	82.872	57.432	49.298
A-CE2P Colour	94.036	69.785	64.345
A-CE2P Grayscale	86.124	58.467	50.853
Ours	**88.124**	**63.467**	**57.639**

It is not ideal for grayscale images of ethnic costumes to be used as input for semantic segmentation results, through the experimental observation and analysis, judgment is due to the lack of grayscale image color information, lead to target edge profile is not obvious, for grayscale image segmentation tasks between the edge pixel values difference is not big, will cause the boundary pixels around easily, This will lead to a decrease in accuracy. Therefore, this paper optimized the parameters of the loss function. The main scheme is to improve the contribution of edge loss and edge structure consistency loss by reducing λ_1 and increasing λ_3.

By adjusting the value of the hyper-parameters, the contribution degree of different loss functions was set. By improving the contribution degree of the edge loss and the consistency loss of the edge structure, the learning of the edge boundary of the model was increased. The comparison results are shown in the Table 2.

Table 2. Comparison of different hyper-parameters under loss functions

Parameter Settings	Pixel Acc	Mean Acc	MIoU
$\lambda_1 = 1; \lambda_1 = 1; \lambda_1 = 0.1$	86.124	58.467	50.853
$\lambda_1 = 1; \lambda_1 = 0.9; \lambda_1 = 0.1$	87.343	59.136	52.134
$\lambda_1 = 1; \lambda_1 = 0.8; \lambda_1 = 0.1$	87.524	61.541	55.825
$\lambda_1 = 1; \lambda_1 = 0.8; \lambda_1 = 0.2$(Ours)	**88.124**	**63.467**	**57.639**

5   Conclusion

This paper mainly introduces the semantic segmentation method of the grayscale image of national costume. Then it introduces the composition of the CE2P body parsing framework, including three parts. Then, the enhancement model of CE2P, A-CE2P, is introduced to further optimize the entire network architecture and make the edge features explicitly participate in the optimization iteration. The design of the overall loss function of the model is introduced, and the loss function is discussed. Finally, through the verification and analysis of several groups of experiments, the fine-grained segmentation task of ethnic costume grayscale image was optimized.

Acknowledgment. This work is supported by National Natural Science Foundation of China (No. 61862068), Yunnan Expert Workstation of Xiaochun Cao, and Scientific Technology Innovation Team of Educational Big Data Application Technology in University of Yunnan Province.

References

1. Chen, L.C., Barron, J.T., Papandreou, G., Murphy, K., Yuille, A.L.: Semantic image segmentation with task-specific edge detection using CNNs and a discriminatively trained domain transform. In: Proceedings of the IEEE Conference on Computer Vision and Pattern Recognition, pp. 4545–4554 (2016)
2. Chen, L.C., Papandreou, G., Kokkinos, I., Murphy, K., Yuille, A.L.: Deeplab: semantic image segmentation with deep convolutional nets, atrous convolution, and fully connected CRFs. IEEE Trans. Pattern Anal. Mach. Intell. 40(4), 834–848 (2017)
3. Chen, L.C., Zhu, Y., Papandreou, G., Schroff, F., Adam, H.: Encoder-decoder with atrous separable convolution for semantic image segmentation. In: Proceedings of the European Conference on Computer Vision (ECCV), pp. 801–818 (2018)
4. Dong, J., Chen, Q., Xia, W., Huang, Z., Yan, S.: A deformable mixture parsing model with parselets. In: Proceedings of the IEEE International Conference on Computer Vision pp. 3408–3415 (2013)
5. Gong, K., Liang, X., Zhang, D., Shen, X., Lin, L.: Look into person: self-supervised structure-sensitive learning and a new benchmark for human parsing. In: Proceedings of the IEEE Conference on Computer Vision and Pattern Recognition, pp. 932–940 (2017)
6. Ladicky, L., Torr, P.H., Zisserman, A.: Human pose estimation using a joint pixel-wise and part-wise formulation. In: Proceedings of the IEEE Conference on Computer Vision and Pattern Recognition, pp. 3578–3585 (2013)
7. Li, P., Xu, Y., Wei, Y., Yang, Y.: Self-correction for human parsing. IEEE Trans. Pattern Anal. Mach. Intell. 99, 3349–3364 (2020)
8. Liang, X., Gong, K., Shen, X., Lin, L.: Look into person: joint body parsing & pose estimation network and a new benchmark. IEEE Trans. Pattern Anal. Mach. Intell. 41(4), 871–885 (2018)
9. Liang, X., Xu, C., Shen, X., Yang, J., Liu, S., Tang, J., Lin, L., Yan, S.: Human parsing with contextualized convolutional neural network. In: Proceedings of the IEEE International Conference on Computer Vision, pp. 1386–1394 (2015)
10. Ruan, T., Liu, T., Huang, Z., Wei, Y., Wei, S., Zhao, Y.: Devil in the details: towards accurate single and multiple human parsing. In: Proceedings of the AAAI Conference on Artificial Intelligence, vol. 33, pp. 4814–4821 (2019)
11. Simo-Serra, E., Fidler, S., Moreno-Noguer, F., Urtasun, R.: A high performance CRF model for clothes parsing. In: Cremers, D., Reid, I., Saito, H., Yang, M.-H. (eds.) ACCV 2014. LNCS, vol. 9005, pp. 64–81. Springer, Cham (2015). https://doi.org/10.1007/978-3-319-16811-1_5
12. Zhao, H., Shi, J., Qi, X., Wang, X., Jia, J.: Pyramid scene parsing network. In: Proceedings of the IEEE Conference on Computer Vision and Pattern Recognition, pp. 2881–2890 (2017)

Named Entity Recognition of Wa Cultural Information Resources Based on Attention Mechanism

Xiangxu Deng[1,2], Shu Zhang[1(✉)], Jun Wang[1,2], and Ken Chen[1,3]

[1] Key Laboratory of Education Informatization for Nationalities,
Ministry of Education, Yunnan Normal University, Kunming 650500, China
zhangshu@ynnu.edu.cn
[2] Yunnan Key Laboratory of Smart Education, Yunnan Normal University,
Kunming 650500, China
[3] Logistics Support Service Center, Yunnan Normal University,
Kunming 650500, China

Abstract. Aiming at the problem that the entities in the field of Wa cultural information resources have long length, parallel entities, and no public data set, this paper uses the text information in the Chinese ethnic dictionary Wa nationality volume as the data set, and uses the BERT model to pre-trained the word vector, then extracting the semantic features with the attention mechanism based on the BiLSTM network model, finally, the CRF model is used to predict and output the optimal tag sequence. A method of named entity recognition of Wa cultural information resources based on the attention mechanism is proposed. The experimental results show that the model can effectively identify the entities in the Wa cultural information resources and alleviate the problem of inconsistent entity labels. The recognition accuracy, recall rate, and F value of the Wa cultural information resources corpus are 92.67%, 90.06%, and 91.34% respectively.

Keywords: Wa cultural information resources · Named entity recognition · Attention mechanism · BERT · BiLSTM · CRF

1 Introduction

In the process of named entity recognition of Wa cultural information resources, we are mainly facing the following problems:1) There is no public Wa cultural information resource data set, the scale of the data set and the quality of entity annotation will affect the named entity recognition; 2) As a minority, the language expression of Wa nationality is a very different form of Chinese, and it may have different expressions for the same concept, which makes it difficult to use the existing Chinese training set; 3) Traditional word vector can't solve the problem of polysemous words. For example, "Niutou" of Wa nationality and common sense "Niutou" represent different entities, while traditional word vector will map different "Niutou" to the same vector, which is inconsistent with objective facts.

© Springer Nature Singapore Pte Ltd. 2021
Y. Tan et al. (Eds.): DMBD 2021, CCIS 1453, pp. 300–311, 2021.
https://doi.org/10.1007/978-981-16-7476-1_27

To solve the above problems, Peng Sun. proposed a Tibetan named entity recognition method based on weakly supervised learning [1], through the distribution representation of unlabeled text learning words, the word representation features are constructed to represent the semantic information of words, which are added to the statistical machine learning model of Tibetan name recognition to realize the recognition of Tibetan entities. Lulu Wang et al. proposed a semi-supervised learning based Uyghur named entity recognition method [2], which is based on the conditional random field. By introducing morphological features and unsupervised learning features based on word vectors, the influence of different features on recognition is compared, and the model is optimized. However, the traditional method relies on manually designed feature templates, which not only improves the performance of the model but also reduces the robustness and generalization ability of the whole model [3].

With the improvement of the deep learning algorithm, the deep learning model can fully approximate any complex nonlinear relationship and has strong robustness, memory ability, nonlinear mapping ability, and strong self-learning ability. Moreover, the recognition method based on a single sentence processing unit can't focus on the full-text context and has the problem of inconsistent entity annotation [4]. Weitao Hou et al. proposed a network model [5], which can learn deeper feature information, and has achieved ideal results in many domain entity recognition tasks [6].

In recent years, attention mechanism has been widely applied in the fields of image recognition [7] and natural language processing [8]. Since it mainly imitates the attention mechanism of human beings, it can focus on key information in the case of a limited resource set, thus reducing the attention on useless information. Yuan Li et al. proposed an adversarial learning model [9], which using position encoding and multiple attention mechanisms, combining position encoding and multiple attention mechanisms to better capture the dependence between word orders. Feng Zhao et al. constructed a named entity recognition model based on attention mechanism and convolutional neural network [10]. Aiming at the problem of word segmentation dependence, proposed a word embedding algorithm based on local attention convolution, to reduce the dependence of the model on the word segmentation effect. ALUMNA et al. by adding an attention mechanism to the model framework of BiLSTM-CRF [11], character features of vectors can be effectively learned.

For the task of named entity recognition of Wa cultural information resources, based on the classical network model BiLSTM, this paper introduces a large number of the unlabeled corpus, and through the BERT pre-trained language model, obtains the word vector representation with semantic information. Then enters the attention mechanism, focusing on the keyword information of the entity. Finally obtains the text of the correlation coefficient through the CRF layer. The structure and training parameters of the model are further optimized and improved. The hybrid network model of BERT-BiLSTM-Att-CRF is constructed to realize the accurate recognition of named entities in Wa nationality volume.

So the contributions of this paper is for the task of named entity recognition of Wa cultural information resources, and provided a progressive analysis from existing models to the highly performing BERT-BiLSTM-Att-CRF model, and provided solid experimental data to justify the chosen model.

2   Data Acquisition and Preprocessing

2.1   Data Collection

At present, there is no public data set of named entity recognition of Wa cultural information resources. Therefore, this paper establishes the data set of named entity recognition of Wa cultural information resources through three steps: data collection, data preprocessing, and data annotation. The corpus of this paper is mainly the text corpus of Wa nationality volume, in the dictionary of Chinese ethnic minorities. Take the labeled 400 articles with a total of 2000 sentences as the test set of the experiment, the unlabeled 3000 articles with a total of 120,000 sentences as the training set.

2.2   Data Preprocessing

The corpus of Wa nationality volume contains a large number of stop words and special punctuation marks, which is not conducive to data annotation. Through regular expression and character format normalization in Python, stop words and special punctuation marks in the text are deleted, and sentences are segmented to obtain the standard Wa culture information resource corpus.

2.3   Data Preprocessing

After statistical analysis of the entities in the corpus, this paper divides them into social, geographic, history, customs, religion, language, education, culture, news publishing, science, economy, health care, sports and entertainment, figures, cultural relics, classics, etc. sixteen classes. We use the BIEO labeling scheme to label the corpus, where B is the beginning of the named entity, I is the middle part of the named entity, E is the end of the named entity, and O is the nonentity. The annotation of the corpus is shown in Fig. 1.

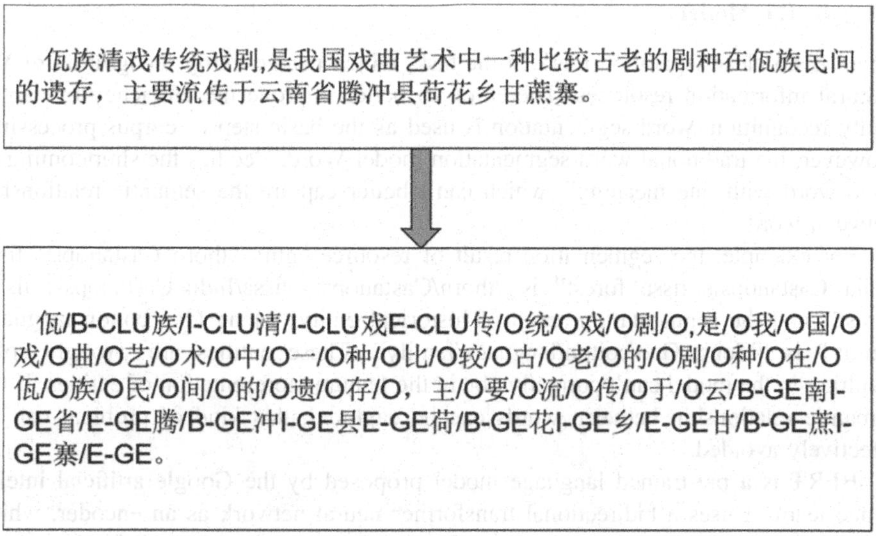

佤族清戏传统戏剧,是我国戏曲艺术中一种比较古老的剧种在佤族民间的遗存，主要流传于云南省腾冲县荷花乡甘蔗寨。
佤/B-CLU族/I-CLU清/I-CLU戏E-CLU传/O统/O戏/O剧/O,是/O我/O国/O
戏/O曲/O艺/O术/O中/O一/O种/O比/O较/O古/O老/O的/O剧/O种/O在/O
佤/O族/O民/O间/O的/O遗/O存/O，主/O要/O流/O传/O于/O云/B-GE南I-
GE省/E-GE腾/B-GE冲I-GE县E-GE荷/B-GE花I-GE乡/E-GE甘/B-GE蔗I-
GE寨/E-GE。

Fig.1. An example of corpus annotations

3 Model Framework

The model in this paper is composed of the BERT embedding model, BiLSTM model, Attention layer, and conditional random field model (CRF). The structure of the model is shown in Fig. 2.

CRF
B
I
E
.....
0
0
Attention
Attention
BiLSTM
LSTM
.....
BERT
BERT
老
寨
河
.....
位
于

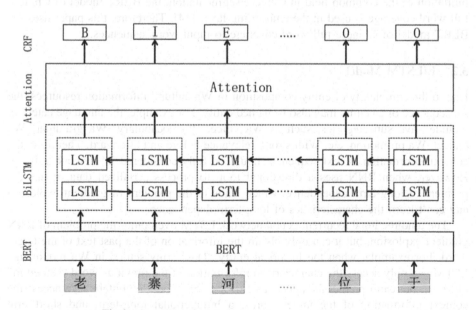

Fig.2. Securities knowledge graph construction process

3.1   BERT Model

There is no clear separation mark in the task, which named entity recognition of Wa cultural information resources. Therefore, to better improve the efficiency of named entity recognition, word segmentation is used as the basic step of corpus processing. However, the traditional word segmentation model Word2Vec has the shortcoming of "one word with one meaning", which can't better capture the semantic relationship between words.

For example, the segmentation result of resource entity "thorn Castanopsis fissa India Castanopsis fissa forest" is "thorn/Castanopsis fissa/India/Castanopsis fissa/ forest", and the segmentation result of historical entity "Meng Gao cotton language family" is "Meng Gao/cotton/language/family". These entities are wrongly split, resulting in the model can't correctly obtain the feature representation of entities. If the semantic relationship between words can be captured, this kind of problem can be effectively avoided.

BERT is a pre-trained language model proposed by the Google artificial intelligence team, it uses a bidirectional transformer neural network as an encoder, which predicts each word can refer to the text information in both directions. With the help of large-scale text corpus, BERT can provide model parameters for natural language processing tasks with small data sets, to improve the training effect [12]. The entities in Wa cultural information resources are usually combined by general words in the general field. The full word coverage model of Chinese by iFLYTEK of Harbin University of technology considers the characteristics of Chinese word segmentation. In the process of covering the corpus, the basic unit is words, and the Chinese data set corpus is used for training. The performance of the words in multiple data set exceeds the original version of BERT [13]. To make up for the defects of Word2vec and the limitation of the common field in Chinese segmentation, the BERT model of Chinese full word coverage is used in the embedding layer [14]. Therefore, this paper uses the BERT model of Chinese full word coverage to input word sequences.

3.2   BiLSTM Model

Due to the complexity of entity composition in Wa cultural information resources, the subsequence of an entity may also be named entity. For example, the language category includes five subcategories, such as Wa voice, Wa vocabulary, Wa grammar, Wa dialect, Wa promotion, etc. With strong relevance before and afterward. Therefore, the context information of text sequence should be fully considered in network training. However, when RNN uses a directional loop to process serialized data, it has the problem of long-term dependence, which leads to the problem of gradient explosion and can't learn the characteristics of long-term dependence.

The unidirectional recurrent neural network LSTM overcomes the problem of RNN gradient explosion, but it can only obtain the information of the past text of the target word. For example, when the historical entity "Daxi army settled in Wa mountain", LSTM can only access the characteristic information of the previous word "settled in" of "Wa", but can't predict the appearance of the next word "mountain". To access the context information of the target words, a bidirectional long-term and short-term memory network (BiLSTM) is constructed. BiLSTM consists of a forward LSTM and a backward LSTM, so the BiLSTM model can learn not only the forward information of the current word but also its backward information. The calculation formula of BiLSTM can be expressed as follows:

$$f_t = \sigma\left(W_f h_{t-1} + U_f X_t + b_f\right) \tag{1}$$

$$i_t = \sigma\left(W_i h_{t-1} + U_i X_t + b_f\right) \tag{2}$$

$$O_t = \sigma(W_o h_{t-1} + U_o X_t + b_o) \tag{3}$$

$$c_t^{\sim} = \tanh(W_c h_{t-1} + U_c X_t + b_c) \tag{4}$$

$$c_t = f_t \odot c_{t-1} + i_t \odot c_t^{\sim} \tag{5}$$

$$h_t = O_t \odot \tanh(c_t) \tag{6}$$

Where σ is the activation function, tanh is the hyperbolic tangent activation function, f_t, i_t, O_t and c_t are the input gate, forget gate, output gate, and memory cell at time t, respectively. $U_{f\sim c}$ and $W_{f\sim c}$ represents the weight matrix corresponding to different control gates, and $b_{f\sim c}$ represents the bias vector. $c_t^{\sim}$ is the intermediate state of the input, x_t and h_t are the input vector and output results at time t, and $\odot$ is the dot product.

The vector x of the BERT layer will be input to the BiLSTM layer as the input vector at time t, and obtained the splicing vector of the hidden layer. After weighting by the tanh activation function, the final output result h_t will be input to the Attention layer.

3.3   Attention Layer

BiLSTM can't highlight the key information mentioned above when calculating the context information, and in the task of named entity recognition, the same entity may have multiple expressions and different location information, which leads to the problem of inconsistent annotation. For example, the description of Bee barrel drum is a percussion instrument, the expression of Wa language is "deng dong ya". Bee barrel drum is handmade by folk, which is divided into father drum, mother drum, and son drum. To make a Bee barrel drum, need to take a section of tree material. Paulownia, kapok, hydrochloric acid trees, etc. peel off the tree skin with a chisel to reinforce the bee barrel drum.

In the text, the Bee barrel drum appears many times in different positions in different sentences, and the label of the "Bee barrel drum" entity is incorrectly labeled or omitted when it is out of context. The attention mechanism has the characteristics of considering the importance of the information in the context. Therefore, given the diversified naming methods and uneven distribution of entities in the Wa cultural information resources, the vector output by BiLSTM is input to the Attention layer. The attention mechanism is used to make the named entity recognition model reduces the attention of irrelevant information, and optimizes resource allocation by assigning different weights to different parts of the input, so that the obtained feature vector is more accurate, and the calculation formula is as follows.

$$g_i = \sum_{j=1}^{N} h_j A_{i,j} \tag{7}$$

$$A_{i,j} = \frac{\exp\left(score\left(W_i, W_j\right)\right)}{\sum_{k=1}^{m} \exp\left(score\left(W_i, W_j\right)\right)} \tag{8}$$

$$score\left(W_i, W_j\right) = \frac{W_a\left(W_i, W_j\right)}{|W_i||W_j|} \tag{9}$$

In the formula, $_j$ is the weight of attention between the current word W_i and the text W_j, h_j is the output of the BiLSTM layer, score (W_i, W_j) represents the similarity score of word W_i and W_j determined by cosine distance, and W_a is the parameter learned in the training process.

3.4 CRF Layer

BiLSTM and Attention layer only consider the long-term context information and don't consider the dependency of tags. Although the output of BiLSTM is the tags of the unit with the highest score, and the tags obtained are all correct tags, BiLSTM and Attention layer can't guarantee the prediction tag is correct, so the tag of the final word can't be determined by the results of BiLSTM and Attention layer. The conditional random field model CRF uses the state transition matrix to obtain the globally optimal tag sequence through the dependency relationship of tags [15]. Let the output matrix of the Attention layer is p, and its dimension is m × k. m is the number of words in the input sentence, and k represents the label collection. The probability formula of y as follows:

$$s(x, y) = \sum_{n}\left(\sum_{i=1}^{m} P_{i,y_i} + \sum_{i=0}^{m} A_{y_i, y_{i+1}}\right) \tag{10}$$

x is the input tag sequence, $_{i,y_{i+1}}$ represents the score of the tag y_i transferred to the tag y_{i+1}, P_{i,y_i} is the score of the i word predicted to be the y_i tag, softmax function is used to get the conditional probability of sequence y, and finally, the sequence with the highest score is used as the final labeling result of the model by Viterbi algorithm.

4   Model Framework

4.1   Experimental Parameter Setting

This experiment uses the operating system of Ubuntu 16.04, the compiler environment of Python 3.7, Anaconda 4.2, TensorFlow 1.3. For the model parameters, our base model is BERT-BiLSTM. the dimension of the word vector is determined to be 768, and the learning rate is set to 0.002. To prevent overfitting of the model, the dropout mechanism [16] is introduced and its value is set to 0.5. Adam is used as its optimization algorithm. The environment configuration and model parameter configuration used in the experiment are shown in Table 1 and Table 2 respectively.

Table 1. Experimental environment configuration

Software and hardware environment	Version
operating system	Ubuntu 16.04
Python	3.7
Anaconda	4.2
Tensorflow	1.3

Table 2. Model parameter configuration

Parameter	Numerical value
Word vector dimension	768
Dropout rate	0.5
Learning rate	0.002
Batch parameters	16
Number of iterations	50

4.2   Evaluation Criteria

In this paper, accuracy P, recall rate R, and F values are used as evaluation indexes [17], the three indexes are defined as:

$$P = \frac{number\ of\ correct\ entities\ identified}{number\ of\ all\ entities\ identified} \times 100 \tag{11}$$

$$R = \frac{number\ of\ correct\ entities\ identified}{number\ of\ all\ labeled\ entities} \times 100\% \tag{12}$$

$$F = \frac{2 \times P \times R}{P + R} \times 100\% \tag{13}$$

4.3   Evaluation Criteria

In the case of not relying on artificial design features, the best experimental results can be achieved by adjusting different model parameters. The ratio of the training set, test set, and valid set is 7:2:1, and there is no overlap of the data set.

Comparative Experimental Analysis of Different Embedding Model. In the case of using the same data set, the Word2vec model and BERT model are used to compare the experiments of different embedding models. The word vector is input into the BiLSTM-Att-CRF model to identify the entity of Wa cultural information resources. The experimental results are shown in Table 3.

Table 3. Experimental results of different embedded models

Embedding model	Model	P	R	R
Word2vec	BiLSTM-Att-CRF	89.78	88.65	89.21
BERT	BiLSTM-Att-CRF	92.67	90.06	91.37

Compared with the Word2vec embedding method, the accuracy of model recognition is improved by 2.89% points by using the BERT model. The analysis results show that entities are wrongly split based on the Word2vec embedding method, which makes it impossible to correctly identify some complex entities. For example, the cultural and artistic entity "Chinese painting Rooster picture" is wrongly split into "Chinese/painting/Rooster /picture". Therefore, under the same data set, the experimental results obtained by using the BERT model are better than those obtained by using the Word2vec model, which shows that the BERT model improves the semantic understanding ability of words.

Comparative Experimental Analysis of Different Chinese Named Entity Recognition Model. In the case of using the same data set and embedding model, different Chinese named entity recognition models are adopted, including the BERT-LSTMCRF model, BERT-BiLSTM-CRF model, and BERT-BiLSTM-Att-CRF model. The experimental results are shown in Table 4. In terms of accuracy P value and F value, the recognition performance of each model for three types of entities in Wa cultural information resource is compared, and the results are shown in Table 4.

Table 4. Experimental results of different models

Model	P	R	R
BERT-LSTM-CRF	84.81	86.74	85.78
BERT-BiLSTM-CRF	90.02	89.72	89.87
BERT-BiLSTM-Att-CRF	92.67	90.06	91.37

Through the above experimental results, it can be seen that the BERT-LSTM-CRF model dynamically plans the optimal sequence labeling through adjacent labels between entities, with an accuracy rate of 84.81%. Compared with the BERT-LSTMCRF model, the accuracy of the BERT-BiLSTM-CRF model is improved by 5.21% points through the context information of the input sequence. Compared with the BERT-BiLSTM-CRF model, because of the addition mechanism, the BERTBiLSTM-Att-CRF model pays more attention to finding more relevant information with the current output, to obtain the similarity coefficient between entities in the text. Its accuracy, recall rate, and F value are improved.

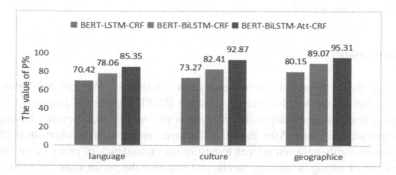

Fig. 3. The comparison of the value P in the experiment.

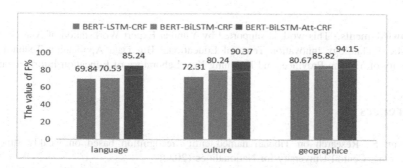

Fig. 4. The comparison of the value F in the experiment.

Figure 3 and Fig. 4 shows the P and F values of the three models for the recognition rate of language, culture, and geography. The entity recognition rate of the three models for culture and geography is relatively high, while the entity recognition rate for language is relatively low. Due to the single structure of the LSTM model, the BERTLSTM-CRF model can't obtain rich feature information for complex language entities. The recognition rates of P and F are 70.42% and 69.84% respectively.

The analysis shows that culture and geography are composed of more conventional words, such as folk dance and plant resources, and this obvious character information improves the accuracy of such entity recognition. The language entity is mostly the Wa language, and its language expression is very different from Chinese. For example, the "wind custom song" in Chinese corresponds to "Luodai Biao" in the Wa language, which increases the difficulty of entity recognition. Therefore, such entities need to improve the complexity of the model, to obtain more abundant feature information.

The recognition rate of cultural and geographical entities is 82.41% and 89.07% respectively, and the recognition rate of language entities is 78.06%, which is 9.14% and 8.92% higher than the BERT-BiLSTM-CRF model. The information of forward and backward sequence is extracted by the BiLSTM hidden layer, which improves the recognition rate of complex entities in entity recognition, but the entity labels are still inconsistent in the model.

5   Conclusion

Aiming at the problem of named entity recognition of Wa cultural information resources, the whole word coverage Chinese BERT pre-trained language model is introduced to enhance the dependency between two words and alleviate the impact of word segmentation errors. After the BiLSTM layer, an attention mechanism is added to obtain the similarity between entities to ensure the consistency of entity labels, to avoid the situation of wrong or missing labels, and improve the performance of model entity recognition. The experimental results show that the BERT-BiLSTM-Att-CRF model has high accuracy and recall rate in the named entity recognition of Wa cultural information resources, and its F value is 91.37%, which verifies the effectiveness of the model.

Acknowledgments. This work is supported by Yunnan Expert Workstation of Xiaochun Cao, Scientific Technology Innovation Team of Educational Big Data Application Technology in University of Yunnan Province, and Kunming Key Laboratory of Education Informatization.

References

1. Peng, S.: Research on Tibetan named entity recognition based on weakly supervised learning. Central University for Nationalities (2020)
2. Lulu, W.: Named entity recognition based on deep neural network. J. Chin. Inf. Process. **33** (03), 64–70 (2019)
3. Habibi, M., Weber, L., Neve, M.: Deep learning with word embeddings improves biomedical named entity recognition. Bioinformatics **33**(14), i37–i48 (2017)
4. Pengfei, Z., Chunjiang, Z.: Named entity recognition of Chinese agri-cultural text based on attention mechanism. Trans. Chin. Soc. Agric. Mach. **52**(01), 185–192 (2021)
5. Weitao, H., Donghong, J.: Research on clinic event recognition based Bi-LSTM. Appl. Res. Comput. **35**(07), 1974–1977 (2018)
6. Tong, F., Luo, Z.: A deep network-based integrated model for the disease named entity recognition. In: IEEE International Conference on Bioinformatics and Biomedicine, p. 618621 (2017)
7. Shibo, J., Jing, X., Yanfang, L.: Text-to-single image method based on self-attention. Comput. Eng. Appl. **3**(01), 183–391 (2021)
8. Lei, S., Yi, W., Ying, C.: Review of attention mechanism in natural language processing. Data Anal. Knowl. Discov. **4**(05), 1–14 (2020)

9. Yuan, L., Lei, M.: Chinese named entity recognition for social media. J. Chin. Inf. Process. **34**(08), 61–69 (2020)

10. Feng, Z., Jian, H.: LAC-DGLU: named entity recognition model based on CNN and attention mechanism. Comput. Sci. **47**(11), 212–219 (2020)

11. Alina, T.: Boosting Arabic named-entity recognition with multi-attention layer. IEEE Access **7**, 46575–46582 (2019)

12. Mingyi, M.: BERT named entity recognition model with the self-attention mechanism. CAAI Trans. Intell. Syst. **15**(04), 772–779 (2020)

13. Habibi, M., Weber, L., Neves, M., Wiegandt, D.L., Leser, U.: Deep learning with word embeddings improves biomedical named entity recognition. Bioinformatics (Oxford England) **33**(14), i37–i48 (2017)

14. Pengbo, Y.: Panetc.Clickbait recognition research based on BERT-BiGA model. Data Anal. Knowl. Discov. (24) (2021)

15. Tongqiang, J.: Food safety named entity recognition based on bert and attention mechanism. Sci. Technol. Eng. **21**(03), 1103–1108 (2021)

16. Srivastava, N.: Dropout: a simple way to prevent neural networks from overfitting. J. Mach. Learn. Res. **15**(1), 1929–1958 (2014)

17. Gri, M.: Character neural network for biomedical named entity recognition. J. Biomed. Inform. **70**, 85–91 (2017)

Semantic Similarity Retrieval System Based on the Chinese Minority Dictionary Wa Volume

Xiangdong Meng[1,2] (iD), Jun Wang[1,2(✉)] (iD), Yiping Liufu[1,2] (iD),
and Zhaoxiang OuYang[3]

[1] Key Laboratory of Education Informatization for Nationalities,
Ministry of Education, Yunnan Normal University, Kunming 650500, China
[2] Yunnan Key Laboratory of Smart Education, Yunnan Normal University,
Kunming 650500, China
[3] School of Information, Dehong Teachers' College, Mangshi 678400, China

Abstract. With the rapid development of information retrieval technology, related research has also made great progress. However, in the specific field of minority information resources, the problem of insufficient scalability has caused users to retrieve the accurate information required by the specific field still very difficult. We use the Word2vec method to calculate the semantic similarity of specific vocabulary based on the "The Chinese Minority Dictionary Wa Volume (abbreviated as Wa Volume)" and Chinese Wikipedia. Finally, we experimentally verify that the semantic similarity based on the Wa Volume in the field of ethnic minorities is higher than that based on Chinese Wikipedia.

Keywords: Ethnic information · Wa nationality · Semantic similarity

1 Introduction

1.1 Research Background

As an important part of the network information platform, the information retrieval system plays an irreplaceable role in online information acquisition. Nowadays, the related research about retrieval system has also made great progress. But in the specific field of information resources, the problem of insufficient scalability makes it very difficult for users to retrieve the accurate information needed in the specific field.

In response to the above problems, this paper uses the Chinese Minority Dictionary Wa Volume combined with Word2vec method to calculate semantic similarity, in order to partially promote the development of the retrieval system in the field of ethnic minorities. "Wa Volume" is an encyclopedia that reflects the society, history, language and culture of the Wa nationality. "Wa Volume" contains certain peculiarities, and the frequency of certain special words is different from that of Baidu Encyclopedia. At the same time, the calculation of semantic similarity is a very important basic research work in Chinese information processing. The current retrieval system does not have enough expansion when searching in a specific field. Therefore, we calculate the

© Springer Nature Singapore Pte Ltd. 2021
Y. Tan et al. (Eds.): DMBD 2021, CCIS 1453, pp. 312–326, 2021.
https://doi.org/10.1007/978-981-16-7476-1_28

semantic similarity of the "Wa Volume" to search the words are expanded enough to make the search results better in the field of ethnic minorities.

1.2 Related Work

Since Word2vec [1] was proposed, it can successfully solve the problem of dimensionality of text features. Word2vec provides two training models, CBOW and Skip-gram. Combining hierarchy normalization and negative sampling optimization technology, Word2vec can quickly and efficiently express words into vectors.

At the same time, the emergence of Word2vec provides the possibility to quickly obtain the semantic features of natural language, thereby promoting the development of related research in the field of natural language processing [2]. BENGIO et al. [3] proposed to use neural networks to construct language models, which solved the problem of N-gram model to a certain extent. MIKOLOV et al. [4] pointed out that the vectors trained using the tool Word2vec are low-dimensional and continuous, and the semantic similarity between words can be judged by calculating the cosine distance between these vectors. Li Xiao et al. [5] obtained word vectors based on the Word2Vec model training corpus, and then calculated the subject, predicate, and object vector similarity based on syntactic analysis, and assigned different weight coefficients to design a sentence similarity algorithm.

1.3 Research Significance

Semantic similarity refers to the degree of similarity between two concepts, and usually refers to the common characteristics between the two concepts themselves [6]. Semantic similarity calculation has a wide range of applications in information retrieval, data mining, machine translation, document copy detection and other fields [7] [8]. This article innovatively combines the Word2vec method with xxx to calculate semantic similarity, which is different from the previous semantic similarity calculations for Chinese Wikipedia. At the same time, due to the particularity of the data content of the Chinese Minority Dictionary Wa Volume, it will show higher-quality semantic similarity in special words related to ethnic minorities. This view is also confirmed in Sect. 5. The smooth development of this work can also play a certain degree of perfection in the development of the retrieval system of minority-related information.

2 Data Training Based on Word2vec

2.1 Word2vec Model Principle

The Word2vec tool mainly includes two models: skip-gram and continuous bag of words, referred to as CBOW, and two efficient training methods: negative sampling and hierarchical normalization. Word2vec provides a method of using distributed vectors to represent text [9]. The overall network structure of Word2vec is shown (see Fig. 1):

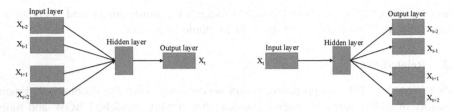

Fig. 1. Word2vec overall network structure (The picture on the left shows the CBOW model, the picture on the right shows the Skip-gram model)

2.2   CBOW Model

The CBOW (Continue Bags of Word) model, is characterized by using the context of a word as input to predict the word (target) [10]. The network structure diagram is shown (see Fig. 2), which can predict the target through CBOW:

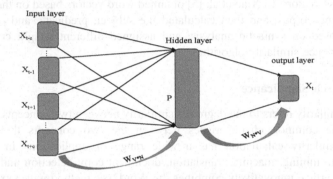

Fig. 2. Detailed network structure diagram of CBOW

Among them, the total number of words in the text is V, X_{t-1}, X_{t+1}, X_{t-c} and X_{t+c} are all one-hot representations of words. This part is the input of the CBOW model, Xt is the output of the model, and the target is X_t. X_{t-c} is the c-th word on the left of the target, X_{t+c} is the c-th word on the right of the target, W_{V*N} and W'_{N*V} are the weight matrix. The middle hiddened layer P_{1*N} is expressed as:

$$P = \frac{1}{2c} \sum_{-c \leq j \leq c \& j \neq 0} X_{t+j} * W_{V*N} \tag{1}$$

After obtaining P_{1*N}, go through the weight matrix W'_{N*V} and the softmax function to obtain the output X_t with the final dimension of $1*N$.

At the same time, our maximum optimization goal in the CBOW model is:

$$L = \frac{1}{T} log P(X_t | X_{t-c}...X_{t+c}) \tag{2}$$

2.3   Skip-Gram Model

Skip-gram is the reverse process of CBOW. As shown in the figure below, the characteristic of the model is that a given vocabulary (target) is used as an input and a prediction of the context of the current word is output [5]. The network structure diagram is shown (see Fig. 3), which can predict context through Skip-gram.

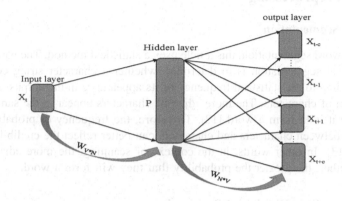

Fig. 3. Skip-gram detailed network structure diagram

Among them, the total number of words in the text is V, X_t is the input of the model, X_{t-1}, X_{t+1}, X_{t-c}, and X_{t+c} are one-hot representations of words. This part is the output of the Skip-gram model, and the target is X_t, X_{t-c} are the c-th vocabulary on the left of the target, X_{t+c} is the c-th vocabulary on the right of the target, W_{V*N} and W'_{N*V} are the weight matrix, and the middle hidden layer P_{1*N} is expressed as:

$$P = X_t * W_{V*N} \tag{3}$$

After P_{1*N} is obtained, the weight matrix W'_{N*V} and the softmax function are used to obtain an output X_{t-1}, X_{t+1}, X_{t-c}, X_{t+c} with a final dimension of $1 * N$.

At the same time, our maximum optimization goal in the CBOW model is:

$$L = \frac{1}{T} \sum_{t=1}^{T} \sum_{-c \leq j \leq c \& j \neq 0} \log P(X_{t+j}|X_t) \tag{4}$$

2.4   Model Training

Since the training of the CBOW model is similar to the training of the Skip-gram model, only the training process of the CBOW model is introduced here. The input layer is $2c$ word vectors in the context of word $w(t)$, and the projection layer vector x_w is the cumulative sum of these $2c$ word vectors. The output layer uses words that have appeared in the training corpus as leaf nodes, and a Huffman tree constructed with the number of times each word appears in the corpus as the weight. In this Huffman tree, there are N (=$|D|$) leaf nodes, which correspond to words in dictionary D and N-1 non-leaf nodes. The result of x_w is predicted by the random gradient ascent algorithm, so that the value of $p(w|context(w))$ is maximized, and $context(w)$ refers to $2c$ words in the context of the word. When the neural network training is completed, it can be calculated the word vector w of all words [11].

3 Data Preprocessing

3.1 Text Segmentation

In terms of word segmentation, this article uses a statistical method. The basic principle of this lexical segmentation is to determine whether a character string constitutes a word according to the statistical frequency of its appearance in the corpus. A word is a combination of characters. The more adjacent characters appear at the same time, the more likely it is to form a word [12]. Therefore, the frequency or probability of co-occurrence between characters and characters can better reflect the credibility of them as words [13]. In other words, in the context of scanning, the more adjacent words appear together, the greater the probability that they will form a word.

3.2 Remove Stop Words and Punctuation

After the word segmentation is completed, it is necessary to remove stop words and punctuation in the text after the word segmentation. Stop words generally refer to words that have no practical meaning in the text but have a greater interference with the results of data mining, such as: "de" "le" "ao" "de" (in Chinese) and other words [14]. In addition, punctuation marks such as "%" and "—" also need to be processed. Removal of stop words can't only reduce the dimensionality of the text, but also effectively improve the efficiency of calculations, and it is also very helpful to improve the accuracy of calculations [15].

4 Semantic Similarity Calculation

In this article, we use the Word2vec model to calculate semantic similarity. When calculating the text similarity, this model obtains the sentence vector representation of the short text by calculating different text representations, and then measures the distance between the sentence vectors of the two short texts to obtain the short text similarity [16]. Common distance measurement methods include cosine distance, Euclidean distance, Manhattan distance and so on [17].

4.1 Semantic Similarity Calculation Based on "Wa Volume"

The data of the "Wa Volume" comes from a University, which contains 25,000 Wa nationality related information. The "Wa Volume" refers to the Wa nationality's "history", "society", "geographical resources", "economy", "traditional education", "ideological economy", "culture and art", "sports entertainment" and other aspects are described in detail. The specific semantic similarity calculation process is shown (see Fig. 4):

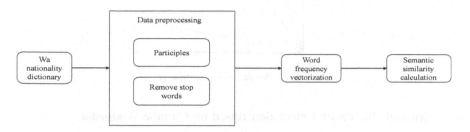

Fig. 4. Semantic similarity calculation process based on the "Wa Volume"

When we calculate the semantic similarity, we need to adhere to a principle, that is: the closer the two words are, the higher the semantic similarity will be, and this is true in actual situations. "The right bank tributary of the Peng River. Located in Zhenkang County, Lincang City, it is adjacent to the Nu River in the north and Myanmar in the west." In this sentence, the words "Mengpeng River" and "Nanpeng River" appear in the text at the same time. And the distance is relatively close. The system will determine that there is a high similarity between the two words.

Since in the Word2vec model, the text is represented by a corresponding vector, the similarity of two texts can be represented by the similarity of their respective vectors. The three vectors (see Fig. 5) in the space shown that r_1 = Mengpeng river, r_2 = Nanpeng river, and r_3 = computer. The angle between the vectors r_1 and r_2 is small, and the angle between r_3 and r_1 and r_2 is relatively large, and finding the degree of similarity between the vectors can be converted to finding the size of the angle between the two vectors. And the similarity is further converted into the cosine value of the included angle. If the included angle between the two vectors is 0°, the cosine value cos0 degrees between the vectors is 1, that is, the current similarity between the two vectors is 1. Similarly, if the angle between the two vectors is 90°, the cosine value 90° between the vectors is 0, that is, the current similarity between the two vectors is 0. Therefore, we can use the cosine value corresponding to the angle formed between the two vectors to represent the similarity between the texts, and the value range is between [0, 1]. The more the cosine value tends to 1, the more the included angle tends to 0°, the higher the degree of similarity between vectors, the more the cosine value tends to 0, the more the included angle tends to 90°, and the lower the degree of similarity between vectors. The cosine similarity calculation formula is defined as follows [18]:

$$\text{sim}(r_1, r_2) = \frac{vec_{r_1} \cdot vec_{r_2}}{||vec_{r_1}|| \cdot ||vec_{r_2}||} \tag{5}$$

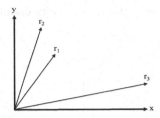

Fig. 5. Angle cosine similarity

4.2   Semantic Similarity Calculation Based on Chinese Wikipedia

Chinese Wikipedia is the Chinese version of the Wikipedia Collaboration Project. Since its official establishment on October 24,2002, it has collected 1,165,780 entries and 54,574 documents.

In Chinese Wikipedia, we also use the Word2vec model to calculate the similarity between texts. Different from the calculation process based on the semantic similarity of "Wa Volume", the semantic similarity based on Chinese Wikipedia requires not only "Participles" and "Remove stop words " in the preprocessing stage, but also "Traditional-Simplified" conversion. The semantic similarity calculation flowchart is shown (see Fig. 6):

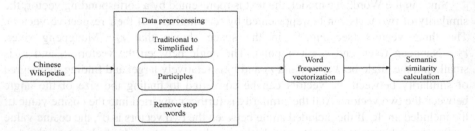

Fig. 6. Semantic similarity calculation process based on Chinese Wikipedia

5   Retrieval System

5.1   Retrieval Based on Chinese Wikipedia

In the calculation of semantic similarity based on Chinese Wikipedia, the preprocessing of the data also includes operations such as word segmentation and removal of stop words. At the same time, the "traditional-simplified" conversion must be performed before this. After preprocessing the data, start training the model and calculate the semantic similarity on the basis of Chinese Wikipedia. We take "Cangyuan (in Chinese)", "Gengma (in Chinese)", "Gengma Dai and Wa Autonomous County (in Chinese)" as examples for input, and the model calculation results are shown in the Table 1, Table 2 and Table 3:

Table 1. The semantic similarity calculation result of "Cangyuan" based on Chinese Wikipedia

Semantic similarity top-10 (in Chinese)	Cangyuan (in Chinese)
Mangshi	0.49
Mianning	0.44
Gengma	0.44
Ruili	0.43
Ruili city	0.42
NaJian county	0.42
Yingjiang	0.41
Yanshuai	0.41
Yunnan Province	0.41
Luxi	0.40

Table 2. The semantic similarity calculation result of "Gengma" based on Chinese Wikipedia

Semantic similarity top-10 (in Chinese)	Gengma (in Chinese)
Yunnan	0.45
Zhenkang	0.44
Cangyuan	0.44
Mangshi	0.44
Zhenkang county	0.43
Yunnan Province	0.42
NaJian county	0.42
Ganya	0.42
Mengding	0.42
Yiliang	0.41

Table 3. The semantic similarity calculation result of "Gengma Dai and Wa Autonomous County" based on Chinese Wikipedia

Semantic similarity top-10 (in Chinese)	Gengma Dai and Wa Autonomous County (in Chinese)
Cangyuan Wa Autonomous County	0.57
Nanjian Yi Autonomous County	0.47
Gengma Town	0.45
Pu'er County	0.45
Jiequ	0.44
Lancang Lahu Autonomous County	0.44
Xiuna County	0.44
Zhanyi County	0.43
Yunnan Province	0.43
Weixin County	0.43

5.2   Retrieval Based on "Wa Volume"

Before the semantic similarity calculation, it is necessary to preprocess the data memory "word segmentation" and "de-stop word". After processing the segmentation and stop words, save the model and calculate the semantic similarity. We use "Cangyuan (in Chinese)" and Enter the words "Gengma (in Chinese)", "Gengma Dai and Wa Autonomous County (in Chinese)" as examples, and the model calculation results are shown in Table 4, Table 5 and Table 6:

Table 4. The semantic similarity calculation result of "Cangyuan" based on the "Wa Volume"

Semantic similarity top-10 (in Chinese)	Cangyuan (in Chinese)
Ximeng	0.91
Lancang	0.90
Shuangjiang	0.81
Gengma	0.76
Agriculture Bureau	0.73
Menglian County	0.72
Gengma County	0.72
Menglian	0.70
Epidemic Prevention Station	0.70
Zhenkang County	0.68

Table 5. The semantic similarity calculation result of "Gengma" based on the "Wa Volume"

Semantic similarity top-10 (in Chinese)	Gengma (in Chinese)
Yongde	0.86
Menglian	0.86
Shuangjiang	0.85
Lancang	0.83
The Belt	0.83
Gengma County	0.79
Today	0.78
Zhenkang	0.76
Dukou	0.76
Cangyuan	0.76

Table 6. The semantic similarity calculation result of "Gengma Dai and Wa Autonomous County" based on the "Wa Volume"

Semantic similarity top-10 (in Chinese)	Gengma Dai and Wa Autonomous County (in Chinese)
Menglian Dai, Lahu and Wa Autonomous County	0.90
Ximeng Wa Autonomous County	0.87
Lancang Lahu Autonomous County	0.86
Cangyuan Wa Autonomous County	0.85
Zhenkang County	0.82
Lincang city	0.79
Court	0.77
Menglian County	0.77
Gengma County	0.77
Deputy governor	0.76

In addition to the above data, the "Wa Volume" dataset also contains special humanistic information for the "Wa (in Chinese)", such as "Sigangli (in Chinese)". The semantic similarity results are shown in Table 7 below:

Table 7. Semantic similarity calculation results of "Sigangli"

Semantic similarity top-10 (in Chinese)	Sigangli (in Chinese)
Legend	0.80
Myth	0.78
Amorous feelings	0.74
Custom	0.74
Walk in	0.73
Folk song	0.73
Ancestors	0.73
Ancient times	0.71
Medicine	0.70
Song	0.70

"Sigangli (in Chinese)" is an ancient legend circulated among the Wa people. "Sigang" means cliff cave, "li" means coming out, "Sigangli" is coming out from the cave, especially the geographical location is in Yuexiu County, Ximeng County. Songxiang Nanxi River across from Burmese is a place named Bagdai near Yancheng. It is also a creation epic of the Wa people [19]. However, this information is not described in corresponding details in the "Chinese Wikipedia" dataset, which leads to a lack of applicability when calculating ethnic minority-specific nouns.

6 Experimental Result

In this paper, data preprocessing such as word segmentation is performed on the data set of "Wa Volume" and the dataset of "Chinese Wikipedia" respectively, and the Word2vec model is used to calculate the semantic similarity of the text. In this article, the words "Cangyuan (in Chinese)", "Gengma (in Chinese)", "Gengma Dai and Wa Autonomous County (in Chinese)" are used for comparison.

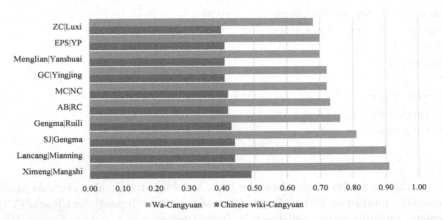

Fig. 7. Comparison of the similarity of "Cangyuan" (Note that orange represents the "Wa Volume" dataset, and blue represents the "Chinese Wikipedia" dataset and the ordinate represents "words" (The former of the coordinate scale corresponds to orange and the latter corresponds to blue), which is the set of top-10 words similar to the sample words, and the abscissa represents "similarity", which is the similarity score. And "AB" means "Agricultural Bureau", "RC" means "Ruili City", "MC" means "Menglian County", "NC" means "Nanjian County", "GC" means "Gengma County", " EPS" means "epidemic prevention station", "YP" means "Yunnan Province", and "ZC" means "Zhenkang County")

Taking "Cangyuan (in Chinese)" as an example, the calculation results of semantic similarity based on two data sets are shown (see Fig. 7). It can be seen from the data that in the semantic similarity calculation based on "Chinese Wikipedia", the words with higher relevance to the word "Cangyuan (in Chinese)" include words such as "Mangshi (in Chinese)", "Mianning (in Chinese)" and "Gengma (in Chinese)", but the correlation between words is about 43%. In the semantic similarity calculation based on the "Wa Volume", the word "Cangyuan (in Chinese)" has high similarity and similarity with words such as "Ximeng (in Chinese)", "Lancang (in Chinese)", "Shuangjiang (in Chinese)", and "Gengma (in Chinese)". Both reached more than 70%.

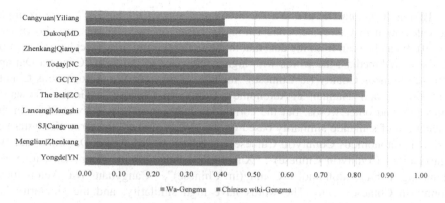

Fig. 8. Comparison of the similarity of "Gengma" (Note that 'SJ' means 'Shuangjiang', 'MD' means 'Mengding', and 'YN' means 'Yunnan')

Taking "Gengma (in Chinese)" as an example, the calculation results of semantic similarity based on two data sets are shown (see Fig. 8). It can be seen from the data that in the semantic similarity calculation based on "Chinese Wikipedia", the words with higher relevance to the word "Gengma (in Chinese)" include words such as "Yunnan", "Zhenkang (in Chinese)" and "Cangyuan (in Chinese)", but the correlation with words is around 44%. In the semantic similarity calculation based on the "Wa Volume", the word "Gengma (in Chinese)" has high similarity with words such as "Yongde (in Chinese)", "Menglian (in Chinese)", "Shuangjiang (in Chinese)" and "Lancang (in Chinese)". Both reached more than 75%.

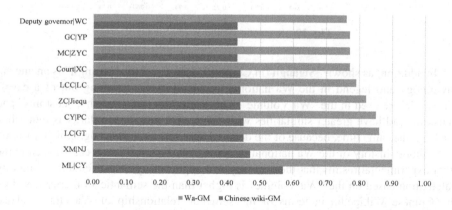

Fig. 9. Comparison of the similarity of "Gengma Dai and Wa Autonomous County" (Where "GM" stands for "Gengma Dai and Wa Autonomous County", "ML" stands for "Menglian Dai Lahu and Wa Autonomous County", "CY" stands for "Cangyuan Wa Autonomous County", "XM" stands for "Ximeng Wa Autonomous County", "NJ" stands for "Nanjian Yi Autonomous County", "LC" stands for "Lancang Lahu Autonomous County", "GT" stands for "Gengma Town", and "PC" stands for "Pu'er County", "ZC" means "Zhenkang County", "LCC" means "Lincang City", "XC" means "Xuna County", "MC" means "Menglian County", "ZYC" means "Zhanyi County", "GC" means "Gengma" County", "YP" means "Yunnan Province", "WC" means "Prestige County")

Taking "Gengma Dai and Wa Autonomous County (in Chinese)" as an example, the calculation results of semantic similarity based on two datasets are shown (see Fig. 9). It can be seen from the data that in the semantic similarity calculation based on "Chinese Wikipedia", the words with higher relevance to the term "Gengma Dai and Wa Autonomous County (in Chinese)" include "Cangyuan Wa Autonomous County (in Chinese)" and "Nanjian Yi Autonomous County (in Chinese)". "Gengma Town (in Chinese)" and other words, but the correlation between words is about 38%. In the calculation of semantic similarity based on the "Wa Volume", the term "Gengma Dai and Wa Autonomous County(in Chinese)" is related to "Menglian Dai Lahu and Wa Autonomous County(in Chinese)", "Ximeng Wa Autonomous County(in Chinese)", "Lancang Lahu Autonomous County(in Chinese)", "Cangyuan Wa Autonomous County(in Chinese)", etc. The words have high similarity, and the similarity has reached more than 75%.

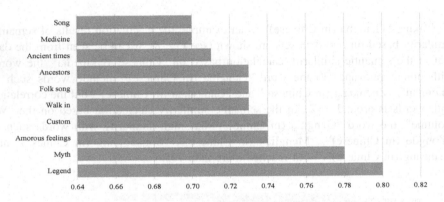

Fig. 10. Semantic similarity of "Sigangli"

In addition, as shown "Sigangli (in Chinese)" (see Fig. 10), "Sigangli" is an ancient mythology and legend in the Wa nationality, which means "coming out of a cave". "Sigangli" are used in the "Wa Volume". The words "legend", "myth", "customs" and "customs" all have greater similarities with "Sigangli", and the similarity is more than 70%. At the same time, because of the detailed description of the geographical location and folklore history of the Wa nationality in the "Wa Volume", so it can be seen in the final experimental results that the accuracy and applicability of the semantic similarity calculation based on the "Wa Volume" is higher than the semantic similarity based on the Chinese Wikipedia in terms of the semantic relationship of Wa ethnic related words.

7   Conclusion

This article starts from the perspective of insufficient expansion of the current retrieval system for specific domain retrieval, with the help of the Word2vec word vector model and related tools, carried out the semantic similarity calculation based on the "Wa Volume", and verified through experiments that the accuracy of the semantic similarity calculation based on the "Wa Volume" was higher than that based on the Chinese Wikipedia. Here, the main work of this article is summarized as follows:

- From the perspective of insufficient expansion of the current retrieval system when searching in a specific field, considering the foreign calculation methods of English and Chinese semantic similarity, they cannot be fully applicable to related problems based on the semantic similarity calculation of the "Wa Volume". The current status of minority information resources research and the status of semantic retrieval are discussed, some problems and shortcomings are pointed out, and the research theme of this article is established on this basis.
- Introduce the related technologies and theories involved in this article, such as the basic theory of information retrieval, the related model of word vectors, and the "Wa Volume" in detail, including the specific content of the Word2vec model and the "Wa Volume". The particularity of "Dictionary" relative to "Chinese Wikipedia". This part of knowledge provides a theoretical basis for the subsequent writing of the thesis.
- Data preprocessing such as word segmentation was performed on the data set of "Wa Volume" and the data set of "Chinese Wikipedia" respectively, and the semantic similarity of the text was calculated using the Word2vec model. And it is verified through experiments that the accuracy of the semantic similarity calculation based on the "Wa Volume" is higher than the semantic similarity calculation based on Chinese Wikipedia in the field of ethnic minorities.

Acknowledgment. This work is supported by Major Science and Technology Project of Yunnan Province (No. 202002AD080001), Yunnan Expert Workstation of Xiaochun Cao, Kunming Key Laboratory of Education Informatization, and Scientific Research Fund Project of Yunnan Provincial Department of Education (No. 2021Y491).

References

1. Mikolov, T., Chen, K., Corrado, G.: Efficient estimation of word representations in vector space. Comput. Sci. **3**(4), 115–126 (2013)
2. Zhou, L.: Research on the working principle and application of Word2vec. Sci. Technol. Inf. Dev. Econ. **25**(02), 145–148 (2015)
3. Bengio, Y., Schwenk, H., Senecal, J.: Neural probabilistic language models. J. Mach. Learn. Res. **3**(6), 1137–1155 (2003)
4. Mikolov, T., Chen, K., Corrado, G.: Efficient estimation of word representations in vector space. Comput. Sci. **3**(4), 186–202 (2013)
5. Li, X., Xie, H., Li, L.: Research on the calculation of sentence semantic similarity based on Word2vec. Comput. Sci. **44**(09), 256–260 (2017)

6. Liu, H., Xu, D.: Ontology-based semantic similarity and correlation calculation research review. Comput. Sci. **39**(02), 8–13 (2012)

7. Wang, C.: A review of text similarity calculation methods. Inf. Sci. **37**(03), 158–168 (2019)

8. Li, R.: Research on semantic-based text similarity calculation method. Beijing University of Technology (2018)

9. Zhang, Q.: Research on Weibo short text classification based on Word2vec. Inf. Netw. Secur. **38**(01), 57–62 (2017)

10. Ma, C.: Research and Application of Chinese Short Text Clustering Algorithm Based on Word2Vec. Chinese Academy of Sciences (2018)

11. Tang, M., Zhu, L., Zou, X.: A document vector representation based on Word2Vec. Comput. Sci. **43**(06), 214–217 (2016)

12. Sun, H.: The design and implementation of a Word2Vec-based efficient vocabulary semantic similarity calculation system. J. Beijing Polytech. Inst. **18**(04), 26–31 (2019)

13. Zhu, L.: Research on text classification based on word2vec word vector. Southwest University (2017)

14. Xue, W.: A text classification method based on word2vec. J. Beijing Inf. Sci. Technol. Univ. (Nat. Sci. Ed.) **33**(01), 71–75 (2018)

15. Ma, Z.: Research on stop word processing and feature selection technology for text classification. Xidian University (2014)

16. Ma, S.: Research on the Calculation Method of Microblog Text Similarity Based on Weighted Word2vec. Xidian University (2019)

17. Wu, Z., Liu, D., Zhang, Q.: Research on similarity calculation of automatic question answering system for customer service. Inf. Technol. **44**(3), 99–103 (2020)

18. Wu, D.: Research and implementation of Chinese text similarity based on word2vec. Xidian University (2016)

19. Zhao, X., Si, G.: The Aesthetic Ideal of Ecological Harmony of the Wa People. Yunnan University, Yunnan (2014)

Short-Term Traffic Condition Prediction Based on Multi-source Data Fusion

Xiaoru Deng[1] , Hui Zhou[1](✉) , Xiaoran Yang[2] ,
and Chunyang Ye[1]

[1] School of Computer Science and Technology,
Hainan University, Haikou 570228, China
{xrdeng, zhouhui, cyye}@hainanu.edu.cn
[2] School of Computer Management,
Hefei University of Technology, Hefei 230009, China

Abstract. Accurate prediction of the short-term traffic condition can help to relieve the pressure of traffic and optimize the intelligent transportation system. Traditional traffic condition prediction is mainly based on historical time-series data only, and some sudden factors such as weather conditions are usually ignored. As a result, the accuracy of prediction is compromised. To address this issue, we propose a recurrent neural network to integrate the information of weather situations and road conditions to predict traffic conditions. Experimental results show that compared to the baseline methods using time-series data only, our proposed method can improve the prediction accuracy up to 5.6%.

Keywords: Short-term traffic condition prediction · Weather situations · Missing value · Recurrent neural network

1 Introduction

The introduction of new issues such as traffic congestion along with the urbanization process has triggered the development of smart city applications. Intelligent traffic system (ITS) [1] is a kind of real-time and accurate transportation operation system, which integrates computer technology, data communication, artificial intelligence, and other advanced technologies. Generally speaking, the short-term traffic condition predict is an important part of the intelligent transportation system. The results of traffic condition prediction are usually applied to optimize the traffic system and avoid traffic jams.

Short-term traffic condition prediction can be regarded as a typical spatio-temporal data mining issue [2]. In general, the traffic data is characterized by complex spatial dependence as well as periodic and dynamic changes over time. In recent years, many methods based on recurrent neural network have been developed to predict the short-term traffic condition. In literature [3], a model based on LSTM is adopted to predict two adjacent roads in Beijing. In another study, a self-learning method based on a Bi-LSTM is proposed by Qu et al. [4] to predict the traffic condition of three locations about 5 km way from the main road. Meanwhile, Feng et al. also proposed an approach to predict the traffic flow at five adjacent points based on the traffic on one road [5].

© Springer Nature Singapore Pte Ltd. 2021
Y. Tan et al. (Eds.): DMBD 2021, CCIS 1453, pp. 327–335, 2021.
https://doi.org/10.1007/978-981-16-7476-1_29

Unfortunately, one major limitation of the aforementioned methods is that they predict the traffic condition based on only a few adjacent roads, which is not suitable for practical application. Nevertheless, in practice, the traffic condition of one road may be affected by not only the adjacent roads, but also others that are not directly connected to the road (e.g., cars may choose an unusual route to bypass a road with an accident).

To address this issue, Wu et al. proposed a LSTM network based on the attention mechanism to simultaneously predict multiple different roads such as expressways, main roads and secondary roads in Nanshan District, Shenzhen [6]. However, due to external disturbances, such as traffic accidents, weather changes, etc., the short-term traffic flow show greater uncertainty. For example, the traffic index status of Qiuhai Avenue in Haikou City on August 9th and August 10th, 2018 as illustrated in Fig. 1(a) are correlated to the rainfall in Fig. 2(b). Here, the larger the value of the traffic index, the worse the traffic capacity of the road, and vice versa. Specifically, as shown in Fig. 1(b), the surface precipitation from 1 pm to 3 pm on August 10th is about 50–60 mm/h. Meanwhile, the corresponding traffic index of this time period is much higher than that of the previous day, and the road capacity becomes very poor, even worse than the evening peak. Our investigation on other roads also confirms that the rainstorm weather has a great impact on the road condition. Therefore, it is incompetent to predict the traffic condition by mining the hidden spatio-temporal patterns from these complex nonlinear time-varying traffic data only. External factors such as the weather should also be considered.

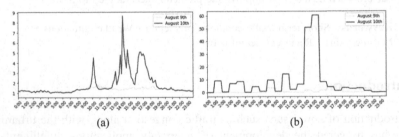

(a)   (b)

Fig. 1. (a) is the two-day traffic index on Qiuhai Avenue in Haikou City on August 9th and 10th, 2018. (b) is the rainfall for two days in Haikou City on August 9th and 10th, 2018.

In this paper, we propose a method to predict the traffic condition based on the fusion of multi-source data. In particular, we fuse the weather situation information and the historical traffic data to predict the traffic condition of multiple road sections simultaneously. The main challenge lies in how to fully explore the impact of weather situation information on road condition, and reduce the noise to predict multiple roads sections at the same time. To address such challenges, we propose an RM-GRU network model to extract multiple road feature information and its corresponding weather feature information at the same time. To reduce the noise, a layer of attention is added to each step to capture the impact of the weather. In general, the major contributions of this paper are two folded: First, we propose a method to fuse the weather situation information and historical traffic data to predict the traffic condition at multiple road sections simultaneously. Second, we conduct extensive experiments to evaluate our proposal. Experimental results show that our approach outperforms the baseline method without concerning the weather factors with an up to 5.6% improvement of the prediction accuracy.

The rest of this paper is organized as follows: Sect. 2 reviews the state-of-the-art research efforts on traffic condition prediction. In Sect. 3, the data preprocessing and our model are introduced. Section 4 evaluates our proposal using extensive experiments. Section 5 concludes the work.

2 Related Work

The prediction model based on mathematical logic was an earlier method used for traffic condition predicting. Then, the time-series related knowledge is adopted to set a prediction model for traffic condition prediction [7]. However, the prediction model based on time-series works well when the traffic condition data changes relatively smoothly. Since the Kalman filter algorithm is proposed, correspondingly, the relatively satisfactory results are the traffic flow prediction algorithm proposed by Okutani et al. [8]. However, these methods cannot reflect the randomness, dynamics, and nonlinearity of traffic flow data, and require a deal of time-series historical traffic flow data when training. Subsequently, research efforts are also devoted to developing some nonlinear theoretical prediction methods. Zhang and Benveniste first proposed a wavelet network under the background of functional nonparametric regression [9]. A fuzzy wavelet neural network with wavelet function as fuzzy membership function is proposed by Guan et al. [10], which estimates the traffic condition in a cycle through fuzzy reasoning. In order to overcome the parameter problem of the traditional non-parametric regression prediction method (NPR) on the huge historical database, a non-parametric regression method K-NN is proposed [11]. The experiment adopting actual highway data shows that the performance of the K-NN method is similar to that of the linear time series method. Later, BP neural network is applied in traffic flow prediction by Cui and Fengying [12]. The results show that it has extent nonlinear mapping and prediction ability. Unfortunately, it has obvious defects in the description of dynamic time characteristics and the input of time series structure.

Due to its ability to remember time-series, RNN is widely applied in time-series predicting. Liu et al. applied RNN to predict traffic condition, due to RNN has the problem of long-distance dependence on previous information and "gradient explosion" [13], the accuracy of the prediction is relatively low. In order to fight the deficiency of standard RNN, the long short-term memory (LSTM) [14] as the improved version of standard RNN, are proposed. Songlin et al. applied LSTM to predict roads and achieves a high prediction effect, but it ignores the temporal and spatial correlation of traffic flow data [15]. In addition, a model based on LSTM network is adopted for predicting traffic flow that makes full use of the weekly/daily periodicity and the temporal and spatial characteristics of traffic flow and introduces an attention-based model, which can automatically learn to determine the importance of traffic flow in different time periods in the past [16]. Further, Hu et al. also proposed a model based on the attention-mechanism to capture the data characteristics of different seasons/months/weeks [17].

Meanwhile, its prediction accuracy can reach about 97%, but it is only for the total number of days and impractical in real-life applications.

To sum up, different from the aforementioned existing work, the model of this paper is designed to predict the roads simultaneously. Moreover, the weather condition is also fused in our model to concern the impact of sudden weather condition on roads with a more accurate prediction.

3   RM-GRU Model

In this section, the model on which the proposed method is based is introduced first, and then the components of the improved structure are introduced in detail, including the attention layer module. Finally, the dataset used in this paper is introduced.

3.1   GRU Model Structure

In recent years, GRU [18] has been widely applied in natural language processing tasks such as speech recognition and time-series prediction. GRU is simpler than the standard LSTM variant model. A GRU cell combines the forget gate and the input gate into a single update gate which also mixes the cell state and the hidden state, and some other changes. Its effect is similar to that of LSTM, but the parameters are nearly one-third less, and it is not prone to overfitting. In order to predict multiple roads simultaneously and better capture the mutual influence of each road, the network model proposed in this paper is designed on the basis of GRU and LSTM network, and the best one is found through comparative experiments.

3.2   RM-GRU Model Structure

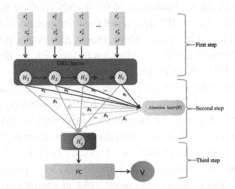

Fig. 2. The overall structure diagram of the RM-GRU model.

The overall structure diagram of the RM-GRU model is shown in Fig. 2. The input of the model is X, which is a matrix of $(p + 1) \times n$, the traffic condition of road p at time t is x^t_p, the condition of all roads at time t is $x(t)$, and the weather condition of these roads at time t is r^t. The predicted target time point is $t + 1$, n is the length of time need to enter, namely the step size. Then the network requires input the historical data includes all the traffic data in the time period $(t\text{-}n + 1, t)$ and the corresponding for weather data.

This paper sets the time step as 12, namely the traffic index of the previous two hours is introduced to predict the road index value of the next ten minutes Y. The fore 40,000 pieces of data for each road conditions are selected, of which apply 28000 data as the training set, and the remaining data as the test set, respectively.

$$X = \begin{bmatrix} x_1^{t-n+1} & x_1^{t-n+2} & x_1^{t-n+3} & \cdots & x_1^{t-1} & x_1^t \\ \vdots & \vdots & \vdots & \vdots & \vdots & \vdots \\ x_p^{t-n+1} & x_p^{t-n+2} & x_p^{t-n+3} & \cdots & x_p^{t-1} & x_p^t \\ r^{t-n+1} & r^{t-n+2} & r^{t-n+3} & \cdots & r^{t-1} & r^t \end{bmatrix} \quad (1)$$

$$Y = \begin{bmatrix} x_1^{t+1} & x_2^{t+1} & \cdots & x_p^{t+1} \end{bmatrix}^T \quad (2)$$

To be specific, the model can be separated into the following three steps.

1) Road traffic index and weather situation data matrix are constructed and normalized as the input into the proposed model.

2) To capture the degrees of influence of different time periods on the traffic condition of the predicted time period, the attention layer is introduced to assign weights to different time periods. H_t' is the attention map obtained by element-wise multiplication of H_t and β_t. Specifically, the hidden state of the GRU is defined as H_t. Meanwhile, the attention mask is defined as β_t.

$$H_t' = \sum_{t=1}^{t} (H_t \otimes \beta_t) \quad (3)$$

3) Finally, to calculate loss and update the parameters through the backpropagation of the model to maximize the prediction effect of the model. the road condition information and weather situation information extracted by the fully connected layer (FC) are combined with a weighted sum to predict the 1×414 road condition information V of the next time window.

3.3 Dataset

In this work, we use the traffic index dataset updated every ten minutes for 414 sections of Haikou City in 2018 provided by DiDi big data platform. Additionally, the corresponding weather data is updated every hour of the year.

DiDi big data platform provides traffic index data updated every 10 min on 414 road conditions with road IDs between 246400 and 246813. The traffic index is defined as follow:

$$p_t = \frac{v}{v_t} \tag{4}$$

where v refers to the average traffic speed at 2.am, v_t is the average traffic speed at time t. The traffic index can reflect the congestion status of the road. The value of p_t is inversely proportional to the degree of traffic condition. The larger the value of p_t, the worse the road capacity, on the contrary, the smoother the road traffic. The original data provided by the platform has many missing data values due to some reasons (such as equipment damage, line failure, storage and processing errors, etc.). More importantly, if the traffic index data with missing values is directly applied to the traffic condition analysis model, the feature of the traffic index data is not explored in-depth. Especially when a lot of data are missing continuously, there is a lot of uncertainty. The filling method used in this paper is to fill in the missing values according to whether the current time data is in working days, peak hours, bad weather, then cycle the average value of this time in a year as the missing value supplement, which is the closest to the original data value to a large extent.

We crawled the weather of Haikou City updated hourly in 2018 as the weather data. The weather indicators include precipitation, visibility, wind speed, and temperature. Since the short-term traffic index data is recorded every 10 min, this paper subdivides weather data into records for every 10 min to make its dimension consistent with the historical short-term traffic index data.

4 Evaluation

4.1 Experimental Setup

In previous work [19], a M-GRU model has been proposed, the missing values of the data are processed by using the average values before and after. To evaluate the impact of the missing value filling method and weather situation on road condition proposed in the study, the previous method is applied as the baseline by this paper. The network parameters were randomly initialized at the beginning, and optimized by the cross-entropy loss and Adam optimizer with a learning rate of 0.001. Each model was trained for 400 epochs, and the batch size was set to 256. The number of GRU step size sets 12, the network layers set 2, and the number of hidden units set 64 and 64 respectively.

To measure the performance, several common performance indicators such as mean absolute error (*MAE*), mean absolute percentage error (*MAPE*), and mean square percentage error (*RMSE*) are selected.

4.2 Experimental Result

In this experiment, the rationality of the model structure was demonstrated by sets of controlled experiments. RM-GRU and RM-LSTM are proposed in this paper. In fact, they have the same network structure. First, to demonstrate the superiority of the missing value filling algorithm proposed in this paper, method of average values before and after as input to train the network. Experimental results are shown in Table 1 (dataA is the filling strategy proposed in this paper, dataB represents the filling method of average value). Second, to demonstrate the necessity of introducing weather conditions into prediction, a dataset containing weather conditions is applied to predict. Table 2 is the performance of comparing different networks on the different dataset (dataR represents the weather features).

Table 1. Filling method results of different missing values.

Model	Dataset	Evaluation index		
		MAE	MAPE (%)	RMSE
M-LSTM	dataB	0.306	18.603	0.943
M-GRU	dataB	0.303	17.197	0.950
M-LSTM	dataA	0.256	15.304	0.958
M-GRU	dataA	**0.245**	**14.673**	0.960

Table 2. Performance of weather feature.

Model	Dataset	Evaluation index		
		MAE	MAPE (%)	RMSE
M-LSTM	dataA	0.256	15.304	0.958
M-GRU	dataA	0.245	14.673	0.960
RM-LSTM	dataA&dataR	0.191	12.506	0.975
RM-GRU	dataA&dataR	**0.183**	**11.562**	0.973

Experiments results demonstrate that the missing value filling strategy proposed in this paper has a higher accuracy than the traditional filling method, and the accuracy is improved by about 2.5%, which can maximize the restoration of historical data. Table 2 shows the MAPE value of our model is 11.562%. Taking into account the impact of weather condition on the road, the model RM-GRU proposed in this paper can achieve an accuracy of 88.44% (1 minus the value of MAPE), which is about 5.6% higher than the baseline method.

5 Conclusion

This paper proposes an RM-GRU model to predict the traffic condition concerning both of traffic historical data and weather conditions. The attention mechanism layer is added to the model to allocate weights for different time steps to reduce the noise. In addition, this paper also uses a new strategy to fill in the missing values of time-series data. Experimental results show that the model can improve the accuracy of the prediction up to 5.6%. Currently, the proposed method still has some limitations. More factors that may affect the traffic condition should be concerned. We plan to investigate the additional factors and design models to further improve the prediction accuracy.

Acknowledgments. This work was supported in part by the Key Research and Development Program of Hainan Province under grant No. ZDYF2020008 the Natural Science Foundation of Hainan Province under the grant No. 2019RC088, 2019CXTD400, and grants from State Key Laboratory of Marine Resource Utilization in South China Sea and Key Laboratory of Big Data and Smart Services of Hainan Province.

References

1. Wang, Y., Goldmines, N., Leclercq, L.: Recent advances in ITS, traffic flow theory, and network operations. Transp. Res. Part C Emerg. Technol. **68**, 507–508 (2016)
2. Nanni, M., Kuijpers, B., Krner, C., et al.: Spatiotemporal data mining. Mob. Data Min. Priv. **27**(3), 187–190 (2008)
3. Li, W., Chen, S., Wang, X., et al.: A hybrid approach for short-term traffic flow forecasting based on similarity identification. Mod. Phys. Lett. B **35**(13), 2150212 (2021)
4. Qu, Z., Li, H., Li, Z., et al.: Short-term traffic flow forecasting method with M-B-LSTM hybrid network. IEEE Trans. Intell. Transp. Syst. **99**, 1–11 (2020)
5. Feng, X., Ling, X., Zheng, H., et al.: Adaptive multi-kernel SVM with spatial-temporal correlation for short-term traffic flow prediction. IEEE Trans. Intell. Transp. Syst. **99**, 1–13 (2018)
6. Wu, P., Huang, Z., Pian, Y., et al.: A combined deep learning method with attention-based LSTM model for short-term traffic speed forecasting. J. Adv. Transp. **2020**(4), 1–15 (2020)
7. Sánchez, J.M., et al.: Predicting using box-Jenkins, nonparametric, and bootstrap techniques. Technometrics **37**(3), 303–310 (1995)
8. Guo, J., Huang, W., Williams, B.M.: Adaptive kalman filter approach for stochastic short-term traffic flow rate prediction and uncertainty quantification. Transp. Res. Part C Emerg. Technol **43**, 50–64 (2014)
9. Zhang, Q., Benveniste, A.: Wavelet networks. IEEE Transp. Neural Netw. **3**(6), 889–898 (1992)
10. Guan, HS., Ma, W.G., Meng, Y.Y.: Traffic flow prediction based on hierarchical genetic optimized algorithm. In: 3rd International Conference on Tractor & Farm Transporter, vol. 37, p. 121 (2008)
11. Davis, G.A., Nihan, N.L.: Nonparametric regression and short-term freeway traffic forecasting. J. Transp. Eng. **117**(02), 178–188 (1991)
12. Cui, F.: Traffic flow prediction based on BP neural network. In: Intelligent Systems and Applications (ISA), pp. 1–4 (2010)
13. Liu, R.R., Hong, F., et al.: Short-term traffic flow prediction based on deep circulation neural network. J. Phys. Conf. Ser. **1176**, 032020 (2019)
14. Hochreiter, S., Schmidhuber, J.: Long short-term memory. Neural Comput. **9**(8), 1735–1780 (1997)
15. Qiao, S., Sun, R., Fan, G., Liu, J.: Short-term traffic flow forecast based on parallel long short-term memory neural network. In: 8th IEEE International Conference on Software Engineering and Service Science (ICSESS), pp. 253–257. IEEE (2017)
16. Wu, Y., Tan, H., Qin, L., et al.: A hybrid deep learning based traffic flow prediction method and its understanding. Transp. Res. Part C Emerg. Technol. **90**(1), 166–180 (2018)
17. Hu, X., Wei, X., Gao, Y., et al.: An attention-mechanism-based traffic flow prediction scheme for smart city. In: 15th IEEE International Wireless Communications & Mobile Computing Conference (IWCMC), pp. 1822–1827. IEEE (2019)

18. Dey, R., Salemt, F.M.: Gate-variants of gated recurrent unit (GRU) neural networks. In: IEEE International Midwest Symposium on Circuits & Systems, pp. 1597–1600 (2017)
19. Jiang, H., Ye, C., Deng, X., et al.: Deep learning for short-term traffic conditions prediction. In: International Conference on Service Science (ICSS), pp. 70–75. IEEE (2020)

Chinese Named Entity Recognition Incorporating Multi-scale Features

Jingxin Liu[1], Jieren Cheng[1,2(✉)], Bo Wu[3(✉)], Dongwan Xia[1], Dengfang Feng[1], and Xiulai Li[1]

[1] School of Compute Science and Technology, Hainan University, Hainan University, Haikou 570228, China
[2] Hainan Blockchain Technology Engineering Research Center, Hainan University, Haikou 570228, China
[3] Hainan Harbor & Shipping Holding CO., LTD., Haikou 570311, China
`wu.bol@coscosshipping.com`

Abstract. Deep learning technology has been widely used in the field of natural language processing, making the deep learning-based Chinese Social Media Named Entity Recognition (NER) method is becoming more and more important. However, the public datasets in the field of Chinese Social Media are small in size, which cannot allow deep learning models to fully learn, resulting in low accuracy of model recognition. At the same time, Chinese Social Media has more new words and abbreviations, which contains a lot of noise. To solve the above problems, we propose a Chinese Social Media NER model based on multi-scale features BiLSTM-CRF, which combines character features, word segmentation features, radical features and pinyin features at the embedding layer to obtain multi-scale semantics information. Then, the acquired features are transferred to the BiLSTM network (CIFG Cell) for encoding, and finally the encoded tags are decoded through the CRF layer to obtain the prediction results. Experimental results prove that the BiLSTM-CRF model based on multi-scale features can improve the accuracy of the model when performing Chinese social media named entity recognition. At the same time, we use CIFG Cell to have higher recognition efficiency than Basic LSTM Cell in network coding. When the model is trained, we use the gradient truncation method and the Dropout layer to further avoid problems such as gradient explosion and model overfitting.

Keywords: BiLSTM-CRF · Named Entity Recognition · Multi-scale features

1 Introduction

With the rapid development of "Internet" and "Big data", Weibo has been become one of the largest social platforms in China, and a large amount of readable data has been accumulated in Weibo. Regarding the important information appearing in Weibo, it is difficult to meet the demand by using manual processing methods to collect massive unstructured network text data. However, the unstructured information in free text is difficult to extract and use directly, which makes the identification of massive unstructured data a difficult problem that needs to be solved urgently.

© Springer Nature Singapore Pte Ltd. 2021
Y. Tan et al. (Eds.): DMBD 2021, CCIS 1453, pp. 336–347, 2021.
https://doi.org/10.1007/978-981-16-7476-1_30

In recent years, the research on NER [1] in the general field has been received extensive attention. It can identify words with actual meanings such as names of people, places, and organizations that appear in unstructured text. NER is the core foundation in the field of Natural Language Processing [2, 3], and is widely used in tasks such as Machine Translation [4, 5], Knowledge Graph [6–8], and Relation Extraction [9, 10].

With the rapid development of deep learning technology [11], Chinese NER has been widely used in Medical [12, 13], Geography [14, 15], Social Media [16, 17] and other fields. However, how to efficiently apply deep learning models to Chinese Social Media to extract entity information from massive unstructured web texts has become a research hot-spot in the field of Chinese Social Media. However, public resources in the field of Chinese Social Media are relatively scarce. The currently recognized dataset is the Weibo NER corpus. The corpus is relatively sparse, which leads to insufficient learning of tag data when the deep learning model is trained, which will result in poor recognition effect. At the same time, the NER task for Chinese social media faces many noisy new words and conventional abbreviations.

In response to these difficult problems, we propose a BiLSTM-CRF model based on multi-scale features to enhance semantic information, so as to achieve the effect of data enhancement. Since we use the BiLSTM-CRF basic model framework, the model uses LSTM in the network coding layer for coding. The biggest disadvantage of this network is the longer training time. In order to optimize this problem, we introduce CIFG Cell instead of Basic LSTM Cell. Compared with the Basic LSTM cell, the CIFG Cell combines the input gate and the forget gate in structure, reducing one step of operation, which can reduce the calculation time of the model to a certain extent.

2   Related Work

In the past, traditional methods have been proposed to improve the accuracy of NER in the Chinese Social Media field. Among them are rule-based methods [18], and statistics-based machine learning methods [19]. For example, Peng Nanyun et al. [16] first released a new corpus for Chinese Social Media, Weibo NER, and proposed a CRF-based NER method for Chinese Social Media.

In recent years, with the development of deep learning, NER methods based on deep learning have gradually become dominant in the field of Chinese Social Media. At present, there are two main ways to improve the performance of NER in the Chinese Social Media field. (1) Improve the performance of text segmentation through joint training models to improve the accuracy of the NER model. (2) Improve the performance of the NER model by introducing external information.

Peng Nanyun et al. [17] jointly trained the word segmentation system and the NER system, and learned the boundary information of Chinese words through the word segmentation system. He Hangfeng et al. [20] proposed a joint training method that takes into account both sentence-level score (F-Score) and label accuracy. This method reduces the loss of the F-Score-driven model in the process of NER, and helps to reduce the impact of noise on Chinese Social Media NER. He Hangfeng et al. [21] proposed a semi-supervised joint model of cross-domain datasets. The model can not only learn information outside the domain based on the similarity of the domain, but also learn unlabeled information in the domain through self-training. The above methods are joint learning related tasks to improve the performance of NER, which will lead to more complex models being trained.

Zhang Yue et al. [22] proposed a Lattice LSTM model, which breaks the traditional Chinese NER model's dependence on word segmentation accuracy, and uses a large amount of external dictionary information to select the most relevant word granularity information to reduce the word segmentation errors. Nie Yuyang et al. [23] proposed a neural network-based NER method. This method obtains expanded semantic information from a large-scale corpus to enhance the semantics of Chinese Social Media. However, these methods all introduce additional data to enhance semantic features, and do not consider the impact of input character context information on recognition.

Starting from the original dataset, we neither use a joint training model nor external resources, but embed radical features and pinyin features on the BiLSTM-CRF model based on word features to further capture semantic features to improve Chinese Social Media accuracy of NER. At the same time, we replaced Basic LSTM Cell with CIFG Cell to improve the efficiency of model recognition.

3 Model

The embedding presentation layer, network coding layer and label decoding layer are designed in the BiLSTM-CRF model based on multi-scale information, and each layer is designed with specific functions, as shown in Fig. 1.

Embedding in the Presentation Layer. Each input Chinese character is converted into a character vector to obtain character information, and word information is obtained through Jieba word segmentation. In addition, radical feature information of Chinese characters and pinyin feature information are added to obtain multi-scale Chinese character information.

Network Coding Layer. Because BiLSTM can better capture context information from the forward and backward directions, the BiLSTM layer is used to model and encode the input sequence. We replaced the Basic LSTM cell with a CIFG cell to reduce the calculation time of the model and improve the efficiency of model recognition.

Label Decoding Layer. Because CRF will consider the dependency relationship between tags when performing tag prediction, so as to obtain the optimal solution. Therefore, the label decoding layer uses CRF to predict entity labels to obtain the most accurate output label sequence.

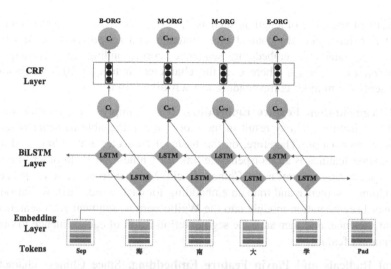

Fig. 1. BiLSTM-CRF model based on multi-scale features

3.1 Embedding Presentation Layer

In order to make the deep learning model have better performance, in the embedding presentation layer, we embed character features, word segmentation features, radical features and pinyin features, as shown in Fig. 2. This embedding method can be used in the field of Chinese Social Media to embed Chinese information from multiple dimensions, which can better obtain semantic information.

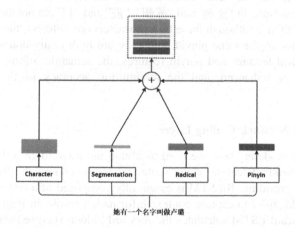

Fig. 2. Four embedding features of the embedding presentation layer

Character Feature Embedding. In order to avoid the impact of Chinese word segmentation errors on Chinese NER, we first extract character features. We use Wikipedia pre-trained character vectors to process the characters input to the model. Formally, we give an input sequence of length n, such as $X_i = (C_1, C_2, ..., C_n)$, where C represents a character, X represents the content of a sentence, and i represents the first few sentences. The character embedding sequence corresponding to this sequence is $C_{100} = (e_1, e_2, ..., e_{100})$, where C is the character content of 100 dimensions, and e represents the number corresponding to each dimension.

Word Segmentation Feature Embedding. If we simply use character vectors as embedding features, it may result in the model not being able to better obtain word boundary information. Therefore, on the basis of character embedding, adding word segmentation features is an indispensable link for Chinese NER. In order to obtain the word segmentation features in the Chinese Social Media corpus, we separate each word in the Chinese sentence and train an embedding for each word. First, we introduce the Jieba word segmentation module into the Weibo corpus, segment each sentence in the Chinese sentence, and then save the segmentation result of each sentence to obtain the segmentation feature.

Radical Radicals and Pinyin Feature Embedding. Since Chinese characters are pictographic characters, the meaning of the characters is closely related to the radicals, so the radicals have a special meaning for a Chinese character. This situation is often reflected in the fact that characters with the same or similar radicals may have similar meanings. For example, although the words "河" and "海" in "黄河" and "南海" are different, they all have the same radical "氵", and they mostly indicate that they are related to water. The "犭" in "野猴" and "小黄狗", they mostly mean a kind of animal. Although Chinese characters are pictographic characters and are greatly influenced by radicals, their meanings are also closely related to pinyin characteristics. Therefore, pinyin information has important meaning for a Chinese character. This situation is often reflected in the fact that characters with the same pinyin may have similar meanings. For example, in "亚洲" and "苏州", "洲" and "州" are not the same word, but their pinyin is "zhōu". Although these two characters are different, they are related to a certain extent due to the same pinyin, and they are both entity nouns and so on. By embedding radical features and pinyin features, the semantic information of Chinese characters can be enhanced, and the recognition accuracy of the model can be improved.

3.2 BiLSTM Network Coding Layer

In the sequence modeling task, we need to obtain the forward embedding feature and the reverse embedding feature of the sentence, so we choose the BiLSTM network architecture for encoding. BiLSTM is essentially composed of a forward LSTM and a backward LSTM, used to capture context information to obtain long-distance dependence. The forward LSTM calculates the forward hidden state sequence to obtain the forward hidden state sequence h_1. The backward LSTM calculates the backward hidden state sequence to obtain the reverse hidden state sequence h_2. Then connect the forward hidden state and the backward hidden state to h to obtain a new multidimensional feature e. In LSTM, we use a LSTM Cell (CIFG) that couples a forget gate and an input gate, as shown in Fig. 3 when the cell is updated. Where x_t represents the input content at the current moment, and C_{t-1} represents the cell state output at the previous moment; f_t is shown in formula (1); h_{t-1} represents the output of the hidden state at the last moment; $\overline{C}_t$ rerepresents the candidate cell state at this moment, as shown in formula (2); C_t represents the updated cell state output at this moment, as shown in formula (3); Ot is shown in formula (4); ht represents the output of the hidden state at this moment, as shown in formula (5). Compared with Basic LSTM Cell, CIFG Cell has three gates (input gate, forget gate, output gate) that need to be calculated, and the input gate and forget gate in CIFG Cell are combined, reducing the calculation of one node to improve the calculation of encoding efficiency.

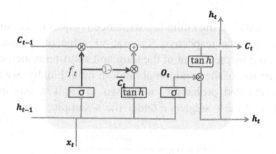

Fig. 3. CIFG structure diagram

$$f_t = \delta(W_f * [h_{t-1}, x_t] + b_f) \tag{1}$$

$$\overline{C}_t = \tanh(W_c * [h_{t-1}, x_t] + b_c) \tag{2}$$

$$C_t = f_t \otimes C_{t-1} \oplus (1 - f_t) \otimes \overline{C}_t \tag{3}$$

$$O_t = \delta(W_o * [h_{t-1}, x_t] + b_o) \tag{4}$$

$$h_t = O_t \otimes \tanh(C_t) \tag{5}$$

3.3   Label Decoding Layer

At the label decoding layer, we choose the CRF model [24]. Its advantage is not to normalize every moment, but to normalize the entire sequence in the end, also called global normalization. However, MEMM [25] is normalized at each moment, also called local normalization. The advantage of global normalization is that it does not calculate the loss of the predicted value and the true value at each moment, because the loss calculation at each moment will cause the previous and next moments to lose the correlation, and the maximum probability is output at each moment. These problems do not exist during model training, because we have processed the data when prepro- cessing, but these problems may exist during model testing, such as the problem of B- PER followed by a B-PER. But there is a transfer feature matrix in CRF, which will consider the order between output adjacent labels, so we choose to use CRF as the output layer of BiLSTM.

The optimization goal of CRF is shown in formula (6), where x represents the x-th training sample, y represents the possible sequence, $Score(x, y)$ is the score that each sequence needs to predict, y_i represents the label at the i-th moment, and y_{i+1} represents the $i+1$th.

$$Score(x, y) = \sum_{i=0}^{m-1} A_{y_i, y_{i+!}} + \sum_{i=1}^{m} P_{i, y_i} \tag{6}$$

The $Score(x, y)$ value of the entire tag sequence is equal to the sum of the scores of each word vector, and the respective $Score(x, y)$ value of the word vector at each position is determined by the output of the long and short-term memory neural network and the transition matrix of the conditional random field. Finally, we use the function to get the global normalized probability is shown in Eq. (7). Among them, $e^{Score(x,y)}$ represents the score of the y sequence under the x sample.

$$P(y/x) = \frac{e^{Score(x,y)}}{\sum_{\tilde{y} \in Y_x} e^{Score(x,\tilde{y})}} \tag{7}$$

4 Experiments

We embed multi-scale features on the basis of the Bi-LSTM-CRF model framework to enhance semantic information and improve the recognition accuracy of the model. At the same time, we replaced CIFG Cell to improve the recognition efficiency of the model. In order to prove the effectiveness of the model, we use the Weibo NER corpus published by Peng and Dredze [16] in the field of Chinese Social Media, experiment with the model by setting different constraints, and discuss the experimental results.

4.1 Datasets

We select the Weibo dataset as the experimental dataset. The Weibo dataset contains four entities: Person, Location, Organization, and Geopolitics. According to the ratio of 1350:270:270 (5:1:1), it is divided into training set, test set, and development set. The details are shown in Table 1 and 2. The proportion of entity tag data in this data set is also relatively small, which often affects the results, and multiple experiments can be performed to adjust the model parameters.

Table 1. Weibo NER dataset information statistics

Weibo NER	Train	Test	Dev	Number of entity types
Characters	73378	270	270	4
Sentences	1350	14703	14336	4

4.2 Parameter Settings

In order to get the best performance of our proposed model, this experiment is used the Tensorflow1.3.1 framework and uses NVIDIA 2080 GPU for training. We selected the specific model parameters are shown in Table 3. The Character feature embedding dimension is set to 100, the Seg feature dimension is set to 20, the Radical feature embedding dimension is set to 50, and the Pinyin feature embedding dimension is set to 50. Droup_keep in the Droupout layer is set to 0.5. The number of layers of BiLSTM is set to 2, the batch size is set to 120, the learning rate is 0.003, and the Epoch is set to 500. In addition, we also use gradient truncation technology in the model to prevent gradient explosion and use Dropout technology to prevent over-fitting. In the gradient truncation technique, [−5, 5] is set as the gradient truncation range. Finally, we use the Adam optimizer to update the gradient.

Table 2. Weibo dataset label statistics

Category	Train	Percentage (%)	Test	Percentage (%)	Dev	Percentage (%)
B-PER	562	0.76	110	0.75	90	0.62
M-PER	475	0.64	90	0.61	67	0.46
E-PER	566	0.77	112	0.75	90	0.62
B-ORG	183	0.25	39	0.26	47	0.32
M-ORG	294	0.39	61	0.41	79	0.55
E-ORG	183	0.25	39	0.26	47	0.32
B-LOC	56	0.08	19	0.13	6	0.04
M-LOC	73	0.09	26	0.18	10	0.07
E-LOC	56	0.08	19	0.13	6	0.04
B-GPE	199	0.27	47	0.31	26	0.18
M-GPE	42	0.06	15	0.10	5	0.04
E-GPE	199	0.27	47	0.31	26	0.18
S-PER	12	0.02	1	0.01	0	0.00
S-GPE	6	0.01	0	0.00	0	0.00
O	70872	96.06	14217	95.79	14010	96.56
Total	73778	100.00	14842	100.00	14509	100.00

4.3 Evaluation Index

As shown in Tabe 4, we compare the three methods [16, 17], and [20] with our method. The experiment uses recall rate (R), accuracy rate (P) and F1 value to evaluate the NER recognition results. Among them, the NER task is more concerned about the recall rate, and the F1 value can be more comprehensively evaluated the performance of the model. The three index calculation formulas are as (8), (9), (10), where TP is the number of samples that recognize the correct samples and are actually correct, FP is the number of samples that recognize the wrong samples but are actually correct, and FN is the number of samples that are recognized The number of wrong samples and actually wrong samples.

$$R = 100\% \times \frac{TP}{FN + TP} \tag{8}$$

$$P = 100\% \times \frac{TP}{FP + TP} \tag{9}$$

$$F_1 = 100\% \times \frac{2PR}{R + P} \tag{10}$$

Table 3. Experimental data statistics

Hyper-parameter	Numerical value
Char_dim	100
Seg_dim	20
Radical_dim	50
Pinyin_dim	50
BiLSTM_layer	2
Learning rate	0.003
Batch size	120
Optimizer	Adam
Droup_keep	0.5
Clip	5.0
Epoch	500

4.4 Comparative Experiment and Analysis

The experimental performance of our comparison model on the Weibo dataset is shown in Table 4. By observing Table 4, we can see that the F_1 value of the Peng and Dredze [19] model is 8.35% lower than ours. The reason for this phenomenon may be that the method based on deep learning can capture words more easily than the method using only CRF Internal deep semantic features. In addition, Peng and Dredze [20] et al. jointly trained the NER task and the word segmentation task to extract fewer word segmentation errors from the corpus. However, because this method only extracts word segmentation features, which are less than our model, the F_1 value is 4.03% lower than our model. Compared with the BiLSTM-CRF model based on the combination of word vectors, we can learn more semantic information more fully in the embedding layer, and reduce the problem of insufficient model learning characteristics due to too small training corpus. Our model uses Wikipedia's pre-trained word vectors to process the words input to the model to obtain new character vector information. At the same time, it uses the Jieba word segmentation tool to obtain the word segmentation information of each sentence, and finally based on the word features Embed the radical features and pinyin features. Compared with the model of Peng [16, 17], the BiLSTM-CRF model based on word embedding, and the model of He and Sun [20], our model can obtain more semantic features in the small-scale Weibo corpus, so that the model can be learned these semantic feature information more fully. During training, we improve training skills, use the method of intercepting gradients to avoid gradient explosion, and use the Dropout layer to prevent over-fitting, which makes the implementation effect better.

Table 4. Comparison of the performance of the model on the Weibo dataset

Models	P	R	F_1
Peng and Dredze [16]	57.98	35.57	44.09
Peng and Dredze [17]	63.33	39.18	48.41
He and Sun[20]	66.93	40.67	49.40
BiLSTM + CRF	58.99	44.93	51.01
Our model (Radical + Pinyin)	**61.58**	**45.66**	**52.44**

Table 5. Experimental performance of ablation experiments on the Weibo dataset

Models	P	R	F_1
BiLSTM-CRF	58.99	44.93	51.01
BiLSTM-CRF+ (Radical)	60.56	45.15	51.73
BiLSTM-CRF+ (Pinyin)	63.58	42.91	51.24
Our model (Radical + Pinyin)	**61.58**	**45.66**	**52.44**

4.5 Ablation Experiment and Analysis

In order to verify the validity of our propose BiLSTM-CRF model based on multi-scale features, we design the following scheme, and conduct experiments and analysis on the Weibo NER corpus, as shown in Table 5.

This table respectively shows the experimental results of the **BiLSTM-CRF** model, **BiLSTM-CRF (Radical)** model, **BiLSTM-CRF (Pinyin)** model, and **BiLSTM-CRF (Radical + Pinyin)** model in the Weibo NER corpus. From the results, it can be seen that the Recall rate and F1 value of the **BiLSTM-CRF** model with embedding radical features and pinyin features are higher than the **BiLSTM-CRF** model, which shows that in the resource-scarce Chinese Social Media field, the embedding radical features and pinyin features can enhance contextual semantic information.

5 Conclusions

Chinese Social Media NER is a basic task of Internet informatization, which can provide powerful support for computer intelligent information extraction and information decision-making. In reality, network text has a large amount of information and involves a wide range of areas. If only human resources are used to recognize named entities in network text data, the recognition efficiency will be very low and many errors may be easily caused. Therefore, it has become a very valuable thing to extract entity tags from network text data intelligently through computers.

The BiLSTM-CRF model based on multi-scale features is proposed and applied to named entity recognition in the field of Chinese Social Media. A large number of experiments show that the proposed model is added with radical features and pinyin features to obtain more Chinese semantic information, which will improve the accuracy of model recognition. At the same time, compared with Basic LSTM Cell, the calculation time of CIFG Cell in the model is reduced by about 20%.

Due to the relatively small Weibo NER dataset, the model is not sufficient trained and the recognition effect is not good. In the future research work, we will introduce joint training models and transfer learning to further improve the model parameters in order to ensure that better models are trained and provided assistance for Chinese social media named entity recognition.

Acknowledgements. This work was supported by the Major science and technology project of Hainan Province (Grant No. ZDKJ2020012), Key Research and Development Program of Hainan Province (Grant No. ZDYF2020040), Hainan Provincial Natural Science Foundation of China (Grant Nos. 2019RC098) and National Natural Science Foundation of China (NSFC) (Grant No. 62162022, 62162024 and 61762033).

References

1. Li, Y., Du, G., Xiang, Y., et al.: Towards Chinese clinical named entity recognition by dynamic embedding using domain-specific knowledge. J. Biomed. Inf. **106**(1), 103435 (2020)
2. Zhong, Q., Tang, Y.: An attention-based BILSTM-CRF for Chinese named entity recognition. In: 2020 IEEE 5th International Conference on Cloud Computing and Big Data Analytics (ICCCBDA). IEEE (2020)
3. Taher, E., Hoseini, S.A., Shamsfard, M.: Beheshti-NER: persian named entity recognition using BERT (2020)
4. Ren, M., Ma, L., Tian, Y., et al.: Research on methods for complex Chinese entity recognition. J. Phys. Conf. Ser. **1576**, 012008 (2020)
5. Patil, N., Patil, A., Pawar, B.V.: Named entity recognition using conditional random fields. Procedia Comput. Sci. **167**, 1181–1188 (2020)
6. Fan, R., Wang, L., Yan, J., Song, W., Zhu, Y., Chen, X.: Deep learning-based named entity recognition and knowledge graph construction for geological hazards. ISPRS Int. J. Geo-Inf. **9**(1), 15 (2019)
7. He, S., Sun, D., Wang, Z.: Named entity recognition for Chinese marine text with knowledge-based self-attention. Multimedia Tools Appl., 1–15 (2021)
8. He, Q., Wu, L., Yin, Y., et al.: Knowledge-graph augmented word representations for named entity recognition. Proc. AAAI Conf. Artif. Intell. **34**(5), 7919–7926 (2020)
9. Ma, Y., Hiraoka, T., Okazaki, N.: Named entity recognition and relation extraction using enhanced table filling by contextualized representations (2020)
10. Schiersch, M., Mironova, V., Schmitt, M., et al.: A German corpus for fine-grained named entity recognition and relation extraction of traffic and industry events (2020)
11. Li, J., Sun, A., Han, J., Li, C.: A survey on deep learning for named entity recognition. IEEE Trans. Knowl. Data Eng. (2020)

12. Wang, C., Wang, H., Zhuang, H., Li, W., Han, S., Zhang, H., Zhuang, L.: Chinese medical named entity recognition based on multi-granularity semantic dictionary and multimodal tree. J. Biomed. Inf. **111**, 103583 (2020)
13. Zhang, R., Gao, Y., Rui, Y., Wang, R., Wenpeng, L.: Medical named entity recognition based on overlapping neural networks. Procedia Comput. Sci. **174**, 27–31 (2020)
14. Xu, F., Li, H., Li, X.: Named entity recognition in the domain of geographical subject. In: 2017 13th International Conference on Natural Computation, Fuzzy Systems and Knowledge Discovery (ICNC-FSKD) (2017)
15. Ma, J., Yuan, H.: Bi-LSTM+CRF-based named entity recognition in scientific papers in the field of ecological restoration technology. Proc. Assoc. Inf. Sci. Technol. **56**(1), 186–195 (2019)
16. Peng, N., Dredze, M.: Named entity recognition for chinese social media with jointly trained embeddings. In: Proceedings of the 2015 Conference on Empirical Methods in Natural Language Processing (EMNLP) (2015)
17. Peng, N., Dredze, M.: Improving named entity recognition for Chinese social media with word segmentation representation learning (2016)
18. Cheng, J., Liu, J., Xu, X., et al.: A review of Chinese named entity recognition. KSII Trans. Internet Inf. Syst. **15**(6), 2012–2030 (2021)
19. Zhang, S., Elhadad, N.: Unsupervised biomedical named entity recognition: experiments with clinical and biological texts. J. Biomed. Inf. **46**(6), 1088–1098 (2013)
20. He, H., Xu, S.: F-score driven max margin neural network for named entity recognition in Chinese social media (2016)
21. He, H., Xu, S.: A unified model for cross-domain and semi-supervised named entity recognition in Chinese social media, vol. 31, no. 1 (2017)
22. Zhang, Y., Yang, J.: Chinese NER using lattice LSTM. In: ACL, pp. 1554–1564 (2018)
23. Nie, Y., Tian, Y., Wan, X., et al.: Named entity recognition for social media texts with semantic augmentation. In: Proceedings of the 2020 Conference on Empirical Methods in Natural Language Processing (EMNLP) (2020)
24. Yiwei, L., Yang, R., Jiang, X., Yin, C., Song, X.: A military named entity recognition method based on pre-training language model and BiLSTM-CRF. J. Phys. Conf. Ser. **1693**, 012161 (2020)
25. Miao, Y., Metze, F.: Improving low-resource CD-DNN-HMM using dropout and multilingual DNN training. In: Proceedings of the Interspeech (2013)

Analysis on the Strategies of Information Technology to Improve Autonomous Learning in Higher Vocational English Teaching

Yu Yan[✉]

Sanya Aviation and Tourism College, Sanya 572000, Hainan, China

Abstract. In the environment of continuous deepening of information technology, higher vocational English classroom has also poured into different teaching modes, to a certain extent, it has played a role in promoting students' autonomous learning ability, teaching efficiency and teaching quality. Higher vocational English teaching must innovate and break through the traditional self, emphasize the effective linkage of content inside and outside the teaching process, using information multimedia platforms to stimulate students' subjective initiative in English learning. For higher vocational students, having a strong autonomous language learning ability is the basis for survival and development in their future careers. This paper mainly analyzes the definition and characteristics of information teaching, the importance and necessity of autonomous learning of higher vocational students, and explain the feasibility of cultivating students' autonomous learning ability through information technology. Meanwhile, not only the effective guidance of teachers and the perseverance of students are needed, but also the schools need to provide abundant educational resources and information technology to enhance students' independent learning and individualized learning capabilities.

Keywords: Information technology · Autonomous learning · Higher vocational English teaching · Strategy inquiry

1 Introduction

Higher vocational education has entered the information age. It relies on modern information technology to build a new education system. Among them, there have been great reforms in educational concepts, educational organization, educational content and educational methods. This information reform is not only equivalent to computer networks, but also includes information from educational hardware to software innovation and development. As an important subject at the stage of higher vocational education, the English teaching of higher vocational education must advance with the times, integrate into the information education model, realize a full range of subject teaching innovation, and create novel and diverse learning methods. In this regard, we should think about how to cultivate students' interest in learning through information education, so that students can independently expand learning content after class, improve learning efficiency, make up for the deficiencies caused by the lack of target language environment, and create conditions for promoting foreign language learning. This article will discuss the cultivation of higher vocational students' autonomous English learning ability under the information technology and how teachers use teaching strategies to assist them. This has a very important guiding role in improving the efficiency of higher vocational English teaching and ensuring that education keeps pace with the times.

2 Basic Connotation of English Innovation Teaching in Higher Vocational College Under the Background of Informationization

In English information teaching in higher vocational colleges, we should make full use of modern information technology such as multimedia facilities and audio-visual education network facilities to optimize the classroom teaching mode and realize the application of information technology in higher vocational English teaching. At present, some colleges and universities have adopted modern teaching methods to effectively promote the application. They have set up special information resources of English education database, English teaching software platform and various professional websites, in order to effectively connect higher vocational English with the Internet, maximize the efficiency of information connection in the whole school. Even some qualified higher vocational colleges have introduced multimedia two-way broadcasting control system, reasonably utilize the comprehensive advantages of high speed and diversified information network, and realize the live broadcast of English teaching in higher vocational colleges. Set up the higher vocational English distance teaching platform, MOOC teaching system, teaching information exchange and feedback platform between students.

In addition, in higher vocational English teaching, a high-quality humanistic system is constructed with the help of the software and hardware of the new powerful information platform, which is very helpful to the innovation of higher vocational English teaching. To a certain extent, it promotes the optimization of efficiency between professional teachers and students' English autonomous learning, encourages students to open up autonomous learning based on unit learning and task-driven goal learning, gradually realizes the informationization and digitization of English teaching, and the overall development of personality.

3 The Concept and Advantages of Autonomous Learning

Higher vocational English teaching is based on the openness principle of the autonomous learning English teaching model, which is conducive to stimulating students' interest in learning English, facilitating students to build interest and confidence in learning English, allowing students to give full play to their initiative, and the principle of interaction is conducive to give full play to the students' sense of competition and cooperation, and learn from each other in group cooperative writing. It can not only stimulate the motivation of self-improvement and competition, but also cultivate the spirit of unity and cooperation. Self-evaluation is an important factor in cultivating students' independent learning ability and lifelong learning ability.

4   Innovative Strategies for Cultivating Students' Autonomous Learning in Higher Vocational English Teaching

Randomly select 200 prestigious vocational students from vocational colleges as the objects of this investigation. A total of 220 questionnaires were sent out in this questionnaire survey, and 216 valid questionnaires were returned to meet the high-efficiency sample number, and relevant data analysis can be carried out. A summary analysis of its admission scores, as shown in the following chart (Fig. 1):

Table 1. Distribution of the number of people in each grade.

	Autonomous scores	Practice scores	Entrance scores	Vocabulary scores
Grade	28–89 points	90–110 points	111–120 points	121 points or more
Percentage	63.89%	31.95%	3.7%	0.46%

Percentage chart of score distribution grades

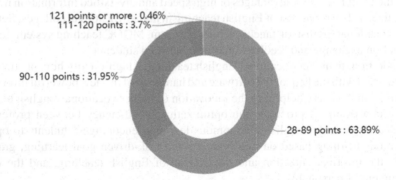

Fig. 1. Percentage chart of score distribution grades

From Table 1, the survey shows that the passing rate of English entrance scores for vocational students is only 36.1%, and less than 20% of students who have mastered more than 1,600 words. Many students have less than 1,000 vocabularies, and some even have only 300 to 500 vocabulary accumulations.

In higher vocational English teaching, how to use the correct guiding method to endow the students with the "stage" of teaching, so as to urge the students to master English learning actively, so as to achieve the purpose of students' autonomous learning. Through many years of English teaching practice and focusing on the new ideas of the teaching process, the innovative characteristics of higher vocational English teaching are highlighted from the two levels of teaching and learning, we can start with the following aspects:

4.1 Adjust the Role of Traditional Teachers

In traditional foreign language teaching, the teacher's role is to "instruct, teach and resolve doubts", while the student's role is to "passively accept knowledge". Cultivating learning autonomy requires teachers and students to readjust their roles. Teachers should change their teaching concepts. The role of a teacher is not only to preach and teach, but also to be a facilitator, mentor, motivator and consultant, information material provider, designer, organizer, and participant in discussions and activities inside and outside the classroom. Students must also change their learning concepts, from "passive learning" to "active learning", overcome the passive dependence of "equality, dependence, and desire", and actively assume the responsibility of learning. In order to improve students' autonomous learning ability, we should reposition the teacher-student relationship and promote students to have a correct attitude towards their own learning.

4.2 Optimize Students' Psychological Quality

The vast majority of vocational students always lack interest in English, and their weak autonomy has always become an obstacle to their learning English. They always lack confidence and timidity in class. In order to eliminate the psychological barriers of students' self-learning in class, we can start from the following aspects: Firstly, create opportunities for students to succeed. Secondly, try to layer teaching as much as possible. Students' learning levels are uneven. For students of different levels, different levels of learning activities can be given. Such as dialogue and text study, the ultimate goal is the use of language. For students with poor language ability, they should recite the original text appropriately, because their key problem is that their language storage is small and the sense of language is not strong, which hinders the organization of spoken English. For students with a solid foundation and rich language, they have the ability to summarize the materials. Organization and reorganization, so they can be asked to repeat the text. Thirdly, try to use the evaluation effect. Education should be oriented towards all students, each student should be able to learn on their own initiative, and teachers should deal with evaluation issues. Teachers should give priority to affirmation and encouragement in the evaluation process. Evaluation is a means to improve students' enthusiasm for independent learning.

4.3 New Strategies for Teaching Creativity

Higher vocational English teachers should know how to flexibly use computer network systems, enrich teaching content through hardware to achieve the effect of optimizing teaching mode, and at the same time propose innovative teaching strategies in all directions. For example, teachers should make reasonable use of personalized online learning systems to guide students to learn in listening, observing, dialogue and thinking, and use voice and video platforms as the carrier of students' English learning activities, so as to replace teachers and let students become the main body of teaching activities. Free play, display individuality and innovation to create a stage. Cultivate students' good English narrative, dialogue, discussion, conversation and debate skills, pay great attention to the complementary with traditional technology and information technology, and consider the introduction of after-school summary content to help students improve their oral expression skills and extracurricular activities, strengthen the English communication and discussion between teachers and students, and constantly improving the English teaching system. In teaching, teachers set up groups for students to find relevant weather information and the dynamic changes of weather in a certain area during the year. Set up typical topics, publish them on the Internet to other teachers and students for discussion, and use subject knowledge as divergence and support points to construct comprehensive courseware. In this process, teachers can help students master the knowledge of network multimedia operations through English, allowing them to learn more independently.

4.4 Learn Innovative Strategies

Teachers need to optimize the learning innovation strategies of higher vocational students under the background of information teaching from the perspective of students, and also give them time and space to learn English knowledge. In practical teaching, humorous classroom learning experience can help students learn English easily in an information environment. For example, in the process of studying Bill Gates class, teachers should give students enough time to learn by themselves. In teaching, we can use computer network to give students the hint of learning activities, stimulate their strong interest in learning, realize learning while thinking, find and solve problems in learning. In teaching, teachers can encourage students to communicate independently by choosing a text and asking questions, for example on a multimedia platform: what do you know about Bill Gates and his company, Microsoft? You know MS and IBM? Do you know that computers work the same way?

The above series of questions is to encourage students to ask and answer each other in the computer network, and to encourage them to express their views, to form a good atmosphere of information learning, innovation and development in the subtle change, and to strive to cultivate a bold and positive spirit in English learning. In the final assignment arrangement, the teacher encourages the students to make full use of the campus network, explain the teacher's video and teaching content in detail, so that the students can use the information equipment skillfully after class and learn to be good at thinking. Teachers need to evaluate students online, realize online teacher-student interaction after class, and improve students' learning initiative.

In this study, the test scores of the two groups of students were counted and analyzed by using SPSS software. The formula applies as follows:

$$\sigma = \sqrt{\frac{\sum_{i=1}^{n}(x_i - \bar{x})^2}{n}} \tag{1}$$

$$S = \sqrt{\frac{\sum_{i=1}^{n}(x_i - \bar{x})^2}{n-1}} \tag{2}$$

$$\sigma_n = \frac{\sigma}{\sqrt{n}} \tag{3}$$

From Table 2, we can see that the performance gap between the two classes of students continues to widen at the end of the first stage. In the process of learning, there

Table 2. Results table

	Reference number	Class average	Highest score	Lowest score	Average increase
Class 1	50	66.4	118	40	9.5
Class 2	50	60.5	110	28	6.7

was progress and improvement, but the differences became more and more obvious. The average score of class 1 is 2.8 points higher than that of class 2, and the average score is 3.3 points higher than the increase in the previous exam. This difference is a testimony to the effectiveness of the classroom. Therefore, we can say that the average score of the students of the class that is engaged in informationization and self-learning ability training is higher than that of the experimental group of students with teachers as the main body.

In the experiment, errors are always inevitable in a single measurement, so we often measure for many times, then use the average value of the measured value to represent the measured quantity, and use the error bar to represent the distribution of the data, in which the height of the error strip is ± standard error. This is the standard deviation.

The data in Table 3 show that the standard deviation of the experimental group is not only larger than that of the control group, but also shows an upward trend, which indicates that the polarization of students in the experimental group is more serious than that of the control group. the reason for this phenomenon mainly lies in the students themselves, because for the experimental group students, the higher vocational English autonomous learning model based on information-based teaching platform It puts forward higher requirements for their autonomous learning ability, self-restraint and time management ability. For those students who have strong autonomous learning ability, self-restraint and time management, they have more autonomous learning times, more homework exercises and more interaction with teachers, and can quickly adapt to this autonomous learning mode. The grades are getting better and better. For those students with poor autonomous learning ability and poor self-restraint and time management, it is difficult for them to adapt to this new model, therefore, their English scores are more and more different from those of the students in the experimental group who have strong autonomous learning ability, self-restraint and proper time management.

Table 3. Establishment result and analysis

	Students' number	Average score	Standard deviation	X value	P value
English testing	114	10.18	2.68	0.592	0.501
English testing	112	10.35	2.51	0.484	0.452

5 Concluding

From the students' test results, the teaching reform of the "two-have-two-nothing" autonomous learning model of English based on the information-based teaching platform is successful, and it is an effective exploration of the information-based teaching reform of English course in higher vocational colleges. Through the implementation of teaching activities through the information-based teaching platform, this teaching model is not only conducive to transforming the subject of teachers' imparting knowledge into the subject of students' autonomous learning, and students carry out autonomous learning anytime and anywhere. Let students change from "want me to learn" to "I want to learn" and "I will learn". Cultivate and improve the sustainable development abilities of higher vocational students, such as autonomous learning ability, self-restraint ability, time management ability and work planning ability, so as to lay a solid foundation for students' lifelong learning. Moreover, it helps to alleviate the problem of shortage of teachers, save teaching resources and costs, and alleviate the contradiction between higher vocational students' heavy professional learning tasks and limited English listening learning hours or even no English listening courses.

In short, in the context of the information age, higher vocational English teaching must innovate and break through the traditional self, emphasize the effective linkage of content inside and outside the teaching process. That is, using information multimedia platforms to stimulate students' subjective initiative in English learning. For higher vocational students, having a strong autonomous language learning ability is the basis for survival and development in their future careers. However, the cultivation of autonomous learning ability does not happen overnight, it requires a long-term process. Not only the effective guidance of teachers and the perseverance of students are needed, but also the schools need to provide abundant educational resources and information technology to enhance students' independent learning and individualized learning capabilities.

References

1. Kim, B.-G.: A study of self-directed English learning strategies of university students for the reinforcement of practical English language skills. Multimedia Assist. Lang. Learn. 16(3), 69–95 (2013)
2. Lee, C.-H.: University students' perceptions and engagement in mobile assisted blended learning in English speaking classes. Clarivate Analytics Web Sci. 21(4), 11–36 (2018)
3. Zhao, S., Miao, G.: Application of English education information management system based on convolution neural network classification algorithm. Int. J. Electr. Eng. Educ. (2020). https://doi.org/10.1177/0020720920940614
4. Sun, X.: Research on the reform of English information-based teaching in higher vocational education under the new media environment. Educ. Teach. Forum 40, 360–361 (2020)
5. Deng, J., Qiao, Z., Wu, A.: Explore the path of the reform of English "three Education" in higher vocational education. Shanxi Educ. (High. Educ.) 09, 45–46 (2020)
6. Hua, C.: The LSCI training mode of public English teachers in higher vocational colleges in the new era–taking Huanggang Vocational and Technical College as an example. J. Huanggang Vocat. Tech. Coll. 22(04), 32–100 (2020)
7. Wang, Y., Zhao, Q.: Exploration on the path of English teaching reform in higher vocational education driven by information-based teaching competition. J. Natl. Netw. Inst. Technol. 23(04), 66–68 (2020)

8. Yiting, P., Jianmei, Z.: Research on the effective ways to improve the Information-based Teaching ability of public English teachers in higher vocational colleges based on TPACK. Economist **08**, 184–185 (2020)

9. Mi, L.: Research on autonomous learning of English listening in higher vocational colleges based on information-based teaching platform. Commun. World **27**(07), 119–120 (2020)

10. Yan, L.: Research on effective English Teaching in higher Vocational Education under the background of Internet+ – a case study of Langfang Yanjing Vocational and Technical College. Mod. Commer. Trade Ind. **541**(20), 197–1999 (2020)

11. Zhang, F.: An analysis of the ways to improve the information-based teaching ability of English teachers in higher vocational colleges. Exch. Sci. Educ. (Mid-Term Issue) **06**, 165166 (2020)

A Data Model Construction Method Based on the Questionnaire Survey

Chaosheng Tang and Heng Zhang

Hainan University, Haikou 570228, China
tcsjk@hainanu.edu.cn

Abstract. A model and application based on the questionnaire survey are presented. After a series of pre-processing of the original survey data, such as de-duplication, missing value and outlier value, the data from the two different data sources are combined and imported into SPSS software. Then, various research variables are extracted according to the research objectives, and the reliability and validity are tested. A structural equation model (SEM) for training willingness is constructed using AMOS software. This model integrates two statistical methods, factor analysis and path analysis, and can well express the direct or indirect effects of other variables on the latent variables of willingness. The results show that individual endeavor expectation is linearly related to subjective norms, which are also the two main factors influencing willingness. Therefore, more publicity and encouragement should be given.

Keywords: Willingness · Pre-processing · AMOS · Structural Equation Model

1 Introduction

There is a strong need to extract latent variables that affect farmers' training willingness through various explicit variables, and to establish multiple linear equations between them and latent variables of training willingness. This paper explores how to effectively induce core latent variables from various explicit variables, and describes the interdependence between them through SEM idea. The model constructed is more in line with general characteristics, which can be further promoted to other fields.

The 13th five year plan for the cultivation and development of new-type professional farmers in China was issued in 2017.Then the relevant national regulations have pointed out the direction and development goal for the training of new-type professional farmers in the future, which also reflects the importance of the training of new-type professional farmers in the new stage. The cultivation of new professional farmers, especially the training of vocational skills and information technology, is an important way to cultivate talents in the Current Rural Revitalization Strategy. Compared with traditional farmers, the willingness of new professional farmers to participate in training is higher. Therefore, it is necessary to explore various factors that affect training intention and establish a relationship model among them.

Y. Tan et al. (Eds.): DMBD 2021, CCIS 1453, pp. 356–366, 2021.
https://doi.org/10.1007/978-981-16-7476-1_32

2 Research Status

Farmers' willingness to participate in training is affected by many factors. Scholars have studied and explored various willingness models from different perspectives, such as Zhai Liming et al. [1]. Based on the data of Guanzhong area in Shaanxi Province as the first-hand data, using binary logistic regression model to study and analyze farmers' willingness to accept new vocational training and the influencing factors, The education level, the scale of land management, the total family population, farmers' confidence in increasing income and the degree of policy concern have important influence on Farmers' participation in the training of new vocational farmers. Fu Xuemei et al. [2] used multivariate logistic model to analyze 304 effective questionnaires of new vocational farmers training trainees in Chengdu, Sichuan Province. The results show that entrepreneurship subsidies, science and technology support, financial support, industrial support and social security subsidies have a significant impact on the satisfaction of new professional farmers' cultivation support policies. Wu Yixiong et al. [3] conducted a questionnaire survey on the agricultural production of new-type professional farmers, and analyzed the factors influencing the agricultural production willingness of new-type professional farmers, such as individuals, agricultural production and management, education and training, and agricultural production willingness, It is found that gender, education level, training time, desire to expand agricultural production, agricultural background, agricultural machinery service mode, unit benefit compared with the local average level and other variables have a statistically significant impact on the new professional farmers' willingness to agricultural production. Hu Wenju et al. [4] took 248 new professional farmers in Yucheng, Ruyang, Shenqiu and other counties of Henan Province as the research objects, and used the logistic regression model to analyze the factors such as gender, age, expenses to be borne and the willingness of distance training of new professional farmers. Wang LINRONG [5] used binary logistic regression model to analyze the influencing factors of training willingness of new-type professional farmers in Hangzhou from two aspects of personal factors and training system of training objects. Ma Yanyan, Li Hongyan [6] taking the survey data in Yinbei area of Ningxia as an example, the binary logistic model was used to conduct regression analysis on the behavior response and influencing factors of farmers' participation in the training of new vocational farmers. The results show that: Farmers' age, education level, cultivated land management, training experience and farmers' awareness of policies have important influence on their willingness to participate in the training of new professional farmers. Based on the survey data of new professional farmers in Heilongjiang Province, Ma Yan, sun Chaoqun et al. [7] used binary logistic regression model to analyze the willingness and influencing factors of new professional farmers to participate in agricultural information training. The results show that: the higher the awareness of the effectiveness of information technology training, the more likely they are to participate in the training; the higher the level of education and income, the higher the demand for agricultural information software application training; the larger the scale of operation of male agricultural cooperatives members are, the more likely they are to participate in the training of agricultural information equipment application; the farmers who are village cadres have the demand for agricultural information policy and knowledge training

Higher. Based on the survey data of Qingdao City, Xu Qian, Xiao Mengmeng [8] used logistic model to analyze the influencing factors of farmers' willingness to vocational skills training from four dimensions of personal characteristics, psychological characteristics, policy characteristics and training characteristics. The results show that education level, training content, policy support and other factors have a significant positive impact on vocational skills training willingness, and the difficulty of access has a significant negative impact on vocational skills training willingness. Based on the questionnaire survey in some areas of Jiangsu Province, Xu Jinhai et al. [9] investigated the different roles of influencing factors of farmers' willingness to agricultural science and technology training service demand by using the extended ordered multi classification logistic model. The results show that farmers' demand for science and technology training services is affected by many factors, such as farmers' individual and family characteristics, the choice of agricultural technology, government services and farmers' risk preference. Xu Hui, Xu Yang, Li Hong et al. [10] obtained first-hand data from 1512 farmers in 7 provinces in China, and used Logistic binary regression model to make an empirical analysis of the effects of 30 indicators in 5 categories on the cultivation of new professional farmers. The results show that 18 factors, such as "whether people often self-study agricultural technology and management knowledge", have a significant impact on the cultivation of new professional farmers under the new normal. Chen Lichang and Chen Jing [11] analyzed the main influencing factors of the cultivation of new professional farmers based on the questionnaire survey data of 89 farmers at fixed observation points in the rural areas of Guangzhou with Logistic model. The results show that there is a negative correlation between age and whether farmers have participated in vocational skills training, while there is a positive correlation between annual per capita family income and the degree of understanding of vocational skills training policies and whether farmers have participated in vocational skills training. Through empirical research on the willingness of new professional farmers to participate in vocational education and training, Wu Zhaoming [12] concluded that the variables such as age, training experience, policy perception, cognition of agricultural quality requirements for professional farmers and professional identity had statistical significance on the willingness of new professional farmers to participate in vocational education and training.

In addition, Zhang Wen, Hao Ying et al. [13] established a structural equation model of influencing factors of rural backbone labor force training willingness. The training content in training characteristics, family income satisfaction in family characteristics and self-awareness ability in personal characteristics are the most important influencing factors. Li still [14] analyzed the willingness and behavior factors of farmers to participate in the training of new professional farmers under the mode of "one village, one product, one subject", and explored the moderating factors of transforming farmers' willingness to participate in training into behavior. On the basis of UTAUT model, Ding Yao and Xu Fang [15] modified the adjustment variables and constructed the hypothesis model of science and technology information service acceptance of new professional farmers in Western China. Through the path analysis of the data obtained from the questionnaire survey, it is found that: performance expectations, effort expectations and convenience conditions significantly affect the willingness and behavior of new professional farmers to use science and technology information services, while the community has no significant impact on the acceptance of science and technology information services of new professional farmers. At the same time, age and education level have a moderating effect on effort expectation.

There are three problems in the existing research:

(1) The dimension of the model research is narrow. And more attention is paid to the influence of single dimension factors on training intention, while the comprehensive effect of multi-dimensional factors is ignored. Training willingness is a complex concept, which is influenced by both subjective factors and non-subjective factors, as well as by rational and irrational factors. Only by integrating different dimensions of factors can the model be expressed more accurately.

(2) The model design method is relatively simple, and the binary regression model is established by using logistic or probit method, which cannot reflect the relatively complex relationship and influence path.

(3) The model lacks the necessary theoretical support, the construction process is not rigorous enough, and the model design process is not easy to popularize and popularize.

Therefore, this paper fully draws on the previous research ideas and methods, according to the design specifications, using descriptive statistics and factor analysis to extract the influencing factors of training willingness. Then on the basis of several classic theoretical models, it constructs a training willingness structure model and carries out empirical analysis, in order to select the cultivation object of new-type professional farmers and improve the training effect, provide reference evidence for better optimizing the farmer training system.

3 Introduction to Relevant Models

3.1 Reliability Test Model

The reliability test model is used to calculate the Cronbach coefficient in the questionnaire survey. The calculation formula is showed as follows:

$$\alpha = \left(\frac{n}{n-1}\right)\left(1 - \frac{\sum s_i^2}{s_t^2}\right) \tag{1}$$

Where α is the reliability coefficient, n is the number of questionnaire questions, s_i^2 is the variance of each test score, and s_t^2 is the variance of the total score of all the test subjects. In exploratory studies, a reliability between 0.70 and 0.98 is considered high reliability, while a reliability lower than 0.35 is considered low reliability and must be rejected. The basic calculation process is showed as follows:

① According to certain requirements, n subjects were selected from the questionnaire. Firstly, the variance S_t^2 of the total scores of these subjects was calculated.

② These people will have a score on each question. Find the variance of these people's scores on each question respectively. s_i^2 (i = 1, 2, ..., n), and find the value of $\sum s_i^2$.

③ The α value is calculated according to the Cronbach coefficient formula.

3.2 Characteristics of Structural Equation Model

Structural equation model is an applied statistical method used to study multiple indexes and variables. It is composed of two parts: the measurement model reflecting the observed variables and latent variables, and the structural model reflecting the relationship between latent variables, respectively corresponding to the measurement Eq. (2) and the structural Eq. (3):

$$y = \Lambda y \eta + \varepsilon$$
$$x = \Lambda x \xi + \delta \tag{2}$$

$$\eta = B\eta + \Gamma\xi + \zeta \tag{3}$$

Where y is a $p \times 1$ vector composed of p endogenous indicators is an $m \times 1$ vector composed of m endogenous latent variables (factors). Λ_y is a $p \times m$ factor load matrix of y at η, and ε is a $p \times 1$ vector composed of p measurement errors. x is a $q \times 1$ vector composed of q exogenous indicators. ξ is composed of n exogenous latent variables (factors) of $n \times 1$ vector. Λ_x is a $q \times n$ factor load matrix of x at Λ, and δ is a $q \times 1$ vector composed of q measurement errors. B is the $m \times m$ coefficient matrix, which describes the mutual influence of the endogenous latent variable η. Γ is the $m \times n$ coefficient matrix, which describes the influence of the exogenous latent variable ξ on the endogenous latent variable η, and ζ is the $m \times 1$ residual vector.

Structural equation model introduces variables that can be directly observed to measure latent variables that cannot be directly measured. It does not need to set the assumption of strict restrictions, while allowing the independent variable and dependent variable measuring error, by simulating observation and computing the correlation coefficient to determine the index of the path, reflect the effect of direct and indirect process between indicators, the relationship between multiple indicators can be clearly seen, In this way, the previous research can avoid using logistic or prohibit to establish binary regression model, but the observation and measurement of potential variables always have a large error, which affects the reliability of data [13].

4 Research Design

4.1 Collection and Pre-processing of Survey Data

In October 2018, we began to conduct research on training institutions, cities, counties and townships in Hainan Province. The research subjects were selected from the rural backbone labor force aged 20–50 years old, using face-to-face questionnaire survey and online questionnaire survey (including two rounds of online questionnaire survey). By October 2019, a total of 430 questionnaires had been collected, including 187 face-to-face questionnaires and 243 online questionnaires. After eight invalid samples were excluded, and the effective rate of the questionnaire reached 98.1%. The proportion of males in the sample was 76.5%. The percentage of females was 24.5%. Those with high school education or above accounted for 52.4%. About 61.2% were involved in local cooperatives or similar organizations. This basically reflects the basic situation of rural backbone labor force in Hainan, with a certain representativeness. In the process of data acquisition, various security mechanisms were used to protect the data from being leaked. At the same time, tools such as Kettle were used to process the original data such as de-duplication, missing values and outliers. In order to obtain the data in the format required by SPSS, the data from two different data sources were merged and transformed.

4.2   Variable Selection and Definition

Using exploratory factor analysis, dimension reduction analysis is carried out on the 9 preset endogenous and exogenous observation variables, and the measurement potential variables are obtained. SPSS software is used to analyze the items. The consistency test results are showed as follows: (1) the kmo value is 0.709, and the chi-square value of Bartlett's sphericity test is 148.802, which indicates that the factors influencing the training willingness are suitable for factor analysis; (2) the contribution rate of cumulative variance is 86.014%, indicating that the explanation of the original variable information is strong enough. The factor load matrix is shown in Table 1 by using the principal component analysis method after six times' maximum orthogonal rotation convergence.

As can be seen from Table 1, the load factor of common factor one is relatively large, which is named "personal characteristics". The loading coefficient of one index of land area to the common factor two is large, which is named "family characteristics". The factor loading coefficient on the three common factors of active registration and publicity is large, which is defined as "training willingness". Improving family life and neighborhood relationship had a larger factor loading coefficient on common factor 4, which was defined as "endeavor expectation". The family encourages and the government encourages the large factor loading coefficient of the common factor five, which is defined as" subjective norm". Among them, personal characteristics, family characteristics, endeavor expectation and subjective norms constitute four premise latent variables in the model of farmers' training willingness, while training willingness is the result latent variable, and the premise latent variable comprehensively affects and determines the result latent variable.

Table 1. Composition matrix after rotation[a].

	Component				
	1	2	3	4	5
Subjective norms of training (from family encouragement) (5)	.899	.255	.097	.036	.098
Subjective norms of training (from government encouragement) (5)	.866	.110	−.154	.248	.079
Training expectations (improving family life) (4)	.107	.905	.005	.103	.094
Training expectations (improving neighborhood relations) (4)	.260	.832	.079	.186	.072
Proficiency of livelihood skills (1)	−.014	.005	.930	.210	.095
Annual income (1)	−.055	.133	.664	.159	.564
Cooperation and publicity of training willingness (3)	.093	.138	.190	.871	.306
Active registration of training willingness (3)	.377	.296	.274	.687	−.217
Family land area of family characteristics (2)	.155	.101	.152	.081	.901

Extraction method: principal component analysis
Rotation method: Caesar normalization maximum variance method[a]
a. The rotation converges after 6 iterations

4.3   Reliability Test

Reliability is the degree of consistency or stability of test data. If the general questionnaire design is good, the reliability value should be higher. In this study, the internal consistency coefficient (Cronbach coefficient) is used to test (as shown in Table 2 and Table 3). The results show that the internal consistency coefficient is 0.791 (greater than 0.7 of the benchmark), indicating that the overall reliability of the questionnaire is good. The internal consistency coefficients of the deleted items in the questionnaire are all above 0.7, which are smaller than the total internal consistency coefficients. In addition, except for the item "proficiency of livelihood skills", the CITC values of other items (the correlation between the revised items and the total) are greater than 0.4, indicating that the reliability of the data is high, and the structural equation modeling could be relied on the data.

Table 2. Reliability statistics.

Cronbach Alpha	Cronbach based on standardization term Alpha	Number of items
.791	.794	9

Table 3. Total statistics.

Item	Scale average after deleting items	Scale variance after deleting items	Revised item and total correlation	Square multiple correlation	Clone Bach alpha after deleting item
Land area of the family (2)	28.11	26.488	.415	.335	.780
Improvement of family life (4)	27.28	26.335	.471	.429	.771
Encouragement of the government (5)	26.81	26.593	.417	.563	.779
Encouragement of the family (5)	27.17	26.188	.533	.582	.763
Improvement of neighborhood relations (4)	27.06	24.539	.567	.509	.757
Enthusiasm for registration (3)	26.60	26.463	.556	.505	.762
Enthusiasm (cooperate with publicity) (3)	26.60	25.377	.589	.476	.755
Proficiency in life skills (1)	26.98	28.760	.364	.476	.784
Annual household income (1)	27.66	25.577	.427	.533	.780

4.4   Structural Equation Model Test

4.4.1   Theoretical Basis and Research Hypothesis

Based on the theory of human capital and motivation, this paper combines qualitative analysis with quantitative analysis, Based on the technology acceptance model (TAM) and task technology adaptation model (TTF), according to the extracted four latent variables, including personal characteristics, family characteristics, training expectations and subjective norms, the "motivation Willingness" path model of farmers' participation in new vocational farmers' training is proposed. Based on the above theoretical model, combined with the actual situation and previous research results, the following assumptions are determined:

H1: Farmers' personal characteristics will have a significant impact on their willingness to participate in the training of new professional farmers.

H2: Farmers' family characteristics will have a significant impact on Farmers' willingness to participate in the training of new professional farmers.

H3: Farmers' training expectations will have a significant positive impact on Farmers' willingness to participate in the training of new professional farmers.

H4: subjective norms will have a significant positive impact on Farmers' willingness to participate in the training of new professional farmers.

4.4.2   Model Construction Fitting and Modification

Through the steps of variable making, data processing, calculation and estimation, the "model fitting degree summary" report can be obtained [16]. Through the output report, we can analyze the indicators related to the fitting degree, and judge whether the model is suitable for the data, so as to further modify the model. Generally speaking, the higher the model fitting degree, the stronger the model availability [17]. We find that the structural equation model based on the pre-set model framework has poor fitting degree, so we use the modified index to modify the model. In view of the phenomenon that the chi-square value calculated by the model is too large and the significant level value is lower than 0.05, the association between the latent variables is increased by releasing restrictions. The error of family characteristics is negative, which violates the estimation analysis rule, so it is removed from the model to simplify the model. Finally, an acceptable structural equation model is obtained, as shown in Fig. 1.

The path coefficient of each latent variable in the model is shown in Table 4. It can be found that each path coefficient is greater than the significance level of 0.05, indicating that personal characteristics, subjective norm, and endeavor expectation all have a significant impact on the willingness of training.

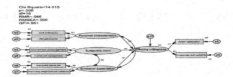

Fig. 1. Structure Model of training willingness of new type professional farmers

Table 4. Standardized regression weight: (Group number 1-default model).

Path	Estimate
Training willingness ← Personal characteristics	0.20
Training willingness ← Subjective norm	0.35
Training willingness ← Endeavor expectation	0.37

4.4.3   Model Adaptability Test and Interpretation

Through the operation and modification of the model, the final standard model fitting index and the actual comparison are shown in Table 5. It is found that except the RMR value is slightly higher than the standard value, the other items meet the requirements, indicating that the modified model has good fitting degree. In addition, the results of path hypothesis test show that hypothesis H1, H3 and H4 are tested, and they are significant at the level of 0.001. The H2 hypothesis is adjusted to the model because the standard coefficient is a small negative value, which shows that family characteristics have little influence on willingness.

Table 5. Standard and actual structural equation fit index.

Judgment index		Fitness standard	Actual test results
Absolute fit index	DF	<3.00	0.875
	P	>0.05	0.598
	GFI	>0.90	0.951
	RMR	<0.05	0.086
	RMSEA	<0.1	0.000

DF: the ratio of chi square value to degree of freedom, the closer to 0, the better the fit between model and data; P: significance, greater than 0.05, the quasi suitability of model and data can be identified; GFI: goodness of fit index, between 0–1, the closer to 1, the model is better; RMR: generally less than 0.05 is better; RMSEA: the square root of average square error, less than 0.05, the model fitting degree is good.

5   Conclusion

In this paper, online and offline methods are used to obtain the personal data of the new professional farmers. During the investigation and analysis, the corresponding protection measures are taken for the secret information related to the individuals, and the structural equation model of the influencing factors of the training willingness of the new professional farmers is established. The model fits well and the influencing factors of farmers' training willingness are showed as follows: endeavor expectation > subjective standard > personal characteristics. There is a high correlation between endeavor expectation and subjective norms, indicating that individuals' desire to work hard is encouraged by government and family. Second, there is a correlation between personal characteristics and effort expectations. People with higher incomes are more likely to look forward to improving their living conditions. In addition, the most prominent willingness of farmers to participate in training is "active registration". This paper takes the rural backbone labor force in some areas of Hainan Province as the research object. Due to the diversity of survey methods and the limitation of sample size, the results may have some limitations. Therefore, each place should make the choice according to the local actual situation.

By means of factor analysis and path analysis, this paper has completed the practical process of integrating several regression equations between latent variables into a simultaneous equation. It also provides a reference for the in-depth analysis by introducing latent variables to materialize the variables that cannot be observed in the study of social and economic life, which cannot be measured with specific indicators, such as willingness, social atmosphere, loyalty, etc.

Acknowledgments. This work was supported by the Hainan Provincial Natural Science Foundation (618ms025); the major scientific project of Hainan Province (ZDKJ2020012).

References

1. Zhai, L., Xia, X., Sun, Y.: Analysis of farmers' willingness to participate in the training of new vocational farmers and its influencing factors – a survey of four cities in Guanzhong, Shaanxi Province. Vocat. Tech. Educ. **835**(21), 55–59 (2016)
2. Fu, X., Chen, G., Zhuang, T., Zhi, Y.E.: Analysis on the influencing factors of satisfaction with the cultivation and support policies for new professional farmers – based on the survey of 304 farmers participating in the training in Chengdu. Jiangsu Agric. Sci. **44**(08), 540–544 (2016)
3. Wu, Y.: Influencing factors and countermeasures of agricultural production willingness of new professional farmers based on binary logistic model. Contemp. Econ. Manage. **261**(11), 40–49 (2016)
4. Hu, W., Liu, S.: Analysis of the willingness of new professional farmers to receive distance training based on logistic model. Adult Educ. **363**(04), 55–59 (2017)
5. Wang, L.: Analysis on influencing factors of training willingness of new vocational farmers – Zhejiang. Agric. Sci. **058**(011): 2055–2057, 262 (2017)
6. Ma, Y., Li, H.: Analysis of farmers' willingness response to the training of new vocational farmers and its influencing factors – taking the survey data of 265 households in Yinbei area of Ningxia as an example. Northwest Popul. **039**(004), 99–104,111 (2018)
7. Ma, Y., Sun, C., Ma, W.: Study on the influencing factors of agricultural informatization training willingness of new professional farmers. Heilongjiang Agric. Sci. **03**, 91–97 (2020)
8. Xu, Q., Xiao, M.: A study on the influencing factors of the willingness of new vocational farmers to train their skills: a case study of Qingdao. J. Qingdao Univ. Sci. Technol. (Soc. Sci. Edn.) **36**(01), 1–7 (2020)
9. Xu, J., Jiang, N., Qin, W.: An empirical study on the demand willingness and performance of farmers' agricultural science and technology training service: a case study of Jiangsu Province. Agric. Econ. Issues **35**(012), 66–72 (2011)
10. Xu Hui, X., Yang, L.H., et al.: A study on the influencing factors and precision cultivation of new professional farmers – based on the survey data of 63 townships (towns) in 21 counties (cities, districts) in 7 provinces. J. Jiangxi Univ. Finan. Econ. **117**(03), 88–96 (2018)
11. Chen, L., Chen, J.: Econometric analysis of the influencing factors of the cultivation of new professional farmers – based on the survey of farmers in the fixed observation point in the rural areas of Guangzhou. J. Agric. Econ. **012**, 39–41 (2019)
12. Wu, Z.: Study on the improvement mechanism of vocational education and training willingness of new professional farmers. Adult Educ. **9**, 58–63 (2020)
13. Zhang, W., Hao, Y., Zhang, G.: Research on Influencing Factors of rural backbone labor force training willingness – empirical test based on structural equation model. Agric. Econ. **04**, 66–68 (2013)
14. Li, Q.: Research on the willingness and behavior of farmers to participate in the training of new professional farmers – based on the mode of "one village, one product, one subject". Hubei Agric. Mech. **04**: 46–49 (2018)
15. Ding, Y., Xu, F.: A study on the willingness to use science and technology information services of new professional farmers in Western China. Libr. Sci. Res. **10**, 58–67 (2019)
16. Rong, T.: Amos and Research Methods. Chongqing University Press, Chongqing (2010)
17. Huang, J.: Research on the Relationship Between Key Livelihood Factors of Landless Farmers and the Construction of Structural Equation Model. Economic Science Press, Beijing (2017)

Automatic Coloring Method for Ethnic Costume Sketch Based on Pix2Pix Network

Huifeng Wang[1,2], Juxiang Zhou[1,2(✉)], Jianhou Gan[1,2], and Wei Zou[1,2]

[1] Key Laboratory of Education Informatization for Nationalities,
Ministry of Education, Yunnan Normal University, Kunming 650500, China
[2] Yunnan Key Laboratory of Smart Education,
Yunnan Normal University, Kunming 650500, China

Abstract. Ethnic minority costume culture is an indispensable part of ethnic minority culture and an important content of ethnic minority culture protection and inheritance. It plays a very important role in Chinese traditional culture. The coloring of minority costume sketches has many practical application environments. It is a research topic with scientific significance and application prospects. On the basis of coloring the sketches of ethnic minority costumes on the GAN network, this paper proposes a coloring model of ethnic clothing sketches based on the Pix2Pix network, which can automatically colorize ethnic clothing sketches. The network is implemented based on the CGAN network. Among them, the ResNet is used as the network Generator. In order to achieve the constraints on the target image generation process and further ensure the coloring effect of the generated image, we use the ethnic minority costume sketch as a "label" input in the Generator, and the L1 loss is used as the loss function. The network is trained on the data set constructed in this paper. In order to verify the effectiveness of the network, we compared it with a variety of coloring methods. The results show that the peak signal-to-noise ratio reaches 24.061 and the structural similarity reaches 0.820, which further verifies that the coloring method proposed in this paper has good coloring performance.

Keywords: Sketch coloring · Pix2Pix · ResNet

1 Introduction

With the continuous development of artificial intelligence, more and more sketches of ethnic minority clothing are collected and organized. Sketches are a visual expression that is composed of a few lines and can be executed quickly. The sketches of ethnic costumes are rendered stably and efficiently, combining the style of ethnic minority costumes with modern people's aesthetics to innovate, and apply them to the design of ethnic minority costumes. This modern costume with national characteristics will contain the beautiful meaning of ethnic

© Springer Nature Singapore Pte Ltd. 2021
Y. Tan et al. (Eds.): DMBD 2021, CCIS 1453, pp. 367–381, 2021.
https://doi.org/10.1007/978-981-16-7476-1_33

minority elements, but also in line with the aesthetics of most people, providing a new direction for the inheritance and development of ethnic minority costume culture [4].

Most of the traditional coloring methods require manual interaction and professional equipment processing, which is very difficult. Moreover, manual correction is also required if the coloring effect is not good. The early image colorization tasks mainly focus on grayscale images, and great progress has been made in the study of grayscale image colorization so far [10]. However, in the aspect of clothing, most of the current research focuses on the coloring of gray images and clothing sketches. For example, Liu Bo [6] uses generative adversarial networks to realize the coloring of ethnic clothing accessories, jackets, and trouser legs, but there are not many studies on the coloring of the overall ethnic clothing sketches.

The emergence of artificial intelligence provides a new idea for the coloration of ethnic minority clothing. If the "virtual labor force" of artificial intelligence can be fully utilized, a deep learning framework will be integrated to construct a deep learning-based ethnic costume based on the colors and styles of ethnic minority costumes. The sketch coloring model realizes the rapid and reasonable coloring of ethnic clothing sketches, provides technical support for the research on the integration of ethnic clothing color elements in clothing design, and can be applied and promoted in the field of clothing auxiliary design. In this way, in the process of making ethnic minority costumes, people can select their favorite colors for processing and production according to the generated color images of ethnic minority costumes, thereby increasing the diversity of ethnic minority costumes and providing a new theoretical basis for better inheritance of ethnic minority costumes.

The contribution of this paper has the following three aspects. 1. Proposed an automatic coloring method of ethnic costume sketches based on Pix2Pix network, which realized the conversion of ethnic costume sketches to real images. 2. On the basis of Pix2Pix network, the generator structure is replaced with Resnet to further improve the coloring effect of the model. 3. The network input is modified to a high-definition rectangular image of 512×1024 to improve the resolution and make the clothing image generated after coloring of the sketch more in line with modern aesthetics.

1 Proposed an automatic coloring method of ethnic costume sketches based on Pix2Pix network, which realized the conversion of ethnic costume sketches to real images.
2 On the basis of Pix2Pix network, the generator structure is replaced with ResNet to further improve the coloring effect of the model.
3 The network input is modified to a high-definition rectangular image of 512×1024 to improve the resolution and make the clothing image generated after coloring of the sketch more in line with modern aesthetics.

2   Methods

Currently, the generative adversarial networks (GAN) have achieved good results for image coloring. In the case of not many data sets, GAN networks can often get a good result. Recently, researchers have performed image coloring tasks on maps, cartoons and architectural images, but there are still few research achievements on the coloring of clothing sketches. In order to better build the coloring model of minority costume sketches, this paper starts with the construction of the data set, then uses the GAN with better effect in the image staining task to carry out the experiment. Finally, based on GAN analysis and improvement, a better coloring effect of the ethnic minority sketch coloring model is constructed.

2.1   GAN

GAN based on unsupervised learning methods was first proposed by Ian Good-fellow in 2014 [3]. The traditional generative model, which lacks the penalty for generating images, will have a variety of other image generation when generating the target image, and the effect is not satisfactory. However, GAN is very different from the traditional generative network. In the training, the generators and judges are repeatedly trained by using the confrontation method, and finally the data close to the real samples are generated in the game. The network structure is shown in Fig. 1.

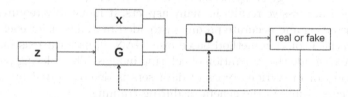

Fig. 1. The GAN network structure. xxx

The specific technical process of generative admittedly network structure is as follows: firstly, random noise z is input into the generator G, and the false sample G(z) is generated through the training of generator, and G(z) should be very similar to the real image. Then, the G(z) generated by the generator and the real image x are input into the discriminant D at the same time. At this time, the discriminant shall accurately discriminate the input G(z) and x and predict the results. Finally, the result of the discrimination is true or false feedback is given to the generator, and the coloring effect of the GAN model is shown in Fig. 2.

Since GAN [6] generates images through the antagonization between generator and discriminator in the training process, there is no limitation of other conditions in the network input except random noise, so there is a phenomenon of more confusing color and a large gap with the real image when performing the ethnic minority sketch coloring task.

Fig. 2. The GAN model coloring effect. (Color figure online)

2.2   CGAN

In order to solve the above problem of the automatic coloring of minority costume sketches that cannot be output deterministically in accordance with the required colors, someone proposed a method of image classification according to the color conditions given by users. Although the method to classify the image has achieved impressive results in many aspects, it inevitably requires accurate color information and accurate prompts provided by the user for each step. The semi-supervised coloring method based on CGAN [9] uses the existing image as a reference to guide the generation of coloring images. The coloring performance of the generator on various types of data sets is demonstrated by supervising the input constraints in the generator during training.

According to the ethnic costumes sketch data set constructed in this paper, paired ethnic clothing data have been obtained. On this basis, the semi-supervised network CGAN is used to color the ethnic costume sketches. The training process of CGAN is basically not very different from the original GAN. The difference is just because the data output by the model is better constrained by the input label y, which requires a longer training iteration so that the model can better learn the correspondence between the label y and the generated number. The label y is spliced to the feature map generated by each layer of the generator and the discriminator. The coloring effect of the CGAN network model is shown in Fig. 3.

According to the coloring effect of the sketch, it can be clearly seen that the color distribution of the real image of ethnic minority clothing can be roughly rendered, and the color distribution of the colored image and the real image is also relatively close. However, for the more complex image rendered color will still appear variegation and detail part distortion phenomenon, and the rendered color is vaguer.

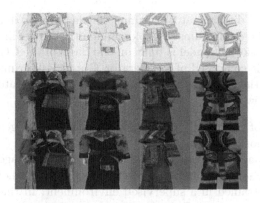

Fig. 3. The CGAN model coloring effect. (Color figure online)

2.3 Construction of Coloring Model of Ethnic Minority Clothing Based on Pix2Pix

Since a condition y is added to both the generator and the discriminator in the CGAN model, the additional information we can use for the coloring task of ethnic minority clothing sketch is the real color image corresponding to ethnic minority clothing sketch. A recently proposed GAN model is a classical paper that applies GAN to supervised images to image translation. The proposed GAN model is abbreviated as Pix2Pix [5], and the Pix2Pix network structure is shown in Fig. 4.

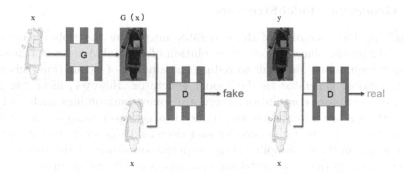

Fig. 4. The Pix2Pix network structure. (Color figure online)

The entire Pix2Pix2 model structure is also divided into two parts: generator and discriminator, but certain adjustments have been made in the generator part. In the generator, the ethnic minority clothing sketch x will be input as the 'label', and the discriminator will use the PatchGAN with better effect. In the training process, the sketch of ethnic minority clothing input into the generator will also have certain constraints on the generation of the target image.

The generator and discriminator continue to play games during training, and finally generate the ethnic minority color image that looks like the real one.

The Pix2Pix coloring model is built on the basis of the CGAN network. The overall structure is composed of a generator G and a discriminator D, which is used to complete the conversion between images. The generator and discriminator are set as follows:

(1) In the input of the model, the control condition of the generator is changed to ethnic minority clothing sketch.
(2) The discriminant function is to distinguish the real image from the colored image and return the predicted results, so that the whole coloring framework can be trained in a supervised environment. In the Pix2Pix network structure, the generator G does not consider the existence of noise, even if the input noise is ignored. Pix2pix fits the pixel probability distribution of the target image in the training set, and ethnic minority costume sketch is used as a 'constraint condition' in the training process.

In Pix2Pix, the control condition of the input discriminator also changed from 'classification label' to the ethnic minority costume sketch. As a 'condition', the sketch should be stitched together with the real image or the target image generated by the generator and sent to the discriminator. This also explains why the input of the generator should be interpreted as a 'condition' more comprehensively. In this way, after the above changes made to Pix2pix, the whole model changed from the process of "input noise and output image" to the process of 'input sketch and output target image'.

2.4   Generator Model Structure

In Pix2Pix, the resolution of the generator output by the global generator is 1024×512 pixels. Since the output resolution of the global generator meets the data size requirement, in order to reduce the amount of calculation, this article uses the global generator as the model generator. However, after the global generator undergoes convolution, there are some shortcomings such as loss of part of the feature information and reduced target positioning accuracy. Based on this, this paper uses the encoder and decoder to generate feature maps of the same size in the up-sampling stage, superimposes them at the corresponding positions, and performs convolution operations to effectively fuse the shallow and deep features of the image to generate. The network structure of the device is shown in Fig. 5.

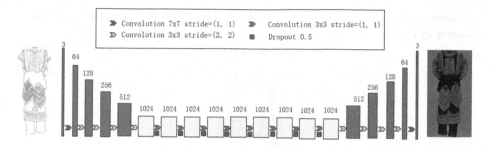

Fig. 5. The coloring model structure. (Color figure online)

The generator consists of a series of down samples (Downsample), a set of residual blocks (Residual Block) and a series of up samples (Concatenate-Upsample). The specific data flow of the model is as follows: (1) First, input the label map into the convolutional layer with a size of 7×7, a number of convolution kernels of 64, and a step size of 1, and the results are input into the BN layer for normalization processing. (2) The output data of the BN layer is then down-sampled 4 times, in which a convolutional layer with a convolution kernel size of 3×3 and a step size of 2 is set, and after each downsampling operation, the convolutional layer channel. The number is doubled, and the image features are input to the BN layer for normalization. (3) The 9 small yellow squares in Fig. 5 represent the residual block. After downsampling, the tensor is input into the residual block for residual calculation. The convolution operation includes the use of 3×3, A convolution layer with 1024 convolution kernels and a step size of 2 performs operations, and inputs the result to the BN layer for normalization. (4) Next upsampling is performed 4 times, mainly for deconvolution operation, and the number of channels of the convolutional layer will be reduced by half after each upsampling. The size of the deconvolution layer is 3×3, and the step size is 2. The results of deconvolution are input to the BN layer for normalization [1].

In addition, before each feature is input to the upsampling process, it will jump up with the corresponding feature in the downsampling process, thereby doubling the number of channels, so the stitched feature tensor must be input to the convolution kernel with a size of 3 × 3. In the convolutional layer with a step size of 1, the number of feature channels is restored to the number before the jumper. Finally, the image is generated by the output of a convolution layer with a convolution kernel number of 3, a size of 7 × 7, and a step size of 1.

The Pix2Pix method compares the Encoder-Decoder structure with U-Net, which was earlier selected as a generator by Pix2Pix because it uses a multi-scale fusion for cross-layer connection and achieves good results. Because ResNet can well solve the problem of neural network gradient disappearance, when it appears, most GAN adopts the "residual block" as the ResNet version of the component generator, so the method in this paper also adopts RESNET as the generator. ResNet is composed of multiple ResnetBlocks, and the structure is shown in Fig. 6.

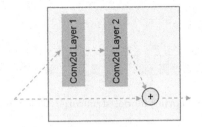

Fig. 6. The ResnetBlock.

A total of 9 ResnetBlocks are included in the generator. Each residual block is composed of two convolution layers. The convolution layer uses the convolution kernel size of 3×3 and stride of 1. The information before the convolution operation is added to the feature information extracted by the other side after the two-layer convolution operation as the output of the residual block. In order to ensure that the input attributes of the previous layer can also be used in the subsequent layer, the output information of the network will not be less and less than the gradient disappearance problem.

2.5   Discriminator Model Structure

The discriminator model adopts the PatchGAN structure, and the data processing process of the PatchGAN structure is as follows: (1) Divide the data into multiple patches of size N×N, and judge whether it is true or false. (2) Take the average of all patch results in each data, and output this value as the final result, so that a faster scale can be achieved to punish the network model. The PatchGAN structure consists of 5 convolutional layers. The first 4 convolutional layers complete the extraction of features, and the last layer is a convolution calculation, which is used to match the one-dimensional output to realize the judgment of the true and false of the image. A single feature value represents the true and false degree of a certain part in the target image or generated image. In addition, PatchGAN has fewer parameters and runs faster than discriminating the entire image. The discriminator structure is shown in Fig. 7.

2.6   Objective Function

CGAN can be supervised to generate images in the training process, and the principle is also very simple. GAN is to fit the probability distribution of the data, while CGAN is to fit the probability distribution under the conditions. The training optimization objective function of the original GAN network is as follows (1):

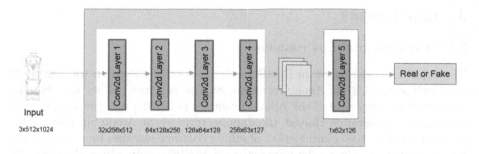

Fig. 7. The Discriminator model structure.

$$\min_{G} \max_{D} \; V(D,G) = E_{\mathrm{x} \sim p_{\mathrm{data}}} \times [\log D(\mathrm{x})]$$
$$+ E_{\mathrm{z} \sim p_{\mathrm{z}}\mathrm{z}}[\log(1 - D(\mathrm{G}(\mathrm{Z})))] \tag{1}$$

Among them, $\max_D V(D,G)$ is that when the generator parameters are fixed, the parameters of the discriminator are optimized through the cross-entropy loss function to maximize the value of the discriminator, so that the performance of the discriminator will be optimal. $\min_G \max_D V(D,G)$ means that on the basis of the optimal performance of the above discriminator, the parameters of the discriminator are fixed, and the generator is optimized through the cross-entropy loss function, and the value of the generator is minimized, so that the performance of the generator will also reach the optimal. The loss function of the CGAN network is shown in formula (2):

$$L_{\mathrm{cGAN}}(G,D) = E_{x,y}[\log D(\mathrm{x},\mathrm{y})]$$
$$+ E_{\mathrm{x},z}[\log(1 - D(\mathrm{x}),\mathrm{G}(\mathrm{x},\mathrm{z}))] \tag{2}$$

In addition to using the loss function of CGAN in our network structure, we also calculate the loss between the generated image and the real image, assuming (x, y) is a real image pair. It is assumed that y is a real picture, and x is a contour image. Then the L1 loss function formula between the generated image and the real image is shown in (3):

$$L_{\mathrm{L1}}(G) = E_{x,y,z}[\|y - G(x,z)\|_1] \tag{3}$$

The calculation method of L1 loss is to calculate the absolute value of the difference between the real B group (target style) picture and the fake B group picture generated by the generator pixel by pixel and then average. In the formula, x refers to group A (original style) pictures, y refers to group B (target style) pictures, and z refers to Gaussian distributed noise in the input generator.

The total loss of the Pix2Pix network is the sum of the loss function of the CGAN network and the L1 loss, as in formula (4):

$$L_{pix2pix} = \arg \min_{G} \max_{D} L_{\mathrm{cGAN}}(G,D) + \lambda L_{\mathrm{L1}}(G) \tag{4}$$

3   Experiments

3.1   Experimental Environment

The coloring model based on Pix2Pix is trained on the Pytorch framework [2], and optimized with the Adam optimizer [8], the parameter is set to 2 batches, the initial learning rate of the Adam optimizer is 0.0002, and the learning rate is 50 times per iteration Halved, the impulse term of the Adam optimizer is 0.5. In order to make the coloring effect of ethnic costume sketches more in line with human aesthetics, the model parameters of Pix2Pix were adjusted so that the input and output of the model were both 512*1024. The specific experimental environment settings are shown in Table 1.

Table 1. Experimental environment.

Operating system	Ubuntu16.04
Programming language	Python3.5
Deep learning framework	Pytorch1.5
Other related libraries	Cudnn, CUDA10.2, numpy1.16.3
CPU	Intel Xeon Gold 5118
GPU	NVIDIA GeForce RTX 2080 Ti

3.2   Data Set

The ethnic minority clothing sketch data constructed in this paper comes from two aspects: one is the 1,935 ethnic minority clothing sketches obtained by using the clothing sketch automatically generated model constructed by this laboratory, and then some unclear outlines and missing details are removed on this basis. Many sketches, and finally 1,650 high-resolution sketch images of ethnic minority costumes. The second is for the collected ethnic costume images, after artificial outline, 130 ethnic costume sketch images were obtained. After sorting and summarizing this article, a total of 1780 sketch images of ethnic minority costumes have been obtained, of which some color images of ethnic minority costumes and some sketch images of ethnic minority costumes are shown in Fig. 8(a) and Fig. 8(b), respectively. In the end, this paper divides the obtained ethnic clothing sketch images into two subsets of training set and test set according to the ratio of 4:1, including 1,424 in the training set and 356 in the test set.

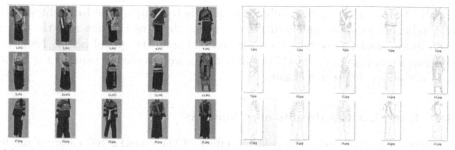

(a) The color images of ethnic costumes.   (b) The sketches of ethnic costumes.

Fig. 8. The color images and sketches of ethnic costumes. (Color figure online)

3.3 Evaluation Index

In order to better evaluate the correlation between the target image and the real image, and intuitively reflect the coloring effect of the sketch, the quantitative evaluation criteria in this paper are PSNR (peak signal-to-noise ratio) and SSIM (structure similarity) two indicators [11]. PSNR is the most common objective evaluation index based on error-sensitive images. It does not take into account the visual characteristics of the human eye, that is, the human eye is more sensitive to contrast differences with lower spatial frequencies, and the human eye is more sensitive to differences in brightness contrast. Sensitivity is higher than chromaticity [7], and the surrounding neighboring areas will affect the results from the human eye's perception of an area. Therefore, there will often be differences between human subjective feelings and the evaluation results obtained. The PSNR image quality evaluation index measures whether the signal is distorted, and its unit is dB. The larger the value, the smaller the distortion, and the better the sketch coloring effect. To calculate PSNR, you need to calculate the MSE (the mean square error between the target image and the real image). Set a size as the real image I and the target image K, then the mean square error (MSE) can be defined as formula (5):

$$MSE = \frac{1}{mn} \sum_{i=0}^{m-1} \sum_{j=0}^{n-1} [I(i,j) - K(i,j)]^2 \tag{5}$$

After the mean square error is calculated, we can calculate the PSNR according to the value of MSE, as shown in formula (6):

$$PSNR = 10 \cdot \log_{10} \left(\frac{MAX_I^2}{MSE} \right) \tag{6}$$

Among them, is the maximum possible pixel value of the image. If each pixel is represented by 8-bit binary, then is 255. Usually, if the pixel value is represented by B-bit binary, then $MAX_I = 2^B - 1$

The SSIM image quality evaluation index is to compare the three dimensions of brightness, contrast and structure between the target image and the generated image, and finally take their average value as the global SSIM. From the comparison of PSNR and SSIM two indicators, we can see the value of the sketch coloring under different methods.

3.4   Experimental Results and Analysis

In order to further verify the coloring effect of the constructed coloring model, this paper uses GAN, CGAN, CycleGAN and Pix2Pix network models for training, and then compares the coloring effect. The coloring effect of each coloring model is shown in Fig. 9. The first row on the left in the figure is the sketch of ethnic minority clothing, followed by the GAN method staining effect and the CGAN method staining effect. The first row on the right side is the CycleGAN staining effect, followed by the Pix2Pix method staining effect and the real image of ethnic minority clothing.

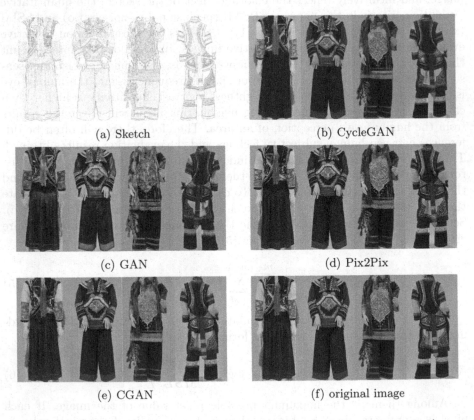

Fig. 9. The coloring effects under different methods. (Color figure online)

Through the coloring effect of GAN, CGAN network, CycleGAN network and Pix2Pix network, it can be seen that GAN has no limitation of other conditions due to the fact that the generator and discriminator compete with each other to generate images during the training process, so in the test process, because the overall contour of ethnic clothing has not appeared in the training, the color of the generated image is more confusing. The color rendered by CGAN is mostly blurred, and the distortion is more serious. For the CycleGAN network coloring effect is clearer, but some rendered colors are very abrupt, and the coloring phenomenon appears unreasonable. As for the coloring effect of Pix2Pix network model is close to the original image, the target image after coloring is very clear, and it is close to the original image.

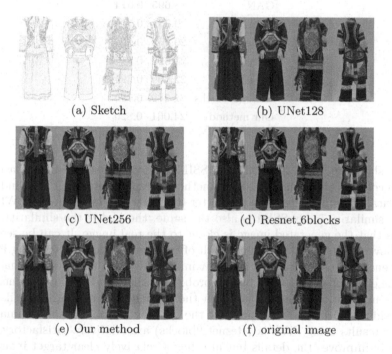

(a) Sketch   (b) UNet128

(c) UNet256   (d) Resnet_6blocks

(e) Our method   (f) original image

Fig. 10. The coloring effects under different generator structures in the Pix2Pix model. (Color figure online)

In order to better verify the coloring effect of the network constructed in this paper, the generator is replaced with Unet128, Unet256 and Resnet_6blocks for experimental comparison. The experimental results are shown in Fig. 10. The first line in Fig. 10 represents the sketch of ethnic minority clothing, followed by the generator using Unet128, the generator using Unet256, and the generator using Resnet_6blocks. This paper methods and the last line of real images.

From the above experimental results, it can be seen that the effect of sketch coloring can be achieved by selecting different generators on the basis of the coloring network model constructed in this paper, and because the input of the network is a high-resolution reference image, there are few cases of blurring in the generated image. Among the several generator structures, the method and the choice of using Unet128 generator sketch coloring sharpness is the highest, but although the Unet128 coloring model ensures the sharpness of the generated image, the rendered color is sometimes not reasonable, so in comparison, the generated image in this paper is closer to the real image.

Table 2. The sketch shading effect under different methods.

Method	PSNR	SSIM
GAN	18.695	0.614
CGAN	20.731	0.719
CycleGAN	20.408	0.698
Unet_128	23.800	0.817
Unet_256	22.609	0.791
Resnet_6blocks	21.289	0.795
Our method	24.061	0.820

As shown in Table 2, PSNR and SSIM indexes are selected to measure the sketch coloring effect under different methods, respectively. For PSNR index, the numerical value indicates that the better the generated image quality. While the image similarity index SSIM is also the same, the higher the similarity, which proves that the generated image is closer to the real image. It can be seen from the above results that the output result of the image generated by using Pix2Pix (the generator uses Unet128) is approximately close to the original image, and has the effect of clear details, but its problem is that it adds a lot of unnecessary details in addition, which is far from the original real image in details. Since the residual block can better preserve the detailed information of the image, the output results using Pix2Pix (Resnet_9blocks) are relatively satisfactory, which not only improves the details but also has a relatively clear target image. The generated image is close to the real image, achieving a good coloring effect.

4   Conclusion

This paper proposes an automatic coloring method of ethnic minority clothing sketches based on Pix2Pix is proposed, and a network model for automatic coloring of ethnic minority clothing sketches is constructed. The original image is input as a constraint condition in the model generator to constrain the generation process of the target image, so as to make the generated colored image more reasonable. By adding L1 constraint to the objective function to improve the clarity of coloring effect maps, a generator model of ResNet structure is used to retain the bottom contour information of ethnic minority clothing sketches and color images. In addition, a generator and discriminator confrontation is used for ground training to construct the mapping relationship between ethnic minority clothing sketches and color images. Finally, a model that can be used to coloring general ethnic minority clothing sketches is produced, to realize the automatic coloring of ethnic minority clothing sketches. Compared with GAN [3], CGAN and CycleGAN, the results show that the coloring model constructed in this chapter can reasonably stain the draft of ethnic minority clothing, while maintaining high clarity.

Acknowledgement. This work is supported by National Natural Science Foundation of China (No. 61862068), Yunnan Expert Workstation of Xiaochun Cao, and Scientific Technology Innovation Team of Educational Big Data Application Technology in University of Yunnan Province.

References

1. Bhujel, A., Pant, D.R.: Dynamic convolutional neural network for image super-resolution. J. Adv. Coll. Eng. Manage. **3**, 1–10 (2017)
2. Gao, R., Sun, Z., Li, W., Pei, L., Hu, Y., Xiao, L.: Automatic coal and gangue segmentation using u-net based fully convolutional networks. Energies **13**(4), 829 (2020)
3. Goodfellow, I., et al.: Generative adversarial networks. Commun. ACM **63**(11), 139–144 (2020)
4. Hong, F., Wang, X.: The application of national costume elements in modern fashion design. In: Proceedings of the 2010 International Conference on Information Technology and Scientific Management, pp. 114–116 (2010)
5. Isola, P., Zhu, J.Y., Zhou, T., Efros, A.A.: Image-to-image translation with conditional adversarial networks. In: Proceedings of the IEEE Conference on Computer Vision and Pattern Recognition, pp. 1125–1134 (2017)
6. Liu, B., Gan, J., Wen, B., LiuFu, Y., Gao, W.: An automatic coloring method for ethnic costume sketches based on generative adversarial networks. Appl. Soft Comput. **98**, 106786 (2021)
7. Loussaief, S., Abdelkrim, A.: Machine learning framework for image classification. In: 2016 7th International Conference on Sciences of Electronics, Technologies of Information and Telecommunications (SETIT), pp. 58–61. IEEE (2016)
8. Mehta, S., Paunwala, C., Vaidya, B.: Cnn based traffic sign classification using adam optimizer. In: 2019 International Conference on Intelligent Computing and Control Systems (ICCS), pp. 1293–1298. IEEE (2019)
9. Mirza, M., Osindero, S.: Conditional generative adversarial nets. arXiv preprint arXiv:1411.1784 (2014)
10. Pham, V.D., Bui, Q.T.: Spatial resolution enhancement method for landsat imagery using a generative adversarial network. Remote Sens. Lett. **12**(7), 654–665 (2021)
11. Setiadi, D.R.I.M.: PSNR vs SSIM: imperceptibility quality assessment for image steganography. Multimed. Tools Appl. **80**, 8423–8444 (2021)

Multi-Model Fusion Based NOx Emission Prediction for Power Plant Boilers

Kangwei Lin[1], Guangsi Xiong[1], Wenchao Jiang[1(✉)], Hong Xiao[1], Jia Tang[2], and Cong Zhao[1]

[1] School of Computer Science and Technology, Guangdong University of Technology, Guangzhou 510006, China
jiangwenchao@gdut.edu.cn
[2] Guangzhou Yunshuo Technology Development Co., Ltd, Guangzhou 511458, Guangdong, China

Abstract. In view of the complex characteristics of nonlinear and multi operating conditions in the boiler combustion process of power station, a NOx prediction method of boiler combustion process based on Mini-BatchKMeans clustering and Stacking model fusion is proposed. This method optimizes the clustering and division of training sets by applying MiniBatchKMeans clustering algorithm, and establishes the stacking fusion framework prediction model (Stacking-XRLL) based on the XGBoost, Random Forest, LightGBM and the Linear Regression, so as to realize the accurate prediction of NOx emissions under the variable operating conditions of power plant boilers. Taking the NOx emission data of a power plant boiler in Guangdong as an example, the modeling simulation and experiment results shows that compared with the single modeling methods such as the BP, the LSTM and the GRU neural network, the Stacking-XRLL modeling method has higher generalization ability and prediction accuracy, and the average accuracy reaches 99%.

Keywords: Multi-work conditions · MiniBatchKMeans clustering · Stacking-XRLL · Multi-model fusion · NOx emissions

1 Introduction

Although China has been carrying out the reform of power structure in recent years, the coal-fired power plant boiler power generation will still be the most important power generation form in China for a long time. However, the NOx emission from boiler combustion is one of the main pollutants in the atmosphere, which has long affected the air quality and human health [1,2]. With the deepening of China's power system reform and the advancement of energy conservation and emission reduction, power plants pay more and more attention to pollutant emission control [3,4].

In the existing research on NOx emission prediction of power plant boilers, scholars explore the effect of different methods on NOx emission prediction from

© Springer Nature Singapore Pte Ltd. 2021
Y. Tan et al. (Eds.): DMBD 2021, CCIS 1453, pp. 382–396, 2021.
https://doi.org/10.1007/978-981-16-7476-1_34

the perspective of mechanism modeling and data-driven modeling. Li Jingji et al. [5] established a prediction model of NOx emission from circulating fluidized bed boiler by experimental study on the formation mechanism of coke NOx in dense phase zone of circulating fluidized bed boiler, investigating the influence of mass transfer and heat transfer characteristics in dense phase zone on NOx generation. However, due to the different equipment structures of different power plant applications and the complex reaction form and structure, so it is difficult to model by mechanism. With the application and popularization of DCS and SIS systems in power plants, massive on-site operation data can be obtained and saved, which provides the basis for the application of data-driven artificial intelligence modeling methods in the field of NOx emission prediction, such as the combination of the SVM and the RBF neural network [6, 7], the LSTM neural network [8–10], the GRU neural network [11], the partial least squares regression algorithm [12] and hybrid modeling method combined with mechanism analysis, etc. [13–15]. However, the above method does not rely on the process structure and mechanism, and is suitable for nonlinear and complex prediction objects. But in view of the widespread multi-parameter coupling, load adjustment and multi-operating conditions in the combustion process of power station boilers, the prediction accuracy of a single model is difficult to meet the actual demand of industrial applications.

In view of the low accuracy of NOx emission prediction in power plant boiler combustion system under multi-parameter and multi-operating conditions, a NOx prediction method for boiler combustion process based on the combination of MiniBatchKMeans clustering and Stacking model is presented. Firstly, the correlation analysis of boiler operating parameters is carried out, and then the characteristics of boiler operating parameters are screened based on the random forest feature selection algorithm, and then the clustering analysis is carried out for each operating condition. Finally, on the basis of clustering division, in the sample set of multiple operating conditions and the sample set of the same operating condition, the Stacking-XRLL multi-model fusion prediction model is used to forecast NOx emission from power plant boiler. The experimental results show that the prediction accuracy of this model is better than that of the BP, the LSTM and the GRU neural network models under multiple working conditions, with an average accuracy of 99%.

2   Feature Selection Algorithm Based on Random Forest

The boiler combustion system of power station is a typical complex nonlinear system, the combustion mechanism in the furnace is very complex, the influence variables are numerous and the variables also have a complex coupling relationship. There are many kinds of data (44 dimensions) collected from DCS system of power plant unit, including fault-related feature data, unrelated feature data and redundant feature data. In the process of boiler combustion modeling, feature selection based on expert experience and simple correlation analysis can not completely and accurately obtain important features related to failure. How to effectively extract or select useful feature information or rules from high-dimensional data is the basic problem facing power plant boiler combustion process modeling and optimization. The random forest is an integrated machine learning method, which is very robust for noise data and data with missing values, and has a fast learning speed, and its variable importance measurement can be used as a feature selection tool for high-dimensional data. Therefore, this paper uses the bag-out estimation of random forest to sort the characteristic parameters of the boiler combustion process of power station.

In the random forest algorithm, the test samples of each tree are randomly selected from the bag of set s by bagging sampling method, and the remaining Out-Of-Bag (OOB) data samples are represented as set $\bar{s}$. S is defined as the set of s, and $\bar{S}$ is the set of $\bar{s}$. Suppose matrix $X^{m \times p}$ is a test data set with m samples and p features, and y is a m-dimensional response vector, which represents the corresponding class information for each sample. Each feature x_j in the random forest algorithm corresponds to a set of test sets after random permutation features. The importance of features is measured by comparing the classification errors of original features and random permutation features in the OOB test set. When the important features are replaced by random features, the subset discrimination decreases, that is, the OOB classification error increases. When building a T tree, there are T OOB sets as test sets. Then define the feature importance index J_a as shown in formula (1).

$$J_a(x_j) = \frac{1}{T} \sum_{B_k \in S} \frac{1}{|\overline{B_k}|} \left(\sum_{i \in B_k} I\left(h_k^{\overline{x_j}}(i) \neq y_i - I(h_k(i) \neq y_i)\right) \right) \tag{1}$$

In formula (1), y_i is the classification label in the $h_k(i)$ OOB, the I is the indicative function, $h_k(i)$ is the classification attribute of predicting the sample i after training with dataset B_k, and $h_k^{\overline{x_i}}(i)$ is the classification attribute after replacing the feature X_j.

3   Based on MiniBatchKMeans Clustering and Stacking Multi-model Fusion Algorithm Design

3.1   Introduction to Algorithmic Theory

MiniBatchKMeans Clustering Algorithm. The MiniBatchKMeans algorithm is a variant of the K-Means algorithm, clustered using randomly generated subsets of small batch data, greatly reducing computational time, so MiniBatchKMeans maintains cluster accuracy and significantly reduces calculation time when used on large data set samples.

The pseudo code of MiniBatchKmeans algorithm flow is as follows (Table 1):

The distance between the two sample points $\mu = (\mu_1, \mu_2, \mu_3, \ldots, \mu_n)$ and $v = (v_1, v_2, v_3, \ldots, v_n)$ is calculated as shown in formula (2).

$$\text{dist} = \sqrt{\sum_{i=1}^{n} (\mu_i - v_i)^2} \tag{2}$$

Table 1. MiniBatchKMeans algorithm process pseudo-code

---

function MiniBatchKMeans(Input data, number of center points is K) {

    Gets dimension(D) and number(N) of input data;

    The initial centroids of K D-dimensions are randomly generated.;

    while(The algorithm does not converge){

        Building Small Batch Sample Set by Randomly Extracting N Samples from Original Set;

        For N points : Calculate which category each point belongs to;

        For K data center points:

        (1)Find all the data points that belong to your class;

        (2)Modify your coordinates to the center coordinates of these data points;

    }

    Output results;

}

The calculation formula of the ith class center is shown in formula (3):

$$c_{i_q} = \frac{1}{N} \cdot \sum_{x \in C_i} x \tag{3}$$

where C_{iq} represents the class center of the ith class, N_i represents the number of elements in the ith class, and C_i represents the ith class.

When a small batch sample set $X = (X_1, X_2, X_3, \ldots, X_{batch_size})$ with batch size is added, the class center is C_{iq} and the calculation is as formula (4).

$$C_{i_q} = \frac{1}{N_i + batch\_size} \cdot \sum_{x \in C_i \cup X} X \tag{4}$$

In addition, using the sum of squares of errors as the target function for measuring cluster quality, *SSE* definition as formula (5):

$$SSE = \sum_{i=1}^{k} \sum_{x \in C_i} \text{dist}\left(c_{i_q}, x\right)^2 \tag{5}$$

XGBoost Algorithm. Extreme Gradient Boosting (XGBoost) is a distributed general Gradient Boosting library proposed by T Chen in 2016, in this algorithm, the decision tree is used as the ensemble learning model of the base learner, and all CPU cores can be used to build trees in parallel during training. XGBoost improves the calculation method of the objective function on the basis of gradient lifting, which can improve the accuracy of the model. The optimization problem of the objective function is transformed into the problem of finding the minimum value of the quadratic function. The second-order derivative information of the loss function is used to train the tree model. At the same time, the tree complexity is added to the objective function as a regular term, which improves the generalization performance of the model. The objective function definition of XGBoost is as formula (6):

$$J = \sum_{i=1}^{n} L(y_i, \hat{y}_i) + \sum_{k=1}^{k} \Omega(f_k) \tag{6}$$

In the formula (6), y_i is the actual value of target i. $\hat{y}_i$ is the predicted value for target i. $L(y_i, \hat{y}_i)$ is the predicted value for the ith target of y_i and $\hat{y}_i$. $L(y_i, \hat{y}_i)$ is the difference between y_i and $\hat{y}_i$. N is the sample capacity. The $\Omega(f_k)$ is tree complexity. K is the number of sample features.

The iterative results of the objective function in time t are as formula (7):

$$J^{(t)} \approx \sum_{i=1}^{n} \left[L\left(y_i, \hat{y}_i^{t-1}\right) + f_t(x_i) \right] + \Omega(f_t) + C \tag{7}$$

In formula (7), $f_t(x_i)$ is the decision tree complexity where the variable x is computed for the tth iteration. C is a constant.

The loss function is expanded by the second-order Taylor expansion. Assuming that the loss function is the mean square error, the objective function is shown in formula (17):

$$J^{(t)} \approx \sum_{i=1}^{n} \left[L\left(y_i, \hat{y}_i^{t-1}\right) + g_i f_t(x_i) \right] + \frac{1}{2} h_i f_t^2(x_i) + \Omega(f_t) \tag{8}$$

In formula (17), g_i and h_i are the first and second derivatives of the mean square loss function, respectively.

The objective function that can be solved after the quadratic Taylor expansion of the objective function only depends on the first-order and second-order derivatives of each data point on the error function, so that the optimal prediction value can be obtained faster and accurately.

Light GBM Algorithm. The Light GBM algorithm is another evolutionary form of GBDT algorithm. The algorithm uses the depth-constrained leaf-wise strategy to find the node with the largest gain from the current leaf node for splitting, and limits the depth of the tree to prevent overfitting and shorten the time to find the optimal depth tree. At the same time, the same number of splittings can reduce the error and obtain higher accuracy. In the construction process, in order to find the optimal splitting node process, LightGBM uses histogram algorithm, unilateral gradient sampling algorithm and mutual exclusion feature binding algorithm to improve the operation efficiency [16].

In the case of high feature dimension and more samples, the traditional regression prediction algorithm is inefficient, and the accuracy of the final model prediction is not guaranteed. The new deep learning algorithm is slow in processing large data sets, and the accuracy of model prediction is greatly affected by its parameters. The Light GBM algorithm has the characteristics of fast training speed, less memory consumption and high prediction accuracy. It can overcome the shortcomings of both and achieve a balance between training speed and accuracy, which is suitable for industrial real-time prediction system.

Linear Regression Algorithm. Linear regression algorithm is an analysis method to determine the relationship between two or more variables. When the dependent variable is linearly related to the independent variable in regression analysis, it is called linear regression analysis. Linear regression algorithms can be used to analyze the prediction model of data or correlations between data. In the process of solving using linear regression algorithm, it is assumed that the dependent variable and the argument are linearly related, and a sub-equation between the variables is established. By bringing in the data, the equation is solved and the predicted value is obtained. Then build the loss function, and then bring the prediction value and the real value into the loss function, through the target of the loss function requires constant adjustment of the equation parameters, in order to achieve the optimal fit of the data.

Linear equation are defined as formulas (9):

$$\hat{y} = wx + b \tag{9}$$

In formula (9), $\hat{y}$ is the predicted value, x is the characteristic value, w and b are the equation parameters.

The loss function represents the average square distance between the predicted value and the true value, which is the mean square error, as defined in the formula (10):

$$L = \frac{1}{n} \sum_{i=1}^{n} (\hat{y}_i - y_i)^2 \tag{10}$$

In formula (10), $\hat{y}$ is the predicted value, y is the characteristic value, n is the equation parameter.

By combining an linear equation with a loss function, can get:

$$L(w, b) = \frac{1}{n} \sum_{i=1}^{n} (wx_i + b - y_i)^2 \tag{11}$$

Adjusting the parameters of the equation according to the target requirements of the loss function requires that the loss function be minimized.

$$(w^*, b^*) = \mathrm{argmin}_{(w,b)} = \frac{1}{n} \sum_{i=1}^{n} (wx_i + b - y_i)^2 \tag{12}$$

In formula (12), w^* and b^* are the optimal solutions to minimize the loss function.

The solution to the above formula (12) can be done using the least square. By first deriving w and b separately, can get:

$$\frac{\partial L}{\partial W} = 2 \left(w \sum_{i=1}^{n} x^2 - \sum_{i=1}^{n} x_i (y_i - b) \right) \tag{13}$$

$$\frac{\partial L}{\partial W} = 2 \left(nb - \sum_{i=1}^{n} (y_i - wx_i) \right) \tag{14}$$

When the two partial derivative formula (13) and (14) above are equal to zero, the optimal solution to the sum is obtained:

$$W = \frac{\sum_{i=1}^{m} y_i (x_i - \overline{x})}{\sum_{i=1}^{n} x^2 - \frac{1}{n} \left(\sum_{i=1}^{n} x \right)^2} \tag{15}$$

$$b = \frac{1}{n} \sum_{i=1}^{n} (y_i - Wx_i) \tag{16}$$

3.2   Stacking Model Fusion

Stacking is a hierarchical model integration framework. Under the Stacking-based integrated learning approach, the entire model is built in two stages, and the prediction accuracy is improved by passing the prediction results in a learner cascade [17]. In the first stage, the original dataset is firstly sliced and divided into a training set and a test set according to a certain ratio, then suitable base learners are selected to train the training set using cross-validation, and finally each base learner after training is predicted on the validation and test sets. In the first stage, machine learning models with excellent prediction performance should be selected, while ensuring diversity among the models. In the second stage, the prediction results of the base learners are used as the feature data for training and prediction of the meta-learner respectively. The meta-learner combines the features obtained in the previous stage and the labels of the original training set as sample data for model construction and outputs the final Stacking model prediction results. The meta-learner in this stage generally selects simple models with better stability to play the role of overall model performance improvement.

Stacking-based integrated modeling algorithms can improve model prediction accuracy, however, due to the integrated model's nature of incorporating multiple models for modeling, it inevitably reduces execution speed in terms of overall modeling. Therefore, in order to balance the prediction performance and overall modeling speed of Stacking algorithms, XGBoost and RandomForest with high prediction accuracy and LightGBM with excellent prediction performance and low algorithm time complexity are selected as the first layer of Stacking model fusion in this paper. Among them, RandomForest and XGBoost and LightGBM adopt the integrated learning methods of Bagging and Boosting respectively, which have excellent learning ability and rigorous mathematical theory support and have been widely used in various fields. The second layer of the model uses LinearRegression, which is more robust and generalisable, as shown in Fig. 1.

For the power station boiler combustion system in multivariable conditions with non-linear, large lag characteristics, and a single model in a certain degree is difficult to accurately describe the power station boiler combustion system with complex non-linear characteristics of NOx emissions, resulting in the model prediction accuracy is not high. Therefore, in order to improve the accuracy of NOx emission prediction from power station boilers under multiple operating conditions, this paper proposes a modeling method for power station combustion processes based on the MiniBatchKMeans clustering and Stacking multi-model fusion framework, as shown in Fig. 2. The modeling steps are as follows: (1) The pre-processed data is divided into training sets and test sets. (2) Using MiniBatchKMeans algorithm to cluster the parameters of the training sets, save the optimal contour coefficient and clustering center, and get a cluster sample of C_i. (3) For these clustered samples, a Stacking model fusion framework prediction algorithm embedded with multiple machine learning algorithms was constructed to deal with the prediction of NOx under multiple operating conditions using the fusion method shown in Fig. 1, with three machine learning methods, XGBoost, RandomForest and LightGBM, as the first layer base learners for Stacking integrated learning, and LinearRegression as the second layer meta-learners.

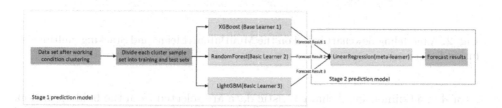

Fig. 1. Stacking model fusion architecture diagram

4   Experimental Results and Analysis

4.1   Experimental Environment and Data

The hardware (computer) required for the experiment is as follows: the central processor is Intel (R) Core (TM) i7-9750H CPU @ 2.60 GHz 2.59 GHz, the computer memory is 16GB RAM, the operating system is Windows 10–64 bit and the graphics processor is NVIDIA GeForce GTX1660Ti 6GB.

The software platform for the experiment in this paper includes: programming language is Python v3.7, Python IDEA is Pycharm v2020.1, Scikit-learn library is v0.22.1, numpy is v1.19.4, pandas is v1.1.4 and matplotlib is v3.3.2.

The data set required to conduct the experiments in this paper is based on a 1000MW supercritical coal-fired power plant unit at a power plant in Guangdong. According to the boiler operation experience and system theory analysis,

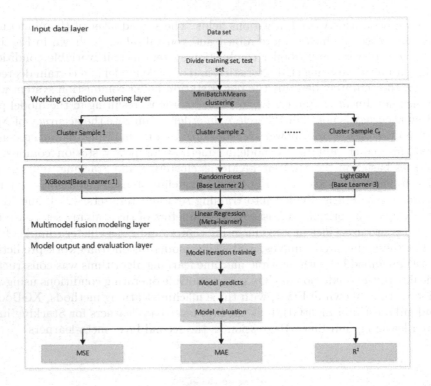

Fig. 2. A modeling flowchart based on the MiniBatchKMeans and Stacking multimodel fusion framework

a total of 44 dimensional characteristic data are selected from the field operation database, such as unit load, coal feed, water flow, exhaust gas temperature, EF2 layer auxiliary air No. 1 angle, F layer fuel air No. 1 angle. The controllable variables includes coal feed(C), water flow rate(F), primary air volume (A1, A2, A3), secondary air volume (S1 $\sim$ S22) and primary air pressure (W1, W2). State variables includes unit load(L), economizer outlet oxygen content (O1 $\sim$ O7), flue gas oxygen content(S) and exhaust gas temperature (T1 $\sim$ T6). The output variable is NOx emission at furnace outlet(NX). The operational data from 1 September 2018 to 7 September 2018 under continuous unit fault-free outage conditions were extracted, with a data collection interval of 60s, and 15,000 samples were finally taken as the data set for the model.

4.2   Feature Correlation Analysis and Selection

(1) Correlation analysis
Through the 15000 sample data collected from the DCS system, the sample data is selected by the correlation analysis method, and the correlation coefficients in the correlation analysis method are used to show the correlation between the

data groups and the correlation between the data groups. The correlation coefficient ranges from $[-1, 1]$, absolute values indicate the degree of correlation, and positive and negative values indicate the direction of correlation. The higher the absolute value, the stronger the correlation between data groups. In this paper, the correlation between variables is measured by the Speedrman correlation coefficient, which is calculated as a formula (17):

$$R = 1 - \frac{6 \sum_{I=1}^{n} |R(Xi_i) - R(Y_i)|^2}{n(n^2 - 1)} \quad (17)$$

In the formula (17), X and Y are two sets of data, n is the number of data per set, $R(X_i)$ and $R(Y_i)$ are ranked after sorting the elements in each set of data.

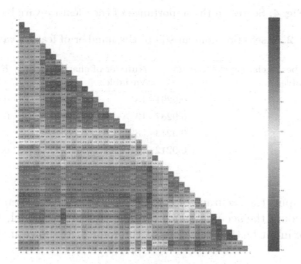

Fig. 3. Data correlation analysis thermal effort

As shown in Fig. 3, we consider the correlation coefficient between 0.0–0.2 to be very weak correlation, 0.2–0.4 to be weak correlation, 0.4–0.6 to be moderate correlation, 0.6–0.8 to be strong correlation, and 0.8–1.0 to be very strong correlation. Therefore, as S1 and S2, S7 and S6, S13 and S14, S17 and S19, T4 and T5 and T6 are all extremely strongly correlated, one of the two variables that are extremely strongly correlated will be retained, so that S1, S7, S13, S17 and T4 are ultimately retained, S2, S6, S14, S19, T5 and T6 are removed.

(2) Feature selection
By analyzing correlations and excluding some features, this section uses a random forest feature selection algorithm to rank the remaining features in terms of feature importance, as shown in Fig. 4.

As shown in Fig. 4 and Table 2, when 38 and 13 feature variables are input into the model, the accuracy of the model is close, and when 8 or fewer feature

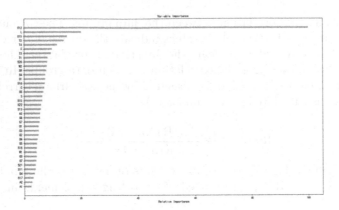

Fig. 4. Scores on the importance of each feature variable

Table 2. A selection comparison of the number of feature variables

Number of characteristic Variables	R^2	Number of characteristic Variables	R^2
38	0.9291	18	0.9144
33	0.9287	13	0.9132
28	0.9213	8	0.8661
23	0.9212	3	0.7551

variables are input, the accuracy of the model decreases significantly. Therefore, taking into account the accuracy and training time of the model, 13 features are selected as the input feature variables of the model, as shown in Table 3.

Table 3. Key parameter information for boiler combustion process after feature screening

Classification	Name
Controlled variable	S16, W2, S13, S4, F, S15, S12
State variable	T1, S, T3, T4, T2, L

4.3   MiniBatchKMeans Work Condition Clustering

The 15,000 samples of steady-state operating conditions were obtained, 12,000 were randomly selected as the training set and the remaining 3,000 were used as the test set, and the training and test sets were guaranteed to cover all typical operating conditions of the unit. After the feature selection analysis, the 13 feature variables were used as input variables to the model and the NOx emissions at the furnace outlet were used as output variables to the model. The initial number of clusters C_f value increases from 2 to 11, and the contour factor S_f under the corresponding C_f value is calculated. When the total contour factor is the largest, the clustering effect is best. The number of clusters $C_f=7$ is determined, and the training set is finally clustered into seven subsets according to the unit load. The result of working condition clustering by MiniBatchKMeans clustering is shown in Table 4.

Table 4. Clustering results for operating conditions

Params	Subset						
	C1	C2	C3	C4	C5	C6	C7
Cluster center unit load/MW	482.55	952.22	756.81	676.46	893.54	586.98	836.01
Sample number	978	7355	1814	1298	1595	737	1223

4.4 Multi-model Fusion Modeling Prediction

Each of the seven subsets was modeled using the multi-model fusion algorithm based on Stacking-XRLL, and the 15,000 sample data obtained, 12,000 as the training set and 3,000 as the test set. Finally, the model is used to make predictions on the test set, and the predicted NOx emission results of boiler furnace outlet are shown in Fig. 5. The model was evaluated using the returned mean absolute error (MAE), mean squared error (MSE) and coefficient of determination (R^2) as shown in Table 5.

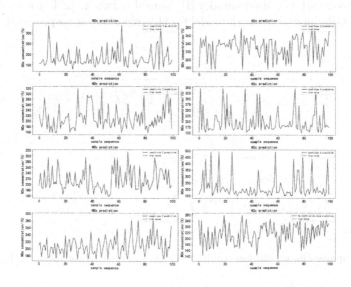

Fig. 5. Predictions for models under different operating conditions

Table 5. Performance comparison of forecast results for different condition models

Condition	MSE	MAE	R^2
No work condition division	38.7455	1.4742	0.9764
Condition1	6.2488	0.5289	0.9966
Condition2	1.3793	0.1065	0.9981
Condition3	0.8866	0.1342	0.9993
Condition4	17.9383	0.5270	0.9913
Condition5	2.7535	0.2648	0.9981
Condition6	1.4448	0.2070	0.9998
Condition7	1.7122	0.1898	0.9979

It can be seen from Fig. 5 and Table 5 that after clustering the boiler operation conditions, the Staking-XRLL model is used to predict the boiler operation conditions in each subset. The experimental results show that the model prediction accuracy of MSE is 38.7455, MAE is 1.4742 and R^2 is 0.9764 before the operation condition division. After the clustering division of boiler operation conditions, the prediction accuracy of each type of conditions has been improved, in which the total mean square error(MSE) is 4.6233, the mean absolute error (MAE) is 0.2797 and the R^2 is 0.9973.

In order to verify the effectiveness of the proposed multi-model fusion algorithm based on Stacking-XRLL, the data under condition 2 is randomly selected from seven conditions as the data set of the model. The Stacking-XTLL model was compared with the single-model BP neural network, LSTM neural network model and GRU neural network model for the experiments respectively, as shown in Fig. 6.

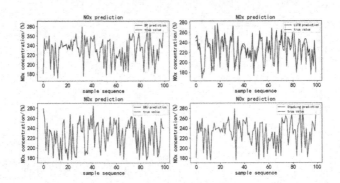

Fig. 6. Compares the prediction results with the different algorithms in the operating conditions

Table 6. Performance comparison of forecast results for different condition models

Model	R^2	MSE	MAE
Stacking-XRLL	0.996	2.875	0.259
BP	0.980	14.420	2.375
GRU	0.913	66.788	3.006
LSTM	0.909	68.795	2.946

It can be seen from Fig. 6 and Table 6 that under the same working condition, the single model of BP neural network is superior to the single model of GRU neural network, and the single model of GRU neural network is superior to the single model of LSTM neural network. However, the multi-model fusion algorithm based on Stacking-XRLL is superior to the BP neural network, GRU neural network and LSTM neural network in both accuracy and generalization ability, where MSE = 2.875, MAE = 0.259 and R^2 = 0.996. Therefore, the experimental results show that the multi-model fusion algorithm (Stacking-XRLL) can effectively and accurately predict NOx emissions at the furnace outlet of power station boilers.

5   Conclusion

To improve the prediction accuracy of NOx emissions from power station boilers under multiple operating conditions, a method combining the MiniBatchKMeans clustering algorithm with a multi-model fusion algorithm (Stacking-XRLL) is proposed. This enables accurate classification of boiler combustion conditions prior to modeling, while ensuring the prediction accuracy of the model during the modeling process. Compared with the single modeling methods of BP neural network, LSTM neural network and GRU neural network, the Stacking-XRLL modeling method has better generalization ability and prediction accuracy, reaching 99%. It solves the problem of low accuracy of NOx emission prediction by a single model under multiple working conditions of boilers and provides an important basis for the accurate control of combustion optimization of power station boilers.

Acknowledgment. This paper is supported by the Key Technology Project of Foshan City in 2019 (1920001001367), National Natural Science and Guangdong Joint Fund Project (U2001201), Guangdong Natural Science Fund Project (2018A030313061, 2021A1515011243), Research and Development Projects of National Key fields (2018YFB1004202), Guangdong Science and Technology Plan Project (2019B010139001) and Guangzhou Science and Technology Plan Project (201902020016).

References

1. Xue, W.B., Xu, Y.L., Wang, J.N., et al.: Ambient air quality impact of emissions from thermal power industry. China Environ. Sci. **36**(05), 1281–1288 (2016)
2. GB 13271–2014 Emission standard of air pollutants for boiler. China Environmental Science Press (2014)
3. Li, Y., Niu, S.: The significance of ultra-low emissions from thermal power plants to environmental protection. Low Carbon World **9**(10), 84–85 (2019)
4. Cheng, H.D., Cao, B.C.: The current situation and development route of ultra-low emission technology in coal-fired power plants. Ind. Innov. **20**, 129–130 (2020)
5. Li, J.J.: Experimental and Modeling Study on NOx Generation Mechanism in Circulating Fluidized Bed Boiler. Tsinghua University (2016)
6. Yu, T.F., Zhang, H.J.: NOx generation prediction model of coal-fired boiler based on SVM and RBF neural network **37**(09), 209–213+316 (2020)
7. Zhang, H.J.: The study of NOx generation prediction model and combustion optimization for coal-fired power plant boilers.Nanchang University (2020)
8. Qing, L., Hongli, H.: Prediction model of the NOx emissions based on long short-time memory neural network. In: 2020 Chinese Automation Congress (CAC). IEEE, pp. 2795–2797 (2020)
9. Yang, G., Wang, Y., Li, X.: Prediction of the NOx emissions from thermal power plant using long-short term memory neural network. Energy **192**, 116597 (2020)
10. Junjie, K., Yuguang, N., Bo, H., et al.: Dynamic Modeling of SCR Denitration Systems in Coal-fired Power Plants Based on a Bi-directional Long Short-term Memory Method. Process Safety and Environmental Protection (2021)
11. Wang, W.G., Zhao, W.J.: NOx emission prediction model based on GRU neural network in coal-fired power station. J. North China Electric Power Univ. (Natural Science Edition) **47**(01), 96–103 (2020)
12. Dong, Z., Ma, N., Li, C.Q.: NOxemission model for coal-fired boilers using partial least squares and extreme learning machine. J. Southeast Univ. (English Edition) **035**(002), 179–184 (2019)
13. Fu, Z.G., Yu, T., Zhou, L.J., et al.: Research and application of the reversed modeling method and partial least-square regression modeling for the complex thermal system. Proc. CSEE **29**(02), 25–29 (2009)
14. Tingting, Y., Kangfeng, M.A., You, L.V., et al.: Hybrid dynamic model of scr denitrification system for coal-fired power plant. In: 2019 IEEE 28th International Symposium on Industrial Electronics (ISIE). IEEE, pp. 106–111 (2019)
15. Gao, X.H.: Hybrid Modeling and Multi-Objective Optimization of Nox Emission and Reheat Steam Temperature for Utility Boilers. Southeastern University (2018)
16. Bian, L.Y., Zhang, L.L., Zhao, K., et al.: Ethereum malicious account detection method based on LightGBM. Netinfo Secur. **20**(04), 73–80 (2020)
17. Shi, J.Q., Zhang, J.H.: Load forecasting based on multi-model by stacking ensemble learning. Proc. CSEE **39**(14), 4032–4042 (2019)

Multi-axis Industrial Robot Fault Diagnosis Model Based on Improved One-Dimensional Convolutional Neural Network

Zongxin Ma[1], Hong Xiao[1(⊠)], Yihao Pan[1], Wenchao Jiang[1,2], Meng Xiong[2], and Zhongtang He[2]

[1] School of Computer Science and Technology,
Guangdong University of Technology, Guangzhou 510006, China
[2] Cloud Computing Center, Chinese Academy of Sciences, Dongguan 523808, Guangdong, China

Abstract. Industrial robots have become indispensable equipment in the automated manufacturing process. However, there are currently few deep learning fault diagnosis methods based on industrial robot operation. Aiming at the problems of low fault diagnosis accuracy and slow speed during the operation of industrial robots, a fault diagnosis model based on an improved one-dimensional convolutional neural network is proposed. To solve the problem of lack of industrial robot fault datasets, this paper uses the method based on random sampling and Mixup data augmentation to enhance data. Then, the model based on the original operation data of industrial robot are trained end-to-end by orthogonal regularization (SRIP) that combines with a one-dimensional convolutional neural network (CNN-1D). The experiment tests the diagnostic accuracy based on 3 million pieces of industrial robot operating data, which includes torque, speed, position, and current. Compared with the WDCNN and CNN-1D models, SRIPCNN-1D method can diagnose industrial robot faults effectively.

Keywords: Multi-axis industrial robot · Fault diagnosis · Convolutional neural network · Orthogonal regularization

1 Introduction

As an important part of the intelligent manufacturing process, industrial robots are widely used in all links of production. When the machine driven system of industrial robots degrades, its working efficiency, positioning accuracy and product quality will be greatly reduced. And then unexpected shutdown will bring huge economic losses. Therefore, it is important to develop an effective fault diagnosis method to monitor the working state of the multi-axis industrial robot. In addition, once a fault occurs, the robot will stop working immediately. So it is difficult to obtain a large number of fault data, which poses a severe challenge to industrial robot fault diagnosis and analysis.

Brambilla et al. [1] proposed a model-based method for robot fault diagnosis. The method detects sensor faults by means of a generalized observer (GOS) scheme, where each GOS input is determined by a Second order synovium law. Finally, the effectiveness of method is verified on a simulation system. Mcintyre et al. [2] proposed a

© Springer Nature Singapore Pte Ltd. 2021
Y. Tan et al. (Eds.): DMBD 2021, CCIS 1453, pp. 397–410, 2021.
https://doi.org/10.1007/978-981-16-7476-1_35

nonlinear dynamic fault diagnosis method based on the robot model. The method requires no acceleration measurement and is independent of the controller. Sabry et al. [3] proposed a fault diagnosis method based on mathematical model. Firstly, a mathematical model of Bode equation vector fitting is established to fit the robot power consumption, then the fault axis is diagnosed by monitoring the energy consumption rate of the robot. However, the actual robot state is difficult to estimate in practice and will change over time. Therefore, the method of model-based robot fault diagnosis is difficult to be used in actual environment.

In recent years, with the development of sensor technology and machine learning technology, more and more data-driven fault detection methods are applied in the field of fault diagnosis. Kim et al. [4] proposed a Phase-based Time Domain Averaging method, which can detect the failure of industrial robot gearboxes in the constant speed area of motion. However, this method is limited to the constant speed range and is not easy to obtain vibration data in the real industrial field. Cheng et al. [5] proposed a gearbox fault detection method based on Gaussian mixture model, which uses industrial robots to cluster normal and fault torque data. Bittencourt et al. [6] used the kernel density estimation method as a wear indicator to monitor the performance of industrial robots performing repeated motions. Algburi et al. [7] developed a health assessment and fault detection system for industrial robots based on rotating encoder signals. Long et al. [8] proposed a hybrid sparse auto-encoder and support vector machine model based on attitude data for multi-joint robot fault diagnosis.

Among all kinds of machine learning algorithms, the performance of fault diagnosis technology based on shallow neural network learning largely depends on whether the extracted fault features are accurate. Therefore, it is more available to use raw signal for fault diagnosis. Wu et al. [9] proposed a motion adaptive minimized output fault detection method for industrial robot gearbox based on torque ripple through one-dimensional residuals convolutional neural network. In this method, the moving average filter is applied to the torque signal to extract the data trend and obtains the torque pulsation in the high frequency band as the residual value between the original signal and the filtered signal. Chang et al. [10] proposed a fault detection algorithm based on neural network. By using neural network to estimate fault torque, the algorithm can detect and diagnose faults effectively. However, these models rarely use the original data of robot controller for analysis, and lack of optimization and practical verification for the fault characteristics of industrial robots.

Once a mechanical axis of a multi-axis industrial robot fails, it will affect the operation state of other axes. Therefore, multi-axis industrial robot fault diagnosis must be integrated with the data of each axis to judge the overall state. In this paper, a new industrial robot fault diagnosis method (SRIPCNN-1D) based on the combination of one-dimensional convolutional neural network and orthogonal regularization (SRIP) [11] is proposed to solve the problem of industrial robot fault diagnosis. Firstly, the industrial robot fault data is enhanced by random sampling and Mixup. Then, the model based on the original operation data of industrial robot are trained end-to-end using orthogonal regularization combined with a one-dimensional convolutional neural network. Finally, the model is used to perform rapid fault diagnosis on the industrial robot. The experimental results show that SRIPCNN-1D model can diagnose industrial robot faults effectively.

2 Multi-axis Robot Fault Diagnosis Model

2.1 Fault Diagnosis Model Structure

Figure 1 shows the fault diagnosis model structure based on the improved one-dimensional convolutional neural network. The model includes two consecutive convolutional layers, a maximum pooling layer, a global pooling layer, and a softmax layer. The model input dimension is consistent with the dimension of industrial robot operation data, and the output dimension is equal to the number of machine failure categories. Orthogonality of weights is a favorable attribute for training convolutional neural networks. The model applies SRIP orthogonality regularization in the convolutional layer to improve the accuracy and convergence stability of the model.

CNN is a feedforward artificial neural network with alternating convolution and sub-sampling layers. This structure shows excellent performance in the field of computer vision and time-frequency signal analysis [12]. CNN is composed of neurons with trainable weights and biases. Each CNN neuron receives some input and performs convolution calculations. The output is each category score [13]. A typical CNN includes an input layer, a convolutional layer, a pooling layer, a fully connected layer, and an output layer. The input layer of CNN can process multi-dimensional data in a standardized form, which is conducive to improving algorithm efficiency and training performance [14].

In the convolution layer, the convolution kernel performs convolution on the output of the previous layer. The convolution layer uses a certain number of filters to obtain data features. The output of each layer is the convolution result of multiple input features. The mathematical model is described as (1) [15, 16].

$$y_i^{l+1}(j) = K_i^l * X^l(j) + b_i^l \tag{1}$$

Among them, K_i^l indicates the weight of the i-th filter kernel of the l-th layer, b_i^l represents the deviation of the i-th filter kernel of the l-th layer, $X^l(j)$ represents the i-th local area of the l-th layer, $y_i^{l+1}(j)$ represents the input $l + 1$ of the i-th neuron in the i-th frame of the layer. * indicates the dot product of the kernel and the local area.

After the convolution operation, the activation function will perform a nonlinear transformation on the logarithmic value output in each convolution. In view of the unstructured nature of industrial robot data, the Relu function is used as the activation function. When the input value is greater than 0, the derivative value of this function is always 1, which solves the problem of model gradient vanishing [16]. The piece wise function Relu is expressed as (2).

$$a_i^{l+1}(j) = f(y_i^{l+1}(j)) = \max\{0, y_i^{l+1}(j)\} = \begin{cases} y_i^{l+1}(j) & y_i^{l+1}(j) \geq 0 \\ 0 & y_i^{l+1}(j) < 0 \end{cases} \tag{2}$$

Among them, $y_i^{l+1}(j)$ represents the convolution operation output value, $a_i^{l+1}(j)$ represents the activation value of $y_i^{l+1}(j)$.

In order to reduce the parameters of neural network, the pooling layer samples the large matrix down into a small matrix through data down-sampling. The pooling method uses maximum pooling and average pooling [9, 17], the expressions are (3, 4).

$$P_i^{l+1}(j) = \frac{1}{w} \sum_{i=t-(j-1)w+1}^{jw} q_i^l(t) \tag{3}$$

$$P_i^{l+1}(j) = \overset{max}{(j-1)W+1 \le t \le jW}\{q_i^l(t)\} \tag{4}$$

Among them, w is the width of the pooling area, $q_i^l(t)$ is the value of the t-th neuron in the i-th feature in the l-th layer, The value range of t is $t \in [(j-1)W+1, jW]$, $P_i^{l+1}(j)$ represents the neuron value of the $l+1$ layer.

The fully connected layer expands the output of the last pooling layer into a one-dimensional vector, which is used as the input of the output layer. A full connection is then established between the input and output [18]. The formula for the fully connected layer is (5).

$$z^{l+1}(j) = f\left(\sum_{i=1}^{m} \sum_{i=1}^{n} W_{i,t,j}^l a_i^l(t) + b_j^l\right) \tag{5}$$

Among them, $W_{i,t,j}^l$ represents the weight between the t-th neuron in the i-th feature of the l-th layer and the j-th neuron in the $l+1$ layer. $z^{l+1}(j)$ represents the logarithm of the j-th neuron in the $l+1$ layer. b_j^l represents the network offset. $a_i^l(t)$ represents the output value of the t-th neuron in the i-th feature of the previous layer l. f represents the activation function Relu.

The output layer uses the softmax classifier to create classification labels. The softmax classifier is a common linear classifier, which is a form of multi-class classification derived from logistic regression [19]. Its mathematical model is shown in (6).

$$Q(j) = soft \max(z^o(j)) = \frac{e^{z^o(j)}}{\sum_{k=1}^{M} e^{z^o(k)}} \tag{6}$$

Among them, $z^o(j)$ represents the logarithm of the output of the j-th neuron in the output layer. M represents the total number of categories.

In order to solve the problems of gradient disappearance or explosion, statistical feature migration, and saddle point diffusion that may occur during training, data regularization is used to limit the parameters of the network layer. It reduces the over-fitting phenomenon. SRIP is introduced to improve the model effect and obtain higher diagnostic accuracy. Assuming the fully connected layer $W \in m \times n$, for the convolutional layer $C \in S \times H \times C \times M$, where S, H, C, and M are respectively the filter width, filter height, the number of input channels and the number of output channels, the C is shaped as a matrix $W' \in m' \times n'$. Among them, $m' = S \times H \times C$, $n' = M$, the regularized convolutional layer realizes orthogonality on the entire filter and promotes the diversity of the filter.

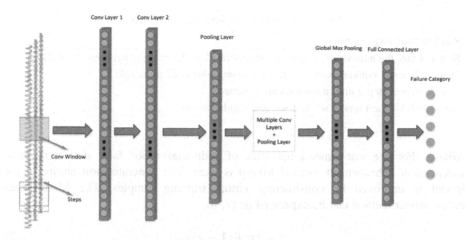

Fig. 1. Schematic diagram of SRIPCNN-1D network model structure

2.2   Data Enhancement

In most fault diagnosis data sets, the number of different types of samples varies greatly, which leads to the poor diagnosis effect of the model for fault types with small number of samples. In order to solve the over-fitting problem in the CNN training process, a data enhancement method based on Mixup is used to process random sampling data, construct virtual training samples and improve the generalization ability of the model. It is divided into random sampling and Mixup.

Random Sampling. Based on the random sampling method, random sampling points are added without setting the offset. On the one hand, the coverage of the training samples is optimized. On the other hand, there is better independence between the before and after samples. The steps of the random sampling algorithm are shown in Table 1. The sampling principle is shown in Fig. 2. Assuming that the original sequence contains M sampling points and L is the sample length, M-L random sampling points can be generated theoretically.

By setting a large sample number N, the random sampling method can expand the number of input samples and alleviate the problems of lack of training samples, category imbalance and over-fitting.

Table 1. Random sampling algorithm steps

Random sampling algorithm:
Step 1: Enter the number of samples to be generated n, the range is between *(1, M-L)*
Step 2: Generate random point 1, select *[random point 1, L]* as sample *1*
Step 3: Repeat step 2 until n samples are generated
Step 4: Divide the training set, test set, and validation set

Mixup. For the one-dimensional data of industrial robot fault detection, data-independent enhancement method Mixup is used. The generalization ability of the model is improved by constructing virtual training samples. The Mixup data enhancement method can be expressed as (7, 8).

$$\hat{x} = \lambda x_i + (1 - \lambda)x_j \tag{7}$$

$$\hat{y} = \lambda y_i + (1 - \lambda)y_j \tag{8}$$

Among them, (x_i, y_i) and (x_j, y_j) are two samples randomly drawn from the training set. λ is the mixing coefficient, $\lambda \in [0, 1]$. $\lambda \sim Beat(\alpha, \alpha)$, $\alpha \in (0, \infty)$. Mixup achieves linear interpolation by mixing feature vectors and their corresponding labels. The interpolation strength of the feature vector and the label can be controlled by the value of the hyper-parameter a.

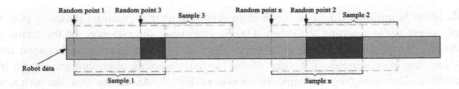

Fig. 2. Schematic diagram of random sampling

2.3   Robot Fault Diagnosis Process

The real-time fault diagnosis process of industrial robot based on SRIPCNN-1D model is shown in Fig. 3. The fault diagnosis process are as follows.

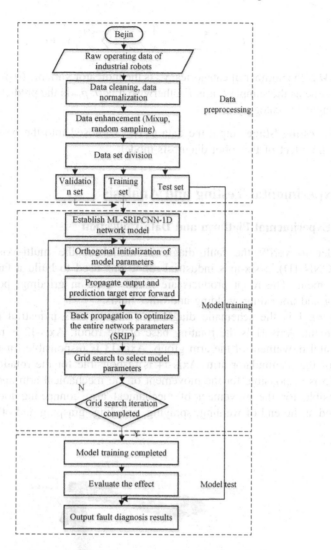

Fig. 3. Process of fault diagnosis model of industrial robot

Data Preprocessing Stage. The real-time operation data of the robot is obtained through the robot operation data acquisition platform. Firstly, the data is cleaned and normalized. Then data enhancement method is used for data expansion. Finally, the data set is divided into training set, verification set and test set.

Model Training Stage. We use orthogonal initialization to avoid gradient explosion or vanishing. The SRIPCNN-1D activation function is Relu, it uses global maximum pooling to achieve dimensionality reduction. Softmax classifier is used to achieve the classification output. The model loss function is the cross-entropy loss function, as shown in Formula (9).

$$L = \frac{1}{N} \sum_i L_i = \frac{1}{N} \sum_i - \sum_{c=1}^{M} y_{ic} \log p_{ic} \tag{9}$$

In (9), M is the number of categories, y_{ic} is the indicator variable (0 or 1). If the category is the same as the sample i, it is 1, otherwise it is 0. p_{ic} is the predicted probability that the sample i is category c.

Model Testing Stage. Input the data to be diagnosed into the best trained model to verify the effect of the robot diagnosis model.

3   Experimental Testing and Analysis

3.1   Experimental Platform and Data Collection

In order to verify the fault diagnosis model of the multi-axis industrial robot (SRIPCNN-1D), a six-axis industrial robot was used to build a fault data collection environment. The robot products are mainly used in grinding, polishing, spraying, loading and unloading, welding and other fields.

Figure 4 is the schematic diagram of the six-axis industrial robot used in the experiment. Axis-J1 is the rotating base of the robot. Axis-J2 is responsible for the horizontal movement of the arm group. Axis-J3 is responsible for the vertical move-ment of the manipulator arm. Axis-J4 is responsible for the rotation of the forearm. Axis-J5 is responsible for the movement of the mechanical arm and wrist. Axis-J6 is responsible for the movement of mechanical arm connecting tools, which can be installed at the end of welding, spraying, grinding, grasping and other tools.

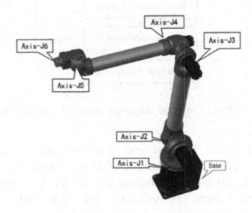

Fig. 4. Six-axis industrial robot model

Robot faults can be divided into robot fault, control system fault, working system fault, drive system fault and so on. The experiment in this paper focuses on the fault of robot body and drive system, such as reducer fault, servo motor fault, etc.

For each robot, there are six joint axis data. Each axis operation data contains 31 characteristic variables. These variables can be divided into two categories. a) robot state data, such as parameter setting, ontology information, firmware version, etc. b) Real-time operation data of the robot, such as feedback torque (tfb), feedback current (flow), feedback velocity (vfb), feedback position (pfb), etc.

Table 2. Industrial robot failure data set

Label	Variable	Axis	Data volume	Situation	Category name
0	tfb, flow, vfb, pfb	1–6	1500,000	Normal	Normal
1	tfb, flow, vfb, pfb	1–6	500,000	3 axis abnormal noise, vibration	Fault1
2	tfb, flow, vfb, pfb	1–6	500,000	2 axis abnormal noise, vibration	Fault2
3	tfb, flow, vfb, pfb	1–6	500,000	4 axis abnormal noise, vibration	Fault3

The fault data set includes data samples of multiple normal or abnormal robots. The fault data includes faults of different axes and faults of different components. The fault data is shown in Table 2. There are two data sample intervals of 4ms and 1s, covering a variety of robot operating data, and the collection time is 120–200 h. These data were collected and stored through the robot fault data acquisition software, with a total of over 3 million pieces of data were collected.

3.2 Data Enhanced Comparative Analysis

In order to verify the influence of different data enhancement methods on the fault diagnosis algorithm, three fault diagnosis models (WDCNN, CNN-1D, SRIPCNN-1D) were tested with different data enhancement methods. The results are shown in Table 3. Each type of fault sample is calculated based on 300,000 records. When the data size is 2000, only 150 samples can be generated, so the sample size is smaller when data enhancement is not used. After using random sampling data enhancement, the number of samples is expanded to 20000, which greatly increases the number of model input.

After experimental comparison, it can be seen from Table 3 that the accuracy of the fault diagnosis algorithm is significantly improved after data enhancement, and the data enhancement method using random sampling combined with Mixup performs best.

Figure 5 is the confusion matrix of the proposed method. The ordinate is the actual label. Each row represents the number of faults of this type and other faults. The total number is 2000, that is, the test is performed under 2000 test samples. The abscissa is the predicted label. Each column indicates the number of faults of this type among all samples. The fault data used includes abnormal vibration faults of industrial robots 2, 3, and 4 axis currently. According to experimental results, in most cases, the correct rate of each type of fault is more than 99%. It shows that the robot fault diagnosis model constructed by SRIPCNN-1D can diagnose fault with higher accuracy and realize fault location.s

3.3   Experimental Results and Analysis

This paper first verifies the feasibility and effectiveness of the data enhancement method for industrial robots, then selects the best model parameters for testing. By comparing with WDCNN and CNN-1D model methods, the effectiveness of SRIPCNN-1D is evaluated.

Table 3. Comparison of results of different data enhancement methods sampled by multiple models

Network model	Data enhancement method	Average diagnostic accuracy
WDCNN [20]	No data enhancement	92. 50
	Random sampling	95. 24
	Mixup	94. 81
	Random sampling + Mixup	96. 37
CNN-1D	No data enhancement	94. 39
	Random sampling	96. 34
	Mixup	95. 47
	Random sampling + Mixup	98. 28
SRIPCNN-1D	No data enhancement	97. 78
	Random sampling	98. 52
	Mixup	97. 65
	Random sampling + Mixup	99. 85

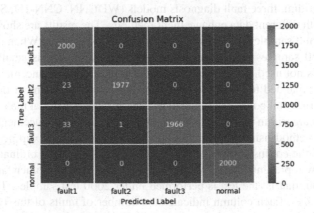

Fig. 5. Confusion matrix

From the comparison in Table 3, the SRIPCNN-1D fault model performs best accuracy among all the above methods. Although WDCNN is effective in bearing fault diagnosis and is used as a benchmark by many scholars, it exists limitations in the field of industrial robot data fault diagnosis. In order to improve the accuracy of rolling bearing fault diagnosis, WDCNN uses a combination of large convolution kernel and small convolution kernel. The large convolution kernel improves the receptive field, but also increases the number of parameters. Moreover, the large convolution kernel is not as good as the multi-layer convolution in terms of feature extraction. The method proposed in this paper using two consecutive convolution kernels can better extract the deep features of industrial robot fault data. This method can also expand the receptive field of model without increasing too many parameters.

In this experiment, $F_1-Score$ index was used to measure the effect of the model. The $F_1-Score$ is also called the balanced F Score. It is defined as the harmonic mean of Precision and Recall. The $F_1-Score$ value of the best output of the model is 1, and the worst output of the model is 0. $F_1-Score$ can be expressed as formula (10).

$$F_1 = 2 \cdot \frac{precision \times recall}{precision + recall} \tag{10}$$

As the method described in Fig. 2, the continuous run data is first divided into data segments. We select 2000 sample points as a fragment and used random sampling and Mixup methods for data enhancement. In order to select the best parameters of the network model, different convolution kernel sizes, number of convolution cores, iteration rounds, pooling methods and data lengths were selected for test comparison. The results are shown in Fig. 6. Among them, parameters of SRIPCNN-1D model are shown in Table 4.

Table 4. SRIPCNN-1D convolutional layer and pooling layer parameters

Network structure	Convolution kernel size	Steps	Number of convolution kernels	Output size
Convolutional layer 1	20	4	70	50 × 70
Convolutional layer 2	20	2	70	25 × 70
Pooling layer	4	4	70	6 × 70

The abscissa axis length represents the data length, and the vertical axis represents the F1-score of the model. The three values corresponding to each curve in Fig. 6 respectively represent the size of convolution kernel, the number of convolution kernel and the pooling mode. For example, "50_100_0" represents the size of convolution kernel is 50, the number of convolution kernel is 100, and the pooling method is global maximum pooling. Among them, parameters of SRIPCNN-1D model are shown in Table 4.

In Fig. 6, Conv + Conv + Pool + Full is the best model. The number of data is 2000. The size and number of filters are 20 and 70 respectively. GlobalMaxPooling1D pooling method is adopted and the maximum number of iterations is 50. The batch size is 100, and the regularization method is SRIP orthogonal regularization. The data action period of the robot is 500 sampling points. When the number of data is 2000, it is about 4 action periods. This shows that the SRIPCNN-1D model can make use of less data for high-precision fault diagnosis.

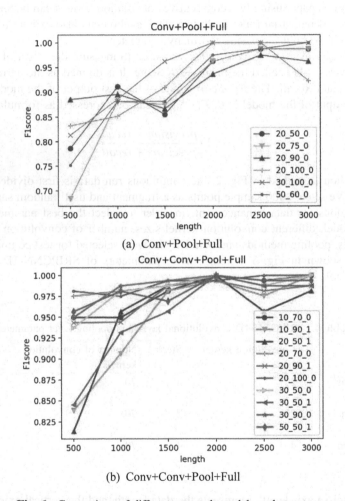

(a) Conv+Pool+Full

(b) Conv+Conv+Pool+Full

Fig. 6. Comparison of different network models and parameters

The model performance of different data length is tested by increasing the action period. The result is shown in Fig. 7. As can be seen from Fig. 7, the accuracy of model increasing by the length of the action is slightly lower than that of the same amount. It indicates that the model has a good feature extraction ability in the actual fault diagnosis, and there is no need to divide the data according to the action.

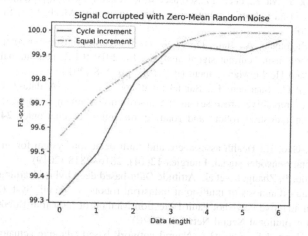

Fig. 7. Comparison of different data length increment methods

4 Conclusion

In this paper, a fault diagnosis model SRIPCNN-1D based on real-time big data analysis of industrial robots was proposed. SRIPCNN-1D used random sampling and Mixup data augmentation to improve model. Based on robot equipment, 3 million pieces of data on torque, speed, position, current and other operational variables were collected. The diagnostic accuracy was tested and compared with WDCNN and CNN-1D models. The results showed that the SRIPCNN-1D method can diagnose industrial robot faults effectively.

Acknowledgements. This paper is supported by the Key Technology Project of Foshan City in 2019 (1920001001367), National Natural Science and Guangdong Joint Fund Project (U2001201), Guangdong Natural Science Fund Project (2018A030313061, 2021A1515011243), Research and Development Projects of National Key fields (2018YFB1004202), Guangdong Science and Technology Plan Project (2019B010139001) and Guangzhou Science and Technology Plan Project (201902020016).

References

1. Brambilla, D., Capisani, L.M., Ferrara, A., et al.: Fault detection for robot manipulators via second-order sliding modes. IEEE Trans. Ind. Electron. **55**(11), 3954–3963 (2008)
2. Mcintyre, M.L., Dixon, W.E., Dawson, D.M., et al.: Fault identification for robot manipulators. IEEE Trans. Robot. **21**(5), 1028–1034 (2005)

3. Sabry, A.H., Nordin, F.H., Sabry, A.H., et al.: Fault detection and diagnosis of industrial robot based on power consumption modeling. IEEE Trans. Ind. Electron. **67**(9), 7929–7940 (2020)
4. Kim, Y., Park, J., Na, K., et al.: Phase-based time domain averaging (ptda) for fault detection of a gearbox in an industrial robot using vibration signals. Mech. Syst. Sig. Process. **138**, 106544 (2020)
5. Cheng, F., Raghavan, A., Jung, D., et al.: High-accuracy unsupervised fault detection of industrial robots using current signal analysis. In: 2019 IEEE International Conference on Prognostics and Health Management (ICPHM), pp. 1–8 (2019)
6. Bittencourt, A.C., Saarinen, K., Sander-tavallaey, S., et al.: A data-driven approach to diagnostics of repetitive processes in the distribution domain – applications to gearbox diagnostics in industrial robots and rotating machines. Mechatronics **24**(8), 1032–1041 (2014)
7. Algburi, R., Gao, H.: Health assessment and fault detection system for an industrial robot using the rotary encoder signal. Energies **12**(14), 2816–2818 (2019)
8. Long, J., Mou, J., Zhang, L., et al.: Attitude Data-based deep hybrid learning architecture for intelligent fault diagnosis of multi-joint industrial robots. J. Manuf. Syst. (2020)
9. Wu: Motion-adaptive Few-shot Fault Detection Method of Industrial Robot Gearboxes Via Residual Convolutional Neural Network (2020)
10. Cho, C.N., Hong, J.T., Kim, H.J.: Neural network based adaptive actuator fault detection algorithm for robot manipulators. J. Intell. Robot. Syst. **95**(1), 137–147 (2019)
11. Bansal, N., Chen, X., Wang, Z.: Can we gain more from orthogonality regularizations in training deep networks? Adv. Neural. Inf. Process. Syst. **31**, 4261–4271 (2018)
12. Jing, L., Zhao, M., Li, P., et al.: A Convolutional neural network based feature learning and fault diagnosis method for the condition monitoring of gearbox. Measurement **111**, 1–10 (2017)
13. Kiranyaz, S., Avci, O., Abdeljaber, O., et al.: 1D convolutional neural networks and applications: a survey. arxiv abs/1905.03554 (2019)
14. Li, D., Zhang, J., Zhang, Q., et al.: Classification of ECG signals based on 1D convolution neural network. In: 2017 IEEE 19th International Conference on E-health Networking, Applications and Services (healthcom), vol. 12, pp. 1–6 (2017)
15. Bengio, Y., Courville, A., Vincent, P.: Representation learning: a review and new perspectives. IEEE Trans. Pattern Anal. Mach. Intell. **35**(8), 1798–1828 (2013)
16. Lin, M., Chen, Q., Yan, S.: Network in network. arXiv preprint arXiv:1312.4400 (2013)
17. Nair, V., Hinton, G.E.: Rectified linear units improve restricted Boltzmann Machines. In: ICML (2010)
18. Ioffe, S., Szegedy, C.: Batch normalization: accelerating deep network training by reducing internal covariate shift. arXiv preprint arXiv:1502.03167 (2015)
19. He, K., Zhang, X., Ren, S., et al.: Deep residual learning for image recognition. In: Proceedings of the IEEE Conference on Computer Vision and Pattern Recognition, pp. 770–778 (2016)
20. Zhang, W.: Study on bearing fault diagnosis algorithm bases on convolutional neural network

Prediction of Oil Temperature for Transformers Using Gated Recurrent Unit

Yuwen Liu(✉)(iD), Yihong Yang(iD), and Yuqing Wang(iD)

School of Computer Science, Qufu Normal University, Rizhao 276800, China

Abstract. The service life of transformer is determined by the insulating materials' aging degree. The factors causing insulation aging are temperature, oxidation and moisture in insulating materials. Among them, temperature is the decisive factor. Therefore, managers need to predict the oil temperature changes in time, which has great significance on maintaining the transformers' lives and ensuring the normal operation of the power system. However, prediction methods are always based on linear regression or artificial neural network. These methods hardly consider the interaction between historical oil temperatures. However, the historical oil temperature is precisely an important factor affecting the future changes of oil temperature. Therefore, we propose an oil temperature prediction model (GRU-OTP) that can simultaneously pay attention to the long-term and short-term effects between historical oil temperatures. In order to pay attention to the short-term effects of historical oil temperature, we add a 5-h time sliding window to preprocess the data. Then, We use the GRU model to explore the long-term effects between historical oil temperatures. Experiments on different transformers show that GRU-OTP model has higher prediction accuracy and applicability.

Keywords: Time series · Gated recurrent unit · Oil temperature prediction

1 Introduction

With the development of science and technology, the production and distribution of electric power resources has become an issue that concerned by people [1]. The electric power resources production needs to ensure the normal operation of transformers, and electric power distribution is to distribute power to different regions for people to use. Therefore, ensuring the normal operation of transformers is the basis for solving the follow-up problems. It is difficult to predict the actual life of transformers directly, because the life of transformers will change with power consumption, environment and temperature. The existing methods are also difficult to predict the long-term and high-precision transformer life based on ultra- long-term real-world data. Therefore, it is necessary to find an effective method to predict the transformers' future service

© Springer Nature Singapore Pte Ltd. 2021
Y. Tan et al. (Eds.): DMBD 2021, CCIS 1453, pp. 411–421, 2021.
https://doi.org/10.1007/978-981-16-7476-1_36

life, which can prevent unnecessary waste of resources and maintain the power system's safe operation. Moreover, sensors are important equipment to monitor and control various parameters during the operation of equipment [26,27]. The oil temperature detected by sensors can reflect the transformer's condition. An effective strategy is to indirectly pridect the transformer's actual condition by predicting the power transformer's oil temperature.

Thermal faults often occur in transformers, which seriously threaten the safe operation of transformers. Oil temperature is an important parameter that can monitor the transformer's operation. Transformer oil fills the whole transformer, which plays the role of insulation and cooling. So the transformer oil is also known as the "blood" of transformer. As the oil temperature increases, the deterioration rate of the transformer will also increase. Therefore, it is an important task for the operation and maintenance personnel to master the oil temperature in time. At present, it is not enough to detect the oil temperature state by using the traditional oil thermometer. If the transformer is not maintained in time when the thermometer detects the abnormality, the irreparable loss may be caused. In addition, the traditional oil thermometer has frequent failures, including internal corrosion, inaccurate temperature indication of thermometer. These factors have brought unstable factors to the operation and maintenance of the transformer.

The oil temperature will change with the use of electricity, and the historical state of oil temperature will affect the future temperature changes. Therefore, the temperature change state of each transformer is often different. Figure 1 shows the temperature variation of the two transformers. It shows that each transformer has its own variation law. This is because each transformer is in a different environment and their specific functions are different. But the same point between transformers is that the oil temperature change is nonlinear, and future oil temperature will be affected by the historical oil temperature. Therefore, an accurate temperature prediction model needs to have the ability to capture the long- and short-term impacts of oil temperature. With the development of deep learning, some deep learning models provides new solutions to some problems [24,25]. Among them, the gated recurrent unit (GRU) [4] is a variant of recurrent neural network (RNN), which can capture the dependencies between historical data well. Therefore, we use the **GRU** and propose an oil temperature prediction model (GRU-OTP). In addition, the oil temperature prediction needs to be time-sensitive. The prediction model should be able to predict the temperature changes in the short term, which can also provide more effective help for the operation and maintenance personnel. Therefore, we use a time sliding window to control the data that mill be input to GRU. Finally, our contributions are summarized as listed below.

– We utilize GRU to capture the time dependence between historical oil temperatures. This method can not only pay attention to the long-term dependence between historical temperatures, but also capture the short-term dependence between historical temperatures.
– In order to make a time-sensitive oil temperature prediction, we add a time sliding window to focus on the influence of short-term oil temperature

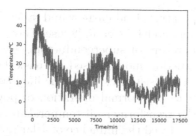
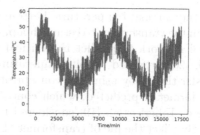

(a) The oil temperature change of trans-   (b) The oil temperature change of transformer 1   former 2

Fig. 1. The oil temperature change of different transformers.

changes. Here, we propose a transformer oil temperature prediction model (GRU-OTP) with high accuracy, which provides a guarantee for maintaining the power system's normal operation.

– We have conducted experiments on two transformer datasets. Temperature prediction is carried out for different transformers and different time intervals. Through comparison with other models, our model is obviously better than other methods.

Other arrangements are as follows. In Sect. 2, we review the oil temperature prediction and other prediction methods. In Sect. 3, we introduce our GRU-OTP model in detail. In Sect. 4, we show the comparative experiment and its results. In Sect. 5, we summarize our work.

2 Related Work

Time series prediction [2,11,21] has always been a research hotspot. By predicting the possible future phenomena, the current state can be adjusted appropriately. In the time series prediction, a common method is to use regression linear model. Quan et al. [16] established support vector regression model to predict reservoir water temperature based on reservoir temperature data. Liu et al. [9] used Gaussian process regression model to predict the capacity of lithium battery. Menon et al. [12] used multiple linear regression to predict the development trend of urban temperature. And there are also some studies using local sensitive hashing technology for prediction [13–15]. However, the above models only used the approximate value to predict the temperature, and could not explore the internal relationship between the temperature changes.

With the emergence of neural network, some researchers began to use neural network to solve the prediction problem [10]. He et al. [5] used artificial neural network (ANN) to predict the temperature of transformer. Liu et al. [3] developed a series of ANN algorithms to predict outdoor temperature. Compared with some linear regression models, experiments show that the NN method is better than linear regression method. Su et al. [18] put forward an ANN method, which uses the ambient temperature, bottom temperature, load current and other factors in the transformer to establish a prediction model. Le et al. [8] used Bayesian neural network to predict the critical temperature of superconductors. Taheri et al. [20] proposed an oil temperature prediction model based on basic heat transfer theory by using the concept of thermal resistance. Thus, the life loss of transformer is predicted, which contributed to the normal operation of power system. Taheri et al. [19] considered that the transformer oil temperature will directly affect the life of transformer. They analyzed the influence of solar radiation on oil temperature by using the concept of thermal resistance. Li et al. [17] established a three-dimensional temperature field model of transformer and used gray neural network to predict temperature, including the top oil temperature, middle temperature and bottom temperature. Pan et al. [22] used Back Propagation (BP) neural network based on Adam optimization to predict transformer oil temperature. They used the historical data of oil temperature as input to predict the transformer's future oil temperature. And Adam optimization algorithm [7] is a stochastic optimization algorithm with excellent performance in deep learning. This model not only improved the accuracy of oil temperature prediction, but also could be applied to different transformers. It provided a reliable basis for maintaining the stable operation of the voltage transformer. Xu et al. [23] used the improved BP neural network model to predict the winter road temperature. They combine dynamic and static prediction methods to predict the temperature, which has great significance on the establishment of road icing early warning system.

However, the above neural network-based methods rarely consider the interaction between historical items. The oil temperature will be affected by historical oil temperature. Therefore, we proposed to use GRU to predict transformer oil temperature. GRU can capture the dependence of oil temperature, and is less prone to gradient disappearance. In addition, in order to focus on the short-term changes of oil temperature, we add a time sliding window to GRU.

3   Gated Recurrent Unit Model for Oil Temperature Prediction

3.1   Problem Definition

Here, we define the symbols we used in this paper.

(1) $OI = \{oi_1, oi_2, ..., oi_m\}$ donates the historical temperature change record of a transformer, where oi_t is the top oil temperature of a transformer at time t.

(2) $TR = \{tr_1, tr_2..., tr_n\}$ donates a set of all transformers. In this paper, we use two different transformers' oil temperature data to demonstrate that our model can be applied to different transformers.

(3) oi_m^n donates the oil temperature of transformer n at time m.

Oil Temperature Prediction. For the transformer, we use the transformer's historical temperature to predict the oil temperature change in the future.

3.2 GRU Model

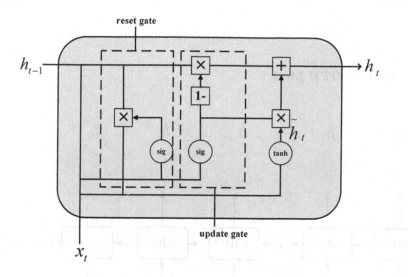

Fig. 2. The GRU model we used in this paper.

The principle of GRU is similar to long short-term memory (LSTM). And they are variants of recurrent neural networks. The GRU unit is shown in Fig. 2. GRU has two gates, update gate and reset gate. It can save the information in the long-term series, and it will not be clear over time. It is worth mentioning that when reset gate = 1 and update gate = 0, GRU is equal to RNN. At time t, we use (1) to calculate the update gate:

$$z_t = \sigma\left(w^{(z)}x_t + u^{(z)}h_{t-1}\right) \tag{1}$$

where x_t represents the t-th component of the input sequence, h_{t-1} donates the information of previous t-1 time step, $w^{(z)}$ and $u^{(z)}$ represent the weight of the update gate. The update gate transforms the information of x_t and h_{t-1}, adds them and inputs them into sigmoid function. Again, we use (2) to calculate the reset gate:

$$r_t = \sigma\left(w^{(r)}x_t + u^{(r)}h_{t-1}\right) \tag{2}$$

where x_t and h_{t-1} are the same as in (1), $w^{(r)}$ and $u^{(r)}$ represent the weight of the reset gate. The calculation of the update gate and the reset gate is the same, but the parameters and functions of these two gates are different. Then, candidate status calculation expression is as follows:

$$h'_t = \tanh\left(wx_t + r_t \odot uh_{t-1}\right) \tag{3}$$

Finally, we calculate the information that needs to be passed to the next unit. In this process, we need to use the update gate. This process can be expressed as follows:

$$h_t = z_t \odot h_{t-1} + (1 - z_t) \odot h'_t \tag{4}$$

3.3   *GRU − OTP* Model

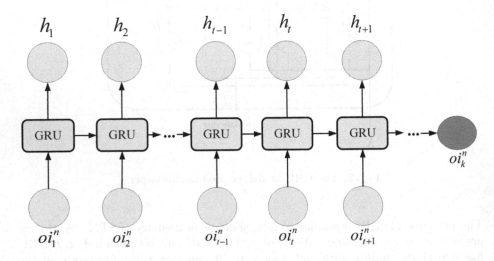

Fig. 3. The basic architecture of $GRU - OTP$.

In this section, we introduce the implementation of our model. The basic diagram of GRU-OTP model is shown in Fig. 3. Firstly, for the oil temperature of the transformer to be predicted, we input the collected historical temperature into the GRU according to the time series. First, we input the oil temperature sequence to the update gate in turn. For the oil temperature at time t, we add it with the previous GRU unit output, and then we input them to the sigmoid activation function. Therefore, the calculation formula of GRU update gate used in this paper is as follows:

$$Z_t = \sigma \left(W^{(Z)} oi_t^n + U^{(Z)} H_{t-1} \right) \tag{5}$$

where oi_t^n represents the transformer's temperature at time t, H_{t-1} represents the hidden information of the previous unit, $W^{(Z)}$ and $U^{(Z)}$ represent the weight of the update gate we used. Then, the calculation process of reset gate is the same as that update gate, and the calculation is as follows:

$$R_t = \sigma \left(W^{(R)} oi_t^n + U^{(R)} H_{t-1} \right) \tag{6}$$

where $W^{(Z)}$ and $U^{(Z)}$ represent the weight of the reset gate we used. Then, we use the following (7) to calculate what the current GRU unit needs to remember.

$$H'_t = \tanh\left(W oi^n_t + R_t \odot U H_{t-1}\right) \tag{7}$$

Finally, the (8) can be used to calculate the output of the current GRU unit. Through the model's training, we can finally get the transformer oil temperature oi^n_k at time k.

$$H_t = Z_t \odot H_{t-1} + (1 - Z_t) \odot H'_t \tag{8}$$

GRU can capture the long time dependence of temperature series. Again, in order to pay attention to short-term changes of oil temperature, we processed the data before entering it into GRU. We added a time sliding window for oil temperature data. The time sliding window can reflect the short-term change of oil temperature as a whole. Moreover, we choose the appropriate size for the time sliding window through experiments. Finally, the algorithm of GRU-OTP model is shown in Algorithm 1.

Algorithm 1. GRU-OTP model

Require: $OI = \{oi_1, oi_2, ..., oi_m\}$: temperature set, $TR = \{tr_1, tr_2\}$: transformer set
Ensure: RMSE of GRU-OTP model.
   //Training of GRU-OTP model
1: **for** i = 1 to m-5 **do**
2:    Add sliding window to oil temperature records $(oi_i - oi_{i+5} \rightarrow oi_{i+6})$
3: **end for**
   //Initialize parameter set P
4: **for** j = 1 to 2 **do**
5:    **for** i = 1 to m-5 **do**
6:      Randomly select a batch of check-in records
7:      Train the optimal P
8:    **end for**
9: **end for**
   //Calculate RMSE
10: **for** predicted $oi^{n'}_k$ **do**
11:    RMSE $= \sqrt{\frac{1}{N}\sum_{i=1}^{N}\left(oi^{n'}_k - oi^n_k\right)^2}$
12: **end for**
13: **return** RMSE of GRU-OTP model.

---

4 Experiments

4.1 Dataset and Evaluation Index

We used the oil temperature data of two real transformers [28]. The transformer oil temperature is detected every hour for two years, including 17420 data points.

We take the first 80% of the dataset as the training set and the last 20% as the test set.

RMSE is used to measure the deviation between the predicted value and the real value. Iis formula is as follows:

$$\text{RMSE} = \sqrt{\frac{1}{N} \sum_{i=1}^{N} (oi_k^{n\prime} - oi_k^{n})^2} \tag{9}$$

where $oi_k^{n\prime}$ donates the predicted oil temperature and oi_k^{n} donates the real oil temperature.

4.2 Parameters

The parameters setting will affect the GRU-OTP model's performance. Therefore, it is necessary to set better parameters for the model. We set the time sliding window's size to 5-h, 10-h, 15-h and 20-h respectively. It can be seen from Fig. 4 that the RMSE of the test set no longer decreases with the time sliding window increases. Therefore, we set the sliding window = 5-h. The embedding dimension of GRU also affects the model's performance. We set the embedding dimensions to 20, 40, 60, 80 and 100 respectively. As can be seen from Fig. 5, when the embedding dimension = 100, the model's RMSE is the lowest.

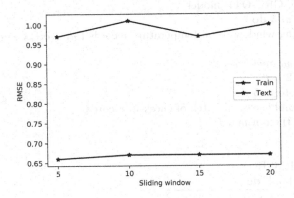

Fig. 4. The sliding window size influence on GRU-OTP performance.

4.3 Results

We compare GRU-OTP model with RNN model and LSTM [6] model. In addition, we have performed oil temperature predictions on two different transformers, and the experimental results are shown in Fig. 6. In the first transformer, RNN model's RMSE = 0.7, LSTM model's RMSE = 0.67, GRU-OTP model's RMSE = 0.66. In the second transformer, RNN model's RMSE = 1.19, LSTM model's RMSE = 0.98, GRU-OTP model's RMSE = 0.89. Therefore, It shows that GRU-OTP model can be applied to different transformers and achieve better performance.

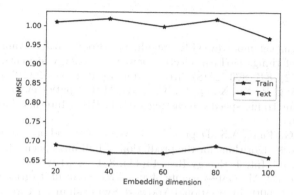

Fig. 5. The embedding dimension influence on GRU-OTP performance.

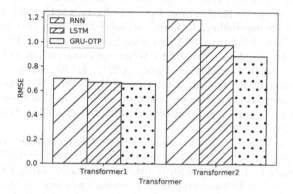

Fig. 6. Prediction accuracy comparison.

5   Conclusion

We propose a GRU-OTP model for transformer oil temperature prediction. Considering the influence of historical oil temperature on future oil temperature, we introduce the time sliding window concept to focus on the short-term influence between historical oil temperatures, and use GRU to focus on the long-term influence between historical oil temperatures. Experiments have proved the effectiveness and feasibility of our model.

In future work, we will consider more influencing factors to predict the life of transformers, coordinate power resource allocation and maintain the stable operation of power system.

Acknowledgment. This work was supported by the National Natural Science Foundation of China (No. 61872219).

References

1. Bedi, G., Venayagamoorthy, G.K., Singh, R., Brooks, R.R., Wang, K.C.: Review of internet of things (IoT) in electric power and energy systems. IEEE Internet Things J. **5**(2), 847–870 (2018). https://doi.org/10.1109/JIOT.2018.2802704
2. Dai, F., Huang, P., Xu, X., Qi, L., Khosravi, M.R.: Spatio-temporal deep learning framework for traffic speed forecasting in IoT. IEEE Internet Things Mag. **3**(4), 66–69 (2020)
3. Demirezen, G., Fung, A.S., Deprez, M.: Development and optimization of artificial neural network algorithms for the prediction of building specific local temperature for hvac control. Int. J. Energy Res. **44**(11), 8513–8531 (2020)
4. Dey, R., Salem, F.M.: Gate-variants of gated recurrent unit (gru) neural networks. In: 2017 IEEE 60th International Midwest Symposium on Circuits and Systems (MWSCAS), pp. 1597–1600. IEEE (2017)
5. He, Q., Si, J., Tylavsky, D.J.: Prediction of top-oil temperature for transformers using neural networks. IEEE Trans. Power Delivery **15**(4), 1205–1211 (2000)
6. Hochreiter, S., Schmidhuber, J.: Lstm can solve hard long time lag problems. In: Advances in Neural Information Processing Systems, pp. 473–479 (1997)
7. Jais, I.K.M., Ismail, A.R., Nisa, S.Q.: Adam optimization algorithm for wide and deep neural network. Knowl. Eng. Data Sci **2**(1), 41–46 (2019)
8. Le, T.D., Noumeir, R., Quach, H.L., Kim, J.H., Kim, J.H., Kim, H.M.: Critical temperature prediction for a superconductor: a variational bayesian neural network approach. IEEE Trans. Appl. Supercond. **30**(4), 1–5 (2020). https://doi.org/10.1109/TASC.2020.2971456
9. Liu, K., Hu, X., Wei, Z., Li, Y., Jiang, Y.: Modified gaussian process regression models for cyclic capacity prediction of lithium-ion batteries. IEEE Trans. Transp. Electrification **5**(4), 1225–1236 (2019). https://doi.org/10.1109/TTE.2019.2944802
10. Liu, Q., et al.: A fully connected deep learning approach to upper limb gesture recognition in a secure fes rehabilitation environment. Int. J. Intell. Syst. **36**(5), 2387–2411 (2021)
11. Liu, Y., et al.: An attention-based category-aware gru model for the next poi recommendation. Int. J. Intell. Syst. **36**(7), 3174–3189 (2021)
12. Menon, S.P., Bharadwaj, R., Shetty, P., Sanu, P., Nagendra, S.: Prediction of temperature using linear regression. In: 2017 International Conference on Electrical, Electronics, Communication, Computer, and Optimization Techniques (ICEECCOT), pp. 1–6 (2017). https://doi.org/10.1109/ICEECCOT.2017.8284588
13. Qi, L., Wang, R., Hu, C., Li, S., He, Q., Xu, X.: Time-aware distributed service recommendation with privacy-preservation. Inf. Sci. **480**, 354–364 (2019)
14. Qi, L., Zhang, X., Dou, W., Hu, C., Yang, C., Chen, J.: A two-stage locality-sensitive hashing based approach for privacy-preserving mobile service recommendation in cross-platform edge environment. Futur. Gener. Comput. Syst. **88**, 636–643 (2018)
15. Qi, L., Zhang, X., Dou, W., Ni, Q.: A distributed locality-sensitive hashing-based approach for cloud service recommendation from multi-source data. IEEE J. Sel. Areas Commun. **35**(11), 2616–2624 (2017)
16. Quan, Q., Hao, Z., Xifeng, H., Jingchun, L.: Research on water temperature prediction based on improved support vector regression. Neural Comput. Appl., 1–10 (2020). https://doi.org/10.1007/s00521-020-04836-4
17. Shuqing, L., Ding, C., Qunhui, Q., Jianli, S., Weiming, X., Xiao, S.: Transformer winding hot-spot temperature prediction based on the grey neural network. Automation & Instrumentation, p. 04 (2017)

18. Su, X., Pan, C., Yang, X., Zou, J.: Application of elman neural network in top oil temperature prediction of transformer. In: 2018 IEEE International Conference on High Voltage Engineering and Application (ICHVE), pp. 1–4 (2018). https://doi. org/10.1109/ICHVE.2018.8641891

19. Taheri, A.A., Abdali, A., Rabiee, A.: A novel model for thermal behavior prediction of oil-immersed distribution transformers with consideration of solar radiation. IEEE Trans. Power Delivery **34**(4), 1634–1646 (2019). https://doi.org/10.1109/ TPWRD.2019.2916664

20. Taheri, A.A., Abdali, A., Rabiee, A.: Indoor distribution transformers oil temperature prediction using new electro-thermal resistance model and normal cyclic overloading strategy: an experimental case study. IET Generation, Transmission Distribution **14**(24), 5792–5803 (2020)

21. Wang, F., Zhu, M., Wang, M., Khosravi, M.R., Ni, Q., Yu, S., Qi, L.: 6g-enabled short-term forecasting for large-scale traffic flow in massive IoT based on time-aware locality-sensitive hashing. IEEE Internet Things J. **8**(7), 5321–5331 (2021). https://doi.org/10.1109/JIOT.2020.3037669

22. Wenxia, P., Kun, Z., Tianao, G., Congchuang, G.: Neural networks applied in the prediction of top oil temperature of transformer. In: 2019 International Joint Conference on Neural Networks (IJCNN), pp. 1–7 (2019). https://doi.org/10.1109/ IJCNN.2019.8852072

23. Xu, B., Dan, H.C., Li, L.: Temperature prediction model of asphalt pavement in cold regions based on an improved BP neural network. Appl. Therm. Eng. **120**, 568–580 (2017)

24. Xu, X., Liu, X., Yin, X., Wang, S., Qi, Q., Qi, L.: Privacy-aware offloading for training tasks of generative adversarial network in edge computing. Inf. Sci. **532**, 1–15 (2020)

25. Xu, X., et al.: Service offloading with deep q-network for digital twinning empowered internet of vehicles in edge computing. IEEE Trans. Ind. Inform., 1 (2020). DOI: https://doi.org/10.1109/TII.2020.3040180

26. Xu, X., Wu, Q., Qi, L., Dou, W., Tsai, S.B., Bhuiyan, M.Z.A.: Trust-aware service offloading for video surveillance in edge computing enabled internet of vehicles. IEEE Trans. Intell. Transp. Syst. **22**(3), 1787–1796 (2021). https://doi.org/10. 1109/TITS.2020.2995622

27. Xu, X., Yao, L., Bilal, M., Wan, S., Dai, F., Choo, K.K.R.: Service migration across edge devices in 6g-enabled internet of vehicles networks. IEEE Internet Things J., 1 (2021). https://doi.org/10.1109/JIOT.2021.3089204

28. Zhou, H., et al.: Informer: beyond efficient transformer for long sequence time-series forecasting. In: The Thirty-Fifth AAAI Conference on Artificial Intelligence, AAAI 2021, Virtual Conference. vol. 35, pp. 11106–11115. AAAI Press (2021)

Towards Making More Reliable Cardiotocogram Data Prediction with Limited Expert Knowledge: Exploiting Unlabeled Data with Semi-supervised Boosting Method

Jiaming Hong[1,2], Chen Qin[1], Yun Huang[3(✉)], and Yin Zhou[4(✉)]

[1] School of Medical Information Engineering, Guangzhou University of Chinese Medicine, Guangzhou, China
[2] Guangdong Key Laboratory of Big Data Analysis and Processing, Guangzhou, China
[3] Software College, Jishou University, Zhangjiajie, China
huangyun109@sina.com
[4] School of Computer Science, Shenzhen Institute of Information Technology, Shenzhen, China

Abstract. Cardiotocography (CTG) is frequently used as a method of diagnosing fetal distress during pregnancy and delivery, including listening to Fetal Heart Rate (FHR) and monitoring Uterine Contractions (UC). Many scholars have contributed to classify CTG data through machine learning methods, intending to reduce the consuming-time and mistakes during obstetricians' identification. In this study, we used repeated holdout cross-validation for data pre-processing and classified the CTG dataset as a normal class and pathological class. Sensitivity, specificity, accuracy, and AUC were involved to measure the performance of the models. According to the results of ASSEMBLE AdaBoost and AdaBoost, we can conclude that ASSEMBLE AdaBoost is robust in the classification of CTG data. Training with few labeled data and amounts of unlabeled data, ASSEMBLE AdaBoost achieved an accuracy of over 90%, which was superior to AdaBoost.

Keywords: Cardiotocography · SVM · AdaBoost · Semi-supervised learning · Machine learning · Ensemble learning

1 Introduction

In the early nineteenth century, de Kergeradee first pointed out that it might be clinically useful to listen to the baby's heartbeat (Grant 1989a). It could be used to observe fetal life and multiple pregnancies. From then on, different approaches of listening to the fetal heart were invented to improve outcomes for the fetus and reduce the heartache for gravida. Cardiotocography (CTG) is widely used in fetal health monitoring. It is a technique for recording Fetal Heart Rate (FHR) and Uterine Contractions (UC) synchronously during pregnancy, typically in the third trimester to evaluate maternal and fetal well-being [1, 2].

© Springer Nature Singapore Pte Ltd. 2021
Y. Tan et al. (Eds.): DMBD 2021, CCIS 1453, pp. 422–435, 2021.
https://doi.org/10.1007/978-981-16-7476-1_37

Most pregnant women are prone to choose remote monitoring to monitor the health of the fetus because it has the advantages of simplicity, safety, effectiveness and reduction of time and space costs. After collecting CTG data, the central station would send the data to specialists. However, a doctor would probably make mistakes if he/she marks the sample on his/her own. The deficient interpretation of CTG data led to unnecessary surgical intervention. To ensure the accuracy of diagnosis and reduce the error rate at the same time, more than an expert is needed to mark the sample repeatedly. This complex procedure makes the human and time cost of labeling data extremely high [3].

Although the quantity of real clinical CTG data is limited and the fetal distress is difficult to be artificially classified, various machine learning methods for CTG data classification were proposed by scholars. Mei-Ling Huang, Yung-Yan Hsu [4] predicted fetal distress using discriminant analysis, decision tree, and artificial neural network. The accuracies of DA, DT and ANN were 82.1%, 86.36%, and 97.78%, respectively. Paul Fergus et al. [5] trained deep learning classifier, random forest classifier, fishers linear discriminant analysis classifier in conjunction with synthetic minority oversampling technique (SMOTE). The results indicated that applying a deep learning classifier could achieve 94% for sensitivity, 91% for specificity, and 99% for AUC. Sundar C. et al. [6] implemented a CTG data classification system using a supervised artificial neural network (ANN). In the case of normal and pathological records, it could give good precision, recall, and f-score, but poor performance in the case of suspicious records. Syed Ahsin Ali Shah et al. [7] combined bagging approach with three traditional decision trees algorithms (random forest, Reduced Error Pruning Tree (REPTree) and J48) to identify normal and pathological fetal state using CTG data. All three classifiers have shown nearly similar classification accuracies on full features set, while random forest performed slightly better (94.7%).

In similar studies, AdaBoost is also regarded as an excellent method. Esra Mahsereci Karabulut et al. [8] applied a Based Adaptive Boosting Approach to CTG data. The most remarkable result belonged to the decision-tree based AdaBoost algorithm with 0.861 kappa statistics and 95.01% accuracy. Yang Zhang and Zhidong Zhao [9] showed the performance of hybrid PCA and AdaBoost for classifying fetal state. The experiment indicated that selecting 5 features improves classification accuracy for AdaBoost as compared to full features (98.6% for the former and 93% for the latter).

Esra Mahsereci Karabulut et al. [8] and Yang Zhang, Zhidong Zhao [9] employed ten-fold cross validation technique to assess their models, and Paul Fergus et al. [5] used five-fold cross validation, and Mei-Ling Huang, Yung-Yan Hsu [4] trained models with 80% dataset. In this paper, we applied the ASSEMBLE method to the CTG dataset. The proportion of training data in ASSEMBLE Adaboost was just 60%. Since the unlabeled data method was applied, the percentage of the labeled data we needed was no more than 10%, which was superior to the methods mentioned before.

The ASSEMBLE method combines the semi-supervised method and ensemble method. Unlike supervised method, the semi-supervised method selects unlabeled examples in each iteration, having less requirement for the quantity of labeled data. In the NIPS 2001 competition on semi-supervised datasets, ASSEMBLE based on decision tree won the first place. Kristin P. Bennett et al. [10] trained the ASSEMBLE estimator based on neural networks and the ASSEMBLE AdaBoost estimator based on decision tree using breast-cancer-wisconsin, pima-indians diabetes, and letter-recognition drawn from the UCI Machine Learning repository. The experiment exposed that the performance of ASSEMBLE surpassed that of AdaBoost. Considering the robustness of the ASSEMBLE AdaBoost based on decision tree, we applied it to the classification of the CTG dataset.

Criteria such as sensitivity, specificity, accuracy, AUC are considered to measure the performance of the classifiers. We compared the performance of the ASSEMBLE AdaBoost algorithm and the AdaBoost algorithm. The ASSEMEMBLE AdaBoost classifier achieved 0.97 for sensitivity, 0.64 for specificity, 0.90 for accuracy, 0.81 for AUC, while the classifier based on supervised AdaBoost achieved 0.94 for sensitivity, 0.73 for specificity, 0.86 for accuracy, 0.84 for AUC, indicating that the ASSEMBLE AdaBoost classifier did better in classifying CTG data, especially for the normal class.

2   Meterial and Methods

2.1   Dataset

In this study, we used the Cardiotocography (CTG) dataset which is publicly available at "The Data Mining Repository of University of California Irvine (UCI)". This dataset includes 21 attributes and 2126 instances which is 1655 normal, 295 suspicious and 176 pathologic. All attributes are numeric. The CTG dataset consists of the measurement of Fetal Heat Rate (FHR) and Uterine Contraction (UC) features. By using the given attributes data, doctors can evaluate maternal and fetal well-being during pregnancy and before delivery [11].

Attribute Information:

- LB—FHR baseline(beats per minute)
- AC—# of accelerations per second
- FM—# of fetal movements per second
- UC—# of uterine contractions per second
- DL—# of light decelerations per second
- DS—# of severe decelerations per second
- DP—# of prolonged decelerations per second
- ASTV— percentage of time with abnormal short term variability
- MSTV—mean value of short term variability
- ALTV—percentage of time with abnormal long term variability
- MLTV—mean value of long term variability
- Width—width of FHR histogram
- Min—minimum of FHR histogram
- Max—maximum of FHR histogram
- Nmax—# of histogram peaks
- Nzeros—# of histogram zeros
- Mode—histogram mode
- Mean—histogram mean
- Median—histogram median
- Variance—histogram variance

- Tendency—histogram tendency
- CLASS—FHR pattern class code (1 to 10)
- NSP—fetal state class code (N = normal; S = suspect; P = pathologic).

Class Information: Table 1. shows the descriptions of a three-class fetal state classification.

Table 1. Descriptions of fetal state classification

Class information	Description
Normal	All four features fall into the reassuring category
Suspicious	Features fall into one of the non-reassuring categories and the reassuring category and the remainder of the features are reassuring
Pathological	Features fall into two or more of the non-reassuring categories and the reassuring category or two or more abnormal categories

2.2 Data Pre-processing

Cross Validation. The performance of the algorithms should be estimated overall, thus repeated holdout cross-validation was involved as a way of splitting dataset for training set and test set [12]. Meanwhile, a fixed ratio was used in the of the split of the CTG dataset. The overall performances of the classifiers were determined after the predictions of the testing subset on several split.

Dataset Standardization. Feature standardization is widely used in machine learning. The magnitude difference among the data is so large that the machine learning estimators can not correctly learn the feature with a small magnitude, so the data is supposed to be standardized. Z-scores were adopted as the standard scores, derived by the mean and the standard deviation of each feature. Assume $z = \frac{x - \bar{x}}{\sigma}$, where z is the z-score of the feature, x is the feature vector, $\bar{x}$ is the mean of that feature vector, and σ is its standard deviation.

2.3 Classification

AdaBoost. The Adaptive Boosting (AdaBoost) algorithm is the most popular boosting ensemble method and has made great success in enhancing the accuracy of the best learner. It is a machine learning algorithm that first introduced by Freund and Schapire in 1995 [13]. AdaBoost is underlying the theory of Boosting (Schapire 1999). The advantages of this algorithm are it is fast, easy to implement and except for the number of iterations there are no parameters to set. Moreover, AdaBoost can process noisy data and identify outliers.

The idea behind AdaBoost is to maintain repeatedly a distribution or set of weights over the training set in a series of iterations and combine into a weighted majority vote to get high accuracy. The algorithm focuses on the sample incorrectly classified. Each sample is given the same weight in the first round of iteration. In the next iteration, the algorithm will increase the weights of samples misclassified by the base classifier in the last iteration and decrease the weights of samples correctly classified. In the weighted voting system, each base weak classifier holds different power. The base classifiers with a low error rate will get higher weights and high error rate one will get lower weights. After certain times of iterations, the algorithm combines the base weak classifiers and build a strong classifier to get the final classification result. The Ada-Boost algorithm is presented in nine steps below:

1. Input: training set $T = \{(x_1, y_1), (x_2, y_2), \ldots, (x_n, y_n)\}$; $x_i \in X \in R_n$, $y \in \{-1, +1\}$
2. Initialise the weights of $D_i = (w_{1,1}, w_{1,2}, \ldots, w_{1,i})$, $w_{1,i} = \frac{1}{N}$, $i = 1, 2, \ldots, N$
3. for m = 1, 2, ..., M
4. Train weak classifier $G_m(x)$ using distribution D_m
5. Get weak hypothesis with its error rate:

$$e_m = \sum_{i=1}^{N} w_{m,i} I(G_m(x_i) \neq y_i) \tag{1}$$

6. Get the weight of weak classifier $G_m(x)$:

$$\alpha_m = \frac{1}{2} \log \frac{1-e_m}{e_m} \tag{2}$$

7. Update:

$$w_{m+1,i} = \frac{w_{m,i}}{z_m} exp(-\alpha_m y_i G_m(x_i)), \quad i = 1, 2, \ldots, 10 \tag{3}$$

$$z_m = \sum_{i=1}^{N} w_{m,i} exp(-\alpha_m y_i G_m(x_i)) \tag{4}$$

where z_m is a normalization factor (chosen so that D_{k+1} will be a distribution).

8. Output final hypothesis:

$$F(x) = sign\left(\sum_{i=1}^{N} \alpha_m G_m(x)\right) \tag{5}$$

The AdaBoost algorithm requires user little prior knowledge which makes medical practitioners manage to concentrate on other more important aspects. However, it can fail to improve the performance of the base classifiers when there are insufficient data.

ASSEMBLE AdaBoost. Semi-supervised learning is a method to train a model with a limited number of labeled data and many unlabeled data [14]. Using a semi-supervised method to improve performance has become popular in the field of machine learning [15].

There are three typical semi-supervised hypotheses: Cluster Assumption, Continuity Assumption and Manifold Assumption. Cluster Assumption is a smoothness assumption means that two samples of close neighbors in a high-density region are more likely to share a label. Semi-supervised methods adopting Cluster Assumption vary from Co-training method, TSVM, to ASSEMBLE [16].

ASSEMBLE assigns "pseudo-classes" to the unlabeled data using the existing ensemble and construct the next base classifier using both the labeled and pseudo-labeled data. Classification boosting corresponds to maximizing the margin measured on labeled data, while ASSEMBLE can be regarded as maximizing the margin in function space of both the labeled and unlabeled data.

Let the labeled training data L and unlabeled training data U. Assume $x_1 \ldots x_n$ be the 21-dimensional points and $y_1 \ldots y_n$ to be the labels, where $y \in \{-1, +1\}$, with n being the number of the samples. $f_j(x)$ denotes the mean of base classifiers where f_j is the jth classifier in the ensemble. The ensemble classifier $F(x)$ is constructed by a linear combination of the J base classifiers $F(x) = \sum_{j=1}^{J} w_j f_j(x)$ where w_j is the weighting term for the jth classifier. For labeled data points, the margin is $y_i(F_t(x_i) + w_{t+1}f_t(x_i))$, where y_j is the true label of the point. For unlabeled data points, the margin is $|(F_t(x_i) + w_{t+1}f_t(x_i))|$, where y_j is the pseudo-class of the point. If the point of labeled data is correctly classified, the margin is positive, and negative if wrongly classified.

The ASSEMBLE cost for AdaBoost:

$$\sum_{i \in labeled} \alpha_i M(y_i(F_t(x_i) + w_{t+1}f_t(x_i)))$$
$$+ \sum_{i \in unlabeled} \alpha_i M(|(F_t(x_i) + w_{t+1}f_t(x_i))|) \tag{6}$$

where α_i is used to weight the data and $M(x) = e^x$. M is a monotonically decreasing function, thus,

$$M(y_i(F_t(x_i) + w_{t+1}f_t(x_i))) \geq M(|(F_t(x_i) + w_{t+1}f_t(x_i))|) \tag{7}$$

and

$$\sum_i \alpha_i M(y_i(F_t(x_i) + w_{t+1}f_{t+1}(x_i))) \tag{8}$$

provides an upper bound on the true cost function.

As a result, pseudo-cost function must strictly decrease if the upper bound decrease. Moreover, if the model is not optimal, the strictly decrease of the pseudo-cost function is always possible.

Table 2. Process of the ASSEMBLE Adaboost

Algorithm: ASSEMBLE AdaBoost
1   $Let\ l := |L|\ and\ u := |U|$
2   $Let\ y_i := c\ where\ c\ is\ predicted\ by\ SVM\ for\ i \in U$
3   $Set\ D_1(i)$
4   $Let\ f_1 := \mathcal{L}(L + U, Y, D_1)$
5   $for\ t := 1\ to\ T\ do$
6   $\quad Let\ \hat{y}_i := f_t(x_i), i = 1 \dots l + u$
7   $\quad \epsilon = \sum_i D_t[y_i \neq \hat{y}_i], i = 1 \dots l + u$
8   $\quad If\ \epsilon > 0.5\ then\ Stop$
9   $\quad \omega_t = 0.5 * log(\frac{1-\epsilon}{\epsilon})$
10 $\quad Let\ F_t := F_{t-1} + \omega_t f_t$
11 $\quad Let\ y_i = F_t(x_i)\ if\ i \in U$
12 $\quad Let\ D_{t+1}\ as\ \frac{\alpha_i e^{-y_i F_{t+1}(x_i)}}{\sum_j \alpha_j e^{-y_j F_{t+1}(x_j)}}\ for\ all\ i$
13 $\quad S = Sample(L + U, l, D_{t+1})$
14 $\quad f_{t+1} = \mathcal{L}(S, Y, D_{t+1})$
15 $end\ for$
16 $return\ F_{T+1}$

The process of the ASSEMBLE Adaboost has been shown in Table 2. T is the number of the algorithm training iteration. $\mathcal{L}(S, Y, D_{t+1})$ is an algorithm to construct a base learner according to the data points S with current labels Y and D_{t+1} calculated from current distribution D_t.

Although AdaBoost performs as well in some properties as the ASSEMBLE AdaBoost, ASSEMBLE is an alternative for the experiment. AdaBoost tends to overfit while for the ASSEMBLE AdaBoost, maximizing the margin in function space of training data can prevent overfitting. Samples used for training are the same, thus ASSEMBLE AdaBoost has similar computational complexity with AdaBoost.

Figure 1 illustrates the detailed flow chart of the ASSEMBLE AdaBoost algorithm applied in this study.

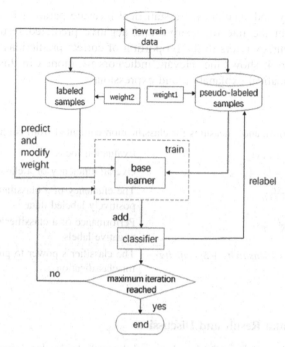

Fig. 1. Flow chart of ASSEMBLE AdaBoost

3 Result and Discussion

3.1 Performance Evaluation Indexes

There are some valuable performance evaluation parameters for classification according to the result. In this study, positive refers to the normal class and negative refers to the pathological class. The confusion matrix has four basic indicators, which are true positives (TP), true negatives (TN), false positives (FP) and false negatives (FN), represents true classification for positive sample, true classification for negative sample, false classification for positive samples and false classification for negative samples, respectively. The confusion matrix is used to compute the efficiency of a classifier, shown in Table 3.

Table 3. Confusion matrix

Predicted	Actual	
	Positive (normal)	Negative (pathological)
Positive	TP	FP
Negative	FN	TN

The sensitivity and specificity are statistical measure parameters of classification, and they represent the rate of positive and negative predicted results respectively. Classification accuracy refers to the proportion of correct predictions in all classification results. Table 4. shows the relevant indicators mentioned in this paper with the respective mathematical explanation and expressions.

Table 4. Performance measures for classification computed from confusion matrix

Measure	Formula	Evaluation focus
Accuracy	$\frac{TP+TN}{TP+TN+FP+FN}$	Overall efficiency of a classifier
Sensitivity (Recall)	$\frac{TP}{TP+FN}$	The efficiency of a classifier to categorize positively labeled data
Specificity	$\frac{TN}{TN+FP}$	Performance of a classifier when categorize negative labels
AUC	$\frac{1}{2} * (Sensitivity + Specificity)$	The classifier's power to prevent misclassification

3.2 Experimental Result and Discussion

Firstly, we combined the suspicious class and the pathologic class as negative class and the normal class was positive class. After that, we standardized the dataset using z-scores. The whole dataset was divided into training set and testing set and the proportion of testing set was fixed at 40%. Then, randomly divided the training set and test set 10 times. We separated training set into labeled data and unlabeled data and used Support Vector Machine (SVM) to train labeled data. We assigned "pseudo-classes" to unlabeled data.

Secondly, we set the initial weights of training data in the ASSEMBLE AdaBoost algorithm. Due to the data imbalance in the CTG dataset, we set multiple parameters to set the weights of the data. The total weights of labeled data accounted for 0.2 of the total weights of the training set. In labeled data, the rate of the total weights of the data labeled -1 to the total weights of the data labeled 1 was 0.5. In unlabeled data, the rate of the total weights of the wrongly classified data to the total weights of the correctly classified data was 0.55. The ratio of labeled data weights in total weights of training data was 0.2.

Finally, repeated holdout cross-validation was used as a model of performance evaluation on changing the ratio of labeled data to unlabeled data in the training set. To simulate the real situation that the quantity unlabeled data is far more than the quantity of labeled data, we set 0.1, 0.15, 0.2, 0.25 as the proportion of labeled data in training set respectively. In cross-validation, we chose Decision Tree as the base classifier and got the results to make a comparison between AdaBoost and ASSEMBLE AdaBoost.

To sum up, Fig. 2 shows the detailed flow chart of the whole procedure applied in this study.

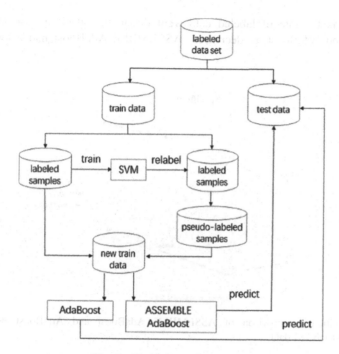

Fig. 2. Flow chart of this study

Figure 3 compares the variation of AUC of the AdaBoost algorithm and the ASSEMBLE AdaBoost algorithm. Under the four proportions of labeled data, AUC of ASSEMBLE AdaBoost (from 80.181% to 82.55%) was lower than that of AdaBoost (from 84.299% to 88.456%). In Fig. 4, the specificity of ASSEMBLE AdaBoost (from 62.783% to 67.239%) was significantly lower than that of AdaBoost (from 73.39% to

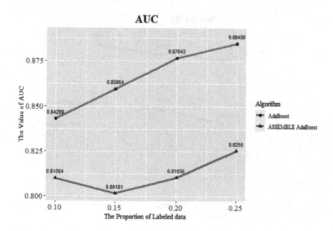

Fig. 3. AUC comparison of ASSEMBLE AdaBoost and AdaBoost with different proportions of labeled data

80.434%). As the rate of labeled data went down, the specificity of ASSEMBLE AdaBoost and AdaBoost all decreased. ASSEMBLE AdaBoost had a low value of specificity.

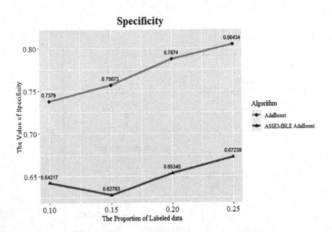

Fig. 4. Specificity comparison of ASSEMBLE AdaBoost and AdaBoost with different proportions of labeled data

Figure 5 visually presents that the sensitivity of ASSEMBLE AdaBoost (from 97.582% to 97.87%) was higher than that of AdaBoost (from 94.814% to 96.549%). With the decline of the proportion of labeled data, the sensitivity of AdaBoost decreased but the sensitivity of ASSEMBLE AdaBoost did not change much, stable at about 97%. In addition, Fig. 6 shows that with the reduction of the proportion of labeled data, the accuracy of ASSEMBLE AdaBoost had a little change (from 90.903% to 89.265%), while there was a big drop in the accuracy of AdaBoost (from 90.676% to 86.602%).

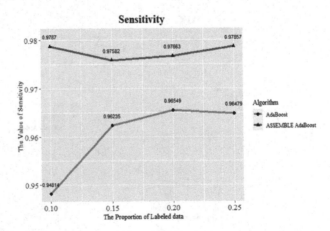

Fig. 5. Sensitivity comparison of ASSEMBLE AdaBoost and AdaBoost with different proportions of labeled data

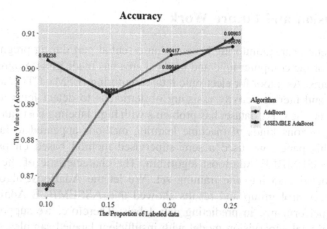

Fig. 6. Accuracy comparison of ASSEMBLE AdaBoost and AdaBoost with different proportions of labeled data

Table 5 is the experimental results when the rate of labeled data was 0.1. The amount of labeled data was the least, which could perfectly reflect the performance between ASSEMBLE AdaBoost and AdaBoost. Among the data in Table 3, ASSEMBLE AdaBoost had the maximum value of accuracy (90.238%) and sensitivity (97.87%). However, AdaBoost had the lowest accuracy (86.602%) and sensitivity (94.814%). Although the AUC of ASSEMBLE AdaBoost was less than that of Ada-Boost, they had a small difference (3.25%). The specificity of ASSEMBLE AdaBoost had a similar situation.

Table 5. Results of the 2 algorithms where the rate of labeled data is 0.1

Measure	Algorithm	
	AdaBoost	ASSEMBLE AdaBoost
Specificity	0.7379	0.64217
Sensitivity	0.94814	0.9787
AUC	0.84299	0.81044
Accuracy	0.86602	0.90238

It could be directly concluded that when the number of unlabeled data increase in the future and the number of labeled data is still small, the classification accuracy of ASSEMBLE AdaBoost for normal class can be stable at a relatively high value.

4 Conclusion and Future Work

Nowadays, fetal heart monitoring becomes an essential part during pregnancy and the combination of the computer field and medical area has made great progress in clinical support systems. As a tool for electronic fetal monitoring (EFM), CTG can continue to record FHR and uterine activity assisting obstetricians to detect fetus abnormal patterns. However, the CTG dataset has problems with high labeling costs and few labeled data. Hence, various kinds of machine learning methods appeared to label the CTG dataset. In this paper, we used a semi-supervised method based on pseudo-classes named the ASSEMBLE AdaBoost algorithm. The characteristic of the algorithm is adding unlabeled data into the training set. We let the AdaBoost algorithm be the experimental control group and results showed that ASSEMBLE AdaBoost had an outstanding performance in predicting data labels. Therefore, we suppose that when establishing a fetal supervision model with insufficient labeled samples, we could use ASSEMBLE AdaBoost to improve the effect instead of manual annotation.

Furthermore, an imbalanced dataset is another important issue that needs to discuss. In this study, we found that there is an imbalanced distribution of data in the CTG dataset that leads to ASSEMBLE AdaBoost's poor learning effect of negative class. As the training set becomes more and more unbalanced, the results of the Boosting algorithm will rely more and more on the base classifier [17]. That is to say, if the performance of the base classifier of the Boosting algorithm is poor, then the combination of Boosting will not be exceptional. In the future, further research needs to be conducted on reducing the effect of the unbalanced data and improving the AUC. AUCBoost [18], an algorithm applying AUC to the weight of the learning data and the classifier, can replace Adaboost to achieve the goal.

Acknowledgments. This work is partially supported by a grant from the Natural Science Foundation of Guangdong Province (grant no. 2018A0303130055), the Opening Project of Guang-dong Province Key Laboratory of Big Data Analysis and Processing at Sun Yat-sen University (No. 202001) and the Social Science Project of Guangzhou University of Chinese Medicine grants 2020SKYB05 and 2020SKXK25.

References

1. Jing, D., Zhenya, W.: Incremental fault diagnosis: exploiting unlabelled data with semi-supervised ensemble learning. In: 2017 13th IEEE International Conference on Electronic Measurement & Instruments (ICEMI), Yangzhou, pp. 7–14 (2017)
2. Alfirevic, Z., Devane, D., Gyte, G.M.L.: Continuous cardiotocography (ctg) as a form of electronic fetal monitoring (efm) for fetal assessment during labour. Cochrane Database Syst. Rev. 5(3), CD006066 (2006)
3. Kothari, R., Jain, V.: Learning from labeled and unlabeled data. In: International Joint Conference on Neural Networks. IEEE (2002)
4. Huang, M.-L., Hsu, Y.-Y.: Fetal distress prediction using discriminant analysis, decision tree, and artificial neural network. J. Biomed. Sci. Eng. 05(9), 526–533 (2012)

5. Fergus, P., Hussain, A., Al-Jumeily, D., Huang, D.-S., Bouguila, N.: Classification of caesarean section and normal vaginal deliveries using foetal heart rate signals and advanced machine learning algorithms. Biomed. Eng. Online **16**(1), 89 (2017)
6. Sundar, C., Chitradevi, M., Chitradevi, M., Geetharamani, G.: Classification of cardiotocogram data using neural network based machine learning technique. Int. J. Comput. Appl. **47**(14), 19–25 (2012)
7. Shah, S.A.A., Aziz, W., Arif, M., Nadeem, M.S.A.: Decision trees based classification of cardiotocograms using bagging approach. In: 2015 13th International Conference on Frontiers of Information Technology (FIT), Islamabad, pp. 12–17 (2015)
8. Karabulut, E.M., Ibrikci, T.: Analysis of cardiotocogram data for fetal distress determination by decision tree based adaptive boosting approach. J. Comput. Commun. **2**, 32–37 (2014)
9. Zhang, Y., Zhao, Z.: Fetal state assessment based on cardiotocography parameters using PCA and AdaBoost. In: 2017 10th International Congress on Image and Signal Processing, BioMedical Engineering and Informatics. IEEE (2017)
10. Bennett, K.P., Demiriz, A., Maclin, R.: Exploiting unlabeled data in ensemble methods. In: Proceedings of the 8th ACM SIGKDD International Conference on Knowledge Discovery and Data Mining, KDD 2002, pp. 289–296. Association for Computing Machinery, New York (2002). https://doi.org/10.1145/775047.775090
11. Silwattananusarn, T., Kanarkard, W., Tuamsuk, K.: Enhanced classification accuracy for cardiotocogram data with ensemble feature selection and classifier ensemble. J. Comput. Commun. **4**, 20–35 (2016). https://doi.org/10.4236/jcc.2016.44003
12. Kohavi, R.: A study of cross-validation and Bootstrap for accuracy estimation and model selection. In: International Joint Conference on Artificial Intelligence. Morgan Kaufmann Publishers Inc. (1995)
13. Quinlan, R.J.: Bagging, Boosting, and C4.5. In: Proceedings of the 13th National Conference on Artificial Intelligence (1996)
14. Liu, J.W., Liu, Y., Luo, X.L.: Semi-supervised learning methods. Chin. J. Comput. **38**(8), 1592–1617 (2015)
15. Mallapragada, P.K., Jin, R., Jain, A.K., Liu, Y.: Semiboost: boosting for semi-supervised learning. IEEE Trans. Pattern Anal. Mach. Intell. **31**(11), 2000–2014 (2009)
16. Hou, J., Mao, Y., Sun, J.: Semi-supervised separability-maximum boosting. Nanjing Li Gong Daxue Xuebao/J. Nanjing Univ. Sci. Technol. **38**(5), 675–681 (2014)
17. Joshi, M.V., Agarwal, R.C., Kumar, V.: Predicting rare classes: can boosting make any weak learner strong? (2002)
18. Li, Y., Wang, L.: AUC-based boosting method for the classification of rare classes. J. Yunnan Univ. (Nat. Sci.) **S2**, 313–318 (2007)

A Label Propagation Algorithm Combining Eigenvector Centrality and Label Entropy

Shucan Pan[1], Wenchao Jiang[1(✉)], Sui Lin[1], and Dongjun Ning[2]

[1] School of Computer Science and Technology,
Guangdong University of Technology, Guangzhou 510006, China
jiangwenchao@gdut.edu.cn
[2] Taotall Technology Development Co., Ltd, Guangzhou 510635, China

Abstract. Aiming at the strong randomness and low accuracy problem caused by fuzzy boundaries of overlapping communities, a label propagation algorithm combining eigenvector centrality and label entropy (ECLE-LPA) is proposed. The K-kernel iteration factor and the eigenvector centrality of the node are used to calculate the node influence. In the propagation process, the label entropy and the closeness of the node are calculated to update the node label list, and the corresponding label memberships in this label list. These can overcome the overlapping community fuzzy boundaries recognition problem. The experimental results show that in the real network such as Les, Pollbooks, Football, Polblogs, Netscience, the EQ value of ECLE-LPA algorithm is generally increased by 1%–3% compared with the contrast algorithm. In the artificial network with fuzzy community structures, the NMI value of ECLE-LPA is more than10% higher than the contrast algorithm.

Keywords: Complex network · Overlapping community · K-kernel iteration factor · Label propagation · Eigenvector centrality · Label entropy

1 Introduction

In the scientific researches and industries, the things and their connections can be represented by complex network structures [1–3] that the things represent nodes, and connections between them represent edges, such as the social network [4], transportation networks, scientist cooperation network and biological networks [5, 6]. With the increase of interaction between nodes, the relationship between nodes becomes more complex and the network becomes denser. In order to research these networks more accurately, the network community structure as a reflection of the underlying laws and characteristics of the network is essential [7–9]. Community structure detection is to divide the complex real network into a communities formed by the node set composed of network nodes. The structural division of networked communities accepted by most researchers is based on a concept defined by Newman and Gievan [10]: nodes within the same community are relatively closely connected, while nodes between different communities are relatively sparse.

In recent years, many algorithms have been proposed for network community detection. According to the number of communities witch the network nodes, they can

© Springer Nature Singapore Pte Ltd. 2021
Y. Tan et al. (Eds.): DMBD 2021, CCIS 1453, pp. 436–451, 2021.
https://doi.org/10.1007/978-981-16-7476-1_38

be divided into non-overlapping community detection algorithm [11–13] and overlapping community detection algorithm. In the non-overlapping community detection algorithm, a node can only belong to one community, while in the overlapping community detection algorithm, a node can belong to multiple communities. For non-overlapping community detection algorithms, there are SVDCNMF community detection algorithm based on singular value decomposition and non-negative matrix decomposition [11], BLDLP community detection algorithm based on balanced link density [12] and LPA-FCM community detection algorithm based on label propagation and fuzzy C-means [13]. For overlapping community detection algorithms, there are ICDCA algorithm for user interaction based on cascading analysis [14], ENCOD algorithm for overlapping community detection based on integrated disjoint community structure [15], NSGA2 algorithm for overlapping community detection based on multi-objective optimization [16] and PSOCD algorithm for parallel self-organizing overlapping community detection algorithm [17]. The real network usually has a large number of complex node relations. Nodes with the same attribute are linked to each other through these node relations. Nodes with multiple attributes can belong to multiple communities in the community division, resulting in community boundary overlap. However, for the increasingly fuzzy network node relations many algorithms are powerless, the accuracy of their community detection is significantly reduced.

Label propagation algorithm is often used in network community detection because of its nearly linear time complexity. However, the methods do not make full use of the global and local characteristics of nodes to measure the influence of nodes more effectively, which leads to the low quality of the fixed node ordering sequence. In addition, the simple label propagation strategy based on the influence of neighbor nodes has been difficult to deal with the network structure with fuzzy community structure. Because of these reasons, the community detection on the network with fuzzy community structure is characterized by high randomness and low precision.

Aiming at the problems of high randomness and low precision of existing label propagation algorithms in fuzzy community networks, a label propagation algorithm combining eigenvector centrality and label entropy was proposed. It improves the order of node label propagation in the process of label propagation and the strategy of label propagation based on the influence of neighbor nodes. In the first stage, the K-kernel iteration factor and eigenvector centrality of the nodes in the network are calculated, and the node influence N_i is defined in combination with these two characteristics. Through the node influence, a more accurate node ranking can be obtained to ensure the stability of the sequence of node label propagation. In the second stage, firstly, Rough Cores [18] algorithm is improved based on node influence to initialize the label list of each node in the network and the corresponding node label membership degree. Secondly, in the process of label propagation, the label entropy of the current node and the neighbor node and the closeness between the neighbor node and the node are calculated to update the label list of the current node and its corresponding node label membership degree, so as to realize the label propagation from the neighbor node to the current node. Thirdly, remove redundant labels from the new current node label list. Then, at the end of each iteration, delete the small label community surrounded by the large label community. Finally, continue iterating until the community structure is stable.

2   The ECLE-LPA Algorithm

2.1   Node Influence

Traditional label propagation algorithms, such as COPRA, SLPA and DLP, the randomness of node's label iteration update order is an important reason that leads to the unstable results of its community division. We use the global feature K-kernel iteration factor of the node and the local feature eigenvector centrality to define the node influence N_i, and then determine the updating order of the node according to this node influence, so as to improve the stability of the community detection results.

The K-kernel decomposition algorithm proposed in Literature [19] is used to calculate the global network importance index K-shell (Ks) value of network nodes.

Definition 1 (K-kernel iteration factor δ). Node u is a node in network $G = (V, E)$, then the K-kernel iteration factor of the node can be expressed as follow:

$$\delta(u) = Ks(u) + \frac{n_{Ks}(u) - 1}{m_{Ks}} \tag{1}$$

Where, $Ks(u)$ is the Ks value of node u, m_{Ks} is the number of iterations when the Ks value is calculated, and $n_{Ks}(u)$ is the number of iterations when node u is deleted in m_{Ks} iteration.

The K-kernel iteration factor $\delta(u)$ is based on Ks value, the first term of Eq. (1) represents the node Ks value, which ensures the isolation of nodes with different Ks values. The second term further subdivides nodes with the same Ks value.

Considering that the influence of neighbor nodes will also affect the current node, this paper uses the eigenvector centrality to further calculate the influence of nodes.

Definition 2 (eigenvector centrality EC). Given an undirected, unweighted graph $G = (V, E)$, an adjacency matrix $A = (a_{u,v})$, if u and v have an edge, then $a_{u,v} = 1$, otherwise $a_{u,v} = 0$, then the function of eigenvector centrality EC of the node is expressed as:

$$EC(u) = \frac{1}{\lambda} \sum_{v \in N(u)} EC(u) = \frac{1}{\lambda} \sum_{v \in V} a_{u,v} EC(v) \tag{2}$$

$N(u)$ is the set of neighbor nodes of node u, and λ is a constant. $EC(u)$ is the eigenvector centrality of node u.

The eigenvector centrality of a node is an improvement of local characteristic centrality, which further reflects the centrality degree of its neighbor nodes.

After transformation, Eq. (2) can be transformed into:

$$AX = \lambda X \tag{3}$$

The component x_u of vector X corresponds to the eigenvector centrality value $EC(u)$ of node u, and X is the eigenvector corresponding to different eigenvalues of adjacency matrix A.

Since the eigenvector centrality is positive and non-zero, according to Perron-Frobenius theorem, vector X can only be the eigenvector corresponding to the maximum eigenvalue of the adjacency matrix A. Therefore, the eigenvector corresponding to the maximum eigenvalue obtained by the power iteration method can be used in this paper to obtain the eigenvector centrality value $EC(u)$ of each node in the network.

Definition 3 (node influence NI). Node u is a node in the graph $G = (V, E)$, $\delta(u)$ is the k-kernel iteration factor of node u, and $EC(u)$ is the eigenvector centrality of node u, then the node influence of node u can be expressed as:

$$NI(u) = \frac{\delta(u)}{\max_{v \in V}(\delta(v))} \times EC(u) \tag{4}$$

Since the value range of k-kernel iteration factor $\delta(u)$ is obviously larger than eigenvector centrality $EC(u)(EC(u) \in (0, 1))$, the measurement of node influence will be more biased to $\delta(u)$. Therefore, the first term of Eq. (4) first normalizes of $\delta(u)$ of the node with the maximum value so that its value range is consistent with that of $\delta(u)$, which also ensures that the node influence $Ni(u)$ can well reflect the global importance and local importance of the node in the network.

2.2 Initialization of Node Label

Definition 4 (node label membership degree $W_u(l)$). The strength of node u having label l is called node label membership degree $W_u(l)$, that is, the membership degree of node u to the community C represented by label l, and the sum of all node label membership degrees of each node is 1.

In order to reduce the number of labels during node initialization, speed up algorithm convergence and reduce label redundancy, this paper uses improved Rough Cores [18] algorithm based on node influence to initialize node labels, as the pseudocode shown in algorithm 1:

Algorithm 1: initNodeCommunityMessage (G, descendQueue)

Input: the network $G = (V, E)$, Descending $descendQueue$ of node sequences based on node influence.

Output: The initialization label for each node (Initialized network community structure)

While $descendQueue$ is not null:

$u_{max}=descendQueue.getNextNode()$; //Gets the node with the maximum influence that is not labeled.

$u_{nmax}=getBigestNINeighbor(u_{max})$// Gets the most influential node in u_{max}'s neighbor nodes that is not labeled

if u_{nmax} is $null$:

$L_{u_{max}} = (L_{u_{max}}, Id_{u_{max}})$;// Add the node ID of u_{max} as a label to the u_{max} label list

$descendQueue.remove(u_{max})$;// Removes the u_{max} node from the descendQueue

$continue$;// Go back to the beginning of the While loop

end if

$CS = getCompleteSubgraph(u_{max}, u_{nmax})$;

foreach $v \in CS$:

$L_v = (L_v, Id_{u_{max}})$; // Add the ID of node u_{max} as the label to the label list of nodes v

$descendQueue.remove(v)$; // Removes the v node from the descendQueue

end for

end while

foreach $v \in V$://Initializes the node label membership

$s = getSize(L_v)$// Gets the number of initialization labels for node v

foreach $l \in L_v$:

$w_v(l) = \frac{1}{s}$;

end for

end for

2.3 Label Propagation Rules Based on Node Label Entropy

Due to community overlap, nodes at the edge of the community have more labels and basically the same node label membership degree, which leads to increased uncertainty of the node belonging to a certain community. This uncertainty can be measured by information entropy. The greater the information entropy, the greater the uncertainty. This information entropy is called label entropy in this paper.

Definition 5 (node label entropy $H(u)$) Node u is a node in the graph $G = (V, E)$, $L(u)$ is a label set owned by node u in the iteration process, $w_u(l)$ is the node label membership degree of node u to the label l, then the node label entropy can be expressed as

$$H(u) = -\sum_{l \in L_u} w_u(l) \ln w_u(l) \tag{5}$$

Where, the sum of $w_u(l)$ of all the labels of node u is 1.

From the above analysis and Eq. (5), it can be concluded that the node label entropy gradually increases from the inside of the community to the edge of the community.

The measurement method of node closeness proposed by Eustace et al. [20] is introduced to measure the closeness $I_{u,v}$ of node u to neighbor node v, which improves the method of measuring node closeness by Jaccard coefficient.

Definition 6 (Node intimacy $I_{u,v}$). Node u and v are two adjacent nodes in the graph $G = (V, E)$. The intimacy of these two nodes can be expressed as:

$$H(u) = -\sum_{l \in L_u} w_u(l) \ln w_u(l) \tag{6}$$

where, $\gamma(u) = N(u) \cup \{u\}$, $N(u)$ is the neighbor node set of node u.

This paper defines the label entropy to identify the location of the node in the community. The closer the node is to the community center, the lower the label entropy of the node and the neighbor node. Therefore, node's label update direction prefers to follow the node with low label entropy. Meanwhile, node intimacy is used to distinguish the different influences of neighbor nodes on the current node's label update.

The specific node label propagation rules in this paper are as follows:

1. The network nodes are sorted in ascending order according to their influence, and the ascending sequence (ascendQueue) obtained is taken as the node update order. It reduces the randomness of the update process.
2. In the process of label propagation, the label list of each node u in the ascendQueue is updated in an orderly and asynchronous manner, and the label list of nodes u is set to be L_u after this label propagation:

$$L_u = L_u' \cup \left(\cup_{v \in Ng(u)} L_v \right) \tag{7}$$

$Ng(u)$ is a neighbor node set of u, and L_u' is the label list of u before this label propagation Then the node label membership degree $W_u(l)(l \in L_u)$ corresponding to each label l in L_u is:

$$w_u(l) = \frac{\frac{1}{H_u'+\varepsilon} \times I_{u,u} \times w_u'(l) + \sum_{v \in Ng(u)} \frac{1}{H_v'+\varepsilon} \times I_{u,u} \times w_v(l)}{\frac{1}{H_u'+\varepsilon} \times I_{u,u} + \sum_{v \in Ng(u)} \frac{1}{H_v+\varepsilon} \times I_{u,u}} \tag{8}$$

Where, H_u' and $w_u'(l)$ are the label entropy and node label membership before the node u label list is updated, and ε is a smooth constant to prevent the denominator from being zero.

3. In order to reduce label redundancy, the label list L_u obtained by Eq. (7) and (8) is used to remove the labels with low label membership degree of adaptive threshold α. First, the labels in L_u are sorted in descending order of membership degree, and then the nodes with the largest membership difference between two adjacent labels are found. The average value of the membership degree of these two labels is taken as the adaptive threshold α of L_u, and the labels in L_u whose membership degree is less than α are deleted.

4. Finally, the membership degree of node labels remaining in L_u is normalized, as shown in Eq. (9), and the membership degree of node labels updated in this paper is obtained:

$$w'_u(l) = \frac{w_u(l)}{\sum'_l \in L(u) w_u(l')} \tag{9}$$

2.4 Algorithm Description and Analysis

Based on the above defined node influence, node initialization label rule and label propagation rule, this paper designs a Label Propagation Algorithm combining Eigenvector Centrality and Label Entropy (ECLE-LPA). The specific algorithm steps are as follows:

Given a connected undirected and unweight network $G = (V, E)$, and the maximum number of iterations T, ECLE-LPA algorithm is used to output the findings of overlapping communities, and each node has a label list. Nodes with the same label form a community, while nodes with different labels belong to different communities, resulting in community overlapping.

1. **Calculate node influence:** K-kernel iteration factor and eigenvector centrality of each node are respectively calculated by Eq. (1) and (3), and node influence is calculated by Eq. (4) in combination with these two node attributes.
2. **Node label initialization:** The nodes are sorted in descending order according to the node influence, and the labels are initialized according to the initialization rule of **Algorithm 1**, and the membership degree of the initial node labels corresponding to the corresponding label is allocated.
3. **Node label propagation:** According to the node influence, the nodes are sorted in ascending order. According to the order of nodes in this sequence, the label propagation update based on node label entropy is carried out for each node according to the Eq. 5, 6, 7, 8, 9, and then the redundant labels with low label membership degree are deleted. At the end of each iteration, delete the smaller communities surrounded by the larger communities, and proceed to the next iteration. Iterate continuously until the number of iterations reaches T or when the label of the maximum label membership degree of each node remains unchanged.

3 Output the Labels List for Each Node

3.1 Time Complexity Analysis

A given network $G = (V, E)$, V is G the node set, $n = |V|$, E is a set of G edge, $m = |E|$. The time complexity of K-kernel iteration factor of each node u calculated by Eq. (1) is $O(n)$, the time complexity of power iteration method to calculate the eigenvector centrality is $O(n^2)$, and the time complexity of computing the node influence is $O(n)$. The nodes are sorted twice according to the node influence, and the average time complexity is $O(2n)$. In one iteration, the time to calculate the label entropy and intimacy of the neighbor nodes of all nodes is $O(2l_u m)$ and $O(2m)$ respectively, where l_u is the average number of labels of nodes. According to Eq. (7) and (8), the time complexity of updating the label information of nodes is $O(2l_u m)$, and the time complexity of label removal after each iteration of each node is $O(l_u^2)$, and the total time of label removal is $O(nl_u^2)$. The time for deleting small communities surrounded by large communities is $O(l^2 n)$, where l is the number of tags in this iteration. Therefore, the total time complexity of ECLE-LPA algorithm is $O(n + kn^2 + n + t(2n + 4l_u m + 2m + nl_u^2 + l^2 n))$, and t is the number of iterations of this label propagation. Since k, l, l^2 and t are far less than n, and the number of edges m in a complex network is proportional to the number of points n. In general, the adjacency matrices of the real network are all sparse matrices, and most of elements are 0. Therefore, Power iteration method's time complexity in this case is $O(2m)$, Finally, the complexity of this algorithm is $O(n)$. In the worst case, if the number l of groups is n, the maximum time complexity is $O(n^3)$.

4 Experiment and Analysis

4.1 The Experimental Dataset

In Real network data include Zachary's Karate Club, Les Miserables, Books About Us Politics, American Football Games College Foot-ball, Political Blogs and Coauthorships in Network Science. The relevant information of the above network is shown in Table 1:

Table 1. Real network dataset information

Network	Node	Edge
Karate [21]	34	78
Les Miserables [21]	77	254
Polbooks [21]	105	441
Football [21]	115	613
Polblogs [21]	1490	19022
Netscience [21]	1588	2742

The data of the artificial network is generated by the artificial network generation tool LFR Benchmark, which was proposed by Lancichinetti et al. The generated network has many characteristics similar to the real network, the different parameters can output different properties of the network, is widely used in the research of complex network in the study of specific characteristics.

Different networks can be generated by adjusting the input of different parameters. Specific parameters set in this paper are shown in Table 2:

Table 2. LFP manual network parameter setting

Id	N	k	maxk	minc	maxc	on	om	mu
S1	1000	10	50	10	50	100	4	0.1–0.65
S2	3000	10	50	10	50	100	4	0.1–0.65
S3	6000	10	50	10	50	100	4	0.1–0.65

N represents the number of nodes in the network, k represents the average degree of nodes, $maxk$ represents the maximum degree of nodes, $minc$ represents the minimum community size in the network, $maxc$ represents the maximum community size in the network, on represents the number of overlapping nodes, om represents the number of communities to which the overlapping nodes belong. mu represents the ratio of the number of edges connected by all nodes in the network to other community nodes and to the number of edges connected by all nodes in the community to which they belong. The larger the value of mu is, the more chaotic the network is, the less clear the community structure is. The value range of mu in this paper is $[0.1, 0.65]$. Each value interval is 0.05, and the fuzzy degree of generated artificial network community structure is controlled by controlling mu value.

4.2   Experimental Evaluation Method

For the real network, the extended module degree function EQ [22] is used to evaluate the accuracy of the division of overlapping communities. It is based on the difference between the network node distribution in the completely random structure distribution and the detected community structure distribution. The higher the EQ value of modularity, the better the community division. Its expression is as follows Eq. (10):

$$EQ = \frac{1}{2m} \sum_{i \in C} \sum_{u \in c_i, v \in c_i} \frac{1}{Q_u Q_v} \left(A_{uv} - \frac{k_v k_u}{2m} \right) \tag{10}$$

where, m represents the number of edges in the network, C represents the number of communities divided, Q_u represents the number of communities that node u belongs to, A_{uv} represents whether there is an edge between u and v, if there is an edge, $A_{uv} = 1$, otherwise, $A_{uv} = 0$, and k_u represents the degree of node u.

For artificial network, Normalized Mutual Informational NMI [23] was adopted to measure the difference between the community structure divided by the algorithm in this paper and the real community structure. The larger the NMI value, the more accurate the community discovery result is, and the closer it is to the real community structure. Its expression is shown in Eq. (11):

$$NMI(X|Y) = 1 - \frac{1}{2} \left(H(X|Y)_{norm} + H(Y|X)_{norm} \right) \tag{11}$$

where, X and Y represent the results of the division of the two communities, which in this paper refer to the real community structure and the community structure discovered by the algorithm.

4.3   Visual Analysis on the Sample Network

This paper takes Fig. 1 as a sample network to conduct a visual analysis of ECLE-LPA algorithm. The example network can be artificially divided into two overlapping communities, $C_1 = (1, 2, 3, 4, 5)$ and $C\_2 = (4, 6, 7, 8, 9)$, where node 4 is the overlapping node. The algorithm in this paper is used to divide them as follows:

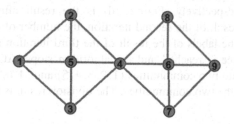

Fig. 1. Sample network

Table 3 shows the calculation results of δ, EC and Ni for the sample network nodes, and obtains ascending and descending sequences sorted according to Ni. Nodes with the same Ni are sorted according to ID. The ascending sequence is $aQueue = (1 - 9 - 2 - 3 - 7 - 8 - 5 - 6 - 4)$. It can be seen that, based on K-kernel iteration factor, Ni added with EC further distinguishes node 1 from node 2 and node 3, and similarly distinguishes other nodes.

Table 3. The K-nuclear iteration factor, eigenvector centrality and node influence of the sample network.

NodeID	1	2	3	4	5	6	7	8	9
δ	0.857	0.875	0.857	1	1	1	0.857	0.875	0.857
EC	0.5	0.586	0.586	1	0.709	0.709	0.586	0.586	0.5
NI	0.428	0.502	0.502	1	0.709	0.709	0.502	0.502	0.428

Figure 2 shows how this paper's label propagation process is applied to the sample network, with the smoothing constant $\varepsilon = 0.01$. The label initialization results of a sample network based on a descending sequence (*dQueue*) are shown in Fig. 2a. Compared with other algorithms that directly initialize each node label using node ID, the label initialization strategy proposed in this paper can effectively reduce redundant labels in the iteration process. In Fig. 2a, we can already find the initial community information divided by four labels, and three overlapping nodes 4, 5 and 6. Begin the first label propagation iteration based on the ascending sequence aQueue. Taken node 5 as an example. From Eq. (7), the label entropy of each node in the set $\gamma(5) = \{1, 2, 3, 4, 5\}$ is $H(\gamma(5)) = \{0.0, 0.0, 0.0, 0.6931, 0.6931\}$. The intimacy between node 5 and set $\gamma(5)$ is obtained by Eq. (6) as set $I_{5,\gamma(5)} = \{0.6, 0.6, 0.6, 0.6, 1.0\}$. According to Eq. (8) and (9), the updated label set of node 5 in this time is $L(5) = \{3 = 0.6309, 4 = 0.3501, 6 = 0.0188\}$. Cut off the redundant labels with low node label membership in $L(5)$ The maximum label membership difference is taken as the threshold $\alpha = 0.18445$. Since $w_5(6) = 0.0188 < \alpha$, the label 6 of $L(5)$ is deleted. The remaining labels are $L(5) = \{3 = 0.6309, 4 = 0.3501\}$. Finally, normalize $L(5)$ to get $L'(u) = \{3 = 0.6431, 4 = 0.3568\}$. Similarly, the labels of other nodes and the corresponding label membership can be updated.

Figure 2(b) and Fig. 2(c) show the results of the first and second iterations of the example network, respectively. Figure 2(d) is the result after the third iteration. Compared with the result of the second iteration, the number of labels and the number of nodes owned by the labels of the result of the third iteration remain unchanged. At this time, convergence is reached and the algorithm stops. At this time, the sample network is divided into two communities $(1, 2, 3, 4, 5)$ and $(4, 6, 7, 8, 9)$, where 4 is the overlapping node of the two communities. The division result is the same as the author expected.

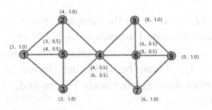

(a) label initialization result of the sample network

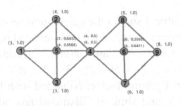

(b) results of the first iteration of the ECLE-LPA algorithm

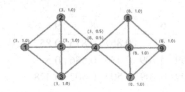

(c) results of the second iteration of the ECLE-LPA algorithm

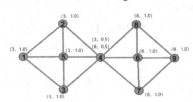

(d) results of the third iteration of the ECLE-LPA algorithm

Fig. 2. Label propagation process of ECLE-LPA on the sample network

4.4   Practical Analysis on the Real Network

In order to evaluate the effectiveness of the ECLE-LPA algorithm on the real network, the following experiment selects three overlapping community discovery algorithms based on label propagation for comparison, LPANNI, DLPA, and COPRA.

Since both COPRA and DLPA are unstable community detection algorithms, the final result is the best result in 100 runs. The community overlap parameter v of COPRA algorithms has different values with different network. The value of the in parameter of the DLPA algorithm has different values according to different networks. Analyzed by LPANNI's original paper, the path length threshold α is set to 3. The maximum number of iterations T of all algorithms in this experiment is 50. The smoothing constant ε of the ECLE-LPA algorithm is 0.01. Table 4 shows the community division results of the above four algorithms for the real network. It can be seen from Table 4 that under the evaluation criteria of EQ, except that the performance on the Karate network is slightly inferior to that of the LPANNI algorithm, ECLE-LPA has the highest EQ value on other networks. It can be seen from the Polblogs network that the LPANNI algorithm cannot identify the fuzzy network of the community, while the ECLE-LPA and DLPA algorithms have a certain recognition effect on the fuzzy network of the community, and the effect of ECLE-LPA is slightly better than that of DLPA. Visible ECLE-LPA algorithm can improve the accuracy of the label propagation algorithm in overlapping community detection in real network.

Table 4. Comparison of EQ values of different algorithms on real network data sets

Network	ECLE-LPA	LPANNI	DLPA	COPRA
Karate	0.4451	0.4488	0.4269	0.3776
Les	0.5584	0.5419	0.5478	0.4645
Polbooks	0.5364	0.5158	0.5217	0.4960
Football	0.6112	0.6047	0.5894	0.5265
Polblogs	0.4281	0.0089	0.4266	0.1935
Netscience	0.8773	0.8642	0.8484	0.6243

4.5   Experimental Analysis on LFR Benchmark Artificial Network

The comparison algorithms on the artificial network generated by the LFR benchmark are still LPANNI, DLPA, and COPRA.

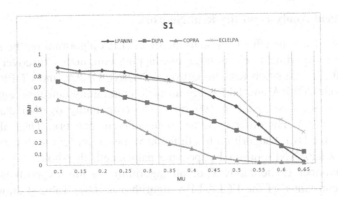

Fig. 3. The algorithm is compared in NMI of the 1000 - scale network

Since the value of the *om* parameter is 4 in the generated network, the *v* of the COPRA algorithm is set to a fixed value of 4. Since the in parameter of the DLPA algorithm is mostly 6 in the real network, *in* can be set to a fixed value of 6. The values of other parameters are the same as those in the real network. The experimental results on the artificial network are shown in Fig. 3, Fig. 4, and Fig. 5, respectively corresponding to three networks of different sizes, S1, S2, and S3, and the different levels of confusion of networks of the same size are adjusted by adjusting *mu*.

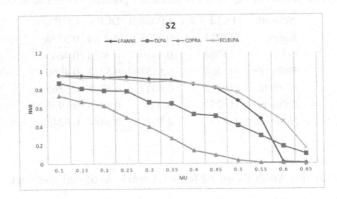

Fig. 4. The algorithm is compared in NMI of the 3000 - scale network

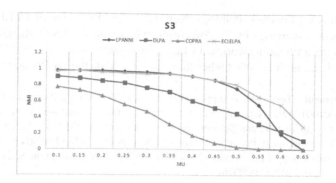

Fig. 5. The algorithm is compared in NMI of the 6000 - scale network

From Figs. 3, 4, and 5, it can be seen that with the continuous increase of *mu*, the degree of confusion in the network continues to increase, and the accuracy of community detection, that is, the NMI value, of the four algorithms is constantly declining. However, the decline speed of the ECLE-LPA and LPANNI algorithms is much slower than that of the DLPA and COPRA algorithms, showing a relatively flat curve, and the NMI of the first two algorithms is significantly higher than the latter two algorithms in different *mu*. In comparison between the ECLE-LPA and LPANNI algorithms, on the artificial network where *mu* is in the interval of [0.1, 0.45], it can be seen from the NMI value that these two algorithms are comparable in the accuracy of community detection, and both are at the same level. With a high accuracy of NMI greater than 0.7, even their accuracy NMI values exceed 0.85 on S2 and S3 networks. On the artificial network with the value of *mu* in the interval of [0.45, 0.65], the ECLE-LPA algorithm shows its community detection ability in networks with fuzzy community structure. In this interval, the NMI curve of the LPANNI algorithm drops quickly, while the curve of the ECLE-LPA algorithm drops relatively slowly. It can be concluded that the ECLE-LPA algorithm and the LPANNI algorithm perform better than the DLPA and COPRA algorithms in networks with obvious network community distribution; In a network with fuzzy community distribution, the community discovery ability of the ECLE-LPA algorithm is significantly better than that of the LPANNI algorithm.

5   Conclusion

To overcome the high randomness and low accuracy problems of the overlapping community detection algorithm based on label propagation in the fuzzy community structure network, a label propagation algorithm that combining the eigenvector centrality and label entropy (ECLE-LPA) is proposed. In this algorithm, the node influence is defined by calculating the K-kernel iteration factor and eigenvector centrality. Based on this node influence, a more accurate node sorting sequence is obtained, and a more stable community detection result is obtained through label propagation. The nodes are initialized by the improved Rough Cores algorithm, which effectively reduces label redundancy and speeds up the convergence of the algorithm. In the real network such as Les, Pollbooks, Football, Polblogs, Netscience, the EQ value of ECLE-LPA algorithm is generally increased by 1%-3% compared with the LPANNI, the DLPA and the COPRA. In the artificial network with fuzzy community structures, the NMI value of ECLE-LPA is more than 10% higher than the LPANNI, the DLPA and the COPRA.

Acknowledgement. This paper is supported by the Key Technology Project of Foshan City in 2019 (1920001001367), National Natural Science and Guangdong Joint Fund Project (U2001201), Guangdong Natural Science Fund Project (2018A030313061, 2021A1515011243), Research and Development Projects of National Key fields (2018YFB1004202), Guangdong Science and Technology Plan Project (2019B010139001) and Guangzhou Science and Technology Plan Project (201902020016).

References

1. Watts, D.J., Strogatz, S.H.: Collective dynamics of 'small-world' networks. Nature (1998)
2. Dorogovtsev, S.N., Mendes, J.: Evolution of networks: from biological nets to the internet and www. OUP Catalogue **57**(10)**, 81–82 (2013)**
3. Albert, R., Barabasi, A.L.: Statistical mechanics of complex networks. Rev. Modern Phys. **74**(1), xii (2001)
4. Kun, H., Yingru, L. et al.: Hidden community detection in social networks. Inf. Sci.: Int. J. **425**, 92–106 (2018)
5. Sah, P., Singh, L.O., Clauset, A., et al.: Exploring community structure in biological networks with random graphs. BMC Bioinformatics **15**(1), 220 (2014)
6. Atay, Y., Koc, I., Babaoglu, I., et al.: Community detection from biological and social networks: a comparative analysis of metaheuristic algorithms. Appl. Soft Comput. **50**(C), 194–211 (2017)
7. Su and, J., Havens, T.C.: Fuzzy community detection in social networks using a genetic algorithm. In: IEEE International Conference on Fuzzy Systems
8. Xie, J., Kelley, S., Szymanski, B.K.: Overlapping community detection in networks: The state-of-the-art and comparative study. ACM Comput. Surveys **45**(4), 43.1–43.35 (2013)
9. Okamura, Y., Obayashi, T., Kinoshita, K.: Comparison of gene coexpression profiles and construction of conserved gene networks to find functional modules. PLoS ONE (2015)
10. Newman, M.E.J. Girvan, M.: Finding and evaluating community structure in networks. Phys. Rev. E Vol. **69**, 026113 (2004)
11. Lu, H., Sang, X., Zhao, Q., et al.: Community detection algorithm based on nonnegative matrix factorization and pairwise constraints. Phys. A (2019). https://doi.org/10.1016/j.physa.2019.123491
12. Jokar, E., Mosleh, M.: Community detection in social networks based on improved label propagation algorithm and balanced link density. Phys. Lett. A **383**(8), 718–727 (2019)
13. Zheng, H.D., Hong, H.Q., et al.: A complex network community detection algorithm based on label propagation and fuzzy C-means. Phys. A **519**, 217–226 (2019)
14. Luo, L.B., Liu, K.X., Guo, B.: User interaction-oriented community detection based on cascading analysis. Inf. Sci. **510**, 70–88 (2020)
15. Chakraborty, T., Ghosh, S., Park, N.: Ensemble-based overlapping community detection using disjoint community structures. Knowl.-Based Syst. **163**, 241–251 (2019)
16. Ebrahimi, M., Shahmoradi, M.R., Heshmati, Z., et al.: A novel method for overlapping community detection using multi-objective optimization. Phys. A-Stat. Mech. Appl. **505**, 825–835 (2018)

17. Sun, H.L., Jie, W., Loo, J., et al.: A parallel self-organizing overlapping community detection algorithm based on swarm intelligence for large scale complex networks. Future Gener. Comput. Syst. **89**, 265–285 (2018)
18. Wu, Z.H., Lin, Y.F., Gregory, S., et al.: Balanced multi-label propagation for overlapping community detection in social networks. J. Comput. Sci. Technol. **27**(3), 468–479 (2012)
19. Kong, H., Kang, Q., Liu, C., et al.: An improved label propagation algorithm based on node intimacy for community detection in networks. Int. J. Modern Phys.B 32(25) (2018)
20. Tong, C., Niu, J., Wen, J., et al.: Weighted label propagation algorithm for overlapping community detection. In: Proceedings of ICC 2015–2015 IEEE International Conference on Communications, pp. 1238–1243 (2015)
21. Newman, M.E.J.: Network data from Mark Newman's home page. (2013). http://www.personal.umich.edu/~mejn/netdata/. Accessed 10 May 2018
22. Shen, H., Cheng, X., Cai, K., et al.: Detect overlapping and hierarchical community structure in networks. Phys. A **388**(8), 1706–1712 (2008)
23. Yang, Z., Wang, X., Zhong, J.: Representational learning for fault diagnosis of wind turbine equipment: a multi-layered extreme learning machines approach. Energies **9**(6), 379 (2016)

MI-HGRU: A Combine Method of Mutual Information and HGRU Neural Network for Boiler NOx Emission Prediction

Kangwei Lin[1], Hong Xiao[1(✉)], Wenchao Jiang[1,2], Jianren Yang[2], Cong Zhao[1], and Jiarong Lu[1]

[1] School of Computer Science and Technology, Guangdong University of Technology, Guangzhou 510006, China
[2] Guangzhou Yunshuo Technology Development Co., Ltd, Guangzhou 511458, Guangdong, China

Abstract. Accurately predicting NOx emissions during boiler combustion is of significance for the operation and control of the boiler combustion systems in coal-fired power plants. According to the characteristics of the boiler combustion process with strong disturbances, highly nonlinear and multivariate coupling, a fusion model based on mutual information variable selection and Hyperopt optimized GRU neural network (MI-HGRU) is proposed. The method can accurately select the parameters of boiler combustion process base on mutual information feature selection algorithm. A GRU neural network prediction model with Hyperopt optimization is established to achieve accurate prediction of NOx emission during boiler combustion. The modeling experiment was using a NOx emission dataset from a power plant boiler in Guangdong. The experimental results show that the MI-HGRU method has higher generalization ability and prediction accuracy than the RBF, LSSVM, RNN and LSTM neural networks, with an average accuracy of 99.4%.

Keywords: Combustion process · Mutual information · GRU (gated recurrent unit) neural network · Hyperopt optimization · Nox emission

1 Introduction

Despite China's ongoing reform of its power structure in recent years, coal-fired power station boiler generation will remain the dominant form of power generation in China for a long time to come. However, NOx emitted by boiler combustion is one of the main pollutants in the atmosphere, which has long affected air quality and further affected human health [1,2]. As China's power system reform continues to deepen and energy conservation and emission reduction continues to advance, power plants are paying more and more attention to the issue of pollutant emission control.

© Springer Nature Singapore Pte Ltd. 2021
Y. Tan et al. (Eds.): DMBD 2021, CCIS 1453, pp. 452–467, 2021.
https://doi.org/10.1007/978-981-16-7476-1_39

In the existing research on NOx emission prediction of power plant boiler combustion process, some researchers have built models based on combustion and heat transfer mechanism to achieve prediction. Li [3] through the experimental study on the formation mechanism of coke NOx in dense phase zone of CFB boiler, the influence of mass and heat transfer characteristics on NOx formation in dense phase zone was investigated, and the NOx emission model of boiler was established. Gao et al. [4] through the analysis of the formation mechanism of NOx, taking the fuel NOx produced by CFB boiler combustion as the main body, the mathematical modeling and simulation method are used to establish the prediction model of NOx emission in coal-fired boilers. In fact, the NOx emission of power plant boiler combustion engineering is affected by numerous factors. Due to the complexity, uncertainty, strong coupling and nonlinearity of combustion process, the use of mechanism modeling has certain assumptions and simplifications for modeling objects. Therefore, it is difficult to achieve the accuracy and reliability of meeting industrial needs through mechanism modeling.

In recent years, with the maturity of storage technology and the development of artificial intelligence technology, data-driven modeling method has become more and more common. Zhang et al. [5] established the prediction model of NOx emissions based on the least squares support vector machine (LSSVM), and optimized the parameters of the LSSVM by the difference algorithm. However, it did not select the feature of the data set, which was easy to problems such as over-fitting of the model and long modeling time. Yang [6] based on the LSTM neural network model, the NOx emission prediction model of coal-fired boilers is established. The prediction results of the model have little fluctuation, but the structure is complex, and there are many super parameters that need to be optimized. Hong et al. [7] effectively predicted the power generation efficiency and NOx emission concentration based on the BP/RBF neural network, but when there were a large number of data sets in the actual industry, the training time of the model was long and the generalization was not good enough.

In order to improve the prediction accuracy of NOx in the combustion process of power station boilers while enhancing the generalisation capability and robustness of the model, a modeling approach based on a combination of mutual information and Hyperopt optimised GRU neural network (MI-HGRU) is proposed in this paper. Firstly, the mutual information algorithm is used to select the multi-parameter and multi-variable features of the boiler combustion process, and then the optimal feature subset of the input model is determined. Finally, the GRU neural network and Hyperopt parameter optimization algorithm are used to establish the NOx emission prediction model of power station boiler combustion process. The experimental results show that the MI-HGRU model outperforms the RBF, LSSVM, RNN and LSTM neural network models in terms of prediction accuracy, with an average accuracy of 99.4%.

2   Overview of Methodology

2.1   Feature Selection Algorithm Based on Mutual Information

Accurate variable selection is the basis of model building and control optimization. The actual boiler combustion is in a dynamic process of variable
working conditions, and because the DCS system stores a multi-variable, high-
dimensional and massive time series data, the current working conditions are
related to the historical working conditions, and the method of predicting the
NOx emissions of thermal power plants by time series prediction is extended.
If only the data at the current moment are analyzed and modeled, the input-
output relationship of the object cannot be fully described, and there must be
deviations in the prediction results. Therefore, it is of great significance to accurately select the key parameters affecting the combustion process of coal-fired
power plant boilers. In this paper, the boiler combustion process parameters are
multi-variable and high-dimensional time series data, and the mutual information feature selection algorithm based on filtering is adopted. The effectiveness
of this method in the selection of key parameters of boiler combustion process
is verified by experiments.

The feature selection algorithm based on mutual information uses mutual
information to find features that are highly correlated to the class and have low
redundancy among features. Mutual information (MI) is a measure of the degree
to which a random variable in two random variables X and Y changes itself due
to the change of another random variable [8,9], and its calculation method is as
follows:

$$I(X, Y) = -\iint_{x,y} p(x,y) \lg \frac{p(x,y)}{p(x)p(y)} dxdy. \tag{1}$$

In formula (1), $p(x,y)$ is the joint probability distribution of X and Y. $p(x)$
and $p(y)$ are the marginal probability distributions of X and Y, respectively.
Mutual information (MI) can quantify the correlation between two random variables. When the mutual information is 0, it means that X and Y are independent of each other. The larger the mutual information, the higher the correlation
between X and Y [10].

2.2   NOx Emission Prediction Modeling of Boiler Combustion
Process Based on MI-HGRU Algorithm

Since the combustion process of power plant boilers is a continuous process
flow, the current working condition will be affected by the superposition of the
working condition time series of the first N cycles. Therefore, the data of boiler
combustion process collected by DCS system have the characteristics of randomness, hysteresis and time series. After considering the above characteristics, this
paper will build a prediction model of NOx of power plant boiler combustion
process based on the GRU neural network.

The GRU model is a variant of the LSTM neural network and also a time-
cycle neural network, which is suitable for processing and predicting important

events and regular characteristics with relatively long interval and delay in time series. By introducing memory neurons, the GRU model can deeply mine long-period continuous time series data, and can overcome the prediction error caused by the superposition of boiler continuous combustion adjustment conditions. At the same time, the GRU model uses a 'gate' structure, which greatly avoids the problem of gradient disappearance and can more effectively analyze long-term dependencies. The GRU model reduces the number of gates in the unit and simplifies the unit complexity on the LSTM model. Figure 1 shows the internal structure of the GRU unit, it combines the forget gate and the input gate into a single update gate, whose function is to determine how much information in the hidden state of the previous time step is transferred to the current hidden state. There is also a reset gate in GRU. The calculation operation is similar to the update gate, but the weight matrix is different. The role is to determine how much information the hidden state of the previous time step needs to be forgotten. At the same time, the GRU also mixed cell state and hidden state, as well as other changes, making the GRU have fewer parameters and lower computational cost.

In the GRU network model, x_t and h_t denote the input and output of the GRU network at time t, respectively, where h_t is calculated iteratively by the following equation:

$$z_t = \sigma \left(W_{hz} h_{t-1} + W_{xz} x_t + b_z \right), \tag{2}$$

$$r_t = \sigma \left(W_{hr} h_{t-1} + W_{xr} x_t + b_r \right), \tag{3}$$

$$\tilde{h}_t = \tanh \left(r_t * W_{hh} h_{t-1} + W_{xh} x_t + b_h \right), \tag{4}$$

$$h_t = (1 - z_t) * h_{t-1} + z_t * \tilde{h}_t. \tag{5}$$

Where z_t, r_t is the output of the update gate and the reset gate, respectively. W_{hz} is the matrix of weights output to the update gate at time $t-1$. W_{xz} is the matrix of weights input to the update gate at time t. W_{hr} and W_{xr} are the weight matrices of the output at time $t-1$ and the input to the reset gate at time t, respectively. The results of these two gates pass through a sigmoid function, and the range is [0–1]. $\tilde{h}_t$, h_t are candidate hidden states and hidden states, respectively, which control how much information has been forgotten and how much information has been saved in the last hidden state h_{t-1}. W_{hh} and W_{xh} are the weight matrices of the output at time $t - 1$ and the input to the candidate hidden state at time t, respectively. The results of the candidate hidden state pass through a *tanh* function. b_z, b_r and b_h represent the bias values of update gate, reset gate and candidate hidden states.

Therefore, in this paper, based on the mutual information feature selection algorithm and the GRU neural network model, we propose the MI-HGRU method for predicting NOx emissions during combustion in power station boilers. The model combines the advantages of the mutual information feature selection algorithm and the GRU neural network model, and its overall framework is shown in Fig. 1, which includes three parts: the input layer, the hidden layer and the output layer. The input layer mainly preprocesses the original data such as feature selection, data standardization and data set partitioning to meet the input requirements of the model. The hidden layer constructs a four-layer GRU recurrent neural network. The internal structure of the unit is reflected in Fig. 1. Adam optimization algorithm is used for model training, and Hyperopt is used for model parameter optimization algorithm. Then the model is trained based on the training set. The output layer predicts the data according to the model learned by the hidden layer, and restores the previously preprocessed data after scaling, and then evaluates the performance of the model.

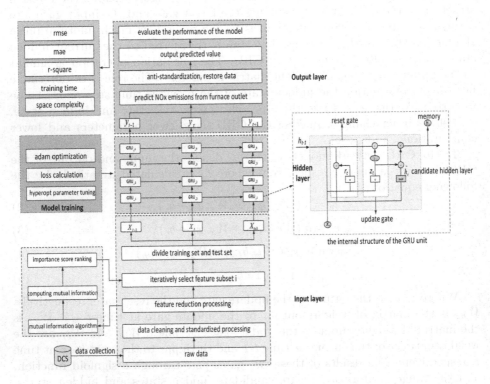

Fig. 1. Furnace exit NOx forecasting framework based on MI-HGRU model

In order to further improve the prediction accuracy of the model, this paper proposes to optimise the hyperparameters of the GRU neural network model using the Hyperopt hyperparameter optimisation method. Hyperopt-based automated hyperparameter tuning is used to find the value that minimises the objective function by building a substitution function (probabilistic model) based on the past evaluation results of the objective function. The method differs from a random or grid search in that it refers to the previous evaluation results when trying the next set of hyperparameters, thus saving a lot of useless work. For the deep learning model, if the traditional parameter tuning algorithms such as genetic algorithm [11,12], grid search [13,14] and random search [15,16] are used, it will take several hours or even days to complete the training and evaluate the model. The Hyperopt hyperparameter tuning algorithm can therefore help the GRU model to be tuned quickly for parameters.

3   Experimental Results

3.1   Experimental Environment

The hardware (computer) required for the experiment is as follows: the central processor is Intel (R) Core (TM) i7-9750H CPU @ 2.60 GHz 2.59 GHz, the computer memory is 16 GB RAM, the operating system is Windows 10–64 bit and the graphics processor is NVIDIA GeForce GTX1660Ti 6 GB.

The software platform required for the experiment in this paper includes: programming language is python v_3.7, python IDEA is pycharm v_2020.1, scikit-learn library is v_0.22.1, numpy is v_1.19.4, pandas is v_1.1.4, matplotlib is v_3.3.2, deep learning platform is tensorflow-gpu v_2.0.0 and neural network training library is cuDNN v_7.6.5.

3.2   Model Data and Initial Parameter Setting

Experimental Data. The data set required for the experiment in this paper is based on the boiler combustion system of a 1000 MW power plant in Guangdong. According to the operation status of the system and expert experience analysis, from the DCS system to select the total coal feed, total fuel quantity, primary air volume (3 detection points), secondary air volume (22 detection points), primary air pressure (2 detection points), unit load, outlet oxygen (A, B each 3 detection points), exhaust gas temperature (A, B each 3 detection points) and furnace outlet NOx emission concentration, a total of 43 parameter variables. The steady-state operation data of the unit in the boiler combustion system of the power station from August 1, 2018 to August 7, 2018 were selected. The data were collected once every 60 s, and 10000 samples were finally taken as the data set of the model.

Initial Parameters of the Model. In the MI-HGRU model proposed in this paper, due to the excessive model parameters involved, the initial parameters of the model are preliminarily determined according to the parameter setting experience of the deep learning neural network in the preliminary experiment, as shown in Table 1. In Sect. 3.5 of this chapter, Hyperopt algorithm is used to optimize the parameters of the MI-HGRU model proposed in this paper.

Table 1. Initial parameters of NOx emission prediction model based on MI-HGRU for boiler combustion process

Parameter name	Parameter value
batch_size	64
dropout_rate	0.5
first_neurons	128
second_neurons	128
third_neurons	64
four_neurons	32
learning_rate	0.01

3.3   Data Feature Selection Analysis

From the 43 dimensions boiler parameters collected by DCS, through many investigations and exchanges with experts from power grid companies and combustion mechanism analysis, it is concluded that NOx produced in the combustion process of power plant boilers is mainly divided into three types: fuel type, thermal type and rapid type. In general, the main factors affecting the NOx emissions of coal-fired boilers are coal quality characteristics, air content and so on, but in the actual power plant boiler combustion process, the coal quality will not change generally. Therefore, in the 43 dimensions boiler parameters collected by DCS, the secondary air volume (22 dimensions) is selected as the input variable of the model, and the NOx emission at the furnace outlet is selected as the output variable of the model. At the same time, in order to improve the performance of the model and prevent the complexity of the model, the mutual information algorithm is established to reduce the second dimension of the selected secondary air volume (22 dimensions), and find out the effective part of the original data that can express the data characteristics. As shown in Fig. 2, the estimation results of mutual information between each feature and the target are obtained. If the feature and the target are independent, the mutual information is equal to 0, and the greater the mutual information, the stronger the dependence. The mutual information results between each feature and label are sorted by mutual information analysis, and the feature subset is constructed according to the sorting results. As shown in Table 2, the feature subset has 22 groups. Using the constructed feature subset as the input feature of the GRU neural network, the time step of the GRU model is set to 5, the iterative training period is 3000, and the RMSE and R^2 are used as the performance evaluation indexes of the model. When the feature subset is 10, that is, when the feature variables with mutual information estimator ranking in the top 10 are selected as the input of the model, the performance is the best. Therefore, considering comprehensively, we make a trade-off between the complexity of the model and the fitting effect, and finally reduce the original data to 10 dimensions.

Based on the above analysis, as shown in Table 3, the 10-dimensional characteristics of secondary air volume (L2 layer burn-out air volume, DE1 layer auxiliary air volume, BC2 layer auxiliary air volume, U2 layer burn-out air volume, L1 layer burn-out air volume, U1 layer burn-out air volume, BC21 layer auxiliary air volume, AB2 layer auxiliary air volume, B layer fuel air volume and EF1 layer auxiliary air volume) are selected as input variables, and the NOx

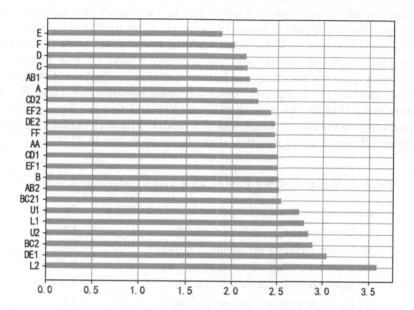

Fig. 2. The amount of mutual information between features and tags

Table 2. Performance comparison results of different feature subsets

Dimension	R^2	RMSE	Dimension	R^2	RMSE
22	0.9025	13.0722	11	0.8862	14.2086
21	0.8499	16.8887	**10**	**0.9101**	**13.0731**
20	0.9021	13.4738	9	0.8972	13.3931
19	0.8968	13.9998	8	0.8858	14.0166
18	0.8598	15.4775	7	0.9021	13.7085
17	0.8491	16.0593	6	0.9035	13.5359
16	0.8816	14.9963	5	0.8865	14.3121
15	0.8962	13.3717	4	0.8553	17.1826
14	0.8738	15.3013	3	0.8749	15.8478
13	0.8721	14.7993	2	0.8799	14.3040
12	0.8630	16.0413	1	0.8999	13.2326

emission concentration at the outlet of the furnace is used as the output variable of the model, with a total of 10000 records.

3.4   Analysis of Experimental Results

In order to verify the advantages of mutual information feature selection algorithm in the modeling method proposed in this paper in feature selection. Under the condition of the same data set (secondary air volume 22 dimension), the same time step (time step 5), the same neural network structure (GRU neural network) and the same training cycle (iterative training cycle 3000), with the maximum information coefficient feature selection method, random forest feature selection method, gradient boosting tree feature selection method and CART feature selection method are compared. The root mean square error (RMSE), mean absolute error (MAE), decision coefficient (R^2) and training time are used as the performance evaluation indexes of the model. The performance comparison results of different feature selection algorithms are shown in Table 4.

Table 3. Ten-dimensional features after mutual information reduction

Parameter name/unit	Symbol
L2 layer burn off air volume/(m^3/h)	L2
DE1 layer auxiliary air volume/(m^3/h)	DE1
BC2 layer auxiliary air volume/(m^3/h)	BC2
U2 layer burn-out air volume/(m^3/h)	U2
L1 layer burn-out air volume/(m^3/h)	L1
U1 layer burn-out air volume/(m^3/h)	U1
BC21 layer auxiliary air volume/(m^3/h)	BC21
AB2 layer auxiliary air volume/(m^3/h)	AB2
B layer fuel air volume/(m^3/h)	B
EF1 layer auxiliary air volume/(m^3/h)	EF1
NOx mass concentration at furnace outlet/(mg·m^{-3})	NOx

Table 4. Performance comparison of different feature selection methods on GRU model

Feature selection method	Dimension after feature selection	RMSE	MAE	R^2	Training time/unit(s)
MIC	9	16.1662	6.6990	0.8683	1507 s
RF	12	16.8712	7.6750	0.8463	2306 s
GBDT	8	15.5529	5.8712	0.8627	1272 s
CART	14	14.3224	5.7417	0.8817	2579 s
Mutual information	**10**	**13.0731**	**5.3507**	**0.9101**	**2239 s**

It can be seen from Table 4 that the performance of the random forest feature selection algorithm on the GRU model after feature selection is the worst, and the gradient lifting tree feature selection method is superior to other feature selection algorithms in feature dimension reduction. The performance of filtering feature selection algorithm based on mutual information in feature dimension reduction is equivalent to that of the gradient lifting tree feature selection method. However, the features selected by the mutual information feature selection algorithm are the best in the GRU model, the RMSE is 13.0731, MAE is 5.3507 and R^2 is 0.9101. In summary, the feature selection method based on mutual information adopted in this paper has stronger advantages in feature selection.

After determining the optimal input features for the model through the mutual information feature selection algorithm, the GRU model was compared with RBF, LSSVM, RNN and LSTM neural network models in order to further fully validate the performance of the GRU model for NOx emission prediction in power station boiler combustion process, and the experimental results are shown in Table 5 and Fig. 3(a) to Fig. 3(e).

Table 5. Performance comparison of different model structures

Model	RMSE	MAE	R^2	Training time/unit(s)	Space complexity
RBF	27.329	18.503	0.615	8 s	150 KB
LSSVM	23.577	17.747	0.654	29 s	374 MB
RNN	15.531	7.029	0.867	3989 s	835 KB
LSTM	11.252	4.088	0.931	3739 s	3.08 MB
GRU	**6.326**	**2.412**	**0.972**	**3548 s**	**2.34 MB**

As can be seen from Fig. 3(a) to Fig. 3(e) and Table 5, the RBF model has the least satisfactory prediction results. Although the R^2 of the LSSVM model is somewhat better than that of the RBF model, the spatial complexity of the LSSVM model is greater. Among the deep learning methods, the RNN model has the lowest spatial complexity, but the gradient disappearance occurs, which makes its accuracy unsatisfactory. GRU is a simplified structure of LSTM with faster training speed and fitting effect. Its RMSE is 6.326, MAE is 2.412 and R^2 is 0.972, which are better than RBF model, LSSVM model, RNN model and LSTM model. The experimental results show that the GRU model has higher prediction accuracy.

From the comparison experiments in Table 5, it can be determined that the GRU neural network model is the best performer for NOx emission prediction from the combustion process of power station boilers. Since GRU model is a time series recurrent neural network model, in order to verify the prediction accuracy and fitting effect of GRU model under different time steps. The preliminary time step parameter adjustment experiment will be carried out and lay the experimental foundation for Hyperopt hyperparameter optimization. The experimental results are shown in Table 6.

Table 6. Comparison of time step selection for GRU neural network model

GRU model (iterative training 3000)	RMSE	MAE	R^2	Training time/unit(s)
Time Step = 5	16.314	5.338	0.861	2502 s
Time Step = 10	14.585	5.104	0.876	2718 s
Time Step = 24	14.134	4.205	0.891	3076s
Time Step = 32	**6.326**	**2.412**	**0.972**	**3548 s**
Time Step = 48	7.317	3.263	0.965	4357 s

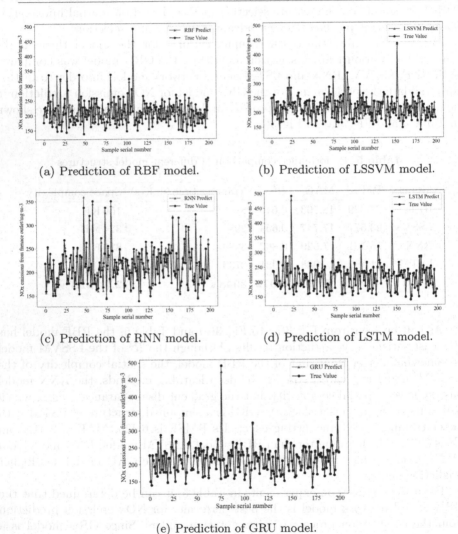

(a) Prediction of RBF model.

(b) Prediction of LSSVM model.

(c) Prediction of RNN model.

(d) Prediction of LSTM model.

(e) Prediction of GRU model.

Fig. 3. Result graph of performance comparison of different models

As shown in Table 6, when the time step is set small, the training time of the model is the shortest, but the accuracy of the model is not yet optimal. As the time step increases, the accuracy of the model improves, but the training time also increases. When the time step is set to 32, the RMSE and the MAE of the model prediction results are the smallest, and the R^2 reaches the optimum. However, the time step is set too long, resulting in reduced model predictions due to the reduced effectiveness of the model back propagation and the increased difficulty of training. Therefore, in Sect. 3.5, Hyperopt parameter tuning algorithm will be used to find the optimal time step value.

3.5   Parameter Tuning

In order to further improve the prediction accuracy of the model, seven hyperparameters of the GRU model are optimized based on Hyperopt hyper-parameter optimization algorithm. Firstly, the value of non-critical parameters is fixed: the iteration period of model training is 3000, the time step is 5, the loss function is the mean square error (MSE), the model optimization algorithm is Adam, and the model activation function uses tanh except the last layer using linear. Then set the domain space, that is, the range of seven hyperparameters: batch_size ϵ {16, 32, 64, 128, 256}, dropout_rate ϵ {0.3, 0.5, 0.8}, first_neurons ϵ {16, 32, 64, 128, 256}, second_neurons ϵ {16, 32, 64, 128, 256}, third_neurons ϵ {16, 32, 64, 128, 256}, four_neurons ϵ {16, 32, 64, 128, 256}, learning_rate ϵ {0.01, 0.001, 0.0001}. Finally, the objective function in Hyperopt is defined as minimizing loss. The optimization algorithm uses Tree Parzen Estimator, and the result history uses Trials object to store basic training information. The model tuning results are shown in Table 7 and Table 8.

Table 7. Results of superparameter tuning of the prediction model based on GRU neural network

Algorithm	Model parameters						
	batch_size	dropout_rate	first_neurons	second_neurons	third_neurons	four_neurons	learning_rate
Initial parameters	64	0.5	128	128	64	32	0.01
Grid-search	16	0.3	128	64	32	256	0.01
Random search	16	0.3	16	128	16	256	0.01
Hyperopt	16	0.3	64	128	64	256	0.01

Table 8. Performance comparison of different hyperparameter tuning algorithms corresponding to GRU model

Methods	RMSE	MAE	R^2	Training time/unit(s)	Space complexity
Grid-search	15.187	5.527	0.872	1711 s	3.76 MB
Random search	13.889	5.163	0.892	2039 s	3.20 MB
Hyperopt	**11.992**	**4.430**	**0.914**	**1333 s**	**4.33 MB**

As can be seen from Table 7 and Table 8, the prediction accuracy of the GRU neural network model is improved compared to the initial model parameter conditions(as shown in Table 6 for a time step of 5) after model parameter tuning by grid search, random search and Hyperopt hyperparameter tuning algorithm. However, Hyperopt tuning is the best performer in terms of model performance improvement. The prediction accuracy of the GRU model optimized by Hyperopt is as follows: the RMSE is 11.92, which is reduced by 4.322, the MAE is 4.30, which is reduced by 0.908 and the R^2 is 0.914, which is increased by 5.3%.

For the GRU neural network model, as it is a time-series recurrent neural network model, the step size of the time series has a large impact on the prediction results of the model. As can be seen from Table 6, the GRU model performance gets better as the time step gets larger. However, if the time step is set too large, the accuracy of the GRU model is reduced due to problems such as gradient disappearance when the GRU model gradients are back-propagated. Therefore, in order to find the optimal time step parameter(sequence_length) for the model, the time step finding range was set at [1,50]. The Hyperopt hyperparameter tuning algorithm was used to find the optimal time step parameters(sequence_length) and the experimental results are shown in Fig. 4 and Fig. 5.

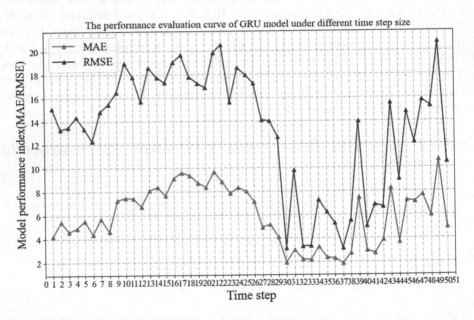

Fig. 4. GRU neural network under different time step conditions MAE and RMSE value changes

As can be seen from Fig. 4 and Fig. 5, the performance of the GRU neural network reaches an optimal value when the time step is set to 37, with the RMSE of 3.131, the MAE of 1.856 and the R^2 of 0.994. Compared with the GRU neural network model before optimization, the RMSE of the GRU neural network model decreased by 3.195, the MAE decreased by 0.556, and the R^2 increased by 2.2%. Therefore, it is verified that the Hyperopt hyperparameter tuning algorithm is effective for parameter optimization of the GRU neural network model.

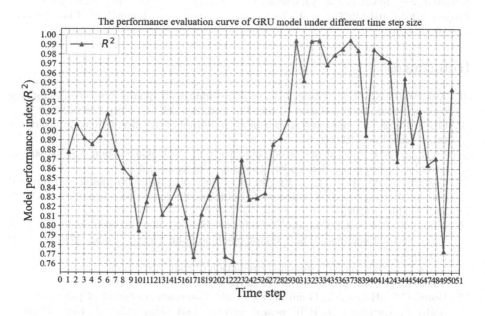

Fig. 5. Change of R^2 value of GRU neural network under different time steps

4 Conclusion

In order to improve the prediction accuracy of NOx emissions in coal-fired power plant boiler combustion process, a modeling method(MI-HGRU) combining mutual information feature selection algorithm and Hyperopt optimized GUR neural network model is proposed. The proposed MI-HGRU prediction modeling method can accurately select the characteristic variables of boiler combustion process and reduce the complexity of the model. Moreover, the GRU model was optimized by Hyperopt hyper-parameter optimization algorithm. The RMSE of GRU neural network model was reduced by 3.195, the MAE was reduced by 0.556, and the R^2 was improved by 2.2%, reaching 99.4%. Compared with the RBF model, LSSVM model, RNN model and LSTM model, the GRU model has better generalization ability and prediction accuracy, which can be effectively applied to the prediction of NOx emission at the furnace exit of power station boiler combustion process and provides an important basis for the accurate control of power station boiler combustion optimization.

Acknowledgment. This paper is supported by the Key Technology Project of Foshan City in 2019 (1920001001367), National Natural Science and Guangdong Joint Fund Project (U2001201), Guangdong Natural Science Fund Project (2018A030313061, 2021A1515011243), Research and Development Projects of National Key fields (2018YFB1004202), Guangdong Science and Technology Plan Project (2019B010139001) and Guangzhou Science and Technology Plan Project (201902020016).

References

1. Xue, W.B., Xu, Y.L., Wang, J.N., et al.: Ambient air quality impact of emissions from thermal power industry. China Environ. Sci. **36**(05), 1281–1288 (2016)
2. GB 13271–2014 Emission standard of air pollutants for boiler. China Environmental Science Press (2014)
3. Li, J.J.: Experimental and Modeling Study on NOx Generation Mechanism in Circulating Fluidized Bed Boiler. Tsinghua University (2016)
4. Gao, M.M., Yu, H.Y., Lyu, J.F., et al.: Study on prediction model and optimal control of nitrogen oxides emission of circulating fluidized bed. Clean Coal Technol. **26**(03), 46–51 (2020)
5. Zhang, H., Zhe, C.C., Ren, P.: Model for predicting boiler nitrogen oxide emissions based on least squares support vector machine. Jilin Electric Power **47**(03), 18–20 (2019)
6. Yang, Q.: Study on NOx emission prediction of coal - fired boiler based on LSTM. Mech. Electr. Inf. **2019**(05), 21–22 (2019)
7. Hong, C.S., Huang, J., Guan, Y.Y., et al.: Combustion control of power station boiler by coupling BP/RBF neural network and fuzzy rules. J. Eng. Thermal Energy Power **36**(04), 142–148 (2021)
8. Peng, H., Long, F., Ding, C.: Feature selection based on mutual information criteria of max-dependency, max-relevance, and Min-redundancy. IEEE Trans. Pattern Anal. Mach. Intell. **27**(8), 1226–1238 (2005)
9. Vergara, J.R., Estévez, P.A.: A review of feature selection methods based on mutual information. Neural Comput. Appl. **24**(1), 175–186 (2014)
10. He, F., Xiao, H.: Information entropy feature selection method to locate the cause of head narrowing of hot rolled strip. J. Eng. Sci. **37**(S1), 45–50 (2015)
11. Tao, Z., Huiling, L., Wenwen, W., et al.: GA-SVM based feature selection and parameter optimization in hospitalization expense modeling. Appl. Soft Comput. **75**, 323–332 (2019)
12. Nikbakht, S., Anitescu, C., Rabczuk, T.: Optimizing the neural network hyperparamters utilizing genetic algorithm. J. Zhejiang Univ. Sci. A (Appl. Phys. Eng.) **22**(06), 407–426 (2021)
13. Ghawi, R., Pfeffer, J.: Efficient hyperparameter tuning with grid search for text categorization using kNN approach with BM25 similarity. Open Comput. Sci. **9**(1), 160–180 (2019)
14. Xu, C., Li, S.Q., Li, Z.F., et al.; Application of reliefF-SVM with hyperparameter optimization in fault diagnosis of refrigerant charge. Chin. J. Refrigeration Technol. **41**(01), 17–22+34 (2021)

15. Torres, J.F., Gutiérrez-Avilés, D., Troncoso, A., et al.: Random hyper-parameter search-based deep neural network for power consumption forecasting[C]//International Work-Conference on Artificial Neural Networks, pp. 259–269. Springer, Cham (2019)
16. Andonie, R., Florea, A.C.: Weighted random search for CNN hyperparameter optimization. Int. J. Comput. Commun. Control **15**(2) (2020)

An MOEA/D-ACO Algorithm with Finite Pheromone Weights for Bi-objective TTP

Lei Yang[1,2(✉)], Xiaotian Jia[1], Rui Xu[1], and Jiale Cao[1]

[1] College of Mathematics and Informatics, South China Agricultural University, Guangzhou 510642, China
[2] Guangdong Provincial Key Laboratory of Food Quality and Safety, South China Agricultural University, Guangzhou 510642, China

Abstract. The Travelling Thief Problem is a complex logistics planning problem composed of the Travelling Salesman Problem and the Knapsack Problem. The Bi-objective TTP needs to optimize the two goals of the time spent on the journey and the total value of the item picked up. There are two dimensions to be considered in the solution space, which is more difficult to deal with. The original solution method has some limitations. This paper proposes a MOEA/D-ACO algorithm based on finite pheromone weights, which constructs distance-related weights when pheromone weights are initialized and adjusts the weights to improve the effect and efficiency of the ant's search path. Then a new weighted Tchebycheff aggregation method was designed. By adjusting the parameters to control the proportion of the two aggregation methods, the advantages of weighted sum method and Tchebycheff aggregation method are integrated to improve the quality of the algorithm. Then we introduced the method of dynamic adjustment of ant neighbor number and adaptive mutation operator to improve the convergence speed and the quality of the solution. The experiment result indicates that our algorithm has competitive performance comparing with the well-known optimization algorithms GA£¬ISA, ISA-Local, and NSGA-II on Bi-objective TTP benchmark datasets.

Keywords: Finite pheromone weights · MOEA/D-ACO · Bi-objective TTP · Adaptive mutation operator

1 Introduction

The Travelling Thief Problem (TTP) [1] is a typical representative of many practical logistics problems, which is a complex problem composed of the two sub-problems Travelling Salesman Problem (TSP) [2] and the Knapsack Problem (KP) [3] proposed by Bonyadi in 2013. The definitions of single-objective TTP was given in Bonyadi's paper, which laid the foundation for further research on this issue.

The Bi-objective TTP not only needs to minimize the time spent in the journey, but also needs to maximize the total value of the items picked up. Many scholars use evolutionary algorithms, dynamic programming, etc. to solve the Bi-objective TTP, but the solution effect is not ideal. The MOEA/D-ACO algorithm proposed by Ke in 2013 [4], which has been used by many researchers to solve different problems due to its

© Springer Nature Singapore Pte Ltd. 2021
Y. Tan et al. (Eds.): DMBD 2021, CCIS 1453, pp. 468–482, 2021.
https://doi.org/10.1007/978-981-16-7476-1_40

excellent performance. However, it is difficult for the parameters set in advance to change with the algorithm, which affects the convergence speed and the quality of the solution set of the algorithm.

This paper proposes a new MOEA/D-ACO algorithm based on finite pheromone weights (MOACO-PW), which is used to solve the Bi-objective TTP. The rest of this paper is organized as follows. Background knowledge of Bi-objective TTP is summarized in Sect. 2. Section 3 introduces the details of our proposed algorithms. In Sect. 4, systematic experiments are conducted to verify the effects of the proposed algorithm. Finally, Sect. 5 is conclusion of whole paper.

2 Bi-objective TTP

Bi-objective TTP needs to consider both the time spent in the journey and the total value of the item picked up, and its goal is to minimize the time function $f(\pi, z)$ and maximize the value $g(z)$ of the item picked up. It can also be transformed into minimizing both the negative form $-g(z)$ of the time function and the item value function $f(\pi, z)$ at the same time. Using matrix $A^{m \times n} = (a_{i,j})$ to allocate items to each city π_i, the thief can pick up items from each city he visited and pack them into backpack, the maximum capacity of the backpack is Q. The travel speed of the thief depends on the current backpack weight W, which is obtained by the following formula (1).

$$W(i, \pi, z) = \sum_{k=1}^{i} \sum_{j=1}^{m} a_j(\pi_k) w_j z_j \tag{1}$$

The function $a_j(\pi_k)$ has the following definition, for each item j, if the item is selected in the city π_k, it returns 1, and if it is not selected, it returns 0, v is the travel speed, and its value remains in the range $v = (v_{min}, v_{max})$. The travel speed is calculated as follows formula (2).

$$v(w) = \begin{cases} v_{max} - \dfrac{w}{Q} \cdot (v_{max} - v_{min}) & \text{if } W \leq Q \\ v_{min} & \text{otherwise} \end{cases} \tag{2}$$

The city distance is represented by a matrix $D^{n \times n} = (d_{i,j})$, where $i, j \in \{1, ..., n\}$ and $d_{i,j} = d_{j,i}$, and the path of the thief's visit is represented by a vector $\pi = (\pi_1, \pi_2, ..., \pi_n) \in P^n$, where π_i is the i-th city visited by the thief, and $\pi_1 = 1$ is usually specified. The Bi-objective TTP is defined as follows formula (3).

$$\min_{\pi, z} F(\pi, z)$$

$$F(\pi, z) = (f(\pi, z), -g(z))$$

$$\min f(\pi, z) = \sum_{i=1}^{n-1} \frac{d_{\pi_i, \pi_{i+1}}}{v(W(i, \pi, z))} + \frac{d_{\pi_n, \pi_1}}{v(W(i, \pi, z))}$$

$$\max g(z) = \sum_{j=1}^{m} z_j b_j \qquad (3)$$

$$\text{s.t.} \pi = (\pi_1, \pi_2, ..., \pi_n) \in P^n$$

$$\pi_1 = 1$$

$$z = (z_1, ..., z_m) \in B^m$$

$$\sum_{j=1}^{m} z_j w_j \leq Q$$

There are two main algorithms for Bi-objective TTP: Greedy Algorithm (GA) and Independent Sub-Problem Algorithm (ISA). The former uses exhaustive search to find TSP and fixes the tour. Then it uses exhaustive search to solve KNP. The latter uses Lin-Kernighan heuristic to find TSP, and fixes the tour. Then it uses Q-segment of KNP greedy solution to KNP. However, the quality and efficiency of these algorithms need to be improved.

3   An MOEA/D-ACO Algorithm with Finite Pheromone Weights(MOACO-PW)

3.1   Weight Tchebycheff Aggregation Strategy

The Tchebycheff aggregation method transforms the process of individuals approaching the optimal Pareto front surface to the individual evolving and optimizing along the λ to the reference point z^* until they intersect with the optimal Pareto front surface. The intersection point O is the optimal solution of the multi-objective sub-problem. In this paper, a weighted Tchebycheff aggregation method is proposed, in which ρ is designed, and the ratio of the two aggregation methods is controlled by adjusting ρ to improve the solution quality of the algorithm. The weight Tchebycheff aggregation method is calculated as shown in the following formula (4).

$$\min g^{AT}(x|\lambda, Z^*) = \rho \cdot max_{1 \leq i \leq m}\{\lambda_i|f_i(x) - Z^*|\} + (1 - \rho) \sum_{i=1}^{m} \lambda_i f_i(x) \qquad (4)$$

By optimizing the aggregation ratio parameter ρ, the convergence speed and solution quality of the algorithm can be improved.

3.2   Weight Vector Adjustment Method

When the shape of the optimal Pareto surface is close to $f_1 + f_2 + \dots + f_m = 1$, the distribution of the optimal solution will be extremely uneven. As shown in Fig. 1.

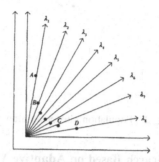

Fig. 1. Deviation occurs between uniform sampling and Pareto surface

According to the Pareto optimal solution x, the weight vector can be calculated, as shown in the following formula (5).

$$\lambda_i = \frac{1}{f_i(x) - z_i} [\sum_{i=1}^{m} \frac{1}{f_i(x) - z_i}]^{-1} \tag{5}$$

The optimal solution of the single objective sub-problem corresponding to the weight vector $\lambda = (\lambda_1, \lambda_2, \dots, \lambda_m)$ is the Pareto optimal solution x. Figure 2 shows that the clustering divides the non-dominated population into 3 parts. Because the shape of the optimal Pareto surface has a certain gap with the surface enclosed by the initial uniform weight, the D, E regions are not easy to be searched. So we have improved the generation of weight vectors. The specific method is listed as follows: Firstly, judge the area where the offspring are located, which is the result of the classification of the non-dominated population. If it is judged that the offspring individuals are still in the area where the parent individuals are located, which indicates that the current population evolution can also be affected by the weight vector. And then adjust the weight vector, which is $\lambda = \lambda - \varepsilon^*$. The adjusted weight vector will ensure the deep search of the population, and the optimal. The ability to search for solutions will also increase. If the offspring leave the area of the parent, which means that the current population evolution cannot be affected by the weight vector, and the weight vector is regenerated according to formula (5) to continue iterating.

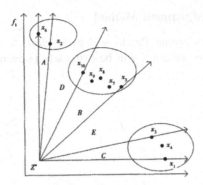

Fig. 2. Population clustering after trial

3.3　Ant Neighborhood Search Based on Adaptive Mutation Operator

The number of ant neighbors will affect the convergence speed and effect of the solutions. This paper designs an adaptive mutation operator, which can adaptively adjust the number of ant neighbors based on the evolutionary algebra. The code of the ant neighborhood search algorithm based on the adaptive mutation operator is shown in Algorithm 1.

Algorithm 1 Search_neighbor Function

Input:
　　λ the weight vector,
　　iter the number of groups,
　　max_gen the maximum number of generations
Output: set *result* the neighborhood of each weight vector
　　function SEARCH_NEIGHBOR($\lambda, iter, max\_gen$)
　　　　$T_0 = 0$
　　　　$T = T_0 2^{\exp\left(1 - \frac{G_{max}}{1 + G_{max} - G}\right)}$
　　　　for j in $\{1, ... \lambda.length\}$ **do**
　　　　　　for i in $\{1, ... \lambda.length\}$ **do**
　　　　　　　　$distance[i] = |\lambda_i - \lambda_j|$
　　　　　　end for
　　　　#returns the index value of the array value sorted from smallest to largest
　　　　　　$temp = $ ARGSORT($distance$)
　　　　#take the first T index
　　　　　　$result.add(temp[:T])$
　　　　end for
　　　　return *result*
　　end function

3.4   A Method of Updating Finite Pheromone Weights Based on Distance Weighting

In this paper, the weights related to distance are designed in the initialization pheromone, so that the cities which are closer to the current city have a higher probability of being selected. In the initial stage of the iteration, the weight $q1$ is introduced when the pheromone is initialized, which makes the pheromone concentration in cities closer to city l where the current ant is located than in cities farther away. The initial pheromone concentration is shown in formula (6).

$$\tau_{k,l}(0) = \max\{1, pow(q1, max(c_l^j)/(K * c_{k,l}^j))\} \tag{6}$$

The update of pheromone draws on the maximum and minimum ant colony system, and sets the finite pheromone weight. The pseudo code of the finite pheromone update method based on distance weighting is shown in Algorithm 2.

Algorithm 2 Pheromone Function

Input:
  K the number of groups,
  $city$ the number of cities,
  q_1 the weight value
  $pathTable$ the cities where ants crawl
  N the number of ants
  $distmat1$ the distance between cities
Output: $pheromoneTable$ the pheromone matrix
  function PHEROMONE($K, city, q_1, pathTable, N, distmat1$)
    for m in $\{1,...K\}$ **do**
      for i in $\{1,...city\}$ and j in $\{1,...city\}$ **do**
        $pheromoneTable[m][i][j] = 1$
      end for
    end for
    for j in $\{1,...N/K\}$ **do**
      $start = pathTable[j][0]$
      for i in $\{1,...city\}$ **do**
        if $start! = i$ **then**
          $ad = distmat1[start][i]$ $ap = $ MAX($distmat1[start]$)
          $pheromoneTable[0][start][i] = $ MAX($q_1^{\frac{ap}{K*ad}}, 1$)
        end if
      end for
    end for
    return $pheromoneTable$
  end function

3.5   Algorithm Framework

We firstly define the information related to the N ants of MOEA/D-ACO: In N solutions $x^1, ..., x^N \in \Omega$, the x^i is the current solution of sub-problem i; F^i in $F^1, ..., F^N$ is the function value of x^i, that is, $F^i = F(x^i)$; τ^j in $\tau^1, ..., \tau^K$ is the current solution pheromone weights of group j ants; $\eta^1, ..., \eta^N$, where η^i is the heuristic information weight of sub-problem i, which is predetermined before searching; EP contains the external archive of all non-dominated solutions found so far. The basic process of the algorithm in this paper is listed as follows.

(1) the Basic Settings:

① the Settings of N and $\lambda^1, .., \lambda^N$: N is controlled by H, and each component of $\lambda^1, .., \lambda^N$ selects a value from the following set: $\{0, \frac{1}{H}, ..., \frac{H-1}{H}, 1\}$, so there are $N = C_{H+m-1}^{m-1}$ weight vector combinations.

② the Settings of the Number of Subgroups:

In order to set the number of the subgroup for each ant, we used the above method to set K and the weight vector $\xi^1, \xi^2, ..., \xi^K$ of each subgroup and calculated the vector with the smallest distance $\xi^1, \xi^2, ..., \xi^K$ for $\lambda^1, \lambda^2, .., \lambda^N$.

③ the Settings of Neighborhood: Calculating the neighborhood of the weight vector based on Euclidean distance.

④ Heuristic Information and Pheromone: The n-dimensional real-valued vector is used to represent the pheromone and heuristic information, and the pheromone weight of subgroup j is shown in formula (7).

$$\tau^j = (\tau_1^j, \tau_2^j, ..., \tau_n^j) \tag{7}$$

Where τ_k^j represents the value of the item k picked up by the subgroup j in the previous search. The heuristic information weight of the ant i is shown in formula (8).

$$\eta^i = (\eta_1^i, \eta_2^i, , ..., \eta_n^i) \tag{8}$$

The η_k^i represents the prior value of item k selected by ant i. The relevant definitions are as follows: k, l in the pheromone weight $\tau_{k,l}^j$ of each group j means that city k and city l are connected; k, l in the heuristic information weight $\eta_{k,l}^i$ of an ant i means that it connects city k and city l. Each independent solution x represents the order of a city.

(2) Initialization: For $i = 1, ..., N$, the initial solution x^i of the sub-problem i is generated and set $F^i = F(x^i)$. For $i = 1, ..., N$, the initialization the heuristic information weight of ant i is $\eta_{k,l}^i = \frac{\sum_{j=1}^m \lambda_j^i b_j}{\sum_{j=1}^m \lambda_j^i c_{k,l}^j}$, where $c_{k,l}^j$ represents the distance between city k and city l in the j-th target, and b_j represents the value of item j. As for $j = 1, 2, ..., k$, τ^j represents the pheromone weight of j, which is needed to be initialized. Then initialize EP, which is the set of all non-dominated solutions in $\{F^1, ..., F^N\}$. Finally initialize Z^* for $i = 1, 2, ..., m$, $Z_i^* = min\{f_i(x)|x \in \Omega\}$.

(3) Constructing New Solutions£°As for $i = 1, ..., N$, assuming that ant i belongs to the j-th group, and the current solution is $x^i = (x_1^i, ..., x_n^i)$, the ant i will construct a new solution $y^i = (y_1^i, y_2^i, ..., y_n^i)$ in the following way.

① For all $k, l = 1, ..., n$ (n is the number of cities), specify

$$\phi_{k,l} = [\tau_{k,l}^i + \Delta * x'^i * In(x^i, (k, l))]^\alpha * (\eta_{k,l}^i)^\beta \qquad (9)$$

The Δ£¬α£¬β are all controlling parameters and greater than 0. $\phi_{k,l}$ represents the attractiveness of the route between city k and city l to ant i, that is, the degree of preference. If the solution x^i includes city k and city l, then the function $In(x^i, (k, l))$ is 1, otherwise it is 0.

② The ant i finds an arbitrary city as the starting point firstly. And then starts to create the route. Assuming that the current location of ant i is city l and it has not yet completed all the cities, it will choose city k from the set of cities C that has never been walked. If $C \neq \emptyset$, a number from (0,1) will be randomly generated first. If this number is less than the control parameter r, ant i chooses the city with the largest ϕ value as the next city k from the city set C that has never been completed. If the random number is greater than the control parameter r, a city is randomly selected from C as the next city k according to the roulette principle. Then remove the city k from the set C. If the set C is an empty set, a new solution can be obtained, otherwise repeat the above steps. In formula (9), τ_k^j is the k-th component of the pheromone weight shared by all ants in the subgroup j. x'^i also indicates that item k is selected in the current solution of subproblem i. x'^1 is the private information of Ant i. Therefore, $\Delta * x'^i * In(x^i, (k, l))$ combines subgroups and private information. This combination is represented by the pheromone of ant i on item k and city k and city l.

(4) Updating Reference Points Z^*: To $i = 1, 2, ..., m$, $Z_i^* = min\{f_i(x) | x \in \Omega\}$.

(5) Updating EP: The constructed new solutions are applyed to update the external archive EP. As for $i = 1, ..., N$, if there is no vector in EP that can dominate $F(y^i)$, add $F(y^i)$ to EP and delete the vector dominated by $F(y^i)$ in EP.

(6) Terminating: If the problem-specific stopping conditions are met, the program is stopped and EP is output, and the algorithm can return a complete and feasible solution. The introduction of current solution information can promote communication between ants and neighbors, so that ants in different groups can also cooperate. The solution distribution obtained in this way will be more even.

(7) Updating Pheromone Weights: As for $j = 1, 2, ..., k$, the pheromone weights of the j-th group are updated by using the function constructed by the ants in the j-th group in step 2 and the new solution information added to the EP in step 4, and the algorithm draws on the maximum and minimum ant colony system (MMAS), MMAS effectively solves the shortcomings of high pheromone concentrations in certain paths that make the algorithm fall into local optimum. τ_{max} and τ_{min} are used to limit the range of pheromone.

(8) Updateing x^i: As for $i = 1, ..., N$, the ant i looks for the solution y, which is the solutions with the smallest $g(\cdot | \lambda^i, Z^*)$ among all the new solutions. These new

solutions are constructed by its neighbors and have not been used to replace other old solutions. If $g(y|\lambda^i, Z^*) < g(x^i|\lambda^i, Z^*)$, x^i will be replaced with y and new solutions will be recreated.

4 Experiment and Result Analysis

4.1 DataSet

This paper designs two datasets, one is a customized datasets: the number of cities in different datasets can be 10, 20, 50, and 100, and each city can have 1, 5, and 10 items. According to the maximum capacity, backpacks are divided into small backpacks ($c = 0.2$), medium backpacks ($c = 0.5$) and large backpacks ($c = 0.8$), that is, the backpack capacity $Q = c \sum_{i=1}^{m} w_i$ is dynamic. Set the speed range of the thief's travel V_{min} and V_{max}. The name of the TTP datasets is as follows: multi-number of cities-number of items in each city-type of backpack.

For all mutli-cluster-X datasets, 100 cities were assigned to X different clusters. And only one item is allocated to each city, and the backpack is a medium backpack. The other is the Polyakovskiyet datasets: 9 medium/large examples in the comprehensive TTP benchmark developed by Polyakovskiyet are used, as shown in Table 1.

Table 1. Bi-objective TTP Benchmark datasets

Datasets	N	m	Q	KP type	R
a280_n279	280	279	25936	bsc	01
a280_n395		395	63701	usw	05
a280_n790		790	126202	unc	10
fnl446_n446	446	446	87150	bsc	01
fnl446_n230		223	18205	usw	05
fnl446_n600		600	102441	unc	10
pla338_n338	338	338	91521	bsc	01
pla338_n404		404	77184	usw	05
pla338_n809		809	153960	unc	10

In Table 1, according to the value/weight ratio of the items, three different methods are used to construct the backpack component of each item using boundary strong correlation (bsc), uncorrelation of similar weight(usw) and uncorrelated (unc). The number of items available in each city (R), of which no items are placed in the first city.

4.2 Experiments and Analysis

The experimental parameters of this paper: the number of ants $N = 24$, the number of ant groups $K = 3$, the number of initialized ant neighbors $T_0 = 10$, the pheromone volatilization coefficient $\rho = 0.95$, the pheromone factor $\alpha = 1$, the heuristic function factor $\beta = 2$, the disturbance coefficient $r = 0.9$, the maximum number of iterations $G_{max} = 3000$, the pheromone weight $q_1 = 1.5$, the probability selection weight $q_2 = 2$,. the control parameter $\Delta = 0.05 * \tau_{max}$, the weight vector adjustment control parameter $g_d = 5$, the reference point of the HV index $Ref = (30000, 30000)$ initialize the weight vector $\lambda_i^j = (\lambda_1^j, \lambda_2^j, .., ., \lambda_m^j (\sum_{i=1}^m \lambda_i^j = 1, j = 1, 2..., N)$, and it is a value that is not repeated from $\{\frac{0}{N-1}, \frac{1}{N-1}, ..., \frac{N-1}{N-1}\}$.

For the Bi-objective TTP, the algorithm is compared from the HV index of the comprehensive quality evaluation method of the solution set, the algorithm convergence speed, the coverage rate and the distribution degree, and the running time. The larger the HV value, the better.

The normalized results of the HV index of the median Pareto frontier of MOACO-PW and other algorithms on the custom dataset are shown in Fig. 3. The algorithm is executed 30 times to get the average value, and each run iterates 100,000 times.

According to the results in Fig. 3, the average HV index of MOACO-PW in most datasets is higher than other algorithms, and it also shows that optimizing independent sub-problems does not show better results than independent sub-problems.

Figure 4 shows the HV index performance comparison between MOACO-PW and the MOEA/D-ACO on 10 custom datasets. The algorithm is executed 30 times to get the average value, and both stop after 1000 generations.

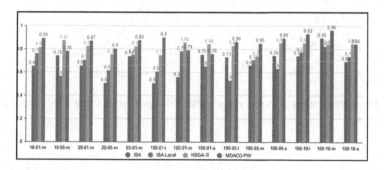

Fig. 3. The normalized results of the four algorithms HV indicators

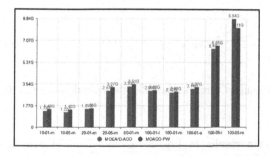

Fig. 4. Comparison of HV indicators of the two algorithms

It can be seen from Fig. 4 that the average value of the HV index of MOACO-PW is higher on the custom datasets. Figures 5, 6, and 7 show the comparison of the Pareto frontier results of MOACO-PW and MOEA/D-ACO after being randomly run 1000 times on 6 custom datasets. The algorithms are executed 30 times to get the average value.

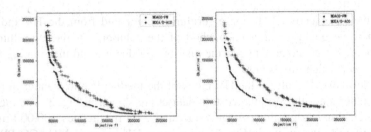

Fig. 5. The average result of Pareto surface after the algorithms are run 1000 times on 10-05-m and 20-05-m

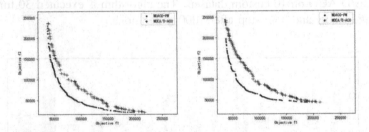

Fig. 6. The average result of Pareto surface after the algorithms are run 1000 times on 50-01-m and 100-01-s

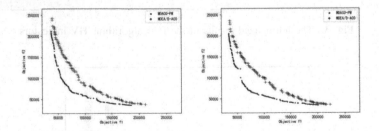

Fig. 7. The average result of Pareto surface after the algorithms are run 1000 times on 100-05-l, 100-10-m

According to the results in Fig. 5, 6, and 7 the Pareto frontier obtained by MOACO-PW in different city scales on the standard datasets has a more uniform and better solution set, which is substantially close to the standard Pareto frontier. Figures 8, 9 and 10 show the comparison of the average growth process of the HV

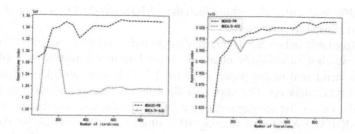

Fig. 8. The HV index change process of the algorithms running 1000 times on 10-05-m and 20-05-m

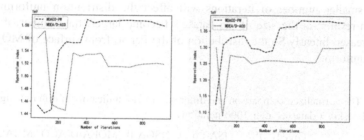

Fig. 9. The HV indicator change process of the algorithms running 1000 times on 50-01-m and 100-01-s

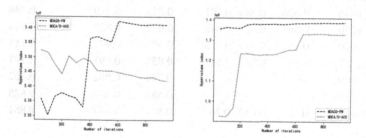

Fig. 10. The HV index change process of the algorithms running 1000 times on 100-05-l and 100-10-m

index with the increase of the number of iterations after MOACO-PW and MOEA/D-ACO are randomly run 1000 times on 6 custom datasets. According to the results of Figs. 8, 9 and 10, the HV index changes rapidly with the number of iterations, which shows that the optimization of pheromone initialization and the restriction on pheromone update effectively improve the convergence speed of the solution.

In addition, the results in Fig. 10 show that the HV value of MOACO-PW in the mutli-0100-10-m datasets initially stabilized at a relatively high level, which verifies that the convergence of the algorithm has been greatly improved. Table 2 shows the HV index performance comparison of Polyakovskiyet's large-scale datasets to

MOACO-PW and other algorithms including MOEA/D-ACO. Among them, mutli-0010-01-m is used as a reference.

The algorithms below are averaged after 30 independent runs. The "-" means that the result was not successfully obtained. According to the results in Table 2, the 6 algorithms mentioned in this paper are in the HV indicators on 9 large datasets and a custom reference datasets. The improved algorithm works well in most cases. Figures 11, 12 and 13 show the comparison of the Pareto frontier average results of MOACO-PW and MOEA/D-ACO after running 1000 times on 9 Polyakovskiyet datasets randomly. Both algorithms are run independently for 30 times to obtain the average value of the objective function.

Seen from Figs. 5, 6, and 7 and Figs. 11, 12 and 13, The Pareto front surface of MOACO-PW is closer to the ideal point compared with MOEA/D-ACO. This shows that the smaller number of iterations will affect the distribution uniformity of the algorithm results.As the size of the datasets become larger, the number of iterations have increased linearly.So the distribution of the Pareto front surface of MOACO-PW is more uniform.

Table 2. The normalized comparison and difference of HV indicators of different algorithms on the Polyakovskiyet datasets after 1000 iterations

Datasets	Greedy	ISA	ISA-Local	NSGA-II	MOEA/D-ACO	MOACO-PW
a280_n279	0.5624	0.612	0.57	0.825	0.851	**0.874**
a280_n395	0.79	0.541	0.663	0.721	**0.872**	0.815
a280_n790	0.616	0.437	0.501	0.735	0.781	**0.792**
fnl446_n446	0.626	0.586	0.691	0.553	0.719	**0.798**
fnl446_n230	0.591	0.487	0.648	0.672	**0.823**	0.804
fnl446_n600	0.381	0.55	0.316	0.697	0.672	**0.717**
pla338_n338	-	0.777	0.515	**0.858**	0.791	0.791
pla338_n404	-	-	-	0.744	**0.802**	0.802
pla338_n809	-	-	-	0.581	0.613	**0.628**
mutli-0010-01-m	0.462	0.652	0.76	0.814	0.847	**0.851**

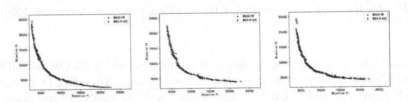

Fig. 11. The Pareto front surface after the algorithms are run 1000 times on a280_n279 (_n395, _n790)

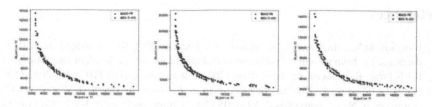

Fig. 12. Pareto front surface after the algorithms are run 1000 times on fnl446_n446(_n230, _n600)

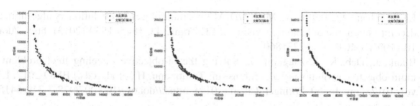

Fig. 13. Pareto front surface after the algorithms are run 1000 times on pla338_n338(_n404, _n809)

5 Conclusions and Future Work

After analyzing the shortcomings of existing algorithms in dealing with the Bi-objective TTP, this paper proposes a MOEA/D-ACO algorithm based on finite pheromone weights, which constructs distance-related weights when pheromone weights are initialized. Then a new weighted Tchebycheff aggregation method was designed, and a method of dynamically adjusting the number of ant neighbors and an adaptive mutation operator are introduced. By comparing experiments with other algorithms, it is concluded that this algorithm has a better effect in solving the Bi-objective TTP. However, the algorithm still has some areas for improvement: the use of the datasets specification problem when solving the Bi-objective TTP, the dividing line of the number of algorithm iterations, the number of averages, and the solution of multi-dimensional targets need further study.

Acknowledgment. This work was partially supported by the Natural Science Foundation of Guangdong Province of China (Grant No. 2020A1515010691), Science and Technology Project of Guangdong Province of China (Grant No. 2018A0124), National Natural Science Foundation of China (Grant Nos. 61573157 and 61703170), and Guangdong Provincial Key Laboratory of Food Quality and Safety (Grant No. 2020B1212060059).The authors also gratefully acknowledge the reviewers for their helpful comments and suggestions that helped to improve the presentation.

References

1. Bonyadi, M.R., Michalewicz, Z., Barone, L.: The travelling thief problem: the first step in the transition from theoretical problems to realistic problems. In: Evolutionary Computation. IEEE Press, Piscataway, pp. 1037–1044 (2013). https://doi.org/10.1109/CEC.2013.6557681
2. Gutin, G., Punnen, A.: The traveling salesman problem and its variations. Paradigms Comb. Optim. Prob. New Approaches **4**, 193–205 (2007). https://doi.org/10.1002/9781118600207.ch7
3. Kellerer, H., Pferschy, U., Pisinger, D.: Introduction to NP-Completeness of Knapsack Problems, pp. 483–493. Springer, Heidelberg (2004). https://doi.org/10.1007/978-3-540-24777-7_16
4. Ke, L., Zhang, Q., Battiti, R.: MOEA/D-ACO: a multiobjective evolutionary algorithm using decomposition and antcolony. Cybern. IEEE Trans. **43**, 1845–1859 (2013). https://doi.org/10.1109/TSMCB.2012.2231860
5. Blank, J., Deb, K., Mostaghim, S.: Solving the bi-objective traveling thief problem with multi-objective evolutionary algorithms. In: Trautmann, H., et al. (eds.) EMO 2017. LNCS, vol. 10173, pp. 46–60. Springer, Cham (2017). https://doi.org/10.1007/978-3-319-54157-0_4
6. Chagas, J.B.C., Blank, J., Wagner, M., Souza, M.J.F., Deb, K.: A non-dominated sorting based customized random-key genetic algorithm for the bi-objective traveling thief problem. J. Heuristics **27**(3), 267–301 (2020). https://doi.org/10.1007/s10732-020-09457-7
7. Cheng, J., Zhang, G., Li, Z., et al.: Multi-objective ant colony optimization based on decomposition for bi-objective traveling salesman problems. Soft. Comput. **16**, 597–614 (2012). https://doi.org/10.1007/s00500-011-0759-3
8. Hui, L., Zhang, Q.: Multiobjective optimization problems with complicated Pareto sets, MOEA/D and NSGA-II. IEEE Trans. Evol. Comput. **13**, 284–302 (2009). https://doi.org/10.1109/TEVC.2008.925798
9. Wu, J., Polyakovskiy, S., Wagner, M. et al.: Evolutionary computation plus dynamic programming for the bi-objective travelling thief problem. In: Proceedings of the Genetic and Evolutionary Computation Conference. ACM, New York, pp. 777–784. (2018). https://doi.org/10.1145/3205455.3205488
10. Mei, M.A., Hecheng, L.I.: Hybrid genetic algorithm for solving new optimization model of TTP. Comput. Eng. Appl. **54**(6), 156–160 (2018)
11. El Yafrani, M., Martins, M., Wagner, M., Ahiod, B., Delgado, M., Lüders, R.: A hyperheuristic approach based on low-level heuristics for the travelling thief problem. Genet. Program Evolvable Mach. **19**(1–2), 121–150 (2017). https://doi.org/10.1007/s10710-017-9308-x

Lightweight Object Tracking Algorithm Based on Siamese Network with Efficient Attention

Hanhua Yu and Qingling Liu[(✉)]

Harbin Engineering University, Harbin, China
{yuhanhua, liuqingling}@hrbeu.edu.cn

Abstract. Siamese networks have drawn great attention in visual tracking in recently years because they have a good balance between accuracy and speed. However, in most Siamese trackers, their backbone networks used as feature extractor are relatively shallow and narrow like AlexNet, which does not take full advantage of deep neural networks. In this paper, we propose a lightweight Siamese network object tracking algorithm based on efficient attention mechanism to enhance tracking robustness and accuracy. Firstly, we modify MobileNetV2 and use it as our backbone network, it can reduces the parameters and calculation amount drastically and upgrades the speed of training and testing. Secondly, attention mechanism weighted the feature maps in channels and spatial use for distributing the contribution of the different response maps. Thirdly, different level features are fused for the purpose of obtaining more robust results. The experiments show that our tracker can improve both the accuracy and speed on three benchmarks, including OTB2015, VOT2018 and TrackingNet.

Keywords: Object tracking · Siamese network · Lightweight · Attention mechanism

1 Introduction

In computer vision field, object tracking task is a basic research direction which aims to predict the position of an object in need in the whole image sequence when its location was given only in the first frame. How to achieve real-time tracking is vital problem, it can be apply into many scenes such as autopilot, intelligent robotics and remote collaboration.

Modern trackers include two directions approximately. The first direction is correlation filter based methods, which takes good advantages of circular correlation and performing operations in the Fourier domain to get a regressor. It makes these methods can tracking online and update the weights of filters simultaneously and efficiently. After the correlation filter based method conducted in Fourier domain, then these methods are used widely by researchers. Recently, correlation filter based methods for the purpose of improving the accuracy by using deep features, but it largely increased the amount of parameters and calculations result in reducing the speed during tracking. Another direction of modern trackers focuses on use robustness deep features by convolution network and keeping the model updated. However, because these trackers

© Springer Nature Singapore Pte Ltd. 2021
Y. Tan et al. (Eds.): DMBD 2021, CCIS 1453, pp. 483–497, 2021.
https://doi.org/10.1007/978-981-16-7476-1_41

do not use the domain specific information well, performance of these trackers is always worse than correlation filter based trackers.

In recently years, Siamese networks based trackers have attracted great attention because of well-balanced between speed and accuracy. These Siamese network based trackers regard the object tracking task as a similarity mapping problem by do cross-correlation operation with the feature maps which extracted from the template branch and the search branch. However, these trackers still use narrow and shallow network like AlexNet [1] as their backbone.

Aiming at the above problems, this paper proposes a Siamese network object tracking algorithm based on lightweight backbone and efficient attention modules. The contributes of this method is mainly reflected in the following three aspects:

(1) The improved lightweight network MobileNetV2 [2] is used as the feature extraction backbone network, which eliminates the impact of the filling operation on the tracking model, and adjusts its network structure to adapt to the tracking algorithm;
(2) In order to obtain features that are more conducive to the model, efficient channel attention and spatial attention modules are designed to promote the network's model ability of discrimination;
(3) The cross-correlation results of different layers are fused for weights averaging to generate a score response map to take full advantage of low-level and high-level information to improve the performance and robustness of the model.

Our network framework is shown in Fig. 1.

2   Related Work

In this section, we will introduce some latest trackers, especially those the trackers based on Siamese network. We also introduce developments of attention mechanism in recently years simultaneously. Object tracking as a computer vision task has a rapid improvement in the past ten years because of the construction and metrics of new benchmark datasets and tracking methodologies has been greatly improved. These new benchmark datasets has become standardized testing platform for comparing with other mainstream algorithms. The tracking challenge competition held every year continuously promotes the improvement of tracking performance. All these advancements promote researchers to propose many novel tracking algorithms.

Since ten years ago, correlation filters based algorithm have been appeared and got good results by using the detection-based target framework. Cyclic convolution used in correlation filters to distinguish objects and backgrounds by training filters. Bolme et al. [3] proposed Minimum Output Sum of Squared Error (MOSSE), using correlation filters method to object tracking task firstly. The idea of correlation filters followed the development of the Circulant Structure with Kernels (CSK) [4], Kernel Correlation Filter (KCF) [5] and the Efficient Convolution Operator (ECO) [6]. The DeepSRDCF proposed by Danelljan et al. [7] uses the convolution layer features to replace the traditional feature. Ma et al. [8] by analyzing the characteristics of backbone network VGGNet [9] introduced the Hierarchical Convolutional Features (HCFT).

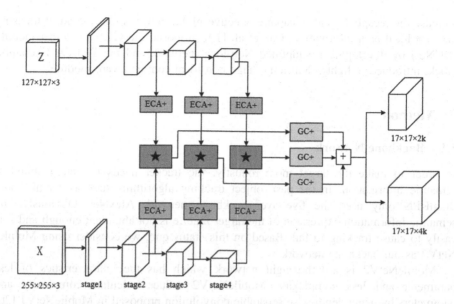

Fig. 1. Framework of Siamese network based on efficient attention modules. Our backbone network including four stages (see it in Sect. 3.1), we have list it one by one, ECA+ denote the efficient channel attention module we designed (see it in Sect. 3.2), GC+ denote the efficient spatial attention module we designed (see it in Sect. 3.2), ★ denote adjust and correlation operation.

Siamese network algorithm was proposed by Luca Bertinetto et al. [10] which conclude two branches and weight-sharing backbone network, those used to calculate the similarity between the search branch and template branch to distinguish the similar objects. DSiam [11] design a feature transformation which not only ease the object appearance deformation problem efficient but also reduce background interference. SASiam [12] introduces multiple attention mechanisms to make the tracking model more robust to the object. In order to achieve object regression more accuracy, SiamRPN [13] from object detection task introduces the Region Proposal Network (RPN) into the Siamese network. DaSiamRPN [14] then by using a distractor-aware module upgrade the tracker's discrimination ability to distinguish the positive samples and negative samples.

In recently years, researchers have applied attention mechanisms to convolution neural networks to strengthen their robustness. It gets good performance in object detection task and introduce it into object tracking task. Hu et al. [15] use the feature of the global average pooling operation to calculate the attention between channels.

Woo et al. [16] use max pooling and average pooling to calculate the channel attention, and use a 2D convolution to compute spatial attention and combine it finally. Wang et al. [17] proposed an Efficient Channel Attention module (ECANet) which does not reduce dimensions by summarizing Hu's work shortcomings. Wang et al. [18] designed a Non-local Neural Network, a non-local operation that calculates the response of a certain location as the weighted summation of all location features to increase the receptive field to capture effective global information instead of focusing only on local area information. Cao et al. [19] proposed the Global Context module (GCNet) by developing a simplified Non-local network and the Squeeze-Excitation block, introduces a lightweight long-range non-local context-aware module.

3   Method

3.1   Backbone Network

In order to make the target more robustly, the tracker needs to obtain abundant semantic information. In the past, object tracking algorithms such as SiamFC and SiamRPN only used the five-layer backbone network AlexNet. Obviously, the semantic information expression of the target feature is not abundant enough and it is easily to cause tracking to fail. Based on this status quo, we consider using Mobile-NetV2 as our backbone network.

MobileNetV2 is a lightweight network which has the characteristics of less parameter and less complexity. MobileNetV2 reduce calculate complexity and parameters by using depth-wise separable convolution proposed in MobileNetV1 [20] to replace standard convolution, and refers to ResNet [21] structure build out inverted residual network block. In the trade-off between accuracy and speed using depth-wise separable convolution and inverted residual block, the accuracy will be reduced a bit, but the speed can be greatly improved.

In order to enable MobileNetV2 to effectively solve the object tracking problem, the network has been improved in the following three aspects:

(1) Deleting 2 convolution layers with stride of 2, and change the total stride of the network from 32 to 8. The original MobileNetV2 network was proposed for classification and detection tasks, it reduces the input size of 224×224 to output size of 7×7. But in tracking tasks, the size of the input of the Siamese network is small, input size is 127×127 in template branch and input size is 255×255 in search branch, reducing the stride appropriately can effectively retain enough feature information in the deep feature map to make the network adapted to tracking tasks;

(2) Cropping the feature maps that influenced by padding operation. The padding will cause the maximum response point in the feature map to shift, and the maximum response in score map obtained when the similarity measurement is done will also have a large deviation. In order to reduce the influence of padding on the tracker, the outermost feature of the feature map is removed by cropping operation after every inverted residual block;

(3) Changing the stride of convolutions with 3×3 filters in bottleneck to 1.The original network uses a convolution layer with a step size of 2 to reduce the resolution of the feature map to half of the original. It is easy to lose the edge information of the image, which is not conducive to tracking. Therefore, we changes the stride of all convolutions with 3×3 filters in bottleneck to 1, and uses the maximum pooling layer to reduce the resolution of the feature map as an alternative.

The specific backbone network structure is shown in Table 1.

Table 1. Backbone network structure.

Stage	Convolution layer	Stride	Padding	For exemplar	For search
Input				$127 \times 127 \times 3$	$255 \times 255 \times 3$
Stage 1	Conv3 $\times$ 3	2	1	$60 \times 60 \times 64$	$124 \times 124 \times 64$
Stage 2	maxpool2 $\times$ 2	2	0	$30 \times 30 \times 64$	$62 \times 62 \times 64$
	Bottleneck	1	1	$28 \times 28 \times 64$	$60 \times 60 \times 64$
	Bottleneck	1	1	$26 \times 26 \times 64$	$58 \times 58 \times 64$
Stage 3	Bottleneck	1	1	$24 \times 24 \times 128$	$56 \times 56 \times 128$
	Bottleneck	1	1	$22 \times 22 \times 128$	$54 \times 54 \times 128$
	Bottleneck	1	1	$20 \times 20 \times 128$	$52 \times 52 \times 128$
Stage 4	Bottleneck	1	1	$18 \times 18 \times 256$	$50 \times 50 \times 256$
	maxpool2 $\times$ 2	2	0	$9 \times 9 \times 256$	$25 \times 25 \times 256$
	Bottleneck	1	1	$7 \times 7 \times 256$	$23 \times 23 \times 256$
	Bottleneck	1	1	$5 \times 5 \times 256$	$21 \times 21 \times 256$

3.2   Attention Mechanism

In this section, we introduce the attention mechanism conclude channel attention and spatial attention, which makes the process of feature extraction faster. The channel attention mechanism focuses on the contribution of each channel, and spatial attention mechanism focuses on the contribution of each location primarily. The attention modules we designed can hardly affect the tracking speed while improving the tracking performance. For details, see Sect. 4.3 of the ablation experiment.

Efficient Channel Attention Module. Refer to ECANet, we improve the channel attention and design an efficient channel attention module we call it ECA+. Putting input features into global average pooling layer and global max pooling layer to calculate the channel weights in the case of keeping interactive learning in high dimensions. Firstly, calculate the global average pooling values and global max pooling values of every input channel. Then, calculate interactive information between adjacent channels, through a sigmoid activate layer and calculate the weighted summation. Last, calculate input features and weights multiply in channel-wise to achieve the effect of enhancing the original features. The designed efficient channel attention module ECA+ is shown in Fig. 2.

It can be shown by the following equation:

$$\tilde{x}_i = \{\lambda_A \sigma(\sum_{j=1}^{k} \alpha^j G_A^j(c_i)) + \lambda_M \sigma(\sum_{l=1}^{k} \beta^l G_M^l(c_i))\} \bullet x_i \tag{1}$$

In Eq. (1), c_i denote the ith channel, G_A and G_M denote the global average pooling operation and global max pooling operation, respectively. Calculate the information learned by the interaction between adjacent channels through summation, and $\sigma()$ denote sigmoid function. λ_A and λ_M are weights in summation. Content in brackets are weights calculated by using the module designed.

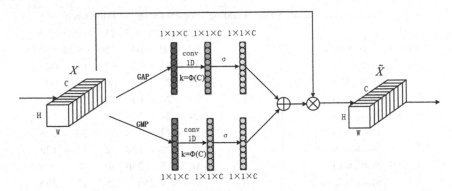

Fig. 2. Efficient channel attention module

Efficient Spatial Attention Module. Refer to GCNet, we improve the spatial attention and design an efficient spatial attention module we call it GC+. The network can effectively perceive the context information of the target, thereby enhancing the estimation of the target state. Firstly, we use a convolution with 1×1 filter to get spatial information and do matrix multiplication with tiled input features to get non-local context. Then, two continuously convolution layers and a layer-normalization layer between that used to ease optimization. Last, using a spatial max pooling layer generates pixel-wise weights. The designed efficient spatial attention module GC+ is shown in Fig. 3.

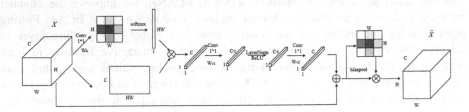

Fig. 3. Efficient spatial attention module

It can be shown by the following equation:

$$\tilde{x}_i = (x_i + w_i) \bullet \max_{i=1}^{C}(x_i + w_i) \tag{2}$$

Equation (2) denotes the final result after summation and a spatial max pooling.In Eq. (2), w_i is the result of the bottleneck transform conclude a layer normalization layer between two convolution layers which filter size both 1×1, It can be shown by the following equation:

$$w_i = W_{v2} \bullet \text{ReLU}[LN(W_{v1} \bullet \sum_{j=1}^{N_p} \alpha_j x_j)] \quad (3)$$

In Eq. (3), α_j is the result of the first matrix multiplication denotes the weight for global attention pooling, It can be shown by the following equation:

$$\alpha_j = \frac{e^{W_k x_j}}{\sum_{m=1}^{N_p} e^{W_k x_m}} \quad (4)$$

3.3 Feature Fusion

Features extracted from the first two stages contain abundant low level appearance information such as color and shape, these are all indispensable for object localization but lacking of enough semantic information; features extracted from the last two stages contain abundant semantic information that can response special scenarios like scale variation or occlusion better. In general, these high-level features are more sensitive to object detection and low-level features are more sensitive to object localization.

In deeper convolution layers, the resolution of the feature maps are getting lower and it is more difficult to see the low level features on the images, but the boundary between the object and the background become more conspicuous. It denotes the high level feature maps is helpful in object classification.

In order to further improve the robustness of the algorithm, this paper makes improvements based on SiamRPN. The cross-correlation results of template and search based on the feature maps generated by channel attention and spatial attention are weighted and averaged. For details, see Sect. 4.3 of the ablation experiment.

4 Experiments

4.1 Experimental Details

We pre-trained the parameters of our networks on ImageNet and use it to initialize the weights. During training period, the weights of the first convolution layer was frozen, and the weights of other layers are fine-tuned from back to front gradually. After every five epochs, every layers weights in bottleneck were unfrozen. As same as in SiamRPN, we set testing epochs to 50. Reducing the learning rates from 10^{-2} to 10^{-6} logarithmically, respectively. The weight decay and the momentum are set to 10^{-4} and 0.9. We use the GOT-10K dataset as our training dataset. Following the conventional, the size of input image in template branch is 127×127 pixels, and the size of input image in search branch is 255×255 pixels.

The embedding function $\phi_\theta(z)$ in template branch is computed only once at the first frame, and the parameters were frozen, then is continuously matched to subsequent features $\phi_\theta(x)$ from search branch. In order to response scale variations problem, Siamese searches for the object over three scales $1.0482^{\{-1, 0, 1\}}$ and updates the scale by linear interpolation with a factor of 0.3629 to provide damping. We set the anchor aspect ratio general five scales [1/3, 1/2, 1, 2, 3]. Our backbone network and whole model are implemented in visual environment Python 3.7 and PyTorch 1.1.0. The experiments are conducted on a PC with an Nvidia GeForce RTX2080 GPU and an Intel 10600KF CPU.

4.2   Comparison Experiments

OTB Benchmark. OTB2015 is a widely used tracking dataset that contains 100 fully annotated sequences, including 26 Gy sequences and 76 color sequences, and different sequences including different attributes in 11 tracking challenges. It uses Precision and Success(AUC) scores as the main two evaluation indicators. Precision rate represents the percentage of the error between the center point coordinate of the bounding-box predicted by the algorithm and the center point coordinate of the ground-truth frames to the total number of frames at the threshold of 20. When the IoU exceeds the set threshold, the prediction of the current frame is regarded as a success, and the percentage of the total number of frames successfully predicted to the total number of frames is the Success rate.

We choose four Siamese network trackers - SiamRPN, GradNet [22], SiamDW [23], SiamFC and three correlation filters trackers – SRDCF [24], DeepSRDCF, Staple [25] as our tracker's comparisons on the OTB2015. Table 2 shows the result of comparsion with other mainstream algorithms on OTB2015, Fig. 4 shows the Precision plots and Success plots of comparsion with other mainstream algorithms on OTB2015.

We compare our tracker on the testing dataset OTB2015 with the mainstream trackers. Figure 4 shows that our tracker produces leading result in overlap success. Compared with the recent SiamRPN, our tracker outperforms 2.9% in success and 3.4% in precision.

Compared with the Siamese network based methods, the reason for the higher tracking success rate and accuracy of the algorithm in this paper is that the backbone network used in this paper is deeper, the extracted features have stronger semantic expression ability for the target, and the network after the optimized strategy is more suitable for tracking tasks. The introduction of the attention mechanism makes the characteristics of both branches extraction make full use of the semantic information of the target to be tracked and the foreground and background, and it has a certain degree of robustness to the target's illumination changes and scale changes.

Compared with correlation filters based methods, not only the tracking accuracy and success rate are greatly increased but also the speed has a improvement. Correlation filter based methods, its better accuracy and success rate benefit from the online training and real-time update of the tracker, but the online training process is very time-consuming, so its speed is slow, which cannot meet the real-time tracking requirements.

Table 2. Comparison of test results of different algorithms on the OTB2015 dataset

	AUC	Precision
Ours	0.658	0.881
GradNet	0.639	0.861
DeepSRDCF	0.635	0.851
SiamRPN	0.629	0.847
SiamDW	0.627	0.828
SRDCF	0.598	0.789
Staple	0.587	0.783
SiamFC	0.578	0.772

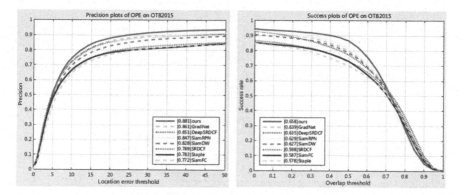

Fig. 4. Comparison of precision and success rates of different algorithms on the OTB2015 dataset

VOT Benchmark. VOT2018 are more challenging dataset that contain 60 color sequences, and the ground-truth of each sequence is marked by a rotating regression box. The evaluation indicators of the testing dataset include Accuracy (A) refers to the average overlap rate of the tracker under a single sequence, Robustness (R) refers to the number of failures under a single test sequence, it is regarded as a failure when the overlap rate is zero. The most important evaluation indicator is Expected Average Overlap (EAO) which refers to the expected value of non-reset overlap of the tracker on a short-term sequence as a combination of accuracy and robustness. The higher Accuracy and EAO represents the better performance, and the lower Robustness represents the better performance on the contrary. Table 3 shows the result of comparsion with other mainstream algorithms on VOT2018, Fig. 5 shows the EAO plots of comparsion with other mainstream algorithms on VOT2018.

Table 3. Comparison of test results of different algorithms on the VOT2018 dataset

	Accuracy	Robustness	EAO
Ours	0.586	0.256	0.394
MFT	0.505	0.140	0.385
SiamRPN	0.566	0.276	0.383
UPDT	0.536	0.184	0.378
DeepSTRCF	0.523	0.215	0.345
SASiam	0.566	0.258	0.337
CPT	0.506	0.239	0.339
DRT	0.519	0.201	0.356

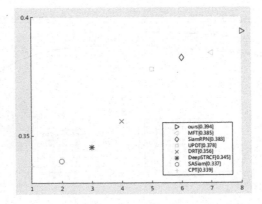

Fig. 5. Comparison of EAO of different algorithms on the VOT2018 dataset

From Table 3, it shows that our tracker has achieved the best performance in terms of EAO and accuracy. Compared with the top-ranked Siamese network tracker SiamRPN, our method produces a significant gain of 2.0% in terms of robustness. Nevertheless, since the template is not updated in the Siamese network, the robustness of our tracker is still worse than the correlation filters method that relies on online updates. Because the correlation filters based methods update the template online, its speed is slow even cannot achieve tracking in real-time.

Therefore, in order to further illustrate our tracker have a good balance between accuracy and speed, we compare the EAO and speed with some mainstream object tracking algorithms. Speed use Frame-Per-Second (FPS) as evaluation indicator. Figure 6 shows the result of comparison between EAO and speed on VOT2018.

It can obtain from Fig. 6 that compare with other mainstream algorithm, our tracker not only gets good performance but also keeps high speed on VOT2018, in general, we get the best performance in the trade-off between speed and accuracy. It can be attributed to the two lightweight attention modules we designed in our network, which not only makes our tracker get more robust but also keeps our model slim.

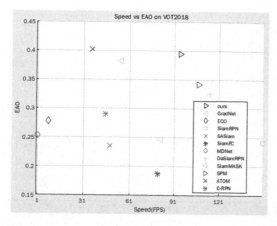

Fig. 6. Comparison of EAO and speed of different algorithms on the VOT2018

TrackingNet Benchmark. The recently released dataset TrackingNet include training dataset and testing dataset provides a large amount of data to assess trackers. We evaluate our tracker on its testing dataset with 500 videos. TrackingNet uses three metrics success (AUC), precision (Precision) and normalized precision (P_{norm}) as evaluation indicators. Success and precision are same as OTB benchmark, normalized precision is calculating by normalizing the precision over the size of the ground truth bounding box. Table 4 shows the result of comparsion with other mainstream algorithms on TrackingNet, Fig. 7 shows the P_{norm} plots of comparsion with other mainstream algorithms on TrackingNet.

Table 4. Comparison of test results of different algorithms on the TrackingNet dataset

	AUC	Precision	P_{norm}
Ours	0.678	0.652	0. 763
DaSiamRPN	0.638	0.591	0.733
ECO	0.554	0.492	0.618
CSRDCF	0.534	0.480	0.622
CFNet	0.578	0.533	0.654
MDNet	0.606	0.565	0.705
SiamFC	0.571	0.533	0.663

Table 4 demonstrates the comparison results in some mainstream trackers, showing that our tracker achieves the best results. Especially, our tracker outperform DaSiamRPN with AUC score, Precision score and P_{norm} score by 4.0%, 6.1% and 3.0%, respectively.

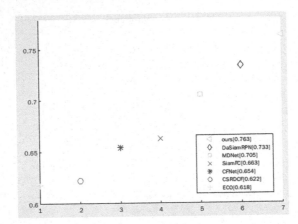

Fig. 7. Comparison of P_{norm} of different algorithms on the TrackingNet dataset

4.3   Ablation Study

Attention Modules. In order to illustrate the effectiveness of the two lightweight modules we designed, an ablation experiment was carried out, using the same training data and method. Based on the absence of ECA+ and GC+ modules, we trained only ECA+ and only GC+, and we also trained ECA and GC modules without any improvement and tested on the OTB2015 and VOT2018 datasets. From Table 5, we can compare and analyze:

Table 5. Attention modules ablation experiment OTB2015 and VOT2018

	ECA	GC	ECA+	GC+	OTB2015 Success	VOT2018 EAO	FPS
(i)					0.631	0.373	110
(ii)	√				0.635	0.378	107
(iii)		√			0.637	0.379	104
(iv)			√		0.639	0.382	102
(v)				√	0.646	0.388	100
(vi)	√	√			0.642	0.385	99
(vii)			√	√	0.651	0.394	98

Compared with lines (i)(ii)(iv), after adding the ECA module to the original benchmark network, the OTB2015 success rate (Success) and the VOT2018 expected average overlap rate (EAO) only increased by 0.4% and 0.5% respectively, while the designed ECA+ module can increase by 0.8% and 0.9% respectively;

Compared with lines (i)(iii)(v), the success rate of OTB2015 and the expected average overlap rate of VOT2018 are only increased by 0.6% and 0.6% respectively after adding the GC module to the original benchmark network, while the designed GC + module can increase by 1.5% and 1.5% respectively;

Compared with line (i)(vi)(vii), after adding ECA and GC modules to the original reference network, the success rate of OTB2015 and the expected average overlap rate of VOT2018 are only increased by 1.1% and 1.2% respectively, while the designed ECA+ and GC+ modules can increase by 2.0% and 2.1% respectively.

It can be seen from the speed comparison that the impact is small. Furthermore, it proves that the two lightweight modules designed in this paper—ECA+ and GC+ do not bring much computational overhead while improving performance.

Features Fusion. In order to illustrate the effectiveness of the fusion operation of feature maps, an ablation experiment was carried out, using the same training data and method. Table 6 shows the results on different combination of feature maps on OTB2015 and VOT2018.

Table 6. Features fusion ablation experiment OTB2015 and VOT2018

	Stage 2	Stage 3	Stage 4	OTB2015 Success	VOT2018 EAO
(i)	√			0.599	0.313
(ii)		√		0.617	0.336
(iii)			√	0.622	0.349
(iv)	√	√		0.634	0.360
(v)	√		√	0.628	0.356
(vi)		√	√	0.639	0.372
(vii)	√	√	√	0.651	0.394

Compare with line (i)(ii)(iii), use feature maps from stage 2 or stage 3 or stage 4 separately, the performance is related to the depth of backbone network, the performance of using stage 4 separately is best, but using single stage feature maps cannot get satisfactory result even though we modify the MobileNetV2 as our backbone network that make feature extraction get better;

Compare with line (iv)(v)(vi), use feature maps from stage 2 or stage 3 or stage 4 pairwise combination, we found that the combination of stage 2 and stage 4 get the worst result, combination of stage 3 and stage 4 get the best result. This result was unexpected, in our predict result of combination of stage 2 and stage 3 should be the worse, the reason for this result needs follow-up research;

Comparing line (vii) with above lines, combine all these three stages can get the best result, it confirm our method which fuse the different layers feature maps can makes classification and localization more accuracy.

In general, by replace the backbone from AlexNet to MobileNetV2 and fusing different stage feature maps makes performance better. It proves our method is effective and it has a room to improve for further research.

5 Conclusion

The proposed object tracking algorithm based on efficient attention modules can effectively learn the abundant information and local context information of the object under the action of the two lightweight modules designed to deal with the serious deformation of the object and the complex environment interference, and will not bring computational overhead. Our tracker has got top-ranked performance on OTB2015, VOT2018 and TrackingNet, it has a good improvement than other mainstream algorithms. While maintaining good tracking performance, the ultra-small parameter amount has great advantages over other mainstream algorithms in the application scenarios of mobile or embedded devices.

References

1. Krizhevsky, A., Sutskever, I., Hinton, G.E.: Imagenet classification with deep convolutional neural networks. In: Advances in Neural Information Processing Systems, pp. 1097–1105 (2012)
2. Sandler, M., Howard, A., Zhu, M., Zhmogino, A., Chen, L.: MobileNetV2: inverted residuals and linear bottlenecks. In: Proceedings of the IEEE Conference on Computer Vision and Pattern Recognition (CVPR), New York, pp. 4510–4520. IEEE (2018)
3. Bolme, D.S., Beverideg, J.R., Draper, B.A.: Visual object tracking using adaptive correlation filters. In: 2010 IEEE computer society Conference on Computer Vision and Pattern Recognition (CVPR), New York, pp. 2544–2550. IEEE (2010)
4. Henriques, J.F., Caseiro, R., Martins, P., Batista, J.: Exploiting the circulant structure of tracking-by-detection with kernels. In: Fitzgibbon, A., Lazebnik, S., Perona, P., Sato, Y., Schmid, C. (eds.) ECCV 2012. LNCS, vol. 7575, pp. 702–715. Springer, Heidelberg (2012). https://doi.org/10.1007/978-3-642-33765-9_50
5. Henriques, J.F., Caseiro, R., Martins, P.: High-speed tracking with kernelized correlation filters. In: IEEE Transactions on Pattern Analysis and Machine Intelligence, pp. 583–596 (2015)
6. Danelljan, M., Bhat, G., Shahbaz, K.F.: ECO: Efficient convolution operators for tracking.In: Proceedings of the IEEE Conference on Computer Vision and Pattern Recognition (CVPR), New York, pp. 6638–6646. IEEE (2017)
7. Danelljan, M., Hager, G., Shahbaz, K.F.: Convolutional features for correlation filter based visual tracking. In: Proceedings of the IEEE International Conference on Computer Vision Workshops (ICCV), New York, pp. 58–66. IEEE (2015)
8. Ma, C., Huang, J., Yang, X.: Hierarchical convolutional features for visual tracking. In: Proceedings of the IEEE International Conference on Computer Vision (ICCV), New York, pp. 3074–3082. IEEE (2015)
9. Simonyan, K., Zisserman, A.: Very deep convolutional networks for large-scale image recognition. arXiv preprint arXiv:1409.1556 (2014)
10. Bertinetto, L., Valmadre, J., Henriques, J.F., Vedaldi, A., Torr, P.H.S.: Fully-convolutional siamese networks for object tracking. In: Hua, G., Jégou, H. (eds.) ECCV 2016. LNCS, vol. 9914, pp. 850–865. Springer, Cham (2016). https://doi.org/10.1007/978-3-319-48881-3_56
11. Guo, Q., Feng, W., Zhou, C.: Learning dynamic siamese network for visual object tracking. In: IEEE International Conference on Computer Vision (ICCV), New York, pp. 1763–1771. IEEE (2017)

12. He, A., Luo, C., Tian, X.: A twofold Siamese network for real-time object tracking. In: Proceedings of the IEEE International Conference on Computer Vision (CVPR), New York, pp. 4834–4843. IEEE (2018)
13. Li, B., Yan, J., Wu, W.: High performance visual tracking with siamese region proposal network. In: Proceedings of the IEEE Conference on Computer Vision and Pattern Recognition (CVPR), New York, pp. 8971–8980. IEEE (2018)
14. Zhu, Z., Wang, Q., Li, B., Wu, W., Yan, J., Hu, W.: (2018) Distractor-Aware Siamese Networks for Visual Object Tracking. In: Ferrari V., Hebert M., Sminchisescu C., Weiss Y. (eds.) Computer Vision – ECCV 2018. ECCV 2018. Lecture Notes in Computer Science, vol 11213. Springer, Cham
15. Hu, J., Shen, L., Sun, G.: Squeeze-and-excitation networks. In: Proceedings of the 2018 IEEE Conference on Computer Vision and Pattern Recognition (CVPR), New York, pp. 7132–7141. IEEE (2018)
16. Woo, S., Park, J., Lee, J.Y., Kweon, I.S.: CBAM: Convolutional Block Attention Module. In: Ferrari, V., Hebert, M., Sminchisescu, C., Weiss, Y., (eds.) Computer Vision – ECCV 2018. ECCV 2018. Lecture Notes in Computer Science, vol. 11211. Springer, Cham (2018)
17. Wang, Q., Wu, B., Zhu P.: ECA-net: efficient channel attention for deep convolutional neural networks. In: Proceedings of the IEEE Conference on Computer Vision and Pattern Recognition (CVPR), New York, pp. 11534 –11542. IEEE (2020)
18. Wang, X., Girshick, R., Gupta, A., He, K.: Non-local neural networks. In: IEEE Conference on Computer Vision and Pattern Recognition (CVPR), New York, pp. 7794–7803. IEEE (2018)
19. Cao, Y., Xu, J., Lin, S., Wei, F., Hu, H.: GCnet: non-local networks meet squeeze-excitation networks and beyond. In: Proceedings of the IEEE International Conference on Computer Vision Workshops (ICCV), New York, pp.1971–1980. IEEE (2019)
20. Howard, A.G., Zhu, M.: Chen, B.: MobileNets efficient convolutional neural networks for mobile vision applications. https://arxiv.org/abs/1704.04861
21. He, K., Zhang, X., Ren, S., Sun, J.: Deep residual learning for image recognition. In: Proceedings of the IEEE Conference on Computer Vision and Pattern Recognition (CVPR), New York, pp. 770–778. IEEE (2016)
22. Li, P., Chen, B., Ouyang, W.: GradNet: gradient-guided network for visual object tracking. In: Proceedings of the IEEE/CVF International Conference on Computer Vision ICCV (ICCV), New York, pp. 6162–6171. IEEE (2019)
23. Zhang, Z., Peng, H.: Deeper and wider Siamese networks for real-time visual tracking.In: 2019 IEEE Conference on Computer Vision and Pattern Recognition (CVPR), New York, pp. 4591–4600. IEEE (2019)
24. Danelljan, M., Hager, G., Khan, F.S.: Learning spatially regularized correlation filters for visual tracking. In: 2015 IEEE International Conference on Computer Vision(ICCV), New York, pp. 4310–4318. IEEE (2015)
25. Bertinetto, L., Valmadre, J., Golodetz, S.: Staple: complementary learners for real-time tracking.In: 2016 IEEE Conference on Computer Vision and Pattern Recognition (CVPR), New York, pp. 1401–1409. IEEE (2016)

Author Index

Printed in the United States
by Baker & Taylor Publisher Services